Welcome to Colorado

A playground for nature lovers and outdoor enthusiasts, Colorado has majestic landscapes, raging rivers, and winding trails perfect for activities from biking to rafting. Skiers flock to the slopes here for the champagne powder and thrilling downhill runs while urban adventures await in cool cities like Denver, Boulder, and Aspen. This book was produced during the COVID-19 pandemic. As you plan your upcoming travels to Colorado, please confirm that places are still open and let us know when we need to make updates by writing to us at this address: editors@fodors.com.

TOP REASONS TO GO

★ **Mountains:** The stunning views from the state's many commanding peaks can't be beat.

★ **Outdoor Activities:** Hiking, biking, horseback riding, and fishing are all excellent.

★ **Local Flavors:** Grass-fed meats, microbrews, green chilies, and stream-raised trout.

★ **Hip Cities:** Cosmopolitan Denver, trendy Boulder, and glamorous Aspen entice.

★ **Skiing:** Fluffy powder, top-notch runs, and posh resorts draw skiers of all levels.

★ **National Parks:** Rocky Mountain, Mesa Verde, Great Sand Dunes, and Black Canyon of the Gunnison.

Contents

MAPS

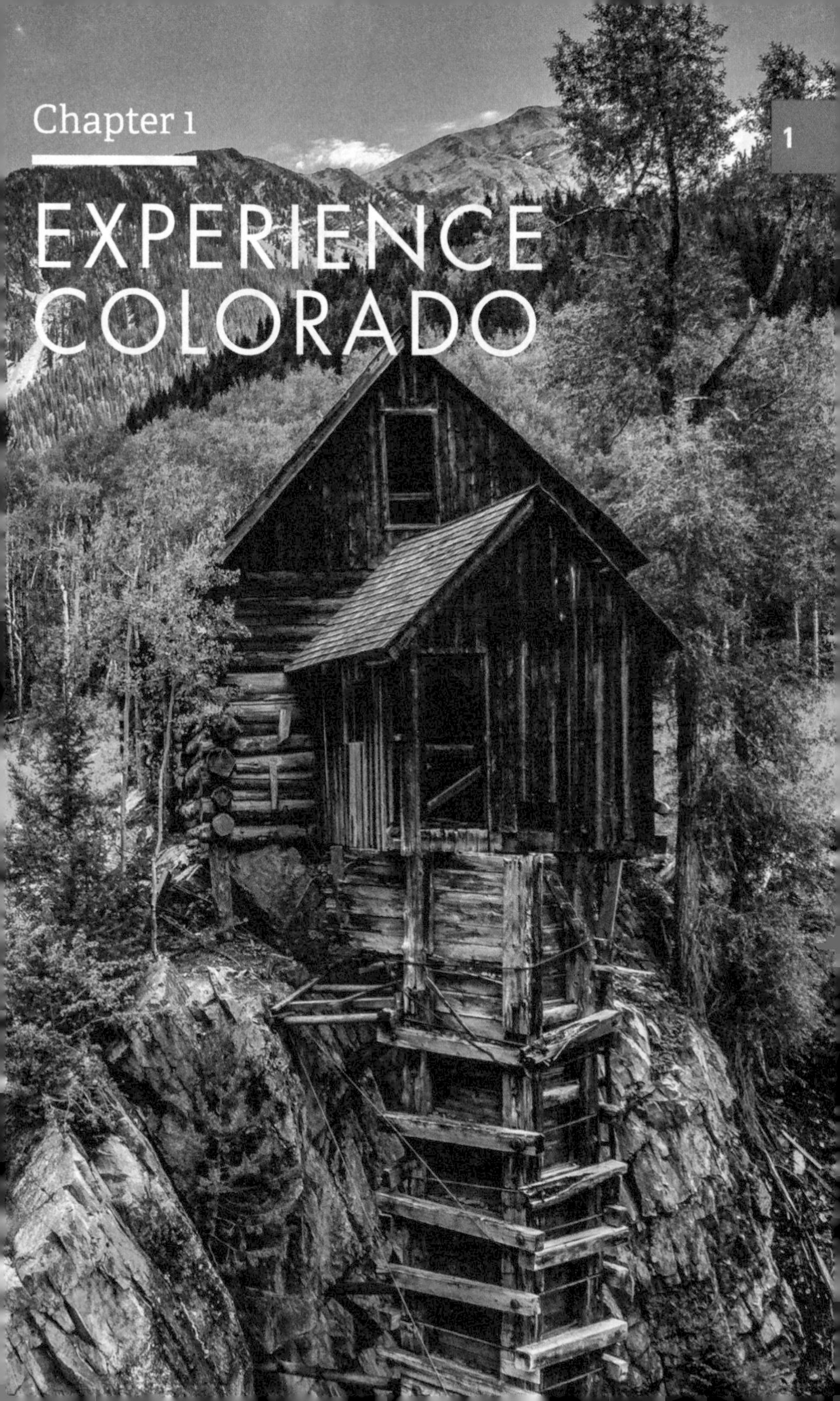

Chapter 1

EXPERIENCE COLORADO

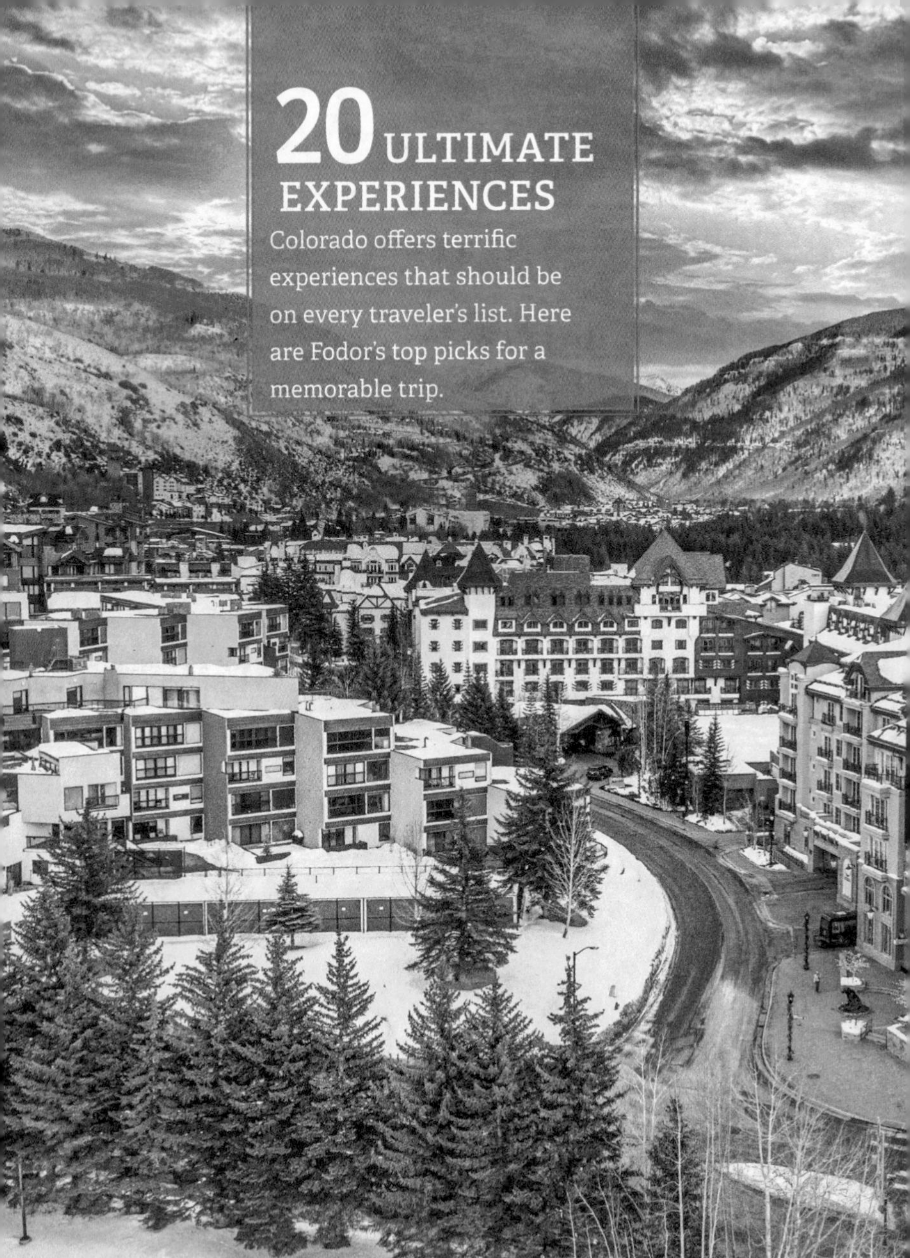

1 Vail

Swiss-inspired chalet architecture and global dining bring the ambience of the Alps to Colorado at the base of the state's largest ski resort. *(Ch. 6)*

2 Mesa Verde National Park

Wandering through some of the nearly 600 ancient Puebloan dwellings carved into high sandstone cliffs at this park is truly awe-inspiring. *(Ch. 12)*

3 Microbrews

Coloradans craft some superb microbrews. Pop into local establishments for tours and tastings, or take away a growler for an outdoor picnic. *(Ch. 3--13)*

4 Dude Ranches

Staying at a dude ranch is a true Western experience. Guests can ride horses through gorgeous terrain and then dine family-style on grass-fed meat. *(Ch. 11)*

5 Wildlife Spotting

Colorado's national parks offer excellent opportunities to spot all kinds of wildlife, from the small (marmots, pika) to the large (bear, moose, elk). *(Ch. 1, 9)*

6 Hot Springs

Relax in one of many mineral hot springs throughout the state. Some have developed into resorts with spas while others remain off the beaten path. *(Ch. 10, 13)*

7 Great Sand Dunes National Park

You'll feel like you're on the moon as you travel across the giant dunes at the base of the Sangre de Cristo range. Hit the slopes on sled or sandboard for the complete experience. *(Ch. 13)*

8 Mountain Biking

From half-day rides to multiday excursions, Colorado's mountains and deserts offer some of the country's most sought-after mountain bike trails. *(Ch. 11)*

9 Hiking

No matter where you're based in Colorado, the best way to experience the Rockies is to enter on foot. Wildlife, alpine lakes, and wildflowers await to reward your effort. *(Ch. 9)*

10 Scenic Drives and Train Trips

Eye-opening vistas of dramatic canyons, verdant forests, and undulating landscapes await on ground journeys around the state. *(Ch. 3–13)*

11 Fishing

Hook a walleye or rainbow trout on a fishing expedition, whether guided or on your own. Many lakes and reservoirs are stocked, while fishing in rivers offers a more natural experience. *(Ch. 3–10)*

12 White-Water Rafting

There's no better way to experience true a wilderness adventure than to hop on a raft and float through the Royal Gorge, Dinosaur National Monument, or a section of the high Rockies. *(Ch. 3–13)*

13 Marijuana Tourism

Take in a cannabis experience in a controlled setting with marijuana cooking classes, guided experiences like "puff and paint" classes, and 420-friendly hotels. *(Ch. 1)*

14 Pikes Peak

The inspiration for the song "America the Beautiful," Pikes Peak beguiles with its breathtaking views. Take the world's highest cog train all the way to the summit. *(Ch. 13)*

15 Denver

Colorado's capital boasts historic museums, walkable neighborhoods, parks, breweries, and quaint cafés, as well as live music to rival coastal cities. *(Ch. 3)*

16 Black Canyon of the Gunnison National Park

Hike above or into a towering canyon surrounding the Gunnison River with opportunities for kayaking, rock climbing, and more. *(Ch. 11)*

17 Dinosaur National Monument

Step into history by viewing preserved fossils and petroglyphs here. Rafting, hiking, and camping can take you deep into the monument's canyons and expansive backcountry. *(Ch. 10)*

18 Aspen

One of the U.S.'s fabled resort towns, Aspen defines glitz, glamour, and glorious skiing. Top-notch restaurants and high-end shops provide diversions year-round. *(Ch. 7)*

19 Rocky Mountain National Park

This premier national park boasts lush forests, alpine lakes, snowcapped peaks, and more than 350 miles of hiking trails. With any luck, you'll spot bighorn sheep, elk, and mule deer. *(Ch. 9)*

20 Old West Mining Towns

Relive the boom times of the West in the state's lively mining communities. Many historic buildings have been converted into museums and hotels. *(Ch. 11)*

WHAT'S WHERE

1 **Denver.** Colorado's capital and largest city, Denver is unmatched in its combination of urban fun and easy access to outdoor recreation.

2 **Side Trips From Denver.** Scenic highway I–70 ascends into the foothills through historic towns like Golden, Idaho Springs, and Georgetown.

3 **Breckenridge and Summit County.** The ski resorts of Keystone, Breckenridge, Copper Mountain, and Arapahoe Basin cluster near I–70 as it rises in the Rockies. Lake Dillon and its port towns attract summer visitors.

4 **Vail Valley.** The largest ski resort in Colorado, the beautiful valley at the base of Vail sits in a narrow corridor bounded by steep peaks.

5 **Aspen and the Roaring Fork Valley.** Glitzy Aspen is a serious skiing draw while Victorian charmer Glenwood Springs centers on a massive hot springs pool.

6 **Boulder and North Central Colorado.** Boulder balances high-tech with bohemia while Estes Park abuts Rocky Mountain National Park's eastern entrance.

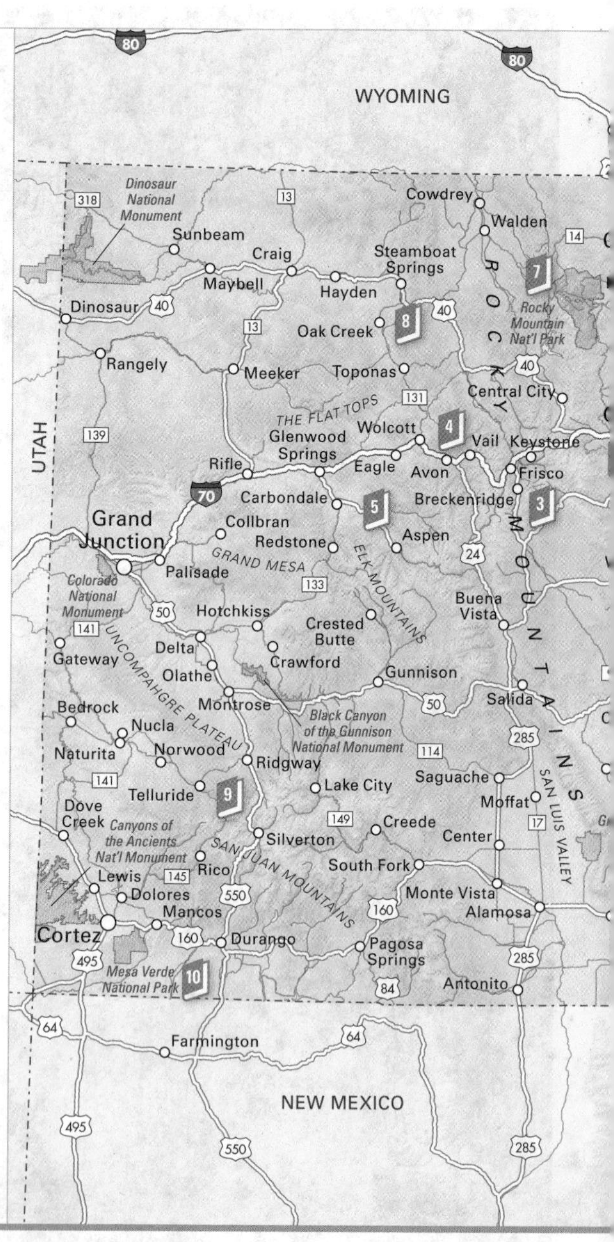

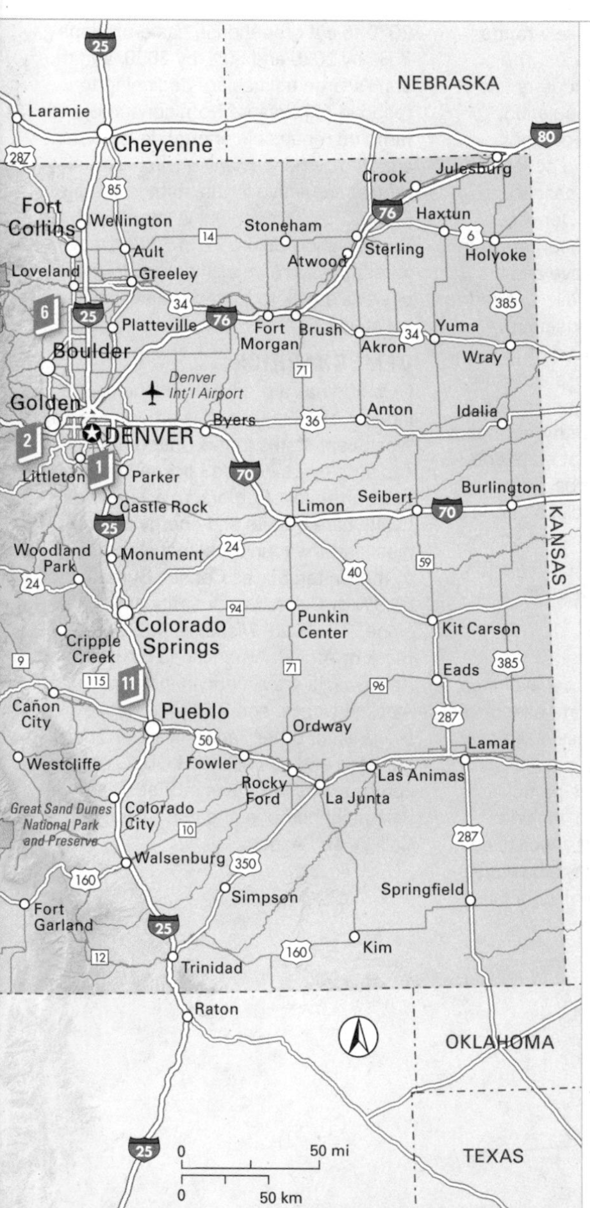

7 Rocky Mountain National Park. The wilderness and alpine tundra here welcome wildlife and outdoor enthusiasts year-round.

8 Steamboat Springs and Northwest Colorado. Where the Rockies transition into an arid desert, Grand Junction is the region's hub. Nearby are the Colorado and Dinosaur National Monuments and Steamboat Springs.

9 Telluride and Southwest Colorado. Evergreen-clad peaks and red desert beckon outdoor enthusiasts to mountain-biking birthplace Crested Butte, Black Canyon of the Gunnison, and idyllic Telluride.

10 Mesa Verde National Park. This protected series of canyon ruins provides a peek into the lives of the Ancestral Pueblo people who made their homes among the cliffs.

11 Colorado Springs and South Central Colorado. Colorado Springs' mineral waters still flow. To the south, explore Great Sand Dunes National Park and Preserve and the surrounding San Luis Valley.

Colorado Today

POLITICS

After generations as a swing state, Colorado has moved decisively to the left over the past two decades. The long-dominant extraction industry has given way to a booming population of young professionals and outdoor recreationists, reshaping the economy around adventure tourism, cannabis, and a budding tech scene. Denver, Boulder, and many of the resort areas in the Rockies trend progressive and are welcoming to all stripes, while Colorado's rural areas remain more conservative. However, no matter where you travel, environmental stewardship is an issue that binds otherwise divergent ideologies. The state's natural beauty, abundant wildlife, and vast amounts of state and federal open land form the backbone of politics in Colorado—regardless of one's personal politics, Coloradans are staunch defenders of public lands. By and large, the state is also LGBTQ+ friendly.

ENVIRONMENTALISM AND SUSTAINABILITY

Building on Colorado's political evolution, voices ranging from corporate executives to citizen activists are increasingly vocal in support of sustainability initiatives in the state. The ski industry is particularly outspoken. Aspen Ski Co. includes renewable energy and sustainability as a core focus of the company's business model, with Vail Resorts making similar pledges for its multiple destinations. Governor Jared Polis released a plan in 2020 to cut greenhouse gas emissions 25% by 2025 and 50% by 2050, and the state's large utilities are beginning to respond to pressure from consumers to ramp up renewable energy development and deployment. Many environmental groups are active in the state including Sierra Club, Protect Our Winters, and Conservation Colorado. In 2020, Denver voters passed a small increase to the city's sales tax to fund sustainability initiatives.

DEMOGRAPHICS

Colorado has a median household income of $69,000 and is among the 15 wealthiest states in the United States. Top employers include Lockheed Martin, the University of Colorado, a variety of health-care outlets and energy companies, and the tourism sector. According to the United States Census Bureau, 86.9% of Coloradans identify as White alone, 21.8% are Hispanic, 4.6% are Black or African American, 3.5% are Asian, 1.6% are American Indian or Alaskan Native, and 0.2% are Native Hawaiian or other Pacific Islander. There are large and established LGBTQ+ communities in Denver's Cheesman Park neighborhood and in Boulder, Fort Collins, and Aspen.

Colorado with Kids

Colorado is an outdoor adventure playground that offers memorable experiences for both adults and kids, with its many mountains, waterways, parks, lakes, and bustling urban areas. In the winter, families can whoosh down the state's many ski slopes, while in summer they can hike through its numerous trails and then gather around a campfire at night.

There are a few things to remember when traveling with kids in Colorado. Throughout much of the state, you will be at a high altitude, which will affect every member of the family. Make sure children drink plenty of water, are protected from the sun, and have plenty of down time.

Stock up on sunscreen, water, and extra food if you plan to undertake a family hike. Keep an eye on all members of your group when enjoying the outdoors and watch that no one strays too close to rivers or mountain overlooks.

WHERE TO GO

Cheyenne Mountain Zoo, Colorado Springs. This superlative zoo is loaded with interactive exhibits that allow kids to really learn about the animals they are seeing. Animal lovers can feed giraffes by hand and more daring tykes can soar in a gondola that flies over the zoo.

Children's Museum of Denver, Denver. One of the best children's museums in the country, the Children's Museum of Denver has an impressive range of hands-on exhibits. There's a fire station with a fire truck and pole, and an assembly line where kids can design and build various items.

Dinosaur Journey, Fruita. What kid isn't intrigued by dinosaurs? This museum provides interactive experiences for curious young ones: they can look for fossils in a mock quarry, examine dino prints, and be wowed by animatronic dinosaurs.

Georgetown Loop Railroad, Georgetown. This 3-mile narrow-gauge loop ascends over 640 feet of mountainous terrain between the mining towns of Georgetown and Silver Plume. It feels as if you're being transported back to an earlier era as the steam engine slowly chugs up the tracks.

Glenwood Caverns Adventure Park, Glenwood Springs. This once-sleepy resort town, renowned for its hot springs, has transformed itself into one of the state's best family vacation spots. The Glenwood Caverns Adventure Park has a thrilling alpine coaster, a fun zipline ride, and a roller coaster that overhangs a cliff. Add in several caves, two rivers, and miles of hiking trails and your family is guaranteed to stay busy.

Great Sand Dunes National Park, San Luis Valley. While the largest sand dunes in the United States may seem entirely out of place amid the state's soaring mountains, they provide unique adventures for families. Kids enjoy amazing hikes, nighttime stargazing, tours to spot the bison in the southwest part of the park, and, if they're particularly adventurous, climbing the massive dunes.

What to Eat and Drink in Colorado

CRAFT BEER

More than 400 breweries call Colorado home. Craft beer is a cultural staple throughout the state, with nearly every mountain town featuring at least one brewery and most restaurants serving a variety of local brews. Denver also hosts the annual Great American Beer Festival, which draws brewers from across the country each October.

TROUT

Rainbow trout is a staple on farm-to-table menus across the state, typically filleted and pan-seared or baked with lemon, garlic, and pepper. Trout dishes are a source of local pride as no fish species is more common in Colorado's rivers or kitchens.

BEEF AND BISON

Rural Colorado is comprised of vast stretches of open rangeland and the state follows a charter allowing open grazing on much of its public lands. As a result, Colorado raises great cattle and bison—try the Denver steak, a marbled shoulder cut beloved in steak houses. Bison burgers are also a popular, healthier alternative to ground beef common in burger joints throughout the state.

CHILE VERDE

No single dish is more popular in Colorado than the breakfast burrito. Chile verde—green chile—is its defining ingredient and it's what separates a good burrito from the run-of-the-mill one, and this semi-spicy sauce is quite versatile. Even many classy dinner spots serve house-made chile verde. Both crisp and smoky, it can be served vegetarian but often comes with chunks of pork.

COLORADO-STYLE PIZZA

Popularized by Beau Jo's restaurant in Idaho Springs, Colorado-style pizza features a thick, braided crust and is known locally as "Mountain Pie." No matter your toppings of choice, dip the towering crust in honey as no bread-stick satisfies in quite the same way.

LOCAL WINES

The wine country surrounding Palisade in western Colorado offers more than two dozen vineyards and tasting rooms to choose from. Popular varietals include Merlot, Chardonnay, Cabernet Sauvignon, and Sauvignon Blanc. The region is also known for its orchards so fruit-forward wines are common.

Lamb chops

ROCKY MOUNTAIN OYSTERS
Restaurants serving Rocky Mountain oysters beg you to try before you judge. This quirky appetizer consists of bull testicles breaded, fried, and served with cocktail sauce for dipping.

LAMB
Advocates of lamb chops and ragù boast that Colorado raises and serves lamb on par with New Zealand's best. Lamb is a popular entrée at steak houses and Western-style saloons in Denver and Colorado Springs, as well as in resort areas.

PALISADE PEACHES
Sweet and juicy Palisade peaches are a rite of passage in Colorado during the late summer months. Peach shacks set up shop along highways and busy intersections, but nothing beats the fun of picking your own bag of peaches at an orchard in Colorado's Grand Valley.

COFFEE
Coffee-shop culture is strong in Colorado, with locally roasted beans available in cafés and markets.

OLATHE SWEET CORN
Coloradans rush to farmers' markets to stock up on the sweet corn grown outside the tiny town of Olathe. Bountiful in mid-to-late summer, sweet corn is perfect right off the grill, eaten straight from the cob.

What to Buy

PUEBLO CHILIES
Take home the flavor of Colorado's favorite breakfast with Pueblo chilies, available roasted and by the pound. Farms around the city of Pueblo grow the renowned chilies and ship them by the truckload to markets throughout the state.

LOCAL ART
Take home a piece of mountain-inspired wall art or photography to commemorate your trip. Denver's Arts District on Santa Fe hosts Colorado's premiere First Friday event and has a gallery row populated by big-name artists and local celebrities. In the high country, artists host galleries and showings in Aspen and Vail during winter and summer seasons.

WALLAROO HATS
With 300 days of sunshine per year, a sun hat is the perfect accessory in the Centennial State. Wallaroo Hats makes them Rocky Mountain-style, with a wide brim and a dose of open-range class that falls somewhere between John Denver and Nathaniel Rateliff (it doesn't get more Colorado than that).

PEACH-INFUSED ANYTHING
Palisade peaches make their way into seemingly everything in Colorado from pies and ice cream to craft beer and wine. A bottle of peach wine makes the perfect gift or souvenir with the promise of a sweet toast among friends.

HAMMOND'S CANDIES
Hammond's dark and milk chocolate bars fly off shelves in specialty and gift shops around the state. Other sweet treats include candy canes, licorice, and old-style rolled lollipops. Visit the factory in Denver or look for their treats at Denver International Airport and elsewhere in the state.

ROCKY MOUNTAIN CHOCOLATE FACTORY
A staple in mountain towns and shopping districts, Rocky Mountain Chocolate Factory is a must-try for every sweet tooth. Their retail shops are perfect for unique treats and unforgettable fudges. Insider's tip: when shopping for others, splurge on a caramel apple for yourself.

Stranahan's Colorado Whiskey

SPYDER SKI GEAR
Skiing is an iconic Colorado activity, especially when donning a jacket from Boulder-based Spyder. The classic Black Widow logo has been a staple on the slopes since the ski apparel company was founded in 1978.

CELESTIAL SEASONINGS TEA
Even if you don't drink tea on the regular, a tour of the Celestial Seasonings factory and shop in Boulder is a popular experience and an easy way to remember Colorado each time you fire up the kettle in your home kitchen.

STRANAHAN'S COLORADO WHISKEY
While craft beer is still Colorado's most popular alcoholic beverage, distilleries like Stranahan's have also been making their mark. Located in Denver, Stranahan's has been producing small-batch whiskeys since 2004. It was the first modern microdistillery to legally make whiskey in the state.

Best Outdoor Adventures in Colorado

SNOWBOARDING AT KEYSTONE
Near Breckenridge and Copper Mountain, Keystone has many beginner and intermediate offerings and is small enough to navigate easily. For the avid snowboarder, Keystone's Area 51 terrain park is the industry standard for jumps and rails.

HORSEBACK RIDING IN COLORADO SPRINGS
Ideal for visitors who have only a short time in the area but long to do a half-day trail ride, Academy Riding Stables brings red rock country up close at the Garden of the Gods, with pony rides for kids and hay wagon or stagecoach rides for groups.

VISITING A DUDE RANCH
One of the finest ranches in the state, the C Lazy U Guest Ranch in Granby offers a relaxing upscale experience, from daily horseback rides with a horse chosen for the duration of the visit to supervised kids' activities and chef-prepared meals, deluxe accommodations, a spring-fed pool, fly-fishing, and an on-site spa.

HIKING IN ROCKY MOUNTAIN NATIONAL PARK
In the Bear Lake Road section of the park, a network of trails threads past alpine lakes, waterfalls, aspens, and pines. Stroll 1 mile to Sprague Lake on a wheelchair-accessible path, or take a four-hour hike past two waterfalls to Mills Lake, with its views of mighty Longs Peak.

FLY-FISHING IN THE GUNNISON RIVER
In Almont, a tiny hamlet near Crested Butte and, more importantly, near the headwaters of the Gunnison, they live fly-fishing. Go on a guided excursion or head out on your own.

CONQUERING GRAY'S PEAK
It can take a full day to climb a Fourteener, one of Colorado's 58 peaks above 14,000 feet. Gray's Peak is challenging but manageable for experienced hikers. The trail passes through an open valley before heading up across a ridge to a summit that rewards hikers with views of the entire Front Range.

SKIING IN VAIL
Those looking for the big-resort experience head to Vail, where modern comforts and the esteemed back bowls mean a dizzying variety of runs and every possible convenience, all laid out in a series of contemporary European-style villages.

MOUNTAIN BIKING IN CRESTED BUTTE
Pearl Pass is the storied birthplace of mountain biking (check out the museum devoted to it in town). If your legs are not quite ready for that 40-mile, 12,700-foot challenge, there are plenty of paths more suitable to mere mortals.

RAFTING THE ARKANSAS RIVER
The Arkansas rages as a Class V or murmurs as a Class II, depending on the section and the season. It's *the* white-water rafting destination in the state. Join a tour passing through the Royal Gorge if you only have time for one outing.

TROUT FISHING IN THE ROARING FORK RIVER
Uninterrupted by dams from its headwaters to its junction with the Colorado, the Roaring Fork is one of the last free-flowing rivers in the state, plus it has a healthy population of 12- to 18-inch trout.

Best Wildlife in Colorado

COYOTES

These omnivores weigh about 30 pounds, distinguishing them from much larger wolves, and thrive throughout the western United States. They travel alone or in small packs and, with rare exceptions, pose little threat to humans, although you'll hear their loud cries when nearby.

ELK

Elk congregate where forest meets meadows, summering at high elevations before migrating lower in winter. In September and October, bulls attract a "harem" of mating partners by bugling, a loud and surreal whistling.

BIGHORN SHEEP

Clambering along rocky ledges, muscular bighorn sheep fascinate with their ability to travel so easily where the rest of us can't. In winter the docile herd animals descend to lower elevations. Rams have heavy, curled horns, while ewes' horns are short and slightly bent.

MARMOT

A few species of marmots like to live high up among granite rock piles of talus slopes and along riverbanks, so if you see them, it's likely to be along high-country trails. The rocky strongholds help protect these furry ground squirrels from such natural predators as eagles and hawks.

MOOSE

Feeding on fir, willows, and aspens, the moose is the largest member of the deer family: the largest bulls stand 7 feet tall at the shoulders and weigh up to 1,600 pounds. Distinctive characteristics include its antlers, which lie flat like palmate satellite dishes. Keep your distance if you come upon a moose; they are notoriously territorial and protective of their offspring.

BLACK BEARS

So common in Colorado that residents in some areas must chase them out of garbage cans and backyards, the black bear is in a constant battle for space and food. "Black" refers to the species, not the color, so don't be confused if you see gold, tan, or rust; it's the same family. In any case, the way not to see one is to hike loudly, especially in Rocky Mountain National Park and other heavily forested areas from mid-March to November. Hang a bear bag while camping and pack out your trash.

Black bears

MOUNTAIN LIONS
Although the mountain lion is an occasional predator, chances are you won't see him at most of the parks. They're tawny colored, can be 8 feet long, and weigh up to 200 pounds. They're capable of taking down a mule deer or elk.

MULE DEER
Often seen in meadows and forests are mule deer, with their black-tipped tails and pronounced antlers. Their name comes from the shape of their ears, which resemble mules' ears. Their unusual gait—all four feet can hit the ground at once—gives them an advantage over predators, as they move faster over scrubby terrain and can change directions instantly. Watch for them at peak feeding times at dawn and dusk.

BISON
The shaggy, grouchy American bison may not be the West's most charismatic ungulate, but it's certainly the most iconic. A bison can reach 6 feet at the shoulder, and males can weigh a ton (females weigh about 1,000 pounds). Bulls and cows both have short, curved horns, which they'll use to gore predators (or tourists who get too close).

PIKA
These small, mountain-dwelling mammal are similar to rabbits, except they have short, round ears. With short limbs and very round bodies, pikas can usually be found in boulder fields. They're also quite cute; Pikachu from Pokémon is loosely based on one.

Microbrews in Colorado

Colorado is crazy for microbrews. Since the first microbrewery opened in Boulder in 1979, the state has wholeheartedly embraced the craft beer movement. Currently there are more than 400 establishments making fresh beer throughout the state. With a senator and former governor who once was a brewer (John Hickenlooper), a family that helped define American brewing (the Coors), and a youthful demographic, craft beer is as much a part of the lifestyle in Colorado as the outdoors.

While most towns have their own brewpub or brewery, many of the most popular ones are located in three cities in the Front Range of the Rocky Mountains: Denver, Fort Collins, and Boulder. Many breweries have attached restaurants or host food trucks that offer everything from pub grub to upscale cuisine. Much like wineries, they offer tasting flights, which allow visitors to sample the full range of their beers.

The Great American Beer Festival, the country's largest and most prestigious beer festival, attracts brews from more than 2,000 breweries across the country each fall in downtown Denver. For a list of the microbrews in the state, visit the Colorado Brewers Guild (🌐 *coloradobeer.org*).

WHERE TO GO

Aspen Tap, Aspen. One of the most beautiful places in the state, Aspen is home to a local brewery (Aspen Brewing Company) that turns out some fine beers. Independence Pass Ale pays homage to the 12,000-foot-high pass and "back road" into town that is closed all winter due to snow. The taproom is open daily noon–midnight.

Avery Brewing Company, Boulder. The beers at Avery Brewing Company range from big bold IPAs to subtly smooth porters. Their state-of-the-art, technologically advanced brewery has a suspended catwalk that allows you to take your own self-guided tour while sipping a cold one.

Boulder Beer Company, Boulder. Learn about Colorado's first craft brewery on the free tours and tastings at Boulder Beer Company. You can grab a bite to eat afterward at the brewhouse's pub; in summer, you can enjoy the grub and suds on the patio.

Crooked Stave Artisan Beer Project, Denver. When owner Chad Yakobson opened his brewery in the Denver neighborhood of LoDo he had one plan: to create superior sour and experimental beers. His barrel-aged beers are proof of his success.

Elevation Beer Co, Poncha Springs. In Chaffee County, surrounded by 14,000-foot peaks and next to the Arkansas River headwaters, Elevation makes some of the state's best barrel-aged and specialty beers. The tasting room is open daily noon–8.

Upslope Brewing Company, Boulder. Upslope's Craft Lager is an easy way to introduce yourself to Colorado's expansive selection of craft beers. Their diverse roster features Belgian, German, and experimental brews, available in their two taprooms open daily until 10 pm.

Ska Brewing Company, Durango. Ska Brewing's popular Modus Hoperandi earned its spot atop Colorado's roster of smooth-drinking IPAs, and this happening brewery is the hub for craft beer activity and events in southern Colorado. Their diverse roster of brews also includes a popular blonde ale and red ale.

Recreational Marijuana

Colorado voters approved recreational marijuana in 2012, the first state in the United States to do so, with stores opening to the public on January 1, 2014. While many states have followed suit over the past several years, Colorado's role as the first has given it the time necessary to become a true weed tourism destination. Although use is legal statewide, Denver is generally the jumping-off point for visitors interested in a legal cannabis experience. Use of marijuana is permitted only on private property; smoking outside or in public is considered a crime and is strictly forbidden. This leaves visitors with limited options of where to consume, with the primary option being cannabis-friendly hotels.

⚠ Each individual's tolerance of and reaction to marijuana may be different. Staff members at dispensaries are accustomed to answering questions and can make recommendations based on personal preference and experience level. First-timers should stick to traditional marijuana flower as it is easier to control the amount of intake, and the accompanying high often wears off faster than with ingested products such as "edibles."

CANNABIS-FRIENDLY HOTELS

A number of hotels throughout Denver have made selected rooms available to those wishing to vaporize the plant. These hotels typically withhold their logo and name from booking websites, often due to the hotel's affiliation with a corporate parent or brand. Potential guests are able to see the location of the hotel and all other booking details but are not advised of the hotel name until after booking is confirmed. Upon check-in at the front desk, guests receive a vaporizer for their room, but must purchase cannabis separately from one of the state's many recreational marijuana stores. Hotel rooms are available through 🌐 *www.coloradopotguide.com*, and 🌐 *www.coloradocannabistours.com*.

DISPENSARIES

Cannabis stores are known as "dispensaries" throughout the state. Recreational dispensaries serve all customers over age 21. Medical dispensaries serve only those possessing a Colorado medical marijuana card, which is only available to Colorado residents. While cannabis is legal throughout Colorado, certain municipalities, often in suburban and rural areas, do not allow recreational sales. In larger cities, recreational dispensaries are commonplace and marked with a green cross. Customers must be 21 years of age with proper state-issued identification to gain entry. The amount a person is legally allowed to purchase is dependent on residency; Colorado residents with a valid ID may buy up to 1 ounce of marijuana per day, while those with an out-of-state ID may purchase a quarter-ounce of marijuana. No personal information is collected, and your ID is used only for proof of age and residency.

⚠ Driving while high is against the law, and legal limits have been established for the amount of THC a driver can have in their system. You can drive legally while possessing marijuana in a vehicle the same way you can with alcohol; it just needs to be sealed.

Colorado Harvest Company, Denver. Colorado Harvest Company offers a wide range of products ranging from traditional marijuana flower to infused gels, tinctures, edible candies and foods, and topical lotions. Their three locations in the Denver area specialize in high-quality service and frequently offer weekly specials. The flagship store on South Broadway Boulevard is part of Denver's "Green Mile," home to more cannabis centers than any similar stretch in the world. 🌐 *www.coloradoharvestcompany.com*

Ballpark Holistic Dispensary, Denver. Located downtown near the baseball stadium, this dispensary is a long-time player in Denver's cannabis culture. Both medical and recreational options are available. Their staff, many of whom have been on board for years, is knowledgeable and courteous. Ballpark Holistic Dispensary is convenient if you're staying in a "green hotel" in the downtown area. 🌐 *www.ballparkdispensary.com*

Native Roots. Native Roots operates multiple locations across Colorado and is known for their wide selection and streamlined shopping process. Their locations along the I–70 and I–25 corridors are convenient for those making their way across the state. Keep in mind that cannabis must be kept in a sealed container, which is provided upon purchase. 🌐 *www.nativerootsdispensary.com*

PRIVATE TOURS

Marijuana-infused dining experience. One of the more creative ways to experience Colorado's cannabis culture is to hire a private chef to prepare a private fine-dining experience. Full-service upscale meals are prepared for groups large and small by the chefs of Colorado Cannabis Tours. Menus are personalized, and the experience is as educational as it is delicious. 🌐 *www.coloradocannabistours.com*

The Original Colorado Cannabis Tour. With this company, you can tour a cannabis grow facility, visit dispensaries, see top views in the mountains near Denver, and experience cannabis, all on a 3½-hour tour. Guides show visitors the nuts and bolts of the cannabis industry and provide a safe space to sample and learn about cannabis culture. Packages, including 420-friendly hotel rooms, are available. Transportation is included, with pick-ups and drop-offs from your hotel or accommodations. 🌐 *www.coloradocannabistours.com*

Full-service city tours. For those curious about how Colorado's cannabis industry functions, but not necessarily wanting to partake in cannabis themselves, a guided tour is the best option. Options are available to tour growing facilities and dispensaries and often include general tourist hot spots such as Red Rocks Amphitheatre and Mount Evans as well. Transportation including pick-up and drop-off from your hotel or accommodation are included. 🌐 *www.coloradopotguide.com*

What to Watch and Read Before Your Trip

THE SHINING BY STEPHEN KING

Inspired by the real-life, supposedly haunted Stanley Hotel in Estes Park, *The Shining* chronicles a writer who turns on his family after holing up in a mountain hotel laden with dark secrets. Jack Nicholson stars in the equally chilling film of the same name.

CENTENNIAL BY JAMES MICHENER

This historical novel chronicles a series of events that take place in eastern Colorado. Though most of the events themselves—and the towns in which they happen—are fictitious, the book offers a thoughtful look into the cowboy and ranching history of an oft-overlooked part of the Centennial State.

PLAINSONG BY KENT HARUF

Another novel set in eastern Colorado, *Plainsong* tells a captivating but rough-and-tumble story of love, lust, and loneliness in Colorado's remote eastern plains. The common theme binding characters together is a longing for something beyond their past, each handling their plight in a unique manner.

FIRE IN THE HOLE BY SYBIL DOWNING

The Colorado coalfield war of the early 1900s pitted a state militia against picketing civilians. In this novel, Downing uses fictitious happenings built around pinpointed historical references to capture the emotion and lasting strife caused by the conflict that rocked the state, from oil country to Denver.

ON THE ROAD BY JACK KEROUAC

Jack Kerouac and his crew gallivanted the streets of downtown Denver in the late 1940s and early 1950s, resulting in this book that has inspired a scene of nomadic beat writers with a knack for uncovering the city's true grit and character through their taste for wild living.

BLACKKKLANSMAN

Based on the memoir of Ron Stallworth, the 2018 Spike Lee film *BlacKkKlansman* enacts the real-life struggles of the Colorado Springs police department as they infiltrated the area's Ku Klux Klan chapter in the 1970s—led by a Black officer and his Jewish colleague posing as a member.

SOUTH PARK

The Colorado town of Fairplay inspired the fictitious mountain village of South Park in this adult comedy cartoon television series, starring a group of curious and foul-mouthed elementary schoolers. Stuck in a floating timeline, they offer sarcastic—but eerily relevant—takes on current events and societal taboos.

COMMUNITY

This cult classic television sitcom follows a crew of community college students in their quest to find themselves. In the ficitional Colorado town of Greendale, the show's main character is intent on his own premonitions but slowly realizes there's value in the world beyond the way he sees it.

BUTCH CASSIDY AND THE SUNDANCE KID

Professional train robbers Butch Cassidy and Harry Longabaugh live out their Wild West dreams and elude the law in this classic 1969 film. Along the way, the pair spend time hiding out in western Colorado; loosely based on a true story, the two are believed to have hidden vast sums of loot in the high country.

THE RANCH

Among its accomplishments, the Netflix television series *The Ranch* silenced any who doubted Ashton Kutcher could hack it on a Colorado cattle ranch. The show tells the story of a working ranch family and the estranged mother of Kutcher's character, the owner of a local saloon. Though most of the show was shot in California, opening and other exterior shots were filmed in Ouray, Naturita, and other parts of western Colorado.

MORK AND MINDY

This classic television series from the late 1970s and early 1980s starred Robin Williams as Mork, an extraterrestrial living in the attic of Mindy (Pam Dawber) in Boulder. On assignment to gather intelligence on Earth-bound humanity, Mork spends most of his time simply trying to comprehend what is happening around him.

THE HATEFUL EIGHT

This 2015 modern Western film, filmed outside of Telluride, tells a post-Civil War tale of a diverse cast of characters who all end up stuck in a remote haberdashery after a massive blizzard. None of them trust each other, and Wild West chaos ensues in a way that only Quentin Tarantino could dream up.

Chapter 2

TRAVEL SMART

Updated by
Tim Wenger

★ **CAPITAL:**
Denver

POPULATION:
5.8 million

LANGUAGE:
English

$ CURRENCY:
U.S. Dollar

AREA CODES:
303, 719, 970, 720

EMERGENCIES:
911

DRIVING:
On the right side of the road

ELECTRICITY:
120-240 v/60 cycles; plugs have two or three rectangular prongs

TIME:
2 hours behind New York

WEB RESOURCES:
www.colorado.com
www.colorado.gov

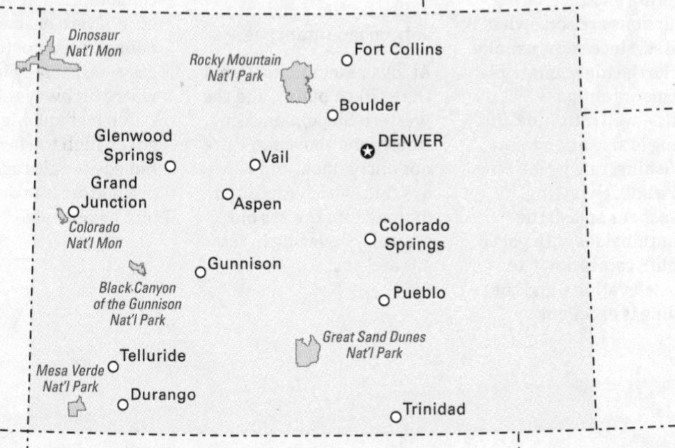

Know Before You Go

As one of the United States' most popular destinations, Colorado has dozens of notable attractions and can even be a little overwhelming for a first-time visitor. Here are some key tips to help you navigate your trip, whether it's your first time visiting or your twentieth.

WHEN TO GO

The Colorado you experience will depend on the season you visit. Ski resorts buzz from December to early April, especially around Christmas and Presidents' Day. Many of the same big resorts are popular summer destinations for downhill mountain biking, hiking, and scenic chairlift rides. Hotels book up early in summer, especially in July and August, and hikers crowd the backcountry.

If you don't mind capricious weather, rates drop and crowds tend to thin in spring and fall. Spring's excursions are somewhat limited, since snow usually blocks the high country—and mountain-pass roads—well into June. But spring is also a good time for fishing, rafting, birding, and wildlife-viewing. In fall, aspens splash the mountainsides with gold, wildlife comes down to lower elevations, and the angling is excellent.

WEATHER

Summer in the Rocky Mountains begins in late June. Days are warm, with highs often in the 80s; nighttime temperatures fall to the 40s and 50s. Afternoon thunderstorms are common over the higher peaks. Fall begins in September; winter creeps in during November, and deep snows arrive by December. Temperatures usually hover near freezing by day, thanks to the warm mountain sun, and drop overnight, occasionally reaching below zero. Winter tapers off in March, though snow lingers into April on valley bottoms and into July on mountain passes.

At lower elevations (Denver, the eastern plains, and the Western Slope), summertime highs above 100°F are not uncommon, and winters are cold, with highs often dipping into the 20s but typically hovering in the 30s and 40s.

ADJUSTING TO THE ALTITUDE

With a mean elevation of 6,800 feet above sea level, Colorado has the highest average altitude of any U.S. state. The three things to consider with high-altitude travel are altitude sickness, dehydration, and sunburn. If you are coming from sea level and plan to visit the mountains, it's worth taking a day or two in Denver or another lower-elevation area to acclimate. Either way, take it easier than usual. Drink plenty of water and avoid alcohol. Always wear sunscreen and protective clothing. Sunglasses and a hat also are must-haves at higher elevation.

If you experience altitude sickness, you may feel dizzy and weak and find yourself breathing heavily—signs that the thin mountain air isn't giving you your accustomed dose of oxygen. Take it easy, and rest often for a few days until you're acclimatized. Throughout your stay, drink plenty of water and watch your alcohol consumption. If you experience severe headaches and nausea, see a doctor. It's easy—especially in a state where highways climb to 11,000 feet and higher—to go too high too fast. The remedy for altitude-related discomfort is to descend into heavier air.

SKI RESORTS WITHOUT THE SNOW

Colorado's most popular mountain resorts offer more adventures in the summer than in winter. At resorts like Copper Mountain and Steamboat, alpine coasters wind down the mountainside and provide even more thrill for the buck than the traditional alpine slide. Kids enjoy rock-climbing walls and trampolines, and families make their way through enjoyable Frisbee and minigolf courses. But no mountain town does summer quite like Telluride, where festivals and scenic golf courses (where your drive sails a good deal longer in the thin air) complement resort experiences. You'll feel like a true "mountain bum" as you take the gondola from downtown Telluride up into Mountain Village, where more dining, trailheads, and family-friendly activities await.

LAND OF THE LOST

Colorado definitely has a thing for dinosaurs—no surprise, considering that the state sits on prime dino real estate, with plenty of sandstone and shale perfect for preservation. Dinosaur Ridge, close to Morrison, features a trail where you can see, touch, and photograph Jurassic-period bones and Cretaceous footprints. Both the Denver Museum of Nature & Science and the University of Colorado Museum of Natural History have collections of fossil specimens. Other attractions, such as the Denver Botanic Gardens and Red Rocks Amphitheatre, offer regular dino-theme events. There's even a town called Dinosaur, which sits near Dinosaur National Monument in the northwest part of the state. Parfet Prehistoric Preserve east of Golden and Picketwire Canyonlands south of La Junta have hiking trails with extensive sets of dinosaur tracks.

HIKING SAFETY

There are few real hazards to hiking, but a little preparedness goes a long way. Route out your hike beforehand, and know your limits—make sure the terrain you are about to embark on does not exceed your abilities. It's a good idea to check the elevation change on a trail before you set out—a 1-mile trail might sound easy, until you realize how steep it is—and be careful not to get caught on exposed trails at elevation during afternoon thunderstorms in summer. As a general rule, avoid open terrain above treeline if it appears a storm is moving in. Bring layers of clothing to accommodate changing weather, and always carry enough drinking water. Make sure someone knows where you're going and when to expect your return.

SMOKING AND MARIJUANA LAWS

Cigarette smoking is prohibited in Colorado's public places, including restaurants and bars, but since January 2014, Colorado has allowed the legalized sale, possession, cultivation, and use of recreational marijuana for persons 21 years of age and older. It is important to note that the law varies between residents and visitors, and statutes are subject to change by the year. The industry is highly regulated and taxed by the state government, but certain municipalities statewide have their own local ordinances banning the sale of marijuana outside of prior medicinal laws that date back to 2000.

Retail marijuana must be purchased at authorized dispensaries, which are available in most major cities and towns, but not all outlets provide both recreational and medicinal marijuana. All use, be it smoked or consumed in edibles like drinks or candies, must take place in private residences or in the increasingly popular "420-friendly" hotels or other rentals. It is prohibited to smoke or consume marijuana in any public space. Consumption in motor vehicles or public transportation is also illegal. When in doubt, do your research before partaking. Be aware that transporting marijuana through airports or neighboring states currently remains a federal crime.

Getting Here and Around

Denver is Colorado's hub; the state's two major interstates, I–25 and I–70, intersect here, and most of the state's population lives within a one- or two-hour drive of the city. The high plains expand to the east from Denver, and the western edge of the metro area ends at the foothills of the Rocky Mountains. A corridor of cities along I–25 parallels the foothills from Fort Collins to Pueblo, and the most lonely stretches of highway are in the eastern portion of the state on the plains. Although air, rail, and bus service connects Denver to many smaller cities and towns, a car is the most practical way to explore the state.

Air

It takes about two hours to fly to Denver from Los Angeles or Dallas, and 2½ hours from Chicago. From New York and Boston the flight is about 4½ hours. If you'll be checking skis, arrive at the airport earlier than normal.

AIRPORTS

The major air gateway to the Colorado Rockies is Denver International Airport (DEN), usually referred to by its nickname, DIA. It's about 25 miles northeast of downtown Denver and 45 miles from Boulder. Flights to smaller resort-town airports generally connect through it. Inclement weather, fairly common in winter, occasionally delays or cancels flights. In recent years, the airport has expanded its restaurant offerings to include higher-end spots like Elway's steak house and the Denver Chophouse, but also includes more casual fare. The Westin Hotel at DIA is adjacent to the main concourse, with additional hotel options 7 miles west.

Colorado Springs Airport (COS) has direct flights from many major cities and is slightly less subject to bad winter storms than Denver. The airport is sometimes still open when bad weather closes other airports (especially those in the ski towns). Some of the major airlines and their subsidiaries serve communities around the state: Grand Junction (GJT), Durango (DRO), Steamboat Springs (HDN), Gunnison–Crested Butte (GUC), Montrose (MTJ), Telluride (TEX), Aspen (ASE), and Vail (EGE).

GROUND TRANSPORTATION

If you are driving, the best route from Denver International Airport to Denver, the ski resorts, or the mountains is to drive west on I–70. If coming from south Denver, bypass some traffic by using the E–470 tollway, which you can access west of the airport. It connects to I–25 both south and north of Denver. When flying into Colorado Springs, take I–25 north and south. Vail, Aspen, Telluride, and the surrounding towns are accessible on Highway 24 without going through Denver.

RTD, the city's public transit, runs a commuter train from the airport to Union Station in the heart of downtown. The train picks up just outside the main terminal underneath the Westin Hotel, with departures running every 15 minutes during busy times and every half hour otherwise. Visit their booth in the main terminal for destinations, times, and tickets ($10.50 per person). There are taxis and various private airport shuttles to cities along the Front Range from the airport, and some offer door-to-door service. Many hotels and ski resorts have their own buses; check with your lodging or ski resort to see if they offer service. The Ground Transportation Information Center is on the fifth level of the main terminal, and can direct travelers to companies' service counters.

FLIGHTS

Denver International Airport (DEN) has direct flights from most major U.S. cities, as well as quite a few smaller ones, especially in the West. A few international carriers serve Denver with nonstop flights from London, England; Frankfurt, Germany; Tokyo, Japan; Reykjavik, Iceland; as well as Canadian cities like Vancouver, Toronto, and Montréal. United Airlines, Southwest Airlines, and Frontier Airlines (based in Colorado) are Denver's largest carriers, with the most flights and the longest list of destinations. Colorado Springs is served by Allegiant Airlines as well as by most major domestic airlines. United Express and Great Lakes Airlines connect Denver with smaller cities and ski resorts within Colorado.

Bus

Traveling by bus within the Denver–Boulder region is fairly easy with RTD, because the coverage of the area is dense and most routes are not too circuitous. The free 16th Street MallRide and the light-rail routes within Denver make travel to and from downtown attractions easy.

Bustang, an intercity coach service run by the Colorado Department of Transportation, connects Denver with cities across the state including Grand Junction, Colorado Springs, and Durango. It also serves the mountain corridor along I–70 to connect passengers with local bus services to ski resorts and lodging.

Mountain Metropolitan Transit serves the Colorado Springs area. Epic Mountain Express offers both shared-ride shuttles and private-car airport services from Denver International Airport and Eagle County Regional Airport.

Car

Car travel within the urban corridor north and south of Denver can be congested, particularly weekday mornings and afternoons. Weekends, too, can have quite a bit of traffic, particularly along I–70 between Denver and the high mountains. Heavy traffic is not limited to ski season or bad weather. It is nearly a matter of course now for eastbound I–70 to be heavily congested on Sunday afternoons. If you are returning to Denver International Airport for a Sunday afternoon or evening flight, allow more than enough time to reach the airport.

PARKING

On-street metered parking as well as by-the-hour garages and lots are fairly plentiful in larger cities. Meters take coins and credit cards almost everywhere.

ROAD CONDITIONS

Colorado offers some of the most spectacular vistas and challenging driving in the world. Roads range from multilane blacktop to barely graveled backcountry trails; from twisting switchbacks considerately marked with guardrails to primitive campgrounds with a lane so narrow that you must back up to the edge of a steep cliff to make a turn. Scenic routes and lookout points are clearly marked, enabling you to slow down and pull over to take in the views.

One of the more unpleasant sights along the highway is roadkill—animals struck by vehicles. Deer, elk, and moose may try to get to the other side of a road just as you come along, so watch out for wildlife on the highways. Exercise caution both for the sake of the animal in danger and your car, which could be totaled in a collision.

Getting Here and Around

WINTER DRIVING

Modern highways make mountain driving safe and generally trouble-free even in cold weather. Although winter driving can occasionally present real challenges, road maintenance is good and plowing is prompt. However, in mountain areas tire chains, studs, or snow tires are essential. If you're planning to drive into high elevations, be sure to check the weather forecast and call for road conditions beforehand. Even main highways can close. Between Dotsero and Morrison, Traction Law may be in effect in winter, which requires tires to have at least 3/16 inch of tread.

It's a good idea to carry an emergency kit and a cell phone, but be aware that the mountains can disrupt service. If you do get stalled by deep snow, do not leave your car. Wait for help, run the engine only if needed, and remember that assistance is never far away. Winter weather isn't confined to winter months in the high country (it's been known to snow in July), so be prepared year-round.

CAR RENTALS

Rates in most major cities run about $70 to $95 a day and $490 to $660 a week for an economy car with air-conditioning, automatic transmission, and unlimited mileage. Rates can vary greatly from company to company, so it's worth comparing online. Keep in mind that if you're venturing into the Rockies you'll need a little oomph in your engine to get over the passes. If you plan to explore any back roads, an SUV is the best bet, because it will have higher clearance. Unless you plan to do much mountain exploring, a four-wheel drive is usually needed only in winter.

To rent a car in Colorado you must be at least 25 years old and have a valid driver's license; most companies also require a major credit card. Some companies at certain locations set their minimum age at 21, and then add a daily surcharge. In Colorado, child-safety seats or booster seats are compulsory for children under five (with certain height and weight criteria).

You'll pay extra for child seats ($5–$13 a day), and usually for additional drivers (about $10 per day). When returning your car to Denver International Airport, allow 15 minutes (30 minutes during busy weekends and around the holidays) to return the vehicle and to ride the shuttle bus to the terminal.

 Train

Amtrak connects several stations in Colorado to both coasts and major American cities. The *California Zephyr* and the *Southwest Chief* pass three times per week with east- and west-bound trains that stop in Denver, Winter Park, Granby, Glenwood Springs, Grand Junction, and Trinidad. There are also several scenic narrow-gauge sightseeing railroads all over the state.

Essentials

Activities

The Colorado Rockies are one of America's greatest playgrounds. Information about Colorado's recreational areas and activities is provided in each regional section.

BICYCLING

Most streets in the larger cities have bike lanes and separated bike paths, and Denver, Boulder, Fort Collins, Durango, Crested Butte, and Colorado Springs are especially bike-friendly. Cities and biking organizations often offer free maps.

The Rockies are a favorite destination for bikers. Wide-open roads with great gains and losses in elevation test (and form) the stamina for road cyclists, while riders who prefer pedaling fat tires have plenty of mountain and desert trails to test their skills. Many cyclists travel between towns (or backcountry huts or campsites) in summer. Unmatched views often make it difficult to keep your eyes on the road.

BIKE RENTALS

Thanks to the popularity of the sport here, it's usually easy to find a place that rents bicycles, both entry-level and high-end. Bike shops are also a good bet for information on local rides and group tours.

SAFETY

On the road, watch for trucks and stay as close as possible to the side of the road, in single file. On the trail, ride within your limits and keep your eyes peeled for hikers and horses (both of which have the right of way), as well as dogs. Always wear a helmet and carry plenty of water.

FISHING

Fact: trout do not live in ugly places. Hence it is in Colorado, with unbridled beauty, towering pines, rippling mountain streams, and bottomless pools that blue-ribbon trout streams thrive, much as they were when Native American tribes, French fur trappers, and a few thousand miners first placed a muddy footprint along their banks.

MAKE THE MOST OF YOUR TIME

To make the best use of a limited vacation, consider hiring a guide. You could spend days locating a great fishing spot, learning the water currents and fish behavior, and determining what flies, lures, or bait the fish are following. A good guide will cut through the options, get you into fish, and turn your excursion into an adventure complete with a full creel.

If you're not inclined to fork over the $250-plus that most quality guides charge per day for two anglers and a boat, your best bet is a stop at a reputable fly shop. They'll shorten your learning curve, tell you where the fish are, what they're biting on, and whether you should be "skittering" your dry fly on top of the water or "dead-drifting" a nymph.

KNOW THE RULES

Fishing licenses, available at tackle shops and a variety of stores, are required in Colorado for anyone over the age of 16. Famed fisherman Lee Wolff wrote that "catching fish is a sport. Eating fish is not a sport." Most anglers practice "catch and release" to maintain productive fisheries and to protect native species. A few streams are considered "private," in that they are stocked by a local club; other rivers are fly-fishing or catch-and-release only.

Essentials

HIKING

Hiking is easily the least expensive and most accessible recreational pursuit. While gear such as trekking poles, expensive boots, and water filtration systems are recommended for "conquering Fourteeners" and multiday backpacking treks, all that's really essential are sturdy athletic shoes, water, and the desire to see the landscape under your own power.

Hiking in the Rockies is a three-season sport that extends as far into fall as you're willing to tromp through snow, though in the arid desert regions it's possible to hike year-round without snowshoes. One of the greatest aspects of this region is the wide range of hiking terrain, from high-alpine scrambles that require stamina to flowered meadows that invite a relaxed pace to confining slot canyons where flash floods are a real danger.

HORSEBACK RIDING

Horseback riding in the Rocky Mountains can mean a quick trot on a paved trail through craggy red rocks or a weeklong stay at a working dude ranch, where guests rise at dawn and herd cattle from one mountain range to another. Horse-pack trips are great ways to visit the backcountry, because horses can travel distances and carry supplies that would be impossible for hikers.

WHAT TO WEAR

Clothing requirements are minimal. A sturdy pair of pants, a wide-brim sun hat, and outerwear to protect against rain are about the only necessities, but a long-sleeve shirt is also recommended. Ask your outfitter for a list of things you'll need. June through August is the peak period for horse-pack trips.

CHOOSING A DUDE RANCH

Dude ranches fall roughly into two categories: working ranches and guest ranches. Working ranches, where you participate in such activities as roundups and cattle movements, sometimes require experienced horsemanship. Guest ranches offer a wide range of activities in addition to horseback riding, including fishing, four-wheeling, spa services, and cooking classes. At a typical dude ranch you stay in log cabins and are served family-style meals in a lodge or ranch house; some ranches now have upscale restaurants on-site, too. For winter, many ranches have snow-oriented amenities.

When choosing a ranch, consider the level of physical activity your group is after and whether the place is family-oriented or adults only. Check on the length-of-stay requirements and what gear, if any, you are expected to bring. Working ranches plan around the needs of the business, and thus often require full-week stays for a fixed price, while regular guest ranches operate more like hotels.

RAFTING

Rafting brings on emotions as varied as the calm induced by flat waters surrounded by stunning scenery and the thrill and excitement of charging a raging torrent of foam. Beginners and novices should use guides, but experienced rafters may rent watercraft.

CHOOSING A GUIDE

Seasoned outfitters know their routes and their waters as well as you know the road between home and work. Many guides offer multiday trips in which they do everything, including searing your steak and rolling out your sleeping bag. Waters are ranked from Class I (the easiest) to Class VI (think Niagara Falls). Ask your guide about the rating on your route before you book. Remember, ratings can vary greatly throughout the season due to runoff and weather events.

"Raft" can mean any number of things: an inflated raft in which passengers do the paddling; an inflated raft or wooden dory in which a licensed professional does the work; a motorized raft on which some oar work might be required. Be sure you know what kind of raft you'll be riding—or paddling—before booking.

Wear a swimsuit or shorts and sandals and bring along sunscreen and sunglasses. Outfitters are required to supply a life jacket for each passenger that must be worn. Most have moved to requiring helmets, as well. Early summer, when the water is highest, is the ideal time to raft, although many outfitters stretch the season, particularly on calmer routes.

SKIING AND SNOWBOARDING

The champagne powder of the Rocky Mountains can be a revelation for newcomers. Forget treacherous sheets of rock-hard ice, single-note hills where the bottom can be seen from the top, and mountains that offer only one kind of terrain from every angle. In the Rockies the snow builds up quickly, leaving a solid base that hangs tough all season, only to be layered upon by light, fluffy powder that holds an edge, ready to be groomed into rippling corduroy or left in giddy stashes along the sides and through the trees. Volkswagen-size moguls and half-pipe–studded terrain parks are the norm, not the special attractions.

Many resorts have a wide variety of terrain at all levels, from beginner (green circle) to expert (double black diamond). Turn yourself over to the rental shops, which provide expert help in planning your day and outfitting you with the right equipment. Renting is also a great chance for experienced skiers and snowboarders to sample the latest technology. **■TIP→ Ask about current "demos" available for rent. Demo gear is often of a higher quality than streamlined rental gear and will perform better across the mountain.**

LIFT TICKETS

Shop around for lift tickets before you leave home. Look for package deals, multiple-day passes, and online discounts. Many ski shops also offer discounted lift tickets. The traditional ski season runs from Thanksgiving until early April, with Christmas, New Year's, and the month of March being the busiest times at the resorts.

Skiing the Rockies means preparing for all kinds of weather, sometimes in the same day, because the high altitudes can start a day off sunny and bright but kick in a blizzard by afternoon. Layers help, as well as plenty of polypropylene to wick away sweat in the sun, and a water-resistant outer layer to keep off the powdery wetness that's sure to accumulate—especially if you're a beginner snowboarder certain to spend time on the ground. Must-haves: goggles and plenty of sunscreen, because the sun is closer than you think, and a helmet, because so are the trees.

Dining

Dining in Colorado is generally casual. Dinner hours are typically from 6 pm to 10 pm, but many small-town and rural eateries close by 9 pm. Authentic international food is hard to find outside the big cities and major resort towns.

MEALS AND MEALTIMES

Although you can find all types of cuisine in Colorado's major cities and resort towns, don't forget to try native dishes like trout, elk, and buffalo (the latter two have less fat than beef and are just as tasty). Steak is a mainstay in the Rocky

Essentials

Mountains. Chile verde, also known as green chile, is a popular menu item at Mexican restaurants in Colorado. Many restaurants serve vegetarian items, and some are exclusively vegetarian. Organic fruits and vegetables are also readily available.

RESERVATIONS AND DRESS

Regardless of where you are, it's a good idea to make a reservation if you can. In some places it's expected. We only mention them specifically when reservations are essential (as in, there's no other way you'll ever get a table) or when they are not accepted. For popular restaurants, book as far ahead as you can (often 30 days), and reconfirm as soon as you arrive. Large parties should always call ahead to check the reservations policy.

WINES, BEER, AND SPIRITS

The legal drinking age in Colorado is 21. Colorado liquor laws do not allow anyone to bring their own alcohol to restaurants. You'll find renowned breweries throughout Colorado, including, of course, the nation's second-largest brewer: MillerCoors. There are dozens of microbreweries in Denver, Colorado Springs, Boulder, and the resort towns—if you're a beer drinker, be sure to try some local brews. The wineries in the Grand Junction and Palisade area are earning increased acclaim for their fruit wines and Sauvignon Blancs, with more than two dozen establishments now open for tastings.

Ecotourism

Although neither the Bureau of Land Management (BLM) nor the National Park Service has designated any parts of Colorado as endangered ecosystems, many areas are open only to hikers; vehicles, mountain bikes, and horses are banned. It's wise to respect these closures, as well as the old adage **leave only footprints, take only pictures.** It is considered poor form to pick wildflowers while hiking, and it is illegal to pick columbine, the state flower of Colorado. Recycling is taken seriously throughout Colorado, and you will find yourself unpopular if you litter—which is also illegal—or fail to recycle your cans and bottles.

All archaeological artifacts, including rock etchings and paintings, are protected by federal law and must be left untouched and undisturbed.

Lodging

Accommodations in Colorado vary from the posh ski resorts in Vail, Aspen, and Telluride to basic chain hotels and independent motels. Dude and guest ranches often require a one-week stay, and the cost is all-inclusive. Bed-and-breakfasts can be found throughout the state, and there are ample listings on home share sites. Hotel rates peak during the height of the ski season, which generally runs from late November through March or April; although rates are high all season, they top out during Christmas week and in February and March. In summer months, a popular time for hiking and rafting, hotel rates are often half the winter price.

APARTMENT AND HOUSE RENTALS

Rental accommodations are quite popular in Colorado's ski resorts and mountain towns. Condominiums and luxurious vacation homes dominate the Vail Valley and other ski-oriented areas, but there are scads of cabins in smaller, summer-oriented towns in the Rockies and the Western Slope. Many towns and resort areas have rental agencies.

With a direct home exchange you stay in someone else's home while they stay in yours. Some outfits also deal with vacation homes, so you're not actually staying in someone's full-time residence, just their vacant weekend place.

BED-AND-BREAKFASTS

Charm is the long suit of these establishments, which often occupy a restored older building with some historical or architectural significance. They're generally small, with fewer than 20 rooms. Breakfast is usually included in the rates. The owners often manage the B&B, and you'll likely meet them and get to know them a bit. Breakfasts are usually substantial, with hot beverages, cold fruit juices, and a hot entrée. Bed & Breakfast Innkeepers of Colorado prints a free annual directory of its members.

GUEST RANCHES

If the thought of sitting around a campfire after a hard day on the range is your idea of a vacation, consider playing dude on a guest ranch. Wilderness-rimmed working ranches accept guests and encourage them to pitch in with chores and other ranch activities; you might even be able to participate in a cattle roundup. Most dude ranches don't require previous experience with horses. Luxurious resorts on the fringes of small cities offer swimming pools, tennis courts, and a lively roster of horse-related activities such as breakfast rides, moonlight rides, and all-day trail rides. Rafting, fishing, tubing, and other activities are usually available at both types of ranches. In winter, cross-country skiing and snowshoeing keep you busy.

Lodgings can run the gamut from charmingly rustic cabins to the kind of deluxe quarters you expect at a first-class hotel. Meals may be sophisticated or plain but hearty. Be sure to check with the ranch for a list of items you might be expected to bring. If you plan to do much riding, a couple of pairs of sturdy pants, boots, a wide-brim hat to shield you from the sun, and outerwear that protects from rain and cold should be packed. Nearly all dude ranches in Colorado offer all-inclusive packages: meals, lodging, and generally all activities. Weeklong stays cost between $1,300 and $4,000 per adult, depending on the ranch's amenities and activities.

Packing

For the most part, informality reigns in the Centennial State; jeans, sport shirts, and T-shirts fit in almost everywhere. No matter what your vacation plans are, don't forget to pack sunscreen, lip balm with SPF, sunglasses, and a cap or hat. The sunshine is intense at Colorado's altitude, and there are plenty of souvenirs available that you'll prefer over a sunburn.

Essentials

If you plan to spend much time outdoors, and certainly if you go in winter, choose clothing appropriate for cold and wet weather. Cotton clothing, including denim, can be uncomfortable when it gets wet or when the weather's cold. Better choices are clothing made of wool or any of a number of synthetics that provide warmth without bulk and maintain their insulating properties when wet. It's not a bad idea to save your shopping for when you arrive in Colorado, where you'll find a huge selection of suitable clothing and gear.

In summer you'll probably want to wear shorts during the day. Because early morning and night can be cool, particularly in the mountains, pack a sweater and a light jacket. For walks and hikes, you'll need sturdy footwear. Boots should have thick soles and plenty of ankle support; if your shoes are new and you plan to do a lot of hiking, break them in at home. Bring a day pack for short hikes, along with a canteen or water bottle, and don't forget rain gear, a hat, sunscreen, and insect repellent.

In winter, prepare for subzero temperatures with good boots, warm socks and liners, long underwear, a well-insulated jacket, and a warm hat and mittens. Layers are the best preparation for fluctuating temperatures.

Safety

Although Colorado is considered to be generally safe, travelers should take ordinary precautions—unfortunate incidents can happen anywhere. At your hotel, lock your valuables either in the hotel's safe or in the safe in your room, if one is available. Be aware of your surroundings, and keep your wallet and passport in a buttoned pocket, or keep your handbag in front of you where you can see it. At night, avoid dimly lighted areas as well as those where there are few people. Consider a taxi ride to your hotel if it is a long walk or you are alone.

Regardless of the outdoor activity or your level of skill, safety must come first. When hiking or taking part in any other outdoor activity, it's best (and often more fun) to go in pairs or small groups. If you do hike, cycle, kayak, or backcountry ski alone, it is essential that you tell someone where you are going and when you plan to return, whether it's a park ranger or the host of your B&B. Let them know, of course, when you've returned safely.

Many trails are at high altitudes, where oxygen is scarce. They're also frequently desolate. Hikers and bikers should carry emergency supplies in their backpacks. Proper equipment includes a flashlight, a compass, waterproof matches, a first-aid kit, a knife, a space blanket, and a light plastic tarp for shelter. Backcountry skiers should add a repair kit, a blanket, avalanche equipment including a beacon and probe, and a lightweight shovel to their lists. Always bring extra food and a canteen of water, as dehydration is a real danger at high altitudes. Never drink from streams or lakes, unless you boil the water first or purify it with tablets. Giardia, an intestinal parasite, may be present.

When in any park, give all animals their space. If you want to take a photograph, use a long lens rather than a long sneak to approach closely. Approaching an animal can cause stress and affect its ability to survive the sometimes brutal climate. In all cases, remember that animals have the right-of-way; this is their home, you are the visitor.

COVID-19

COVID-19 brought all travel to a virtual standstill in 2020, and interruptions to travel have continued into 2021. Although the illness is mild in most people, some experience severe and even life-threatening complications. Once travel started up again, albeit slowly and cautiously, travelers were asked to be particularly careful about hygiene and to avoid any unnecessary travel, especially if they are sick.

Older adults, especially those over 65, have a greater chance of having severe complications from COVID-19. The same is true for people with weaker immune systems or those living with some types of medical conditions, including diabetes, asthma, heart disease, cancer, HIV/AIDS, kidney disease, and liver disease.

Starting two weeks before a trip, anyone planning to travel should be on the lookout for some of the following symptoms: cough, fever, chills, trouble breathing, muscle pain, sore throat, new loss of smell or taste. If you experience any of these symptoms, you should not travel at all.

And to protect yourself during travel, do your best to avoid contact with people showing symptoms. Wash your hands often with soap and water. Limit your time in public places, and, when you are out and about, wear a face mask that covers your nose and mouth. Indeed, a mask may be required in some places, such as on an airplane or in a confined space like a theater, where you share the space with a lot of people.

You may wish to bring extra supplies, such as disinfecting wipes, hand sanitizer (12-ounce bottles were allowed in carry-on luggage at this writing), and a first-aid kit with a thermometer.

Given how abruptly travel was curtailed in March 2020, it is wise to consider protecting yourself by purchasing a travel insurance policy that will reimburse you for any cancellation costs related to COVID-19. Not all travel insurance policies protect against pandemic-related cancellations, so always read the fine print.

Visitor Information

Almost every town, county, and resort area has its own tourist office.

Great Itineraries

Denver, Boulder, and Rocky Mountain National Park, 7 Days

DAYS 1–3: DENVER

Denver is filled with folks who stopped to visit and never left. After a few days in the Mile High City and surrounding metro area it's easy to see why: Colorado's capital has a lot going on, including a thriving cultural scene, restaurants representing every ethnicity, plenty of sunshine, and outdoor options galore, all set beneath a stunning backdrop of snowcapped peaks.

After you've settled into your hotel, head downtown, or, if you're already staying there—always a good option to explore the city—make your way to Lower Downtown, or **LoDo.** The historic district is home to many of the city's famous brewpubs, art galleries, and **Coors Field,** as well as popular restaurants and some of the area's oldest architecture.

Hop on the free MallRide, the shuttle bus run by RTD, to head up to the 16th Street Mall, a pedestrian-friendly, shopping-oriented strip that runs through the center of downtown. From there you can walk to **Larimer Square** for more shopping and restaurants. You can also visit the **Denver Art Museum, Union Station, the History Colorado Center, the Colorado State Capitol, the Molly Brown House,** and the **U.S. Mint.**

Logistics: Light-rail is an excellent way to navigate the city. Vending machines at each station for the RTD Light Rail service show destinations and calculate your fare ($3–$5.25 depending on the number of zones crossed). Children under age five ride free when accompanied by a fare-paying adult. RTD buses also provide an excellent way to get around.

DAY 4: BOULDER

Boulder takes its fair share of ribbing for being a Birkenstock-wearing, tofu-eating, latter-day hippie kind of town, but the truth is that it is healthy, wealthy, and exceedingly popular. Stroll along the **Pearl Street Mall** and sample the excellent restaurants and shops, catching one of the dozens of street performers; or head just outside the city to tour **Celestial Seasonings,** the tea manufacturer; or to **Chautauqua Park** to hike in the shadow of the dramatic Flatiron Mountains. In winter, Eldora Mountain Resort is a 21-mile jaunt up a steep, switchback-laden road with no lift lines as payoff. The University of Colorado campus here means there is a high hip quotient in much of the nightlife.

Logistics: You can take the Flatiron Flyer bus to Boulder from Denver's Union Station, but it's just as easy to drive up U.S. 36 (one hour or less by car). If you're going to go beyond the Pearl Street Mall in Boulder, it's nice to have a car once you're there.

DAYS 5–7: ROCKY MOUNTAIN NATIONAL PARK

Rocky Mountain National Park (RMNP) is a year-round marvel, a park for every season: hiking in the summer, spotting elk in the fall, snowshoeing in winter, and snapping photos of wildflowers in spring. There are several hikes that shouldn't be missed in the park. For lovely scenery, opt for the one that goes from **Bear Lake to Emerald Lake.** There are some steep sections along the way, but the spectacular mountain views more than make up for it. Also not to be missed is a drive along **Trail Ridge Road,** the world's highest continuous paved highway. You'll enjoy awesome views of waterfalls, lakes, mountain vistas, glaciers, and emerald meadows. Give yourself four hours to complete the drive, and check the

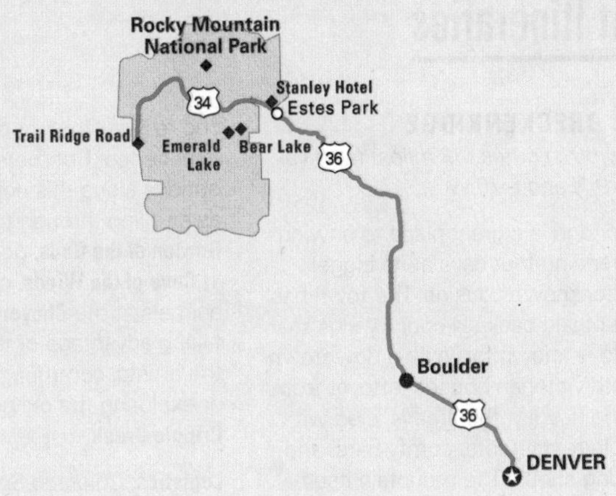

weather conditions before you start. Trail Ridge Road is closed in winter.

There are five campgrounds in the park, but those looking for more comfort should opt for **Estes Park.** This picturesque town is the gateway to RMNP and a worthwhile destination itself, a small town swelling to a large one with the tourists who flock to its Western-theme shops and art galleries. The **Stanley Hotel,** the inspiration for Stephen King's novel *The Shining,* provides great lodging in a historic setting.

Logistics: Estes Park is a hop-skip from Denver and Boulder, about 65 miles northwest of Denver via I–25 and then CO–66 and U.S. 36. To get to RMNP, simply take U.S. 34 or U.S. 36 into the park (a 15-minute drive).

Skiing the Rockies, 5 Days

With its champagne-powder runs and wide variety of alpine terrain, Colorado is a winter paradise. In less than a week, you can ski some of the most iconic resorts in the state.

DAYS 1–2: ASPEN

World-class dining, upscale shopping, and possible celebrity sightings await in Aspen, along with some of the best skiing in North America. Aspen's four ski areas—**Aspen Highlands, Aspen Mountain, Buttermilk,** and **Snowmass**—all have amazing runs through fluffy champagne powder. After an afternoon of whooshing down the slopes, visit some of the fabled restaurants and nightlife options in downtown Aspen, or relax at a hotel spa.

DAYS 3–4: VAIL VALLEY

Roughly 2 hours (102 miles) from Aspen via I–70 W and CO–82 E

The Bavarian-themed village at the base of **Vail Mountain** offers as much as the resorts in the Alps. The back side of the mountain, with its thrilling series of bowls, delivers enough glades and bumps to challenge even the most dedicated skier. But beginners and moderate skiers need not worry; the front side of Vail Mountain has plenty of cruisers to satisfy skiers of all levels. The free shuttle in town runs every 15 minutes and links the three base villages. At night, you can wander along the quaint cobbled streets and pop into the European-style cafés.

Great Itineraries

DAY 5: BRECKENRIDGE

Roughly 50 minutes (38 miles) from Vail via CO–9 N and I–70 W

Breckenridge is a great place to unwind after spending four days at its bigger and better-known cousins. The town has the sort of laid-back ski-country vibe that Colorado is known for. With a downtown filled with Victorian houses leftover from its mining heyday, the area is filled with affordable restaurants, comfy bars, and interesting shops. The mountain itself is one of the larger ski areas in America with five separate peaks offering a variety of terrain from beginner to expert.

Exploring Southwestern Colorado, 10 Days

The southwest corner of Colorado is a study in contrasts. From the soaring peaks of the Sangre de Cristo Mountains to the serene beauty of the San Luis Valley, it is a region that offers a multitude of experiences. It is less crowded than the more popular areas of the state, with more wide-open spaces. As you head across the numerous mountain passes, the gradual changes in fauna and terrain are awe-inspiring.

DAYS 1–2: DENVER

Spend a few days acclimating to the altitude change in Denver, visiting the city's top-notch museums. In preparation for your journey, pop into the massive **REI** flagship store in the Central Platte Valley neighborhood.

DAYS 3–4: COLORADO SPRINGS AND NEARBY

The Colorado Springs area is dominated by 14,115-foot **Pikes Peak**—the inspiration for the song "America the Beautiful"—and getting to its summit, whether by cog railway, foot, or car, is a memorable experience. But there are other worthy options along this popular corridor, such as strolling through the red rocks of the **Garden of the Gods,** peeking at the tunnel in **Cave of the Winds,** checking out the animals at the **Cheyenne Mountain Zoo,** taking advantage of the healing vibes in the artists' community at **Manitou Springs,** or exploring the old gold-mining town of **Cripple Creek.**

Logistics: Colorado Springs is 70 miles south of Denver on I–25. You'll enjoy mountain views on most of the drive; Pikes Peak is visible on clear days. Take U.S. 24 west from I–25 to reach Manitou Springs; follow CO–67 south from U.S. 24 west to visit Cripple Creek.

DAY 5: SALIDA

Surrounded by the Collegiate Peaks, **Salida** is a good jumping-off point for the many outdoor activities available in this mountainous region. Salida is also a haven for artists who specialize in Western-oriented themes and grassroots sensibilities.

Logistics: Take CO–115 south from Colorado Springs to Canyon City; continue west on U.S. 50 toward Salida. As you head into Salida the Sangre de Christo Mountains offer stunning views.

DAY 6: BLACK CANYON OF THE GUNNISON NATIONAL PARK

From Salida head west on U.S. 50 toward Montrose, and then continue north on CO–347 to **Black Canyon of the Gunnison National Park.** The trip takes about 2½ hours. This national park offers sheer cliffs rising more than 2,000 feet above the river and stunning views that rival the Grand Canyon. Stay overnight in nearby **Montrose,** about 15 miles west of the park.

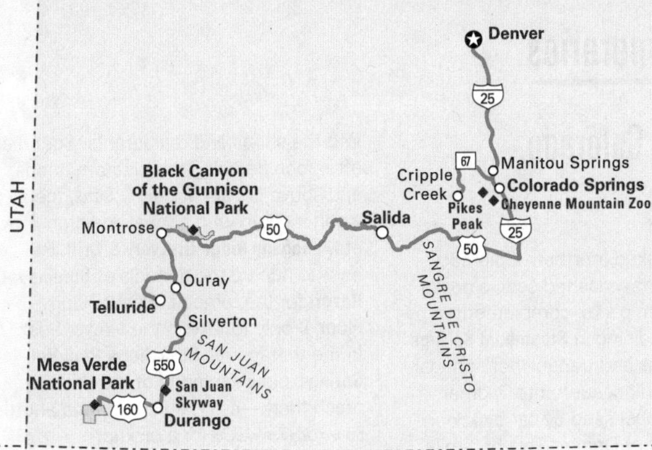

DAYS 7–8: TELLURIDE AND NEARBY

Telluride, though famous for its film and bluegrass festivals, presents a less glitzy face than other ski resorts like Aspen and Vail, but is still well worth the visit. The **San Juan Skyway,** a 236-mile loop that connects Durango, Telluride, Ouray, and Silverton, is a gloriously scenic drive that winds you through mountains, alpine forests, and wildflower meadows.

Logistics: To get to Telluride from Montrose head south on U.S. 550 to Ridgeway, continue west on CO–62 toward Placerville, and then head south on CO–145 to Telluride. The entire journey is roughly 66 miles and takes about 90 minutes.

DAY 9: MESA VERDE NATIONAL PARK

Mesa Verde National Park safeguards the 1,400-year-old cliff dwellings of the Ancestral Pueblo. Take a ranger-led tour to the primary cliff-dwelling sites like the **Balcony House, Cliff Palace,** and **Spruce Tree House.** Make time for the **Chapin Mesa Archaeological Museum,** where you can learn the history of the Ancestral Pueblo culture. Afterward, drive to Durango to spend the night.

Logistics: Mesa Verde is a 1½-hour drive from Telluride, heading south on CO–145. From Mesa Verde head east on U.S. 160 toward Durango, an approximately one-hour drive.

DAY 10: DURANGO

Durango is an Old West mining town that has retained much of its Victorian charm. Mountain bikers make it a mission to try their mettle on the tough trails surrounding the town; in winter, the **Purgatory at Durango Mountain Resort** routinely has deep powder and short lift lines.

Logistics: To get back to Denver head east from Durango on U.S. 160 until you get to Walsenburg (approximately four hours); then head north on I–25 to Denver. Telluride and Durango have airports with limited service from major carriers.

Great Itineraries

Northern Colorado, 5-7 days

Often overlooked, northern Colorado is a gem of snow-dashed scenic peaks and lush green parks, complemented by farm-to-table dining in **Steamboat Springs** and **Fort Collins** and tranquil hot springs. The area is a dinosaur hunter's dream, and is easily accessed by car by taking I–70 west out of Denver. This 550-mile round-trip journey offers something for all ages and interests, and provides the perfect opportunity to relax. Without the crowds, there's no need to rush between attractions or hit the road first thing in the morning.

DAYS 1–2: DINOSAUR NATIONAL MONUMENT

Dinosaur National Monument celebrates Colorado's history as a thriving hub for dinosaurs. From the main entrance of U.S. 40, Harpers Corner Road provides a mellow and scenic cruise through the monument, offering gorgeous views of the canyon and both the Yampa and Green rivers that wind their way through the park. There are many points to stop for a quick hike and picnic along the way. Be sure to grab a map at the entrance and don't forget to pack a lunch.

Logistics: To get to the park, take I–70 to Silverthorne and head north on CO–9 to U.S. 40 West. Allow two days to do the drive, with a night in Steamboat Springs breaking it up.

DAYS 3–4: STEAMBOAT SPRINGS

Steamboat Springs is everything you picture a Colorado mountain town to be: rustic and charming but lively in the summer and winter seasons, with a dose of Old West flair provided by the surrounding ranching community. Stay downtown and walk along Lincoln Avenue, ducking into the shops and restaurants. Spend an afternoon perusing the western goods and souvenirs at **FM Light & Sons,** then wash it down with a meal and craft brew at **Mahogany Ridge Brewery & Grill.** Be sure to ride up the gondola at **Steamboat Resort** for the famous Sunset Happy Hour, if only to take in the views. Soak in the therapeutic **Strawberry Park Hot Springs,** but be mindful of the drive to reach them—call The Hot Springs Shuttle ☎ *970/879–4688* for a pickup.

Logistics: Plan to spend two nights in Steamboat Springs so as not to rush yourself. The drive from there to Fort Collins is nothing short of an event in itself. Along CO–14, you'll pass through State Forest State Park and the Arapahoe & Roosevelt National Park before dropping into the jagged walls of the Poudre Canyon on the way into town, a trip that takes about 3½ hours.

DAYS 5–6: FORT COLLINS

Like Boulder, Fort Collins is a thriving college town, home to the Colorado State University campus, but the city offers a number of under-the-radar treasures that are unique to its northern Colorado location. Indie art and music abound in venues and galleries downtown, often situated next to bustling restaurants and pubs where diners prefer the cool air of outdoor patios. This town is as bike-crazy as they come, and you can join the fun by renting a bike and pedaling through the triangular **Old Town** and arts district. Sample a Fat Tire Amber Ale at the famous **New Belgium Brewery** or mosey through the storefronts and galleries, having dinner at one of the many restaurants along the downtown strip.

Logistics: Fort Collins is about 1½ hours north of Denver. Take I–25 south straight into downtown Denver, but turn off at the E–470 toll road in Thornton if heading to the airport.

On the Calendar

Year-Round

First Friday Art Walk. Anchored by the Arts District on Santa Fe, Denver's three arts districts pull out all stops for a monthly celebration complete with music, food trucks, and street performers. ✉ *Denver* ☎ *720/773–ADSF* 🌐 *www.denversartdistrict.org/first-friday*.

Jazz Aspen Snowmass. Top names from jazz to rock perform outdoors in the beautiful Roaring Fork Valley. ✉ *Aspen* ☎ *970/920–4996* 🌐 *www.jazzaspensnowmass.org*.

Summer

Bravo! Vail Valley Music Festival. This festival brings national orchestras to venues around the valley from mid-June through early August. ✉ *Vail* ☎ *877/812–5700* 🌐 *www.bravovail.org*.

Telluride Film Festival. You'll find movie premieres, workshops, and the chance to rub elbows with celebs at this film fest that typically occurs in late August and early September. ✉ *Telluride* ☎ *510/665–9494* 🌐 *www.telluridefilmfestival.org*.

Vail Dance Festival. For two weeks every summer, all types of dance are presented in this series at the beautiful Vilar Center in Beaver Creek or the Gerald R. Ford Amphitheater in Vail. ✉ *Vail* ☎ *888/920–2787* 🌐 *www.vaildance.org*.

Fall

Colorado Mountain Winefest. This event brings together local wines and spirits alongside live music, food, and craft vendors in Palisade's enormous Riverbend Park on a Sunday in mid-September. 🌐 *www.coloradowinefest.com*.

Chili and Frijoles Throwback Fest. This a weekend celebration of the chili pepper takes place in Pueblo, Colorado each fall in late September. The event features food and drink vendors, music, and of course, plenty of green chili. 🌐 *www.festival.pueblochamber.org*.

Great American Beer Festival. Since 1982, Denver's Great American Beer Festival has been the country's leading event showcasing diverse craft brews from across the United States. Part tasting event and part private competition, it brings together brewers and drinkers every fall for the chance to sample 4,000 different beers from over 800 of the nation's finest breweries. ☎ *303/447–0816* 🌐 *www.greatamericanbeerfestival.com*.

Telluride Blues and Brews. A variety of musical genres complement craft beers and artists at this September tradition. ✉ *Telluride* ☎ *970/728–8037* 🌐 *www.tellurideblues.com*.

Winter

National Western Stock Show. For 16 days each January, Denver hosts the world's largest stock show, with over 15,000 animals, bull riders, horse shows, livestock competitions, and more. Considered the Super Bowl of livestock shows, it's the perfect introduction to rodeo life, exploring the region's connection to agriculture and agribusiness. ✉ *4655 Humboldt St., Denver* ☎ *303/296–6977* 🌐 *www.nationalwestern.com*.

Best Tours

Aspen Expeditions. This company leads outdoor adventures from guided day hikes to multiday mountain climbing summits. Their local focus is on the central mountains in and around Aspen and the greater Roaring Fork Valley. ✉ *133 Prospector Rd., Aspen* ☎ *970/925–7625* 🌐 *www.aspenexpeditions.com* 🎫 *From $230.*

Culinary Connectors. Offering Denver-based culinary tours of the city's best restaurants, cafés, and craft-beer havens, each tour with Culinary Connectors is a private event that must be scheduled in advance. ☎ *303/495–5487* 🌐 *www.culinaryconnectors.com* 🎫 *From $34.*

Denver Free Walking Tours. Guided walking tours through downtown Denver from the State Capitol building are offered by Denver Free Walking Tours as are audio guides for self-guided walking tours. Tours meet daily in summer and weekends in winter. ☎ *720/372–3849* 🌐 *www.denverfreewalkingtours.com.*

Denver Microbrew Tour. This company offers guided historical walking tours of downtown breweries, paired with cultural highlights including Denver history and graffiti and public art. ☎ *303/578–9548* 🌐 *www.denvermicrobrewtour.com* 🎫 *From $50.*

Lizard Head Cycling Guides. This company leads both road and mountain bike tours throughout Colorado, ranging from day rides to multiday expeditions. ☎ *970/728–5891* 🌐 *www.lizardheadcyclingguides.com.*

OARS. For multiday rafting trips on the Yampa and Green rivers and hiking vacations in Chaco Canyon, Mesa Verde National Park, Ute Mountain Tribal Park, and National Bridges Monument, try OARS. ☎ *800/346–6277* 🌐 *www.oars.com/colorado.*

Pali-Tours. This company takes visitors wine tasting through the greater Palisade region. Both standard and customized tours are available, and they can also include mountain biking or rafting add-ons. ☎ *970/697–8134* 🌐 *www.pali-tours.com.*

Victor Emanuel Nature Tours. With several multiday Colorado-based birding tours in the spring and summer that include accommodations and meals, Victor Emanuel Nature Tours is the company for bird-lovers. ☎ *512/328–5221, 800/328–8368* 🌐 *www.ventbird.com* 🎫 *From $3,895.*

Did You Know?

The Denver Botanic Gardens features different themed gardens, showcasing flora from several different regions.

Contacts

Activities

BICYCLING

CONTACTS Bicycle Colorado. ☎ *303/417–1544* 🌐 *www.bicyclecolorado.org.*

DUDE RANCHES

CONTACTS Colorado Dude Ranch Association. 🌐 *www.coloradoranch.com.*

FISHING

CONTACTS Colorado Parks and Wildlife. ☎ *303/297–1192* 🌐 *cpw.state.co.us.*

HIKING

CONTACTS Colorado Mountain Club. 🌐 *www.cmc.org.*

RAFTING

CONTACTS Colorado River Outfitters Association. ☎ *720/260–4135* 🌐 *www.croa.org.*

SKIING AND SNOWBOARDING

CONTACTS Colorado Ski Country USA. ☎ *303/825–7669* 🌐 *www.coloradoski.com.*

Air

AIRPORT INFORMATION

Colorado Springs Airport (COS). ☎ *719/550–1900* 🌐 *www.coloradosprings.gov/flycos.* **Denver International Airport (DEN).** ☎ *800/247–2336* 🌐 *www.flydenver.com.*

Bus

BUS INFORMATION

Bustang. ☎ *800/900–3011* 🌐 *www.ridebustang.com.* **Epic Mountain Express.** ☎ *970/754–7433* 🌐 *www.epicmountainexpress.com.* **Mountain Metropolitan Transit.** ☎ *719/385–7433* 🌐 *coloradosprings.gov/mountain-metro.* **RTD.** ☎ *303/299–6000* 🌐 *www.rtd-denver.com.*

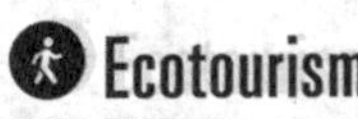

Ecotourism

CONTACTS National Park Reservation Service. ☎ *877/444–6777* 🌐 *www.recreation.gov.* **U.S. Bureau of Land Management.** ☎ *303/239–3600* 🌐 *www.blm.gov/co.*

Lodging

APARTMENT AND HOUSE RENTALS

LOCAL RENTAL AGENCIES Colorado Mountain Cabins & Vacation Home Rentals. ☎ *719/636–5147, 866/425–4974* 🌐 *www.coloradomountaincabins.com.* **Colorado Vacation Directory.** ☎ *303/499–9343, 888/222–4641* 🌐 *www.coloradodirectory.com.*

BED-AND-BREAKFASTS

RESERVATION SERVICES Bed & Breakfast Innkeepers of Colorado. 🌐 *www.innsofcolorado.org.*

GUEST RANCHES

INFORMATION Colorado Dude & Guest Ranch Association. ☎ *866/942–3472* 🌐 *www.coloradoranch.com.*

Train

INFORMATION Amtrak. ☎ *800/872–7245* 🌐 *www.amtrak.com.*

Visitor Information

CONTACT Colorado Tourism Office. ☎ *800/265–6723* 🌐 *www.colorado.com.*

Chapter 3

DENVER

Updated by
Kyle Wagner

Sights ★★★★★ | Restaurants ★★★★★ | Hotels ★★★★★ | Shopping ★★★★☆ | Nightlife ★★★★☆

WELCOME TO DENVER

TOP REASONS TO GO

★ **Denver Art Museum:** Visitors are treated to Asian, pre-Columbian, and Spanish Colonial works along with a world-famous collection of Native American pieces.

★ **Denver Botanic Gardens:** Creatively arranged displays of more than 15,000 plant species from around the world draw garden enthusiasts year-round.

★ **Larimer Square:** Specialty stores, superior people-watching, and some of the city's top restaurants and nightlife bring tourists and locals alike to the city's oldest area.

★ **LoDo:** Lower downtown's appeal lies in its proximity to Coors Field, the innovative and multi-use Union Station, and the convenient and free 16th Street Mall shuttle. Shops and galleries are busy during the day, and it's also a hot spot at night.

★ **Red Rocks Park and Amphitheatre:** Even if you aren't attending a concert, the awe-inspiring red rocks of this formation-turned-venue are worth a look, and there are hiking trails nearby.

1 Central Business District. The true center of Denver's downtown.

2 LoDo and Five Points. The city's cultural mecca, with its highest concentration of restaurants and bars.

3 Capitol Hill and Civic Center. A charming area with the State Capitol building and the Golden Triangle Arts district at its center.

4 City Park and Around. A 330-acre oasis that also serves as a jumping-off point for the Denver Zoo and the Denver Museum of Nature & Science.

5 Greater Denver. A collection of neighborhoods east, west, north, and south of the city center, including Cherry Creek and the Central Platte Valley.

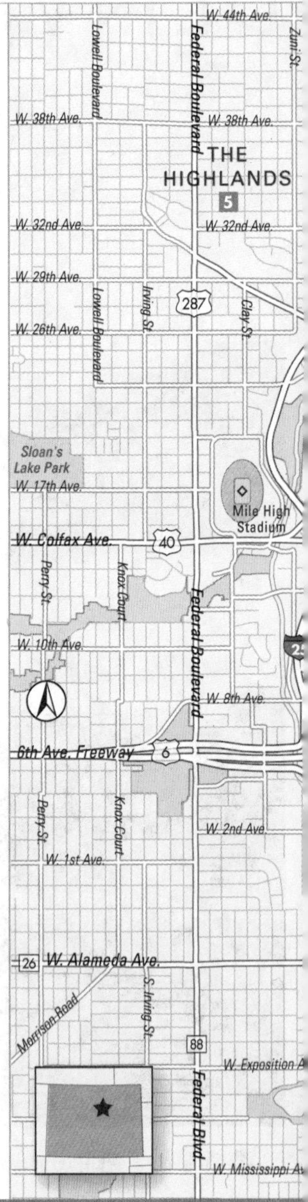

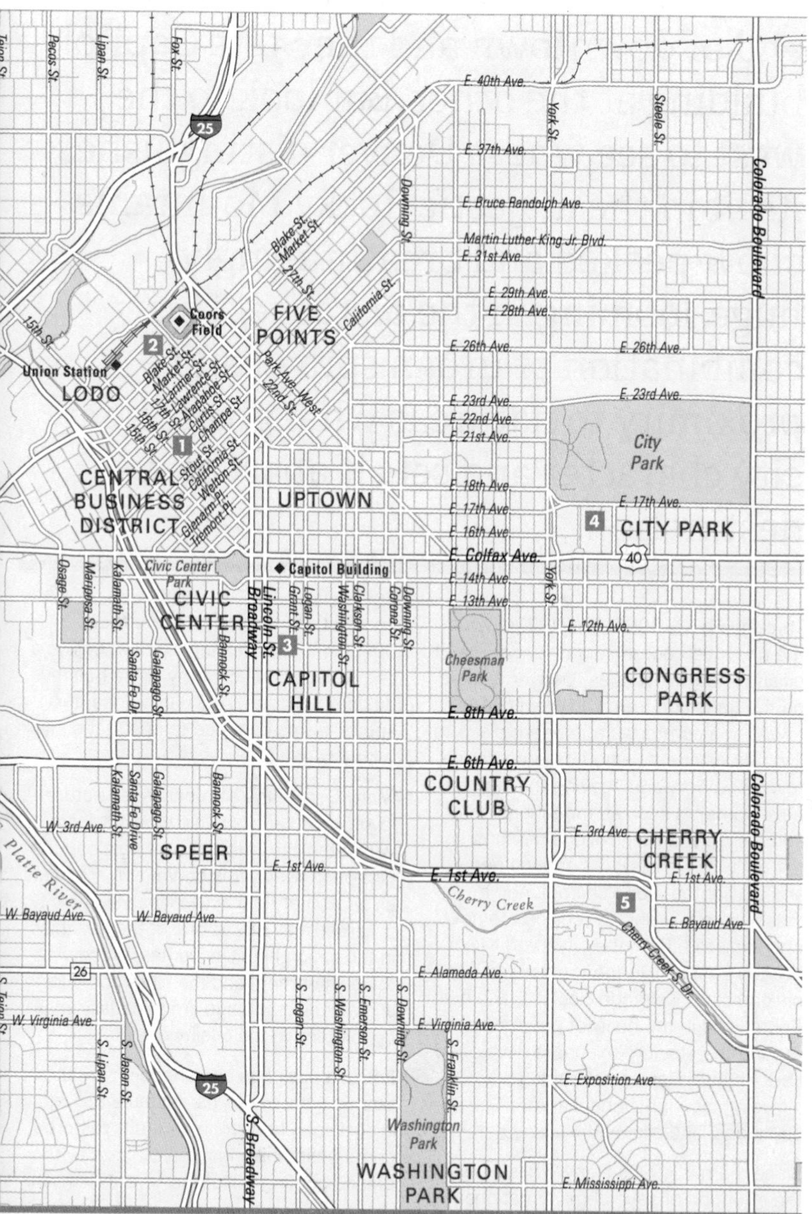
Pecos St.
Lipan St.
Fox St.
E. 40th Ave.
York St.
Steele St.
E. 37th Ave.
Colorado Boulevard
Downing St.
E. Bruce Randolph Ave.
Blake St.
Market St.
Martin Luther King Jr. Blvd.
E. 31st Ave.
27th St.
California St.
E. 29th Ave.
E. 28th Ave.
FIVE POINTS
15th St.
Coors Field
E. 26th Ave.
E. 26th Ave.
Union Station
LODO
Blake St.
Market St.
Larimer St.
Lawrence St.
17th St.
Arapahoe St.
Curtis St.
Champa St.
16th St.
15th St.
Park Ave. West
22nd St.
E. 23rd Ave.
E. 22nd Ave.
E. 21st Ave.
E. 23rd Ave.
City Park
CENTRAL BUSINESS DISTRICT
Stout St.
California St.
Welton St.
Glenarm Pl.
Tremont Pl.
UPTOWN
E. 18th Ave.
E. 17th Ave.
E. 16th Ave.
E. 17th Ave.
CITY PARK
E. Colfax Ave.
Civic Center Park
Capitol Building
Osage St.
Mariposa St.
Kalamath St.
CIVIC CENTER
Lincoln St.
Broadway
Grant St.
Logan St.
Washington St.
Clarkson St.
Corona St.
Downing St.
E. 14th Ave.
E. 13th Ave.
York St.
E. 12th Ave.
Santa Fe Dr.
Galapago St.
Bannock St.
CAPITOL HILL
Cheesman Park
CONGRESS PARK
E. 8th Ave.
E. 6th Ave.
COUNTRY CLUB
Kalamath St.
Santa Fe Drive
Galapago St.
Bannock St.
W. 3rd Ave.
SPEER
E. 3rd Ave.
CHERRY CREEK
Platte River
E. 1st Ave.
E. 1st Ave.
E. 1st Ave.
Cherry Creek
W. Bayaud Ave.
W. Bayaud Ave.
E. Bayaud Ave.
Cherry Creek S. Dr.
26
E. Alameda Ave.
S. Logan St.
S. Washington St.
S. Emerson St.
S. Downing St.
W. Virginia Ave.
E. Virginia Ave.
S. Franklin St.
S. Lipan St.
S. Jason St.
25
E. Exposition Ave.
S. Broadway
Washington Park
WASHINGTON PARK
E. Mississippi Ave.

You can tell from its skyline alone that Denver is a major metropolis, with a Major League Baseball stadium at one end of downtown and the State Capitol building at the other. But look to the west to see where Denver distinguishes itself in the majestic Rocky Mountains, snow-peaked and breathtakingly huge, looming in the distance. This combination of urban sprawl and proximity to nature is what gives the city character and sets it apart as a destination.

Throughout the 1960s and 1970s, when the city mushroomed on a huge surge of oil and energy revenues, Denver worked on the transition from Old West "cow town" to a comfortable, modern place to live. The city demolished its large downtown Skid Row area, paving the way for developments such as the Tabor Center and the Auraria multicollege campus. In the early 1990s mayors Federico Peña and Wellington Webb championed a massive new airport to replace the rickety Stapleton. Then the city lured Major League Baseball, in the form of the purple-and-black Colorado Rockies, and built Coors Field in the heart of downtown. Around the stadium, planners developed LoDo, a business-and-shopping area including hip nightclubs, Larimer Square boutiques, and bike and walking paths.

Since the mid-1990s Denver has caught the attention of several major national corporations looking to move their operations to a thriving city that enjoys a relatively stable economy and a healthy business climate. And win or lose, the sports teams continue to imbue the city with a sense of pride.

Many Denverites are unabashed nature lovers who can also enjoy the outdoors within the city limits by walking along the park-lined river paths downtown. (Perhaps as a result of their active lifestyle, the city is named annually as one of the healthiest in the nation.) For Denverites, preserving the environment and the city's rich mining and ranching heritage are of equally vital importance to the quality of life.

LoDo, a business-and-shopping area, buzzes with jazz clubs, restaurants, and art galleries housed in carefully restored century-old buildings; more recently, the up-and-coming RiNo (the River North Arts

District) has begun to rival LoDo with its contemporary art galleries, food halls, brewpubs, and concert venues. The culturally diverse populace avidly supports the Denver Art Museum, the Denver Museum of Nature & Science, the Museo de las Americas, and the History Colorado Center. The Denver Performing Arts Complex is the nation's second-largest theatrical venue, bested in capacity only by New York's Lincoln Center. An excellent public transportation system, including a popular, growing light-rail system and 85 miles of bike paths, makes getting around easy.

Planning

When to Go

Denver defies easy weather predictions. Although its blizzards are infamous, snowstorms are often followed by beautiful spring weather just a day or two later. Ski resorts are packed from roughly October to April, and Denver itself often bears the traffic. Summers are festival-happy, with a rock-concert slate and films on the big screen at nearby Red Rocks Park and Amphitheatre. Local bands and nationally known acts perform at venues around the city such as City Park and Civic Center Park. Perhaps the best times to visit, though, are spring and fall, when the heat isn't so intense, the snow isn't so plentiful, and crowds are relatively thin. Ski resorts are still as scenic, but less expensive.

Getting Oriented

Denver's downtown is laid out at a 45-degree angle to the rest of the metro area. Interstate 25 bisects Denver north to south, and I–70 runs east to west. University Boulevard is a major north–south road and Speer Boulevard is a busy diagonal street. Most Denverites are tied to their vehicles, but the light-rail works well if you're going to certain areas.

If you're staying downtown, you can visit LoDo, Capitol Hill, RiNo, and Larimer Square by walking or using the light-rail or the free Mall shuttle. The Central Platte Valley can be accessed by taking the Mall shuttle all the way north to the end and then walking across the pedestrian-only Millennium Bridge. You will need a car to get to Cherry Creek or City Park, however, but once there, those sections also are easy to explore on foot.

Planning Your Time

An easy way to organize the first day of a visit to Denver is to start at one end of the pedestrian-friendly downtown and work your way to the other using the free 16th Street Mall shuttle. The Central Platte Valley neighborhood (a short walk across Millennium Bridge), LoDo, and RiNo sit at one end, with Larimer Square on the way toward Capitol Hill at the other. Along the way, a few blocks' walk from the Mall can take you to attractions such as the Denver Art Museum, the History Colorado Center, and the U.S. Mint.

A car or bus ride is necessary to visit City Park or Cherry Creek, but once there, these areas also are easily navigated on foot and can offer a second day's worth of attractions, including the Denver Zoo, Denver Botanic Gardens, and the Denver Museum of Nature & Science at City Park, and the plethora of shopping and restaurants of Cherry Creek North.

Getting Here and Around

AIR

Denver International Airport (DEN) is 15 miles northeast of downtown, but it usually takes about a half hour to 45 minutes to travel between them, depending on the time of day. It's served by most major domestic carriers and many international ones. Arrive at the airport with plenty of time before your flight, preferably two hours; the airport's check-in and security-check lines are particularly long.

Between the airport and downtown, Super Shuttle makes door-to-door trips. The region's public bus service, Regional Transportation District (RTD), runs SkyRide to and from the airport; the trip takes 50 minutes, and the fare is $9–$26 each way. There's a transportation center in the airport just outside baggage claim. A taxi ride to downtown costs $60–$70.

AIRPORTS Denver International Airport. *(DEN) ✉ 8500 Peña Blvd. ☎ 800/247–2336 🌐 www.flydenver.com.*

AIRPORT TRANSFERS Regional Transportation District/SkyRide. *☎ 303/299–6000 for route and schedule information 🌐 www.rtd-denver.com.* **Super Shuttle.** *☎ 303/370–1300 🌐 www.supershuttle.com.*

BUS

In downtown Denver, a free shuttle-bus service, called the Free MallRide, operates about every 10 minutes from 5 am weekdays (5:30 am Saturday; 6:30 am Sunday and holidays) until 1:19 am, running the length of the 16th Street Mall (which bisects downtown) and stopping at one-block intervals. In addition, the Free MetroRide offers weekday rush-hour service between Union Station and Civic Center Station, making limited stops along 18th and 19th Streets. If you plan to spend much time outside downtown, a car is advised, although Denver has one of the best city bus systems in the country.

The region's public bus service, RTD, is comprehensive, with routes throughout the metropolitan area. The service also links Denver to outlying towns such as Boulder, Longmont, and Nederland. You can buy bus tokens at grocery stores or pay with exact change on the bus. Fares vary according to time and zone. Within the city limits, buses cost $2.80.

CONTACTS RTD. *☎ 303/299–6000, 800/366–7433 🌐 www.rtd-denver.com.*

CAR

Rental-car companies include Advantage, Alamo, Avis, Budget, Dollar, Enterprise, E-Z Rent-A-Car, Fox, Hertz, Payless, Sixt, Thrifty, and National. All have airport and downtown representatives.

Reaching Denver by car is fairly easy, except during rush hour. Interstate highways 70 and 25 intersect near downtown; an entrance to I–70 is just outside the airport.

■ **TIP→ When you're looking for an address within Denver, make sure you know whether it's a street or avenue.** Speer Boulevard runs alongside Cherry Creek from northwest to southeast through downtown; numbered streets run parallel to Speer and most are one-way. Colfax Avenue (U.S. 40, with U.S. 287 routed alongside as well) runs east–west through downtown; numbered avenues run parallel to Colfax. Broadway runs north–south. Other main thoroughfares include Colorado Boulevard (north–south) and Alameda Avenue (east–west). Try to avoid driving in the area during rush hour, when traffic gets heavy. Interstates 25 and 225 are particularly slow during those times; although the Transportation Expansion Project (T-REX) added extra lanes, a light-rail system along the highways, bicycle lanes, and other improvements, expansion in the metro area outpaced the project.

Finding an open meter has become increasingly difficult in downtown Denver, especially during peak times such as Rockies games and weekend nights. Most meters have two-hour limits until 10 pm and cost $1 per hour. The city has made it easier to pay by switching most meters to accept debit/credit cards as well as change. In addition, there's no shortage of pay lots for anywhere from $3 to $29 per day.

RIDE-SHARING SERVICES

Hailed solely via smartphone app, car services in the metro area give taxis a ride for their money, particularly because the ride can be considerably cheaper and arrive faster. The downside, though, is that at peak times, Uber and Lyft prices soar to "surge pricing." Expect to pay about 81¢–$1 base and 24¢–28¢ a minute and 83¢–$1.25 per mile at nonpeak times and up to four times as much during surge pricing.

TAXI

Taxis can be costly and difficult to simply flag down compared to some major metropolitan areas; instead, you usually must call ahead to arrange for one. Cabs are $2.50–$3.50 minimum and $2.25–$2.80 per mile, depending on the company. However, at peak times—during major events, and at 2 am when the bars close—taxis are very hard to come by.

CONTACTS Freedom Cab. ☎ *303/444–4444* 🌐 *www.freedomcabs.com.* **Metro Taxi.** ☎ *303/333–3333* 🌐 *www.metro-transportationdenver.com.* **Yellow Cab.** ☎ *303/777–7777* 🌐 *www.denveryellow-cab.com.*

TRAIN

Historic Union Station in the heart of downtown has undergone extensive redevelopment and features an open-air train hall behind the refurbished historic building, where passengers once again can hop aboard the California Zephyr as it stops in Denver on its runs between Chicago and San Francisco.

RTD's Light Rail service's 11 lines and 113 miles of track links southeast, southwest, west, and east Denver to downtown, including service from Union Station. The peak fare is $3 within the city limits.

CONTACTS Amtrak. ✉ *Union Station, 1701 Wynkoop St.* ☎ *800/872–7245* 🌐 *www.amtrak.com.* **RTD Light Rail.** ☎ *303/299–6000* 🌐 *www.rtd-denver.com.*

Restaurants

As befits such a diverse crossroads, Denver lays out a dizzying range of eateries. Head for LoDo, the Highland District, the RiNo Art District, or south of the city for the more inventive kitchens. Try Federal Street for cheap international eats—especially Mexican and Vietnamese—and expect authentic takes on classic Italian, French, and Asian cuisines. Throughout Denver, menus at trendy restaurants focus on locally sourced, organic, and healthier options; Denver's top chefs continue to gain the attention of national food magazines and win culinary competitions, but between the increased exposure and the rapid influx of residents, prices have skyrocketed to match or exceed those of larger cities.

Hotels

Denver's lodging choices include the stately Brown Palace, bed-and-breakfasts, and business hotels. Unless you're planning a quick escape to the mountains, consider staying in or around downtown, where most of the city's attractions are within walking distance. Many of the hotels cater to business travelers, with accordingly lower rates on weekends—many establishments slash their rates in half on Friday and Saturday. The hotels in the vicinity of Cherry Creek are about a 10- to 15-minute drive from downtown.

Restaurant and hotel reviews have been shortened. For full information, visit Fodors.com. Restaurant prices are the average cost of a main course at dinner or, if dinner is not served, at lunch. Hotel prices are the lowest cost of a standard double room in high season, excluding service charges and 14.85% tax.

What It Costs

$	$$	$$$	$$$$
RESTAURANTS			
under $15	$15–$22	$23–$30	over $30
HOTELS			
under $125	$125–$200	$201–$300	over $300

Visitor Information

The Visitors and Information Center is operated by VISIT Denver, the Convention and Visitors Bureau. It's located downtown at the corner of 16th and California. They also have self-guided walking-tour brochures.

CONTACTS Lower Downtown District, Inc.. ☎ *303/605–3510* 🌐 *www.lodo.org.* **VISIT Denver, The Convention and Visitors Bureau.** ✉ *1575 California St., LoDo* ☎ *303/892–1505, 800/233–6837* 🌐 *www.denver.org.*

Tours

Denver History Tours
BUS TOURS | FAMILY | Personalized, guided tours of historic Denver are available, as are tours to select surrounding areas along the Front Range, in buses (for groups only) and on walking tours for a minimum of two people; prices and times vary according to the tour. Guides are knowledgeable locals eager to tailor the tour to individual tastes and interests, and work to accommodate varying fitness levels within a group. Trains, the Old West, the Art District on Santa Fe, and "haunted" Denver are particular specialties. ✉ *Denver* ☎ *720/234–7929* 🌐 *www.denverhistorytours.com* 🎫 *From $20.*

Denver Microbrew Tour
WALKING TOURS | This guided walking tour in LoDo includes beer sampling at several microbreweries and a comprehensive history of local beer making as well as Denver's history; a swing through Coors Field is also included. The fee covers the samples along the way and a voucher for a full pint, as well. A newer tour on Sundays through the hip arts district RiNo (River North) includes cider tastings, too (but not Coors Field). The guides are all beer enthusiasts who thoroughly enjoy sharing beer trivia, and can recommend anything beer-related in Denver. ✉ *Denver* ☎ *303/578–9548* 🌐 *www.denvermicrobrewtour.com* 🎫 *From $50.*

Gray Line
BUS TOURS | This company offers the usual expansive and exhaustive coach tours of anything and everything, from shopping in Cherry Creek to visiting Rocky Mountain National Park. Tours last from 3 to 10 hours, and lunch is sometimes included at a local eatery. Guides run the gamut from informed-to-a-point (yet enthusiastic) to expert locals. ✉ *Denver* ☎ *800/472–9546, 303/539–8502* 🌐 *www.grayline.com* 🎫 *From $55.*

Activities

Denver is a city that can consistently and enthusiastically support three professional sports teams, but it has more than that—the Colorado Rockies, Colorado Avalanche, Denver Broncos, Denver Nuggets, and Colorado Rapids (soccer). Until recently, the Nuggets and Rapids had been the odd teams out, as the Rockies, Avalanche, and Broncos have all reached or won championships in their respective sports. But here and there the Nuggets have come close to catching up, and fans patiently await their year.

What's great about Denverites is that most aren't just spectators. After a game, they go out and do stuff—hiking, bicycling, kayaking, and, yes, playing team sports themselves. The city and its proximity to outdoor pursuits encourage a fit lifestyle.

BASKETBALL

Ball Arena

BASKETBALL | From November to April, the Denver Nuggets play at Ball Arena (formerly Pepsi Center); from October to April, the Colorado Avalanche play there, too. The 19,000-seat arena is also the primary indoor venue for large musical acts such as U2, The Weeknd, and Justin Timberlake. Tours of the facilities are available several days a week. ✉ *1000 Chopper Cir., Auraria* ☎ *303/405–1100* 🌐 *www.ballarena.com.*

BICYCLING

Evo

BICYCLING | This facility just south of downtown repairs road and mountain bikes and rents them for $30 to $80 a day. ✉ *860 Broadway, Golden Triangle* ☎ *303/831–7228, 866/386–1590* 🌐 *www.evo.com.*

Cherry Creek Bike Path

BICYCLING | A well-kept path runs from Cherry Creek Shopping Center past Larimer Square downtown and to the confluence of the South Platte River alongside the peaceful creek of its name. ✉ *Cherry Creek, LoDo.*

Deer Creek Canyon

BICYCLING | Running through forested foothills southwest of Denver near the intersection of C–470 and Wadsworth Boulevard, the Deer Creek Canyon trail system is popular with mountain bikers. ✉ *C–470 and Wadsworth Blvd., 13388 Grizzly Dr., Littleton* 🌐 *www.jeffco.us/1208/Deer-Creek-Canyon-Park.*

Denver Parks Department

BICYCLING | With more than 663 miles of off-road paths in and around the city to choose from, cyclists can move easily between urban, mountain, and rural settings. Denver Parks Department has suggestions for bicycling and jogging paths throughout the metropolitan area's 250 parks, including the popular Cherry Creek and Chatfield Reservoir State Recreation areas. ✉ *Denver* ☎ *720/913–0696* 🌐 *www.denvergov.org/parks.*

High Line Canal

BICYCLING | Seventy-one miles of mostly dirt paths through the metropolitan area run along the scenic canal at almost completely level grade. ✉ *Auraria, Cherry Creek, LoDo* 🌐 *www.denverwater.org.*

Matthews/Winters Park

BICYCLING | West of the city, paved paths wind through Matthews/Winters Park near both Golden and Morrison. It's dotted with plaintive pioneer graves amid the sun-bleached grasses, thistle, and columbine. ✉ *South of I–70 on CO 26, 1103 County Hwy. 93, Golden* 🌐 *www.jeffco.us/1292/Matthews-Winter-Park.*

South Platte River

BICYCLING | Eighteen miles of paved paths run along the river as it heads into downtown. ✉ *Central Platte Valley, LoDo* 🌐 *www.greenwayfoundation.org.*

FOOTBALL

Empower Stadium at Mile High

FOOTBALL | The team that introduced America to quarterback (and now general manager) John Elway—the National Football League's Denver Broncos—plays September through December at Empower Stadium at Mile High (formerly Broncos Field at Mile High). Every game has sold out for more than 30 years, so tickets are not easy to come by. ✉ *1701 Bryant St., Exit 210B off I–25, Sun Valley* ☎ *720/258–3000* 🌐 *www.denverbroncos.com.*

GOLF

CITY-OWNED PUBLIC COURSES

Eight courses—City Park, Harvard Gulch, Evergreen, Kennedy, Overland Park, Wellshire, and Willis Case, along with Aqua Golf, a water driving range—are operated by the City of Denver and are open to the public. Green fees for all range from $26 to $48; Kennedy, Overland Park, and Harvard Gulch offer night golf. For advance reservations golfers must use the City of Denver Golf Reservation System (on the Web or by phone) up to seven days in advance. For same-day tee times you can call the starters at an individual course. Reservations can be made up to 14 days in advance with a Denver Golf Loyalty card, free by visiting any Denver golf course location.

Aqua Golf

GOLF | **FAMILY** | Two 18-hole miniature golf courses and a water driving range make this a fun spot for families and those looking to spend some time practicing. There are loaner clubs, as well as table tennis for those who don't golf. The clubhouse has a small snack bar, but you're also allowed to bring in your own food. *501 Florida Ave., Overland* *720/865–0880* *cityofdenvergolf.com* *$9 for 18 holes of miniature golf; $6 for 40 balls.*

City Park

GOLF | Since 1913, City Park's tree-lined public course at the north end of the park has been a popular go-to for an urban golf experience. After a nearly three-year renovation, the course reopened in 2020 with a more player-friendly design that still evokes its historic Parkland style. The course sports a full-size driving range and a clubhouse with a public restaurant. The Denver Zoo and Denver Museum of Nature & Science are almost within putting distance, so those in the group who don't want to golf have options. *2500 York St., City Park* *303/295–2096* *www.cityofdenvergolf.com* *$28 weekdays, $39 weekends* *18 holes, 6703 yards, par 70.*

Evergreen Golf Course

GOLF | Situated 30 minutes from Denver and at an altitude of 7,220 feet (which is why it opens a month later than the other city golf courses, in June), this public course offers golfers even more bang for their buck in terms of yardage—but they may feel the extra exertion of walking along this rolling, public 18-hole executive course, as well. With its setting along Bear Creek in the midst of a pine-heavy forest, the course is a favorite byway for elk. *29614 Upper Bear Creek Rd.* *303/865–6430* *www.cityofdenvergolf.com* *$26 weekdays, $38 weekends* *18 holes, 4877 yards, par 69.*

Harvard Gulch

GOLF | For golfers on a time crunch, this 9-hole, par-3 beginners course—the longest hole is 110 yards—in South Denver is ideal. Low-key, walkable, and completed in about an hour, the course features mountain views and tidy greens. If you're serious about golf etiquette—including wearing appropriate attire, replacing divots, and yelling "fore"—this is probably not the right course for you. Most folks here are just learning, but it's hard to beat the price and the convivial atmosphere. *660 Iliff Ave., South Denver* *720/865–0450* *www.cityofdenvergolf.com* *$9* *9 holes, 891 yards, par 27.*

Kennedy Golf Course

GOLF | The sprawling, rolling hills of this course feature magnificent mountain views and plenty of putting practice on the greens. Technically located in suburban Aurora southeast of Denver, the 27-hole regulation course has quite a bit of variety, with the short, tight Creek nine; longer, wider West nine; and a combination of both in the Babe Lind nine—any two of which can be combined to make up your 18 holes. Miniature golf is on-site, as well. *10500 E. Hampden Ave., Aurora* *720/865–0720* *www.cityofdenvergolf.com* *$36 weekdays, $48 weekends* *West Course: 9 holes, 3455 yards, par 36; Creek Course: 9 holes, 3304 yards, par 35; Babe Lind Course: 9 holes, 3580 yards, par 36.*

Overland Park

GOLF | Touted as the oldest continuously operating golf course west of the Mississippi—it was once the Denver Country Club—Overland Park has appealing city and mountain views as well as narrow but open fairways; small, easily read and well-bunkered greens; and fast play. The course is peppered with trees but sports only one water hazard, and the flat terrain makes for a fairly effortless walk. *1801 S. Huron St., Overland* *303/865–0430* *www.cityofdenvergolf.com* *$36* *weekdays, $48 weekends* 🏌 *18 holes, 6676 yards, par 72.*

Wellshire Golf Course

GOLF | Designed in 1926 by Donald Ross and famously played by Ben Hogan, Wellshire Golf Course is known for its classic layout; small, slightly elevated greens; and intermittent mountain views. The foliage-heavy course is mostly flat and contains a handful of water hazards; fairways are narrow and sometimes run parallel to each other. The Wellshire has retained some of its old-time country club charm in the clubhouse and restaurant. ✉ *3333 S. Colorado Blvd., South Denver* ☎ *303/865–0440* 🌐 *www.cityofdenvergolf.com* 🎫 *$36 weekdays, $48 weekends* 🏌 *18 holes, 6541 yards, par 72.*

Willis Case

GOLF | Out of Denver's city-owned golf courses, arguably the best mountain views can be found at Willis Case, whose old-growth-covered, beautifully landscaped, gently rolling terrain can be found right off I–70. The first tee feels as if you are aiming straight for the Rockies, and the sloping fairways, guarded greens, and strategically placed bunkers make for moderately challenging play. The clubhouse is a local favorite for a meal or cocktails with a view. ✉ *4999 Vrain St., North Denver* ☎ *720/865–0700* 🌐 *www.cityofdenvergolf.com* 🎫 *$36 weekdays, $48 weekends* 🏌 *18 holes, 6306 yards, par 72.*

NON–CITY-OWNED COURSES

With their sprawling layouts and impressively appointed greens, these public clubs merit a special look over their city-operated counterparts simply because of their more rural settings. On any Denver-area course, though, out-of-town golfers should keep in mind that the high altitude affects golf balls as it does baseballs—which is why the Rockies have so many more home runs when they bat at home. It's generally agreed that your golf ball will go about 10%–15% farther in the thin air here than it would at sea level.

Arrowhead Golf Club

GOLF | Designed by Robert Trent Jones Sr. and Jr., this private course with rolling terrain is set impressively among red sandstone spires. It's 45 minutes from downtown in Roxborough State Park, which means that any members of your group who don't want to golf can hike nearby. The slow-paced play is made up for by allowing more time to spend looking at the spectacular scenery. ✉ *10850 Sundown Trail, Littleton* ☎ *303/973–9614* 🌐 *www.arrowheadcolorado.com* 🎫 *$80 weekdays, $130 weekends* 🏌 *18 holes, 6636 yards, par 72.*

★ Ridge at Castle Pines North

GOLF | Tom Weiskopf designed this 18-hole course with great mountain views and dramatic elevation changes. It's ranked among the nation's top 100 public courses. It's in Castle Rock, about 45 minutes south of Denver on I–25. One of the course's distinguishing features is its commitment to pace of play; a series of programs have been implemented to help golfers stick to a schedule without cramping golfing styles. ✉ *1414 Castle Pines Pkwy., Castle Rock* ☎ *303/688–4301* 🌐 *www.playtheridge.com* 🎫 *$55 weekdays, $80 weekends* 🏌 *18 holes, 7013 yards, par 71* ✍ *Reservations essential.*

Riverdale Golf Courses

GOLF | It's two golf courses in one: Riverdale has the Dunes, a Scottish-style links course designed by Pete and Perry Dye that sits on the South Platte River and offers railroad ties, plenty of bunkers, and water; while the Knolls has a more gnarly, park-inspired layout. Both courses are shaded by plenty of trees, and you can't beat the price for this public facility maintained as pristinely as a private one. While you're here, be sure to peruse the on-site Colorado Golf Hall of Fame showcases. ✉ *13300 Riverdale Rd., Brighton* ☎ *303/659–4700* 🌐 *www.riverdalegolf.com* 🎫 *Knolls $28 weekdays, $33 weekends; Dunes $25 weekdays,*

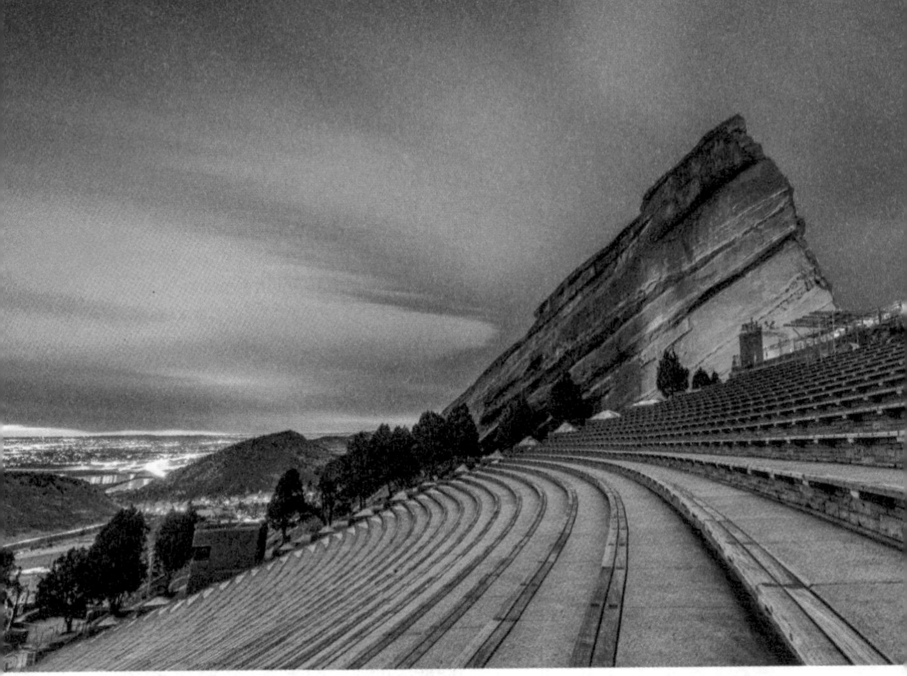

Red Rocks Park and Amphitheatre is one of the state's best places for concerts and for hiking.

$49 weekends ⛳ *Knolls: 18 holes, 6771 yards, par 71; Dunes: 18 holes, 7064 yards, par 72.*

HIKING

Green Mountain

HIKING/WALKING | Part of Jefferson County Open Space and a piece of William Frederick Hayden Park (City of Lakewood), Green Mountain is the first named foothill as you head west from Denver toward the mountains. The easy, mostly exposed trails here afford panoramic views of downtown Denver, Table Mesa, Pikes Peak, and the Continental Divide from the top (895 feet in elevation gain). There are multiple trails from several trailheads, including a 6½-mile loop and a 3-mile loop. You must share the experience with bikers and dogs (as well as other critters). ✉ *Lakewood* ✣ *I–70 west to CO 470 to W. Alameda Pkwy., turn left to trailhead entrance* 🌐 *www.lakewood.org/HaydenPark.*

Mount Falcon Park

HIKING/WALKING | Looking down on Denver and across at Red Rocks, this park is amazingly tranquil, laced with meadows and streams, and shaded by conifers. The 12.2 miles of trails are well marked. ✉ *Aurora* ✣ *Off Rte. 8, Morrison exit, or U.S. 285, Parmalee exit* 🌐 *www.jeffco.us/1332/Mount-Falcon-Park.*

★ Red Rocks Park and Amphitheatre

HIKING/WALKING | Fifteen miles southwest of Denver, Red Rocks Park and Amphitheatre is a breathtaking wonderland of vaulting oxblood-and-cinnamon-color sandstone spires. The outdoor music stage is in a natural 9,000-seat amphitheater (with perfect acoustics, as only nature could have designed). Visit even when there's no show. The 5-mile scenic drive offers a glorious glimpse of the 868 acres of sandstone, and there are picnic and parking areas along the way for photos and a rest. If you're feeling particularly spunky, follow the locals' lead and run the steps for a real workout. The Trading Post loop hiking trail, at 6,280 feet, is 1½ miles long and quite narrow with drop-offs and steep grades. ✉ *18300 W. Alameda Pkwy., Morrison* ✣ *I–70 west to Exit 259, turn left to park entrance* 🌐 *www.redrocksonline.com.*

Roxborough State Park

HIKING/WALKING | An easy, wheelchair-accessible 2-mile loop trail in this 4,000-acre park goes through rugged rock formations; there are also myriad harder hikes that offer striking vistas and a unique look at metropolitan Denver and the plains. ✉ *Littleton* ✣ *I–25 south to Santa Fe exit, take Santa Fe Blvd. south to Titan Rd., turn right and follow signs* 🌐 *cpw.state.co.us/placestogo/parks* 🎫 *$9 day pass.*

HOCKEY

Colorado Avalanche

HOCKEY | This wildly popular Denver-based National Hockey League team won the Stanley Cup in 1996 and beat the New Jersey Devils for an encore in 2001. It continues to be beloved by locals and plays October to April in a packed 19,000-seat Ball Arena. ✉ *1000 Chopper Pl., Auraria* ☎ *303/428–7645* 🌐 *www.coloradoavalanche.com.*

STOCK SHOWS

National Western Stock Show

RODEO | **FAMILY** | Thousands of cowpokes retrieve their string ties and worn boots and indulge in two weeks of hootin', hollerin', and celebratin' the beef industry during the National Western Stock Show each January.

Whether you're a professional rancher or bull rider, or just plan to show up for the people-watching, the Stock Show is a rich, colorful glimpse of Western culture. The pros arrive to make industry connections, show off their livestock, and perhaps land a few sales. The entertainment involves nightly rodeo events, presentations of prized cattle (some going for thousands of dollars), and "Mutton Bustin'." The latter is one of those rowdy rodeo concepts that usually has no place in a genteel metropolis like Denver: kids, ages five to seven, don huge hockey-goalie helmets and hold for dear life onto the backs of bucking baby sheep. At the trade show you can buy hats and boots as well as yards of beef jerky and quirky gift items.

The yearly event is held at the National Western Complex. Just be sure to call first and ask for directions; although parking is plentiful it can move around based on volume and livestock needs, and the Complex, usually home of straightforward sporting and entertainment events, becomes a labyrinth of lots and shuttles during the Stock Show. Daily admission prices depend on the day's events. ✉ *National Western Complex, 4655 Humboldt St., Elyria* ✣ *East of I–25 on I–70* ☎ *303/296–6977, 866/464–2626 for tickets* 🌐 *www.nationalwestern.com* 🎫 *$12–$25.*

WATER SPORTS

Chatfield marina rents sailboats, powerboats, and Jet Skis June through August, while the Marina at Cherry Creek specializes in pontoons and paddle sports.

Chatfield Marina

WATER SPORTS | Fifteen miles south of downtown and on the fringes of the Rocky Mountains, Chatfield Marina attracts wakeboarders, water-skiers, stand-up paddleboarders, and tubers. ✉ *Chatfield State Park, Littleton* ☎ *303/791–5555* 🌐 *www.chatfieldmarina.com.*

Pelican Bay at Cherry Creek

WATER SPORTS | Southeast of Denver, Pelican Bay at Cherry Creek serves the 850-acre reservoir of the same name, a sailing hot spot, offering boat and paddle sports rentals. ✉ *Cherry Creek State Park, 4800 S. Dayton St., Greenwood Village* ☎ *303/741–2995* 🌐 *pbcherrycreek.com.*

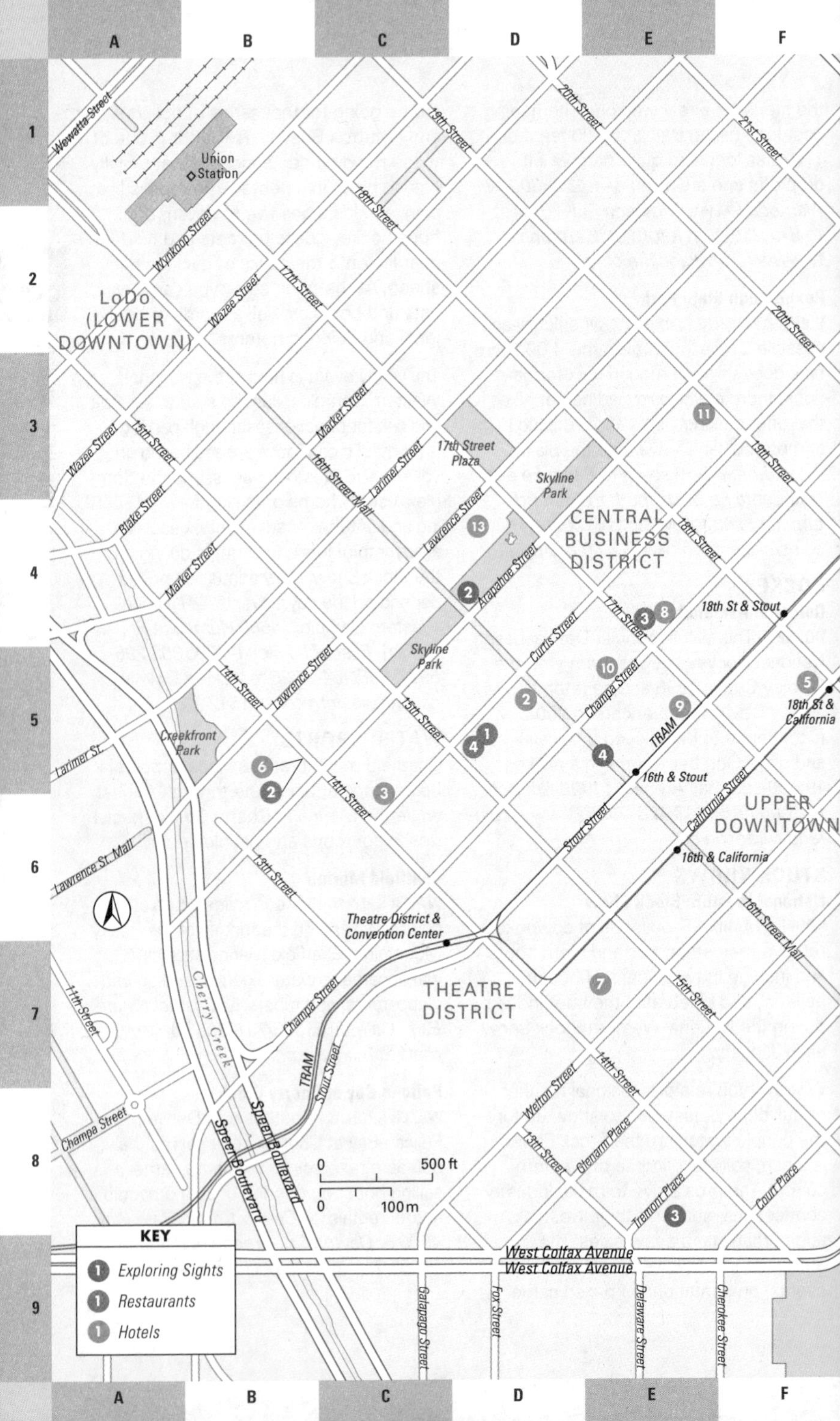

A B C D E F
1 2 3 4 5 6 7 8 9
LoDo (LOWER DOWNTOWN)
CENTRAL BUSINESS DISTRICT
UPPER DOWNTOWN
THEATRE DISTRICT
Union Station
17th Street Plaza
Skyline Park
Creekfront Park
Cherry Creek
18th St & Stout
18th St & California
16th & Stout
16th & California
Theatre District & Convention Center
TRAM
Wewatta Street
Wynkoop Street
Wazee Street
Blake Street
Market Street
Larimer Street
Larimer St.
Lawrence Street
Lawrence St. Mall
Arapahoe Street
Curtis Street
Champa Street
Stout Street
California Street
Welton Street
Glenarm Place
Tremont Place
Court Place
11th Street
13th Street
14th Street
15th Street
16th Street Mall
17th Street
18th Street
19th Street
20th Street
21st Street
Speer Boulevard
West Colfax Avenue
Galapago Street
Fox Street
Delaware Street
Cherokee Street
0 500 ft
0 100 m
KEY
Exploring Sights
Restaurants
Hotels

Sights

1 Brown Palace....................... **G6**
2 Daniels & Fisher Tower........... **D4**
3 Denver Firefighters Museum...... **E8**
4 16th Street Mall..................... **E5**

Restaurants

1 Dazzle at Baur's.................... **D5**
2 The Nickel........................... **B5**
3 Panzano.............................. **E4**
4 Sam's No. 3......................... **D5**

Hotels

1 Brown Palace....................... **G6**
2 Courtyard Denver Downtown Marriott............... **D5**
3 The Curtis—A Doubletree by Hilton Hotel....................... **C6**
4 Grand Hyatt......................... **G6**
5 Hilton Denver City Center.......... **F5**
6 Hotel Teatro........................ **B5**
7 Hyatt Regency Denver at Colorado Convention Center...... **E7**
8 Kimpton Hotel Monaco............ **E4**
9 Magnolia Hotel...................... **E5**
10 Renaissance Denver Downtown Hotel.................... **E5**
11 The Ritz-Carlton, Denver........... **E3**
12 Sheraton Denver Downtown Hotel.................. **G8**
13 Westin Denver Downtown....... **D4**

Built in 1892, Brown Palace is Denver's most historic hotel.

Central Business District

Downtown Denver is really made up of two distinct neighborhoods: hip LoDo, and the more business-minded Central Business District. With a more traditional "downtown" look thanks to its many skyscrapers, the CBD has less to offer in terms of restaurants and bars, but it does have a few key sights (like the popular 16th Street Mall) along with the city's highest concentration of hotels.

Sights

★ Brown Palace

HOTEL—SIGHT | The grande dame of Denver hotels was built in 1892, and is still considered the city's most prestigious address. Famous guests have included President Dwight D. Eisenhower, Winston Churchill, and Beyoncé. Even if you aren't staying here, the Brown Palace lobby is a great place to sit on comfortable old couches, drink tea, and listen to piano standards (or harp, during afternoon tea). Reputedly this was the first atrium hotel in the United States; its ornate lobby and nine stories are crowned by a Tiffany stained-glass window. ✉ *321 17th St., LoDo* ☎ *303/297–3111* 🌐 *www.brownpalace.com.*

Daniels & Fisher Tower

BUILDING | This 330-foot-high, 20-floor structure emulates the Campanile of St. Mark's Square in Venice, and it was the tallest building west of the Mississippi when it was built in 1909. William Cooke Daniels originally commissioned the tower to stand adjacent to his five-story department store. Today it's an office building with a cabaret in the basement as well as the city's most convenient clock tower. It's particularly striking—the clock is 16 feet high—when viewed in concert with the fountains in the adjacent Skyline Park. ✉ *1601 Arapahoe St., at 16th St., LoDo* ☎ *303/877–0742* 🌐 *www.clocktowerevents.com.*

Denver Firefighters Museum

MUSEUM | FAMILY | Denver's first firehouse was built in 1909 and now serves as a museum where original items of the trade are on view, including uniforms, nets, fire carts and trucks, bells, and switchboards. Artifacts and photos document the progression of firefighting machinery from horses and carriages in the early 1900s to the flashy red-and-white trucks of today. ✉ *1326 Tremont Pl., LoDo* ☎ *303/892–1436* 🌐 *www.denverfirefightersmuseum.org* 🎫 *$9.*

★ 16th Street Mall

COMMERCIAL CENTER | Outdoor cafés and tempting shops line this pedestrian-only 18-block, 1¼-mile thoroughfare, shaded by red-oak and locust trees. The mall's businesses run the entire socioeconomic range. There are popular meeting spots for business types at places like the Yard House in the Sheraton Hotel; a front-row view of the many street performers and goings-on from restaurants' sidewalk patios; and plenty of fast-food chains. Although some Denverites swear by the higher-end Cherry Creek Shopping District, the 16th Street Mall covers every retail area and is a more affordable, diverse experience. You can find Denver's best people-watching here. Catch one of the free shuttle buses at any corner that run the length of downtown. Pay attention when you're wandering across the street, as the walking area and bus lanes are the same color and are hard to distinguish. ✉ *From Broadway to Chestnut Pl., LoDo* 🌐 *16thstreetmalldenver.com.*

Restaurants

Dazzle at Baur's

$$ | AMERICAN | If it's martinis and jazz you're after, come to this casually elegant space (larger and snazzier after a move to the historic Baur's Building), which features comfort foods with a twist and small plates. Live music most nights makes this a laid-back spot. **Known for:** extensive cocktail roster; mac-and-cheese; Sunday jazz brunch. 💲 *Average main: $19* ✉ *1512 Curtis St., Downtown* ☎ *303/839–5100* 🌐 *dazzledenver.com* ⏲ *Closed Mon. No lunch.*

The Nickel

$$ | MODERN AMERICAN | A basic contemporary American menu offers classics done well at the Nickel, the restaurant located in the Hotel Teatro. Enjoy a top-notch burger, a vegetarian take on Wellington using beets instead of beef, or Mediterranean-style salmon, all while kicking back in sumptuous leather wing chairs. **Known for:** tasty steak frites; pre- and post-theater dining; barrel-aged cocktails. 💲 *Average main: $17* ✉ *1100 14th St., Downtown* ☎ *720/889–2128* 🌐 *www.thenickeldenver.com.*

★ Panzano

$$$ | ITALIAN | This dining room in Hotel Monaco is filled with fresh flowers and windows that let in natural light, making the space cheerful and bright. The focus is on true, multilayered Italian cuisine, such as grilled flatbread topped with cheese, prosciutto, truffle oil, and balsamic vinegar; or risotto made with an ever-changing and ever-pleasing variety of cheeses and fresh produce. **Known for:** house-baked breads; roomy bar; elegant brunch. 💲 *Average main: $30* ✉ *909 17th St., Downtown* ☎ *303/296–3525* 🌐 *www.panzano-denver.com.*

Sam's No. 3

$ | DINER | FAMILY | Greek immigrant Sam Armatas opened his first eatery in Denver in 1927, and his three sons use the same recipes their father did in their updated version of his all-American diner, from the famous red and green chilies to the Coney Island–style hot dogs and creamy rice pudding. The retro diner resembles a fancy Denny's, and the bar is crowded with theatergoers and hipsters after dark. **Known for:** heavenly milkshakes; all-day breakfast; old-school horseshoe counter. 💲 *Average main: $14* ✉ *1500 Curtis St., Downtown* ☎ *303/534–1927* 🌐 *samsno3.com.*

Hotels

★ Brown Palace

$$$ | **HOTEL** | This grande dame of Colorado lodging has hosted public figures from President Eisenhower to the Beatles since it first opened its doors in 1892, and the details are exquisite: a dramatic nine-story lobby is topped with a glorious stained-glass ceiling, and the Victorian rooms have sophisticated wainscoting and art deco fixtures. **Pros:** sleeping here feels like being part of history; spacious and comfortable rooms; beautiful full-service spa. **Cons:** restaurants feel dated; parking is expensive and not included; lobby can be chaotic. *$ Rooms from: $254 ✉ 321 17th St., Downtown ☎ 303/297–3111, 800/321–2599 🌐 www.brownpalace.com 241 rooms 🍽 No meals.*

Courtyard Denver Downtown Marriott

$$ | **HOTEL** | This stunning building (it used to be Joslins Department Store) sits right on the 16th Street Mall, which means everything downtown is a few blocks or a free Mall shuttle away. **Pros:** great location and views; deluxe rooms have sofa beds; lobby showcasing art and city history. **Cons:** noisy at night; rooms nothing fancy; chain feel. *$ Rooms from: $180 ✉ 934 16th St., Downtown ☎ 303/571–1114, 888/249–1810 🌐 www.marriott.com 177 rooms 🍽 No meals.*

★ The Curtis — A Doubletree by Hilton Hotel

$$ | **HOTEL** | **FAMILY** | Each floor here has a pop-culture theme, from classic cars to TV to science fiction, and the rooms are spacious and groovy, with speakers for your music and comfy, mod furnishings. **Pros:** across the street from Denver Performing Arts Complex; pet- and kid-friendly; unique and fun decor. **Cons:** can be noisy; high-traffic area; some of the rooms feel small. *$ Rooms from: $199 ✉ 1405 Curtis St., Downtown ☎ 303/571–0300, 800/525–6651 🌐 www.thecurtis.com 338 rooms 🍽 No meals.*

Grand Hyatt

$$$ | **HOTEL** | **FAMILY** | Close to Larimer Square, the theaters, the 16th Street Mall, and the Colorado Convention Center, and with unpretentious, comfortable rooms—downtown hotels don't get much better than this. **Pros:** great views from upper floors; top-notch gym; lavish concierge lounge services. **Cons:** chain-hotel vibe; cavernous space can be overwhelming; disorganized check-in. *$ Rooms from: $249 ✉ 1750 Welton St., Downtown ☎ 303/295–1234, 800/233–1234 🌐 www.grandhyattdenver.com 516 rooms 🍽 No meals.*

Hilton Denver City Center

$$$ | **HOTEL** | Definitely geared toward the business traveler, the Hilton Denver is a three-block walk from the Denver Convention Complex and has 50,000 square feet of meeting space of its own. **Pros:** nice gym and pool; close to the convention center; worthwhile restaurant. **Cons:** noisy at night; bland chain-hotel feel; rooms are small. *$ Rooms from: $229 ✉ 1701 California St., Downtown ☎ 303/297–1300, 800/228–9290 🌐 www.hilton.com 615 rooms 🍽 No meals.*

Hotel Teatro

$$$ | **HOTEL** | Black-and-white photographs, costumes, and scenery from plays that were staged in the Denver Performing Arts Complex across the street decorate the grand public areas of this hotel. **Pros:** great location for theater and other downtown pursuits; excellent restaurants; lovely rooms and public spaces. **Cons:** noisy and chaotic area; costly parking; some rooms are tiny. *$ Rooms from: $299 ✉ 1100 14th St., Downtown ☎ 303/228–1100, 888/727–1200 🌐 www.hotelteatro.com 109 rooms 🍽 No meals.*

Hyatt Regency Denver at Colorado Convention Center

$$ | **HOTEL** | Often confused with the Grand Hyatt, this property, which is near the Convention Center, has rooms with expanded workstations, LCD-screen TVs, and a relaxing palette (slate, beige, pine);

Legalized Marijuana in Denver

How to Purchase

On January 1, 2014, Colorado became the first state to allow legal recreational marijuana sales for any purpose to anyone over 21. Purchasing marijuana in Colorado at a licensed recreational shop is as simple as walking into the store, showing your ID, and buying it in the desired form. Some dispensaries are medical-only, however, and require a doctor-issued medical card for entry, while some buildings are designated as offering medical and recreational.

The amount a person is legally allowed to purchase is no longer dependent on residency; anyone over the age of 21 with a valid ID may buy up to one ounce of marijuana per day. No personal information is collected, and your ID is used only for proof of age.

Recreational marijuana stores are located in cities and towns around the state, but the vast majority of the licenses are held in Denver. Some counties have banned recreational stores. In addition, many cities limit store hours (in Denver, for instance, they can't be open past 10 pm). Call ahead to find out if a shop takes credit or debit cards, as many are still cash-only. *The Denver Post's The Cannabist* and the weekly *Westword* publish online guides that list shops, as well as reviews and information on the latest marijuana products.

Where to Consume

Where to smoke marijuana is considerably more restricted. Marijuana products cannot be consumed on-site at a retail outlet, nor can they be smoked in public spaces, including ski areas or national parks (both of which are on federal lands, where getting caught can result in jail time or hefty fines, as marijuana possession is still illegal under federal law). Under Colorado's Clean Indoor Air Act, weed smoking is banned anywhere that cigarette smoking is also banned. A handful of private cannabis social lounges have opened with membership fees, and some hotels advertise as "cannabis-friendly," meaning they allow consumption in designated smoking areas on-property. References to "420"—a once-obscure, insider allusion to all things marijuana-related—are meant as an indication of an establishment's openness to assisting clientele in procurement or consumption. In 2018, the first public-consumption cannabis café opened in the Lincoln Park neighborhood.

You can drive legally while possessing marijuana in a vehicle the same way you can with alcohol: it just needs to be sealed. Driving stoned is against the law, and legal limits have been established for the amount of THC a driver can have in his or her system. Taking marijuana on a plane is illegal, as is transporting it to another state, even to a state where it's also legal.

Several tour groups offer marijuana-based services that include airport transfers, tours of marijuana-growing operations, transport to recreational shops, and enough time in party-style buses to smoke, consume edible marijuana products and visit local eateries, explore museums and other cultural events, and then get dropped off for a stay at a "cannabis-friendly" hotel.

the hotel caters to business-focused guests. **Pros:** spacious rooms with large workstations; large health club with lap pool; central location. **Cons:** noisy convention atmosphere; chain hotel feel; can be chaotic. *Rooms from: $169 650 15th St., Downtown 303/436–1234 www.hyatt.com 1,100 rooms No meals.*

★ Kimpton Hotel Monaco
$$$ | **HOTEL** | Celebrities and business travelers check into this hip property, which occupies the historic 1917 Railway Exchange Building and the 1937 art moderne Title Building, for the modern perks and art deco–meets–classic French style. **Pros:** one of the pet-friendliest hotels in town; welcoming complimentary wine hour; central location. **Cons:** may be too pet-friendly; hotel has decidedly business rather than romantic feel; popular with partiers. *Rooms from: $260 1717 Champa St., Downtown 303/296–1717, 800/990–1303 www.monaco-denver.com 189 rooms No meals.*

Magnolia Hotel
$$$ | **HOTEL** | The Denver outpost of this Texas-based chain has remarkably spacious, elegant rooms with sophisticated furnishings—some with fireplaces—and warm colors, all built within the confines of the 1906 former American Bank Building. **Pros:** pretty, comfortable rooms; convenient to downtown; good restaurants. **Cons:** although classy, can feel generic; service can be spotty; can be a noisy area at night. *Rooms from: $269 818 17th St., Downtown 303/607–9000, 888/915–1110 www.magnoliahoteldenver.com 297 rooms Free Breakfast.*

Renaissance Denver Downtown Hotel
$$$ | **HOTEL** | The Renaissance's gorgeous hotel lobby is part of the original 1925 Colorado National Bank building, whose 16 vivacious Western-themed murals have been painstakingly restored; rooms are remarkably stylish, with sparkly glitter accents on pillows and blues and browns complementing the plush white linens. **Pros:** central location; mountain views; excellent restaurant and lounge. **Cons:** outside noise heard in certain rooms; slow elevators; some rooms are dark. *Rooms from: $288 918 17th St., Downtown 303/867–8100 www.rendendowntown.com 230 rooms No meals.*

★ The Ritz-Carlton, Denver
$$$$ | **HOTEL** | This beautiful property features warm woods, elaborate glass fixtures, and luxurious details, and the pampering service is typical of the chain. **Pros:** room-service fare delicious and prompt; inviting public spaces; excellent spa. **Cons:** this part of town can be noisy; feels away from the action; very expensive. *Rooms from: $329 1881 Curtis St., Downtown 303/312–3800 www.ritzcarlton.com 202 rooms No meals.*

Sheraton Denver Downtown Hotel
$$ | **HOTEL** | Guest rooms at the ever-bustling Sheraton are roomy and streamlined, with unfussy furniture and nice workstations that appeal primarily to the business traveler. **Pros:** great location; many amenities; heated outdoor pool. **Cons:** front area where cars come in is chaotic; feels like nothing but conventions; lower-floor rooms can be noisy. *Rooms from: $194 1550 Court Pl., Downtown 303/893–3333, 866/716–8134 www.sheratondenverhotel.com 1,236 rooms No meals.*

Westin Denver Downtown
$$$$ | **HOTEL** | This sleek, luxurious high-rise with oversized rooms opens right onto the 16th Street Mall and all the downtown action. **Pros:** convenient location on Mall; multiple dining options; nice pool with great city view. **Cons:** restaurants are uneven; room rates are high; property feels dated. *Rooms from: $329 1672 Lawrence St., Downtown 303/572–9100, 800/937–8461 www.westin.com 430 rooms No meals.*

Bovine Metropolis Theater

COMEDY CLUBS | Eight times a week, a rotating cast of characters offers improv at Bovine Metropolis Theater, which also stages satirical productions and teaches classes in the genre. ✉ *1527 Champa St., Downtown* ☎ *303/758–4722* 🌐 *www.bovinemetropolis.com.*

Dazzle at Baur's

MUSIC CLUBS | This is a cozy, casual spot for live jazz and blues six nights a week downtown. *Downbeat* magazine has named it one of the 100 best jazz clubs in the world. The location, in the historic Baur's Building, offers a classy setting and exceptional acoustics as well as updated takes on classic comfort food before and during shows. ✉ *1512 Curtis St., Downtown* ☎ *303/839–5100* 🌐 *dazzledenver.com.*

Colorado Symphony Orchestra

MUSIC | From September to June, the orchestra performs in the Boettcher Concert Hall, as well as playing ensemble concerts at venues around the city and a popular summer Symphony on the Rocks series at Red Rocks Park and Amphitheatre near Morrison. ✉ *Boettcher Concert Hall, 14th and Curtis Sts., Downtown* ☎ *303/623–7876, 877/292–7979* 🌐 *www.coloradosymphony.org.*

Denver Center Theatre Company

THEATER | Presenting high-caliber repertory theater, including new works by promising playwrights, this company takes over the stage at the Bonfils Theatre Complex, part of the Denver Performing Arts Complex. ✉ *14th and Curtis Sts., Downtown* ☎ *303/893–4100, 800/641–1222* 🌐 *www.denvercenter.org.*

★ Denver Performing Arts Complex

ARTS CENTERS | This huge complex, composed of an impressively high-tech group of theaters, hosts more shows—from classical orchestras to Jay Leno to *Wicked*—than any other performing arts center in the world. Spread over a four-block area, the eight theaters are connected by a soaring glass archway to a futuristic symphony hall. The complex anchors are the round Temple Hoyne Buell Theatre, built in 1991, and the ornate Ellie Caulkins Opera House, which occupies the former Auditorium Theatre built in 1908. The other six theaters include the small Garner Galleria Theatre and the midsize Space Theatre. The symphony, ballet, and opera have their seasons here. The complex has been run by the Denver Center for the Performing Arts since 1972, and 90-minute guided tours that take you behind the scenes are available by reservation Monday and Saturday for $12 per person; customized tours can also be arranged. ✉ *Box office, 1101 13th St., Downtown* ☎ *303/893–4100, 800/641–1222* 🌐 *www.denvercenter.org.*

Opera Colorado

OPERA | World-renowned for its superior acoustics and a Figaro seat-back tilting system that allows attendees to follow the text of the opera, the magnificent Ellie Caulkins Opera House has red-velvet seating and a lyre shape, ideal for full-bodied sound travel. The cherry-wood-accented theater, in the Newton Auditorium, is where Opera Colorado presents its spring season, often with internationally renowned artists. ✉ *1101 13th St., Downtown* ☎ *303/778–1500, 303/468–2030 tickets* 🌐 *www.operacolorado.org.*

Paramount Theatre

CONCERTS | Designed by renowned local architect Temple H. Buell in the art deco style in 1930, the lovingly maintained Paramount in downtown Denver is both an elegant place to see shows and a rowdy, beer-serving party location for rock fans to enjoy large-scale concerts. ✉ *1631 Glenarm Pl., Downtown* ☎ *303/623–0106* 🌐 *www.paramountdenver.com.*

Shopping

Denver Pavilions

SHOPPING CENTERS/MALLS | This three-story, open-air retail and entertainment complex in downtown Denver houses national chain stores like Sephora, H&M, Bath & Body Works, and PacSun. There are also restaurants, including Denver's Hard Rock Cafe, and a 15-screen movie theater, the UA Denver Pavilions. Don't expect distinctive local flavor, but it's a practical complement to Larimer Square a few blocks away. ✉ *16th St. Mall between Tremont and Welton Sts., LoDo* ☎ *303/260–6000* 🌐 *www.denverpavilions.com.*

LoDo and Five Points

Officially, the Lower Downtown Historic District, the 25-plus square-block area that was the site of the original 1858 settlement of Denver City, is nicknamed LoDo. It's home to art galleries, chic shops, nightclubs, and restaurants ranging from Denver's most upscale to its most down-home. This part of town was once the city's thriving retail center, then it fell into disuse. Since the early 1990s LoDo has been transformed into the city's cultural center, thanks to its resident artists, retailers, and loft dwellers who have taken over the old warehouses and redbricks.

Also nearby, the city's newest revitalized area, RiNo (River North Art District), comprises the historic neighborhoods of Globeville, Elyria- Swansea, Five Points, and Cole and has established itself as a solid option for galleries and restaurants.

Sights

★ Black American West Museum and Heritage Center

MUSEUM | The revealing documents and artifacts here depict the vast contributions that Black Americans made to opening up the West. Nearly a third of the cowboys and many pioneer teachers and doctors were Black. One floor is devoted to Black cowboys; another to military troops, including the Buffalo Soldiers. Changing exhibits focus on topics such as the history of Black churches in the West. ✉ *3091 California St., Five Points* ☎ *720/242–7428* 🌐 *www.bawmhc.org* 🎟 *$10* 🕓 *Closed Sun.–Thurs.*

★ Coors Field

BASEBALL/SOFTBALL | The Colorado Rockies, Denver's National League baseball team, play April through October in Coors Field. Because it's set in high altitude and thin air, the park is among the best in the major leagues for home-run hitters—and likewise, one of the worst for pitchers. ✉ *2001 Blake St., LoDo* ☎ *303/292–0200, 800/388–7625* 🌐 *www.coloradorockies.com.*

★ Larimer Square

COMMERCIAL CENTER | This square, on the oldest street in the city, was immortalized by Jack Kerouac in his seminal book *On the Road*. It was saved from the wrecker's ball by a determined preservationist in the 1960s, when the city went demolition-crazy in its eagerness to present a more youthful image. Much has changed since Kerouac's wanderings: Larimer Square's rough edges have been cleaned up in favor of upscale retail and chic restaurants. The Square has also become a serious late-night party district thanks to spillover from the expanded LoDo neighborhood and Rockies fans flowing out from the baseball stadium. Shops line the arched redbrick courtyards of **Writer Square**, one of Denver's most charming shopping districts. ✉ *LoDo* ☎ *303/534–2367* 🌐 *www.larimersquare.com.*

Restaurants

Biker Jim's Gourmet Dogs

$ | **HOT DOG** | **FAMILY** | Quite the character, Biker Jim was hawking his gourmet hot dogs—split down the middle, with Coca-Cola-caramelized onions and a squirt of cream cheese as a topping option—for years on the 16th Street Mall until someone finally convinced him to open his own raucous place. Now he's got two (the second location is at Coors Field) and they're both always packed with folks eager to try a wild boar dog or a duck-cilantro dog. **Known for:** late-night weekend snacks; bizarre but delicious toppings; elk jalapeño cheddar dog. *Average main: $8 ✉ 2148 Larimer St. ☎ 720/746–9355 ⊕ www.bikerjimsdogs.com.*

Bistro Vendôme

$$$ | **FRENCH** | Chef Jennifer Jasinski and her business partner, Beth Gruitch, own several beloved eateries in the area and this classic French bistro, tucked down an alley off the bustling Larimer Square, is equally esteemed. Expect traditional bistro fare done well—think *moules et frites,* escargots, duck confit, rillettes—along with expertly crafted cocktails and an appealing, all-French wine list. **Known for:** perfect herbed pommes frites and French onion soup; inviting bar; Parisian-esque courtyard for outdoor dining. *Average main: $27 ✉ 1420 Larimer St., Larimer Square ☎ 303/925–3232 ⊕ www.bistrovendome.com ⊙ No lunch weekdays.*

Capital Grille

$$$$ | **STEAKHOUSE** | In a town that loves its steaks, the Rhode Island–based chain was taking a chance moving in and pretending to offer anything different from the other high-end big-boy steak houses. That said, Capital Grille—housed in a dark, noisy, broodingly decorated room typical of the genre—has much to recommend it, including a drop-dead Delmonico, textbook French onion soup, and terrific skin-on mashed potatoes. **Known for:** power lunches; excellent steak tartare; best lobster in town. *Average main: $51 ✉ 1450 Larimer St., Larimer Square ☎ 303/539–2500 ⊕ www.thecapitalgrille.com ⊙ Closed Sun.*

★ **Cart-Driver**

$$ | **PIZZA** | Two repurposed shipping containers are the unlikely industrial backdrop for some of the best pizza and oysters in Denver. The owners of Cart-Driver have modeled their casual, unpretentious spot after truck stops in Italy—the Autogrills that focus on putting out simple, easily worked menus that focus on high quality—and the result is crusts that hold their crisp all the way to the center of each pie and briny-fresh oysters, satiny mousses of tuna and chicken liver, and an odd but intriguing roster of canned beers. **Known for:** raucous atmosphere with long waits for a table; clam pizza; house-made chocolate pudding. *Average main: $17 ✉ 2500 Larimer St., Suite 100, RiNo ☎ 303/292–3553 ⊕ www.cart-driver.com.*

Chow Mosro Osteria

$$$ | **ITALIAN** | Brought to LoDo by the same team that owns Barolo Grill, Chow Morso is a much more casual (and less expensive) Italian restaurant that focuses more on everyday food rather than fine dining. That's not to say a visit here doesn't feel special, because the setting is lovely, with mod tables and chairs in blond woods, soft-gray draperies, and the exposed-wood ceiling of the renovated saddlery building. **Known for:** hand-rolled pastas; perfect carbonara; expansive Italian wine list. *Average main: $25 ✉ 1500 Wynkoop St., Suite 101, LoDo ☎ 720/639–4089 ⊕ www.chowmorso.com ⊙ Closed Sun. and Mon. No lunch.*

Coohills

$$$ | **FRENCH** | Classic French cooking is merged with modern techniques and regionally sourced ingredients at this chic, sprawling space that's filled with natural light and offers views of the mountains. Situated at the edge of LoDo and run by the Coohills, a veteran restaurateur couple, the eatery hosts local bands in the summer and has a year-round chef's counter, a large communal table alongside the open kitchen that's

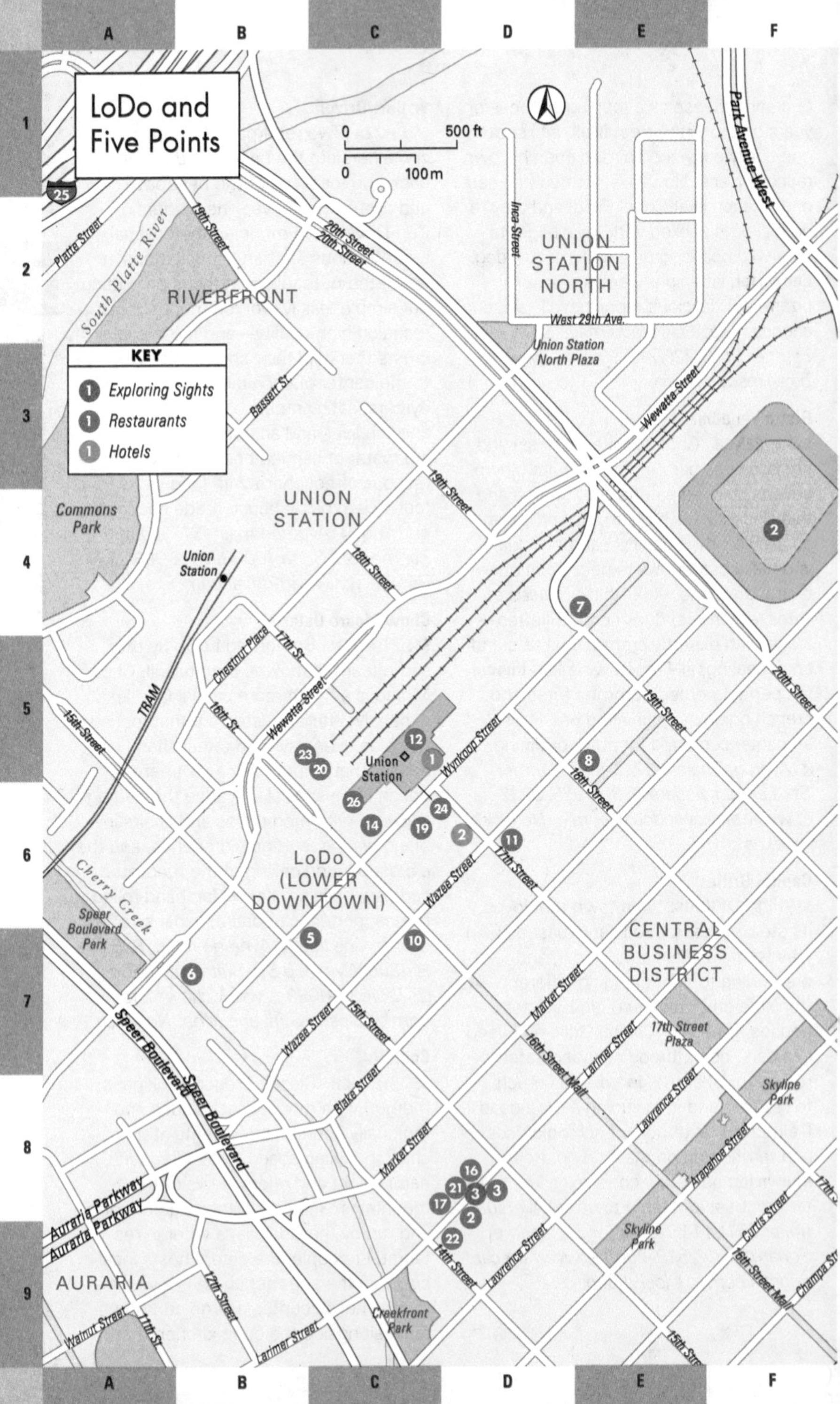
LoDo and Five Points
KEY
Exploring Sights
Restaurants
Hotels
0 500 ft
0 100 m
RIVERFRONT
UNION STATION NORTH
UNION STATION
LoDo (LOWER DOWNTOWN)
CENTRAL BUSINESS DISTRICT
AURARIA
Commons Park
Speer Boulevard Park
Union Station North Plaza
17th Street Plaza
Skyline Park
Creekfront Park
Union Station
South Platte River
Cherry Creek
TRAM
Platte Street
19th Street
20th Street
Bassett St.
Inca Street
West 29th Ave.
Park Avenue West
Wewatta Street
18th Street
17th St.
Chestnut Place
16th St.
15th Street
Wynkoop Street
Wazee Street
17th Street
Market Street
16th Street Mall
Larimer Street
Lawrence Street
Arapahoe Street
Curtis Street
Champa Street
Blake Street
14th Street
15th Street
12th Street
11th St.
Walnut Street
Speer Boulevard
Auraria Parkway
A B C D E F
1 2 3 4 5 6 7 8 9

Sights

1 Black American West Museum and Heritage Center..... J7
2 Coors Field.......................... F4
3 Larimer Square D8

Restaurants

1 Biker Jim's Gourmet Dogs........ H5
2 Bistro Vendôme.................... D8
3 Capital Grille........................ D8
4 Cart-Driver............................ J3
5 Chow Morso Osteria B7
6 Coohills B7
7 Denver ChopHouse & Brewery............................... E4
8 Denver Milk Market................ E5
9 Il Posto.................................. J2
10 Illegal Pete's......................... C7
11 Jax Fish House & Oyster Bar..... D6
12 The Kitchen Next Door Union Station........................ C5
13 Marco's Coal Fired Pizzeria....... H5
14 Mercantile Dining & Provisions C6
15 Osaka Ramen J2
16 Osteria Marco........................ D8
17 Rioja D8
18 Snooze H4
19 Stoic & Genuine C6
20 Sunday Vinyl Kitchen and Wine Bar................................ C5
21 TAG D8
22 Tamayo.................................. D9
23 Tavernetta B5
24 Ultreia.................................... C5
25 Work & Class.......................... J3
26 Zoe Ma Ma............................. C6

Hotels

1 The Crawford Hotel................. C5
2 Oxford Hotel........................... D6

Historic Larimer Square is now one of Denver's best places to drink and dine.

set up for tasting menus of 5 to 10 courses with optional wine pairings. **Known for:** free weekly concerts in summer; chef's counter; modern takes on classic French dishes. *Average main: $28 1400 Wewatta St., LoDo 303/623–5700 www.coohills.com Closed Sun. and Mon. No lunch.*

Denver ChopHouse & Brewery

$$$ | **STEAKHOUSE** | Housed in the old Union Pacific Railroad warehouse, the restaurant, similar to the ones in Washington, D.C., and Boulder, is clubby, with dark-wood paneling and exposed brick. The food is basic American, and there's plenty of it: steaks, seafood, pizzas, and chicken served with hot corn bread and honey butter, and "bottomless" salads tossed at the table. **Known for:** pre- and post-game dining; classic brewpub food, including a great steak; sports celebrity sightings. *Average main: $28 1735 19th St., LoDo 303/296–0800 www.denverchophouse.com.*

★ **Denver Milk Market**

$ | **ITALIAN** | As if chef and restaurateur Frank Bonanno didn't have enough on his plate with nine other eateries—including Mizuna, Luca, and Osteria Marco—he opened this market hall containing three bars and 13 food counters. Among the offerings: a reworking of a former Bonanno eatery, Lou's Hot and Naked, and its Nashville-style fried chicken; fresh seafood at Albina by the Sea; wood-fired pizza at Bonnano Brothers Pizzeria; handmade pasta from Mano Pastaria; and boozy milkshakes and freshly crafted soft-serve at Cornicello Gelato. **Known for:** wide variety of vendors; pizza until 3 am; locally sourced food. *Average main: $14 1800 Wazee St., LoDo 303/792–8242 www.denvermilkmarket.com.*

Il Posto

$$ | **MODERN ITALIAN** | The menu, written on a chalkboard on the wall, changes daily at Il Posto (The Place), where chef/owner Andrea Frizzi cooks intricately layered Italian dishes based on what's fresh, often from local farms. Get anything with

foie gras, nasturtiums, or fennel—all of which can be easily paired with the eatery's focused and well-priced Italian-only wine list. **Known for:** savvy sommeliers; great people-watching; lively communal table. *Average main: $20 2601 Larimer St., RiNo 303/394–0100 www.ilpostodenver.com.*

Illegal Pete's

$ | **MODERN MEXICAN** | With nine metro-area locations around Denver and Boulder (the original) and one in Fort Collins, this hip, homegrown chain of burrito joints gives larger operations like Chipotle a run for their money by using hormone-free meats and locally sourced ingredients and by offering five-hour daily happy hours and live music. The burritos are enormous—they even do a tasty fish version—and breakfast burritos (yes, they include chorizo) are nice options. **Known for:** convivial atmosphere late into the night; live music; great breakfast burrito. *Average main: $8 1530 16th St., LoDo 303/623–2169 www.illegalpetes.com No credit cards.*

Jax Fish House & Oyster Bar

$$$ | **SEAFOOD** | A popular oyster bar serves as the foyer to the ever-busy Jax, whose brick-lined back dining room packs in the crowds, especially when there's a ball game at Coors Field three blocks away. A dozen different types of oysters are freshly shucked each day, and main courses make use of fresh catches flown in from both coasts such as ahi tuna, scallops, snapper, and shrimp. **Known for:** East Coast oysters; innovative fish dishes; lively atmosphere with lots of crowds. *Average main: $28 1539 17th St., LoDo 303/292–5767 www.jaxdenver.com No lunch.*

The Kitchen Next Door Union Station

$ | **MODERN AMERICAN** | **FAMILY** | With more reasonably priced offerings and a more casual setting than the other Kitchens in Boulder and Glendale, Next Door's comfortable pub style fits in well at Union Station and provides burgers, sandwiches, and a much-needed selection of healthy salads—the organic kale and apple salad is crunchy and satisfying and part of its proceeds is donated to community school gardens. It's also a great happy-hour stop (daily 2:30–5:30 pm), with snacks for $3 to $6 and drink prices to match. **Known for:** commitment to sustainability; delicious organic kale and apple salad; one of the city's best happy hours. *Average main: $14 1701 Wynkoop St., Suite 100, LoDo 720/460–3730 www.nextdooreatery.com.*

Marco's Coal-Fired Pizzeria

$$ | **PIZZA** | **FAMILY** | Pizzerias often claim to serve authentic Neapolitan pizza, but in this casual, brick-lined place, it's true: Marco's pies come out of the coal-fired ovens with a crispy-crackly crust, generously topped with fresh mozzarella and fresh basil, and just the right amount of homemade sauce made from San Marzano tomatoes. If New York–style is more your thing, they have that, too (try the Bronx, with meatballs). **Known for:** weekend bottomless brunch; cozy downstairs; Nutella pizza and excellent fresh cannolis for dessert. *Average main: $18 2129 Larimer St., Five Points 303/296–7000 www.marcoscfp.com.*

★ Mercantile Dining & Provisions

$$$ | **MODERN AMERICAN** | Brought to you by the same James Beard award–winning chef Alex Seidel of Fruition, Mercantile features the same ingredients from their farm and creamery as well as the emphasis on fresh and local. The pretty space, with its powder-blue upholstery and milky-white walls, calms and invites lingering, ideal for a menu that includes starters doubling as small plates—the bone marrow brûlée has become legendary, and the "provisions" platter pulls from the farm's cheeses and pickles that are also available at the on-site market. **Known for:** the very essence of seasonal dining with farm-fresh ingredients; bone marrow brûlée; creative cocktails and

unique wines. *Average main: $28* *1701 Wynkoop St., Suite 155, LoDo* *720/460–3733* *www.mercantileden-ver.com.*

Osaka Ramen

$ | **JAPANESE** | This spot makes some of the best ramen in town, including a solid shoyu—complete with pork shoulder and a soft egg—and a top-notch *tonkotsu*, with the richness of the pork belly cut with pickled ginger. Although on the small side, the space is casual and comfortable, but it fills up fast. **Known for:** fast service; dessert doughnuts served with salted butter; half-price happy hour. *Average main: $14* *2611 Walnut St.* *303/955–7938* *www.osakara-mendenver.com.*

Osteria Marco

$$$ | **ITALIAN** | **FAMILY** | The Bonannos, whose restaurants number more than a dozen now and are all among the best in town, continue to have success with this reasonably priced, casual eatery. High-backed wooden booths, dish towels as napkins, and exposed-brick walls provide a hip, urban setting below street level for wood-fired pizzas topped with Frank Bonanno's homemade or imported cheeses and house-cured meats. **Known for:** meat and cheese bar; pizzas with thin, crackly crusts; Sunday night roast suckling pig. *Average main: $24* *1453 Larimer St., Larimer Square* *303/534–5855* *www.osteriamarco.com.*

★ Rioja

$$$ | **MEDITERRANEAN** | The restaurant is hip and artsy, with exposed brick and blown-glass lighting, arched doorways, and textured draperies. chef Jennifer Jasinski's intense attention to detail is evident in her tribute to Mediterranean food with contemporary flair. The 2013 James Beard winner for Best Chef Southwest, she also partners with Beth Gruitch to run Stoic & Genuine, Bistro Vendôme, and Ultreia; Gruitch is in charge of the front of the house here too, and together the duo has maintained a remarkably loyal following. **Known for:** classy atmosphere; Rioja-focused wine list; hearty portions. *Average main: $30* *1431 Larimer St., Larimer Square* *303/820–2282* *www.riojadenver.com* *No lunch Mon. and Tues.*

Snooze

$ | **AMERICAN** | The line for this Ballpark neighborhood joint starts just before the 6:30 am weekday opening and sometimes an hour before it opens on weekends, because the lavish breakfasts are well worth the wait. The hollandaise-smothered creations alone—for instance, the Bella!, with Taleggio cheese and prosciutto on toasted ciabatta—are a must-try, and the pineapple upside-down pancakes, with vanilla crème anglaise and cinnamon butter, are exquisite. **Known for:** huge crowds and long waits; filling breakfasts; sugar-bomb French toast. *Average main: $13* *2262 Larimer St., Five Points* *303/297–0700* *www.snoozeeatery.com.*

★ Stoic & Genuine

$$$ | **SEAFOOD** | Known for their eateries Rioja and Bistro Vendôme, Jennifer Jasinski and Beth Gruitch bring fresh seafood and oysters to Union Station in an oddly configured but ultimately comfortable space that features two somewhat cramped raw-bar areas and a row of regular seating, as well as a spacious patio that offers excellent people-watching. The oyster roster is expansive and fresh and comes with a choice of granitas. **Known for:** creative seafood preparations; excellent lobster roll; barbecued octopus. *Average main: $28* *1701 Wynkoop St., LoDo* *303/640–3474* *www.stoicandgenuine.com.*

Sunday Vinyl Kitchen and Wine Bar

$$ | **EUROPEAN** | Hip and happening, Sunday Vinyl was inspired by the Sunday-night-off tradition of listening to records and drinking wine practiced by the owners of Boulder's Frasca, who also own the nearby Tavernetta, which like Sunday

Vinyl is tucked in behind Union Station. The European-style wine bar features an eclectic rotation of music (yes, all on vinyl, played on vintage equipment), chosen for the tony crowds that pack this place nightly. **Known for:** stylish setting; extensive wine list; creative, pan-European small plates. *Average main: $22* *1803 16th St., LoDo* *720/738–1803* *www.sundayvinyl.com* *No lunch weekdays.*

TAG

$$$ | ASIAN FUSION | At first glance, the menu at TAG seems to be all over the place, but after a few bites of chef/owner Troy Guard's eclectic, self-described "continental social food," it all starts to make sense. The dishes are inspired by his Hawaiian upbringing but also draw heavily from Asian and Latin American influences, and the result is a lot of bold flavors that work surprisingly well together. **Known for:** afternoon snacks and cheap drinks; taco sushi; daring dishes. *Average main: $26* *1441 Larimer St., Larimer Square* *303/996–9985* *www.tag-restaurant.com* *Closed Sun. and Mon. No lunch.*

Tamayo

$$$ | MEXICAN | Chef-owner Richard Sandoval brought his popular concept of modern, upscale Mexican cuisine from New York to Denver, and it's just as welcome here. The food is classic Mexican with a twist, such as seafood tacos, *huitlacoche* (edible fungus) dumpling soup, and elaborate moles. **Known for:** tequila flights; mountain views from the patio; bottomless drinks at brunch. *Average main: $24* *1400 Larimer St., Larimer Square* *720/946–1433* *www.eattamayo.com.*

★ Tavernetta

$$$ | FRIULIAN | The modern and elegant Tavernetta features inventive takes on classic Italian dishes (specifically, from the Friuli region) such as homemade pastas, house-cured meats and cheeses, rabbit, quail, and lamb. The appealing, well-varied (and not surprisingly, Italian-heavy) wine list is curated by the multiple sommeliers on staff. **Known for:** impeccable service; perfect lobster tagliatelle; extensive Amari roster. *Average main: $24* *1889 16th St., LoDo* *720/605–1889* *www.tavernettadenver.com.*

Ultreia

$$$ | SPANISH | Mere yards from another of Chef Jennifer Jasinski and business partner Beth Gruitch's popular Union Station restaurant Stoic & Genuine (and blocks from their Larimer Square restaurant Rioja), the Iberian-influenced Ultreia is a charming and lively eatery serving seasonally based Spanish tapas and Portuguese delicacies. The wine list and cocktail roster draw primarily from both regions. **Known for:** trio of cured hams; herbal gin-tonics and sherry; Portuguese egg tart for dessert. *Average main: $30* *1701 Wynkoop St., Suite 125, LoDo* *303/534–1970* *www.ultreiadenver.com.*

Work & Class

$ | LATIN AMERICAN | Well executed in a shipping container in the trendy RiNo Arts District, this restaurant sits guests at a communal table or at one of the two bars, where you can watch the line cooks shred pork for the tender *cochinita pibil* (a savory slow-roasted Yucatán favorite) or cut off haunches of citrus-zesty short ribs—meat comes priced by weight, from a quarter to a full pound. In keeping with the name, the rest of the menu is indeed "regular folks' food," but turned up a notch: think shrimp and grits or cheesy tomato mac spiked with chipotles. **Known for:** Tequila Tuesday deals; the city's best fried chicken; bustling scene (no reservations so expect a wait). *Average main: $13* *2500 Larimer St., Suite 101, RiNo* *303/292–0700* *www.workandclassdenver.com* *Closed Mon. and Tues. No lunch.*

Zoe Ma Ma

$ | **SICHUAN** | Named for the owner's mom, who's also a chef and usually on-site at either this location or the one in Boulder, the fast-casual Zoe Ma Ma offers Chinese homestyle and street food such as dim sum and spicy noodles. Ask for the "secret menu," to access the scallion pancakes and seafood dishes. **Known for:** Sichuan beef noodle soup; super-fast service; patio dining. *Average main: $8* *1625 Wynkoop St., LoDo* *303/545–6262* *www.zoemama.com.*

Hotels

★ The Crawford Hotel

$$$ | **HOTEL** | The lobby here—which guests can view from each floor—is the impressively renovated Union Station, a retro delight of desks with chain-pull lamps, long wooden benches, and constant bustle; the nostalgic sense of being on a train journey is carried elegantly into the 112 rooms, each of which offers a unique layout and design. **Pros:** centralized location; never have to leave Union Station; large choice of excellent restaurants. **Cons:** on the pricey side; lobby chaos at peak times can be jarring; trains whistle constantly. *Rooms from: $225* *1701 Wynkoop St., LoDo* *720/460–3700, 844/432–9374* *www.thecrawfordhotel.com* *112 rooms* *No meals.*

★ Oxford Hotel

$$$ | **HOTEL** | During the Victorian era this hotel was an elegant fixture on the Denver landscape; its comfortable rooms are furnished with French and English period antiques, and civilized touches like complimentary shoe shines, afternoon sherry, and morning coffee remain. **Pros:** prime LoDo location; gorgeous historic setting; great restaurants on-site and nearby. **Cons:** noisy ballpark crowds in season turn LoDo area into a big party; one of the pricier hotels in town; some rooms are tiny. *Rooms from: $260* *1600 17th St., LoDo* *303/628–5400, 833/524–0368* *www.theoxfordhotel.com* *88 rooms* *No meals.*

Nightlife

Comedy Works

COMEDY CLUBS | Denver comics have honed their skills at Comedy Works for more than 30 years, and nationally known performers make it a tour stop. A second location, The Landmark in Greenwood Village, has an upscale lounge and restaurant attached. *1226 15th St., LoDo* *303/595–3637* *www.comedyworks.com.*

Herb's Bar

MUSIC CLUBS | Hidden in the back of a parking lot, the hipster favorite Herb's Bar, known locally by its previous name, Herb's Hideout, is a gloriously nostalgic bar with dim lighting, comfortable booths, and inexpensive cocktails. *2057 Larimer St., LoDo* *303/299–9555* *www.herbsbar.com.*

Mercury Café

MUSIC CLUBS | Tripling as a health-food restaurant with sublime tofu fettuccine, fringe theater, and rock club in a downtown neighborhood, the Mercury Café specializes in acoustic sets, progressive, and newer wave music. Weekly swing and salsa dance lessons upstairs and poetry readings in a side room add to the appeal. Credit cards aren't accepted; there is an ATM on-site. The eatery also prides itself on its self-reliance on solar and wind energy and neighborhood tree and urban garden programs. *2199 California St., Five Points* *303/294–9258* *www.mercurycafe.com* *Closed Mon.*

★ Wynkoop Brewing Company

BREWPUBS/BEER GARDENS | One of the city's best-known bars has anchored LoDo since it was a pre–Coors Field warehouse district. The Wynkoop Brewing Company is now more famous for its founder—former Denver mayor and Colorado governor and current senator John

Hickenlooper—than for its brews, food, or ambience, but it remains a relaxing, slightly upscale, two-story joint filled with halfway-decent bar food, the usual pool tables, and games and beers of all types. ✉ *1634 18th St., LoDo* ☎ *303/297–2700* 🌐 *www.wynkoop.com.*

Shopping

David Cook Fine Art

ART GALLERIES | Historic Native American art and regional paintings, particularly Santa Fe modernists, are David Cook's specialty. ✉ *1637 Wazee St., LoDo* ☎ *303/623–8181* 🌐 *www.davidcookfine-art.com.*

Mudhead Gallery

ART GALLERIES | This gallery in the Titanium Lofts building sells museum-quality Southwestern and Native American art, with an especially fine selection of Santa Clara and San Ildefonso pottery and Hopi kachinas. ✉ *1720 Wazee St., LoDo* ☎ *303/293–0007* 🌐 *www.mudheadgal-lery.com.*

Native American Trading Company

ART GALLERIES | The collection of crafts, jewelry, and regional paintings here is outstanding. ✉ *213 W. 13th Ave., Golden Triangle* ☎ *303/534–0771* 🌐 *www.nativeamericantradingco.com.*

Writer Square

SHOPPING NEIGHBORHOODS | This square is a small but charming and pedestri-an-friendly gathering place with shops and restaurants popular with downtown business types on their lunch breaks. The quirky galleries make for amusing window-shopping. ✉ *1512 Larimer St., LoDo.*

Capitol Hill and Civic Center

These two separate but adjacent neighborhoods both offer a nice taste of Denver's history and culture. Capitol Hill surrounds the gold-domed Colorado State Capitol building and features plenty of bars and restaurants along with historic mansions turned museums. The Civic Center and its vibrant Golden Triangle Arts District has plenty of art galleries and museums, including the Denver Museum of Art.

Sights

Byers-Evans House Museum

MUSEUM | Sprawling and detailed, red and black, this elaborate Victorian went up in 1883 as the home of *Rocky Mountain News* publisher William Byers. Restored to its pre–World War I condition, the historic landmark has occasional exhibitions and regular guided tours. Its main appeal is the glimpse it provides into Denver's past, specifically 1912 through 1924; more recently, the Center for Women's History has taken up residence here, which means an enhanced focus on women's studies and free rotating exhibits. The furnishings are those the Evans family acquired during the 80-some years they lived here. ✉ *1310 Bannock St., Civic Center* ☎ *303/620–4933* 🌐 *www.historycolorado.org* 🎟 *Gallery free; $8 guided house tour.*

Civic Center

CITY PARK | A peaceful respite awaits in this three-block park in the cultural heart of downtown, site of the State Capitol. A 1919 Greek amphitheater is in the middle of one of the city's largest flower gardens, and in summer, it's the site of free bike-in movies at dusk. Festivals such as Cinco de Mayo, Taste of Colorado, and the People's Fair keep things lively here in spring and summer, and on Tuesday,

The Denver Art Museum features a wide array of exhibits.

Wednesday, and Thursday, food trucks offer lunchtime alternatives. The park was born in 1906, when Mayor Robert Speer asked New York architect Charles Robinson to expand on his vision of a "Paris on the Platte." Two of the park's statues, *Broncho Buster* and *On the War Trail*, depicting a cowboy and an Indian on horseback, were commissioned in the 1920s. ✉ *Bannock St. to Broadway south of Colfax Ave. and north of 14th Ave., Civic Center* 🌐 *www.civiccenterconservancy.org* 🎟 *Free.*

Clyfford Still Museum

MUSEUM | Though he showed very little of his work and sold even less during his lifetime, artist Clyfford Still has nonetheless been credited as a significant contributor to the abstract expressionist movement, if not one of the most instrumental in its development. The vast majority of his extensive body of work had been sealed from the public since his death in 1980, but in 2004 his second wife chose Denver as the final resting place for a carefully curated portion—a little more than a hundred works of the more than 2,400 pieces, including paintings, drawings, and sculpture. The nine galleries reveal Still's progression in chronological displays, and true to Still's wishes, it offers no restaurant. Periodically, the museum refreshes the works on display to present a new side of the artist's vision. ✉ *1250 Bannock St., Golden Triangle* ☎ *720/354–4880* 🌐 *www.clyffordstillmuseum.org* 🎟 *$10* 🕒 *Closed Mon.*

★ Denver Art Museum

MUSEUM | **FAMILY** | Unique displays of Asian, pre-Columbian, Spanish Colonial, and Native American art are the hallmarks of this model of museum design. Among the museum's regular holdings are John DeAndrea's life-size polyvinyl painting *Linda* (1983); Claude Monet's dreamy flowerscape *Le Bassin aux Nympheas* (1904); and Charles Deas's red-cowboy-on-horseback *Long Jakes, The Rocky Mountain Man* (1844). The works are thoughtfully lighted, though dazzling mountain views through hallway windows sometimes steal your attention. Imaginative hands-on exhibits, game- and puzzle-filled Family Backpacks, and video corners will appeal to children; the Adventures in Art Center has hands-on art classes and exploration for children and adults. The museum doubled in size with the 2007 opening of the Frederic C. Hamilton building, a 146,000-square-foot addition designed by architect Daniel Libeskind that has prompted debate: some say the glass and titanium design has ruined the view, while others think the building is a work of art in its own right. To the east of the museum is an outdoor plaza—you'll know it by the huge orange metal sculpture—that leads to the Denver Public Library next door. ✉ *100 W. 14th Ave. Pkwy., Civic Center* ☎ *720/913–0130* 🌐 *www.denverartmuseum.org* 🎫 *$13.*

★ Denver Public Library's Central Library

LIBRARY | FAMILY | A life-size horse on a 20-foot-tall chair and other sculptures decorate the expansive lawn of this sprawling complex with round towers and tall, oblong windows. The map and manuscript rooms, Gates Western History Reading Room (with amazing views of the mountains), and Schlessman Hall (with its three-story atrium) merit a visit. Built in the mid-'50s, the library houses a world-renowned collection of books, photographs, and newspapers that chronicle the American West, as well as original paintings by Remington, Russell, Audubon, and Bierstadt. The children's library is notable for its captivating design and its unique, child-friendly multimedia computer catalog. ✉ *10 W. 14th Ave. Pkwy., Civic Center* ☎ *720/865–1111* 🌐 *www.denverlibrary.org.*

History Colorado Center

MUSEUM | FAMILY | The three-story, interactive History Colorado Center serves as the state's de facto historical society. Rotating lobby exhibits welcome visitors with hands-on, offbeat snippets of state history. In addition to revamped versions of the previous collections depicting state history from 1800 to the present, current exhibitions combine technology, artifacts, and multimedia presentations. Milk a life-size replica of a cow, drive a Model T Ford on the plains, or try a virtual ski jump, and then see what you would have looked like in a classroom in the late 1800s. ✉ *1200 Broadway, Civic Center* ☎ *303/447–8679* 🌐 *www.historycolorado.org* 🎫 *$14.*

Molly Brown House

HOUSE | This Victorian celebrates the life and times of the scandalous, "unsinkable" Molly Brown. The heroine of the *Titanic* courageously saved several lives and continued to provide assistance to survivors back on terra firma. Costumed guides and period furnishings in the museum, including flamboyant gilt-edge wallpaper, lace curtains, tile fireplaces, and tapestries, evoke bygone days. The museum collects and displays artifacts that belonged to Brown, as well as period items dating to 1894–1912, when the Browns lived in the house. Tours run every half hour; you won't need much more than that to see the whole place. A bit of trivia: Margaret Tobin Brown was known as Maggie, not Molly—allegedly a Hollywood invention that Brown did not like—during her lifetime. ✉ *1340 Pennsylvania St., Capitol Hill* ☎ *303/832–4092* 🌐 *www.mollybrown.org* 🎫 *$14.*

Museo de las Americas

MUSEUM | The region's first museum dedicated to the achievements of Latinx in the Americas has a permanent collection as well as rotating exhibits that cover everything from Latin Americans in the state legislature to Latin American female artists in the 20th century. Among the more than 3,300 permanent pieces are the oil painting *Virgin of Solitude* (circa 1730) and a Mayan polychrome jar (circa 650–950), as well as contemporary works. In addition to the regular hours, the museum is open (with free admission) the first Friday evening of each month from 5 to 9. ✉ *861 Santa Fe Dr., Lincoln Park* ☎ *303/571–4401* 🌐 *www.museo.org* 🎫 *$8* 🕑 *Closed Sun. and Mon.*

★ State Capitol

GOVERNMENT BUILDING | Built in 1886, the capitol was constructed mostly of materials indigenous to Colorado, including marble, granite, and rose onyx. Especially inspiring is the gold-leaf dome, a reminder of the state's mining heritage. The dome is open for tours weekdays by appointment on the hour and 30 people at a time can go to the top (using a 99-step staircase from the third floor) to take in the 360-degree view of the Rockies. Historical tours and a legislative tour are available. Outside, a marker on the 13th step indicates where the elevation is exactly 1 mile high (above sea level). The legislature is generally in session from January through May, and visitors are welcome to sit in third-floor viewing galleries above the House and Senate chambers. ✉ *200 E. Colfax Ave., Capitol Hill* ☎ *303/866–2604 dome tours* 🌐 *www.colorado.gov/capitol* 🎫 *Free.*

U.S. Mint

GOVERNMENT BUILDING | Tour this facility to catch a glimpse of the coin-making process, as presses spit out thousands of coins a minute. There are also exhibits on the history of money and a restored version of Denver's original mint prior to numerous expansions. More than 14 billion coins are minted yearly, and the nation's second-largest hoard of gold is stashed away here. To schedule a 45-minute tour and prepare for your visit (there are strict security guidelines), visit the Mint's website. Reservations are required for all tours, which are guided (Monday to Thursday from 8:00 to 3:30), free, and available to visitors age seven and older. The gift shop, which sells authentic coins and currency, is in the Tremont Center, across Colfax Avenue from the Mint. ✉ *320 W. Colfax Ave., Civic Center* ☎ *303/405–4761* 🌐 *www.usmint.gov/mint_tours* 🎫 *Free.*

Restaurants

Beast + Bottle

$$ | **MODERN AMERICAN** | A cozy space that's just right for couples and small get-togethers, this Uptown eatery is aptly named for its constantly rotating roster of small plates and handful of entrées that focus on a fish, a couple of meat options, and always one or two vegetarian dishes. The kitchen proclaims a focus on "using the whole animal," with an attempt to introduce diners to new cuts or unusual preparations—they make all the broths and sauces from scraps and bones and offer organ meats in delectable ways. **Known for:** precision cooking; root beer–braised short ribs; unique wine list. 💲 *Average main: $22* ✉ *719 E. 17th Ave., Capitol Hill* ☎ *303/623–3223* 🌐 *www.beastandbottle.com* 🕒 *Closed Mon. No lunch Tues.–Fri.*

Brother's BBQ

$ | **SOUTHERN** | **FAMILY** | Two brothers from England traveled the southern United States on a quest to learn everything there is to know about barbecue, and they decided to share the information with Denver. The result is some of the best 'cue in town, from St. Louis–style ribs to beef brisket, pulled pork, and chicken. **Known for:** ribs slow smoked over hickory; casual setting; tasty side dishes. 💲 *Average main: $10* ✉ *568 N. Washington St., Civic Center* ☎ *720/570–4227* 🌐 *www.brothers-bbq.com.*

Buckhorn Exchange

$$$$ | **STEAKHOUSE** | If hunting makes you queasy, don't enter this Denver landmark and taxidermy shrine, where more than 500 pairs of eyes stare down at you from the walls. The dry-aged, prime-grade Colorado steaks are huge, juicy, and magnificent, as is the game. **Known for:** navy-bean soup; cozy second-floor bar; men's club look. 💲 *Average main: $45* ✉ *1000 Osage St., Civic Center* ☎ *303/534–9505* 🌐 *www.buckhorn.com* 🕒 *No lunch.*

City Cafe

$ | **AMERICAN** | **FAMILY** | Everything is made from scratch at this charming little bakery and café, including the stocks for the French onion soup and other daily restoratives offered alongside the stacked-high sandwiches. Freshly baked for more than a hundred local restaurants, the dozens of varieties of breads are also available to take home or eat at a booth in the light-filled space. **Known for:** excellent baked goods; Christmas stollen (a fruit bread); delicious French dip. *Average main: $9 726 Lincoln St., Downtown 303/861–0809 www.citycafedenver.com Closed Sun. No dinner.*

City O' City

$ | **VEGETARIAN** | Brought to Denver by the same folks who run the vegetarian-friendly WaterCourse, City O' City is a welcoming, casual, three-meals-daily bakery and café that offers gluten-free, vegan, and all manner of other dietary options in a bright, breezy atmosphere. Add cheese and eggs if you like, go macrobiotic, or imbibe from the wine and beer list—there are no judgements here. **Known for:** great coffee; vegan snacks and pastries; artwork from revolving featured artists. *Average main: $14 206 E. 13th Ave., Capitol Hill 303/831–6443 www.cityocitydenver.com.*

CityGrille

$ | **AMERICAN** | Politicians and construction workers rub shoulders while chowing down on the well-crafted sandwiches, soups, and salads at this casual eatery across the street from the State Capitol. CityGrille has earned national attention for both its burger, a half-pounder of ground sirloin, and its chili, a gringo stew of pork, jalapeños, and tomatoes that's spicy and addictive. **Known for:** the famous steakburger; late hours (open until 11 pm); no-frills establishment. *Average main: $12 321 E. Colfax Ave., Capitol Hill 303/861–0726 www.citygrille.com.*

Domo

$$ | **JAPANESE** | Domo's owners pride themselves on fresh flavors and the painstaking preparation of Japanese country foods, as well as one of the largest sake selections in town. Everything is prepared to order, and it's worth the wait: this is where you can find some of Denver's best seafood, curry dishes, and vegetarian fare. **Known for:** patio dining; multicourse wanko sushi; on-site museum and Japanese garden. *Average main: $22 1365 Osage St., Civic Center 303/595–3666 www.domorestaurant.com.*

★ Fruition

$$$$ | **MODERN AMERICAN** | Well-crafted, elegant comfort food made from seasonal ingredients is served in compelling combinations, like roasted pork with fennel, sausage-stuffed squash blossoms, and Colorado lamb loin served with ricotta tortellini. The bonus is that the cheese is made from sheep's milk at chef/owner Alex Seidel's own farm. **Known for:** intimate atmosphere; farm-raised ingredients; potato-wrapped oysters Rockefeller. *Average main: $31 1313 E. 6th Ave., City Park 303/831–1962 www.fruitionrestaurant.com No lunch.*

Luca

$$$ | **ITALIAN** | The restaurant's steel-gray, orange-and-red contemporary decor belies the fact that it's one of the most authentic Italian restaurants in the city. Chef-owner Frank Bonanno summons the memory of his Italian grandmother to re-create small-town Italy through wild boar with pappardelle, goat-stuffed *caramelle* (pasta shaped like candy wrappers), and house-cured capocollo and homemade cheeses. **Known for:** Italian-focused wine list; perfect tiramisu; house-cured meats and cheeses. *Average main: $26 711 Grant St., Capitol Hill 303/832–6600 www.lucadenver.com Closed Mon. and Tues. No lunch.*

★ Mizuna

$$$$ | **MODERN AMERICAN** | Chef-owner Frank Bonanno knows how to transform butter and cream into comforting masterpieces at this cozy eatery with warm colors and intimate seating. His menu is reminiscent of California's French Laundry—witness the foie gras torchon—but his Italian heritage has given him the ability to work wonders with house-made pastas and gnocchi, and he often offers a ragout or other long-stewed sauce. **Known for:** fine French dining; rotating menu; butter-poached lobster. *Average main: $42* *225 E. 7th Ave., Capitol Hill* *303/832–4778* *www.mizunadenver.com* *Closed Sun. and Mon. No lunch.*

Pete's Kitchen

$ | **GREEK** | This old-fashioned, 24/7, greasy-spoon diner specializes in Greek food, huge pancakes, and spicy huevos rancheros. It's a short drive from the Denver Museum of Nature & Science, and it's often packed, particularly on Sunday mornings. **Known for:** convivial atmosphere; smothered burritos; speedy service. *Average main: $11* *1962 E. Colfax Ave., Cheesman Park* *303/321–3139* *www.petesrestaurants.com.*

Potager

$$ | **MODERN AMERICAN** | The menu changes monthly at this industrial-designed restaurant, whose name, French for "kitchen garden," refers to the herb-rimmed back patio. The menu always includes a selection of salads along with fish and a thin-crust pizza from the wood-fired oven. **Known for:** inexpensive wines; French influences; extensive roster of local purveyors. *Average main: $22* *1109 Ogden St., Capitol Hill* *303/832–5788* *www.potagerrestaurant.com* *Closed Mon. No lunch.*

WaterCourse Foods

$ | **VEGETARIAN** | In a town known for its beef, WaterCourse stands out as a devoted vegan eatery in spacious digs uptown. This casual, low-key place serves herbivores three meals a day, most of which are based on fruits, vegetables, whole grains, and meat-like soy substitutes. **Known for:** clever meat substitutes; vegan baked goods; organic wine and local kombucha. *Average main: $14* *837 E. 17th Ave., Capitol Hill* *303/832-7313* *www.watercoursefoods.com.*

Hotels

★ The ART Hotel

$$$$ | **HOTEL** | Each floor of rooms in this nine-story building is dedicated to a different artist, with original art in every room by the artist, as well—you can't miss the entry-level greeting *Wall Drawing #397* by Sol LeWitt or the video art in the elevators that signal this is going to be a unique lodging experience. **Pros:** compelling art collection; comfortable, stylish rooms; incredible views. **Cons:** one of the most expensive hotels in Denver; restaurant still working out the kinks; conventions sometimes overcrowd the hotel. *Rooms from: $375* *1201 Broadway, Civic Center* *303/572–8000* *www.thearthotel.com* *145 rooms* *No meals.*

Capitol Hill Mansion Bed & Breakfast Inn

$$$ | **B&B/INN** | The dramatic turret and intense rust color of this Richardson Romanesque Victorian mansion built in 1891 is enough to draw you into the eight elegantly appointed rooms done in wildflower themes, such as ElkThistle and Forget Me Not. The Gold Banner suite is cheerfully yellow, with a separate sitting room and gas-log fireplace, and it, along with two other rooms, has a view of the Rockies. **Pros:** welcoming hosts; inviting rooms; walking distance to downtown. **Cons:** walls are thin; place feels remote compared to rest of downtown; neighborhood can be noisy. *Rooms from: $254* *1207 Pennsylvania St., Capitol Hill* *303/839–5221, 800/839–9329* *www.capitolhillmansion.com* *8 rooms* *Free Breakfast.*

Queen Anne Inn
$$ | **B&B/INN** | Just north of downtown in the regentrified Clements historic district (some of the neighboring blocks have yet to be reclaimed), this inn made up of adjacent Victorians is a delightful, romantic getaway. **Pros:** lovely rooms; daily wine tastings; hearty breakfast. **Cons:** not right downtown; neighborhood can be noisy; thin walls. *Rooms from: $165* *2147 Tremont Pl., Downtown* *303/296–6666, 800/432–4667* *www.queenannebnb.com* *13 rooms* *Free Breakfast.*

Ramada by Wyndham Denver Downtown
$$ | **HOTEL** | This Ramada is within walking distance of the capitol, as well as nine blocks east of downtown and the 16th Street Mall, and it's one of the few reasonably priced lodgings left so close to the heart of downtown.The spacious rooms in varying shades of brown and beige are filled with prints of Colorado landscapes, and the lobby is dominated by comfy leather couches. **Pros:** very reasonable rates; easy to get downtown; bustling Colfax location appealing during the day. **Cons:** not the safest part of Colfax Avenue late at night; can be noisy; chain feel. *Rooms from: $161* *1150 E. Colfax Ave., Capitol Hill* *303/831–7700, 800/272–6232* *www.ramada.com* *143 rooms* *No meals.*

Warwick Denver Hotel
$$$ | **HOTEL** | **FAMILY** | This stylish midsize business- and family-friendly hotel is ideally located on the edge of downtown, and the spacious rooms have been updated with comfortable beds and the latest in high-tech perks to complement the brass and mahogany furnishings and roomy marble bathrooms. **Pros:** reasonable rates; all rooms have private terraces with city views; rare downtown outdoor swimming pool. **Cons:** more than walking distance from the business district; sometimes attracts large, party-focused groups; walls are thin. *Rooms from: $269* *1776 Grant St., Downtown* *303/861–2000, 800/525–2888* *www.warwickdenver.com* *161 rooms* *No meals.*

Nightlife

Charlie's Denver
BARS/PUBS | Charlie's has country-western atmosphere, music, and dancing, and a drag show at least one night a week. *900 E. Colfax Ave., Capitol Hill* *303/839–8890* *www.charliesdenver.com.*

★ The Church
DANCE CLUBS | Multiple rooms on three floors in a decommissioned church host DJ-spun Goth, indie, and industrial dance music on Sunday nights, as well as progressive trance, hip-hop, and global on Friday, and bachata, reggaeton, salsa, cumbia, and Latin house music on Saturday. *1160 Lincoln St., Capitol Hill* *303/832–2383* *www.coclubs.com/the-church.*

Fillmore Auditorium
MUSIC CLUBS | Denver's classic San Francisco concert hall spin-off looks dumpy on the outside, but it's elegant and impressive inside. Before catching a big-name act such as Rise Against or Marilyn Manson, scan the walls for color photographs of past club performers. *1510 Clarkson St., Capitol Hill* *303/837–0360* *www.fillmoreauditorium.org.*

Hi-Dive
MUSIC CLUBS | This energetic, hip club located in the Baker neighborhood just south of Capitol Hill books a diverse and eclectic range of talented indie rockers. The crowd is young, likes Red Bull, and tends to revel in the discovery of obscure underground music. *7 S. Broadway, Capitol Hill* *303/733–0230* *www.hi-dive.com.*

La Rumba
DANCE CLUBS | DJ-spun, Latin-based dance weekends, with bachata, cumbia, and reggaeton, as well as live salsa Saturday nights and salsa classes nightly, is what's

on deck at La Rumba. ✉ *99 W. 9th Ave., Golden Triangle* ☎ *303/572–8006* 🌐 *www.larumbadenver.com.*

Milk

DANCE CLUBS | One of the city's best dance clubs, the small, Clockwork Orange–styled Milk offers themed nights in its hip, elaborately lighted, multiroom space—Goth, retro, hip-hop—with beloved local DJs taking turns at the table. ✉ *1037 N. Broadway, Civic Center* ✣ *Enter through the alley* ☎ *303/832–8628* 🌐 *coclubs.com/milk.*

Ogden Theatre

MUSIC CLUBS | This classic old theater showcases alternative-rock and hip-hop acts such as The Disco Biscuits, Rainbow Kitten Surprise, and George Clinton & Parliament Funkadelic. ✉ *935 E. Colfax Ave., Capitol Hill* ☎ *888/929–7849, 303/832–1874* 🌐 *www.ogdentheatre.com.*

Performing Arts

Colorado Ballet

DANCE | From September through March, the Colorado Ballet specializes in the classics (including its beloved annual *The Nutcracker*), with performances primarily at the Ellie Caulkins Opera House and the Newman Center for the Performing Arts. ✉ *1075 Santa Fe Dr., Lincoln Park* ☎ *303/837–8888* 🌐 *www.coloradoballet.org.*

Curious Theatre Company

THEATER | Inspiring, innovative, and even edgy theater is held in the same venue in which Curious's founders first met more than 20 years ago—a 19th-century church in Denver's artsy Golden Triangle. Each season begins in September. ✉ *1080 Acoma St., Golden Triangle* ☎ *303/623–0524* 🌐 *www.curioustheatre.org.*

Shopping

★ Tattered Cover Book Store

BOOKS/STATIONERY | A must for all bibliophiles, the Tattered Cover may be the best bookstore in the United States, not only for the near-endless selection (more than 400,000 books on two floors at the Colfax Avenue location and 300,000 in LoDo, along with much smaller versions of the stores at Union Station and Denver International Airport) and helpful, knowledgeable staff, but also for the incomparably refined atmosphere. Treat yourself to the overstuffed armchairs, reading nooks, and afternoon readings and lectures, and stop by the café for an espresso drink and bakery treat at the Capitol Hill site in the renovated historic Lowenstein Theater. ✉ *2526 E. Colfax Ave., Capitol Hill* ☎ *303/322–7727* 🌐 *www.tatteredcover.com.*

City Park and Around

Acquired by the city in 1881, City Park, Denver's largest public space (330 acres), contains rose gardens, lakes, a golf course, tennis courts, and a huge playground. A shuttle runs between two of the city's most popular attractions: the Denver Zoo and the Denver Museum of Nature & Science, both on the site. City Park is east of downtown Denver, and runs from East 17th Avenue to East 26th Avenue, between York Street and Colorado Boulevard.

Sights

★ Denver Botanic Gardens

GARDEN | FAMILY | More than 15,000 plant species from Australia, South Africa, the Himalayas, and especially the western United States compose the horticultural displays in the thoughtfully laid-out theme gardens here. They are at their peak in July and August, when garden enthusiasts could spend half a day here;

the tropical conservatory alone is worth an hour's visit in the off-season. Spring brings a brilliant display of wildflowers to the world-renowned rock alpine garden, primarily in late May and early June. The OmniGlobe simulates the climate and atmospheric changes on Earth; other environmental attractions include a "green roof" atop the café and an extensive interactive children's garden that covers part of the parking structure. Tea ceremonies take place some summer weekends in the tranquil Japanese garden, and artists such as singer-songwriter Melissa Etheridge, jazz musician Herbie Hancock, and blues legend Buddy Guy have performed as part of the summer concert series. ✉ *1007 York St., Cheesman Park* ☎ *720/865–3500* 🌐 *www.botanicgardens.org* 🎫 *$15.*

★ Denver Museum of Nature & Science

MUSEUM | **FAMILY** | Founded in 1900, the museum has amassed more than 775,000 objects, making it the largest natural history museum in the western United States. It houses a rich combination of traditional collections—dinosaur remains, animal dioramas, a mineralogy display, an Egyptology wing—and intriguing hands-on exhibits. In Expedition Health you can test your health and fitness on a variety of contraptions and receive a personalized health profile. The Prehistoric Journey exhibit covers the seven stages of Earth's development. The massive complex also includes an IMAX movie theater and a planetarium, where the Space Odyssey exhibit simulates a trip to Mars. An impressive eating-and-relaxation area has a full-window panoramic view of the Rocky Mountains. ✉ *2001 Colorado Blvd., City Park* ☎ *303/370–6000, 800/925–2250* 🌐 *www.dmns.org* 🎫 *Museum $16.95, IMAX $10.95, planetarium $23.95; $23.95–29.95 for combined pass (any two or all three).*

Denver Zoo

ZOO | **FAMILY** | The state's most popular cultural attraction, this easily navigated property's best-known exhibit showcases man-eating Komodo dragons in a lush re-creation of a cavernous riverbank. Another popular exhibit is The Edge, a series of overhead yards and bridges that allow the Amur (Siberian) tigers to roam 12 feet above visitors. The 10-acre Toyota Elephant Passage houses elephants, gibbons, rhinos, clouded leopards, and tapirs, along with other animals from the Asian continent. The Conservation Carousel ($2) rotates in the center of the 80-acre zoo, with handcrafted endangered species as mounts. A 7-acre Primate Panorama houses 31 species of primates in state-of-the-art environments that simulate the animals' natural habitats. Other highlights include a nursery for baby animals; seal shows; the electric Safari Shuttle, which snakes through the property as you are treated to a lesson on the zoo's inhabitants; and the usual lions, tigers, bears, giraffes, and monkeys. The exhibits are spaced far apart along sprawling concrete paths, so build in plenty of time to visit. ✉ *2300 Steele St., City Park* ☎ *720/337–1400* 🌐 *www.denverzoo.org* 🎫 *Nov.–Feb. $15, Mar.–May $17, Jun.–Oct. $20.*

Hotels

★ Adagio Bed & Breakfast

$$ | **B&B/INN** | After converting to a "Bud + Breakfast" B&B experience, this striking property became famous as a good place to stay if you love music and marijuana, as the Adagio and its sister B&B in Silverthorne are committed to making sure guests can enjoy cannabis during a visit by providing the necessary paraphernalia and a place to use it (note that it is 21-and-over only). **Pros:** pretty, cozy rooms; within driving distance of major attractions; full-meal-plan option

A
B
C
D
E
F
1
2
3
4
5
6
7
8
9
FIVE POINTS
LODO
CENTRAL BUSINESS DISTRICT
THEATRE DISTRICT
UPPER DOWNTOWN
UPTOWN
CIVIC CENTER
CAPITOL HILL
SPEER
Union Station
Speer Boulevard Park
Creekfront Park
Tivoli Quad Public Space
Civic Center Park
Lincoln Memorial Park
La Alma / Lincoln Park
Cherry Creek
TRAM
25th & Welton
20th St & Welton
18th St & Stout
18th St & California
16th & Stout
16th & California
Theatre District & Convention Center
Colfax
10th & Osage
West Colfax Avenue
Speer Boulevard
Broadway
Lincoln Street
East 20th Avenue
East 19th Avenue
East 17th Avenue
East 16th Avenue
West 14th Avenue
West 13th Avenue
West 12th Avenue
West 11th Avenue
West 10th Avenue
West 9th Avenue
West 8th Avenue
West 7th Avenue
West 6th Ave. Ramp
West 6th Avenue
West 5th Avenue
West 4th Avenue
West 3rd Avenue
KEY
Exploring Sights
Restaurants
Hotels
0
1,000 ft
0
200 m

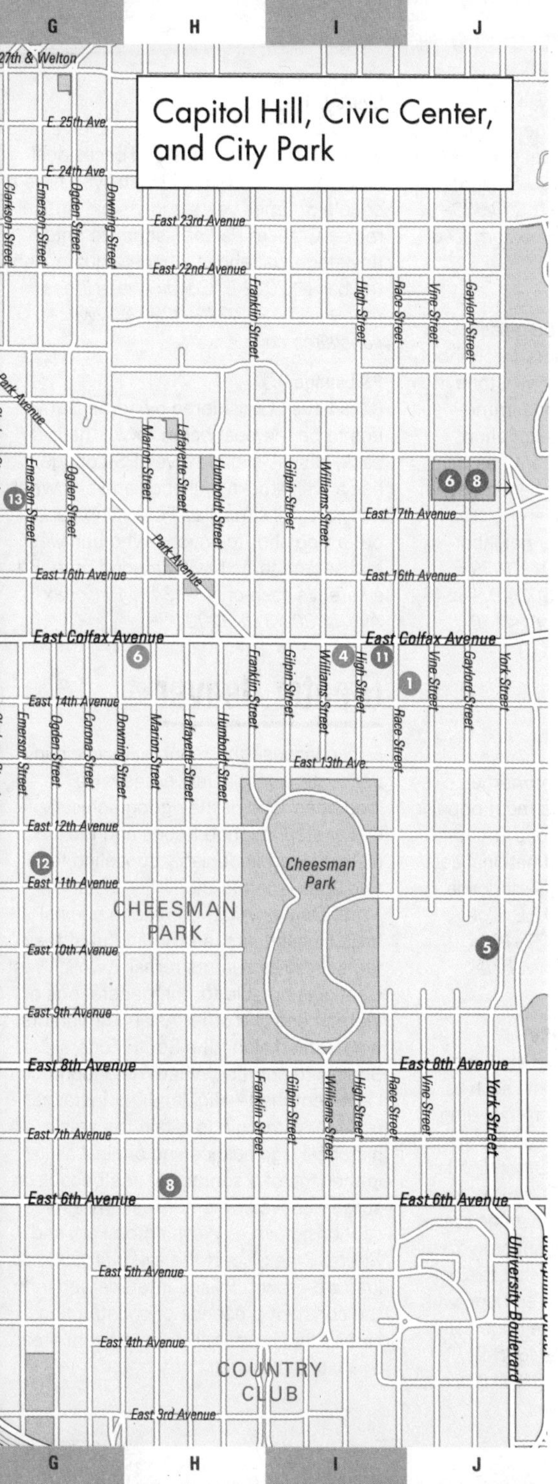

Sights

1 Byers-Evan House Museum D5
2 Civic Center D4
3 Clyfford Still Museum D5
4 Denver Art Museum D5
5 Denver Botanic Gardens J6
6 Denver Museum of Nature & Science J3
7 Denver Public Library's Central Library D5
8 Denver Zoo J3
9 History Colorado Center E5
10 Molly Brown House F5
11 Museo de las Americas B7
12 State Capitol E4
13 U. S. Mint D5

Restaurants

1 Beast + Bottle F3
2 Brother's BBQ F8
3 Buckhorn Exchange A6
4 City Cafe E7
5 CityGrille E4
6 City O' City E5
7 Domo A5
8 Fruition H8
9 Luca E7
10 Mizuna E7
11 Pete's Kitchen I4
12 Potager G6
13 WaterCourse Foods G3

Hotels

1 Adagio Bed & Breakfast I5
2 The ART Hotel D5
3 Capitol Hill Mansion Bed & Breakfast Inn F5
4 Holiday Chalet B&B I4
5 Queen Anne Inn E2
6 Ramada by Wyndham Denver Downtown H4
7 Warwick Denver Hotel E3

G
H
I
J

available. **Cons:** not within walking distance of downtown or Cherry Creek; limited amenities due to size; overpriced. *Rooms from: $199 1430 Race St., Capitol Hill 303/370–6911, 800/533–4640 www.adagiodenverbb.com 6 rooms Free Breakfast.*

Holiday Chalet B&B

$$ | **B&B/INN** | **FAMILY** | Stained-glass windows and homey accents throughout make this 1896 Victorian brownstone in Capitol Hill, the neighborhood immediately east of downtown, exceptionally appealing. **Pros:** each room has full kitchen; delightful teas; enchanting style. **Cons:** parking can be a challenge; creaky house with thin walls; noisy neighborhood. *Rooms from: $129 1820 E. Colfax Ave., Capitol Hill 303/437–8245 www.theholidaychalet.com 10 rooms Free Breakfast.*

Nightlife

Bluebird Theater

MUSIC CLUBS | Of Denver's numerous old-school music hangouts, the most popular is the regally restored Bluebird Theater, which showcases local and national acts, emphasizing rock, hip-hop, Americana, and ambient genres. *3317 E. Colfax Ave., City Park 303/377–1666, 888/929–7849 tickets www.bluebirdtheater.net.*

Hamburger Mary's Bar & Grille

BARS/PUBS | Drag queens rule the scene here on weekends, with events such as "Mary-oke" and the town's premier drag revue, all of which take place on the stage side of this restaurant/club. Other digs farther east on 17th Avenue in City Park feature a sportier, classier look than the previous location, and the restaurant crowd, gay and straight, seems to agree that this bar offers one of the town's best burgers, with tater tots as a side option. The huge patio out back is always a party. *1336 E. 17th Ave., City Park 303/993–5812 www.hamburgermarys.com/denver.*

Lion's Lair

MUSIC CLUBS | The Lion's Lair is a dive where punk-rock bands and occasional name acts—the Black Keys played here a couple of times years ago, as did British rocker Graham Parker—squeeze onto a tiny stage just above a huge, square, central bar. *2022 E. Colfax Ave., Cheesman Park 303/320–9200 www.lionslairco.com.*

PS Lounge

BARS/PUBS | Considered by some Denverites to be the best bar in town, the laid-back, casual, slightly divey PS Lounge has a well-stocked jukebox and an owner, known to all simply as Pete, who hands out a free shot to anyone who behaves and seems to be having a good time. Be aware it's cash-only. *3416 E. Colfax Ave. 303/320–1200.*

Greater Denver

Partly because the mountains so clearly delineate "west," Denverites have long been fond of their geographically designated neighborhoods and the history—and undeniably appealing food traditions—tied to them. For instance, North Denver is famous for its original Italian inhabitants, and a handful of their red-sauce restaurants remain, while West Denver is notable for the generations of Vietnamese and other Asian immigrants who settled along the South Federal Boulevard corridor. Where neighborhoods have gentrified—Highland, for instance—residents struggle to retain the area's historical significance and original allure in the face of a seemingly unstoppable surge of development. Meanwhile, older sections, such as Washington Park and Cherry Creek, sport the awkward look of lush old-growth foliage interspersed with the constant presence of construction cranes that often afflict the affluent areas of a city in the midst of a boom.

Less than a mile west of downtown is the booming Central Platte Valley, with the Highlands neighborhood at its center. Once the cluttered heart of Denver's railroad system, it's now overflowing with attractions. The imposing glass facade of the Broncos' home, Empower Field at Mile High, the stately Ball Arena sports arena (formerly the Pepsi Center), the Downtown Aquarium, and the flagship REI outdoors store are four of the biggest attractions. Hip restaurants, a couple of coffeehouses, and a few small, locally owned shops, including a wine boutique, make it appealing to wander around. The sights in this area are so popular that the light-rail line was extended to connect the attractions with downtown.

The South Platte River valley concrete path, which extends several miles from downtown to the east and west, snakes along the water through out-of-the-way parks and trails. The 15th Street Bridge is particularly cyclist- and pedestrian-friendly, connecting LoDo with sprawling northwest Denver in a seamless way. The most relaxed, and easiest, way to see the area from Memorial Day to Labor Day is on one of the $5 half-hour tours Thursday to Sunday on the **Platte Valley Trolley** (☎ *303/458–6255* 🌐 *www.denvertrolley.org*), which can be accessed by parking at the Children's Museum and catching the streetcar east of the lot by the river.

Sights

★ Children's Museum of Denver

MUSEUM | FAMILY | This is one of the finest museums of its kind in North America, with constantly changing hands-on exhibits that engage children up to about age 10 in discovery. A three-and-a-half-story climbing structure soars through the center of the museum, complete with a bridge and gondola, along with a water area featuring geysers, pumps, and a 30-gallon structure that replicates a toilet flushing. Also among the six indoor playscapes and an outdoor area are a teaching kitchen where kids can cook real food; an art studio staffed by artists in residence; a camping area with a faux fire; a car assembly plant; and Fire Station No. 1, a real fire hall with a pole and kitchen. One of the biggest attractions is the Center for the Young Child, a 3,700-square-foot playscape aimed at newborns and toddlers and their caregivers; or little ones can enter Bubbles Playscape, where science and soap collide in kid-made bubbles up to 6 feet long. ✉ *2121 Children's Museum Dr., off Exit 211 of I–25, Jefferson Park* ☎ *303/433–7444* 🌐 *www.mychildsmuseum.org* 🎟 *$14.*

Downtown Aquarium

MUSEUM | FAMILY | On the north side of the South Platte across from Elitch Gardens, this is the only million-gallon aquarium between Chicago and the West Coast. It has four sections that show aquatic life in all its forms, from the seas to the river's headwaters in the Colorado mountains. The 250-seat Aquarium Restaurant surrounds a 50,000-gallon tank filled with sharks and fish. Other highlights include an expanded stingray touch pool, a gold-panning area, animatronic creatures, and an interactive shipwreck. The aquarium also has a lounge with a weeknight happy hour, and the truly adventurous can learn how to scuba dive or snorkel in the tanks. ✉ *700 Water St., off Exit 211 of I–25, Jefferson Park* ☎ *303/561–4450* 🌐 *www.aquarium-restaurants.com* 🎟 *$23.50.*

Elitch Gardens

AMUSEMENT PARK/WATER PARK | FAMILY | This elaborate and thrilling park was a Denver family tradition long before its 1995 relocation from northwest Denver to its current home on the outskirts of downtown. The park's highlights include hair-raising roller coasters and thrill rides; for younger kids and squeamish parents there are also plenty of gentler attractions such as bumper cars and tea cups. Twister II, an update of

Greater Denver
A
B
C
D
E
F
1
2
3
4
5
6
7
8
9
W. 46th Ave.
W. 44th Ave.
W. 41st Ave.
W. 38th Ave.
W. 35th Ave.
W. 32nd Ave.
W. 29th Ave.
W. 26th Ave.
W. 25th Ave.
W. 20th Ave.
W. 17th Ave.
W. Colfax Ave.
W. 14th Ave.
W. 10th Ave.
W. 8th Ave.
6th Avenue Freeway
W. 3rd Ave.
W. 2nd Ave.
W. 1st Ave.
W. Bayaud Ave.
W. Alameda Ave.
W. Virginia Ave.
W. Exposition Ave.
W. Mississippi Ave.
W. Louisiana Ave.
W. Florida Ave.
Harlan St.
Sheridan Boulevard
Tennyson St.
Lowell Boulevard
Federal Boulevard
Zuni St.
Tejon St.
Pecos St.
Lipan St.
Fox St.
Irving St.
Clay St.
Perry St.
Knox Court
Osage St.
Mariposa St.
Kalamath St.
Santa Fe Dr.
Galapago St.
Bannock St.
Santa Fe Drive
S. Tejon St.
S. Lipan St.
S. Jason St.
S. Irving St.
S. Tennyson St.
Morrison Road
15th St.
16th St.
17th St.
Blake St.
Market St.
Larimer St.
Lawrence St.
Arapahoe St.
Curtis St.
Champa St.
Stout St.
California St.
Welton St.
Glenarm Pl.
Tremont Pl.
S. Platte River
THE HIGHLANDS
LODO
CBD
CIVIC CENTER
SPEER
Sloan's Lake Park
Mile High Stadium
Union Station
Coors Field
Civic Center Park
287
25
95
40
6
88
26
0
1/2 mi
1/2 km
KEY
Exploring Sights
Restaurants
Hotels

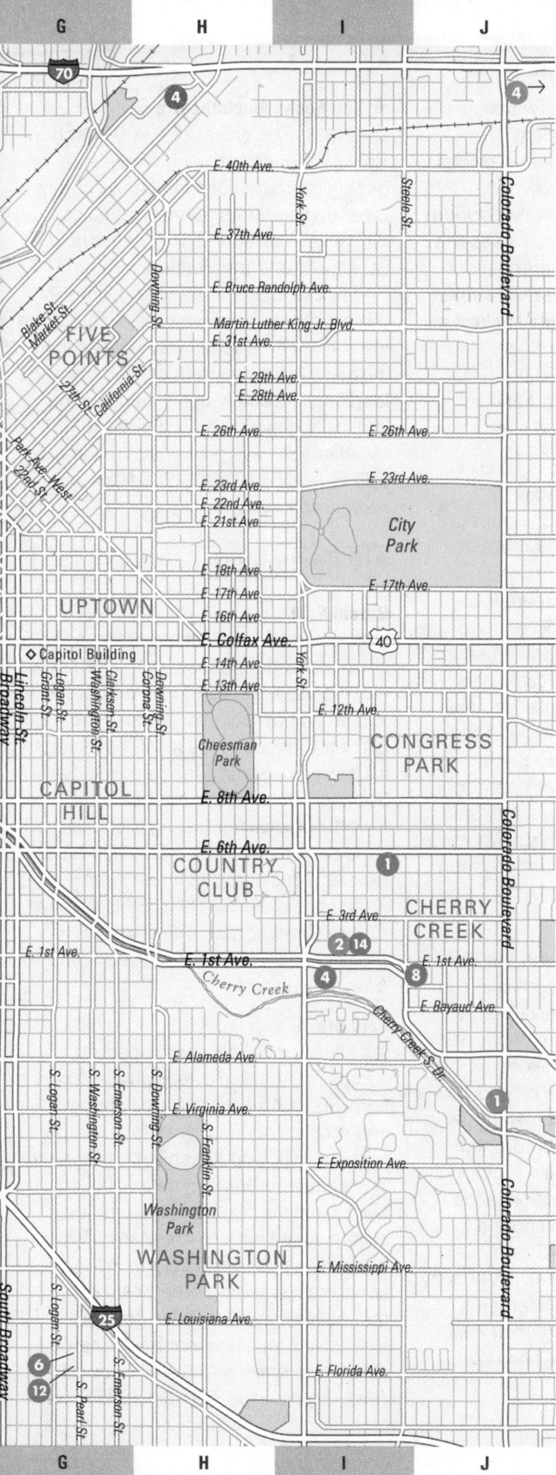

Sights

1 Children's Museum of Denver.... **D4**
2 Downtown Aquarium **E3**
3 Elitch Gardens **E3**
4 Forney Museum of Transportation...................... **H1**
5 Platte River Greenway **E3**
6 Red Rocks Amphitheatre **A4**

Restaurants

1 Barolo Grill **I6**
2 Café Brazil.......................... **C1**
3 El Five **E3**
4 Elway's.............................. **I6**
5 The Fort Restaurant **D9**
6 Izakaya Den **G9**
7 Lola Denver.......................... **E3**
8 Matsuhisa **J6**
9 My Brother's Bar **E3**
10 New Saigon **D8**
11 Pizzeria Locale **C2**
12 Sushi Den........................... **G9**
13 Tacos Tequila Whiskey............ **C2**
14 True Food Kitchen **I6**
15 The Way Back **B1**

Hotels

1 DoubleTree by Hilton Denver Cherry Creek **J7**
2 JW Marriott Denver at Cherry Creek **I6**
3 Lumber Baron Inn & Gardens.... **D2**
4 Westin Denver International Airport................ **J1**

the classic, wooden Mister Twister, is from the original Elitch Gardens, as is a 100-foot-high Ferris wheel that provides sensational views of downtown. A 10-acre water-adventure park is included in the standard entry fee. You can spend a whole day at either the water park or the main park. ■ **TIP→ Locker and stroller rentals are available; discounted tickets are available online.** ✉ *I–25 and Speer Blvd., 2000 Elitch Cir., Auraria* ☎ *303/595–4386* 🌐 *www.elitchgardens.com* 🎫 *$64.99 unlimited-ride pass* ⏲ *Closed late Oct.–Memorial Day.*

Forney Museum of Transportation

MUSEUM | Inside a converted warehouse are an 1898 Renault coupe, Amelia Earhart's immaculately maintained "Goldbug," and a Big Boy steam locomotive, among other historic vehicles. Other exhibits in this eccentric museum consist of antique bicycles, cable cars, and even experimental car-planes. This trivia-laden showcase is outside of the downtown loop: Go north on Brighton Boulevard; the museum is adjacent to the Denver Coliseum on the south side of I–70. ✉ *4303 Brighton Blvd., Globeville* ☎ *303/297–1113* 🌐 *www.forneymuseum.org* 🎫 *$10.*

Platte River Greenway

CITY PARK | **FAMILY** | Just behind the REI flagship store, this serene park is at the center of the South Platte River valley path. Its rocks and rapids are especially attractive in summer to kayakers, bicyclists, and hikers. Sidewalks extend down the South Platte to the east toward the suburbs and west toward the Broncos' home, Empower Field at Mile High. A pathway in yet another direction leads to LoDo. From the park, it's about a 20-minute walk to the 16th Street Mall and Coors Field, which makes it a healthy way to sightsee when the weather is good. ✉ *1615 Platte St., Jefferson Park* 🌐 *www.thegreenwayfoundation.org.*

★ Red Rocks Amphitheatre

CONCERTS | The exquisite 9,000-seat Red Rocks Amphitheatre, amid majestic geological formations in nearby Morrison, is renowned for its natural acoustics, which have awed the likes of Leopold Stokowski and the Beatles. Although Red Rocks is one of the best places in the country to hear live music, be sure to leave extra time when visiting—parking is sparse, crowds are thick, paths are long and extremely uphill, and seating is usually general admission. ✉ *18300 W. Alameda Pkwy., Morrison* ✥ *Off U.S. 285 or I–70* ☎ *720/865–2494* 🌐 *www.redrocksonline.com.*

 Restaurants

Barolo Grill

$$$$ | **ITALIAN** | This restaurant looks like a chichi Italian farmhouse, with dried flowers in brass urns, hand-painted porcelain, and straw baskets everywhere. The food isn't pretentious in the least, however; it's more like Santa Monica meets San Stefano—bold yet classic, healthful yet flavorful. **Known for:** tasting menu with wine pairings; charming fireplace table; excellent duck braised in red wine. 💲 *Average main: $34* ✉ *3030 E. 6th Ave., Cherry Creek* ☎ *303/393–1040* 🌐 *www.barologrilldenver.com* ⏲ *Closed Sun. and Mon. No lunch.*

Café Brazil

$$$ | **BRAZILIAN** | This always-packed spot is worth the trip to Highland for such South American fare as shrimp and scallops sautéed with fresh herbs, coconut milk, and hot chilies or *feijoada completa,* the Brazilian national dish of black-bean stew and smoked meats, accompanied with fried bananas. With its vivid paintings and colorful traditional masks, there's a party style in the festive café. **Known for:** cozy bar; extensive rum selection; fresh seafood. 💲 *Average main: $23* ✉ *4408 Lowell Blvd., Highland* ☎ *303/480–1877* 🌐 *www.*

cafebrazildenver.com ⏲ *Closed Sun. and Mon. No lunch Sat.–Tues.*

El Five

$$ | **MEDITERRANEAN** | Atop a five-story building in the Lower Highland (aka LoHi) neighborhood sits one of the most cosmopolitan restaurants in the area as well as one of its best unobstructed views of the city and mountains (sunset is a nightly show). Diners munch on eclectic takes on Mediterranean tapas, influenced by the cuisines of Africa, Asia, and Europe. **Known for:** seafood paella; herb-based cocktails; unparalleled views. $ *Average main: $22* ✉ *2930 Umatilla St., Highland* ☎ *303/524–9193* 🌐 *www.elfivedenver.com* ⏲ *Closed Mon.–Wed. No lunch.*

Elway's

$$$$ | **STEAKHOUSE** | You won't see the big guy very often here—or at the company's downtown Ritz-Carlton–Denver, Denver International Airport, or Vail locations, either—but that doesn't keep sports fans from packing it in, hopeful. And when the toothy-grinned former Broncos QB (and current executive vice president of football operations) John Elway doesn't show, diners console themselves with some of the best steak-house fare in town, particularly the porterhouse (big enough for half a football team) and the huge side of chunky-creamy Yukon gold mashed potatoes. **Known for:** plush seating; lamb "lollipops"; packed happy hour. $ *Average main: $48* ✉ *2500 E. 1st Ave., Cherry Creek* ☎ *303/399–5353* 🌐 *www.elways.com.*

★ **The Fort Restaurant**

$$$$ | **STEAKHOUSE** | This adobe structure near Red Rocks Amphitheatre, complete with flickering luminarias and a pinyon-pine bonfire in the courtyard, is a perfect reproduction of Bent's Fort, a Colorado fur-trade center. Buffalo meat and game are the specialties. **Known for:** authentic Old West atmosphere complete with costumed characters; gun-powder cocktails; buffalo steaks and Rocky Mountain oysters. $ *Average main: $46* ✉ *19192 Hwy. 8, Morrison* ☎ *303/697–4771* 🌐 *www.thefort.com* ⏲ *No lunch.*

Izakaya Den

$$ | **JAPANESE** | A larger and slightly more reasonably priced offering from the brothers who own Sushi Den next door, Izakaya Den is supposed to be like a Japanese *izakaya*, an informal and inexpensive drinking place where snacks are served. Instead, it's more like a typical upscale American take on a tapas bar, with pricier small plates and an extensive sake roster. **Known for:** reasonably priced sushi; great happy hour; lively atmosphere. $ *Average main: $18* ✉ *1487 S. Pearl St., South Denver* ☎ *303/777–0691* 🌐 *www.izakayaden.net* ⏲ *Closed Sun. and Mon. No lunch Tues.–Fri.*

★ **Lola Denver**

$$ | **MEXICAN** | This casual, modern Mexican eatery with valet parking brings in a young, hip clientele and provides a spectacular view of the city skyline from most of the sunny dining room, bar, and patio. More than 90 tequilas, superior margaritas, and a clever, glass-lined bar area are just a few of the reasons the lovely Lola remains a locals' hangout. **Known for:** Mexican-style weekend brunch; tableside guacamole; heated patio. $ *Average main: $22* ✉ *1575 Boulder St., Highland* ☎ *720/570–8686* 🌐 *www.loladenver.com* ⏲ *No lunch.*

★ **Matsuhisa**

$$$ | **JAPANESE** | World-famous chef Nobu Matsuhisa has restaurants in Vail and Aspen, but this one—a slick, stylish spot serving elegantly presented New Japanese—is his first in Denver. The sushi is both fresh and beautiful, but it's the specialties that truly shine, such as scallops in phyllo pastry with tonkatsu sauce and black truffle-kissed sea bass. **Known for:** private dining rooms; fresh sashimi; beautiful setting. $ *Average main: $28* ✉ *98 N. Steele St., Cherry Creek North* ☎ *303/329–6628* 🌐 *www.matsuhisarestaurants.com* ⏲ *No lunch weekends.*

My Brother's Bar

$ | **BURGER** | Down the street from the REI store, on the corner along the bicycle path on 15th Street, My Brother's Bar is a homey neighborhood tavern that serves microbrews, burgers—buffalo and beef—and sandwiches of all kinds until 1:30 am. The bar's name isn't on the facade, so look for the street number. **Known for:** late-night dining; classical background music; inviting outdoor space. *Average main: $8* *2376 15th St., Highland* *303/455–9991* *www.mybrothersbar.com* *Closed Sun.*

New Saigon

$$ | **VIETNAMESE** | Denver's best Vietnamese restaurant is always crowded with folks trying to get at their crispy egg rolls, shrimp-filled spring rolls, and cheap but hefty noodle bowls. With nearly 200 dishes on the menu—priced and portioned for sharing—this vast, avocado-color eatery has everything Vietnamese covered, including 30-some vegetarian dishes and 10 with succulent frogs' legs. **Known for:** seafood dishes; exhaustive menu of Vietnamese classics; Vietnamese iced coffee. *Average main: $17* *630 S. Federal Blvd., West Denver* *303/564–5938* *www.newsaigon.com.*

Pizzeria Locale

$ | **PIZZA** | **FAMILY** | This casual pizzeria is a franchised offshoot of the original in Boulder. They had set out to make inexpensive pizza the way it was done in Italy 150 years ago: in under two minutes in a blistering-hot oven, with a light, thin, bubbly crust, and sparingly topped with fresh ingredients. **Known for:** sausage and broccolini pizza and other unique ingredients; kid-friendly setup; butterscotch pudding for dessert. *Average main: $8* *3484 W. 32nd Ave., Highland* *303/302–2451* *www.pizzerialocale.com.*

★ Sushi Den

$$$ | **JAPANESE** | With a sister restaurant in Japan (and another, Izakaya Den, a more casual version just down the street) and owners who import sushi-grade seafood to the United States, it's easy to see why this chic sushi bar is the one Denverites count on to provide the best quality available. The sushi chefs here can meet your every request, and the cooked dishes are just as well prepared—don't miss the steamed fish baskets. **Known for:** inviting patio; impeccable sushi; extensive sake list. *Average main: $28* *1487 S. Pearl St., South Denver* *303/777–0826* *www.sushiden.net* *No lunch weekends.*

Tacos Tequila Whiskey

$ | **MODERN MEXICAN** | Originally a food truck, the name of this taqueria showcases exactly what it specializes in: *queso a la plancha* tacos and seared ahi tuna tacos, with house-made salsas and tangy margaritas. Get to know your fellow diners at the communal tables or the long bar, or sit on the patio that opens from the dining area through the garage door. **Known for:** street-style tacos; festive patio; tequila cocktails. *Average main: $8* *3300 W. 32nd Ave., Highland* *720/502–4608* *www.tacostequilawhiskey.com* *No lunch Mon.*

True Food Kitchen

$$ | **CONTEMPORARY** | Holistic health guru Dr. Andrew Weil has opened restaurants in select locations in Arizona and California, and this venture in Cherry Creek, where his intensive focus is on anti-inflammatory preparations and antioxidant ingredients prepared with an international flair, has met with great success. Don't expect all-vegetarian, however; the menu offers plenty of meat, particularly lean bison and turkey, as well as fish, but there are also tempeh and other meat substitutes. **Known for:** house-made soda and trendy cocktails; healthy desserts; unique kids' menu. *Average main: $20* *2800 E. 2nd Ave., Cherry Creek* *720/509–7661* *www.truefoodkitchen.com.*

The Way Back

$$ | **FUSION** | Whimsical, eclectic dishes are the hallmark of the Way Back, a fun and funky eatery with secluded booths, polished woods, and black leather couches.

The global fare, mostly small plates, sports a heavily Asian influence, but you're also likely to come upon unfamiliar ingredients like trout roe, yak, and *rousong* (fluffy, dried pork). **Known for:** well-crafted cocktails; spacious back patio; monthly Test Tuesday, with experimental dishes and flavors. *Average main: $20 3963 Tennyson St., Highland 970/682–6888 www.thewaybackdenver.com Closed Sun. and Mon. No lunch.*

Hotels

DoubleTree by Hilton Denver Cherry Creek

$$ | **HOTEL** | The Cherry Creek shopping district is 4 miles away, and the major museums and the zoo are a five-minute drive from this bustling hotel, which provides coveted mountain views from many of its rooms. **Pros:** good for business travelers; location bridges gap for folks who want both museums and downtown; free shuttle on weekdays. **Cons:** not walking distance to any attractions; far from downtown; can be noisy. *Rooms from: $139 455 S. Colorado Blvd., Cherry Creek 303/388–5561, 800/388–6129 www.hilton.com 269 rooms No meals.*

JW Marriott Denver at Cherry Creek

$$$$ | **HOTEL** | The hip atmosphere and location smack in the middle of Cherry Creek's shopping district has made this upscale outpost of the Marriott family popular with tourists and locals alike. **Pros:** one of the most sought-after spas in town; great location for shopping; bus to downtown a block away. **Cons:** chain-like; feels far from downtown; very pricey. *Rooms from: $449 150 Clayton La., Cherry Creek 303/316–2700 www.marriott.com 196 rooms No meals.*

Lumber Baron Inn & Gardens

$$ | **B&B/INN** | The Keller family has made a plush, stylish, and romantic bed-and-breakfast out of a dilapidated Highland apartment building originally constructed for a lumber baron and his family in the 1890s. **Pros:** romantic, appealing mix of historic and modern; intimate spaces; happening neighborhood. **Cons:** not downtown; usually have to book well in advance; rooms feel dated. *Rooms from: $159 2555 W. 37th Ave., LoDo 303/477–8205, 888/214–2790 www.lumberbaron.com No credit cards 5 rooms Free Breakfast.*

Westin Denver International Airport

$$$ | **HOTEL** | This on-site airport hotel offers impressively soundproofed accommodations, local art throughout the rooms and the hotel itself, and some of the best views of the mountains and the plains in the state. **Pros:** only hotel right at the airport; stunning views; soundproofing so outstanding you won't realize you're next to an airport. **Cons:** feels rather isolated; until TSA rules change, only the Westin's restaurants are accessible; train periodically breaks down. *Rooms from: $285 8300 Peña Blvd., Cherry Creek 303/317–1800 www.marriott.com 559 rooms No meals.*

Nightlife

Gothic Theatre

MUSIC CLUBS | Sitting south of downtown, this theater came of age in the early '90s, with a steady stream of soon-to-be-famous alternative-rock acts such as Nirvana and the Red Hot Chili Peppers. It still showcases the old and new, from the Hives to T-Pain and Neko Case, but also operates as a community venue for theater, music, and charity events. *3263 S. Broadway, Englewood 303/789–9206 www.gothictheatre.com.*

Grizzly Rose

DANCE CLUBS | Classic-rock bands are big here, as are country acts big and small. The Grizzly Rose has miles of dance floor, hosts regional and national bands, gives two-step dancing lessons, and sells plenty of Western wear, from cowboy boots to spurs. Sunday nights are for all ages until 11 pm. ✉ *5450 N. Valley Hwy., I–25 at Exit 215, Globeville* ☎ *303/295–1330* 🌐 *www.grizzlyrose.com.*

Herman's Hideaway

MUSIC CLUBS | In a south Denver neighborhood, down-home Herman's Hideaway showcases mostly local rock, with a smattering of reggae and blues thrown in. ✉ *1578 S. Broadway, Overland* ☎ *303/777–5840* 🌐 *www.hermanshideaway.com.*

Skylark Lounge

BARS/PUBS | A vintage-style poolroom is just one reason to stop by the beloved Skylark Lounge, which counts live music, pinball machines, comfortable seating, and friendly staffers among its many charms. ✉ *140 S. Broadway, South Denver* ☎ *303/722–7844* 🌐 *www.skylarklounge.com.*

Stampede Mesquite Grill & Dance Emporium

DANCE CLUBS | This suburban country club and bar is a cavernous boot-scooting spot, with dance lessons and a restaurant. ✉ *2430 S. Havana St., Aurora* ☎ *303/696–7686* 🌐 *www.stampedeclub.net* ⏲ *Closed Sun.–Tues.*

Performing Arts

Bug Theatre Company

THEATER | Based in Denver's trendy Highland neighborhood, this small nonprofit theater produces cutting-edge, original works. ✉ *3654 Navajo St., Highland* ☎ *303/477–5977* 🌐 *www.bugtheatre.org.*

Shopping

Cherry Creek

SHOPPING NEIGHBORHOODS | In a pleasant, predominantly residential neighborhood 2 miles from downtown, the Cherry Creek shopping district has retail blocks and an enclosed mall. ✉ *Cherry Creek.*

Cherry Creek North

SHOPPING NEIGHBORHOODS | Just north of the Cherry Creek Shopping Mall is Cherry Creek North, an open-air development of tree-lined streets and shady plazas with art galleries, specialty shops, and fashionable restaurants. ✉ *Between 1st and 3rd Aves. from University Blvd. to Steele St., Cherry Creek* ☎ *303/394–2904* 🌐 *www.cherrycreeknorth.com.*

Cherry Creek Shopping Center

SHOPPING CENTERS/MALLS | At Milwaukee Street, the granite-and-glass behemoth Cherry Creek Shopping Center holds some of the nation's top retailers. Its more than 160 stores include Free People, Burberry, H&M, Tiffany & Co., Louis Vuitton, Neiman Marcus, and Macy's. ✉ *3000 E. 1st Ave., Cherry Creek* ☎ *303/388–3900, 866/798–0889* 🌐 *www.shopcherrycreek.com.*

Park Meadows

SHOPPING CENTERS/MALLS | The upscale Park Meadows is a mall designed to resemble a ski resort, with a 120-foot-high log-beam ceiling anchored by two massive stone fireplaces. The center includes more than 100 specialty shops. On snowy days, "ambassadors" scrape your windshield while free hot chocolate is served inside. ✉ *I–25, 5 miles south of Denver at County Line Rd., Littleton* 🌐 *www.parkmeadows.com.*

★ REI

SPORTING GOODS | Denver's REI flagship store, one of four such shops in the country, is yet another testament to the city's adventurous spirit. The store's 94,000 square feet are packed with all stripes of outdoors gear and some special extras: a climbing wall, a mountain-bike track, a white-water chute, and a "cold room" for gauging the protection provided by coats and sleeping bags. There's also a Starbucks inside. Behind the store is the Platte River Greenway, a park path and water area that's accessible to dogs, kids, and kayakers. ✉ *1416 Platte St., Jefferson Park* ☎ *303/756–3100* 🌐 *www.rei.com.*

Chapter 4

SIDE TRIPS FROM DENVER

Updated by
Kyle Wagner

Sights ★★★★☆ Restaurants ★★☆☆☆ Hotels ★★★☆☆ Shopping ★★☆☆☆ Nightlife ★★☆☆☆

WELCOME TO SIDE TRIPS FROM DENVER

TOP REASONS TO GO

★ **Hit the slopes at Winter Park Resort:** There's a blocked-off area for beginners, an outstanding children's program, and chutes and in-bounds off-piste–style terrain for experts.

★ **Ride the Georgetown Loop Railroad:** Peering out the window at the steep mountainside and the rickety trestle bridge on the vintage train ride from Georgetown to Silverplume provides an eye-opening lesson in 1800s transportation.

★ **Tour the Molson Coors Brewery:** An entertaining (and free) tour ends with an informal tasting. You'll see the steeping, roasting, and milling of the barley, then tour the Brew House where the "malt mash" is cooked in massive copper kettles.

★ **Explore Mount Evans:** The highest paved road in the United States leads to the summit of 14,264-foot-high Mount Evans, and you can drive or bike nearly to the top or hike as much or as little of it as you like, passing mountain goats, bighorn sheep, and other animals along the way.

The Front Range mountains, the easternmost mountains in Colorado, stretch more than 180 miles from the Wyoming border to Cañon City. The Continental Divide flows along much of the northern portion of this spine, which includes several "Fourteeners," 14,000-foot or higher peaks. A boon for high-country lovers, the Rockies near Denver are easily accessed from the metro area via I–70, Colorado's major east–west interstate, or U.S. 285, the major route heading southwest into the mountains toward Fairplay in the now infamous South Park, one of the largest high-altitude valleys in the country. (Trey Parker, co-creator of the animated sitcom *South Park,* went to Evergreen High School.) Interstate 70 stitches together Denver, Golden, Idaho Springs, and Georgetown before crossing the Continental Divide through the Eisenhower Tunnel, right next to Loveland Ski Resort.

1 Golden. Once the territorial capital of Colorado and now home to Molson Coors Brewery.

2 Evergreen. An upscale community where Denverites go to beat the heat.

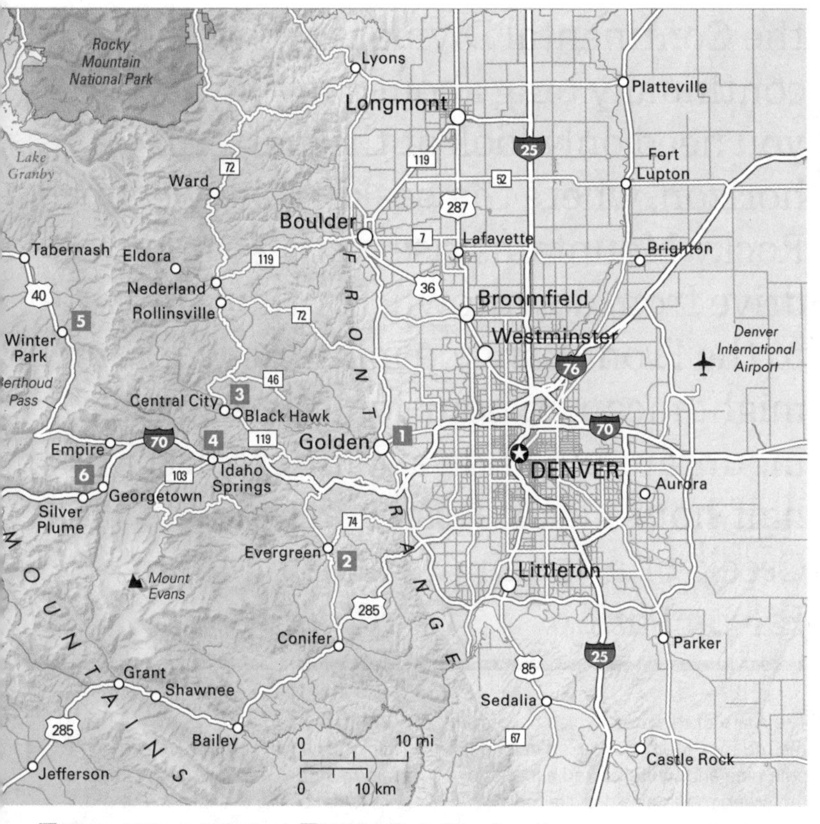

3 Central City and Black Hawk. The area's gambling mecca.

4 Idaho Springs. The first mining town of the Colorado Gold Rush.

5 Winter Park. One of the most accessible ski resorts from Denver.

6 Georgetown. A one-time silver mining boom town.

If you have ever wondered why folks living along the Front Range—as the area west of Denver and east of the Continental Divide is known—continually brag about their lifestyles, you need only look at the western horizon, where the peaks of snowcapped Rocky Mountains rise just a 35-minute drive from downtown. For those drawn to the Front Range, a morning workout might mean an hour-long single-track mountain-bike ride at Winter Park, a half-hour kayak session in Golden's Clear Creek, or a 40-minute hike in Mount Falcon Park.

The allure of this area, which rises from the red-rock foothills cloaked in lodge-pole pine and white-barked aspens to the steep mountainsides draped with the occasional summer snowfields, has brought increasing recreational pressures as mountain bikers, equestrians, hikers, dog lovers, hunters, and conservationists all vie for real estate that is increasingly gobbled up by McMansion sprawl. On the Front Range the days of the elitist "Native" bumper stickers are long since gone; almost everyone here is from somewhere else. Finding an outdoor paddling, climbing, or skiing partner is about as difficult as saying hello to the next person you meet on the trail.

MAJOR REGIONS

Rocky Mountain Foothills. Less than 40 minutes from the city's heart, there are fast, cooling escapes in the mountain towns of Golden, Morrison, and Evergreen. Try your luck at the gaming towns of Central City and Black Hawk, or explore the former mining town of Idaho Springs. If you want to head into the High Country for a few hours, take the Molson Coors tour in Golden, then head up to the Buffalo Bill Museum. If you want to climb even higher, take a walk around the lake in the center of Evergreen and visit some of the local shops in the tiny downtown area.

Continental Divide Area. Colorado's gold- and silver-mining heritage is the highlight of Georgetown, within an hour's drive of Denver along I–70. Highway 40 climbs northwest from I–70, west of Idaho Springs, making a switchback ascent up Berthoud Pass before dropping into the resort town of Winter Park. Nearby Loveland is smaller, but one of the locals' favorite ski areas because of its proximity to Denver.

Planning

When to Go

Summers are hot in the city, but when you go higher up in the Front Range the days may be warm, but the nights are cool. It's a time of year when many hikers and bikers head for the higher peaks. Heavy traffic on I–70 during weekends and holidays has become a sad fact of life for those wanting to explore the Front Range and Colorado's High Country. Slowdowns peak on Friday and Sunday afternoons when stop-and-go jams are the norm, particularly around Idaho Springs and Georgetown. Winter weekend and holiday traffic fares little better, with regular slowdowns in the morning rush to the Summit County ski resorts and afternoon returns.

Many locals claim that the best times to visit Colorado are the spring "mud season" and autumn, when the tourists are gone and the trails are empty. In spring the Front Range mountains are carpeted with fresh new growth, while late September brings the shimmering gold of turning aspens. The interstate is well maintained. It's rare, but atop the mountain passes and at the Eisenhower Tunnel it's possible to see a bit of snow during the summer.

Getting Here and Around

AIR

Denver International Airport is east of Denver, about a 35-minute taxi ride from the city center and a two-hour drive from the Continental Divide when the roads are clear and traffic is normal.

CONTACTS Denver International Airport (DEN). ☎ *800/247–2336* 🌐 *www.flydenver.com.*

AIRPORT TRANSFERS Home James. ☎ *833/274–3397 shuttle service from Denver International Airport to Winter Park and Grand County* 🌐 *www.ridehj.com.*

CAR

The most convenient place to rent a car is at Denver International Airport. You can save money if you rent from the other offices of major car companies, but you'll have to take a shuttle or taxi to the city locations.

The hardest part about driving in the High Rockies is keeping your eyes on the road, what with canyons, mountain ridges, and animals to distract your attention. Some of the most scenic routes aren't necessarily the most direct, like the spectacular Loveland Pass.

Although it is often severely overcrowded on weekends and holidays, I–70 is still the quickest and most direct route from Denver to the High Rockies. It slices through the state, separating it into northern and southern halves. Idaho Springs is along I–70. Winter Park is north of I–70, on U.S. 40 and over Berthoud Pass, which has gorgeous views but also has many hairpin turns. U.S. 285 is the southwest route to Buena Vista, Salida, and the High Rockies. Any mountain road or highway can be treacherous when a winter storm blows in. Drive defensively, especially downhill to Denver and Dillon where runaway truck ramps see a fair bit of use.

Gasoline is readily available along I–70 and U.S. 285, but not so in more-remote areas like Mount Evans and Guanella Pass. Blinding snowstorms can appear out of nowhere on the high passes at any time of the year. In the fall, winter, and early spring, it's a good idea to bring chains and a shovel along. Road reports and signage on the highways will indicate whether chains or four-wheel-drive vehicles are required. Keep your eyes peeled for wildlife, especially along the stretch of I–70 from Idaho Springs to the Eisenhower Tunnel. Bighorn sheep, elk, and deer frequently graze along the north side of the highway.

Parks and Recreation Areas

Arapaho & Roosevelt National Forests
Much of the northern Front Range region is within the Arapaho & Roosevelt National Forests. The **Indian Peaks Wilderness Area** is northwest of Denver and encompasses a rugged area of permanent snowfields, alpine lakes, and peaks reaching 13,000 feet and higher. It's a popular wilderness area for Denver and Front Range residents because it's easily reachable for overnight trips. Some of the trailheads on the eastern side are about one hour from Boulder and almost two hours from Denver. Because 90% of the people enter from the east side of the forests, visitors entering from the west side will find more solitude. ✉ *Fort Collins* ☎ *303/541–2500* 🌐 *www.fs.usda.gov/arp.*

Clear Creek
For Class II to IV rafting and kayaking, try Clear Creek Rafting Company, which offers rafting on Clear Creek near Idaho Springs and on the Arkansas River during the early spring snowmelt season and throughout the summer. ✉ *350 Whitewater Rd., Idaho Springs* ☎ *800/353–9901* 🌐 *www.clearcreekrafting.com.*

Golden Gate Canyon State Park
Just west of Golden, Golden Gate Canyon State Park has great hiking and wildlife-viewing, and offers some of the best car camping in the metro area. ✉ *Golden* ☎ *303/297–1192* 🌐 *cpw.state.co.us.*

Jefferson County Open Space Parks
Most recreational lands in the foothills west of Denver are protected by Jefferson County Open Space Parks. These relatively small county parks are heavily used and have excellent hiking, mountain-biking, and horse-riding trails. ☎ *303/271–6511* 🌐 *www.jeffco.us.*

Meyer Ranch Park
A homestead in the early 1870s, Meyer Ranch is now one of the most popular hiking areas in Jefferson County Open Space, as well as a sledding mecca in the winter and a leaf-peeping spot in fall. The park offers more than 4 miles of trails winding through meadows of wildflowers and small, hilly stands of lodgepole pine and aspens; biking and horseback riding also are allowed. ■ **TIP→ There is a scenic picnic area along Owl's Perch Trail.** The park is open from one hour before sunrise to one hour after sunset. Address is for parking lot. ✉ *10508 S. Turkey Creek Rd.* ✥ *30 mins west of Denver off Hwy. 285* ☎ *303/271–5925 Jeffco administrative office* 🌐 *www.jeffco.us.*

Restaurants

Front Range dining draws primarily from the Denver metro area; you'll find standard chains, mom-and-pop restaurants, upscale dining, and good international food choices like Mexican and Thai, with the occasional Middle Eastern restaurant thrown in.

Hotels

In summertime, out-of-state and regional visitors flock to Georgetown and Idaho Springs to explore the rustic ambience, tour a mine, and hike or mountain bike on trails that thread the mountainsides; or to Golden to tour the Molson Coors Brewery. You won't find megaresorts or grand old lodges; but there are bed-and-breakfasts, condominiums, a few nice hotels in Golden, and some chain properties. Winter Park Resort has a mix of hotels and motels, plus a few upscale ranches. In Black Hawk and Central City, where gambling is allowed, there are several big hotels with casinos on the main floor, plus a few smaller casinos tucked into historical storefronts.

Restaurant and hotel reviews have been shortened. For full information, visit Fodors.com. Restaurant prices are the average cost of a main course at dinner or, if dinner is not served, at lunch, excluding 7.1%–8.9% tax. Hotel prices are the lowest cost of a standard double room in high season, excluding service charges and 8.9% tax.

What It Costs

	$	$$	$$$	$$$$
RESTAURANTS	under $15	$15–$22	$23–$30	over $30
HOTELS	under $125	$125–$200	$201–$300	over $300

Visitor Information

CONTACTS Clear Creek County Tourism Bureau. ☎ *303/567–4660, 866/674–9237* 🌐 *www.clearcreekcounty.org.*

Golden

15 miles west of Denver via I–70 or U.S. 6 (W. 6th Ave.).

Golden was once the territorial capital of Colorado. City residents have smarted ever since losing that distinction to Denver by "dubious" vote in 1867, but in 1994 then-Governor Roy Romer restored "ceremonial" territorial-capital status to Golden. While the growth boosted by the high-tech industry as well as the Molson Coors Brewery and the Colorado School of Mines has slowed down, it remains a top draw for outdoors and history enthusiasts. Locals love to kayak along Clear Creek as it runs through Golden; there's even a racecourse and a white-water park on the water.

GETTING HERE AND AROUND

Golden is a 30-minute drive from downtown Denver via U.S. 6. Downtown Golden is compact and easily walkable. You may want to drive to the Colorado School of Mines area of town; it's about a mile away from the downtown area, and you'll want a car to reach the Buffalo Bill Museum, which is several miles away. The parking area for the Molson Coors tours is within walking distance of downtown.

TIMING

You can explore downtown and tour the Molson Coors Brewery in three hours or so.

VISITOR INFORMATION Greater Golden Chamber of Commerce. ✉ *1010 Washington Ave.* ☎ *303/279–3113* 🌐 *www.goldenchamber.org.*

If you love beer, be sure to visit Coors Brewery in Golden, the world's largest single-site brewery.

Sights

Bradford Washburn American Mountaineering Museum

MUSEUM | Even if you never intend to go climbing, you may enjoy learning about lofty adventures showcased at the American Mountaineering Museum here. Visual exhibits display photos and items from experiences climbing some of the world's highest mountains. Artifacts from famous climbs are alongside exhibits about the 10th Mountain Division—men who fought in Italy in World War II, some of whom founded several of Colorado's ski resorts. ✉ *710 10th St.* ☎ *303/996–2755* 🌐 *www.mountaineeringmuseum.org* 🎫 *$7.*

★ **Buffalo Bill Museum and Grave**

MUSEUM | **FAMILY** | The drive up **Lookout Mountain** to the Buffalo Bill Museum and Grave provides a sensational panoramic view of Denver that alone is worth the price of admission. It was this view that encouraged Bill Cody—Pony Express rider, cavalry scout, and tireless promoter of the West—to request Lookout Mountain as his burial site. Adjacent to the grave is a small museum with art and artifacts detailing Cody's life and times, as well as a souvenir shop. The grave is 100 yards past the gift shop on a paved walkway. ✉ *987½ Lookout Mountain Rd.* ✣ *Rte. 5 off I–70 Exit 256, or 19th Ave. out of Golden* ☎ *303/526–0744* 🌐 *www.buffalobill.org* 🎫 *$5.*

Colorado Railroad Museum

MUSEUM | **FAMILY** | Just outside Golden is the Colorado Railroad Museum, a must-visit for any train lover. More than 100 vintage locomotives and cars are displayed outside the museum. Inside the replica-1880 masonry depot are historical photos and memorabilia of Puffing Billy (the nickname for steam trains), along with an astounding model train set that steams through a miniature-scale version of Golden. In the Roundhouse you can witness a train's restoration in progress, and in winter, the popular tale of *The Polar Express* is theatrically performed. ✉ *17155 W. 44th Ave.* ☎ *800/365–6263* 🌐 *www.coloradorailroadmuseum.org* 🎫 *$10.*

★ Coors Brewery

WINERY/DISTILLERY | Thousands of beer lovers make the pilgrimage to the venerable Coors Brewery (formerly the MillerCoors Brewery) each year. Founded in 1873 by Adolph Coors, a 21-year-old German stowaway, today it's the largest single-site brewery in the world and part of Molson Coors. The free self-paced tour explains the malting, brewing, and packaging processes. Informal tastings are held at the end of the tour, and you can buy souvenirs in the gift shop. A free shuttle runs from the parking lot to the brewery. ✉ *13th and Ford Sts.* ☎ *303/277–2337, 866/812–2337* 🌐 *www.coorsbrewerytour.com* ⏲ *Closed Sun. in winter* ☞ *Children under 18 must be accompanied by an adult.*

Golden History Museum & Park

HISTORIC SITE | **FAMILY** | Two properties—the Golden History Center, and Clear Creek Golden History Park (formerly Clear Creek History Park)—have combined under the name of Golden History Museum & Park. The park interprets the Golden area circa 1843–1900 via restored structures and reproductions, including a teepee, prospector's camp, one-room schoolhouse, and cabins. It is also populated with live chickens and bees. On select days, guides in period clothing lead 45-minute tours, but you can stroll the park and peek into the buildings anytime. There's also a research center and an interactive area for kids. ✉ *11th and Arapahoe Sts.* ☎ *303/278–3557* 🌐 *www.goldenhistory.org* 🎫 *Free* ⏲ *Museum closed Tues.*

12th Street

HISTORIC SITE | A National Historic District, Golden's 12th Street has a row of handsome 1860s brick buildings. ✉ *Golden.*

Restaurants

★ Woody's Wood Fired Pizza

$$ | **PIZZA** | **FAMILY** | Woody's has a full menu, with pastas, chicken, calzones, and burgers, but it's the pizza, with its smoky, wood-charred crust, that's the big draw. Woody's is so popular that the pies are always just out of the oven. **Known for:** honey dip for the crust; beer cheese soup; lots of crowds. 💲 *Average main: $17* ✉ *1305 Washington Ave.* ☎ *303/277–0443* 🌐 *www.woodysgolden.com.*

Hotels

Golden Hotel

$$$ | **HOTEL** | Right in the heart of Golden, this hotel is a comfortable place to stay midway between downtown Denver and the mountains, where the rooms have beds covered by high-quality bedding with triple sheeting, backed by a faux-leather chocolate-colored headboard. **Pros:** downtown, riverside setting; spacious rooms; great personal products. **Cons:** caters to businesspeople; often understaffed; can be noisy from parties. 💲 *Rooms from: $237* ✉ *800 11th St.* ☎ *800/233–7214, 303/279–0100* 🌐 *www.thegoldenhotel.com* 🛏 *62 rooms* 🍽 *No meals.*

Activities

GOLF

★ Fossil Trace Golf Club

GOLF | Created by James Engh, this spectacular 18-hole course is set into an old quarry. You play along fairways that have been set into deep gouges in the earth created when the quarry was mined, and you hit past pillars of sandstone to reach some of the greens. Along the way, players can stop to look at fossils of triceratops' footprints in an aeons-old rock wall, and relics of old clay-mining equipment. ✉ *3050 Illinois St.* ☎ *303/277–8750* 🌐 *www.fossiltrace.com*

$90 weekdays, $100 weekends. 18 holes, 6831 yards, par 72.

HIKING

Mount Falcon Park

HIKING/WALKING | This park is a great way to explore the true foothills of the Front Range, and the comparatively low elevation makes it a good warm-up for higher ventures. Early in the morning mule deer can be seen grazing on the adjacent slopes. Take the **Turkey Trot Trail** from the east parking lot in the Morrison Town Park marked with a "hikers only" sign. The trail winds 1¾ miles up the east face of Mount Falcon through brushy slopes before curving behind the mountain up a forested draw to top out at around 7,000 feet. The trail loops back around and connects to the Castle Trail for a 1¼-mile easy return to the parking lot. Allow about 90 minutes. ⚠ **Stay on the path to avoid critters, including rattlesnakes, that lie in the grass.** *Jefferson County Open Space, start at east parking lot www.jeffco.us/parks.*

Evergreen

20 miles southwest of Golden via U.S. 6 east, Hwy. 470, I–70 west, and Hwy. 74 (Evergreen Pkwy.); 28 miles west of Denver.

Once a quiet mountain town, today Evergreen is a tony community filled with upscale, extravagantly designed homes. The downtown core remains rustic in feel, however, and on warm-weather weekends it's filled with tourists and Denverites escaping the city heat. Visitors browse the eclectic mix of shops and mingle with locals walking their dogs on the path, which circles Lake Evergreen.

GETTING HERE AND AROUND

It's a 45-minute drive from downtown Denver. Once you're in the heart of town, it's easy to find parking and explore on foot.

FESTIVALS

Evergreen Jazz Fest

FESTIVALS | The annual, multiday Evergreen Jazz Fest in July features musicians from around the country, such as New York's popular The Brain Cloud. Ticket prices vary; concerts are offered in five venues around town. *Evergreen www.evergreenjazz.org From $30.*

Sights

Hiwan Heritage Park and Museum

MUSEUM | Built between 1890 and 1930, this restored log cabin shows a popular and relaxed mountain summertime lifestyle. The museum, which includes three other buildings, has an exceptional collection of Southwestern Indian artifacts, and there's a short trail around the pretty property's 4 acres. *4208 S. Timbervale Dr. 720/497–7650 www.jeffco.us/1251/Hiwan-Heritage-Park Free.*

Restaurants

Dandelions Café & Bakery

$ | **VEGETARIAN** | Nearly everything at Dandelions is made from scratch, from the ginger-infused limeade and lemon-tarragon salad dressing to the honey oat bread and superb gluten-free brownies. The small dining area is inviting and open to the kitchen, where the owners cook as they chat with the customers. **Known for:** super-friendly owners; individual pizzas; gluten-free pancakes. *Average main: $10 1552 Bergen Pkwy. #305 303/674–5000 www.dandelionsevergreen.com Closed Sun. No dinner.*

Saigon Landing

$$ | **VIETNAMESE** | Gracious service and exceptional Vietnamese food have made Saigon Landing an Evergreen favorite. The dining room, decorated with imported knickknacks, serves as a relaxing and romantic backdrop for live piano music on the weekends. **Known for:** owners who chat with guests; exotic dishes such as frog's legs and grilled quail; tempura-fried

ice cream. $ *Average main: $18 ✉ 28080 Douglas Park Rd. ☎ 303/674–5421 🌐 www.saigonlanding.com.*

The Wildflower Cafe

$ | AMERICAN | FAMILY | This tiny but friendly café serves breakfasts so scrumptious that there's a line out the door most days. It's well worth the wait, especially for the jalapeño-studded huevos rancheros Benedict. **Known for:** kids' dinosaur-shaped pancakes; great espresso; Thursday-night Asian-fusion specials. $ *Average main: $13 ✉ 28035 Hwy. 74 ☎ 303/674–3323 🌐 www.wildflowerevergreen.com ⏲ No dinner Fri.–Wed.*

Hotels

★ Highland Haven Creekside Inn

$$$ | B&B/INN | Within walking distance of downtown Evergreen, this inn has a combination of standard and luxury rooms, suites, and cottages set alongside Bear Creek, where guests can go trout fishing. **Pros:** mountain town locale but only 35 minutes from downtown Denver or Georgetown; very quiet; romantic, particularly the adult Tree House. **Cons:** bathrooms tend to be small; you'll have to walk or drive into Evergreen; rates are high. $ *Rooms from: $290 ✉ 4395 Independence Trail ☎ 303/674–3577 🌐 www.highlandhaven.com 18 rooms 🍽 Free Breakfast.*

Shopping

Evergreen Gallery

ART GALLERIES | This gallery has an excellent collection of contemporary decorative and useful ceramics, art glass, photographs, and other fine craft work. ✉ *28195 Hwy. 74 ☎ 303/674–4871 🌐 www.theevergreengallery.com.*

Activities

SPAS

TallGrass Aveda Spa and Salon

SPA/BEAUTY | Tucked at the end of a windy road, the warmly rustic TallGrass is remote enough that you may see deer or elk outside as you wait for your treatment. Scrubs are a top pick to slough off skin dried by the Colorado climate, and the CBD-enhanced Recovery Massage uses roller to target stress and muscle fatigue. Note that prices are higher for services on weekends, but the spa also offers last-minute discounts. A healthy spa lunch can be added to the experience. ✉ *997 Upper Bear Creek Rd. ☎ 303/670–4444 🌐 www.tallgrassspa.com ☞ $120 50-min massage, $355 half-day escape. Hair salon, steam room. Services: Aromatherapy, waxing, body wraps, facials, massage, nail services.*

Central City and Black Hawk

18 miles west of Golden via U.S. 6 and Hwy. 119; 38 miles west of Denver.

Changes to the gambling laws created a "gold rush" to Black Hawk and Central City, allowing the casinos to stay open 24/7 and offer craps and roulette; the betting limit was also raised to $100. The two former mining towns edge up against each other with more than two dozen casinos, several of which are topped by big hotels.

Central City offers a fleeting sense of what the original mining town looked like. Many of the casinos there are in buildings dating from the 1860s—from jails to mansions—and their plush interiors have been lavishly decorated to re-create the Old West era, a period when this town was known as the "Richest Square Mile on Earth." Black Hawk looks like builders stuck a load of glitzy hotels and casinos right in the middle of once-quiet mountainous terrain. The biggest casinos are in newer buildings in Black Hawk; hotel deals are common.

GETTING HERE AND AROUND

Both towns are about a 45-minute drive from Denver. If you want to start in Black Hawk, take the narrow and winding Highway 119. If you'd rather start in Central City, head up I–70 and take the wide Central City Parkway. Bus transportation is also available from Denver and Golden through most of the casinos and the Opera House.

Gilpin History Museum

MUSEUM | At the Gilpin History Museum, photos and reproductions, as well as vintage pieces from different periods of Gilpin County history, paint a richly detailed portrait of life in a typical rowdy mining community. *228 E. 1st High St., Central City 303/582–5283 www.gilpinhistory.org $6 Closed Mon. By appointment only Oct.–Memorial Day.*

Restaurants

White Buffalo Grille

$$$$ | STEAKHOUSE | Inside Black Hawk's Lodge Casino, this upscale spot serves steaks, seafood such as honey-bourbon-glazed salmon, a top-notch burger, and Colorado rack of lamb. The views from the all-glass enclosure on a bridge above Richmond Street are divine. **Known for:** reasonably priced steaks; romantic setting with great views; well-made desserts, including a delicious carrot cake. *Average main: $35 Lodge Casino, 240 Main St., Black Hawk 303/582–6375 www.thelodgecasino.com Closed Tues. and Wed. No lunch.*

Central City Opera House

ARTS VENUE | Opera has been staged at the Central City Opera House, the nation's fifth-oldest opera house, almost every year since opening night in 1878. Lillian Gish has acted, Beverly Sills has sung, and many other greats have performed here. Performances are held in summer only. *124 Eureka St., Central City 303/292–6700, 800/851–8175 Denver box office www.centralcityopera.org.*

SPAS

Ameristar Casino Resort Spa Black Hawk

SPA—SIGHT | The upscale hotel Ameristar upped the ante for size and amenities, and nowhere is the opulence more apparent than in the modern but restful Ara Spa, which offers aromatherapy and hot stone massages, a variety of tub soaks, and a detox wrap. Before or after treatment, guests can take advantage of the steam room, sauna, and whirlpool; if you aren't indulging in a treatment, a $50 day-use fee weekdays garners use of the water amenities, including the steam room and whirlpool (but not on weekends). The well-equipped fitness center and rooftop pool are added incentives to spend the day; use is free by leaving your photo ID. *111 Richman St., Black Hawk 720/946–4300, 866/667–3386 www.blackhawkameristar.com $120 50-min massage, $350 3-hr, 3-treatment spa package. Hair salon, sauna, steam room. Services: Aromatherapy, body wraps, facials, hydrotherapy, massage.*

The Mount Evans Scenic and Historic Byway will take you to the summit of Mount Evans by car.

Idaho Springs

11 miles south of Central City via Central City Pkwy. and I–70; 33 miles west of Denver via I–70.

Colorado prospectors struck their first major vein of gold here on January 7, 1859. That year local mines dispatched half of all the gold used by the U.S. Mint—ore worth a whopping $2 million. Today the quaint town recalls its mining days, especially along portions of Colorado Boulevard, where pastel Victorians will transport you back to a century giddy with all that glitters.

GETTING HERE AND AROUND

After taking one of the I–70 Idaho Springs exits, it's hard to get lost, because the central part of this small town is bordered by the highway on one side and landlocked by a steep mountainside just a few blocks away. Head to the center of town, park, and walk around.

Sights

Argo Gold Mine & Mill

FACTORY | **FAMILY** | During gold-rush days the Argo Gold Mine & Mill processed more than $100 million worth of the precious metal. To transport the ore from mines in Central City, workers dug through solid rock to construct a tunnel to Central City, 4½ miles away. When completed in 1910 the Argo Tunnel was the longest in the world. During a tour of the mine and mill, guides explain how this monumental engineering feat was accomplished. Admission includes the small museum and a gold-panning lesson. ✉ *2350 Riverside Dr.* ☎ *303/567–2421* 🌐 *argomilltour.com* 🎫 *$25.*

Charlie Taylor Waterwheel

BUILDING | Near Indian Hot Springs Resort is a 600-foot waterfall, Bridal Veil Falls. The imposing Charlie Taylor Waterwheel—the largest in the state—was constructed in the 1890s by a miner who attributed his strong constitution to the fact that he never shaved, took baths, or kissed women. ✉ *Idaho Springs ✥ South of Idaho Springs on I–70 🌐 www.historicidahosprings.com.*

Indian Hot Springs Resort

HOT SPRINGS | FAMILY | Idaho Springs presently prospers from the hot springs here at Indian Hot Springs Resort. Around the springs, known to the Ute natives as the "healing waters of the Great Spirit," are geothermal caves that were used by tribes as a neutral meeting site. The hot springs, a translucent dome–covered mineral-water swimming pool, mud baths, and geothermal caves are the primary draws for the resort. You don't need to be an overnight guest to soak in the mineral-rich waters; day rates start at $22 for the geothermal cave baths (depending on type of bath and day of week), $24.50 for outdoor Jacuzzi baths, and $18 for the pool. The plain but comfortable spa offers massages and facials. ✉ *302 Soda Creek Rd.* ☎ *303/989–6666* 🌐 *www.indianhotsprings.com* 🎫 *Varies by bath and pool; prices higher on weekends.*

★ Mount Evans Scenic and Historic Byway

SCENIC DRIVE | The incomparable Mount Evans Scenic and Historic Byway—the highest paved road in the United States—leads to the summit of 14,264-foot-high Mount Evans. This is one of only two Fourteeners in the United States that you can drive up (the other is her southern sister, Pikes Peak). More than 7,000 feet are climbed in 28 miles, and the road tops out at 14,134 feet, 130 feet shy of the summit, which is a ¼-mile stroll from the parking lot. The toll road winds past placid lakes and through stands of towering Douglas firs and bristlecone pines. This is one of the best places in the state to catch a glimpse of shaggy white mountain goats and regal bighorn sheep. Small herds of the nimble creatures stroll from car to car looking for handouts. Feeding them is prohibited, however. Keep your eyes peeled for other animals, including deer, elk, and feather-footed ptarmigans. ✉ *U.S. Forest Service fee station, State Rd. 3 ✥ From Idaho Springs, State Rd. 103 leads south 14 miles to the entrance to Hwy. 5, which is the beginning of the scenic byway* ☎ *303/567–3000* 🎫 *$10.*

Oh-My-Gawd Road

VIEWPOINT | Although most travelers heading to Central City take the new highway from I–70, adventurous souls can take the Oh-My-Gawd Road. Built in the 1870s to transfer ore, this challenging drive climbs nearly 2,000 feet above Idaho Springs to Central City. After traveling along a series of hairpin curves you arrive at the summit, where you are treated to sweeping views of Mount Evans. The dusty road is often busy with mining traffic, so keep your windows up and your eyes open. ✉ *Hwy. 279 ✥ From Idaho Springs (Exit 240), drive west through town on Colorado Blvd. Turn right on 23rd Ave., left on Virginia St., and right at Virginia Canyon Rd. (Hwy. 279).*

Phoenix Gold Mine

MINE | At the Phoenix Gold Mine a seasoned miner leads tours underground, where you can wield 19th-century excavating tools or pan for gold. Whatever riches you find are yours to keep. ✉ *Off Trail Creek Rd.* ☎ *303/567–0422* 🌐 *www.phoenixgoldmine.com* 🎫 *$22; $12 for tour only.*

★ St. Mary's Glacier

VIEWPOINT | This is a great place to enjoy a mountain hike and the outdoors for a few hours. From the exit, it's a beautiful 10-mile drive up a forested hanging valley to the glacier trailhead. The glacier, technically a large snowfield compacted in a mountain saddle at the timberline, is thought to be the southernmost glacier in the United States. During drought years it all but vanishes; a wet winter creates a wonderful Ice Age playground throughout the following summer. Most visitors are content to make the steep ¾-mile hike on a rock-strewn path up to the base of the glacier to admire the snowfield and sparkling sapphire lake. The intrepid hiker, with the right type of gear, can climb up the rocky right-hand side of the snowfield to a plateau less than a mile above for sweeping views of the Continental Divide. Because of its proximity to Denver, St. Mary's Glacier is a popular weekend getaway for summer hikers, snowboarders, and skiers. There are two pay parking lots with about 140 spaces between them; the cost is $5 per vehicle per day, with restrooms and trash facilities available at both. Don't look for a St. Mary's Glacier sign on I–70; it reads "St. Mary's Alice," referring to the nearby ghost towns. ✉ *Idaho Springs* ✥ *I–70 Exit 238, west of Idaho Springs.*

Restaurants

Beau Jo's Pizza
$$ | PIZZA | FAMILY | This always-hopping pizzeria is the area's original après-ski destination: be prepared for a wait on winter weekends, because Denverites often stop in Idaho Springs for dinner until the traffic thins. Topping choices for the famous olive oil–and-honey pizza crust range from traditional to exotic—andouille sausage, Hatch green chile, tofu—and they've added a decent version of a gluten-free crust, as well. **Known for:** popular honey crust; family-friendly atmosphere; hamburger pizza. $ *Average main: $15* ✉ *1517 Miner St.* ☎ *303/567–4376* ⊕ *www.beaujos.com.*

Tommyknocker Brewery & Pub
$ | AMERICAN | Harking back to gold-rush days, this casual bar and restaurant is usually filled with skiers in winter and travelers or Denverites year-round who want to meet high country friends halfway. The beers have a distinctly local flavor and straightforward names like Cream Ale and Nut Brown. **Known for:** the spot to take a break from I–70 traffic; group and family gatherings; house-made root beer. $ *Average main: $14* ✉ *1401 Miner St.* ☎ *303/567–2688* ⊕ *www.tommyknocker.com.*

Shopping

The Wild Grape
GIFTS/SOUVENIRS | This store is filled with an eclectic collection of gift items and souvenirs and an outstanding collection of greeting cards. ✉ *1435 Miner St.* ☎ *303/567–4670.*

Winter Park

36 miles west of Idaho Springs; 67 miles west of Denver via I–70 and U.S. 40.

Winter Park Resort is easily navigable from the small village at the base anchored by Zephyr Mountain Lodge and the Fraser Crossing and Founders Pointe condominiums. The Village Cabriolet—an open gondola—takes day skiers from a big parking lot to one end of the village, and they must walk past most of the shops, restaurants, and bars before reaching the lifts at the base of the resort.

GETTING HERE AND AROUND

In winter you can catch a ride on shuttle buses that move between the resort and the town of Winter Park, a few miles away. But in summer you'll need a car to vacation here. Amtrak stops at nearby Fraser and Granby.

WHEN TO GO

From late November to mid-April good snow attracts winter-sports lovers. Winter Park is equally popular in summer with hikers, bicyclists, and golfers, but has few tourist attractions besides its natural beauty. Mountain bikers flock here because of the diversity of the trails and the growing emphasis on downhill mountain biking.

VISITOR INFORMATION Winter Park/Fraser Valley Chamber of Commerce. ✉ *78841 U.S. 40* ☎ *970/726–4221, 800/903–7275* ⊕ *www.playwinterpark.com.* **Winter Park Resort.** ✉ *100 Winter Park Dr.* ☎ *800/977–7669, 970/726–5514* ⊕ *www.winterparkresort.com.*

Carvers

$ | **AMERICAN** | Long a local and Denverite favorite for breakfast, this casual joint makes Belgian waffles that are as delicious as the variety of Benedicts and scrambles with fresh orange or grapefruit juice (not to mention great coffee). Lunch is also served. **Known for:** local crowd; cinnamon rolls made fresh daily; good Bloody Marys. *Average main: $12* *Kings Crossing Center, 78336 U.S. 40* *970/726–8202* *No dinner.*

Deno's Mountain Bistro

$$$ | **AMERICAN** | A sizable selection of beers from around the world helps make this casual establishment the liveliest spot in town, but what sets it apart is a wine list that's comprehensive and fairly priced—a rarity in low-key Winter Park. The cellar full of fine vintages is a labor of love for Deno and his son, the powerhouse duo behind the restaurant. **Known for:** location in a former stagecoach stop; wine cellar that can be reserved for private parties; standard bistro fare like steak and lobster ravioli. *Average main: $30* *78911 U.S. 40* *970/726–5332* *www.denoswp.com* *No lunch weekdays.*

★ The Dining Room at The Lodge at Sunspot

$$$$ | **AMERICAN** | Reached via chairlift during the day and gondola at night, this massive log-and-stone structure set at 10,700 feet above sea level is a real stunner, with views of the surrounding mountains, including the peaks marching along the Continental Divide. A prix-fixe menu includes game and fish, while Douglas-fir beams, Southwestern rugs on the walls, and a huge stone fireplace in the bar add to the rustic charm. **Known for:** perfect elk tenderloin dish; incredible mountain views; charming wood-burning fireplace. *Average main: $60* *Top of Zephyr Express Lift* *970/726–1446* *www.winterparkresort.com.*

Hernando's Pizza and Pasta Pub

$$ | **PIZZA** | **FAMILY** | Bring along a dollar bill that you're willing to leave on the wall—it will join thousands of others that have been drawn on, written on, and tacked up in rows around and above the bar. There's nothing fancy here, just good pasta and pizzas. **Known for:** pizza crust the size of your fist; garlic breadsticks; raucous surroundings. *Average main: $15* *78199 U.S. 40* *970/726–5409* *www.hernandospizzapub.com* *No lunch.*

★ Devil's Thumb Ranch

$$$$ | **RESORT** | **FAMILY** | Many visitors come to this 6,500-acre ranch outside Winter Park for unrivaled cross-country skiing, with 75 miles of groomed trails, but they wind up staying for the resort's comfort and privacy. **Pros:** terrific cross-country skiing and horseback riding; top-notch restaurant; gorgeous rooms and spacious cabins. **Cons:** in winter getting there can be rough; one of the pricier properties in the state; must drive to eat in any other restaurant or cook your own meals. *Rooms from: $339* *3530 County Rd. 83, Tabernash* *800/933–4339* *www.devilsthumbranch.com* *102 rooms* *No meals.*

Iron Horse Resort

$$$ | **RENTAL** | On the banks of the Fraser River, this condo-style hotel is ski-in ski-out, but it's removed from the resort's base village. **Pros:** truly ski-in ski-out; quiet location; indoor-outdoor heated pool. **Cons:** isolated area, so you must drive to the base village or to town for restaurants and shops; must create your own nightlife; some condos are nicer than others. *Rooms from: $265* *101 Iron Horse Way* *970/726–8851, 800/621–8190* *www.ironhorse-resort.com* *126 suites* *No meals.*

★ **StayWinterPark**

$$$ | **RENTAL** | The premier source for luxury condos, town homes, and multibedroom, million-dollar homes on the fairways at Pole Creek and at the base of Winter Park offers luxury homes for large groups at prices that are often comparable to regular condos. **Pros:** luxe accommodations; ideal for families; many properties have hot tubs. **Cons:** pricey during ski season; some properties far from resort; lodging options vary. *Rooms from: $220* *800/215–6535* *www.staywinterpark.com* *158 properties.*

Vasquez Creek Inn

$$ | **B&B/INN** | The owners of Devil's Thumb Ranch bought the little Gasthaus Eichler alongside Vasquez Creek and remodeled it in a similar vein, softening the rooms with puffy pillows atop remarkably comfortable beds and recasting in creams, golds, and rusts. **Pros:** comfortable rooms; great restaurant; walking distance to town. **Cons:** on weekends the streets in front of the hotel can be busy; restaurant noise can reach rooms; no elevator. *Rooms from: $135* *78786 U.S. 40* *970/722–1188* *www.vasquezcreekinn.com* *15 rooms* *Free Breakfast.*

Vintage Hotel

$$ | **HOTEL** | **FAMILY** | Right next to the Village Cabriolet lift, the Vintage is the best value if you want to be close to the resort base, and most of its comfortable rooms look out onto the mountains. **Pros:** from door to base village in five minutes on the cabriolet; great value; most rooms have fireplaces. **Cons:** its popularity means it can get noisy; you'll need to drive or take a shuttle to the town of Winter Park; some rooms feel dated. *Rooms from: $152* *100 Winter Park Dr.* *970/726–8801, 800/472–7017* *www.winterparkresort.com/plan-your-trip/lodging/vintage-hotel* *118 rooms* *No meals.*

Wild Horse Inn

$$ | **B&B/INN** | Tucked into the woods on the way to Devil's Thumb Ranch, this mountain retreat is a bit off the beaten path, but your reward is complete relaxation. **Pros:** quiet at night; on-site massage therapist; rooms have private balconies overlooking the forest. **Cons:** it's a 10- to 15-minute drive to Winter Park; must create your own nightlife; the largest, loveliest room is on the first floor near the entrance area. *Rooms from: $180* *1536 County Rd. 83* *970/726–0456* *www.wildhorseinn.com* *10 rooms* *Free Breakfast.*

Zephyr Mountain Lodge, Fraser Crossing, Founders Pointe, and Parrys Peak Lofts

$$$ | **RENTAL** | These are all condo complexes—some with individual hotel rooms, too—that are in the village at the base a short walk from the base lifts. **Pros:** close to the lifts; fireplaces in most units; close to restaurants and bars. **Cons:** no air-conditioning and only limited air circulation in the units; will need a car or shuttle to head into town; owned units vary in decor. *Rooms from: $240* *Zephyr Mountain Lodge, 201 Zephyr Way* *800/729–7907, 970/726–5514* *www.zephyrmountainlodge.com* *232 rooms* *No meals.*

Nightlife

Fisher's Bar

BARS/PUBS | For a bit of local color, head down to Fraser and the rustic and inviting Fisher's Bar. Owned by a local brother-and-sister duo, this bar and eatery is filled with local memorabilia and antiques, as well as lots of TVs, which draw sports-loving crowds. Locals still show up for the cheap beer during happy hour, as well as for the excellent burgers. *401 Zerex St.* *970/726–9250.*

Eisenhower Memorial Tunnel

As you travel west along I–70 you'll reach one of the world's engineering marvels, the 8,941-foot-long Eisenhower Memorial Tunnel. Most people who drive through take its presence for granted, but until the first lanes were opened in 1973 the only route west through the mountains was the perilous Loveland Pass, a heart-pounding roller-coaster ride. In truly inclement weather the Eastern and Western slopes were completely cut off from each other. Authorities first proposed the tunnel in 1937. Geologists warned about unstable rock, and through more than three decades of construction, their direst predictions came true as rock walls crumbled, steel girders buckled, and gas pockets caused mysterious explosions. When the project was finally completed, more than 500,000 cubic yards of solid granite had been removed from Mount Trelease. The original cost estimate was $1 million; by the time the second bore was completed in 1979 the tunnel's cost had skyrocketed to $340 million. Today there can be a long wait during busy weekends because so many travelers use I–70.

Ullrs Tavern

BARS/PUBS | This tavern provides the closest thing to real nightlife in the area. Ullrs Tavern's small, somewhat ramshackle space attracts a younger crowd, with live music on the weekends, a DJ other nights, and a handful of pool tables. A small grill inside the tavern called The Spot ($) serves decent pub grub, including sandwiches and wings. ✉ *78415 U.S. 40* ☎ *719/238–6500* 🌐 *ullrs-tavern.com.*

Winter Park Pub

BARS/PUBS | The under-30 crowd tends to hang out at the lively Winter Park Pub, grooving to local bands. ✉ *78260 U.S. 40* ☎ *970/726–4929.*

Shopping

Cooper Creek Square

SHOPPING NEIGHBORHOODS | **FAMILY** | This square is filled with inexpensive souvenir shops and fine jewelers, upscale eateries and local cafés, plus live entertainment all summer in the courtyard. ✉ *47 Cooper Creek Way* ☎ *970/460–9800* 🌐 *coopercreeksquare.com.*

Activities

BACKCOUNTRY SKIING

Berthoud Pass

SKIING/SNOWBOARDING | South of Winter Park, Berthoud Pass is a hard place to define. At the top of the pass there is a former downhill skiing area—its lifts have been removed—that is popular with some backcountry skiers. There's no regular avalanche control on these former runs. Skiers and snowboarders venturing in must have their own rescue equipment, including beacons, shovels, and probes. Backcountry skiing on the slopes of the former ski area or anywhere else on Berthoud Pass is only for very experienced, well-conditioned, and properly prepared skiers and riders. You must check current avalanche conditions before starting out, although that's no guarantee. In addition to skiing the slopes of the former ski areas, many people pull into parking areas elsewhere alongside the highway over Berthoud Pass and go cross-country or backcountry skiing. At many spots along the highway you'll see signs warning of avalanche blasting at any time with long-range weaponry. (This blasting is done to help prevent

Winter Park is great for skiers and snowboarders alike.

avalanches from covering the highway.) ✉ *U.S. 40* 🌐 *berthoudpass.com.*

DOWNHILL SKIING AND SNOWBOARDING

★ Winter Park

SKIING/SNOWBOARDING | This ski park is really two interconnected areas: Winter Park and Mary Jane, both open to skiers and snowboarders. Between the two peaks there are four distinct skiable sections: Winter Park; the "Jane"; Vasquez Ridge, which is primarily intermediate cruising; and Vasquez Cirque, which has seriously steep in-bounds off-piste terrain. Pick a meeting place for lunch in case you and your friends get separated.

The skiing on the Winter Park and Vasquez Ridge trails is generally family-friendly, and there are segregated areas for beginners. Winter Park's runs promise lots of learning terrain for beginners and easy cruising for intermediates. On busy weekends Vasquez Ridge is a good place for escaping crowds, partly because this area is a bit more difficult to find, but the run-outs can be long.

Mary Jane is famous for its bumps and chutes, delivering 1,766 vertical feet of unrelenting moguls on a variety of trails, although there are a couple of groomed intermediate runs. Experts gravitate toward the far end of the Jane to runs like Trestle and Derailer, or to Hole-in-the-Wall, Awe, and other chutes. Expert skiers and riders seeking inbound off-piste–style terrain hike over to the Vasquez Cirque.

The resort's Eagle Wind terrain has advanced steeps and deeps tucked among the trees. Panoramic Express, the highest six-person lift in North America, provides access to above-the-tree-line skiing at Parsenn Bowl, Perry's Peak, and Forever Eva, as well as terrain and gladed sections. The pitch in many areas of Parsenn's is moderate, making the bowl a terrific place for intermediate skiers to try powder and crud-snow skiing.

The resort's Rail Yard, with its superpipe and terrain parks, is specially designed for freestylers. A progressive park system allows skiers and snowboarders to start small and work their way up to the bigger and more difficult features. There is also a limited-access park, the Dark Territory, which is for experts only and requires an additional fee. **Facilities:** 143 trails; 3,081 acres; 3,060-foot vertical drop; 26 lifts. ✉ *100 Winter Park Dr.* ☎ *800/729–7907, 970/726–5514* 🌐 *www.winterparkresort.com* 🎟 *Lift ticket $165.*

LESSONS AND PROGRAMS

National Sports Center for the Disabled

SKIING/SNOWBOARDING | Winter Park is home to the National Sports Center for the Disabled, one of the country's largest and best programs for skiers with disabilities. ☎ *970/726–1518* 🌐 *www.nscd.org.*

Winter Park Ski and Ride School

SKIING/SNOWBOARDING | For adult skiers and snowboarders, the Winter Park Ski and Ride School has half-day lessons starting at $149. Daylong children's programs, which include lunch, start at $199. ✉ *Balcony House* ☎ *800/729–7907* 🌐 *www.winterparkresort.com.*

RENTALS

Winter Park Resort Rentals

SKIING/SNOWBOARDING | This rental agency rents skiing and snowboarding gear from its Village location and west Portal location and includes free overnight storage. Rental equipment is also available from shops downtown. ✉ *Zephyr Mountain Lodge, 201 Zephyr Way* ☎ *970/726–1664 Village location, 970/726–1662 west Portal location.*

GOLF

Golf Granby Ranch

GOLF | This 18-hole course is nestled against the Rocky Mountains. The original course by Michael Asmundson was redesigned by the Nicklaus Design firm to turn it into a more walkable course; two "family holes" were added to offer a golf experience for novices. The back nine is fraught with interesting challenges and fast greens. ✉ *1000 Village Rd., Granby* ☎ *970/887–2709, 888/850–4615* 🌐 *www.granbyranch.com* 🎟 *$85 weekdays, $130 weekends* ⛳ *18 holes, 7123 yards, par 72.*

Pole Creek Golf Club

GOLF | Designed by Denis Griffiths, Pole Creek has three 9-hole, par-36 courses and fantastic views of the mountains. You can play any combination of 18 holes, but try to get on the Ridge 9, which has particularly challenging holes with slippery greens and one of the best views in the state. The on-site eatery Bistro 28 ($$) serves three well-executed meals daily. ✉ *6827 County Rd. 51* ☎ *970/887–9195, 800/511–5076* 🌐 *www.polecreekgolf.com* 🎟 *$95 weekdays, $109 weekends* ⛳ *Meadow/Ranch: 18 holes, 3074 yards, par 36; Ranch/Ridge: 18 holes, 3143 yards, par 36; Ridge/Meadow: 18 holes, 3377 yards, par 36.*

HIKING

Byers Peak

HIKING/WALKING | At 12,804 feet, Byers Peak is one of the tallest mountains overlooking Fraser, and the highest point in the Byers Peak Wilderness Area. The trail climbs the northern ridge of Byers through lodgepole pine and Engelmann spruce forests before entering the spaciousness of the alpine tundra at around 11,200 feet. Climbers are rewarded with views of the Indian Peaks Wilderness, the Gore Range, and Middle Park. The trail is only 1½ miles, but it climbs 2,400 feet. If you aren't used to it, high altitude can catch you off guard. Bring plenty of water and slather on the sunscreen. In summer an early morning start is best. Afternoon thunderstorms are frequent, and you should never be above the tree line during a storm with lightning. Plan on three hours for the round-trip hike. ✉ *Sulphur Ranger District, Arapaho & Roosevelt National Forests* ☎ *970/887–4100.*

HORSEBACK RIDING

Cabin Creek Stables at Devil's Thumb Ranch

HORSEBACK RIDING | For leisurely horseback-riding tours of the Fraser Valley, your best bet is Cabin Creek Stables at Devil's Thumb Ranch. ✉ *3530 Hwy. 83, Tabernash* ☎ *800/933–4339* 🌐 *www.devilsthumbranch.com* 🎟 *From $125.*

MOUNTAIN BIKING

Trestle Bike Park Shop

BICYCLING | This shop gives tips about the best trails and rents a huge fleet of downhill and cross-country mountain bikes in the summer, which makes it the perfect stop on the way to the Trestle Bike Park, 40 miles of trails for all skill levels located in Winter Park Resort. They also offer half-day bike clinics. ✉ *In the Village at Winter Park* ☎ *800/729–7907 for reservations, 970/726–5514* 🌐 *www.trestlebikepark.com.*

Vasquez Creek

BICYCLING | Winter Park is one of the leading mountain-biking destinations in the Rockies, with some 30 miles of trails crisscrossing the main part of the resort in two bike parks and 600 more miles off the beaten path. Vasquez Creek is an easy but fun 4½-mile trail that runs along a forest of blue spruce, fir, and aspen. The trail sticks to dirt roads with easy grades; the elevation gain is barely 600 feet. For more serious bikers the side trails have challenging climbs and rewarding vistas. ✉ *Trailhead: parking garage next to the visitor center at the junction of U.S. 40 and Vasquez Rd.*

SNOW TUBING

Fraser Snow Tubing Hill

SNOW SPORTS | **FAMILY** | You can slide down this hill on an oversize inner tube and then hop on a magic carpet for a ride up to the top to do it all over again. When you get cold, head into the warming hut nearby. The hill is lighted at night. ✉ *455 County Rd. 72* ✣ *Hwy. 72 and Fraser Valley Pkwy.* ☎ *970/726–5954* 🌐 *frasertubinghill.com* 🎫 *$25 per hour; $30 for 90 minutes.*

SNOWMOBILING

Grand Adventures

SNOW SPORTS | This company offers snowmobile rentals and guided tours. Rates range from $150 per hour to $230 for a full-day tour. ✉ *81699 U.S. 40 S* ☎ *970/726–9247, 800/726–9247* 🌐 *www.grandadventures.com.*

TRACK SKIING

Devil's Thumb Ranch

SKIING/SNOWBOARDING | About 8 miles northwest of Winter Park, Devil's Thumb Ranch grooms about 75 miles of cross-country trails. Some skiing is along fairly level tree-lined trails; some is with more ups and downs and wide-open views. The ranch has rentals, lessons, and backcountry tours. ✉ *3530 County Rd. 83, Tabernash* ☎ *970/726–5632* 🌐 *www.devilsthumbranch.com* 🎫 *Trail fee $22.*

Snow Mountain Ranch

SKIING/SNOWBOARDING | Twelve miles northwest of Winter Park, Snow Mountain Ranch has an 80-mile track system that includes almost 3 miles of trails lighted for night skiing. The ranch is a YMCA facility (with discounts for members) and has added bonuses such as a sauna and an indoor pool. Lessons, rentals, and on-site lodging are available. **■ TIP→ No trail fee for overnight guests.** ✉ *1101 County Rd. 53, Granby* ☎ *970/887–2152, 888/613–9622* 🌐 *www.snowmountainranch.org* 🎫 *Trail fee $22.*

Georgetown

32 miles southwest of Winter Park via U.S. 40 and I–70; 50 miles west of Denver via I–70.

Georgetown rode the crest of the silver boom during the second half of the 19th century. Most of the impeccably maintained brick buildings that make up the town's historic district date from that period. Georgetown hasn't been tarted up, so it provides a true sense of what living was like in those rough-and-tumble times. It's a popular tourist stop in the summertime. Be sure to keep an eye out for the state's largest herd of rare bighorn sheep that often grazes alongside I–70 in this region.

The historic Georgetown Loop Railroad crosses the 95-foot-high Devil's Gate Bridge.

GETTING HERE AND AROUND

Just west of where I–70 and U.S. 40 intersect, the downtown historic area is just a few blocks long and a few blocks wide, so park and start walking.

TIMING

Georgetown is close enough to attract day-trippers from Denver, but much of the summer the town is filled with vacationers who have come here to ride the Georgetown Loop Railroad. Weekdays are quieter than weekends.

VISITOR INFORMATION Georgetown. ✉ *Georgetown City Hall, 404 6th St.* ☎ *303/569–2405* 🌐 *georgetown-colorado.org.* **Loveland Snow Report.** ☎ *800/736–3754, 303/571–5580* 🌐 *www.skiloveland.com.*

Sights

★ Georgetown Loop Railroad

TRANSPORTATION SITE (AIRPORT/BUS/FERRY/TRAIN) | **FAMILY** | This 1920s narrow-gauge train connects Georgetown with the equally historic community of Silver Plume. The 6-mile round-trip excursion takes about 70 minutes, and winds through vast stands of pine and fir before crossing the 95-foot-high Devil's Gate Bridge, where the track actually loops back over itself as it gains elevation. You can add on a tour of the **Lebanon Silver Mill and Mine,** which is a separate stop between the two towns, as well as meals in the dining car. In fall and around the holidays, special trains run, including popular rides with Santa. ✉ *646 Loop Dr.* ☎ *888/456–6777* 🌐 *www.georgetownlooprr.com* 🎫 *$27.95 for train; $37.95 with mine tour.*

Guanella Pass Scenic Byway

VIEWPOINT | South of Georgetown, the Guanella Pass Scenic Byway treats you to marvelous views of the Mount Evans Wilderness Area. Along the way—while negotiating some tight curves, especially as you head down to Grant—you'll get close views of Mount Evans as well as Grays and Torrey's peaks—two Fourteeners. It takes about 40 minutes to cross the 22-mile dirt and asphalt road. ✉ *Hwy. 381.*

Hotel de Paris

HOTEL—SIGHT | The elaborate Hotel de Paris, built almost single-handedly by Frenchman Louis Dupuy in 1878, was one of the Old West's preeminent hostelries. Now a museum, the hotel depicts how luxuriously the rich were accommodated: Tiffany fixtures, lace curtains, and hand-carved furniture re-create an era of opulence. ✉ *409 6th St.* ☎ *303/569–2311* 🌐 *www.hoteldeparismuseum.org* 🎟 *$8.*

Restaurants

The Alpine Restaurant and Bar

$ | **PIZZA** | **FAMILY** | The thin-crust brick-oven pizzas and ingredient-packed stromboli and calzones draw families and groups to the casual, bustling Alpine, which serves lunch and dinner and offers live music Thursday to Saturday. Kids love the operating model train that winds around the restaurant overhead, and adults love the cozy bar. **Known for:** Wednesday-night trivia; warm cookie à la mode; extensive beer roster. 💲 *Average main: $14* ✉ *1106 Rose St.* ☎ *303/569–0200* 🌐 *alpinerestaurantgeorgetown.com* 🕒 *Closed Tues.*

Hotels

Georgetown Mountain Inn

$$ | **HOTEL** | **FAMILY** | Next door to the Old Georgetown Railroad, this basic inn has rooms decorated with Western-style wood furniture and Southwestern blankets. **Pros:** right by the station for the Georgetown Loop railroad; pine-paneled walls and log headboards feel authentically Colorado; indoor pool. **Cons:** several blocks away from historic downtown; some noise; some rooms feel dated. 💲 *Rooms from: $130* ✉ *1100 Rose St.* ☎ *303/569–3201, 800/884–3201* 🌐 *www.georgetownmountaininn.com* *33 rooms* *No meals.*

Hiking the Continental Divide

The Continental Divide, that iconic geographic division that sends raindrops to either the Atlantic or Pacific Ocean, makes a worthy pilgrimage for day hikers and backpackers alike in summer. The easiest way to reach the divide is to drive up U.S. 6 over Loveland Pass at the Eisenhower Tunnel on I-70 and park on top of the divide. Hiking trails lead both east and west along the divide. Bring cash or a check for the $5 parking fee, and carpool if you can—parking is limited and tight during nice weather.

Hotel Chateau Chamonix

$$ | **B&B/INN** | With its log exterior and green roof, this hotel doesn't look exceptional for the region outside, but inside it's a lovely property put together with care by local owners. **Pros:** some rooms overlook a stream and have a two-person hot tub on a porch; rooms have espresso-cappuccino machines; owners often greet you with a glass of wine. **Cons:** on a busy main street; not within easy walking distance to downtown; thin walls and noisy overhead floors. 💲 *Rooms from: $180* ✉ *1414 Argentine St.* ☎ *303/569–1109, 888/569–1109* 🌐 *www.hotelchateauchamonix.com* *10 rooms* *Free Breakfast.*

Shopping

Grizzly Creek Gallery

LOCAL SPECIALTIES | This gallery has wonderfully scenic large-scale photographs of the Rockies and wildlife. ✉ *512 6th St.* ☎ *303/569–0433* 🌐 *www.grizzlycreekgallery.com.*

DOWNHILL SKIING AND SNOWBOARDING

Loveland Ski Area

SKIING/SNOWBOARDING | Because of its proximity to Denver (an hour's drive), lack of resort facilities and hotels, and few high-speed lifts, Loveland Ski Area is often overlooked by out-of-staters, but that's just the way locals like it. Loveland has some of the highest runs in Colorado spread across a respectable 1,800 acres serviced by 12 lifts. It's split between Loveland Valley, a good place for beginners, and Loveland Basin, a good bet for everyone else. Loveland Basin has excellent glade and open-bowl skiing and snowboarding, especially on the 2,210-foot vertical drop. Best of all, it opens early and usually stays open later than any other ski area except Arapahoe Basin. **Facilities:** 94 trails; 1,800 acres; 2,210-foot vertical drop; 12 lifts. ✉ *Georgetown* ✣ *I–70 Exit 216, 12 miles west of Georgetown* ☎ *303/571–5580, 800/736–3754* 🌐 *www.skiloveland.com* 🎫 *Lift ticket $89.*

LESSONS AND PROGRAMS

Loveland Ski School

SKIING/SNOWBOARDING | This ski school offers 2½-hour group "Newcomer Packages" beginning at 10 am and 1 pm for $140 including all rental gear and an all-day lift ticket. Advanced half-day lessons (a maximum of four people per group) are $140 or $155 with rental gear. ✉ *Georgetown* ☎ *303/571–5580 ext. 170* 🌐 *www.skiloveland.com.*

RENTALS

Loveland Rental Shop

SKIING/SNOWBOARDING | Loveland Rentals has two on-mountain locations, at the basin next to the Sport Shop and in the valley next to the restaurant. You can purchase sport packages for $45, and performance packages for $55. Snowboard packages start at $45; helmets run $12. ✉ *Georgetown* ☎ *303/571–5580 ext. 113 Basin Rental Shop, 303/571–5580 ext. 155 Valley Rental Shop* 🌐 *www.skiloveland.com.*

Chapter 5

BRECKENRIDGE AND SUMMIT COUNTY

Updated by
Lindsey Galloway

Sights ★★★☆☆ | Restaurants ★★☆☆☆ | Hotels ★★☆☆☆ | Shopping ★☆☆☆☆ | Nightlife ★★☆☆☆

WELCOME TO BRECKENRIDGE AND SUMMIT COUNTY

TOP REASONS TO GO

★ **Festival fun:** Breckenridge hosts numerous festivals, including the aptly named Spring Fever Festival in March and April, and the weeklong Ullr Fest honoring the snow god in winter.

★ **Mining heritage:** It was gold that built Colorado in the 1800s, and this legacy is alive and well in the rejuvenated mining town of Leadville.

★ **Mountain waters:** Nothing beats a day of lake kayaking or fishing among the many wooded islets on Lake Dillon, the reservoir that is the heart of Summit County.

★ **Skiing choices:** You won't find more choices to ski and ride within snowball-throw's distance of one another than in Summit County, many a mere hour's drive from the Denver Metro Area.

★ **Trail biking:** Sure, there are plenty of singletrack rides, but the real draw is the glorious paved bike trail that runs from Dillon up and over the mountains to Vail.

The great east–west Colorado corridor I–70 cleaves through the heart of Summit County, punching west from Denver past Idaho Springs and Georgetown. The traffic here can be heavy and fast; everyone is in a hurry to make it through the Eisenhower Tunnel, the traditional gateway to Summit County. Those with an extra half hour and a yearning for hairpin turns, shaggy mountain goats, and 100-mile views opt for U.S. 6 over Loveland Pass and the Continental Divide. As it drops into the Summit County Basin on the west side of the divide, U.S. 6 passes Arapahoe Basin and Keystone Ski Resort before merging with I–70. Both roads skirt Dillon Reservoir, with its shoreline communities of Dillon and Frisco. The highway quickly disappears back into a narrow mountain valley and climbs to Copper Mountain and then up and over Vail Pass.

1 **Keystone.** A laid-back mountain town with the state's largest night skiing operation.

2 **Arapahoe Basin.** Summit County's first ski area.

3 **Dillon.** Home to one of the state's largest man-made reservoirs.

4 **Frisco.** One of the area's more affordable towns.

5 **Breckenridge.** A mining town turned skiing and snowboarding destination.

6 **Copper Mountain.** A thriving resort town.

7 **Leadville.** The highest incorporated city in the country.

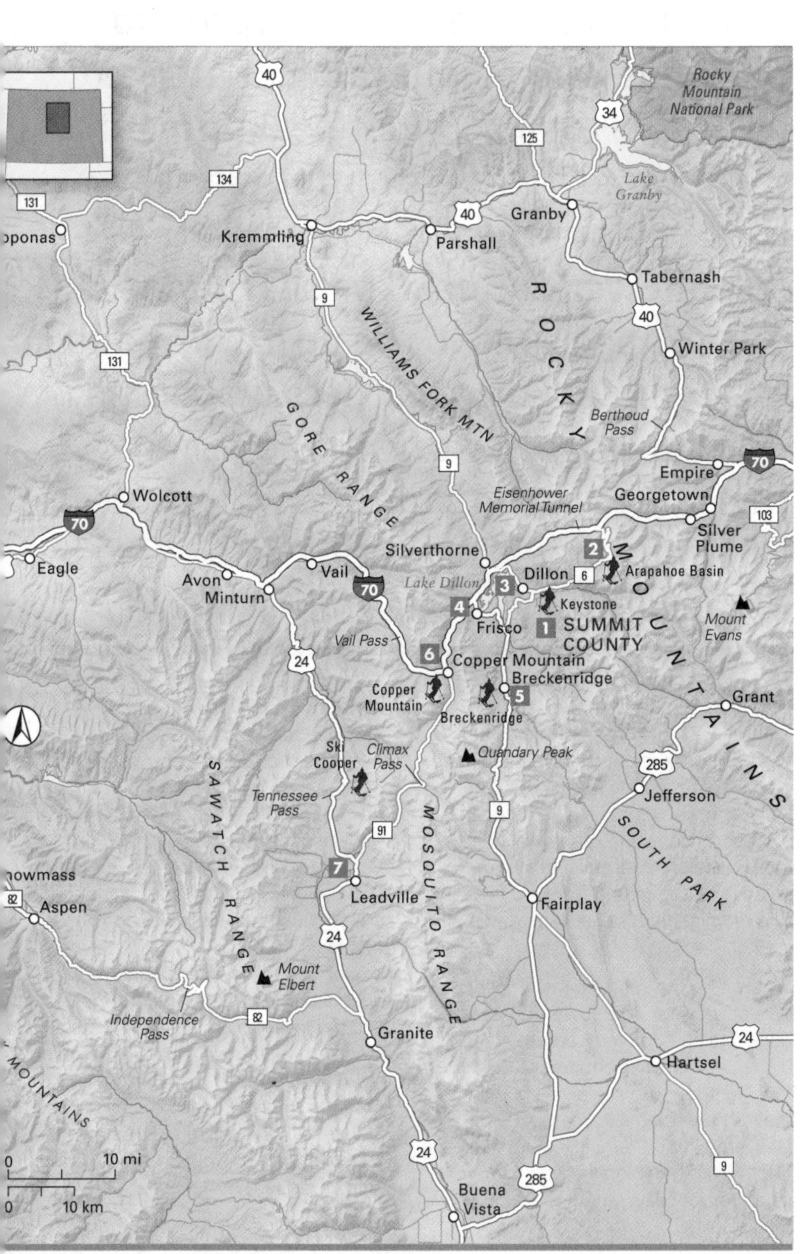
Rocky Mountain National Park
Lake Granby
Granby
Kremmling
Parshall
Tabernash
Winter Park
WILLIAMS FORK MTN
ROCKY
GORE RANGE
Berthoud Pass
Empire
Georgetown
Silver Plume
Eisenhower Memorial Tunnel
Wolcott
Eagle
Avon
Minturn
Vail
Silverthorne
Lake Dillon
Dillon
Arapahoe Basin
Keystone
Frisco
SUMMIT COUNTY
MOUNTAINS
Mount Evans
Vail Pass
Copper Mountain
Breckenridge
Grant
Ski Cooper
Climax Pass
Quandary Peak
Tennessee Pass
Jefferson
SAWATCH RANGE
MOSQUITO RANGE
SOUTH PARK
Leadville
Fairplay
Aspen
Mount Elbert
Independence Pass
Granite
Hartsel
MOUNTAINS
Buena Vista
0 10 mi
0 10 km

Summit County, a mere hour's drive from the Denver Metro Area on a straight shot up I–70, is Denver's playground. The wide-open mountain park ringed by 13,000- to 14,000-foot peaks greets westbound travelers minutes after they pop out the west portal of the Eisenhower Tunnel. The sharp-toothed Gore Range rises to the northwest and the Tenmile Range gathers up behind Breckenridge. Resting in the center of this bowl are the sapphire waters of Dillon Reservoir, an artificial lake fed by Blue River.

In winter, Summit County is packed with tourists and Front Range day-trippers skiing the steeps at Breckenridge, Keystone, Arapahoe Basin, and Copper Mountain. The high density of first-rate ski resorts generally keeps lift lines low, particularly on weekdays. In summer, the steady westbound traffic is mostly SUVs stacked high with kayaks and mountain bikes.

Summit County, as its name implies, is relatively high. The town of Breckenridge sits at 9,603 feet, and the resort's highest ski lift tops out just shy of 13,000 feet. Visitors from sea level should take their time getting acclimated. Even Denverites find themselves breathless in the thin air. Drink lots of water and rest your first few days; there will be plenty of time to play.

MAJOR REGIONS

Keystone and Arapahoe Basin. Just 90 miles west of Denver over Loveland Pass or through the Eisenhower Tunnel, Keystone and Arapahoe Basin are among the closest ski resorts to the Front Range. Given their location hugging the Continental Divide's western flank—both are surrounded by high-altitude peaks topping 12,000 feet—they are also among the highest resorts in the state. They tend to attract more of a local—and hardier—ski crowd, and hikers in summer. Keystone is an intimate resort town but "A-Basin" is little more than a ski area. You can reach both by taking I–70 across the divide to Dillon and then following U.S. 6 south and east up the narrow valley.

Lake Dillon and Breckenridge. Lake Dillon, a 3,233-acre artificial reservoir with four narrow arms and almost 27 miles of shoreline, sits at the heart of Summit County. The lake is guarded on the northwest by the steep Gore Range and on the southwest by the Tenmile Range (a part of the Mosquito Range), and to the east by the Continental Divide. Along the northern shore sit Dillon and her sister town Silverthorne, while Frisco hugs a southwest arm of the lake. Skiers will bypass these towns for Breckenridge, the largest ski area in Summit County. "Breck" has a blend of authentic Colorado character with a flashy dose of upscale lodges and high-end condos.

Copper Mountain and Leadville. Farther west on I–70, Copper Mountain makes up for a lack of mountain charm with its near-perfect ski mountain. Skiers head here because the runs make sense—you can start easy and progress to harder slopes without having to crisscross the mountain. It also offers the largest expanse of skiing in Summit County. The high-altitude mountain town of Leadville will leave you breathless, both from the thin air and from the gorgeous views of Colorado's highest peak, 14,440-foot Mount Elbert. Although it has a small ski resort (Ski Cooper) and plenty of snowmobiling trails, this rustic mining town is more popular as a summer base for hiking forays to Mount Elbert.

Planning

When to Go

Summit County is a haven for winter enthusiasts: the resorts of Arapahoe Basin and Breckenridge—and nearby Loveland in Clear Creek County—are so high that the ski season often dawns here weeks before it does in the rest of the state, with Arapahoe Basin and Loveland competing to see who has the longest season, which can begin as early as October and end as late as July. The altitude also means that it can snow on any day of the year, so be prepared. Traffic, particularly on the I–70 approaches to the Eisenhower Tunnel and the Georgetown-to–Idaho Springs stretch, moves at a snail's pace around weekend rush hours—noon to 10 pm on Friday and all day Sunday.

Getting Here and Around

AIR

Denver International Airport (DEN) is the gateway to the attractions and ski resorts in Summit County. The airport is an hour's drive from the Continental Divide along I–70.

To and from Summit County (Breckenridge, Copper Mountain, Dillon, Frisco, and Keystone), use Colorado Mountain Express and 453 Taxi, which have regular service to and from the Denver airport.

AIRPORT CONTACTS Denver International Airport (DEN). ✉ *8500 Pena Blvd., Denver* ☎ *800/247–2336* 🌐 *www.flydenver.com.*

AIRPORT TRANSFER CONTACTS Epic Mountain Express. ☎ *970/754—7433, 800/525–6363* 🌐 *www.epicmountain-express.com.* **453-Taxi.** ☎ *970/453–8294* 🌐 *453taxi.com.*

BUS AND SHUTTLE

All the resorts run free or inexpensive shuttles between the ski villages and the slopes. Summit Stage provides free public transportation to town and ski areas, in and between ski areas in Summit County.

CONTACTS Summit Stage. ☎ *970/668–0999* 🌐 *www.summitcountyco.gov/586/Transit-Summit-Stage.*

CAR

The hardest part about driving in the High Rockies is keeping your eyes on the road. A glacier-carved canyon off to your left, a soaring mountain ridge to your right, and there, standing on the shoulder, a bull elk. Some of the most scenic routes aren't necessarily the most direct. The Eisenhower Tunnel sweeps thousands of cars daily beneath the mantle of the Continental Divide, whereas only several hundred drivers choose the slower, but more spectacular, Loveland Pass. Some of the most beautiful byways, like the Mount Evans Scenic and Historic Drive, are one-way roads.

Although it is severely overcrowded, I–70 is still the quickest and most direct route from Denver to Summit County. The interstate slices through the state, separating it into northern and southern halves. Breckenridge is south of I–70 on Highway 9; Leadville and Ski Cooper are south of I–70 along U.S. 24 and Highway 91.

Gasoline is readily available along I–70 and its arteries, but when venturing into more remote areas be sure that you have enough fuel to get there and back. Blinding snowstorms can appear out of nowhere on the high passes at any time of the year. Chains aren't normally required for passenger vehicles on highways, but it's a good idea to carry them. A shovel isn't a bad idea, either.

Parks and Recreation Areas

Summit County is perched in a 9,000-foot-high park (a wide valley surrounded by peaks) with Lake Dillon at its recreational heart.

The Blue River, which bisects the county south to north and is the lifeblood of Lake Dillon, has gold-medal fishing beginning below Lake Dillon to the Green Mountain Reservoir.

Arapaho National Forest
The wild Gore Range northwest of Lake Dillon is protected within the Eagles Nest Wilderness Area, administered by the Arapaho National Forest. As in all wilderness areas in Colorado, motorized or mechanized vehicles (forestry-speak for mountain bikes) are prohibited. You can tackle the backcountry peaks on your own two feet or on horseback. ☎ *970/295–6600* 🌐 *www.fs.usda.gov/arp.*

Restaurants

Whereas the restaurants in the celeb resorts of Aspen and Vail mimic the sophistication and style of New York and Los Angeles, Summit County eateries specialize in pub food and Mexican cuisine for calorie-hungry hikers, skiers, and boaters, with the exception of a few more urbane spots in Breckenridge. You won't find much sushi here, but you will find fish tacos, shepherd's pies, and burgers with every imaginable topping. Hearty, reasonably priced comfort food is served at a number of cozy brewpubs along with handcrafted local suds like Dam Straight Lager, Avalanche Ale, and Backcountry Brewery. *Restaurant reviews have been shortened. For full information, visit Fodors.com.*

Hotels

Summit County is a great place for history buffs looking for redone Victorian mining mansions–cum–bed-and-breakfasts, and budget hunters who want affordable rooms close to the slopes. Note that many accommodations do not have air-conditioning—beware that rooms with southern exposures warm up quickly. Summer nights, however, are often cool enough in the mountains that opening the windows will do the trick. *Hotel reviews have been shortened. For full information, visit Fodors.com.*

BACKCOUNTRY HUTS

The backcountry offers something more comfortable than camping. Several huts are available (primarily fully stocked cabins) for individual or group rentals in both summer and winter, some accessible only by foot. Some are rustic, historic buildings without electricity, but others are modern and inviting. Almost all have wood stoves and solar lights and come equipped with cooking utensils.

Summit County Huts Association
SKIING/SNOWBOARDING | The Summit County Huts Association has five backcountry cabins where skiers can spend the night (two are open for summer hikers). One popular touring route for backcountry skiing is the trip to Boreas Pass, just south of Breckenridge. The 6½-mile-long trail follows the route of a former railroad, with good views of distant peaks along the way. ✉ *524 Wellington Rd., Breckenridge* ☎ *970/925–5775* 🌐 *www.summithuts.org.*

10th Mountain Division Hut Association
SKIING/SNOWBOARDING | There are cabins available through the 10th Mountain Division Hut Association near Eagle, Vail, Leadville, and Breckenridge. ✉ *Breckenridge* ☎ *970/925–5775* 🌐 *www.huts.org.*

CAMPING

Despite the abundant amount of federal and state land that checkerboards the High Rockies, finding an established campsite is surprisingly difficult along the I–70 corridor. From Memorial Day to Labor Day, campsites fill up quickly, especially on weekends and holidays. To improve your chances, call to reserve a campsite or arrive well before noon. Established car-camping sites generally have restrooms, water pumps, trash cans, and firepits. Open fires are only allowed when the danger of wildfires is low. Wilderness devotees who don't relish the idea of a neighborhood of tents can easily escape into the vast backcountry. As long as you're 200 feet away from a water source, you can pitch your tent anywhere.

Restaurant prices are the average cost of a main course at dinner or, if dinner is not served, at lunch, excluding 7.75%–12.7% tax. Hotel prices are the lowest cost of a standard double room in high season, excluding service charges and 8.8%–12.1% tax.

What It Costs

$	$$	$$$	$$$$
RESTAURANTS			
under $15	$15–$22	$23–$30	over $30
HOTELS			
under $125	$125–$200	$201–$300	over $300

Keystone

8 miles southeast of Dillon via U.S. 6; 69 miles west of Denver.

One of the region's most laid-back destinations, Keystone is understandably popular with families and, as the state's largest night skiing operation (with lifts running until 8 pm), has long been a local favorite. Its trails are spread across three adjoining peaks: Dercum Mountain, North Peak, and the Outback. Through the years, as the resort added more runs, it morphed from a beginner's paradise on Keystone Mountain to an early-season training stop for the national ski teams that practice on the tougher and bumpier terrain on North Peak. Keystone also has full-day guided snowcat tours. Today it's a resort for all types of skiers and riders, whether they prefer gentle slopes, cruising, or high-adrenaline challenges on the Outback's steep bowls.

The planners were sensitive to the environment, favoring colors and materials that blend inconspicuously with the natural surroundings. Lodging, shops, and restaurants are in Lakeside Village, the older part of the resort, and in River Run, a newer area at the base of the gondola that has become the heart of Keystone. Everything here is operated by Keystone, which makes planning a vacation one-stop shopping.

GETTING HERE AND AROUND

The easiest way to travel to and around Summit County is to rent a car at Denver International Airport. Catching one of the numerous shuttles up to the ski areas and then taking advantage of the free transportation by Summit Stage (taxi service is also available) is a more economical route, but requires patience and a good timetable. You'll want a car to reach both resorts, but once there both Keystone and A-Basin are easily navigated on foot.

VISITOR INFORMATION

CONTACTS Keystone Snow Report. ☎ *970/496–4111 Press 1* 🌐 *www.keystoneresort.com/the-mountain/mountain-conditions/snow-and-weather-report.aspx.*

WHEN TO GO

From late October to late April winter sports rule. But Keystone is quickly becoming a magnet in summer as well, with a small lake for water sports, mountain biking and hiking trails, two highly respected golf courses, and outdoor concerts and special events.

Restaurants

★ Alpenglow Stube

$$$$ | EUROPEAN | The competition has heated up in recent years, but Alpenglow Stube remains among the finest mountaintop restaurants in Colorado. The exposed wood beams, a stone fireplace, and floral upholstery make it elegant and cozy. **Known for:** outstanding wine list; ragout of blue crab; weekend brunch with complimentary mimosas. *$ Average main: $46* ✉ *100 Dercum Sq.* ☎ *970/496–4386* 🌐 *www.keystoneresort.com* ⏲ *Closed late Apr.–early June and mid-Sept.–late Nov.*

Inxpot

$ | AMERICAN | A blend of books, coffee, martinis, and some of the best breakfast and lunch sandwiches you can get your hands on make this cozy shop a local favorite. Collages covering ceiling tiles and worn couches give this spot its character, and the après-ski rehashing over hot buttered rum and wine samplings bring in the community. **Known for:** lively atmosphere; smoked salmon breakfast sandwich; warm cocktails for the après-ski crowd. *$ Average main: $10* ✉ *195 River Run Rd.* ☎ *970/262–3707* 🌐 *www.inxpot.com.*

Keystone Ranch

$$$$ | AMERICAN | This 1930s homestead was once part of a working cattle ranch, and cowboy memorabilia is strewn throughout, nicely blending with stylish throw rugs, antler chandeliers, and a trophy mount. The gorgeous and massive stone fireplace is a cozy backdrop for dessert, or sipping an aperitif or after-dinner coffee. **Known for:** Colorado cheese and charcuterie board; seared pheasant; signature Grand Marnier soufflé. *$ Average main: $48* ✉ *Keystone Ranch Golf Course, 1239 Keystone Ranch Rd.* ☎ *970/496–4386* 🌐 *www.keystoneresort.com* ⏲ *Closed Sun. and Mon.*

Kickapoo Tavern

$$ | AMERICAN | This rustic bar and grill has local microbrews on tap and big portions of home-style dishes like piled-high burgers, sandwiches, and giant, stuffed burritos perfect for skiers, hikers, or cyclists recovering from a day on the mountain. The central location, pleasant outdoor patio, and live music keep the place hopping both après-ski and après–night ski. **Known for:** outdoor patio scene; live music and events; hearty portions of pub food. *$ Average main: $18* ✉ *129 River Run Rd.* ☎ *970/468–0922* 🌐 *www.kickapootavern.com.*

Ski Tip Lodge Restaurant

$$$$ | MODERN AMERICAN | In this ski lodge dating from the 1880s, the four-course, prix-fixe dinner is a favorite for its Colorado-spun American cuisine. Main courses have included whiskey sage–glazed Muscovy duck, peppered bacon-wrapped buffalo tenderloin, and thyme-seared wild

Alaskan halibut. **Known for:** homemade bread and soup; seasonal venison; creme brûlée. *Average main: $80 0764 Montezuma Rd. 970/496–4950, 800/354–4386 www.keystoneresort.com No lunch.*

Hotels

Keystone Lodge & Spa

$$ | **RESORT** | The cinderblock structure gives no hint of the gracious, pampered living just inside the door. **Pros:** one of the larger properties in the resort; lovely on-site spa; dog-friendly. **Cons:** rooms are small; hot tubs get crowded; limited housekeeping. *Rooms from: $150 22101 U.S. 6 877/753–9786, 970/496–4500 www.keystoneresort.com 152 rooms No meals.*

Ski Tip Lodge

$$$ | **B&B/INN** | Opened as a stop along the stagecoach route back in the 1880s, this property was turned into the state's first ski lodge in the 1940s by skiing pioneers Max and Edna Dercum. **Pros:** updated rooms; on-site restaurant; cozy and romantic. **Cons:** small rooms; not near the lifts; some rooms are noisy. *Rooms from: $260 0764 Montezuma Rd. 970/496–4950, 877/753–9786 www.keystoneresort.com 10 rooms Free Breakfast.*

Nightlife

Goat Soup and Whiskey

BARS/PUBS | Across from Mountain View Plaza, the Goat Soup and Whiskey is filled year-round with twenty- and thirtysomethings drinking whiskey and beer after a day on the mountain. There's live music during ski season and pool tournaments that draw crowds to the laid-back bar. *22954 U.S. 6 970/513–9344 www.soupandwhiskey.com.*

Snake River Saloon

BARS/PUBS | Live music with rock-and-roll leanings makes the Snake River Saloon a good spot to stop for a beer. The fun-loving crowd spans all ages. *23074 U.S. 6 970/468–2788 www.snakeriversaloon.com.*

Activities

DOWNHILL SKIING AND SNOWBOARDING

★ Keystone Resort

SKIING/SNOWBOARDING | **FAMILY** | What you see from the base of the mountain is only a fraction of the terrain you can enjoy when you ski or snowboard at Keystone. There's plenty more to Keystone Mountain, and much of it is geared to novice and intermediate skiers, but full-day guided snowcat tours cater to higher-level skiers on some of the state's steepest terrain. Its trails are spread across three adjoining peaks: Dercum Mountain, North Peak, and the Outback. The Schoolmarm Trail has 3½ miles of runs where you can practice turns. Dercum Mountain is easily reached from the base via high-speed chairs or the River Run gondola. You can ski or ride down the back side of Dercum Mountain to reach North Peak, a mix of groomed cruising trails and ungroomed bump runs. A family ski trail with green/blue trails through the woods and kid-friendly features, like tunnels and bridges, is a mountain favorite.

If you prefer to bypass North Peak, the River Run gondola is a short walk from the Outpost gondola, which takes you to the Outpost Lodge (home to the Alpenglow Stube, which, at 11,444 feet above sea level, is advertised as the "highest gourmet restaurant in the country"). From here there are two easy downhill runs to the third mountain, appropriately named the Outback because of its wilderness setting. Some glades have

Keystone Resort is one of the more laid-back of Colorado's ski resorts.

trees thinned just enough for skiers and riders who are learning to explore gladed terrain; other sections are reserved for advanced skiers.

One of the most popular non-skiing or -boarding sports at Keystone is tubing at Adventure Point.

Rental packages (skis, boots, and poles, or snowboards and boots) start at around $50 per day for a basic package but increase quickly for high-performance gear. **Facilities:** 128 trails; 3,149 acres; 3,128-foot vertical drop; 20 lifts. ✉ *Keystone* ☎ *800/239–1639* 🌐 *www.keystoneresort.com* 🎫 *Lift ticket $159.*

GOLF

Keystone Golf

GOLF | With 36 challenging holes spread across two 18-hole courses situated at 9,300 feet, Keystone lures golfers as soon as the snow melts. **Keystone Ranch,** designed by Robert Trent Jones Jr., has a links-style front nine; the back nine has a traditional mountain-valley layout. Holes play past lodgepole pines, meander around sage meadows, and include some carries across water. **The River Course** is a par-71 stunner designed by Michael Hurdzan and Dana Fry. The front nine runs around the Snake River, whereas the back nine threads through a stand of lodgepole pines. Dramatic elevation changes, magnificent views, bunkers, and water hazards combine to test golfers of all abilities. Add magnificent views of the Continental Divide and Lake Dillon, and it's easy to see why this course is so popular. ✉ *1239 Keystone Ranch Rd.* ☎ *800/464–3494* 🌐 *www.keystonegolf.com* 🎫 *Keystone Ranch, $160; The River Course, $180* 🏌 *Keystone Ranch: 18 holes, 7017 yards, par 72; The River Course: 18 holes, 6886 yards, par 71* 🕓 *Closed mid-Oct.–mid-May.*

ICE-SKATING

Keystone Lake Ice Rink

ICE SKATING | **FAMILY** | In winter, 5-acre Keystone Lake freezes to become the largest Zamboni-maintained outdoor ice-skating rink in North America. You can rent skates, sleds, or even hockey sticks for an impromptu game. Lessons in figure skating and hockey are available. Weather permitting, skating runs from late November to early March. The smaller Dercum Square ice rink is also available in River Run. ✉ *Decatur Rd.* ☎ *800/354–4386* 🌐 *www.keystoneresort.com* 🎟 *From $15.*

NORDIC SKIING

Keystone Nordic Center

SKIING/SNOWBOARDING | This center has more than 9 miles of groomed trails and access to more than 35 miles of packed trails available for skiing and snowshoeing through the White River National Forest. Cross-country, skating, snowshoeing, family tubing, and telemark lessons and rentals are available. ✉ *155 River Course Dr.* ☎ *970/496–4275* 🌐 *www.keystoneresort.com.*

SPAS

Spa at Keystone Lodge

SPA/BEAUTY | Beyond a deceiving cinderblock stairwell, this spa is blessedly warm and naturally lighted. It includes 11 treatment rooms where guests can layer on signature treatments like the Altitude Massage that pairs massage with oxygen to relieve negative elevation effects. Guests sip complimentary champagne or Tazo tea before their treatments in the relaxation room. Arrive ahead of time to properly unwind or jump-start your relaxation with a quick steam or sauna. Use of the outdoor heated pool, indoor and outdoor Jacuzzis, dry sauna, steam room, and fitness facilities are complimentary. ✉ *Keystone Lodge & Spa, 22101 U.S. 6* ☎ *970/496–4118* 🌐 *www.keystoneresort.com.*

Bighorn Sheep 

Keep your eyes peeled on the northern slopes of I–70 as you drive up to Summit County from Denver (your right side). Herds of bighorn sheep congregate around Georgetown, often right off the highway.

Arapahoe Basin

6 miles northeast of Keystone via U.S. 6.

Arapahoe Basin was the first ski area to be built in Summit County. It has changed—but not too much—since its construction in the 1940s, and most of A-Basin's dedicated skiers like it that way. It's America's highest ski area, with a base elevation of 10,780 feet and a summit of 13,050 feet. Many of the runs start above the timberline, ensuring breathtaking views (and the need for some extra breaths). Aficionados love the seemingly endless intermediate and expert terrain and the wide-open bowls that stay open into June (sometimes July). "Beachin' at the Basin" has long been one of the area's most popular summer activities.

Because A-Basin is on U.S. Forest Service land, there is no resort lodging. The closest place to stay is 5 miles down the road in Keystone, which is accessible by the free Summit Stage bus. Nevertheless, the dining here is on par with what you might expect at bigger resorts. Starting around December, don't miss the Moonlight Dinner Series put on by Black Mountain Lodge's chef Christopher Rybak, a prix-fixe meal that rotates themes like "A Night in France" and "Randonnée Dinner," which ends with a moonlit ski. On New Year's Eve, ski, snowshoe, or hike to the mountain for a themed dinner under the moon.

GETTING HERE AND AROUND

Given the remoteness of Arapahoe Basin, a car is the best way to go.

VISITOR INFORMATION

CONTACTS Arapahoe Basin Snow Report. ☎ *970/468–0718* 🌐 *www.arapahoebasin.com.*

WHEN TO GO

Skiing is the highlight here. That said, winter in this high-country spot can begin in early October and last into June. In the summer, go hiking or mountain biking, or sign up for Yoga on the Mountain and the 6.8-mile Cirque Series Trail Run (and its after-party).

Restaurants

Black Mountain Lodge

$$ | **AMERICAN** | Located mid-mountain, Black Mountain Lodge serves up hearty skier fuel like the staff-favorite BBQ brisket burrito and homemade bison stew. Even non-skiers and summer visitors can enjoy the scenic views on the expansive patio with a passenger lift ticket on the Black Mountain Express. **Known for:** bacon Bloody Marys; full moon–themed dinners (only times dinner is offered); large patio with mountain views. $ *Average main: $18* ✉ *Arapahoe Basin Mid-Mountain, 28194 U.S. 6, Dillon* ☎ *970/468–0718* 🌐 *www.arapahoebasin.com* ⏲ *No dinner.*

Activities

DOWNHILL SKIING AND SNOWBOARDING

Arapahoe Basin

SKIING/SNOWBOARDING | What makes Arapahoe Basin delightful is also what makes it dreadful in bad weather: its elevation. Much of Arapahoe's skiing is above the tree line, and when a storm moves in, you can't tell up from down.

If that sounds unpleasant, consider the other side of the coin: on sunny spring days Arapahoe is a wonderful place, because the tundra surrounded by craggy peaks is reminiscent of the Alps. Intermediate-level skiers can have a great time here on the easier trails. But A-Basin is best known for its expert challenges: the East Wall, a steep face with hike-to terrain; Pallavicini, a wide tree-lined run; and the West Wall, from which skiers of varying degrees of bravado like to launch themselves. After a long battle with the U.S. Forest Service, A-Basin won permission to install snowmaking machines that supplement about 125 of the skiable acres. Daily snowboard and ski-rental packages (skis, boots, and poles) start at $45. Ski stores in Breckenridge, Dillon, and Frisco are even cheaper. **Facilities:** 145 trails; 1,428 acres; 2,530-foot vertical drop; 9 lifts. ✉ *28194 U.S. 6, Keystone* ☎ *970/468–0718, 888/272–7246* 🌐 *www.arapahoebasin.com* 🎫 *Lift ticket from $99.*

LESSONS AND PROGRAMS

Arapahoe Basin Snowsports

SKIING/SNOWBOARDING | Regular classes and ski clinics, including telemark skiing, snowboarding, alpine skiing, and private lessons for all ages, are available throughout the winter. ☎ *970/468–0718* 🌐 *www.arapahoebasin.com/lessons-rentals/snowsports.*

Dillon

73 miles west of Denver via I–70.

Dillon can't seem to sit still. Founded in 1883 as a stagecoach stop and trading post for men working in the mines, Dillon has had to pack up and move three times since. It was first relocated to be closer to the Utah and Northern Railroad, and then to take advantage of the nearby rivers. Finally, in 1955, bigwigs in Denver

While swimming in Lake Dillon is not permitted, boating, canoeing, and kayaking are allowed.

drew up plans to dam the Blue River so they could quench the capital's growing thirst. The reservoir would submerge Dillon under more than 150 feet of water. Once again the town was dismantled and moved, this time to pine-blanketed hills mirrored in sapphire water. Residents agreed that no building in the new location would be taller than 30 feet, so as not to obstruct the view of the reservoir, which is appropriately called Lake Dillon.

Dillon now blends with neighboring Silverthorne, where dozens of factory outlets are frequented by locals and travelers vying for bargains. Combined, the two towns have hotels, restaurants, and stores galore.

GETTING HERE AND AROUND

Private car is the best way to explore Dillon, although in summer a network of bicycle trails around the reservoir makes pedaling an attractive option.

VISITOR INFORMATION

CONTACTS Summit Chamber of Commerce. ☎ *970/668–2051* 🌐 *www.summitchamber.org.*

WHEN TO GO

Dillon is a hub for all seasons. In winter, during ski season, Dillon is the place to get gas, groceries, and directions before heading to Keystone, Arapahoe Basin, Breckenridge, or Copper. Beginning with the snowmelt in May, Dillon unfolds as a center for hiking, biking, and water sports. Dillon also is home to Summit County's largest farmers' market every Friday in warmer weather.

Sights

★ Lake Dillon

BODY OF WATER | Resting in the heart of Summit County at 9,017 feet is the Front Range's answer to a day at the beach—beautiful Lake Dillon and her two ports, Dillon, just off I–70 on the south, and Frisco, off I–70 and Highway 9 on the west. The lake is actually backed up by a 231-foot earth-filled dam that fills the valley where Dillon once sat. During the frequent Western droughts, when water levels can drop dramatically, collectors wander along the exposed shores hunting for artifacts from this Rocky Mountain Atlantis. Below the mile-long dam the Blue River babbles past the outlet shopping haven and turns into miles of gold-medal fly-fishing waters on its journey north. There are more than 27 miles of gravel beaches, marshes, peninsulas, and wooded islets for picnickers to enjoy, many accessible from a 7½-mile paved trail along the northern shores, or from the informal dirt paths elsewhere. Gaze out at the deep blue waters from **Sapphire Point Lookout** (a short ½-mile hike on the south side of the lake) any nice day, and you'll see a flotilla of motorboats, sailboats, canoes, kayaks, and sailboarders dancing in the waves. In winter the frozen waters are enjoyed by ice anglers and cross-country skiers. Because the lake is a drinking-water source, swimming is not permitted, and the lake is patrolled vigorously by Summit County sheriffs. ✉ *Dillon.*

Restaurants

★ Dillon Dam Brewery

$$ | AMERICAN | At this popular brewery, one of the largest brewpubs in the Rockies, you can belly up to the horseshoe-shaped bar and sample ales and lagers while you munch on burgers, sandwiches, or pub grub. The menu is steps above average bar food with plenty of vegetarian and gluten-free options. **Known for:** house-brewed beers; customizable, piled-high nachos (make sure to top with pork green chile); large, two-story dining room anchored by the bar. 💲 *Average main: $16* ✉ *100 Little Dam St.* ☎ *970/262–7777* 🌐 *www.dambrewery.com.*

Red Mountain Grill

$$ | SOUTHWESTERN | FAMILY | The colorful decor of this American Southwest joint is something you'll remember. High-backed chairs ring the tables, stone buttresses arch toward vaulted ceilings, and mobiles of round- and star-shaped metal lights dangle above. **Known for:** outdoor patio with funky decor; bistro burger with blue cheese mousse, fig jam, bacon, and port wine reduction; secret southwestern flair in most dishes. 💲 *Average main: $15* ✉ *703 E. Anemone Trail* ☎ *970/468–1010* 🌐 *www.redmountaingrill.com.*

Activities

BICYCLING

Summit County attracts cyclists with its 55 miles of paved bike paths and extensive network of backcountry trails. There are dozens of trailheads from which you can travel through gentle rolling terrain, up the sides of mountains, and along ridges for spectacular views. Starting in Dillon, you could bike around the reservoir to Frisco. From there you could ride the Blue River Pathway, largely along the river, to Breckenridge. Or you could ride through beautiful Tenmile Canyon all the way to Copper Mountain. If you're really fit, you could even continue your ride over Vail Pass and down into Vail Village.

BOATING

Boats rented from the Frisco Bay and Dillon marinas are not permitted to beach; the aluminum pontoons are easily damaged on the rock and gravel shores.

Dillon Marina

BOATING | At Dillon Marina you can rent a kayak, stand-up paddleboard, sailboat, pontoon boat, or runabout to play on the water, or take sailing lessons at the on-site school. Reserve ahead in high season. ✉ *Take I–70 Exit 205 to U.S. 6, and follow signs to the marina, 150 Marina Dr.* ☎ *970/468–5100* 🌐 *www.townofdillon.com/marina.*

Frisco Bay Marina

BOATING | FAMILY | This marina is less crowded than Dillon and has quick access to the numerous pine-cloaked islands along the western shores. Here you can rent pontoon boats, fishing boats, canoes, and kayaks. ✉ *267 Marina Rd., Frisco* ☎ *970/668–4334* 🌐 *www.townoffrisco.com/play/frisco-bay-marina/general-info.*

FISHING

Cutthroat Anglers

FISHING | A favorite with locals, Cutthroat Anglers has a pro shop chock-full of gear for avid fly-fishermen. Their wade trips are good for beginners; full-day float-trip adventures are a favorite for those with a bit more experience. The wade trip is available in half-day and full-day versions. ✉ *400 Blue River Pkwy., Silverthorne* ☎ *970/262–2878* 🌐 *www.fishcolorado.com.*

GOLF

Raven Golf Club at Three Peaks

GOLF | A technically challenging layout and rich, natural beauty, including stands of pine and aspen trees and visiting elk and deer herds, make this one of the state's best mountain courses. All 18 holes have dramatic views of the Gore Mountain range. ✉ *2929 Golden Eagle Rd., Silverthorne* ☎ *970/262–3636* 🌐 *www.ravenatthreepeaks.com* *$169* *18 holes, 6386 yards, par 72.*

Frisco

9 miles north of Breckenridge via Hwy. 9.

Keep going past the hodgepodge of strip malls near the interstate and you'll find that low-key Frisco has a downtown district trimmed with restored B&Bs. The town is removed from the ski lifts, but is a low-cost lodging alternative to pricier resorts in the surrounding communities.

GETTING HERE AND AROUND

Private car is the best way to arrive in Frisco, but the town is compact enough for walking or biking.

Sights

Historic Park & Museum

MUSEUM VILLAGE | FAMILY | This sprawling museum re-creates Frisco's boom days. Stroll through 11 buildings dating from the 1880s, including a fully outfitted one-room schoolhouse, a trapper's cabin with snowshoes and pelts, the town's original log chapel, and a jail with an exhibit on mining. ✉ *120 Main St.* ☎ *970/668–3428* 🌐 *www.townoffrisco.com* *Free.*

Restaurants

Butterhorn Bakery & Café

$ | AMERICAN | There's usually a wait at this popular breakfast and lunch spot, where meals are cheap, portions are large, and the coffee is perfect. Snag a seat on the patio on weekends when the restaurant can get packed and loud. **Known for:** eggy bread; homemade cakes and baked goods to go; lively spot. *Average main: $10* ✉ *408 Main St.* ☎ *970/668–3997* 🌐 *www.butterhornbakery.com* *No dinner.*

Hotels

Frisco Lodge

$$ | B&B/INN | This 1885 stagecoach stop has morphed into a European-style boutique hotel complete with a chalet facade and a garden courtyard. **Pros:** great location on Main Street; outdoor hot tub and fireplace; courtyard garden. **Cons:** street noise audible; thin walls; some rooms have shared baths. *Rooms from: $159* ✉ *321 Main St.* ☎ *800/279–6000* 🌐 *www.friscolodge.com* *18 rooms* *Free Breakfast.*

Hotel Frisco

$$ | **B&B/INN** | This Main Street hostelry is a great home base for skiers wanting to hit Breckenridge, Copper, Keystone, and Arapahoe Basin. **Pros:** centrally located; quaint, charming decor; friendly staff. **Cons:** small bathrooms; no elevator; fees for parking. *Rooms from: $169 ✉ 308 Main St. ☎ 970/668–5009 ⊕ www.hotelfrisco.com 20 rooms No meals.*

Nightlife

Moose Jaw

BARS/PUBS | The Moose Jaw is a locals' hangout. Pool tables and arcade games beckon, and a plethora of old-time photographs, trophies, and newspaper articles makes the barn-wood walls all but invisible. *✉ 208 Main St. ☎ 970/668–3931 ⊕ www.moosejawfrisco.com.*

Activities

FISHING

Trouts Fly Fishing

FISHING | Float, wade, or shore fish the Colorado or Arkansas River on guided fly-fishing trips on private and public lands with this outfitter. If you're lucky, you may catch 10- to 20-inch rainbow and brown trout. *✉ 309 B Main St. ☎ 888/453–9171, 970/668–2583 ⊕ www.troutsflyfishing.com.*

Breckenridge

22 miles southwest of Keystone via U.S. 6, I–70, and Hwy. 9.

Breckenridge was founded in 1859, when gold was discovered in the surrounding hills. For the next several decades the town's fortunes rose and fell as its lodes of gold and silver were discovered and exhausted. Throughout the latter half of the 19th century and the early 20th century, Breckenridge was famous as a mining camp that "turned out more gold with less work than any camp in Colorado," according to the *Denver Post.* Dredging gold out of the rivers continued until World War II. Visitors today can still see evidence of gold-dredging operations in the surrounding streams.

At 9,603 feet above sea level and surrounded by higher peaks, Breckenridge is the oldest continuously occupied town on the Western Slope. Much of the town's architectural legacy from the mining era remains, so you'll find stores occupying authentic Victorian storefronts, and restaurants and bed-and-breakfasts in Victorian homes. Surrounding the town's historic core, condos and hotels are packed into the woods and along the roads threading the mountainsides toward the base of Peak 8.

GETTING HERE AND AROUND

Most people arrive by car or a shuttle from Denver International Airport. Getting around is easiest by car, but can also be done by local shuttles and taxis.

CONTACTS Breckenridge Free Ride. *☎ 970/547–3140 ⊕ www.breckfreeride.com.*

VISITOR INFORMATION

CONTACTS Breckenridge Snow Report. *☎ 970/496–4111 ⊕ www.breckenridge.com.* **Breckenridge Tourism Office.** *✉ 111 Ski Hill Rd. ☎ 970/453–2913 ⊕ www.gobreck.com.*

TOURS

Breckenridge Heritage Alliance

GUIDED TOURS | **FAMILY** | The Breckenridge Heritage Alliance leads lively tours of downtown Breckenridge, one of the largest National Historic Districts in the state. *✉ 203 S. Main St. ☎ 970/453–9767 ⊕ www.breckheritage.com From $5.*

WHEN TO GO

The ski season runs from November to April, but festivals and warm-weather activities attract visitors year-round.

FESTIVALS

Festivals run rampant here, and it's rare to show up when locals aren't celebrating. Among the best festivals are the annual tribute to the Norse god of winter, Ullr Fest (usually in December or January), and the International Snow Sculpture championships in winter (usually January). Summer events include the Breckenridge Summer Beer Festival (July), the Breckenridge Food and Wine Festival (late July), and the National Repertory Orchestra (*www.nromusic.com*) performances at the Riverwalk Center near the center of town.

Sights

★ Breckenridge Downtown Historic District

HISTORIC SITE | Downtown Breckenridge's Historic District is one of Colorado's largest, with about 250 buildings on the National Register of Historic Places. The district is roughly a compact 12 square blocks, bounded by Main, High, and Washington Streets and Wellington Road. There are some 171 buildings with points of historical interest, from simple log cabins to Victorians with lacy gingerbread trim. *Breckenridge* *www.townofbreckenridge.com.*

Country Boy Mine

MINE | **FAMILY** | When gold was discovered here in 1887, the Country Boy Mine became one of the region's top producers—lead and zinc, which were vital for U.S. efforts in World War I and World War II, were big here, too. The gold mine tour takes visitors more than 1000 feet deep into the mountain. Visitors can pet the donkeys that roam the area, pan for keepable gold, or go on a treasure hunt with a metal detector. The mine has a 55-foot ore chute slide, historic buildings, and plenty of mining artifacts. *0542 French Gulch Rd.* *970/453–4405* *www.countryboymine.com* *Gold panning $20; tours $35* *Closed Wed. and Thurs. in fall and winter.*

Edwin Carter Discovery Center

MUSEUM | **FAMILY** | The Edwin Carter Discovery Center is dedicated to the 19th century miner-turned-environmentalist who helped to create Denver's Museum of Nature and Science. Look for realistic stuffed animals and interactive exhibits like the hands-on taxidermy workbench. *111 N. Ridge St.* *970/453–9767* *www.breckheritage.com/museums* *Free, or $5 donation.*

Restaurants

Blue Moose

$ | **AMERICAN** | Locals flock here for the hearty breakfasts of eggs, oatmeal, pancakes, and much more, so you can expect a wait unless you get there early. Neither the food nor the decor is fancy, and the service—while friendly—can be slow. **Known for:** popular so there's often a wait; hearty breakfasts; cash only. *Average main: $10* *540 S. Main St.* *970/453–4859* *No credit cards* *No dinner.*

Downstairs at Eric's

$ | **AMERICAN** | **FAMILY** | Loud and fun best describes this place, which is popular among locals and visitors of all ages. Kids hang out in the arcade while their folks watch sports on the big-screen TVs. **Known for:** sporting events bring in huge crowds; arcade games; wings. *Average main: $13* *111 S. Main St.* *970/453–1401* *www.downstairsaterics.com.*

Sancho Tacos

$ | **MEXICAN** | The tacos, house salsa and guac, frozen margaritas, and tequila are everything you hope for when you spot the Day-of-the-Dead skull on the sign of this lively dining room in central Breck. Locals rave about happy hour and visitors dig the funky toppings and unique tacos like fried chicken, duck confit, and sweet potato. **Known for:** happy hour drink specials; duck confit taco; central location on La Cima Mall. *Average main: $4* *500*

The slopes at Breckenridge are spread across five interconnected mountains.

S. Main St. ☎ 970/453–9493 ⊕ www.sanchotaco.com.

Hotels

Grand Colorado on Peak 8

$$$$ | RESORT | FAMILY | Breckenridge's newest crown jewel, the Grand Colorado sprawls the base of Peak 8, with walk-out access to the Rocky Mountain and Colorado Superchair lifts. **Pros:** huge aquatics area with hot tubs and pools; rooftop bar with great views; shuttle service to town. **Cons:** some rooms can be loud; time-share offers are plentiful and pricey; resort signage lacking in spots. *$ Rooms from: $329 ✉ 1627 Ski Hill Rd ☎ 970/547–8788 ⊕ www.grandcolorado.com ⇨ 253 condos 🍴 No meals.*

Lodge at Breckenridge

$$$$ | HOTEL | This lodge more than compensates for its location on a mountainside beyond the downtown area with breathtaking views of the Tenmile Range from nearly every angle. **Pros:** great mountain views; complimentary shuttle service; plush bedding. **Cons:** no room service; limited shuttle service in summer; not all rooms include kitchens. *$ Rooms from: $329 ✉ 112 Overlook Dr. ☎ 800/736–1607 ⊕ www.thelodgeatbreckenridge.com ⇨ 45 rooms, 2 houses 🍴 Free Breakfast.*

Activities

BACKCOUNTRY SKIING

They don't call this place Summit County for nothing—mountain passes above 10,000 feet allow relatively easy access to high-country terrain and some of the area's best snow. But remember: avalanche-related deaths are all too common in Summit County. Don't judge an area solely on appearances or the fact that other skiers or snowmobilers have been there before, as even slopes that look gentle may slide. Never head into the backcountry without checking weather conditions, letting someone know where you're going, and wearing appropriate clothing. Always carry survival gear and travel with a buddy.

Dillon Ranger District Office of the White River National Forest

SKIING/SNOWBOARDING | For information on snow conditions and avalanche dangers, contact the Dillon Ranger District Office of the White River National Forest. ✉ *Breckenridge* ☎ *970/468–5400* 🌐 *www.dillonrangerdistrict.com.*

CROSS-COUNTRY SKIING

Breckenridge Nordic Center

SKIING/SNOWBOARDING | This center has more than 18 miles of cross-country ski trails and more than 12 miles of snowshoe trails starting at 9,800 feet. They also offer lessons and guided tours. ✉ *9 Grandview Dr.* ☎ *970/453–6855* 🌐 *www.breckenridgenordic.com.*

DOWNHILL SKIING AND SNOWBOARDING

★ Breckenridge

SKIING/SNOWBOARDING | Affectionately known as "Breck," this mountain attracts skiers and snowboarders with equal fervor, with its terrain parks and an area where you can learn to freeride. The resort's slopes are spread across five interconnected mountains in the Tenmile Range, named Peaks 6, 7, 8, 9, and 10. Peak 6 includes 543 acres, three bowls (two at an intermediate level), and 21 trails to the ski area. The highest chairlift in North America—a high-speed quad lift called Imperial Express SuperChair on Peak 8—tops out at an air-gulping 12,840 feet. Peaks 6, 7, and 8 have above-the-timberline bowls and chutes. The lower reaches of Peak 7 have some of the country's prettiest intermediate-level terrain accessible by a lift. Peak 8 and Peak 9 have trails for all skill levels. Peak 10 has some of the best expert terrain including groomed steeps, challenging moguls, and technical tree chutes.

In line with the town's proud heritage, some runs are named for old mines, including Bonanza, Cashier, Gold King, and Wellington.

Rental packages (skis, boots, and poles; snowboards and boots) start around $45 per day. Save on rentals and find discounted lift tickets by purchasing online at least a week in advance. **Facilities:** 187 trails; 2,908 acres; 3,398-foot vertical drop; 34 lifts. ✉ *1599 Ski Hill Rd.* ☎ *970/453–5000* 🌐 *www.breckenridge.com* 🎫 *Lift ticket $169.*

LESSONS AND PROGRAMS

Breckenridge Ski & Snowboard School

SKIING/SNOWBOARDING | Specialty clinics, traditional lessons, guided sessions, and programs geared to women and children are among the multitude of offerings from Breckenridge Ski & Snowboard School. Ski Girls Rock caters to girls ages 7 to 14 and Elevate teaches groups to conquer steeps, bumps, and park terrain. ✉ *Breckenridge* ☎ *888/576–2754* 🌐 *www.breckenridge.com.*

FISHING

Mountain Angler

FISHING | This company organizes fishing trips on the Colorado, Eagle, Arkansas, Blue, and South Platte rivers year-round. ✉ *311 S. Main St.* ☎ *800/453–4669* 🌐 *www.mountainangler.com.*

GOLF

Breckenridge Golf Club

GOLF | This is the world's only municipally owned course designed by Jack Nicklaus. You may play any combination of the three 9-hole sets: the Bear, the Beaver (with beaver ponds lining many of the fairways), or the Elk. The course resembles a nature reserve as it flows through mountainous terrain and fields full of wildflowers. ✉ *200 Clubhouse Dr.* ☎ *970/453–9104* 🌐 *www.breckenridgegolfclub.com* 🎫 *$117; $59 for 9 holes* 🏌 *The Bear, 9 holes, 3385 yards, par 36; The Beaver, 9 holes, 2945 yards, par 36; The Elk, 9 holes, 3312 yards, par 36.*

KAYAKING

Breckenridge Kayak Park

KAYAKING | FAMILY | With splash rocks, eddy pools, and S-curves, the 1,800-foot Breckenridge Kayak Park is a playground for kayakers. This public park on the Blue River has 15 water features, is free, and generally open from May through August. ✉ *880 Airport Rd.* ☎ *970/453–1734* 🌐 *www.breckenridgerecreation.com/locations/parks-fields/kayak-park.*

RAFTING

Breckenridge Whitewater Rafting

WHITE-WATER RAFTING | This outfitter runs white-water rafting trips on stretches of the Colorado, Arkansas, Eagle, and Blue rivers in Summit County, and Clear Creek on the Front Range. They also offer zipline, rock climbing, fly-fishing, hiking, and horseback tours. ✉ *411 S. Main St.* ☎ *877/723—8464* 🌐 *www.breckenridge-whitewater.com.*

SNOWMOBILING

Good Times Adventures

SNOW SPORTS | This company runs snowmobile and dog-sledding trips on more than 40 miles of groomed trails, through open meadows and along the Continental Divide to 11,585-foot-high Georgia Pass. ✉ *6061 Tiger Rd.* ☎ *970/453–7604, 800/477–0144* 🌐 *www.goodtimesadventures.com.*

Copper Mountain

7 miles south of Frisco via I–70.

Once little more than a series of strip malls, Copper Mountain is now a thriving resort with a bustling base. The resort's heart is a pedestrian-only village anchored by Burning Stones Plaza, which is prime people-watching turf. High-speed ski lifts march up the mountain on one side of the plaza, and the other three sides are flanked by condominiums with retail shops and restaurants on the ground floors. Lodgings extend west toward West Village and east to Center and East villages, where a six-pack high-speed lift ferries skiers.

In winter Burning Stones is filled with skiers on their way to and from the slopes and shoppers browsing for gifts to give to those left at home. In summer people relax on condo balconies or restaurant patios as they listen to free concerts on the plaza or watch athletes inch up the 37-foot-high climbing wall, the largest outdoor climbing wall in the state. Kids can also learn to kayak or float in paddleboats.

GETTING HERE AND AROUND

The easiest way to reach Copper Mountain is by car. The resort is foot-friendly, and there is also a free resort shuttle service around town.

VISITOR INFORMATION

CONTACTS Copper Mountain Snow Report. ☎ *970/968–2100.*

WHEN TO GO

Skiing is from November to mid-April. In summer the resort tends to be quieter, as most visitors gravitate to the Lake Dillon area for hiking and biking.

Hotels

Copper Mountain Resort

$$$$ | RENTAL | FAMILY | Copper Mountain Resort manages the majority of lodging in the area, ranging from standard hotel rooms to spacious condos and town homes. **Pros:** located near expert skiing terrain; wide range of accommodations; includes use of the Copper Mountain Spa & Athletic Club. **Cons:** village can be noisy; quality of rooms varies greatly; novice skiers will have to trek to the West Village. $ *Rooms from: $308* ✉ *509 Copper Rd.* ☎ *970/968–2318, 888/219–2441* 🌐 *www.coppercolorado.com* *460 rooms* *No meals.*

Nightlife

Whether it's a warm afternoon in winter or a cool evening in summer, one of the best places to kick back is at one of the tables spreading across Burning Stones Plaza.

JJ's Rocky Mountain Tavern

BARS/PUBS | The East Village is home to JJ's Rocky Mountain Tavern, the best place for a beer after a long day on the bumps. Local musicians have people dancing on the tables with John Denver and Jimmy Buffet covers during ski season. ✉ *102 Wheeler Circle* ☎ *970/968–3062* 🌐 *www.coppercolorado.com.*

Activities

ATHLETIC CENTERS

Woodward at Copper

SKIING/SNOWBOARDING | **FAMILY** | Hone your best tricks at this massive snowboard, skateboard, and BMX training facility and indoor playground nicknamed "The Barn." Strap on a snowboard or skis specially fitted with wheels to take on the Jumps and Pump track before landing in one of the foam pits. You can also practice tricks on five Olympic trampolines or jump even higher on the Supertramp, one of the first in the world offered at a public gym. There is also space for skateboarders and BMX and mountain-bike riders of all levels. Camps throughout the summer teach children as young as seven how to own the slopes. ✉ *505 Copper Rd.* ☎ *970/968–2318 Ext. 60824* 🌐 *www.coppercolorado.com/woodward/.*

BICYCLING

Gravitee Boardshop

BICYCLING | Hundreds of miles of bike paths weave around Copper Mountain Resort, leading up and down mountainsides and through high-country communities. In summer, find all kinds of organized rides. Gravitee has all the gear you need for cycling in the area. ✉ *Tucker Mountain Lodge, 164 Copper Rd.* ☎ *970/968–0171* 🌐 *www.gravitee.com.*

DOWNHILL SKIING AND SNOWBOARDING

Copper Mountain

SKIING/SNOWBOARDING | This mountain is popular with locals because the resort's 2,490 acres are spread across Union Peak, Copper Peak, and Tucker Mountain where the terrain is naturally separated into areas for beginners, intermediates, and expert skiers and snowboarders, making it easy to pick your slope. On the front side of the mountain, as you move from east to west, trails decrease in difficulty. The back bowls and East Village are home to the best expert terrain, Center Village hosts intermediate terrain, and West Village is where you'll find almost all of the beginner terrain. The Union Creek area contains gentle, tree-lined trails for novices. Several steep mogul runs are clustered on the eastern side and accessible via the Resolution and Alpine lifts. At the top of the resort and in the vast Copper Bowl there's challenging high-alpine terrain. Freeriders gravitate to the Woodward Terrain Parks, including a 22-foot superpipe. Weather permitting, on Friday and weekends, expert skiers can grab a free first come, first served snowcat ride up Tucker Mountain for an ungroomed, wilderness-style ski experience. Rental packages (skis or boards, boots, and poles) start at $40 per day. Purchase your rental equipment in advance over the phone or by booking online for discounts. **Facilities:** more than 142 trails; 2,490 acres; 2,738-foot vertical drop; 24 lifts. ✉ *209 Ten Mile Circle* ☎ *970/968–2882, 800/458–8386* 🌐 *www.coppercolorado.com* 🎫 *Lift ticket $150.*

LESSONS AND PROGRAMS

Copper Mountain Ski and Ride School

SKIING/SNOWBOARDING | **FAMILY** | Copper Mountain's Ski and Ride School has classes for skiers and snowboarders, private lessons, men- and women-only groups, and special competitive lessons (to help you make a quantum leap in skills). Copper's Youth Seasonal Programs, divided into groups based on age and skill level, are designed to both teach and entertain. There's also Kids' Night Out, popular among parents who want an evening without the children. ✉ *Copper Mountain* ☎ *970/968–2318.*

GOLF

Copper Mountain has reasonably priced golf and lodging packages. You can also take a shuttle from the resort to the Raven Golf Club at Three Peaks, about 15 minutes away in Dillon.

Copper Creek Golf Club

GOLF | Right at the Copper Mountain Resort is a course designed by Pete and Perry Dye. The 18-hole course flows up and down some of the ski trails at the base of the mountain and between condos and town homes in the resort's East Village. Rent a golf bike—a bicycle with a bag for your clubs attached to the back end—instead of a cart for a true Colorado experience. ✉ *85 Wheeler Pl.* ☎ *866/286–1663* 🌐 *www.coppercolorado.com* *$89* *18 holes, 5517 yards, par 69.*

Leadville

24 miles south of Copper Mountain via Hwy. 91.

Sitting in the mountains at 10,152 feet, Leadville is America's highest incorporated city. The 70 square blocks of Victorian architecture and adjacent mining district hint at its past as a rich silver-mining boomtown. In the history of Colorado mining, perhaps no town looms larger. Two of the state's most fascinating figures lived here: mining magnate Horace Tabor and his second wife, Elizabeth Doe McCourt (nicknamed Baby Doe), the central figures in John LaTouche's Pulitzer prize–winning opera *The Ballad of Baby Doe.*

Tabor amassed a fortune of $9 million, much of which he spent building monuments to himself and his mistress "Baby Doe." His power peaked when his money helped him secure a U.S. Senate seat in 1883. He married Baby Doe after divorcing his first wife, the faithful Augusta. The Tabors incurred the scorn of high society by throwing their money around in what was considered a vulgar fashion. After the price of silver plummeted, Tabor died a pauper in 1899 and Baby Doe became a recluse, rarely emerging from her tiny, unheated cabin beside the mine entrance. She froze to death in 1935.

GETTING HERE AND AROUND

A car is the only reasonable mode of transportation into Leadville. Once in town, the main street, lined with shops and restaurants, and the cozy surrounding neighborhoods make for pleasant walks in summer.

VISITOR INFORMATION

CONTACTS Leadville Lake County Chamber of Commerce. ✉ *809 Harrison St.* ☎ *719/486–3900* 🌐 *www.leadvilleusa.com.*

WHEN TO GO

It's not that summer never comes to Leadville, it's just that winter never really leaves. This high-altitude town can see snow almost any month, though really only a brief flurry in July and August. In winter Leadville hibernates (except for the nearby Ski Cooper and snowmobile trails), but in summer the town is a popular and cool respite from the heat.

Sights

Healy House and Dexter Cabin

HOUSE | On a tree-lined street in downtown Leadville you'll find the Healy House and Dexter Cabin, two of Leadville's earliest residences. The lavishly decorated rooms of the Healy's clapboard house provide a sense of how the town's upper crust, such as the Tabors, lived and played. ✉ *912 Harrison Ave.* ☎ *719/486–0487* 🌐 *www.historycolorado.org/healy-house-museum-dexter-cabin* *$6* *Closed Sun.–Wed.*

Heritage Museum

MUSEUM | This museum paints a vivid portrait of life in Leadville at the turn of the last century, with dioramas depicting life in the mines. There's also furniture, clothing, and toys from the Victorian era. ✉ *102 E. 9th St.* ☎ *719/486–1878* 🌐 *www.leadvilleheritagemuseum.com* 🎟 *$6.*

Historic Tabor Opera House and Museum

ARTS VENUE | An effort is underway to fully restore the three-story Tabor Opera House that opened in 1879, when it was proclaimed the "largest and best west of the Mississippi." It hosted luminaries such as Harry Houdini, Buffalo Bill, and Oscar Wilde. Shows on the current schedule are mostly music and dance, but there's also a community talent show to give local stars a spotlight on the famous stage. ✉ *308 Harrison Ave.* ☎ *719/486–8409* 🌐 *www.taboropera-house.net* 🕒 *Closed mid-Sept.–late May.*

Leadville, Colorado & Southern Railroad Company

TRANSPORTATION SITE (AIRPORT/BUS/FERRY/TRAIN) | **FAMILY** | Still chugging along is the Leadville, Colorado & Southern Railroad Company, which can take you on a breathtaking 2½-hour trip with views of either wildflowers or fall foliage depending on the time of year. Combo rides include ziplining or rafting adventures. The train leaves from Leadville's century-old depot and travels beside the Arkansas River with views of Mount Elbert, Colorado's highest peak. ✉ *326 E. 7th St.* ☎ *719/486–3936, 866/386–3936* 🌐 *www.leadville-train.com* 🎟 *From $42* 🕒 *Closed early Nov.–late May.*

Mount Elbert

MOUNTAIN—SIGHT | The massive, snow-capped peak watching over Leadville is Mount Elbert. At 14,433 feet it's the highest mountain in Colorado and the tallest peak in the entire Rocky Mountain Range, second in height in the contiguous 48 states only to California's 14,495-foot Mount Whitney. ✉ *Leadville.*

National Mining Hall of Fame and Museum

MUSEUM | **FAMILY** | This museum covers virtually every aspect of mining, from the discovery of precious ore to fashioning it into coins and other items. Dioramas in the beautiful brick building explain extraction processes. ✉ *120 W. 9th St.* ☎ *719/486–1229* 🌐 *www.mininghalloffame.org* 🎟 *$7.*

Restaurants

High Mountain Pies

$$ | **PIZZA** | **FAMILY** | Locals love the pies at this hand-tossed pizza joint, particularly the Crocodile, a barbecue pizza with jalapeños, bacon, cream cheese, and shrimp. Sidle up to the bar, or take advantage of the patio seating in the short Leadville summers. **Known for:** homemade dough; huge ingredient list; friendly staff. 💲 *Average main: $15* ✉ *115 W. 4th St.* ☎ *719/486–5555.*

Treeline Kitchen

$$ | **AMERICAN** | This trendy spot brings a modern touch to the historic mining town's food scene. The menu offers an upscale twist on comfort food faves like fried chicken and the hearty Leadville lamb pasta. **Known for:** trendy cocktails; cool artsy decor; rooftop patio with views for miles. 💲 *Average main: $18* ✉ *615 Harrison Ave.* ☎ *719/293–2200* 🌐 *www.treelinekitchen.com.*

Hotels

Delaware Hotel

$$ | **HOTEL** | This artfully restored 1886 hotel is one of the best examples of high Victorian architecture in the area, so it's no surprise that it's listed on the National Register of Historic Places. **Pros:** loaded with gold-rush character; great mountain views; quirky, unique property. **Cons:** lobby is one large store; no elevator; creaky floors and stairs. 💲 *Rooms from: $129* ✉ *700 Harrison Ave.* ☎ *719/486–1418, 800/748–2004* 🌐 *www.delawarehotel.com* 🛏 *40 rooms* 🍽 *Free Breakfast.*

Twin Lakes Inn & Saloon

$ | **B&B/INN** | You'll be hard-pressed to find better views than at this 1879 inn on the shores of Colorado's largest glacial lake and at the base of Mount Elbert, Colorado's tallest peak. **Pros:** lovely location; excellent restaurant; rooms with mountain views. **Cons:** no air-conditioning; small rooms; shared bathrooms. *Rooms from: $99 6435 E. State Hwy. 82 719/486–7965 www.thetwinlakesinn.com 12 rooms Free Breakfast.*

Activities

CANOEING AND KAYAKING

Twin Lakes Canoe & Kayak Adventures

CANOEING/ROWING/SKULLING | There's no better way to see the high country than by exploring its alpine lakes. Twin Lakes Canoe & Kayak Adventures offers guided tours of Twin and Turquoise lakes to beginners, and equipment rentals to more experienced paddlers and stand-up paddleboarders. *6451 Hwy. 82, about 20 miles south of Leadville 719/251–9961 www.twinlakescanoeandkayak.com.*

DOWNHILL SKIING AND SNOWBOARDING

Ski Cooper

SKIING/SNOWBOARDING | **FAMILY** | Nine miles north of Leadville, Ski Cooper is one of those undiscovered boutique ski areas in the Rockies. The season is a bit shorter than some other resorts, opening in early December and closing early April. It has 400 acres skiable via lift and another 2,600 acres of backcountry powder accessible by snowcat on Chicago Ridge. The 41 trails offer terrain for all levels of skiers. The state's longest magic carpet whisks skiers up the slopes. Rental packages (skis or boards, boots, and poles) start at $40 per day, among the cheapest in the state. **Facilities:** 60 trails; 470 acres; 1,200-foot vertical drop; 5 lifts. *U.S. 24 719/486–3684, 800/707–6114 www.skicooper.com Lift ticket $80.*

LESSONS AND PROGRAMS

Chicago Ridge Snowcat Tours

SKIING/SNOWBOARDING | These tours are for expert backcountry skiers who want the off-piste adventure of scripting their signature across acres of untracked powder. You'll get your fill of a hot lunch, beacons, powder skis or boards, and après-ski refreshments. The terrain has tree glades and open bowls. The runs are up to 10,000 feet long, and some vertical drops top 2,000 feet. *Leadville 719/486–2277 www.skicooper.com/snowcat-skiing From $369.*

Ski Cooper Ski School

SKIING/SNOWBOARDING | This ski school covers the gamut for skiers and snowboarders of all ages and experience levels. A first-timer package with a two-hour lesson, rental equipment, and a magic carpet lift ticket is $99. Kids' lessons range from $69 to $129 including gear, lift tickets, and lunch. *232 County Rd. 29 719/486–2277 www.skicooper.com.*

GOLF

Mt. Massive Golf Course

GOLF | At 9,680 feet, watch your distance increase in the thin mountain air. Just west of Leadville in the Arkansas River valley, this public golf course was opened in the 1930s to the delight of the mining community. True green fairways replaced sagebrush flats after a $50,000 grant in the 1970s heralded an automated irrigation system. *259 County Rd. 5 719/486–2176 www.mtmassivegolf.com $48; $28 for 9 holes 9 holes, 2967 yards, par 36.*

HORSEBACK RIDING

Halfmoon Packing & Outfitting

HORSEBACK RIDING | If you're feeling that it's time to hit the trail, Halfmoon Packing & Outfitting has a stable of horses ready for you. Also ask about wagon rides, stagecoach rides, and overnight trips. *1100 E. Tennessee Rd. 719/486–4570 www.halfmoonpacking.com.*

Chapter 6

VAIL VALLEY

Updated by
Lindsey Galloway

Sights	Restaurants	Hotels	Shopping	Nightlife
★★★☆☆	★★★★☆	★★★★☆	★★☆☆☆	★★★☆☆

WELCOME TO VAIL VALLEY

TOP REASONS TO GO

★ **High-altitude golf:** The thin air at this elevation lets your Titleist fly much farther—enjoy those hero swings at more than a dozen venues.

★ **Romantic meals:** A number of intimate restaurants are hidden away among the peaks, reachable by ski, on horseback, and even by horse-drawn sleigh.

★ **Rugged scenery:** The Gore Range presents some of the most sharp-spined backcountry in the state, with ice-cold tarns, sheer cliffs, and shaggy white mountain goats.

★ **The slopes:** Vail is as real and challenging a ski mountain as you'll find anywhere in the western United States, with the steeps and back bowls to prove it.

★ **Summer festivals:** Check out some of Vail's many cultural activities—summer is full of music, culinary, and dance festivals.

Finding your way around the Vail Valley is relatively easy; the valley runs east and west, and everything you need is less than a mile off the I–70 corridor (and the constant drone of traffic), which parallels the Eagle River. The Gore Range to the north and east is one of the most rugged wilderness areas in Colorado—the peaks are jagged and broken. To the south, the tabled heights of the Sawatch Mountain Range are gentler, and give Vail her superb skiing. Beaver Creek feels more isolated, being set off the highway behind a series of gates that control access to the posh communities within.

1 Vail. European-style cafés and beautifully cobbled streets lined with boutiques are more than just window dressing—Vail is no longer just known for its serious skiing.

2 Beaver Creek. As the entrance gates will remind you, Beaver Creek is the most exclusive skiing community in Colorado. This is resort-to-resort skiing set among gorgeous glades of aspens; it never seems to get crowded.

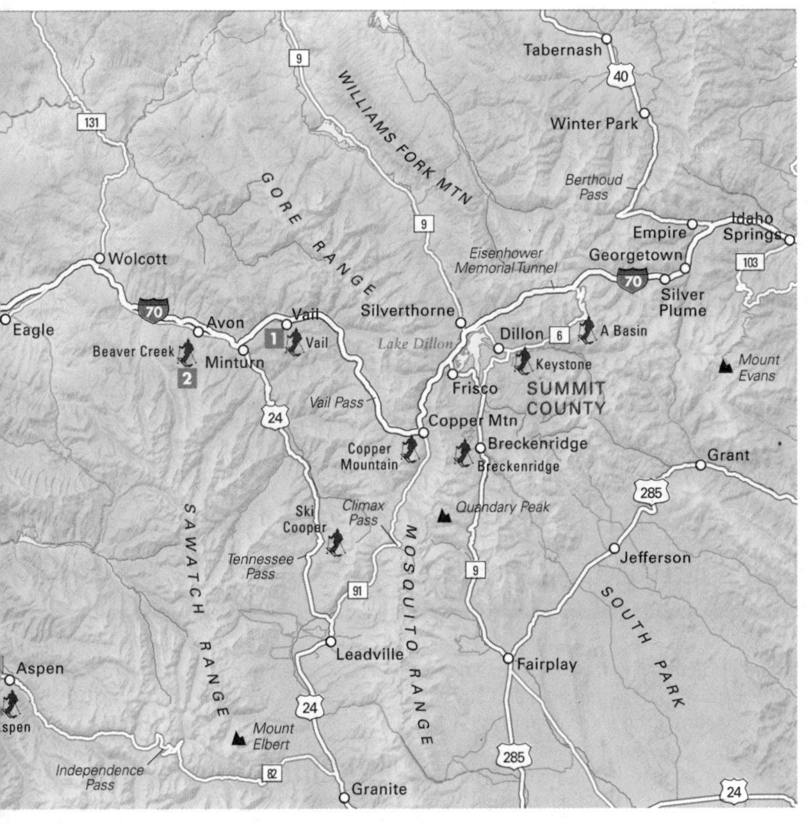
Tabernash
Winter Park
Berthoud Pass
WILLIAMS FORK MTN
GORE RANGE
Empire
Idaho Springs
Georgetown
Silver Plume
Eisenhower Memorial Tunnel
Wolcott
Eagle
Avon
Vail
Silverthorne
Dillon
A Basin
Beaver Creek
Minturn
Lake Dillon
Keystone
Frisco
SUMMIT COUNTY
Mount Evans
Vail Pass
Copper Mtn
Breckenridge
Copper Mountain
Grant
Ski Cooper
Climax Pass
Quandary Peak
SAWATCH RANGE
MOSQUITO RANGE
Tennessee Pass
Jefferson
SOUTH PARK
Leadville
Fairplay
Aspen
Mount Elbert
Independence Pass
Granite

If Aspen is Colorado's Hollywood East, then her rival Vail is Wall Street West. So popular is this ski resort with the monied East Coast crowd that locals sometimes refer to particularly crowded weeks as "212" weeks, in reference to the NYC area code of so many visitors. The attraction for vacationers from all over is the thin, aspen-cloaked Vail Valley, a narrow corridor slit by I–70 and bounded by the rugged Gore Range to the north and east and the tabled Sawatch escarpments to the south. Through it all runs the sparkling Eagle River.

The resorts begin just west of Vail Pass, a saddle well below tree line, and stretch 20 miles through the communities of Vail, Eagle-Vail, Minturn, Avon, Beaver Creek, Arrowhead, and Edwards. The vibe in these places varies dramatically, from Beaver Creek, a gated community of second (and sometimes third) megahomes, to Edwards, a rapidly growing and increasingly affluent worker town, to Vail, filled with styles of lodging, dining, and shopping appealing to many tastes.

In winter this region is famous for the glittering resorts of Vail and Beaver Creek. Between these two areas, skiers and snowboarders have just over 7,000 acres at their disposal, including the unforgettable Back Bowls far beyond the noise of I–70 traffic. In summer these resorts are great bases from which you can explore the high country on foot, horseback, raft, or bike.

Planning

When to Go

Winter is by far the most crowded time in Vail Valley, with early spring seeing the highest number of visitors hoping to catch that blissful blend of thick powder and china-blue skies. Although summer is quickly gaining in popularity, the real deals can be had in the shoulder seasons—late autumn and late spring when the ski slopes are closed. Traffic through the I–70 corridor moves at a good clip unless snows have stacked up truckers putting on chains on either side of Vail Pass. The pass itself is low, and stays below tree line, affording it some protection from drifting and blowing snow.

Getting Here and Around

AIR

Denver International Airport (DEN), the gateway to the High Rockies, is 119 miles east of Vail. It's a 90-minute drive from Vail, but ski traffic can double the time. The Vail Valley is served by Eagle County Airport (EGE), 34 miles west of Vail.

If possible, try snagging a direct flight straight into the Eagle County Airport from your hometown. But if your trip involves a connection through Denver or another hub, it is often faster to rent a car and make the scenic 90-minute drive through the mountains or catch one of the many shuttle services.

AIRPORT CONTACTS Eagle County Airport (EGE). ✉ *219 Eldon Wilson Rd., Gypsum* ☎ *970/328–2680* 🌐 *www.flyvail.com.*

BUS AND SHUTTLE

All the resorts run free or inexpensive shuttles between the ski villages and the slopes. Locals and visitors alike hop the free Town of Vail buses up and down from East Vail to West Vail (a distance of nearly 6 miles, with Lionshead at the center). For trips to Beaver Creek, catch the ECO Transit bus from the Vail Transportation Center in Vail Village, beside the Vail Information Center. Town of Avon buses depart throughout the day from Elk Lot (located near the main gates of Beaver Creek) and Covered Bridge Bus Stop in Beaver Creek. The Bustang West Line service runs along I–70 from Denver to Grand Junction with stops in Eagle and Vail.

CONTACTS Avon/Beaver Creek Transit. ☎ *970/748–4120* 🌐 *www.avon.org.* **Bustang.** ☎ *800/900–3011* 🌐 *www.ridebustang.com.* **ECO Transit.** ☎ *970/328–3520* 🌐 *www.eaglecounty.us/transit/schedules.* **Town of Vail.** ✉ *75 S. Frontage Rd. W, Vail* ☎ *970/477–3456, 866/650–9020* 🌐 *www.vailgov.com/transportation-services.*

CAR

The most convenient place for visitors to rent a car is at Denver International Airport. Most major agencies have offices in Eagle County Airport as well.

Although it is often severely overcrowded, I–70 is still the quickest and most direct route from Denver to Vail. For the first 45 minutes it climbs gradually through the dry Front Range mountains before ducking into the Eisenhower Tunnel. The last 45 minutes are through the high Summit County Basin and up and over the mellow grade of Vail Pass.

Parks and Recreation Areas

The Vail Valley has two wilderness areas in close proximity—the truly untrammeled Eagle's Nest Wilderness Area to the northeast in the Gore Range, and the more popular Holy Cross Wilderness to the southwest.

The Eagle River, whose headwaters are on the north side of Tennessee Pass, is an excellent fishing stream. Public access is easiest upriver of Red Cliff on Forest Service land. There's some superb rafting in Gore Canyon on the Colorado River west of Vail, particularly in spring when the river is boiling with snow runoff.

White River National Forest

The land between the wilderness areas of Eagle's Nest and Holy Cross, including most of the ski resorts' slopes, is part of the White River National Forest. ✉ *Administrative Office, Glenwood Springs* ☎ *970/945–2521* 🌐 *www.fs.usda.gov/whiteriver.*

Restaurants

Unlike the nearby Summit County ski resorts, which pride themselves on standard "mining fare" like surf and turf, Vail has a distinctly European dining style. For the most romantic options, look into a slope-side restaurants where the fixed-course menus and unique transportation (horses in summer and sleighs in winter) make the experience more than just a meal. The farther down-valley you move, the more the prices drop.

Hotels

Vail and Beaver Creek are purpose-built resorts, so you won't find any quaint historic Victorians converted into bed-and-breakfasts here as you will in Breckenridge and Aspen. Instead, Vail lodgings come in three flavors—European chalets that blend with the Bavarian architecture, posh chain resorts up side canyons, and loads of small but serviceable condominiums perfect for families.

Restaurant and hotel reviews have been shortened. For full information, visit Fodors.com. Restaurant prices are the average cost of a main course at dinner or, if dinner is not served, at lunch, excluding 4.4%–8.4% tax. Hotel prices are the lowest cost of a standard double room in high season, excluding service charges and 5.4%–9.8% tax.

What It Costs

$	$$	$$$	$$$$
RESTAURANTS			
under $15	$15–$22	$23–$30	over $30
HOTELS			
under $125	$125–$200	$201–$300	over $300

Vail

100 miles west of Denver via I–70.

Consistently ranked as one of North America's leading ski destinations, Vail has a reputation few can match. The four-letter word means Valhalla for skiers of all skill levels. Vail has plenty of open areas where novices can learn the ropes. It can also be an ego-building mountain for intermediate and advanced skiers who hit the slopes only a week or two a season. Some areas, like Blue Sky Basin, can make you feel like a pro.

Although Vail is a long, thin town spread for several miles along the Eagle River and comprising East Vail, Vail Village, Lionshead in the center, and West Vail, the hub of activity in winter and summer revolves around Vail Village as well as the recently redone Lionshead, which has shops, restaurants, a heated gondola, and even a glockenspiel tower. Vail Village is also a hub of retail and dining with direct lift access to the mountain.

With the blooming of summer columbines come the culture crowds for music and culinary festivals. While the valley teems with visitors, hikers and mountain bikers stream up the steep slopes on foot and via the Eagle Bahn Gondola to head into the network of trails that web the seemingly endless backcountry.

GETTING HERE AND AROUND

The best way to get to the Vail Valley is with a rental car. Once in the valley, a free shuttle makes it easy to get around town, and inexpensive bus service runs between Vail and Beaver Creek.

WHEN TO GO

Vail has grown into a year-round resort, skiing being the main attraction from December through March, and outdoor pursuits like hiking, biking, and fishing the rest of the year. While May and June have pleasant temperatures, many of the hiking and biking trails are still buried beneath snowdrifts. For those interested in seeing wildflowers, mid-July is the time to hit the peaks. The colorful aspen trees generally turn bright gold sometime in September.

FESTIVALS

Vail hosts a wide variety of festivals, starting with the GoPro Mountain Games (🌐 *www.mountaingames.com*), showcasing such sports as kayaking, rafting, and mountain biking. Then there are Taste of Vail, Gourmet on Gore, Spring Back to Vail, Snow Days, Bravo!, and the Vail Dance Festival, to name just a few. There are also free outdoor concerts by up-and-coming musicians, as well as concerts both on and off the mountain by some of the biggest names in the business.

ESSENTIALS

VISITOR INFORMATION Vail Snow Report. ☎ *970/754–4888* 🌐 *www.snow.com.*

TOURS

Nova Guides

ADVENTURE TOURS | Vail's Nova Guides runs Jeep and all-terrain-vehicle tours, as well as fishing and snowmobiling expeditions. ✉ *7088 U.S. 24* ☎ *719/486–2656* 🌐 *www.novaguides.com.*

Timberline Tours

ADVENTURE TOURS | One of the oldest outfitters in the state, Timberline offers guided Jeep and rafting excursions in Vail Valley for every experience and adrenaline level. ✉ *1432 Chambers Ave., Eagle* ☎ *970/476–1414* 🌐 *www.timberlinetours.com.*

Sights

Betty Ford Alpine Gardens

GARDEN | At 8,200 feet above sea level, the Betty Ford Alpine Gardens are the highest botanical gardens in the world. This oasis of columbines, alpine plants, colorful perennials, and wild roses offers stunning views of the Rocky Mountains from meandering pathways that pass beside streams and waterfalls. The gardens are free to the public and open year-round; peak flower season is June through August. Guided tours are available. ✉ *Ford Park, 522 S. Frontage Rd.* ☎ *970/476–0103* 🌐 *www.bettyfordalpinegardens.org* 🎫 *$5 suggested donation.*

Colorado Snowsports Museum and Hall of Fame

MUSEUM | The Colorado Snowsports Museum and Hall of Fame traces the development of skiing and snowboarding throughout the world, with an emphasis on Colorado's contributions. Six galleries include old skis and tows, Olympic displays, ski and snowboard history, and an exhibit on the 10th Mountain Division, an Army division that trained nearby during WWII. ✉ *231 S. Frontage Rd. E* ☎ *970/476–1876* 🌐 *www.snowsportsmuseum.org* 🎫 *$5 suggested donation.*

Restaurants

Almresi

$$$$ | **GERMAN** | Run by the Thoma family, originally from Germany's Black Forest region, Almresi offers authentic German, Austrian, and Swiss dishes in a Rockies-meets-Alps rustic dining room, served by staff outfitted charmingly in lederhosen. Popular dishes include the *griebenschmalz* (a bread made with pork), Alpler macaroni (a Swiss favorite with pasta, bacon, onions, and potatoes and topped with cheddar cheese), and Black Forest cake, all washed down with European wines and German beers. **Known for:** cozy wood cabin dining room; hearty German fare and large portions; kaiserschmarr, Austrian pancakelike pieces with caramelized sugar and cherry compote. $ *Average main: $31* ✉ *298 Hanson Ranch Rd.* ☎ *970/470—4174* 🌐 *www.almresi-vail.com.*

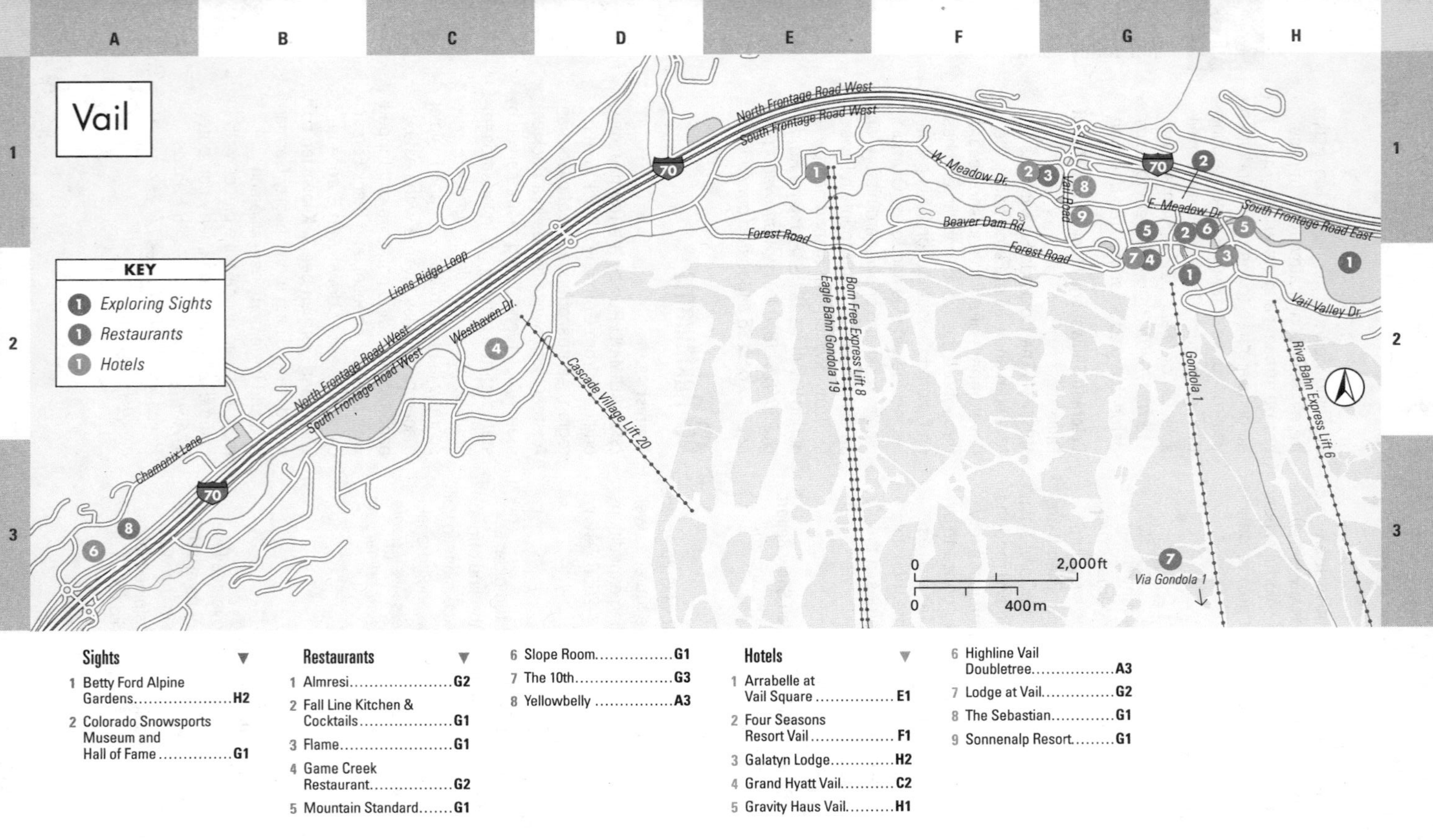

Vail
KEY
Exploring Sights
Restaurants
Hotels
North Frontage Road West
South Frontage Road West
South Frontage Road East
W. Meadow Dr.
E. Meadow Dr.
Vail Road
Beaver Dam Rd.
Forest Road
Vail Valley Dr.
Lions Ridge Loop
Westhaven Dr.
Chamonix Lane
Cascade Village Lift 20
Born Free Express Lift 8
Eagle Bahn Gondola 19
Gondola 1
Riva Bahn Express Lift 6
Via Gondola 1
70
0
2,000 ft
400 m
Sights
1 Betty Ford Alpine Gardens....H2
2 Colorado Snowsports Museum and Hall of Fame....G1
Restaurants
1 Almresi....G2
2 Fall Line Kitchen & Cocktails....G1
3 Flame....G1
4 Game Creek Restaurant....G2
5 Mountain Standard....G1
6 Slope Room....G1
7 The 10th....G3
8 Yellowbelly....A3
Hotels
1 Arrabelle at Vail Square....E1
2 Four Seasons Resort Vail....F1
3 Galatyn Lodge....H2
4 Grand Hyatt Vail....C2
5 Gravity Haus Vail....H1
6 Highline Vail Doubletree....A3
7 Lodge at Vail....G2
8 The Sebastian....G1
9 Sonnenalp Resort....G1

★ Fall Line Kitchen & Cocktails

$$ | **MODERN AMERICAN** | Elevated pub food, rotisserie meats, Asian-fusion (like the duck ramen bowl), and creative craft cocktails somehow marry perfectly on this modern menu. Warm wood paneling and vibrant ski photography decorate the cozy dining room centrally located in Vail Village. **Known for:** hearty meals for après-skiers; trendy cocktail menu; central location. *Average main: $18 232 Bridge St. 970/470–4803 www.falllinevail.com.*

★ Flame

$$$$ | **AMERICAN** | Steaks carved tableside are the highlight of this high-end restaurant in the Four Seasons that provides a luxurious dining experience with surprisingly informal, family-friendly service. Small bites like the spicy tuna tacos or elk corn dogs served with house-made ketchup and aioli are perfect for sharing, which is highly encouraged, but the emphasis is on big here: big windows and a big patio with mountain views; a bar with a big (165-inch) TV; and big bites. **Known for:** aged steaks carved tableside; sophisticated dining room; large terrace dining with a view. *Average main: $65 Four Seasons Vail, 1 Vail Rd. 970/477–8650 www.flamerestaurantvail.com No lunch.*

Game Creek Restaurant

$$$$ | **FRENCH** | Getting to this restaurant is certainly half the fun, as you must catch a gondola up the mountain, then hop on a snowcat to get across Game Creek Bowl during the winter, or shuttle or walk in the summer. The Bavarian-style lodge is members-only for lunch, but open to the public for dinner all year and for an outstanding Sunday brunch in summer. **Known for:** spectacular mountain views; gondola ride to the chalet-style dining room; chef's tasting menu. *Average main: $109 Lion's Head parking garage, 395 S. Frontage Rd. 970/754–4275 Closed Mon. year-round, Sun. in winter, and Tues. and Wed. in summer. No lunch winter and Thurs.–Sat. in summer.*

Mountain Standard

$$$$ | **AMERICAN** | This casual lunch and dinner stop prepares its meat and fish with a deft hand and the age-old way—over an open wood fire. The menu changes often, but usually includes popular dishes such as the spring pea bruschetta, a fall-off-the-bone pork chop with charred okra succotash and cornbread crumble, and a whole Rocky Mountain trout with grilled pole bean salad and smoked almond milk. **Known for:** wood-fired Rocky Mountain trout with chimichurri; creative, seasonal menu; casual, lively setting. *Average main: $34 193 Gore Creek Dr. 970/476–0123 www.mtnstandard.com No credit cards.*

Slope Room

$$$$ | **MODERN AMERICAN** | With spacious glass windows, this sleek, sophisticated space in Gravity Haus looks as if it belongs in a big city, with only the fireplace reminding you that this is Vail. The menu puts a modern spin on the classic steak house, featuring food from Rocky Mountain ranchers and farmers. **Known for:** central location in Vail Village; modern dining room; excellent local steaks. *Average main: $36 Gravity Haus, 352 E. Meadow Dr. 970/476–6836 www.sloperoom.com No lunch.*

The 10th

$$$$ | **AMERICAN** | Find respite from the usual mountain fare at this high-end, high-up restaurant at the base of Look Ma run. A favorite lunch spot for skiers, there are spectacular views of the Gore Range, a cozy bar and lounge with fireplace, a south-facing outdoor deck with heated tables, and hearty pasta and popular meat dishes. **Known for:** on-mountain location; luxury amenities like slippers and hair dryers cater to cold skiers; very popular so can be packed. *Average main: $38 At the base of Look Ma run, Mid-Vail 970/754–1010 Closed Mon.–Thurs. No dinner.*

Yellowbelly

$ | **AMERICAN** | **FAMILY** | Fried-chicken joints usually require several napkins to mop up the grease and a long workout the next day to make up for the indulgence—not so at Yellowbelly. Order the fried white or fried dark plate—this gluten-free recipe is as tasty as it gets without weighing you down. **Known for:** gluten-free fried chicken; delivery and to-go options; affordable eats. *Average main: $8 2161 N. Frontage Rd. W., No. 14 970/343–4340 www.yellowbellychicken.com.*

Hotels

Arrabelle at Vail Square

$$$$ | **RESORT** | Surrounded by shops, restaurants, and galleries, and just steps away from the Eagle Bahn Gondola (which runs right to the top of Vail Mountain), the Arrabelle is a star in Lionshead Village. **Pros:** ski valet and complimentary GoPros to document your adventures; great location; fabulous on-site spa. **Cons:** the valet parking entrance is hard to find; expensive rates; steep service charges added to most purchases. *Rooms from: $1,000 675 Lionshead Pl. 970/754–7777, 866/662–7625 www.arrabelle.rockresorts.com 69 rooms, 29 condos No meals.*

Highline Vail Doubletree

$$$$ | **HOTEL** | **FAMILY** | Located just off I–70 in West Vail, this family-friendly property features large, standard rooms and suites with kitchens and lofts. **Pros:** warm cookies served upon arrival; on-site bar and restaurants; a convenient hub for families. **Cons:** rooms include standard hotel decor; location is 2 miles from skiing and main village; fitness center is crowded with people entering and exiting the pool area. *Rooms from: $516 2211 N. Frontage Rd. 970/476–2739 www.highlinevail.com 116 rooms No meals.*

★ Four Seasons Resort Vail

$$$$ | **RESORT** | **FAMILY** | Rooms at the Four Seasons are large and attractive, in a contemporary alpine style (with warm hickory-wood and limestone accents); every room has at least one gas-burning fireplace and a balcony. **Pros:** large guest rooms with luxurious bathrooms; dedicated ski concierge located right at the Gondola One chairlift; popular on-site dining. **Cons:** a slight walk from slopes; valet and resort fees not included in room rates; some rooms look onto unappealing buildings or parking structures. *Rooms from: $565 1 Vail Rd. 970/477–8600, 800/819–5053 www.fourseasons.com/vail 121 rooms No meals.*

Galatyn Lodge

$$$$ | **RENTAL** | This luxury lodge in a quiet part of Vail Village maintains a low profile, which is just the approach its hard-core skiing regulars prefer. **Pros:** outdoor heated pool; quiet getaway from the lively Vail scene; apartment style lodgings. **Cons:** no children's programs; no restaurant or bar; no fitness center or spa. *Rooms from: $375 365 Vail Valley Dr. 970/479–2418, 800/943–7322 www.thegalatynlodge.com 19 rooms No meals.*

Grand Hyatt Vail

$$$$ | **HOTEL** | With its setting in the quieter west part of town and its dedicated chairlift, the Grand Hyatt Vail suits those more focused on the slopes than the social scene. **Pros:** sleek and polished decor; mountain- and creek-side setting; ski-in ski-out luxury. **Cons:** lobby can be crowded during conferences and events; pricey resort fees and parking; small spa. *Rooms from: $699 1300 Westhaven Dr. 970/476–1234 www.hyatt.com 285 rooms No meals.*

★ Gravity Haus Vail

$$$$ | **HOTEL** | This upscale boutique hotel on Gore Creek is perfectly located for outdoor enthusiasts, but its private fireplaces and feather beds, as well as the sprawling spa and fitness center, may tempt guests to spend the entire stay

indoors. **Pros:** spacious rooms; great fitness club; easy access to town. **Cons:** no hotel-specific parking but valet available; rooms cannot be booked more than six months out; winter valet fee starts at $60 per day. *Rooms from: $599* ✉ *352 E. Meadow Dr.* ☎ *970/476–0700, 888/794–0410* 🌐 *www.gravityhaus.com/locations/vail-haus* *20 rooms, 7 condos* *Free Breakfast.*

Lodge at Vail

$$$$ | HOTEL | One of the first hotels to open in Vail, in 1962, the sprawling lodge is popular with skiers and families because of its fabulous location only 150 feet from the village's main lift, the Gondola One. Ski valets ready your skis every morning and collect your gear for drying in the evening. **Pros:** located near main ski lift; popular steak house, Elway's, on-site; great spa. **Cons:** pricey; quality of rooms varies; some rooms are small and outdated. *Rooms from: $669* ✉ *174 E. Gore Creek Dr.* ☎ *970/754–7800, 877/528–7625* 🌐 *www.lodgeatvail.rockresorts.com* *160 rooms* *No meals.*

★ The Sebastian

$$$$ | HOTEL | FAMILY | Manhattan chic meets Colorado ski lodge at this boutique hotel where you will find the work of Mexican abstract artist Manuel Felguérez throughout, and the lively Frost Bar with its craft cocktails and street-fare–style bites. **Pros:** great location; attention to detail and top-notch service; family-friendly, with pop-up tents in room, a camp, and playroom. **Cons:** many rooms overlook the freeway; some of the town's higher room rates; on-site amenities can be crowded during ski season. *Rooms from: $995* ✉ *16 Vail Rd.* ☎ *970/477–8000, 800/354–6908* 🌐 *www.thesebastianvail.com* *107 rooms* *No meals.*

Sonnenalp Resort

$$$$ | HOTEL | It's the sense of family tradition and European elegance that makes the Sonnenalp Resort the most romantic of all hotels in the faux-Tyrolean village of Vail. **Pros:** classic alpine ambience; romantic atmosphere; spa and beautiful indoor-outdoor pool. **Cons:** removed from lifts; wooden beams can make ceilings feel low; some rooms are small. *Rooms from: $699* ✉ *20 Vail Rd.* ☎ *970/476–5656, 800/654–8312* 🌐 *www.sonnenalp.com* *127 rooms* *No meals.*

Nightlife

Bol

BARS/PUBS | An upscale bar and restaurant with a bowling alley where winter rates start at $100 per hour not including shoes. ✉ *141 E. Meadow Dr., Suite 113* ☎ *970/476–5300* 🌐 *www.bolvail.com.*

Garfinkel's

BARS/PUBS | Near the gondola in Lionshead, Garfinkel's has good service, tons of local flavor, and plenty of TV screens for watching sports. ✉ *536 E. Lionshead Circle* ☎ *970/476–3789* 🌐 *www.garfsvail.com.*

★ Red Lion

BARS/PUBS | This popular spot is a tradition in Vail. It's standing-room-only in the afternoon, and a bit mellower in the evening. Most nights there's guitar or piano music, and there's bingo in the winter. ✉ *304 Bridge St.* ☎ *970/476–7676* 🌐 *www.theredlion.com.*

★ Root and Flower

WINE BARS—NIGHTLIFE | With more than 50 by-the-glass pours of wine (handily categorized by flavor rather than geography), an extensive bottle selection, select draft beers, and a robust list of creative craft cocktails, as well as exquisite boards of cheese and charcuterie and other carefully curated gourmet offerings, Root and Flower is a charming and stylish spot for an elevated après-ski or après-hike drink. ✉ *288 Bridge St, C4* ☎ *970/470–4189* 🌐 *www.rootandflowervail.com.*

Sarah's Lounge

MUSIC CLUBS | Located in Christiania at Vail, this lively spot showcases Helmut Fricker, a Vail institution who plays accordion while yodeling up a storm on Friday evenings in ski season. ✉ *356 E. Hanson Ranch Rd.* ☎ *970/476–5641* 🌐 *www.facebook.com/sarahsbarlounge.*

10th Mountain Whiskey Tasting Room

GATHERING PLACES | Warm your belly with a flight of mountain magic at this industrial-cool but cozy tasting room in the heart of the village. Samples of locally distilled potato vodka, corn moonshine, bourbon, whiskey, and cordial are served up with a history of the 10th Mountain Division. ✉ *227 Bridge St.* ☎ *970/470–4215* 🌐 *www.10thwhiskey.com.*

Activities

ADVENTURE PARKS

Adventure Ridge

LOCAL SPORTS | **FAMILY** | In summer ride the gondola from Lionshead up to Adventure Ridge at Eagle's Nest, the hub of Vail Mountain activities offered through the Epic Discovery park. It's cool and high, and it has the views, especially from the zipline and ropes course. It also has tons of activities like Friday Afternoon Club, live bands, beer, sunset watching, a climbing wall, tubing, an alpine coaster, and scenic hiking and biking trails. Winter activities at Adventure Ridge include snow tubing, kids snowmobiling, and (free) snowshoe tours. ✉ *Atop Front Side of Vail Mountain, Eagle's Nest* ☎ *970/476–9090* 🌐 *www.vail.com.*

BACKCOUNTRY SKIING

★ Paragon Guides

SKIING/SNOWBOARDING | It's a good idea to hire a guide if you're unfamiliar with the area's backcountry trails. Paragon's capable guides can lead you along 300 different trails on snowshoes and skis, including overnight hut trips. ✉ *210 Edwards Village Blvd., Edwards* ☎ *970/827–5363* 🌐 *www.paragonguides.com.*

★ 10th Mountain Division Hut and Trail System

SKIING/SNOWBOARDING | This famed network is one of Colorado's outdoor gems. Its 34 huts are in the mountains near Camp Hale, where the decorated namesake World War II division trained. Skiers and snowshoers in winter (snowmobiles are not permitted to approach the huts) and hikers and mountain bikers in summer tackle sections of the more than 350 miles of trails linking new and rustic cabins on day trips or weeklong expeditions. Apart from the joy of a self-reliant adventure among rugged mountains, travelers enjoy the camaraderie of communal living (there are very few private rooms in the huts), and evenings spent swapping stories by the glow of a wood-burning stove or the twinkle of summer stars. Hut reservations should be made at least a month in advance. ✉ *Vail* ☎ *970/925–5775 for hut reservations* 🌐 *www.huts.org.*

BICYCLING

A popular summer destination for both road bikers and mountain bikers, Vail has a variety of paved bike paths (including one that leads up to Vail Pass), plus dozens of miles of dirt mountain-bike trails. You can take bikes on lifts heading uphill, then head downhill on an array of routes.

Vail Bike Tech

BICYCLING | Known as Vail Ski Tech in the winter, this shop rents and repairs bikes the rest of the year. Best of all, they are only steps from the Eagle Bahn Gondola, a summer gateway to the ski-slope trails. They also offer shuttle service to Vail Pass for downhill mountain biking. ✉ *555 E. Lionshead Circle* ☎ *800/525–5995* 🌐 *www.vailbiketech.com.*

DOWNHILL SKIING AND SNOWBOARDING

★ Vail

SKIING/SNOWBOARDING | Year after year, Vail logs more than a million "skier days" (the ski industry's measure of ticket sales), perpetuating its ranking as one of the most popular resorts in North America.

With its excellent slopes and great restaurants, Vail is one of the most popular ski resorts in the United States.

From the top of China Bowl to the base of the Eagle Bahn Gondola at Lionshead, the resort is more than 7 miles across. The vast acreage is roughly divided into three sections: the Front Side, the Back Bowls, and Blue Sky Basin. Snowboarders will find plenty of steeps on the Front Side, and technical challenges at the Golden Peak or Bwana terrain parks, but they should avoid the Back Bowls, where long catwalks can get slow in the afternoon sun.

Vail's Gondola One is one of the fastest 10-passenger gondolas in the world, clocking in at 1,200 feet per minute. The heated gondola with Wi-Fi and cushioned seats replaced the Vista Bahn. From Mid-Vail, the Mountaintop Express Lift has also been upgraded from a high-speed quad to a high-speed six-passenger chairlift.

Vail is perhaps best known for its legendary **Back Bowls,** more than 3,000 acres of wide-open spaces that are sensational on sunny days. The terrain ranges from wide, groomed swatches for intermediate skiers to seemingly endless bump fields to glades so tight that only an expert boarder can slither between the trees. When there's fresh powder, these bowls beckon skiers intermediate and above.

The **Front Side** of Vail Mountain delivers a markedly different experience. Here there's lots of wide-trail skiing, heavily skewed toward groomed intermediate runs, especially off the Northwood Express, Mountaintop Express, and Avanti Express lifts, as well as the slopes reachable via the Eagle Bahn Gondola. The upper parts of Riva and the top of Look Ma are just a few of the places you'll find skilled skiers. The best show in town is on Highline (you can see it while riding Chair 10), where the experts groove through the moguls and those with a bit less experience careen around the bumps. The other two extremely difficult double-black-diamond trails off this slow lift are the best cruisers on the mountain for skilled skiers.

It takes time (as long as 45 minutes depending on conditions and skier level) to reach **Blue Sky Basin,** made up of three more bowls, but it's worth the effort. Intermediate skiers will find a few open trails with spectacular views of rugged mountain peaks. For advanced and expert skiers, the real fun is playing in glades and terrain with names such as Heavy Metal, Lovers Leap, the Divide, and Champagne Glade. **Facilities:** 195 trails; 5,317 acres; 3,450-foot vertical drop; 31 lifts. ✉ *Vail* ☎ *970/476–5601* 🌐 *www.vail.com* 🎫 *Lift ticket $199.*

Know Your Snow

Vail is known for its "powder": slopes puffed with light, fluffy flakes that make you feel that you are gliding on silk. Ungroomed runs, however, can quickly turn to "crud" as they get "tracked out" (scarred with deep tracks). That's when it's time to hunt up the "corduroy"—freshly groomed runs.

LESSONS AND PROGRAMS

Vail Ski & Snowboard School

SKIING/SNOWBOARDING | FAMILY | This respected operation runs classes, workshops, and clinics for skiers of all levels. Beginners can take three-day courses that include equipment rental and lift passes. Workshops for women, teen sessions, and telemark courses are among the programs targeting specific groups. Family lessons keep your group together and provide individualized instruction. ✉ *250 Vail Rd.* ☎ *970/754–8245* 🌐 *www.vail.com* 🎫 *From $210* ⏲ *Closed in summer.*

RENTALS

Vail Sports

SKIING/SNOWBOARDING | Within steps of the lifts and with 13 locations along the mountainside in Vail Village and Lionshead, this shop rents a wide range of ski gear, including high-end equipment. Prices for skis start at $57. Book online for discounts. ✉ *151 Vail La.* ☎ *970/477–5740* 🌐 *www.vailsports.com.*

FISHING

★ Minturn Anglers

FISHING | FAMILY | Minturn Anglers offers excellent guided fly-fishing, combo horseback and fly-fishing outings, float trips, and cast-and-taste trips (a fly-fishing outing followed by a catered outdoor dining experience) for all experience levels in various locations throughout the Vail Valley. Experienced instructors share their passion for fly-fishing and love of the outdoors (especially fun for novices or families looking for a unique day trip), and the store rents and sells a wide array of gear and bait. ✉ *106 N. Main St., Minturn* ☎ *970/827–9500* 🌐 *www.minturnanglers.com.*

GOLF

Golfers who love to play mountain courses know that some of the best are in Vail Valley. These courses meander through the valleys dividing the area's soaring peaks. The region is home to more than a dozen courses, and there are another half dozen within easy driving distance. It's all just a matter of where you're staying and how much you want to spend. Some courses are only open to members and to guests at certain lodges.

Vail Golf Club

GOLF | The area's municipal course is situated in the White River National Forest with views of the Gore mountains. ✉ *1775 Sunburst Dr.* ☎ *970/479–2260* 🌐 *www.vailclubhouse.com* 🎫 *$105; $75 for 9 holes* ⛳ *18 holes, 6281 yards, par 71* ✍ *Reservations essential.*

HIKING

★ Booth Lake

HIKING/WALKING | This is one of Vail's most popular hikes, so get on the trail early or pick a weekday during the summer high season. It's a sustained 4-mile one-way climb with more than 3,000 feet in

Did You Know?

The hike to Booth Lake will take you to the top of the Eagle's Nest Wilderness, part of the White River National Forest.

elevation gain to Booth Lake at 11,500 feet, right above the tree line. Fit hikers can do this in about seven hours. En route, you can cool off at the 60-foot waterfall; at only 2 miles in, this is also a great spot to turn around if you're seeking an easier hike. The reward for pushing on is a nice view of Booth Lake cradled among the alpine tundra. ✉ *Trailhead: Take Exit 180 from I–70 to end of Booth Falls Rd.*

Eagle's Loop

HIKING/WALKING | FAMILY | This trail starts from atop the Eagle Bahn Gondola at 10,350 feet, but it's a mellow, 1-mile stroll along the mountaintop ridge with panoramic views of the Mount of the Holy Cross. Allow about half an hour. A one-day lift ticket for the 14-minute gondola ride is $39 for adults. Adventurous types may prefer to skip the gondola (and the fee) and hike the intermediate, often steep, 4½-mile trail through aspen trees and wildflowers to the beginning of the Eagle Loop trail. ✉ *Trailhead: Top of Eagle Bahn Gondola.*

OUTFITTERS AND EXPEDITIONS

★ Paragon Guides

HIKING/WALKING | In summer, hiking with llamas is a highlight of this backcountry adventure company's offerings. Llamas carry food, wine, and water on lunch hikes or wine and cheese excursions, and help with overnight packs on hut trips. Paragon Guides also offer rock climbing, mountain biking, and fly-fishing trips in and around Vail Valley. ✉ *210 Edwards Village Blvd., Edwards* ☎ *970/926–5299* 🌐 *www.paragonguides.com.*

NATURE CENTERS

Vail Nature Center

HIKING/WALKING | FAMILY | This nature center occupies a 1940s homestead just across from the Betty Ford Alpine Gardens. In summer, you can sign up for wildflower walks, morning birding expeditions, evening beaver-pond tours, and the "S'mores and More" family campfire program. ✉ *601 Vail Valley Dr.* ☎ *970/479–2291* 🌐 *www.walkingmountains.org/locations/vail-nature-center* ⏲ *Closed mid-Sept.–mid-June.*

SNOWMOBILING

Vail Backcountry Tours

SNOW SPORTS | This snowmobiling outfit offers tours over more than 100 miles of trails with two-hour, half-day, and custom guided tours into the White River National Forest. ✉ *763 Red Sandstone Rd.* ☎ *970/476–7749* 🌐 *www.vailbackcountrytours.com.*

SPAS

RockResorts Spa at The Arrabelle

SPA/BEAUTY | Step into this 10,000-square-foot oasis that mimics the peaceful, mountainous surroundings: cream-colored walls, reclaimed-wood and natural-stone accents bringing the outside in. Arrive early to take advantage of the peaceful setting and the whirlpool, sauna, and eucalyptus steam room, as well as the separate his and hers relaxation rooms with chaise longues. Most treatments use organic ingredients and local flora, such as lavender and mountain juniper. The Fruit and Spice Body Peel and Wrap is the ultimate indulgence, with a hydrating pumpkin peel, cinnamon-sugar scrub, and scalp massage. ✉ *675 Lionshead Pl.* ☎ *970/754–7754* 🌐 *www.arrabelle.rockresorts.com/spa/index.asp.*

Sonnenalp Spa

SPA/BEAUTY | This lovely spa in Sonnenalp Resort is a European-style facility where you can relax on one of the lounge chairs around a crackling fireplace as you sip tea or spa water. Aspen trees stand over the heated outdoor tranquility pool, which has its own waterfall. Quench parched skin with a moisturizing HydraFacial, which diminishes wrinkles and shrinks pores (it's similar to microdermabrasion, but without the redness). You can also reduce altitude headaches with a hit from the oxygen bar. Book ahead for manicures and pedicures—they fill up year-round. ✉ *20 Vail Rd.* ☎ *970/479–5404* 🌐 *www.sonnenalpspa.com.*

The Spa at Four Seasons Vail

SPA/BEAUTY | This 14,000-square-foot, award-winning, full-service spa is the height of decadence. Unwind next to the relaxation lounge's oversized fireplace in the winter or in the relaxation garden during warmer times of year. The grotto-inspired hot tub and cold plunge rotation wake up the body, and a dedicated slumber room lulls you to sleep. A dry cedar sauna and a eucalyptus steam room ends or begins the journey. Aside from the 13 treatment rooms, there are couples' suites with dual massage tables. ✉ *1 Vail Rd.* ☎ *970/477–8600* 🌐 *www.fourseasons.com/vail.*

The Spa at Grand Hyatt Vail

SPA/BEAUTY | Pampering treatments inspired by the natural beauty of the surrounding area include a massage with heated river stones, a Colorado wildflower scrub, and healing hand and foot rubs to pamper after days in mittens and boots. Spa guests also have access to the hotel fitness center next door. ✉ *1300 Westhaven Dr.* ☎ *970/479–5942, 888/824–5772* 🌐 *www.hyatt.com.*

Beaver Creek

12 miles west of Vail; 110 miles west of Denver via I–70.

As with the majority of the area's resorts, the heart of Beaver Creek is a mountainside village. What sets Beaver Creek apart is that it's a series of cascading plazas connected by escalators. In this ultraposh enclave even boot-wearing skiers and snowboard-hauling riders take the escalators from the hotels and shuttle stops on the lower levels. Opened in 1980 as a smaller version of Vail, Beaver Creek has somewhat overshadowed its older sibling in glamour.

Locals know that Beaver Creek is the best place to ski on weekends, when Vail is too crowded, or anytime there's fresh powder. Beaver Creek is just far enough from Denver that it doesn't get the flood of day-trippers who flock to Vail and the other Front Range resorts. The slopes of Beaver Creek Mountain are connected to those of even ritzier Bachelor Gulch. These are close to Arrowhead, creating a village-to-village ski experience like those found in Europe.

GETTING HERE AND AROUND

Driving is the most convenient way to get around Beaver Creek, but there are private shuttles and public buses. Expect to pay for parking.

CONTACTS Avon/Beaver Creek Transit. ☎ *970/748–4120* 🌐 *www.avon.org.*

WHEN TO GO

Beaver Creek's seasons are the same as Vail's; winter is great for snow sports and summer also attracts outdoor enthusiasts.

Restaurants

★ Grouse Mountain Grill

$$$$ | **AMERICAN** | The stately appearance of this Pines Lodge restaurant belies its friendly, welcoming attitude. The fresh, farm-raised, cage-free food philosophy makes for quality ingredients, and the chef here truly knows how to make the food sing. **Known for:** pretzel-crusted pork chop with sweet mustard sauce; farm-fresh ingredients; lovely patio with blankets if you get cold. $ *Average main: $40* ✉ *141 Scott Hill Rd.* ☎ *970/949–0600* 🌐 *www.grousemountaingrill.com* ⏲ *No lunch in summer.*

★ Maya

$$$ | **MODERN MEXICAN** | Oversized windows brighten the already warm space filled with hand-blown glass light fixtures, wood, and Mexican-tile accents, and a bar lined with house-infused tequilas. Guacamole is smashed together tableside, and the skillet pork carnitas and roasted chicken mole dishes are simple reminders that delicious, authentic Mexican isn't confined to hole-in-the-wall outposts. **Known for:** tableside guacamole; smokey mezcal cocktails; outdoor patio with firepits and views of Beaver Creek Mountain. *Average main: $25* *Westin Riverfront Resort & Spa, 126 Riverfront La., Avon* *970/790–5500* *www.westinriverfront.com/maya-beaver-creek.*

Splendido at the Chateau

$$$$ | **MODERN AMERICAN** | With elegant marble columns and clean Italian linens, this posh eatery is the height of opulence. The tasting menu is a perfect sampling of the chef's new American cuisine improved only by the on-site sommelier's perfect wine pairings. **Known for:** elegant dining room; Dover sole with parsley-lemon brown butter; piano bar. *Average main: $35* *17 Chateau La., Beaver Creek Village* *970/845–8808* *splendidorestaurant.com* *Closed mid-Apr.–June, mid-Oct.–mid-Nov., and Mon. and Tues. in summer. No lunch.*

Vin48

$$$$ | **WINE BAR** | Good vino is not hard to find at Vin48, a casual, upscale wine bar in Avon. Enjoying the benefits of Vin48's Enomatic preservation system, you can explore wines by the glass or half glass (with help from an on-staff sommelier) as you go. **Known for:** carefully curated wine list with on-site sommelier; indoor/outdoor dining with large windows that open during warm weather; pork du jour with surprising preparations. *Average main: $32* *48 E. Beaver Creek Blvd., Avon* *970/748–9463* *www.vin48.com* *No lunch.*

Zino Ristorante

$$$$ | **MODERN ITALIAN** | Zino has earned a loyal fan base for its house-made pastas and wood-fired pizzas. The two-story restaurant has a large bar, ideal for lighter bites or a cocktail. **Known for:** pesche e prosciutto pizza with Colorado peaches, prosciutto, balsamic, and an array of cheeses; Colorado lamb Bolognese fettuccine; alfresco dining in the summer. *Average main: $32* *27 Main St., #101, Edwards* *970/926–0777* *www.zinoristorante.com* *No lunch.*

Hotels

Beaver Creek Lodge

$$$$ | **HOTEL** | A large atrium that doubles as an art gallery on the first floor grabs all the attention at this modern hotel a few hundred yards from the lifts. **Pros:** room layouts great for families; good value; friendly service. **Cons:** a short walk to the lifts; fee for parking and resort fee; no spa. *Rooms from: $360* *26 Avondale La., Beaver Creek Village* *970/845–9800* *www.kesslercollection.com/beaver-creek-lodge* *70 rooms* *No meals.*

★ **The Osprey at Beaver Creek, A Rock Resort**

$$$$ | **HOTEL** | You can't get any closer to a ski run in the United States than the Osprey, unless you sleep on the lift. **Pros:** best ski location at Beaver Creek; rooms are fresh and light; romantic atmosphere. **Cons:** often sold out well in advance; some complain of lukewarm showers; despite proximity to the slopes, not every room has a nice view. *Rooms from: $619* *10 Elk Track La.* *970/429–5042, 866/621–7625* *www.ospreyatbeavercreek.rockresorts.com* *45 rooms* *Free Breakfast.*

★ **Park Hyatt Beaver Creek Resort & Spa**

$$$$ | **RESORT** | With magnificent antler chandeliers, and towering windows opening out onto the mountain, the lobby of this slope-side hotel manages to be both cozy and grand. **Pros:** beautiful on-site spa; cozy Colorado mountain vibe; ski-in ski-out location. **Cons:** fee for parking; small rooms; a big-resort feel. *Rooms from: $650* *136 E. Thomas Pl., Beaver Creek Village* *970/949–1234* *www.hyatt.com* *190 rooms* *No meals.*

Pines Lodge

$$$$ | **HOTEL** | This Swiss-style ski-in ski-out lodge is a winner for skiers, combining upscale accommodations with an unpretentious attitude. **Pros:** traditional European chalet decor; slope-side location; on-site ski shop and ski concierge. **Cons:** a short walk to the village; valet parking only; modestly decorated rooms. *Rooms from: $499 ✉ 141 Scott Hill Rd., Beaver Creek Village ☎ 970/429–5043, 855/279–3430 ⊕ www.pineslodge.rockresorts.com 60 rooms, 12 condos, 21 town houses No meals.*

★ **Ritz-Carlton, Bachelor Gulch in Beaver Creek**

$$$$ | **RESORT** | **FAMILY** | Here towering wood beams highlighted by stone fireplaces make for a grand scene in the lobby and on the outdoor terrace where a firepit ties together the cozy scene. **Pros:** the most luxurious property on the mountain; excellent guest service; ski-in ski-out. **Cons:** high altitude (9,000 feet); removed from the Village; special events can crowd public spaces. *Rooms from: $979 ✉ 0130 Daybreak Ridge, Bachelor Gulch Village ☎ 970/748–6200 ⊕ www.ritzcarlton.com 180 rooms No meals.*

Nightlife

Coyote Café

CAFES—NIGHTLIFE | This boisterous spot is a kick-back-and-relax sort of place right on the pedestrian mall, where locals hang out at the bar and enjoy the patio. *✉ 210 The Plaza, Avon ☎ 970/949–5001 ⊕ www.coyotecafe.net.*

Dusty Boot Steakhouse & Saloon

BARS/PUBS | For the best après-ski scene among both visitors and locals, head to this rollicking saloon complete with Wild West decor, including cowboy hats and buffalo skulls over the pinewood bar. When the ski slopes close, the bar is usually packed. *✉ 210 Offerson Rd., Suite 301, Beaver Creek Village ☎ 970/748–1146 ⊕ www.dustyboot.com.*

8100 Mountain Bar & Grill

BARS/PUBS | The faux candlelight, modern chandeliers, and lounge-y vibe lure an upper-crust crowd who knock back favorites from the local craft beer and sparkling cocktail menus. Try the Colorado Wildflower: a mix of local honey, vodka, mint, and fresh-squeezed orange juice. The appetizers are just as delish—consider the shucked oysters with a Colorado hot sauce. *✉ Park Hyatt Beaver Creek Resort, 50 W. Thomas Pl., Beaver Creek Village ☎ 970/949–1234.*

The Met Kitchen

BARS/PUBS | Extensive menus featuring Colorado-made vodka, whiskey, gin, craft beer, and wine bring thirsty travelers here for flights of all types with small plates for pairing. Those with bigger appetites can turn to comforting favorites like chicken and waffles and short ribs, each with its own suggested wine pairing. *✉ 210 Offerson Rd., Suite 201C ☎ 970/748–3123 ⊕ www.themetkitchen.com.*

Performing Arts

Vilar Performing Arts Center

ARTS CENTERS | With gold-color wood paneling and an etched-glass mural re-creating with bold strokes the mountains outside, this dazzling performance venue is itself a work of art. Seating more than 500, the horseshoe-shaped auditorium has great views from just about every seat. Throughout the year there's a stellar lineup of events, including concerts by orchestras and pop stars, great theater, and aerial dancers. In the surrounding plazas you'll find many art galleries. Just walking around Beaver Creek is a feast for the eyes, because sculptures are set almost everywhere you look. *✉ 68 Avondale La. ☎ 970/845–8497, 888/920–2787 ⊕ www.vilarpac.org.*

Smaller yet less crowded than Vail, Beaver Creek is an underrated gem for skiers.

Shopping

Walt Horton Fine Art

ART GALLERIES | Well-known for his expressive, playful bronze sculptures, Walt Horton features several of his own pieces and works by other local oil painters and sculptors in his gallery. ✉ *156 Plaza, Beaver Creek Village* ☎ *970/949–1660* 🌐 *www.walthortonfineart.com.*

Activities

DOWNHILL SKIING AND SNOWBOARDING

Beaver Creek

SKIING/SNOWBOARDING | Beaver Creek is a piece of nirvana, partly because of its system of trails and partly because of its enviable location two hours from Denver. Although only a third the size of Vail, Beaver Creek is seldom crowded. The skiable terrain extends from the runs down Beaver Creek to the slopes around Bachelor Gulch to the network of trails at Arrowhead. You can easily ski from one village to another. The omnipresent and helpful ambassadors are always willing to point you in the right direction, and carry your skis to the liftside.

Beaver Creek has a little of everything, from smoother slopes for beginners to difficult trails used for international competitions. Grouse Mountain, in particular, is famed for its thigh-burning bump runs. Beginners have an entire peak, at the summit of Beaver Creek Mountain, where they can learn to ski or practice on novice trails. Intermediate-level skiers have several long cruising trails on the lower half of Beaver Creek Mountain and in Larkspur Bowl. Both locations also have black-diamond trails, so groups of skiers and snowboarders of varying abilities can ride uphill together. The Birds of Prey runs, like Peregrine and Golden Eagle, are aptly named, because the steepness of the trails can be a surprise for skiers who mistakenly think they are skilled enough to take on this challenging terrain. Terrain parks like the Zoom Room and The Rodeo bring skiers and snowboarders together to practice tricks on technical rails, boxes, stall features, long slides, and jumps.

The slopes of neighboring **Bachelor Gulch** are a mix of beginner and intermediate trails. Here you can often find fresh powder hours after it's gone elsewhere. Many skiers plan to arrive in time for a hearty lunch at Buffalos or an après-ski cocktail in the Buffalo Bar or the Bachelors Lounge at the Ritz-Carlton. There are shuttles handy to take you back to Beaver Creek.

Dependent on conditions, the third village in the area, **Arrowhead,** can have the best and usually the least crowded intermediate terrain. The European concept of skiing from village to village was introduced here in 1996, when Vail Associates decided to connect Arrowhead, Beaver Creek, and Bachelor Gulch via lifts and ski trails. Standard, single-day ski and snowboard rental packages start at $52 for standard equipment. **Facilities:** 150 trails; 1,832 acres; 3,340-foot vertical drop; 25 lifts. ✉ *Beaver Creek* ☎ *800/404–3535* 🌐 *www.beavercreek.com* 🎫 *Lift ticket $199.*

LESSONS AND PROGRAMS

Beaver Creek Ski & Snowboard School

SKIING/SNOWBOARDING | **FAMILY** | At Beaver Creek's excellent ski and snowboard school, special clinics run throughout the year, like workshops for women, teen sessions, and telemark courses. The school boasts numerous beginner through advanced ski and snowboard lessons for all ages, with a focus on small class sizes. ✉ *210 Beaver Creek Plaza* ☎ *866/231—0667* 🌐 *www.beavercreek.com.*

GOLF

Eagle Ranch Golf Club

GOLF | Antique ranch implements scattered throughout this scenic municipal course just 30 minutes from Vail nod to its former life as a working ranch. Caddies like to joke that the perfect club might actually be a fly rod. Arnold Palmer, who designed the 18-hole course, said, "The fairways are very playable and the roughs are not extremely rough." The course is certified as an Audubon Cooperative Sanctuary. ✉ *0050 Lime Park Dr., Eagle* ☎ *970/328–2882* 🌐 *www.eagleranchgolf.com* 🎫 *$109; $65 for 9 holes* ⛳ *18 holes, 6600 yards, par 72* ✍ *Reservations essential.*

HIKING

Missouri Lakes Trail

HIKING/WALKING | This wilderness region southwest of Beaver Creek offers plenty of outdoor adventures. One great hike is the 4½-mile Missouri Lakes trail, a moderate trail in the Holy Cross Wilderness Area. It's easy to access and provides a fun loop through the wilderness with nearly 2,000 feet in elevation gain. See high alpine lakes and great views at the mouth of a mini canyon. Continue on the switchbacks to Fancy Pass and Cross Creek trails for a bird's-eye view of the area. ✉ *Beaver Creek* ✥ *Trailhead: Take exit 171 on I–70 toward Minturn. Turn right onto Hwy. 24 for 13 miles. Turn right onto Homestake Rd. 703 and drive until mile 8.5 and then turn left on Missouri Creek Rd. 704. Turn right and continue 3 miles on the dirt road until the T in the road. Take a left and the trailhead will be on your right.* ☎ *970/827–5715* 🌐 *www.fs.usda.gov/recarea/whiteriver.*

HORSEBACK RIDING

Beaver Creek Stables

HORSEBACK RIDING | Here you can book outings ranging from one-hour rides to all-day excursions. Many trips include a tasty picnic lunch. In the evening, ride your horse to Beano's Cabin for dinner. Horseback-riding lessons are also available. ✉ *93 Elk Track Rd., Avon* ☎ *970/845–7770* 🌐 *www.beavercreekstables.com.*

SPAS

Bachelor Gulch Spa at The Ritz-Carlton

SPA/BEAUTY | Despite being one of the larger spas in the area (with 19 treatment rooms), the spa at Bachelor Gulch cultivates an intimate vibe. Stone-lined grottos ease the day's stress before your treatment even starts. Take a signature soak in the copper tub—alone or with a significant other—or indulge in the miner's mud wrap, a full body exfoliation with a scalp massage, hydrotherapy bath, and massage. The fitness center classes include yoga, Pilates, Barre, Zumba, and stretch recovery (with an option to finish with an alfresco massage once the weather warms up). ✉ *0130 Daybreak Ridge, Avon* ☎ *970/748–6200* 🌐 *www.ritzcarlton.com/en/hotels/colorado/bachelor-gulch/spa* ☞ *$205 for 50-min massage.*

Exhale Spa

SPA/BEAUTY | In the Park Hyatt Beaver Creek, the 30,000-square-foot Exhale Spa—inspired by Roman bathhouses—has a self-guided healing water tour called Aqua Sanitas. Dip in and out of five water rituals, alternating from hot to cold, including a thermal pool, Jacuzzi, rainshower, steam room, and tepidarium bath room with heated loungers. There are a few tables for room-service meals (they're even happy to serve you cocktails and bar drinks). The spa also offers a full range of services, which can be enhanced with additions like relaxing CBD or moisturizing "Climate Rescue" that replaces massage oil with shea butter. The signature "ginger peach cure" treatment comprises a scrub, full-body massage, wrap, and Swiss shower (with 12 jetted nozzles). ✉ *100 E. Thomas Pl.* ☎ *970/748–7500* 🌐 *www.exhalespa.com* ☞ *$190 for 50-min massage.*

TRACK SKIING

Beaver Creek Nordic Center

SKIING/SNOWBOARDING | Lessons, equipment rentals, and guided tours are available here. ✉ *Strawberry Park Condo Bldg., at the bottom of Chair 12* ☎ *970/745–5313* 🌐 *www.beavercreek.com/plan-your-trip/ski-and-ride-lessons/category/nordic-center.aspx* ⏲ *Closed mid-Apr.–mid-Dec.*

Chapter 7

ASPEN AND THE ROARING FORK VALLEY

Updated by
Whitney Bryen

Sights ★★★☆☆

Restaurants ★★★★★

Hotels ★★★★★

Shopping ★★★☆☆

Nightlife ★★★☆☆

WELCOME TO ASPEN AND THE ROARING FORK VALLEY

TOP REASONS TO GO

★ **Fine food:** Restaurants in Aspen, Carbondale, and Glenwood Springs are used to being praised for climbing gastronomic heights, and the dishes that many offer, with ingredients from locally raised Wagyu beef to Russian caviar, are as upscale as the clientele.

★ **Historic hotels:** Thanks to moneyed preservationists, the Victorian Hotel Jerome in Aspen and the Medici-inspired Hotel Colorado in Glenwood Springs still stand.

★ **Hot springs:** Glenwood Springs has been a therapeutic retreat since the Ute Indians called the local hot springs "healing waters."

★ **The mountains:** You'll find postcard Colorado in the 14,000-foot Maroon Bells, especially when these steep-faced peaks are reflected in Maroon Lake.

★ **The Aspen scene:** You'll see it all in Aspen—Hollywood celebs in cowboy boots, high-heeled Brazilians, tanned European ski instructors, and fascinating and friendly locals.

Wedged in a valley between the Elk Mountain palisades to the southwest and the high-altitude massifs of the Sawatch Range in the east, the Roaring Fork Valley is a Rocky Mountain Shangri-la. The charm and beauty of this isolation makes reaching Aspen a scenic journey, but also one that can be frustrating. Aspen's explosive growth hasn't come without some headaches. Despite expanded lanes, Highway 82 quickly clogs with skiers and day commuters.

1 **Aspen.** One of the world's most glamorous ski towns.

2 **Snowmass.** Aspen's more down-to-earth counterpart.

3 **Carbondale.** A town perfect for lovers of both the arts and the outdoors.

4 **Redstone and Marble.** Home to impressive sandstone cliffs and an old mining district.

5 **Glenwood Springs.** A famed spa town home to the world's largest outdoor natural hot-springs pool.

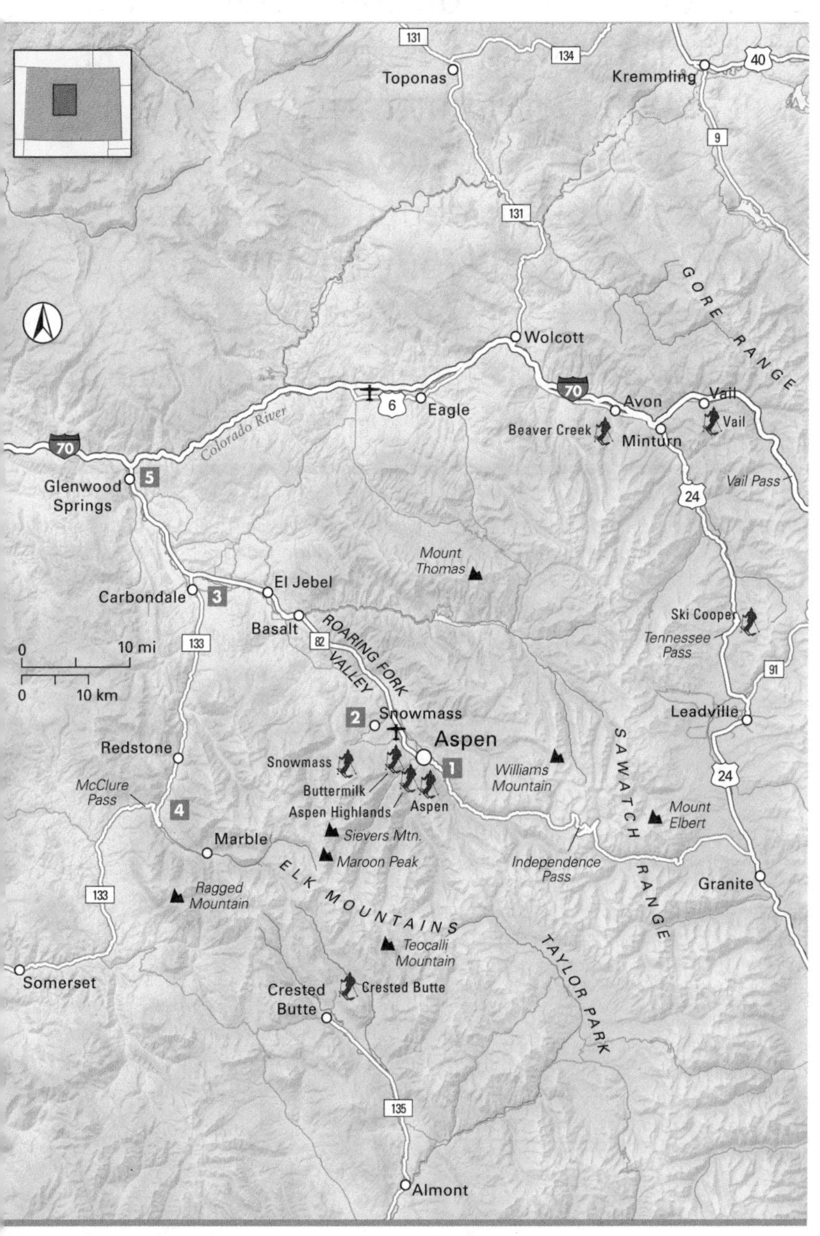
131
134
40
Toponas
Kremmling
9
131
GORE RANGE
Wolcott
70
Avon
Vail
Eagle
6
Colorado River
Beaver Creek
Vail
Minturn
70
Glenwood Springs
5
24
Vail Pass
Mount Thomas
El Jebel
Carbondale
3
Basalt
ROARING FORK VALLEY
82
133
0
10 mi
0
10 km
Ski Cooper
Tennessee Pass
91
Snowmass
2
Leadville
Aspen
SAWATCH RANGE
Redstone
Snowmass
1
Williams Mountain
24
McClure Pass
Buttermilk
Aspen Highlands
Aspen
Mount Elbert
4
Sievers Mtn.
Marble
Maroon Peak
Independence Pass
Granite
ELK MOUNTAINS
133
Ragged Mountain
Teocalli Mountain
TAYLOR PARK
Somerset
Crested Butte
Crested Butte
135
Almont

The Roaring Fork Valley—and Aspen, its crown jewel—is the quintessential Colorado Rocky Mountain High. A row of the state's famed Fourteeners (peaks over 14,000 feet) guards this valley. There are only two ways in or out: over the precipitous Independence Pass in summer or up the four-lane highway through the booming Roaring Fork Valley, which stretches 40 miles from Glenwood Springs to Aspen.

Outside Aspen, Colorado natives regard the city and its mix of longtime locals, newly arrived ski bums, hard-core mountaineers, laser-sculpted millionaires, and tanned celebs with a mixture of bemusement and envy. The "real Aspenites," who came for the snow and stayed for summers, have been squeezed out by seven-digit housing prices. Most have migrated down-valley to bedroom communities such as Carbondale.

The quest for wealth in the valley dates from the mid-1800s, when the original inhabitants, the Ute people, were supplanted by gold prospectors and silver miners, who came to reap the region's mineral bounty. The demonetization of silver in 1893 brought the quiet years, as the population dwindled and ranching became a way of life. Nearly half a century later, the tides turned again as downhill skiing gave new life to Aspen. Today, the Roaring Fork Valley weaves together its past and present into a blend of small-town charm and luxurious amenities, all surrounded by the majestic beauty of central Colorado's 2-million-acre White River National Forest.

MAJOR REGIONS

Aspen. Head here for a dose of the high life in an almost too-pretty town. The aspen-draped Maroon Bells peaks are among the state's most iconic images.

The Roaring Fork Valley. Moving down-valley from Aspen along the Roaring Fork River, past the family resort of Snowmass, is a journey to a much less ritzy Colorado. The landscape changes, too, going from lush aspen groves to the drier Western Slope steppe. Snowmass is a year-round, family resort destination. The historic towns of Glenwood Springs, Carbondale, and Redstone offer pleasant—and less expensive—experiences and have great biking, fly-fishing, and rafting in summer.

Planning

When to Go

Aspen and the Roaring Fork Valley are a year-round destination. If it's skiing you're after, February and March historically have the best snow (deepest base and most terrain open) plus the warmest winter weather. Aspen summers are legendary for their food, music, and art festivals. Nearly 7,000 locals call Aspen home, and the area population swells to more than 14,000 during ski season and to more than 21,000 in summer. June and early July are best for rafting (snowmelt makes for high-octane rapids). Most high-country biking and hiking trails are cleared of snowdrift by mid-June, when brilliant wildflowers emerge and remain in bloom through early August. Mid-September brings hotel-room deals, cooler days, photogenic snow dustings on the Maroon Bells, and flame-orange aspen groves.

Planning Your Time

The drive from Glenwood Springs at the northwest tip of the Roaring Fork Valley to Aspen is less than an hour, making it easy for visitors to set up a base camp, with convenient access to area activities anywhere along "the valley." Carbondale offers local flavor as well as accommodations that are centrally located between the larger towns of Glenwood Springs and Aspen. Snowmass and Aspen are closest to the mountains for winter skiing, but Sunlight Mountain Resort near Glenwood Springs is a less crowded, budget-friendly winter wonderland.

Getting Here and Around

AIR

Aspen/Pitkin County Airport (ASE) is 3 miles from downtown Aspen and 7 miles from Snowmass Village. Airline schedules vary seasonally, but, during ski season, you can count on several daily nonstop flights to and from Denver and regular nonstop flights to and from Dallas, Houston, Chicago, Miami, and Los Angeles.

If you aren't renting a car, your best bet for traveling to and from Aspen and Snowmass Village is Roaring Fork Transportation Authority, which provides bus service from Aspen/Pitkin County Airport to the Rubey Park bus station near the base of the ski mountain. Colorado Mountain Express, a shared-van shuttle service, connects Aspen with Denver International Airport and Eagle County Airport (winter). High Mountain Taxi, based in Aspen, can provide local rides and charter service outside the Roaring Fork Valley.

AIRPORT CONTACTS Aspen/Pitkin County Airport (ASE). ✉ *233 E. Airport Rd., Aspen* ☎ *970/920–5384* 🌐 *www.aspenairport.com.* **Denver International Airport (DEN).** ✉ *8500 Peña Blvd., Denver* ☎ *303/342–2000* 🌐 *www.flydenver.com.* **Eagle County Airport (EGE).** ✉ *217 Eldon Wilson Rd., Gypsum* ☎ *970/328–8600* 🌐 *www.eagle-county.us/airport.*

AIRPORT TRANSFERS Colorado Mountain Express. ☎ *970/754–7433* 🌐 *www.coloradomountainexpress.com.* **High Mountain Taxi.** ☎ *970/925–8294* 🌐 *www.hmtaxi.com.*

BUS AND SHUTTLE

The Roaring Fork Transportation Authority provides bus service up and down the valley, and many resorts have free private shuttles.

SHUTTLE CONTACTS Roaring Fork Transportation Authority. ✉ *0051 Service Center Dr., Aspen* ☎ *970/925–8484* 🌐 *www.rfta.com.*

CAR

In summer, the 160-mile, three-hour drive from Denver to Aspen is a delightful journey up the I–70 corridor and across the Continental Divide through the Eisenhower Tunnel (or by way of the slower, but more spectacular, Loveland Pass), down along the eastern ramparts of the Collegiate Peaks along State Highway 91 and U.S. 24, with a final push on twisty State Highway 82 up and over 12,095-foot Independence Pass.

The scenery, particularly south of Leadville on U.S. 24, is among the best in Colorado, with views to the west of 14,433-foot Mount Elbert, the highest mountain in the state. Independence Pass is closed in winter (the timing depends on snowfall, typically late October to late May), but motorists should always drive cautiously because Colorado's weather can change unexpectedly. Both Highway 82 and I–70, like all Colorado roads, should be driven with caution, especially at night when elk, bighorn sheep, and mule deer cross without warning.

Generally speaking, driving to Aspen from Denver in winter is more trouble than it's worth, unless you plan to stop along the way. The drive west on I–70 and east on Route 82 takes more than three hours at best, depending on weather conditions and, increasingly, ski traffic. On the other hand, the 3-mile drive from the Aspen/Pitkin County Airport (ASE) is a breeze along the flat valley floor. The 70-mile drive from the Eagle County Airport (EGE)—which doesn't cross any mountain passes—is another option. Whenever you visit, the traffic and parking may try your patience.

Parks and Recreation Areas

The Roaring Fork Valley is surrounded by recreational land, wilderness areas, and national forests. To the southeast, in the Collegiate Peaks Wilderness area, more 14,000-foot summits beckon hikers than anywhere else in the Lower 48.

The often overlooked Hunter-Fryingpan Wilderness Area is one of Colorado's hidden secrets—a thin-air spine of unnamed peaks and excellent trout rivers in the Williams Mountains just east of Aspen. On the other side of the Continental Divide, the Hunter-Fryingpan becomes the Mount Massive Wilderness Area, named for Colorado's second-highest peak, which stands 14,421 feet tall. Most of these wilderness areas are encompassed within the much larger—and more fragmented—White River National Forest.

Recreational areas that span the valley offer some of the state's best biking trails, with more than 300 miles of terrain showcasing the idyllic landscape—from the mountain peaks to the valley floor.

Restaurants

Sushi? Coconut curry? Bison and lobster? Colorado's culinary repertoire is at its broadest in Aspen. With all the Hummers and designer handbags come an equal number of menus with high-end ingredients and showy preparations. Plates can be pricey in the area, but many eateries have at least a few moderately priced entrées and a bar menu as a nod to the budget-conscious. *Restaurant reviews have been shortened. For full information, visit Fodors.com.*

Independence Pass

From Memorial Day until the fall flurries, the most beautiful route to Aspen is over Independence Pass. From the Vail–Leadville–Buena Vista corridor on the east side of the Sawatch Mountains, Highway 82 climbs up and over 12,095-foot Independence Pass and switchbacks down to Aspen, along the way passing above the tree line and making some white-knuckle hairpin turns (drive slowly not only to appreciate the scenery, but also because you might have to yield to oncoming traffic in narrow, one-lane sections). The pass divides the Mount Massive Wilderness to the north from the Collegiate Peaks to the south. The trip is not for the fainthearted, given the long, exposed drops and the possibility for snow at any time of the year. At dawn and dusk, elk and mule deer herds can sometimes be seen grazing in the willow thickets beside Lake Creek as it cascades down the eastern flank of the pass. As soon as the autumn snow flies, however, the pass closes, and Aspen becomes a cul-de-sac town accessible by road only via Glenwood Springs.

Hotels

There's no shortage of lodging in Aspen and the Roaring Fork, but you'll pay the highest rates in the state. Downriver alternatives like Carbondale and Glenwood Springs are attractive for budget hunters—but you'll face heavy traffic when commuting to Aspen. Before booking down-valley, however, look for special deals that might include lift tickets and parking. *Hotel reviews have been shortened. For full information, visit Fodors.com. Restaurant prices are the average cost of a main course at dinner or, if dinner is not served, at lunch, excluding 8.2%–8.6% tax. Hotel prices are the lowest cost of a standard double room in high season, excluding service charges and 8.6%–10.7% tax.*

What It Costs

	$	$$	$$$	$$$$
RESTAURANTS	under $15	$15–$22	$23–$30	over $30
HOTELS	under $125	$125–$200	$201–$300	over $300

Aspen

200 miles west of Denver via I–70 and Hwy. 82.

One of the world's fabled resorts, Aspen practically defines glitz, glamour, and glorious skiing. To the uninitiated, Aspen and Vail might be synonymous. Between the galleries, museums, music festivals, and other glittering social events, however, there's so much going on in Aspen that even in winter many people come simply to "do the scene," and never make it to the slopes. Many hotels and restaurants host lively après-ski events.

Aspen History

Originally called Ute City (after its displaced former residents), Aspen was founded in the late 1870s during a silver rush. The most prominent early citizen was Jerome Wheeler, who opened two of Aspen's enduring landmarks: the Hotel Jerome and the Wheeler Opera House. The silver market crashed in 1893, and Aspen's population dwindled from 15,000 to 250 by the end of the Depression. In the late 1930s, the region struck gold when Swiss mountaineer and ski consultant Andre Roche determined that Aspen Mountain would make a prime ski area. By 1941, it had already landed the U.S. Nationals, but Aspen was really put on the world map by Walter Paepcke, who developed the town as a cultural mecca. In 1949, he helped found the Aspen Institute for Humanistic Studies and subsequently organized an international celebration to mark Johann Wolfgang von Goethe's 200th birthday. This paved the way for such renowned annual events as the Aspen Music Festival and the International Design Conference.

At the same time, Aspen is a place where some people live everyday lives, sending their children to school and working at jobs that may or may not have to do with skiing. It is also, arguably, America's original ski-bum destination, a fact that continues to give the town's glamorous facade an underlying layer of humor and texture.

GETTING HERE AND AROUND

The rich arrive by private planes, but almost everyone else arrives in Aspen by car or shuttle bus. Parking is a pricey pain, and traffic, especially on weekends, clogs the streets. The Roaring Fork Transportation Authority has bus service connecting the resort with the rest of the valley. The easiest way to get around Aspen is on foot or by bike. For longer trips, hop aboard the free Aspen Skiing Company shuttles, which connect the Aspen, Buttermilk, and Snowmass base areas.

VISITOR INFORMATION Aspen Chamber Resort Association. ✉ *590 N. Mill St.* ☎ *970/925–1940, 877/702–7736* 🌐 *aspenchamber.org.* **Aspen/Snowmass Snow Report.** ☎ *970/925–1221* 🌐 *www.aspensnowmass.com.*

WHEN TO GO

Aspen is a great place to visit year-round. The summer season, with its festivals, runs from mid-June to Labor Day, and winter season goes from Thanksgiving until the ski lifts close in mid-April.

★ Aspen Music Festival and School
COLLEGE | Focusing on everything from chamber music to jazz, the Aspen Music Festival and School begins on the Thursday before Independence Day and runs for seven weeks. Musicians perform at hundreds of events held at the 2,050-seat Benedict Music Tent, the Victorian Wheeler Opera House, and the Joan and Irving Harris Concert Hall. Tickets are available online. A quarter of the performances are free, and one of the festival's great pleasures is showing up on the free-seating lawn outside the Benedict Music Tent with some friends and a blanket. ✉ *960 N. 3rd St.* ☎ *970/925–9042* 🌐 *www.aspenmusicfestival.com.*

TOURS

Aspen Carriage and Sleigh
CARRIAGE TOURS | A romantic (albeit pricey) way to get acquainted with the backcountry is by taking a private sleigh ride with Aspen Carriage and Sleigh. They also have

more affordable carriage tours around downtown and the historic West End. ✉ *Aspen* ☎ *970/925–3394* 🌐 *www.aspen-carriage.com* 🎫 *From $325 an hour.*

Sights

Aspen Art Museum

MUSEUM | Known for its rotating contemporary exhibits and woven-look exterior design, this non-collecting museum exhibits mainly new pieces from top national and international artists, often commissioned by the museum. Designed by Shigeru Ban, the 33,000-square-foot facility is a three-story glass cube encased in a woven, wood-veneer exterior screen that gives passersby glimpses of the exhibitions. Inside, a glass elevator and an open-plan design create a bright space, and the rooftop sculpture garden and SO Café offer prime views of Aspen Mountain. ✉ *637 E. Hyman Ave.* ☎ *970/925–8050* 🌐 *www.aspenartmuseum.org* 🎫 *Free* ⏲ *Closed Mon.*

Hunter-Frying Pan Wilderness

NATURE PRESERVE | East of Aspen, in the Williams Mountains and lining a stretch of the Roaring Fork River, is an often-forgotten section of the White River National Forest. Overshadowed by the popular Maroon Bells to the west and the Colorado Wilderness of the Holy Cross to the north, the more than 82,000 acres of the Hunter-Fryingpan Wilderness offer 65 miles of hiking trails, excellent trout fishing, and unparalleled seclusion. Elk and mule deer call the area home, and wildflowers abound in July and August. ✉ *Aspen Ranger Station, 806 W. Hallam* ☎ *970/925–3445* 🌐 *www.fs.usda.gov/recarea/whiteriver/recarea/?recid=81105.*

★ Maroon Bells

NATURE SITE | **FAMILY** | The majestic Maroon Bells, twin peaks more than 14,000 feet high, are so colorful, thanks to mineral streaking, that you'd swear they were blanketed with primrose and Indian paintbrush. It's one of the most photographed spots in the country. Before 8 am and after 5 pm in the summer, cars can drive all the way up to Maroon Lake (though vehicles with children in car seats or people with disabilities are allowed to do so at any time). Otherwise, parking is available at the Aspen Highlands garage, where guided bus tours and shuttles leave regularly in summer months. ✉ *White River National Forest, Maroon Creek Rd.* ✣ *10 miles southwest of Aspen.*

Wheeler/Stallard House Museum

MUSEUM | You can get a taste of Victorian high life at the Queen Anne–style Wheeler/Stallard House Museum, which displays memorabilia collected by the Aspen Historical Society and features revolving historical exhibits. Your admission fee also covers entrance to the Holden/Marolt Ranching and Mining Museum (open summer only), a hands-on exploration of Aspen's past housed in an old ore-processing building on the western edge of town. ✉ *620 W. Bleeker St.* ☎ *970/925–3721* 🌐 *www.aspenhistory.org* 🎫 *$10* ⏲ *Closed Sun. and Mon.*

Restaurants

Ajax Tavern

$$$ | **AMERICAN** | So close to the gondola you can keep your boots on while dining, this upbeat restaurant in The Little Nell hotel has big glass windows and a spacious patio with slope-side views. Large wooden beams, red booths, and sleek furnishings define this spot, which is popular both for its location and its hearty surf-n-turf dishes. **Known for:** slope-side patio; Parmesan truffle fries; double cheeseburger made with locally raised Wagyu beef. 💲 *Average main: $27* ✉ *685 E. Durant St.* ☎ *970/920–4600* 🌐 *www.thelittlenell.com.*

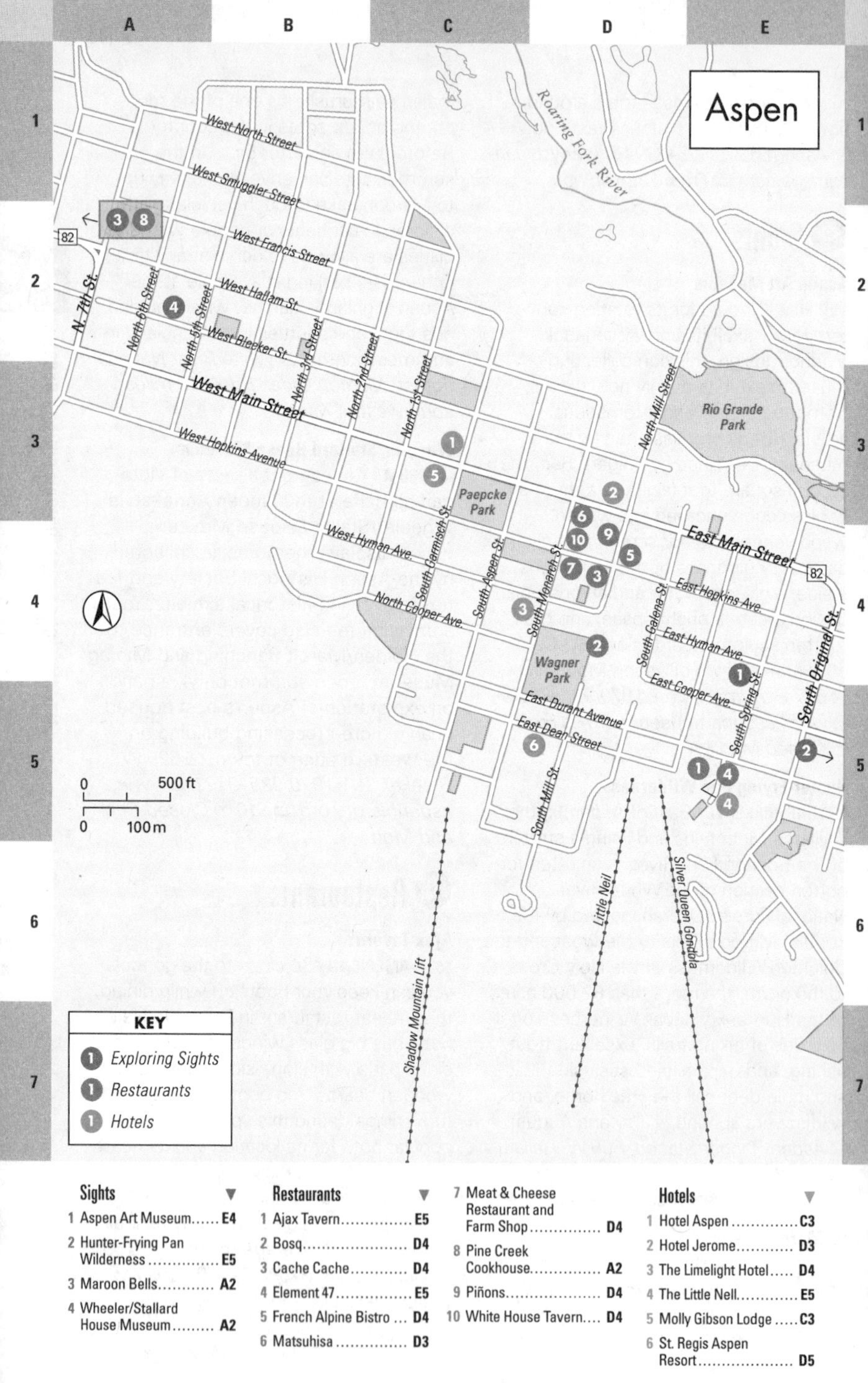

Sights

1 Aspen Art Museum...... E4
2 Hunter-Frying Pan Wilderness E5
3 Maroon Bells........... A2
4 Wheeler/Stallard House Museum......... A2

Restaurants

1 Ajax Tavern............... E5
2 Bosq...................... D4
3 Cache Cache........... D4
4 Element 47.............. E5
5 French Alpine Bistro ... D4
6 Matsuhisa D3
7 Meat & Cheese Restaurant and Farm Shop.............. D4
8 Pine Creek Cookhouse.............. A2
9 Piñons.................... D4
10 White House Tavern.... D4

Hotels

1 Hotel Aspen C3
2 Hotel Jerome............ D3
3 The Limelight Hotel..... D4
4 The Little Nell............ E5
5 Molly Gibson Lodge C3
6 St. Regis Aspen Resort..................... D5

At the base of the Maroon Bells is the lovely Maroon Lake, which attracts lots of wildlife.

★ Bosq

$$$$ | **AMERICAN** | The dining room at Bosq is small and intimate with a rustic-chic setting that's bright in the daytime and dimly lit for a romantic experience at night. The food is equally impressive, melding root vegetables and local meats and fish with bold, and sometimes spicy, surprises like sweet-and-sour eggplant. **Known for:** Peking duck; romantic dining room; lively patio scene. *Average main: $42 ✉ 312 S. Mill St. ☎ 970/710–7299 🌐 www.bosqaspen.com.*

Cache Cache

$$$$ | **MODERN AMERICAN** | With a focus on locally raised meats, Cache Cache brings a Continental influence to sophisticated yet filling entrées that are served on the patio or in the dimly lit room, with its white tablecloths and black chairs. In warmer months, the chic bistro's vegetable accompaniments reflect whatever is freshest from area farms. **Known for:** excellent wine selection; Russian caviar; sensational rotisserie items and desserts. *Average main: $38 ✉ 205 S. Mill St. ☎ 970/925–3835 🌐 www.cachecache.com ⏲ No lunch.*

★ Element 47

$$$$ | **MODERN AMERICAN** | Aspen's elite book tables at this swanky, highly regarded restaurant in The Little Nell hotel not only for the beautifully presented entrées but also for the glass, ceiling-height wine cases stocked by knowledgeable sommeliers who also make tableside recommendations. The seasonal menu highlights locally sourced produce and game, as well as meat raised on Colorado ranches. **Known for:** 20,000-plus bottle wine cellar; local Wagyu beef and rack of lamb; impeccable service. *Average main: $40 ✉ 675 E. Durant Ave. ☎ 970/920–6330 🌐 www.element47aspen.com.*

★ French Alpine Bistro

$$$$ | **FRENCH** | Candlelight makes this bistro romantic, and decorative items such as fur pelts, wooden skis, and European antiques evoke the Swiss chalet where owner and retired pro skier, Raphael Derly, vacationed as a child. The divine, prix-fixe, seasonal menu—with such traditional dishes as escargots, foie gras, boeuf bourguignon, and dessert crepes—is a nod to Derly's upbringing in the south of France. **Known for:** intimate ambience; excellent wine selection; decadent French cuisine. *Average main: $120* *400 E. Hopkins Ave.* *970/925–1566* *www.frenchalpinebistro.com* *No lunch.*

Matsuhisa

$$$$ | **JAPANESE** | Although you shouldn't expect to see celebrity chef Nobu Matsuhisa in the kitchen of his hopping restaurant in an 1887 Victorian house with an elegant downstairs room and a more casual, limited-menu upstairs space, his recipes and techniques are unmistakable. Nobu's sushi rolls and his new-style sashimi are marvelous, his hot dishes delectable, and his prices astronomical. **Known for:** off-menu specialty sushi rolls; caviar-topped seafood tartare; spectacular sake selection. *Average main: $35* *303 E. Main St.* *970/544–6628* *www.matsuhisarestaurants.com/aspen* *No lunch.*

Meat & Cheese Restaurant and Farm Shop

$$ | **AMERICAN** | This shop is the perfect spot for grab-and-go lunches or for creating your own picnic lunch from an array of specialty meats, cheeses, seafood, and produce. The restaurant, with rustic wooden tables and vibrant painted flowers decorating the dark walls, features seasonal, locally sourced dishes made from scratch, with impressive charcuterie boards, sandwiches, and salads that occasionally have an Asian twist. **Known for:** seasonal charcuterie boards; specialty market; kombucha on draft. *Average main: $18* *319 E. Hopkins Ave.* *970/710–7120* *meatcheese.avalancheaspen.com.*

Pine Creek Cookhouse

$$$$ | **MODERN AMERICAN** | In winter, the only way to get to this homey log cabin with breathtaking views of the Elk Mountains is via snowshoe, cross-country ski, or horse-drawn sleigh. In summer, you can drive to the front door, but you should consider hiking here to compensate for the filling American alpine fare. **Known for:** floor-to-ceiling windows with views of the woods; wild game dishes; adventure activities. *Average main: $65* *12500 Castle Creek Rd.* *970/925–1044* *www.pinecreekcookhouse.com* *Closed Tues.*

Piñons

$$$$ | **MODERN AMERICAN** | The open, modern dining room at Piñons combines Old West touches (a rustic-wood decor and a faux-tin ceiling) with a contemporary menu that goes beyond American-style entrées by incorporating selections like sashimi tuna tacos and Russian caviar. The interior fills up fast, but you can eat at the bar, with its budget-friendly, two-course, prix-fixe menu. **Known for:** creative cocktail menu; impeccable service; caviar selection. *Average main: $40* *105 S. Mill St.* *970/920–2021* *www.pinons.net* *No lunch.*

White House Tavern

$$ | **AMERICAN** | The patio outside this cute, white, Victorian house in the heart of Aspen is a fun, lively place to see and be seen. Locals rave about the sandwiches here, and a great beer, wine, and cocktail menu makes the cozy wood-paneled interior perfect on chilly afternoons or evenings. **Known for:** crispy chicken sandwich with spicy slaw; signature margaritas; sceney patio. *Average main: $20* *302 E. Hopkins Ave.* *970/925-1007* *aspenwhitehouse.com.*

Hotel Aspen

$$$ | **HOTEL** | Just a few minutes from the mall and the mountain, this contemporary hotel on the town's main drag takes full advantage of the spectacular view, with huge windows covering its modern exterior. **Pros:** private ski lockers; free parking; hot tubs with mountain views

in some rooms. **Cons:** busy Main Street location; no restaurant; no spa or fitness center. *Rooms from: $208 110 W. Main St. 970/925–3441 www.hotelaspen.com 45 rooms Free Breakfast.*

★ Hotel Jerome

$$$$ | HOTEL | The luxurious Hotel Jerome, first opened in 1889, has an upbeat, private club–like decor that retains the stately hotel's historic integrity but gives it a sumptuous sheen. **Pros:** historic property with modern amenities; central location; top-notch service. **Cons:** small spa and fitness center; very expensive, with rates that do not include the resort fee; located on busy main drag. *Rooms from: $725 330 E. Main St. 970/920–1000, 800/367–7625 hotel-jerome.aubergeresorts.com 93 rooms No meals.*

The Limelight Hotel

$$$$ | HOTEL | FAMILY | This classic is perfect for families who want a taste of luxury without tip-heavy service (guest services such as bellhops are available upon request). **Pros:** family- and pet-friendly; downtown location; complimentary snowshoes. **Cons:** busy and loud, with constant lobby traffic in ski season; often fully booked in high season; self-parking in paid garage. *Rooms from: $450 355 S. Monarch St. 970/925–3025, 855/925–3025 www.limelighthotel.com 126 rooms Free Breakfast.*

★ The Little Nell

$$$$ | HOTEL | Right at the base of the gondola, Aspen's oldest ski-in ski-out hotel features luxurious, modern rooms and superior staff. **Pros:** best location in town; unmatched service; spacious rooms. **Cons:** expensive; difficult to get a room in high season; no spa. *Rooms from: $750 675 E. Durant Ave. 970/920–4600, 888/843–6355 www.thelittlenell.com 92 rooms No meals.*

Molly Gibson Lodge

$$$ | HOTEL | One of the only hotels in Aspen with traditional wood-burning fireplaces, the reasonably priced Molly Gibson feels and smells like a European ski lodge, and its stacks of freshly cut cedar and rustic furniture keep the hotel grounded. **Pros:** central downtown location; lovely outdoor pool area; plush bedding. **Cons:** hotel parking is limited; few rooms with patios; lacks amenities like fitness center and spa. *Rooms from: $229 101 W. Main St. 970/925–3434 www.mollygibson.com 53 rooms Free Breakfast.*

★ St. Regis Aspen Resort

$$$$ | HOTEL | The well-established St. Regis Aspen resembles a mountain chalet that's both stately and contemporary: the lobby and library have rich wood paneling and modern furnishings; the gray-and-brown guest rooms have hardwood floors and large, leather-frame beds; and the elegant bathrooms feature gray marble tile and polished silver fixtures. **Pros:** one of Aspen's most luxurious properties; close to the slopes; ultraposh spa. **Cons:** very expensive; only valet parking; difficult to get a room. *Rooms from: $1101 315 E. Dean St. 970/920–3300, 888/627–7198 www.stregisaspen.com 179 rooms No meals.*

Nightlife

BARS AND LOUNGES

Downtown's East Hyman Avenue is an ideal place for barhopping, with a cluster of nightspots sharing the same street address and additional options for drinking and dancing on the Hyman Avenue Mall.

Aspen Tap

BREWPUBS/BEER GARDENS | Home to Aspen Brewing Company, Aspen Tap serves a small menu of pub food, liquor, wine, and, of course, microbrews from the city's only brewery. The centrally located bar includes a patio that's great for people-watching and sipping an Ajax Pilsner.

✉ *121 S. Galena St.* ☎ *970/710–2461* 🌐 *www.aspenbrewingcompany.com.*

Eric's Bar

BARS/PUBS | Whiskey—and lots of it—is the claim to fame of Eric's Bar, a hip little watering hole that attracts a rowdy crowd. There's also a varied lineup of at least a dozen microbrews and other beers on tap. ✉ *315 E. Hyman Ave.* ☎ *970/920–6707* 🌐 *www.sucasaaspen.com/erics-bar.*

J-Bar

BARS/PUBS | You can't say you've seen Aspen until you've set foot in the historic Hotel Jerome's lively J-Bar, with its textured leather walls and decorative tin ceilings. The centerpiece is the wooden, original, (circa1889) bar, where the Aspen Crud, a bourbon milkshake, was invented during Prohibition. ✉ *Hotel Jerome, 330 E. Main St.* ☎ *970/920–1000* 🌐 *www.hoteljerome.com.*

MUSIC AND DANCE CLUBS

Belly Up Aspen

MUSIC CLUBS | This intimate, live-concert venue has hosted musical acts ranging from country-western legends to '80s rock bands to The Flaming Lips for crowds of just over 400. ✉ *450 S. Galena St.* ☎ *970/544–9800* 🌐 *www.bellyupaspen.com.*

Performing Arts

Jazz Aspen Snowmass

CONCERTS | In June and September, Jazz Aspen Snowmass hosts popular music festivals that feature world-class pop, rock, jazz, and country bands and musicians. JAS also partners with the town of Snowmass Village to bring free concerts to Fanny Hill on Thursday nights in summer. ✉ *Aspen* ☎ *970/920–4996* 🌐 *www.jazzaspensnowmass.org.*

Wheeler Opera House

CONCERTS | This intimate, historic performance hall hosts big-name classical, jazz, pop, and opera performers. Comedy shows and local musical-theater productions also take place here. ✉ *320 E. Hyman Ave.* ☎ *970/920–5770, 866/449–0464* 🌐 *www.wheeleroperahouse.com.*

Shopping

ART GALLERIES

Baldwin Gallery

ART GALLERIES | This modern gallery is the place to see and be seen at receptions for nationally known artists. ✉ *209 S. Galena St.* ☎ *970/920–9797* 🌐 *www.baldwingallery.com.*

Galerie Maximillian

ART GALLERIES | You can find 19th- and 20th-century prints, sculpture, and paintings here—including original Picassos and Chagalls. ✉ *602 E. Cooper Ave.* ☎ *970/925–6100* 🌐 *www.galeriemax.com.*

BOOKS

Explore Booksellers

BOOKS/STATIONERY | Located in a Victorian house, this independent store stocks more than 20,000 books in its multiple rooms and is especially strong in politics, travel, and literature. The upstairs, vegetarian-friendly Pyramid Bistro is the perfect place for a light meal or snack. ✉ *221 E. Main St.* ☎ *970/925–5336 bookstore, 970/925–5338 bistro* 🌐 *www.explorebooksellers.com.*

CLOTHES

Pitkin County Dry Goods

CLOTHING | Founded in 1969, Pitkin County Dry Goods may be one of Aspen's oldest clothing stores, but it carries contemporary, casual apparel for men and women, as well as fun and funky belts, scarves, and jewelry. ✉ *520 E. Cooper Ave.* ☎ *970/925–1681* 🌐 *www.pitkincountydrygoods.com.*

MARKETS

★ Aspen Saturday Market

OUTDOOR/FLEA/GREEN MARKETS | Show up in downtown Aspen any Saturday from mid-June to mid-October, and you can enjoy the Aspen Saturday Market, a sort of farmers' market–meets–arts fair. Tents cluster along the corner of Galena and Hopkins and then extend to the intersection of Hyman and Galena. Everything here is Colorado made (or grown), from pottery and paintings to peppers and peaches. Enjoy live music and ready-made foods to eat on the spot. ✉ *Aspen* 🌐 *www.aspen-saturdaymarket.com.*

SPORTING GOODS

Ute Mountaineer

SPORTING GOODS | This sporting-goods store sells and rents a variety of backcountry gear and also carries outdoor clothing and guidebooks. ✉ *210 S. Galena St.* ☎ *970/925–2849* 🌐 *www.utemountaineer.com.*

Activities

BACKCOUNTRY SKIING

Alfred A. Braun Hut System

SKIING/SNOWBOARDING | The Alfred A. Braun Hut System is one of Aspen's major backcountry networks, with seven huts that sleep 7 to 14 people located near the tree line in the Elk Mountains. They're open in winter only, and reservations for nonmembers can be made beginning in early May through the 10th Mountain Division Hut Association. Take the usual precautions, because the trails cover terrain that's prone to avalanche. ☎ *970/925–5775* 🌐 *www.huts.org* *From $250 for an entire cabin.*

Aspen Alpine Guides

SKIING/SNOWBOARDING | If you're unfamiliar with the hut system in Aspen or are inexperienced in backcountry travel, you should hire a guide. This is a highly reputable company for guiding services. The cost is from $545 per day. ✉ *Aspen* ☎ *970/925–6618* 🌐 *www.aspenalpine.com.*

10th Mountain Division Hut Association

SKIING/SNOWBOARDING | Named in honor of the U.S. Army's 10th Mountain Division, whose troops trained in the central Colorado mountains, this nonprofit organization maintains nearly three dozen backcountry huts, including a handful that are just a few miles from Aspen. You must be in good shape and have some backcountry skiing experience to reach the huts in winter. There is a fair amount of terrain along tree-lined trails, as well as a good bit of high-alpine ups and downs. Accommodations in the huts, which sleep 6 to 20 people vary, but you can count on mattresses and pillows, wood-burning stoves, and utensils for cooking. ✉ *1280 Ute Ave., Suite 21* ☎ *970/925–5775* 🌐 *www.huts.org* *From $37 per person per night; full huts from $270.*

DOWNHILL SKIING AND SNOWBOARDING

Aspen is really four ski areas rolled into one resort. Aspen Highlands, Aspen Mountain (Ajax, to locals), Buttermilk, and Snowmass can all be skied with the same ticket. Three are clustered close to downtown Aspen, but Snowmass is down the valley in Snowmass Village. A free shuttle system connects the four.

★ Aspen Highlands

SKIING/SNOWBOARDING | Locals' favorite Aspen Highlands is essentially one long ridge with trails dropping off either side, with thrilling descents at Golden Horn and Olympic Bowl and hike-in runs at Highland Bowl. The steep and often bumpy cluster of trails around Steeplechase and Highland Bowl makes this mountain one of the best places to be on a good-powder day. Aspen Highlands has a wide-open bowl called Thunder Bowl that's popular with intermediate skiers, as well as plenty of lower-mountain blue runs. The best overall downhill run is Highland Bowl. Besides the comparatively short lift lines and some heart-pounding runs, a highlight of Aspen Highlands is your first trip to the 12,392-foot summit. The view, which includes the Maroon Bells and Pyramid Peak, is the area's most dramatic and one of the best in the country. **Facilities:** 117 trails; 1,040 acres; 3,635-foot vertical drop; 5 lifts. ✉ *Maroon Creek Rd.* ☎ *970/925–1220, 800/525–6200* 🌐 *www.aspensnowmass.com* 🎫 *Lift ticket $179.*

Aspen Mountain

SKIING/SNOWBOARDING | Open since 1946, Aspen Mountain is a dream destination for mogul and steep skiers. Bell Mountain provides some of the best bump skiing anywhere, followed by Walsh's (also a favorite for snowboarders), Hyrup's, and Kristi's. Those wanting long cruisers head to the ridges or valleys: Ruthie's Run and International are the classics. There are no novice-level runs here: this is a resort where nearly half the trails are rated advanced or expert, and a black-diamond trail here might rank as a double black diamond elsewhere. The narrow ski area is laid out on a series of steep, unforgiving ridges with little room for error. Most skiers spend much of the morning on intermediate trails off the upper-mountain quad. Then they head for lunch on the deck of Bonnie's, the popular mid-mountain restaurant. After a big storm, there's snowcat skiing on the back side of the mountain. Many trails funnel into Spar Gulch, so it can be quite crowded late in the day. For an alternate route, head down the west side of the mountain below the Ruthie's chair, and take the road back to the main base area. **Facilities:** 76 trails; 675 acres; 3,267-foot vertical drop; 8 lifts. ✉ *E. Durant Ave.* ☎ *970/925–1220, 800/525–6200* 🌐 *www.aspensnowmass.com* 🎫 *Lift ticket $179.*

★ Buttermilk

SKIING/SNOWBOARDING | **FAMILY** | If you're looking for an escape from the hustle and bustle of Aspen, spend a day at Buttermilk—a family-friendly place where it's virtually impossible to get into trouble. Buttermilk is terrific for novices, intermediates, and freestylers, thanks to the superpipe and Buttermilk Park (which has more than 100 features). A low-key, lighthearted sort of place, it's an antidote to the kind of hotdogging you might encounter at Aspen Mountain. Red's Rover on West Buttermilk is a mellow long run for beginners, while Racer's Edge appeals to speed demons. Among the featured attractions is a hangout for children named The Hideout. The Tiehack section to the east, with sweeping views of Maroon Creek valley, has several advanced runs (though nothing truly expert). It also has superb powder, and the deep snow sticks around longer because many serious skiers overlook this mountain. Buttermilk's allure hasn't been lost on pros, however: it's the longtime host of the Winter X Games. **Facilities:** 44 trails; 470 acres; 2,030-foot vertical drop; 5 lifts. ✉ *W. Buttermilk Rd.* ☎ *970/925–1220, 800/525–6200* 🌐 *www.aspensnowmass.com* 🎫 *Lift ticket $179.*

When Do the Wildflowers Peak?

The Maroon Bells–Snowmass Wilderness Area southwest of Aspen is famed for dramatic cliffs and alpine meadows. The bloom will start first in the valleys and eventually climb above the 11,500-foot tree line. Most Colorado wildflowers reach their peak from just before the summer solstice until mid-July.

LESSONS AND PROGRAMS

Aspen Mountain Powder Tours

SKIING/SNOWBOARDING | This company provides access to 1,100 acres (or up to 12 untracked runs) on the back side of Aspen Mountain via a 12-person snowcat. Most of the backcountry terrain can be handled by confident intermediates, with about 10,000 vertical feet constituting a typical day's skiing. Reservations are required and should be made as early as possible beginning October 1. Full-day trips include a hearty lunch served in a cabin with a woodstove, snacks, wine, chair massages, two guides, and all the skiing you want. ✉ *Aspen* ☎ *970/920–0720* 🌐 *www.aspensnowmass.com* 🎫 *From $600.*

Aspen Skiing Company

SKIING/SNOWBOARDING | Aspen Skiing Company gives lessons at all four mountains. Full-day adult group lessons start at $248 for advance purchase; a private full-day lesson for up to five other people is another option. Beginner's Magic is a package for first-time adult skiers and snowboarders that includes a full-day lesson, lift ticket, and gear rental. Aspen Skiing Company also offers women-only clinics, children's lessons, and freestyle camps just for teens; check availability in advance. ✉ *Aspen* ☎ *970/925–1220, 800/525–6200* 🌐 *www.aspensnowmass.com* 🎫 *From $248.*

RENTALS

Numerous ski shops in Aspen rent equipment. Ski and snowboard rental packages start at around $60 per day and rise to $75 or more for the latest and greatest equipment. Reserve your gear online before you arrive in town to save 10%–20%. For convenience, consider ski-rental delivery to your hotel or condo.

Aspen Sports

SKIING/SNOWBOARDING | This sporting-goods store has a huge inventory of winter gear to choose from. There are three locations in Aspen and three in Snowmass. ✉ *408 E. Cooper Ave.* ☎ *970/925–6331* 🌐 *www.aspensports.com.*

Black Tie Ski Rentals

SKIING/SNOWBOARDING | Reserve your ski or snowboard package online or over the phone, and Black Tie Ski Rentals will deliver your gear directly to your condominium or hotel room. ✉ *Aspen* ☎ *970/925–8544, 800/925–8544* 🌐 *www.blacktieskis.com.*

Four Mountain Sports

SKIING/SNOWBOARDING | Owned by Aspen Skiing Company, Four Mountain Sports has an impressive inventory of ski and snowboard rental equipment and an equally impressive fleet of stores; there are nine locations, including one at the base of all four mountains. ✉ *520 E. Durant Ave.* ☎ *970/920–2337* 🌐 *www.aspensnowmass.com.*

EDUCATION CENTERS

Aspen Center for Environmental Studies *(ACES)*

HIKING/WALKING | **FAMILY** | Workshops run by this nonprofit environmental science education center range from what animals you might find on local trails to mushrooming. ACES naturalist guides offer snowshoe walks in winter or private guides on Aspen Mountain, at Snowmass, and in the historic ghost town of Ashcroft. Summer brings guided hikes in Aspen, Snowmass, and the Maroon Bells, as well as wild yoga and oodles of educational classes for kids, teens, and adults. Its Aspen location is a 25-acre nature preserve on Hallam Lake, but ACES also operates a working farm at Rock Bottom Ranch down-valley between Basalt and Carbondale. ✉ *100 Puppy Smith St.* ☎ *970/925–5756* 🌐 *www.aspennature.org.*

FISHING

★ Aspen Outfitting Company

FISHING | Friendly, expert guides lead rafting, horseback riding, and clay-target shooting adventures, but Aspen Outfitting Company, located inside the St. Regis Aspen, is best known for fly-fishing excursions that provide access to miles of private land just outside of town. Trips include boots and waders, but fish are not guaranteed—they call it fishing, not catching, after all. ✉ *315 E. Dean St.* ☎ *970/925–3406* 🌐 *aspenoutfitting.com* 🎫 *Fly-fishing trips from $325.*

Aspen Trout Guides

FISHING | This company, which is in the Hamilton Sports Shop, runs guided fly-fishing tours of local waterways in Aspen. Half-day trips start at $250. ✉ *520 E. Durant Ave.* ☎ *970/379–7963* 🌐 *aspentroutguides.com.*

Roaring Fork River

FISHING | Fast, deep, and uninterrupted by dams from its headwaters to its junction with the Colorado, the Roaring Fork River is one of the last free-flowing rivers in the state. The healthy populations of rainbow and brown trout—of the hefty, 12- to 18-inch variety—make the Roaring Fork a favorite with anglers. From the headwaters at Independence Pass to within 3 miles of Aspen, most of the river access is on public lands and is best fished in summer and early fall. Downstream from Aspen, the river crosses through a checkerboard pattern of private and public land; it's fishable year-round. 🌐 *cpw.state.co.us/thingstodo/Pages/Fishing.aspx.*

GOLF

Aspen Golf Club

GOLF | Water is featured on nearly every hole at this 18-hole championship course with long greens and views of the Rocky Mountains. Designed by Frank Hummel, Aspen Golf Club is a challenging, parkland-style, municipal course only 2 miles from downtown. The course has a pro shop and a full-service restaurant and bar. It closes December through March and April, depending on the weather. ✉ *39551 Hwy. 82* ☎ *970/429–1949* 🌐 *www.aspengolf.com* 💵 *$68–$104 for 9 holes; $69–$170 for 18 holes* 🏌 *18 holes, 7114 yards, par 71.*

HIKING

Cathedral Lake

HIKING/WALKING | You taste several ecozones as you tackle Cathedral Lake, a 5½-mile round-trip trail. The popular day hike starts gently in aspen and pine groves but has a long, steep climb into a high valley above the tree line. Another series of steep, short switchbacks ascends a headwall, followed by a scree field. From there it's a short walk to a shallow alpine lake cupped by a wall of granite cliffs. In mid-July, the meadows surrounding the lake are colored with blooming wildflowers. You can call the Aspen Ranger Station for additional hiking information and conditions. ✉ *Castle Creek Rd.* ☎ *970/925–3445.*

★ Maroon Bells–Snowmass Wilderness Area

HIKING/WALKING | Aspen excels at high-altitude scenery (seven of the state's Fourteeners are in the Elk Mountains), and nowhere is the iconic image of the Colorado Rockies more breathtaking than in the Maroon Bells–Snowmass Wilderness Area. In summer, shuttle buses take visitors up Maroon Creek Road to the base of the Maroon Bells from 8 am until 5 pm (vehicles with children in car seats or people with disabilities are always permitted). Private cars are allowed at all other times and pay a $10 recreational fee. More ambitious sightseers can select from a number of hiking trails. You can get recommendations based on your ability level from the friendly forest rangers at the Aspen Ranger District office on the west side of town. ✉ *Aspen Ranger District, 806 W. Hallam St.* ☎ *970/925–3319* 🌐 *www.fs.usda.gov/recarea/whiteriver/recarea/?recid=82346.*

HORSEBACK RIDING

Maroon Bells Guide & Outfitters

HORSEBACK RIDING | For day or overnight horseback tours into the spectacular Maroon Bells, try Maroon Bells Guide & Outfitters. Two-hour dinner rides (from $195) culminate with steak or lobster prepared over a campfire. ✉ *3133 Maroon Creek Rd.* ☎ *970/920–4677* 🌐 *www.maroonbellsaspen.com.*

ICE-SKATING

CP Burger Ice Rink

ICE SKATING | For outdoor ice-skating, try this good-size rink across the street from the Rubey Park bus station downtown. Skate rentals are available. In the summer, the rink is transformed into a mini-golf course. Make time for a tasty treat at CP Burger on the rink, which offers burgers, fries, and milkshakes. ✉ *433 E. Durant Ave.* ☎ *970/925–3056* 🌐 *www.cpburger.com.*

KAYAKING

Aspen Kayak & SUP Academy

KAYAKING | Longtime Aspen paddler Charlie MacArthur runs the Aspen Kayak & SUP Academy, where you can learn to roll and drop in on a wave in a kayak. You can also sample stand-up paddling. Group clinics start at $105, and private lessons are $365. ✉ *315 Oak Ln.* ☎ *970/618–2295* 🌐 *www.aspenkayakacademy.com.*

MOUNTAIN BIKING

Aspen Sports

BICYCLING | This store has a wide selection of rental bikes, as well as trail-a-bikes and trailers for kids. ✉ *408 E. Cooper Ave.* ☎ *877/945–7386* 🌐 *www.aspensports.com.*

Hub of Aspen

BICYCLING | Here you can rent high-performance mountain and road bikes and get tips on the best rides in the valley from the passionate local staffers. ✉ *616 E. Hyman Ave.* ☎ *970/925–7970* 🌐 *www.hubofaspen.com.*

RAFTING

Blazing Adventures

WHITE-WATER RAFTING | For the truly adventurous, Blazing Adventures runs mild to wild rafting excursions (prices start at $103) on the Roaring Fork, Colorado, and Arkansas rivers. This outfitter also offers hiking, biking, and Jeep tours. ✉ *555 E. Durant Ave.* ☎ *970/923–4544, 800/282–7238* 🌐 *www.blazingadventures.com.*

SPAS

★ Remède Spa at St. Regis Aspen Resort

SPA/BEAUTY | Be sure to arrive early at Remède Spa to enjoy the extensive amenities here: a co-ed confluence waterfall pool (bring a bathing suit), plus a soothing eucalyptus steam cave, a hot soaking tub, and a cool plunge pool. The customized massage includes aromatherapy, a warm paraffin foot wrap, and a scalp massage on a heated table. Afterward, snuggle under a chenille throw on a chaise in a dimly lit room, where you can breathe pure oxygen through a cannula while sipping champagne. ✉ *315 E. Dean St.* ☎ *970/429–9650* 🌐 *www.stregisaspen.com* ☞ *$250 60-min massage. Hot tubs, nail salon, sauna, steam. Gym with: Cardiovascular machines, free weights, weight-training equipment. Services: Aromatherapy, body wraps, body scrubs, facials, massage, waxing.*

TRACK SKIING

Ashcroft Ski Touring

SKIING/SNOWBOARDING | About 12 miles from Aspen, Ashcroft Ski Touring is sequestered in the high-alpine Castle Creek Valley. The 21 miles of groomed trails are surrounded by the high peaks of the Maroon Bells–Snowmass Wilderness, and a novice section passes by the old ghost town of Ashcroft. Rental gear and guided tours are available. ✉ *11399 Castle Creek Rd.* ☎ *970/925–1044* 🌐 *www.pinecreekcookhouse.com/ashcroft-adventures.*

Aspen Cross-Country Center

SKIING/SNOWBOARDING | Lessons and rentals for track skiing are offered at the center, which acts as a hub for nearly 60 miles of trails maintained by the Aspen/Snowmass Nordic Council. Subsidized by local taxes, the trails are free, making this one of the largest free, groomed, Nordic-trail systems in North America. For a longer ski, try the Owl Creek Trail, connecting the Aspen Cross-Country Center trails with the Snowmass Club trail system. More than 10 miles long, the trail leads through some lovely scenery. Diagonal, skating, and racing setups are available for a fee. ✉ *39551 Hwy. 82* ☎ *970/925–2145* 🌐 *www.aspennordic.com/trails/aspen-cross-country-center.*

Snowmass

9 miles northwest of Aspen via Hwy. 82.

One of four ski mountains operated by Aspen Skiing Company, and one of the best intermediate hills in the country, Snowmass Village has more ski-in ski-out lodgings and a slower pace than Aspen. Snowmass was built in 1967 as Aspen's answer to Vail—a ski-specific resort—and although it has never quite matched Vail's panache or popularity, it has gained stature with age, finding its identity as a resort destination with year-round community activities that inject a village feel.

GETTING HERE AND AROUND

Heading east along Highway 82 toward Aspen, you'll spot the turnoffs (Brush Creek and Owl Creek Roads) to the Snowmass ski area. Snowmass is best navigated with your own car or the free Village Shuttle system. All parking in Snowmass is free during the summer, but there's usually a fee in the winter season.

WHEN TO GO

Snowmass Village is a year-round resort, though the peak times are June through September for hiking and biking and November through April for skiing.

Sights

Treehouse Kids' Adventure Center
LOCAL SPORTS | FAMILY | Interactive, age-appropriate play areas for young children and a full menu of activities for older children and teens make the Treehouse Kids' Adventure Center in the Snowmass Base Village a good headquarters for family fun. Summer camp activities include mountain biking, skateboarding, and mountain boarding. When winter comes, the center serves as an upbeat base camp for ski lessons. ✉ *40 Carriage Way, Snowmass Village* ☎ *970/923–8733* 🌐 *www.aspensnowmass.com/plan-your-stay/kids-programs-child-care.*

Restaurants

New Belgium Ranger Station
$ | **AMERICAN** | It's best to arrive when this place opens for lunch on sunny winter days, since the light-wood tables at this tiny, casual, slope-side restaurant fill up fast with hungry skiers. Patrons squeeze in for soft pretzel rolls with dipping sauces, sandwiches, and snacks, as well as the several beers on tap from Fort Collins–based New Belgium Brewing. **Known for:** Colorado-brewed beer; beer-and-cheese fondue sauce and hazelnut cocoa spread; chili nachos. *Average main: $10* ✉ *100 Elbert Ln., M-115, Snowmass Village* ☎ *970/236–6277* 🌐 *www.rangerstation.org* *No credit cards.*

★ TORO Kitchen & Lounge
$$$$ | **LATIN AMERICAN** | Inside the Viceroy Snowmass hotel, TORO warms up the night after a day of skiing with its craft cocktails, Latin American cuisine, and dining room decorated with wood accents and a fireplace with nearby couches that are the perfect spots for sipping drinks. This spacious restaurant has a daring menu focusing on creative seafood and chops; spicy, smoky flavors pop in many dishes, with milder options for those who can't take the heat. **Known for:** grilled Spanish octopus; chipotle-miso Alaskan black cod; spectacular views of Snowmass. *Average main: $36* ✉ *Viceroy Snowmass, 130 Wood Rd., Snowmass Village* ☎ *970/923–8008* 🌐 *www.viceroyhotelsandresorts.com/en/snowmass/dining_and_nightlife/toro.*

Hotels

Stonebridge Inn
$$$ | **HOTEL** | Slightly removed from the busy Snowmass Village Mall, this hotel has a lobby and bar that are streamlined and elegant—with mood lighting, art that reflects the region's ski history, and rustic lodge furniture—as well as contemporary mountain-style rooms that have rough-hewn paneling, rustic

wooden furnishings, and stone-colored fabrics. **Pros:** quiet location; good on-site restaurant; bus stop outside. **Cons:** not ski-in ski-out; minimal service; small fitness center. *Rooms from: $295* *300 Carriage Way, Snowmass Village* *970/923–2420, 866/939–2471* *www.destinationhotels.com/stonebridge-inn* *90 rooms* *No meals.*

★ Viceroy Snowmass

$$$$ | HOTEL | Perched like a palace atop the hill at the base of the slopes and overlooking the Roaring Fork Valley, the Viceroy Snowmass is the undisputed king of the village in terms of luxury, service, and location. **Pros:** ski-in ski-out; stellar spa; ski valet. **Cons:** a short walk or gondola ride to the main village; small gym; often busy with visitors to the spa and restaurant. *Rooms from: $599* *130 Wood Rd., Snowmass Village* *970/923–8000, 888/235–7577* *www.viceroyhotelsandresorts.com/snowmass* *168 rooms* *No meals.*

The Westin Snowmass Resort

$$$ | HOTEL | FAMILY | The modern, airy Westin has the best location in Snowmass, right on top of Fanny Hill. **Pros:** ski-in ski-out; on-site gourmet restaurant; big, year-round outdoor pool area. **Cons:** no-frills spa; outdoor furniture worn and dated; small balconies. *Rooms from: $299* *100 Elbert Ln., Snowmass Village* *970/923–8200* *www.westinsnowmass.com* *254 rooms* *No meals.*

Nightlife

Venga Venga Cantina & Tequila Bar

BARS/PUBS | A huge patio with warming firepits makes this casual bar and restaurant a prime après-ski location at the edge of the Snowmass Village Mall and the ski hill. Look for happy-hour specials and dozens of tequilas and mezcals to sample into the night. *105 Daly La., Snowmass Village* *970/923–7777* *www.eatvengavenga.com.*

Shopping

Anderson Ranch Arts Center

ART GALLERIES | Pottery, jewelry, and art supplies are sold at ArtWorks, the museum-style gift shop at the Anderson Ranch Arts Center. The center also hosts visiting artists, summer workshops, and art sales. The on-site Cafe Konbini serves grab-and-go noodle bowls and specialty teas inspired by the offerings at Japanese convenience stores. *5263 Owl Creek Rd., Snowmass Village* *970/923–3181* *www.andersonranch.org.*

Activities

DOWNHILL SKIING AND SNOWBOARDING

★ Snowmass

SKIING/SNOWBOARDING | This sprawling ski area is the biggest of the four Aspen-area mountains (Aspen Highlands, Aspen Mountain, Buttermilk, and Snowmass), all of which are connected by a free shuttle system and can be skied with the same ticket. Snowmass includes shops and restaurants, the Elk Camp Gondola, and The Lost Forest activity center. There are six major chairlifts: Elk Camp, High Alpine–Alpine Springs, Big Burn, Sam's Knob, Two Creeks, and Campground. Except for the last two, all these sectors funnel into the pedestrian mall at the base. Snowmass is probably best known for Big Burn, itself a great sprawl of wide-open, intermediate skiing. Experts head to such areas as Hanging Valley Wall and the Cirque for the best turns. For powder stashes among the trees, head to the glades on Burnt Mountain (to the east of Longshot), Hanging Valley, Sneaky's, and Powerline.

At Snowmass nearly 50% of the skiable acres are designated for intermediate-level skiers. The novice and beginning-intermediate terrain on the lower part of the mountain makes it a terrific place for younger children.

Snowmass offers great skiing and one of the most comprehensive snowboarding programs in the country.

Snowmass is four times the size of Aspen Mountain and has triple the black- and double-black-diamond terrain, including several fearsomely precipitous gullies at Hanging Valley. Although only 30% of the terrain is rated expert, this huge mountain has enough difficult runs, including the challenging Powderhorn and the more relaxed Sneaky's Run, to satisfy skilled skiers.

This mountain has one of the most comprehensive snowboarding programs in the country, with the heart of the action in the Headwall Cirque. The terrain map points out the snowboard-friendly trails and terrain parks while steering riders away from flat spots. You'll want to visit Snowmass Park's halfpipe in the Coney Glade area, also known as Makaha Park. **Facilities:** 98 trails; 3,339 acres; 4,406-foot vertical drop; 23 lifts. ✉ *West of Aspen via Brush Creek Rd. or Owl Creek Rd., Snowmass Village* ☎ *970/925–1220, 800/525–6200* 🌐 *www.aspensnowmass.com* 🎟 *Lift ticket $179.*

LESSONS AND PROGRAMS

Aspen Skiing Company

SKIING/SNOWBOARDING | The company runs a top-notch Ski & Snowboard School at Snowmass and Aspen's other mountains. ✉ *Lower Snowmass Village Mall, Snowmass Village* ☎ *970/925–1220, 800/525–6200* 🌐 *www.aspensnowmass.com.*

RENTALS

Numerous ski shops in Snowmass rent equipment. Ski and snowboard rental packages start at around $60 per day and rise to $75 or more for the latest and greatest equipment. Reserve your package online before you arrive in town to save 10%–20%. For convenience, consider ski-rental delivery to your hotel or condo.

Aspen Sports Westin

SKIING/SNOWBOARDING | This sporting-goods store is one of the best-known ski outfitters in Snowmass with three locations in the village, including one inside the Westin Snowmass Resort adjacent to the slopes of Fanny Hill. ✉ *100 Elbert La., Unit M1153, Snowmass Village* ☎ *970/923–6111* 🌐 *www.aspensports.com.*

Four Mountain Sports

SKIING/SNOWBOARDING | Owned by the Aspen Skiing Company, Four Mountain Sports has an impressive rental inventory of premium skis and snowboards and five locations in Snowmass village. ✉ *Snowmass Village Mall, 45 Village Sq., Snowmass Village* ☎ *970/920–2337* 🌐 *www.aspensnowmass.com.*

Incline Ski & Board Shop

SKIING/SNOWBOARDING | Locally owned and operated, Incline Ski & Board Shop is steps from the shuttle-bus stop. Staffers here know the mountains well and offer personalized recommendations based on snowfall and experience. ✉ *1 Village Mall, Snowmass Village* ☎ *800/314–3355* 🌐 *www.inclineski.com.*

MOUNTAIN BIKING

Four Mountain Sports

BICYCLING | Cruiser, street, mountain, downhill, and electric bikes are available along with trail maps and lift tickets so you won't have to ride uphill. For a small fee, you can opt for a one-way journey by dropping your equipment at one of the shop's four valley locations, Woody Creek Tavern, or Tipsy Trout. ✉ *61 Wood Rd., Snowmass Village* ☎ *970/923–0430* 🌐 *www.aspensnowmass.com.*

SPAS

The Spa at Viceroy Snowmass

SPA/BEAUTY | Combo treatments at The Spa at Viceroy Snowmass are dubbed "rituals" and are based on Nordic, Asian, and Ute Indian cultures. Massage or facial "journeys" are offered as well. No matter what your service is called at this (faux) candlelit spa, you'll begin the experience in a dramatic relaxation room. Here, an attendant pours warm water over your feet and dries them with a fluffy towel while you sip tea or champagne. After your treatment, you can soak in a mosaic-tiled hot tub with a waterfall in the locker rooms. ✉ *130 Wood Rd., Snowmass Village* ☎ *970/923–8000* 🌐 *www.viceroyhotelsandresorts.com/en/snowmass* ☞ *$195 60-min massage. Hair salon, hot tub. Gym with: Cardiovascular machines, free weights, weight-training equipment. Services: Aromatherapy, body wraps, body scrubs, facials, massage, Vichy shower, waxing.*

TRACK SKIING

Aspen Snowmass Nordic Trail System

SKIING/SNOWBOARDING | The Aspen Nordic Council maintains more than 60 miles of trails in the Roaring Fork Valley. Probably the most varied, in terms of scenery and terrain, is Trail 60 at the Snowmass Golf Course. For a longer ski, try the Owl Creek Trail, connecting the Snowmass Village trail system and the Aspen Cross-Country Center trails. More than 8 miles long, the trail provides both a good workout and a dose of woodsy beauty, with many ups and downs across meadows and aspen-gladed hillsides. You can take the bus back to Snowmass Village when you're finished. ✉ *Snowmass Village* ☎ *970/429–2039* 🌐 *www.aspennordic.com.*

Carbondale

30 miles northwest of Aspen and 15 miles northwest of Snowmass on Hwy. 82.

The artsy, outdoorsy town of Carbondale sits beneath Mount Sopris (12,965 feet), and its Main Street is lined with century-old brick buildings that house clothing boutiques, art galleries, and excellent restaurants. Locals gather there on the first Friday of every month for an outdoor block party that features music, street performers, artists' receptions, wine tastings, kids' activities, and more.

The paved Rio Grande recreation trail runs through town, and bicycles are the preferred method of commuting for many area employees. Otherwise you'll find Carbondale's fit residents hiking and mountain biking below Mount Sopris's twin summits, fly-fishing the Crystal River, kayaking, rafting, and tubing the Roaring Fork River, and Nordic skiing at Spring Gulch above town.

Restaurants

The Goat Restaurant

$$ | **AMERICAN** | At this lively dinner spot, which draws both foodies and the bar crowd, seasonal salads, pitas, pastas, and other options—from Mediterranean small-bites like hummus and feta to classic American burgers and sandwiches—are made from scratch. The warm wood accents and colorful dishes enhance the ambience, making this a favorite with locals and visitors alike. **Known for:** lively social scene; Med platter including dolmades, quinoa tabbouleh, and more; vegetarian options. *Average main: $16* *995 Cowen Dr., #103* *970/963–4628* *Closed Sun. and Mon.*

SILO

$ | **AMERICAN** | The small but well-prepared menu brings everyone to this small diner just far enough off the main road that it could be easily missed—but do stop for a breakfast burrito stuffed with seasonal veggies or French toast with berry compote. White walls; wooden, metal-ringed tables; and blue chairs create a casual dining area where the wood bartop and high stools are a favorite, though the tiny, outside eating area also fills up fast. **Known for:** casual atmosphere; duck eggs cooked to preference; nitro cold coffee. *Average main: $8* *1909 Dolores Way* *970/963–1909* *www.silocarbondale.com* *No dinner.*

Village Smithy

$ | **AMERICAN** | Locals flock to "the Smithy" for such beloved breakfast items (served daily from 7 am until 2 pm), as scrambles or traditional bacon and eggs. Vegetarians are taken care of with a tasty tofu scramble, fresh spinach and wild mushroom omelets, and deep-fried French toast. **Known for:** great seating on covered porch; locally sourced ingredients; seasonal pancakes. *Average main: $14* *26 S. 3rd St.* *970/963–9990* *www.villagesmithy.com* *No credit cards* *No dinner.*

Hotels

The Distillery Inn

$$$ | **HOTEL** | Sleep above the stills, in one of the spacious, soundproofed, modern rooms—all of which have local art, fireplaces, and large bathrooms with rain showers—atop the Marble Distilling Company. **Pros:** walking distance to Main Street galleries and dining; spacious, luxury bathrooms; free cocktails with your stay. **Cons:** few rooms can make it difficult to get a reservation; no traditional hotel amenities or front desk; busy location with bar customers coming in and out downstairs. *Rooms from: $289* *150 Main St.* *970/963–7008* *marbledistilling.com/the-inn* *5 rooms* *No meals.*

Nightlife

★ Marble Distilling Co.

BARS/PUBS | "Cocktails with a conscience" is the motto at this zero-waste craft distillery named for the famous pieces of marble, from the neighboring town of Marble, used in the filtering process. Stop in the distillery's Marble Bar (there's one in Aspen, too) for a creative cocktail featuring house-made vodka, rye whiskey, bourbon, coffee liqueur, or Gingercello, where fresh-cut ginger adds a twist to the Italian classic. *150 Main St.* *970/963–7008* *marbledistilling.com.*

Activities

BICYCLING

Aloha Mountain Cyclery

BICYCLING | This independent bike shop is the go-to location for year-round tune-ups and purchases, as well as rentals including street and mountain bikes. *580 Hwy. 133* *970/963–2500* *www.alohamountaincyclery.com.*

Located at the base of the mountain, Snowmass Village is a great place to rest after a day of skiing.

FISHING

Alpine Angling

FISHING | Come here for the gear you need to get fishing, including rods, reels, waders, and flies. The smart staff can recommend the best places for visitors to catch (and release) local trout, and the company offers lessons and guided trips. ✉ *995 Cowen Dr., Suite 102* ☎ *970/963–9245* 🌐 *alpineangling.com.*

GOLF

River Valley Ranch Golf Club

GOLF | Jay Moorish designed this course on the banks of the Crystal River. It has lots of water, a constant breeze, and superb—if not downright distracting—views of Mount Sopris. ✉ *303 River Valley Ranch Dr.* ☎ *970/963–3625* 🌐 *www.rvrgolf.com* 🎫 *$49–$60 for 9 holes; $49–$99 for 18 holes* 🏌 *18 holes, 6027 yards, par 72.*

Redstone and Marble

17 miles south of Carbondale via Hwy. 133.

About an hour's drive from Aspen, Redstone is ringed by the impressive sandstone cliffs from which the town draws its name. The entire town, now a National Historic District, was developed in 1902 for coal miners and their families; since the 1930s, it's been known as an artists' colony. Summer brings streams of visitors strolling the main drag, Redstone Boulevard, lined with shops and galleries. In winter, horse-drawn carriages or sleighs carry people along the snow-covered road. A few miles up Highway 133 from Redstone lies Marble, a sleepy town that attracts seekers of rural solitude who make it their summer residence and winter retreat.

GETTING HERE AND AROUND

The best way to reach Redstone and Marble is by car, both because the scenery demands plenty of stops and (more important) there isn't any public transportation available anyway.

WHEN TO GO

Redstone and Marble are popular destinations June through August for hiking in the nearby Elk Mountains and fly-fishing. From September to October, there is usually a brief autumn, which peaks with the blazing turning of the aspen trees. In the winter months, the area offers backcountry skiing and ice climbing.

Sights

Marble

HISTORIC SITE | This hamlet was incorporated in 1899 to serve workers of the Colorado Yule Marble Quarry, whose extraordinary stone graces the Lincoln Memorial and the Tomb of the Unknown Soldier in Washington, D.C. Walk the Marble Mill Park Trail to see remnants of the old marble-processing mill. Other historic sites include a two-story schoolhouse now used by the Marble Historical Society Museum, and a local charter school. Marble is also the gateway to one of Colorado's most-photographed places: the **Crystal Mill.** Set on a craggy cliff overlooking the river, the 1893 mill harkens back to the area's mining past; it's also the perfect place to enjoy a picnic lunch. You need a four-wheel-drive vehicle to get here in good weather (your feet will have to do on rainy days when the road isn't passable). *Marble.*

Restaurants

Slow Groovin' BBQ

$ | **BARBECUE** | A giant smoker sits in front of the two-story wooden structure, with rocking chairs on a large front porch and a line of picnic tables outside. Barbecue sandwiches and platters are what you would expect, served in heaping helpings and coated in messy, delicious sauces. **Known for:** man-eater sandwich with pulled pork and sausage; barbecue their way (they don't adhere to any regional standards); rotating Colorado beers on tap. *Average main: $13 101 W. First St., Marble 970/963–4090 www.slowgroovinbbq.com Closed Nov.–Apr.*

Hotels

Avalanche Ranch

$$ | **RENTAL** | The primary draw of these remote, individually decorated log cabins between Carbondale and Redstone is the three natural hot springs nearby. **Pros:** quiet, remote location; antiques and gift shop; easy access to outdoor adventure. **Cons:** no cell service; no a/c; no in-room TVs. *Rooms from: $190 12863 Hwy. 133, Redstone 970/963–2846 www.avalancheranch.com 13 cabins No meals.*

Crystal Dreams Bed & Breakfast and Spa

$$ | **B&B/INN** | Built in 1994 in the Redstone National Historic District, this three-story, Victorian-style house has charm along with the benefits of modern construction. **Pros:** beautiful views; romantic place for couples; impressive breakfast. **Cons:** cash only; no children under 12; additional charge for one-night stay. *Rooms from: $165 0475 Redstone Blvd., Redstone 970/963–8240 www.crystaldreamsgetaway.com No credit cards 2 rooms Free Breakfast.*

Shopping

Redstone Art Gallery

ART GALLERIES | Watercolor and oil paintings, photography, pottery, woodwork, and jewelry, mostly by Colorado artists, are on display at this gallery. There's also a sculpture garden in the backyard; a fanciful gift shop; and a roster of workshops, classes, and artists' receptions. Hours are limited October through May, so call ahead. *173 Redstone Blvd., Redstone 970/963–3790 www.redstoneart.com.*

Glenwood Springs

40 miles northwest of Aspen via Hwy. 82; 160 miles west of Denver via I–70.

Once upon a time, Glenwood Springs, the famed spa town that forms the western apex of a triangle with Vail and Aspen, was every bit as tony as those chic resorts are today, attracting a faithful legion of the pampered and privileged who came to enjoy the healing waters of the world's largest, outdoor, natural hot-springs pool, said to cure everything from acne to rheumatism. Today, the hot springs, adventure park, recreational activities, and local atmosphere appeal to families and outdoor enthusiasts looking for a fun, casual, and affordable base camp for exploring the valley.

GETTING HERE AND AROUND

The easiest way to arrive is by car on I–70, the main east–west highway in Colorado. Public transportation is more limited in Glenwood Springs than in Aspen, so you'll need a vehicle to explore much beyond the main street. In town, a pedestrian bridge and miles of paved trails along the Colorado River connect downtown restaurants and shopping with North Glenwood, home of the hot-springs pools and the historic Hotel Colorado.

WHEN TO GO

Glenwood Springs comes into its own in the early summer, when rafters, anglers, and spa patrons arrive to sample the attractions of the Colorado River and its underground mineral springs.

ESSENTIALS

VISITOR INFORMATION Glenwood Springs Visitor Center. ✉ *802 Grand Ave.* ☎ *970/945–6580* 🌐 *visitglenwood.com.*

Sights

Glenwood Canyon

CANYON | It took the Colorado River a half-billion years to carve the deep granite, limestone, and quartzite gullies—buff-tint walls brilliantly streaked with lavender, rose, and ivory—of this 16-mile-long canyon. Then, man stepped in, seeking a more direct route west. In 1992, the costly work on I–70 through the canyon east of Glenwood Springs was completed, with much of the expense attributable to the effort to preserve the landscape. When contractors blasted cliff faces, for example, they stained the exposed rock to simulate nature's weathering. Bike the canyon on a paved, riverside recreation path, or try to focus on fishing or rafting the river with views of the canyon walls towering above. ✉ *Glenwood Springs.*

Glenwood Caverns Adventure Park

AMUSEMENT PARK/WATER PARK | **FAMILY** | Glenwood Springs is home to the Historic Fairy Caves (now part of the adventure park), whose subterranean caverns, grottoes, and labyrinths are truly a marvel of nature—the area was touted as the "Eighth Wonder of the World" when it opened to the public in the 1890s. The still-amazing caves are easily accessible year-round via the Glenwood Gondola, which offers a bird's-eye view of downtown, the Colorado River, and surrounding mountains. Choose from two different 40-minute walking tours of the caves, or opt for the crawl-on-your-belly "Wild Tour" spelunking adventure. For a second helping of adrenaline, try the gravity-powered alpine coaster that drops 3,400 feet; plummet 110 feet underground on the Haunted Mine Drop; sail out over 1,300 feet above Glenwood Canyon on a giant swing; or ride a twisty roller coaster that overhangs a cliff. ✉ *51000 Two Rivers Plaza Rd.* ☎ *970/945–4228, 800/530–1635* 🌐 *www.glenwoodcaverns.com* 🎫 *$58.*

Did You Know?

One of the most beautiful ways to see Glenwood Canyon is via the Hanging Lake Trail, which takes you past a gorgeous lake with several waterfalls.

Glenwood Hot Springs

HOT SPRINGS | FAMILY | Even before the heyday of the adjacent Hotel Colorado, Western notables such as gunslinger Doc Holliday came to take advantage of the area's curative spring waters. The smaller pool at Glenwood Hot Springs is 100 feet long and maintained at 104°F. The larger is four times that size and contains more than a million gallons of constantly filtered water that is completely refilled every six hours and maintained at a soothing 90–93°F. Other facilities include a seasonal children's area with a splash pad, fountain, and waterslides; a stellar full-service spa; and a fitness center. ✉ *401 N. River St.* ☎ *970/947–2955, 800/537–7946* 🌐 *www.hotspringspool.com* 🎫 *$29.25.*

★ **Iron Mountain Hot Springs**

HOT SPRINGS | Newer and more relaxing than its famed sibling across town, Iron Mountain Hot Springs is geared to adults looking for a peaceful retreat. Sixteen mineral pools with views of the Colorado River and Mount Sopris are scattered across the hilltop; temperatures vary from 98°F to 108°F. A large family pool, heated to 94°F, encourages young children to stay out of the soaking spas, and soothing music drowns out much of the noise from the nearby kids' area. On-site bars offer a variety of beer and wine for sipping at the pools, and the contemporary locker rooms maintain the property's spalike atmosphere. ✉ *281 Centennial St.* ☎ *970/945–4766* 🌐 *www.ironmountainhotsprings.com* 🎫 *$28.*

Yampah Spa and Vapor Caves

HOT SPRINGS | Part of the Yampah Spa & Salon, the hot springs vapor caves are a series of three underground, geothermal steam baths. Mineral-filled water from a natural hot spring runs about 125°F under the floors of one of the few known natural vapor caves in North America, creating steam temperatures of 112–118°F within the rock chambers, where there are marble benches for you to sit on while you inhale the steam. Each successive chamber is hotter than the last, but you can take a break in an adjacent cooling room or the upstairs solarium when you need it. Spa treatments are also available, including massages, body wraps, and private mineral baths. ✉ *Yampah Spa & Salon, 709 E. 6th St.* ☎ *970/945–0667* 🌐 *www.yampahspa.com* 🎫 *$17 for caves, additional cost for treatments* ☞ *No children under 13.*

Restaurants

Co. Ranch House

$$ | AMERICAN | The Western-inspired, modern dining room with copper tabletops matches the hearty dishes at this centrally located spot with a patio just off the pedestrian walkway. The restaurant serves ranch-raised steaks, chops, and seafood, all of which you can wash down with specialty craft cocktails and microbrews. **Known for:** family-recipe strawberry shortcake in spring and summer; duck wings; elk burger with smoked mozzarella. $ *Average main: $22* ✉ *704 Grand Ave.* ☎ *970/945–9059* 🌐 *coranchhouse.com.*

Grind

$ | BURGER | The owners of this burger joint—a trendy dining room with exposed brick, bright-green seating, and animal drawings on the walls—grind their own beef, lamb, chicken, pork, and buffalo for exquisite gourmet patties. The focus is on locally raised, grass-fed meats and unusual toppings: try the Cordon Bleu chicken burger, or even a vegetarian option. **Known for:** the Hoggfather, with pork, pepperoni, and pizza dust; seared tuna burger; apple and pear side dish. $ *Average main: $10* ✉ *701 Grand Ave.* ☎ *970/230–9258* 💳 *No credit cards.*

Nepal Restaurant

$ | INDIAN | Colorful flags hang from the ceilings over the simple tables and chairs that surround a large fireplace at this little local-favorite eatery. Tucked into a

While it looks like a man-made swimming pool, Glenwood Springs is one of Colorado's best natural hot springs.

strip mall by the highway on the west side of town, it serves wonderfully tasty, authentic Nepalese, Tibetan, and Indian food: try fish *kawab* (marinated overnight and then baked in a tandoor) with a side of buttery *naan* (chewy flat bread). **Known for:** extensive lamb menu; eight kinds of house-made bread; extensive vegetarian options. *Average main: $13* *6824 Hwy. 82* *970/945–8803* *www.nepal-restaurant1999.com.*

The Pullman

$$ | **MODERN AMERICAN** | With its exposed redbrick walls, pendant lighting, loftlike high ceilings, and zinc-topped bar, The Pullman exudes a sophisticated, urban vibe at a location across the street from the Amtrak train station (thus, the name) in Glenwood's historic downtown area. This laid-back restaurant welcomes all types of casual diners with a contemporary American menu that specializes in steak and pork, though the salads and pasta dishes are excellent. **Known for:** the town's fine-dining preference; chicken liver pâté with fruit jam; seasonal meat dishes with decadent toppings. *Average main: $18* *330 7th St.* *970/230–9234* *www.thepullmangws.com* *No credit cards.*

Slope & Hatch

$ | **AMERICAN** | Mix and match tacos and hot dogs at this small, chill spot near the Roaring Fork River that attracts families and outdoor enthusiasts looking to refuel after their adventures. Tacos range from fried fish with pico de gallo to unexpected Asian flavors, and the local, natural casing dogs are equally enticing, including the Glenwood Completo with avocado and ancho remoulade. **Known for:** Carolina dog with pulled pork and chipotle barbecue; Thai veggie tacos; chorizo croquetas with Cajun gravy. *Average main: $9* *208 7th St.* *970/230–9652* *www.slopeandhatch.net.*

Smoke Modern BBQ

$ | **BARBECUE** | House-made bold and tangy, thick and sweet, and smoky and spicy sauces on every table add extra flavor to the traditional barbecue dishes, perfectly prepared in an open kitchen at this casual restaurant with neutral-hue booths, wood tables, and a wall of windows. The mustard sauce pairs perfectly with the smoked chicken wings, and Southern sides and unique cocktails complement the hearty entrées. **Known for:** lively atmosphere; large selection of whiskey and bourbon; pulled pork, brisket, and ribs. *Average main: $14* ✉ *713 Grand Ave.* ✣ *Under the bridge* ☎ *970/230–9796* 🌐 *www.smokemodernbbq.com.*

Hotels

Glenwood Hot Springs Lodge

$$$$ | **HOTEL** | **FAMILY** | Perfectly located, just steps from the Glenwood Hot Springs Pool (which is used to heat the property), the modern lodge has a comfortable lobby with leather chairs and couches and attractive guest rooms decorated in soothing blues, greens, and earth tones. **Pros:** right next to the hot springs; made-to-order breakfast; activity packages available at discounted rates. **Cons:** no restaurant or bar; breakfast is at next-door pool; guests still must walk outside to get to the pool. *Rooms from: $319* ✉ *415 E. 6th St.* ☎ *970/945–6571, 800/537–7946* 🌐 *www.hotspringspool.com* *107 rooms* *Free Breakfast.*

Hotel Colorado

$$ | **HOTEL** | The graceful sandstone colonnades, Italianate campaniles, and historic charm of this hotel dating from 1893 contributed to it being included on the National Register of Historic Places. **Pros:** one of the valley's most historic properties; across the street from the hot springs; courtyard seating at on-site bar and restaurant. **Cons:** no on-site spa or fitness center; some rooms are small; limited parking. *Rooms from: $159* ✉ *526 Pine St.* ☎ *970/945–6511, 800/544–3998* 🌐 *www.hotelcolorado.com* *131 rooms* *No meals.*

Hotel Denver

$$ | **HOTEL** | Right across from the train station, this historic downtown hotel has some rooms that look out on a three-story, New Orleans–style atrium, which is accented by colorful canopies. **Pros:** convenient downtown location; romantic atmosphere; on-site brewpub. **Cons:** no dedicated concierge; no room service; sparse amenities. *Rooms from: $139* ✉ *402 7th St.* ☎ *970/945–6565, 800/826–8820* 🌐 *www.thehoteldenver.com* *73 rooms* *No meals.*

Activities

BICYCLING

Glenwood Canyon Recreation Path

BICYCLING | A concrete trail sandwiched between the Colorado River and highway traffic, Glenwood Canyon Recreation Path runs about 16 miles from Dotsero southwest to Glenwood Springs through the spectacular depths of Glenwood Canyon. The path generally runs below and out of sight of the interstate, and the roar of the river drowns out the sound of traffic. It's closed in the winter months during heavy snow years and occasionally in the spring when water levels are high in the Colorado River. The Ute Trail—a single-track dirt trail—branches off the path, offering a detour at Dotsero for mountain bikers and hikers. Horseshoe Bend, nearly 2 miles from the Vapor Caves, is a perfect picnic spot, since the highway ducks out of sight. ✉ *Glenwood Springs* ✣ *Trailhead: enter path from either the Yampah Spa Hot Springs Vapor Caves in Glenwood Springs or farther east on I–70 at Grizzly Creek rest area.*

OUTFITTERS AND RENTALS

Canyon Bikes

BICYCLING | Canyon Bikes will shuttle you 14 miles up Glenwood Canyon. You can then enjoy the downhill bike ride on the paved Glenwood Canyon Recreation Path. Shuttle rides are $23 per person or $43 including bike rental. ✉ *152 W.*

Rafting the Roaring Fork Valley

The key to understanding white-water rafting is the rating system. Rivers are rated from Class I, with small waves where you really don't need to paddle to avoid anything, to Class VI, where a mistake can be fatal. To confuse matters, rivers often get more difficult when the water level is high (measured in cubic feet of water per second). May and June are peak rafting seasons for those who want the adrenaline rush of fighting spring runoff. By mid-August, many rivers are little more than lazy float trips.

The Roaring Fork, a free-flowing river (no dams), has several different sections that generally range from Class II to Class IV. Because it runs away from major highways through the heart of ranch country, you're liable to see more wildlife than on the Colorado. In June, your guides may point out a nest full of croaking bald eaglets while riding the Cemetery Rapids, a half-mile churning stretch of white water.

The portion of the mighty Colorado that runs through the steep, spectacular walls of Glenwood Canyon alongside I–70 includes the rough-and-tumble Shoshone section, considered Class IV during the peak runoff season, with aptly named rapids like Maneater and Baptism. The lower Colorado has some exciting stretches, too, including Maintenance Shack, a Class III rapid that can flip a large raft when the water is running high. By July and August, you can hit the same rapid sideways or backward and barely get wet. The lower stretches of the Colorado pass by several hidden, and not-so-hidden, shallow hot springs. If you'd like to warm up in them, ask your guides.

6th St. ☎ *970/945–8904, 877/945–6605* 🌐 *canyonbikes.com*.

Sunlight Ski and Bike Shop

BICYCLING | Downtown's Sunlight Ski and Bike Shop rents mountain and comfort bikes, as well as tandem bikes and tag-a-longs for young riders. ✉ *309 9th St.* ☎ *970/945–9425* 🌐 *www.sunlightmtn.com/ski-bike-shop*.

DOWNHILL SKIING AND SNOWBOARDING

Sunlight Mountain Resort

SKIING/SNOWBOARDING | Twenty-five minutes south of Glenwood Springs, Sunlight Mountain Resort is affordable Colorado skiing at its best. Overshadowed by world-class neighbors, the resort sees far less traffic than typical Colorado slopes. Fresh powder, typically skied off at Aspen within an hour, can last as long as two days here on classic downhill runs like Sun King and Beaujolais, and you'll rarely, if ever, stand in lines at the three lifts. A series of double-black steeps on the East Ridge includes three runs named Alligator Alleys for two-time Olympic skier Alice McKennis, who learned to ski at Sunlight. The varied terrain, sensational views, and lack of pretension make Sunlight a local favorite. Lift tickets and lessons cost a fraction of what they do at nearby Aspen, and every slope meets at the bottom base lodge. A terrain park for freestyling skiers and boarders features rails and boxes. For winter-sports enthusiasts who don't want to ride a chairlift, there's a 20-mile network of cross-country ski and snowshoe trails just off the slopes. Parking at the resort is free.

Half-day ski and snowboard lessons (including gear rental and lift ticket) for adults cost $125; full-day lessons are $145. The Children's Center offers lessons for children ages three to six. The resort also has ski-stay-swim packages at a number of Glenwood Springs hotels. The deal includes one night's lodging, a full-day lift ticket for adults, free skiing for kids 12 and under, and a full day at the Glenwood Hot Springs Pool. **Facilities:** 72 trails; 730 acres; 2,010-foot vertical drop; 3 lifts. ✉ *10901 County Rd. 117* ☎ *970/945–7491, 800/445–7931* 🌐 *www.sunlightmtn.com* 🎫 *Lift ticket $65.*

FISHING

Roaring Fork Anglers

FISHING | This shop conducts classes, leads wade and float trips throughout the area, and sells a variety of fly-fishing gear. ✉ *2205 Grand Ave.* ☎ *970/945–0180* 🌐 *alpineangling.com.*

RAFTING

Colorado River

WHITE-WATER RAFTING | When the ski season is over and Colorado's "white gold" starts to melt, many ski instructors swap their sticks for paddles and hit the mighty Colorado River for the spring and summer rafting seasons. Stomach-churning holes, chutes, and waves beckon adrenaline junkies, while calmer souls can revel in the shade of Glenwood Canyon's towering walls. ✉ *Glenwood Springs.*

OUTFITTERS

★ Blue Sky Adventures

WHITE-WATER RAFTING | **FAMILY** | At this outfitter, which shares a shop with Canyon Bikes, you can book a "Pedals & Paddles" package that includes a half-day raft trip with Blue Sky Adventures, followed by a bike rental. ✉ *152 W. 6th St.* ☎ *970/945–6605, 877/945–6605* 🌐 *www.blueskyadventure.com.*

Defiance Rafting Company

WHITE-WATER RAFTING | In addition to half- and full-day trips on the Colorado River, the company offers the "4 O'Clock Special," a late afternoon trip, and a "Raft & Zip Trip" that includes a zipline over the river. ✉ *1308 County Rd. 129* ☎ *970/404–3022* 🌐 *www.raftdefiance.com.*

Whitewater Rafting, LLC

WHITE-WATER RAFTING | The company's tours include the "Double Extreme Shoshone," where you run the area's most hair-raising rapids in a 12-foot, paddle-only raft—twice. ✉ *2000 Devereux Rd.* ☎ *970/945–8477, 800/993–7238* 🌐 *www.coloradowhitewaterrafting.com.*

SPAS

Spa of the Rockies at Glenwood Hot Springs

SPA/BEAUTY | Housed in a 19th-century, sandstone bathhouse at Glenwood Hot Springs, this sprawling, full-service spa pays tribute to the healing pools just outside its doors with a focus on mineral-based treatments. Soothing blues and dark wood decorate the lobby, product shop, and treatment areas. ✉ *415 E. 6th St.* ☎ *877/947–3331* 🌐 *www.spaoftherockies.com* ☞ *$135 60-min massage. Private baths, steam room. Services: Aromatherapy, body wraps, body scrubs, facials, massage, Vichy shower.*

Chapter 8

BOULDER AND NORTH CENTRAL COLORADO

Updated by
Aimee Heckel

Sights ★★★★☆ Restaurants ★★★★☆ Hotels ★★★☆☆ Shopping ★★★☆☆ Nightlife ★★★★★

WELCOME TO BOULDER AND NORTH CENTRAL COLORADO

TOP REASONS TO GO

★ **The arts:** Theater buffs have enjoyed the Colorado Shakespeare Festival's outdoor shows under the stars every summer since 1958, and music lovers engage their ears at the Colorado Music Festival's world-famous performances.

★ **Chautauqua Park:** You can still attend a lecture, silent film, or concert here much like visitors did over a century ago. This is one of Colorado's 25 National Historic Landmarks and the only chautauqua in the nation still running year-round.

★ **Hiking in and around Boulder:** Boulder's 150-plus miles of trails are packed on weekends year-round. The views are spectacular, especially when the wildflowers bloom in spring.

★ **The local breweries:** Basically the Napa Valley of craft beer, you could fill a whole vacation sampling the many award-winning ales, stouts, and lagers on offer.

Outside of Denver, Boulder and Fort Collins are the second and third most prominent cities in the region. Between these two energetic, outdoorsy university towns you'll find the sprawling cities of Loveland and Longmont and a few former coal-mining towns with homey, small-town character (like Louisville, Lafayette, and Erie). To the west are the proud, independent mountain hamlets of Lyons, Nederland, Ward, and Jamestown.

1 **Boulder.** The outdoor adventure capital of a state known for its outdoor adventures.

2 **Longmont.** One of Colorado's brewery hot spots.

3 **Nederland.** A quirky, laid-back mountain town.

4 **Lyons.** A historic small town with great festivals.

5 **Fort Collins.** A college town famous for its beer.

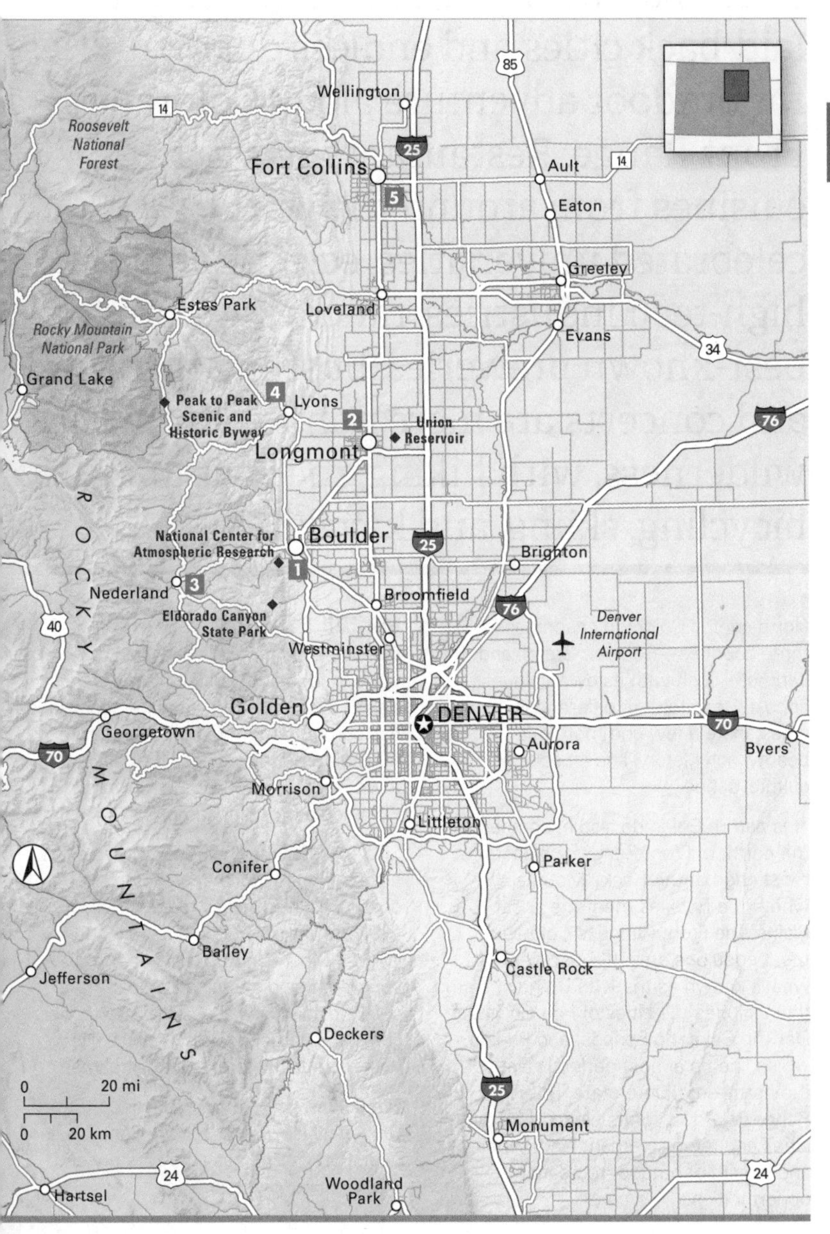
Wellington
Roosevelt National Forest
Fort Collins
Ault
Eaton
Greeley
Estes Park
Loveland
Evans
Rocky Mountain National Park
Grand Lake
Peak to Peak Scenic and Historic Byway
Lyons
Union Reservoir
Longmont
ROCKY MOUNTAINS
National Center for Atmospheric Research
Boulder
Brighton
Nederland
Broomfield
Eldorado Canyon State Park
Denver International Airport
Westminster
Golden
DENVER
Georgetown
Aurora
Byers
Morrison
Littleton
Conifer
Parker
Bailey
Castle Rock
Jefferson
Deckers
0 20 mi
0 20 km
Monument
Hartsel
Woodland Park
1
2
3
4
5
14
85
25
34
76
40
70
24

With spectacular scenery and an equally appealing climate, north central Colorado contains a string of sophisticated yet laid-back cities and endless opportunities for outdoor adventure along Colorado's Front Range. Restaurants serving cuisines from around the world, celebrated universities, eclectic shopping, high-tech industries, ranches, Colorado's best-known breweries, bustling nightlife, and concerts are mere minutes from the wilderness, with hiking, rock climbing, bicycling, skiing, and kayaking.

North central Colorado encompasses three counties—Boulder, Grand, and Larimer—each with its own unique appeal. Despite their differences, these areas share a few common traits: natural beauty, rich history, and an eclectic cultural scene.

This part of Colorado also encompasses the northern Front Range, the easternmost edge of the Rocky Mountains—where the Rockies meet the Great Plains. The Front Range is Colorado's most populous area. It's just west of what's known as the I–25 Corridor, a strip that includes the cities of Fort Collins, Denver, Colorado Springs, and Pueblo, which line up almost perfectly along the north–south interstate. The Front Range is known for its blend of historic cities and towns, verdant landscapes, and wealth of outdoor recreation opportunities.

MAJOR REGIONS

Boulder. Even though every conceivable trend in food and dining, alternative health care, education, and personal style has come through town, Boulder still feels untamed. It's also a lively college town—home to the scenic University of Colorado at Boulder campus.

Side Trips from Boulder. Boulder has a few neighboring towns that are interesting destinations in their own right, well worth a drive and a short stop if not a longer layover. Mountainous Nederland, artsy Longmont, and stunning Lyons all have quirky, distinctive (albeit small) downtown areas and gorgeous surroundings filled with mountains, forests, and streams.

Fort Collins. Famous for Colorado State University, as well as its open spaces and beer, Fort Collins has a rich history and vibrant cultural scene.

Planning

When to Go

Visiting the Front Range is pleasurable in any season. Winter in the urban corridor is generally mild, but can be cold and snowy in the mountainous regions. Snowfall along the Front Range is highest in spring, particularly March, making for excellent skiing but unpredictable driving and potentially lengthy delays. Spring is variable—75°F one day and a blizzard the next—and June can be hot or cool (or both). July typically ushers in high summer, which can last through September, although most 90°F-plus days occur in July and early August and at lower elevations. In the higher mountains, summer temperatures are generally 15°F–20°F cooler than in the urban corridor. Afternoon spring and summer thunderstorms can last 10 minutes or a few hours. Fall brings crisp sunny days and cool nights, some cold enough for frost in the mountains.

Art and music festivals start up in May and continue through September. With them comes an increase in visitor traffic. Spring and summer are typically the best times to fish or watch for wildlife.

Planning Your Time

You could pass a weekend or a month in this area and still leave stones unturned. At a minimum, spend a long weekend in Boulder, exploring the trails, eating and drinking to your heart's content, and people-watching along the Pearl Street Mall. If you have a bit more time, explore the nearby mountain towns of Nederland and Lyons for a few days. In both small towns, hiking trails will reward you with scenic views, alpine lakes, and wildlife, and the historical downtowns are lined with quirky businesses. Or you might venture east and north, respectively, from Boulder to the beer-loving cities of Longmont and Fort Collins, which both boast famous breweries with free tours. It's also easy to explore all these areas on a visit that includes nearby Rocky Mountain National Park.

Getting Here and Around

AIR

Denver International Airport, known to locals as DIA (although its official airport code is DEN), 23 miles northeast of downtown Denver, is the primary commercial passenger airport serving north central Colorado. Boulder and Fort Collins have municipal airports but no commercial service.

Boulder is approximately 45 miles (45 minutes to 1 hour) from Denver International Airport; Fort Collins approximately 70 miles (just over an hour); and Estes Park is about 75 miles (or 1½ hours).

Estes Park Shuttle (reservations essential) serves Estes Park and Rocky Mountain National Park from Denver, Denver International Airport, and Boulder. Groome Transportation serves Fort Collins and Boulder; Super Shuttle Express Ride Denver serves just the city.

AIRPORT CONTACTS Denver International Airport (DEN). ✉ *8500 Peña Blvd., Denver* ☎ *303/342–2000, 800/247–2336* 🌐 *www.flydenver.com.*

AIRPORT TRANSFER CONTACTS Estes Park Shuttle. ☎ *970/586–5151* 🌐 *www.estesparkshuttle.com.* **Groome Transportation.** ☎ *970/226–5533 Fort Collins, 303/997–0238 Boulder* 🌐 *www.groometransportation.com.* **Super Shuttle Express Ride Denver.** ☎ *800/258–3826* 🌐 *www.supershuttle.com.*

BUS

The expansive network of the Regional Transportation District (RTD) includes service from Denver and Denver International Airport to and within Boulder,

Lyons, Nederland, Longmont, and the Eldora Mountain Resort. The Hop bus (part of the RTD network) is a circulator that makes for easy carless travel within Boulder between the university, Boulder Junction, the Twenty Ninth Street shopping area, and the Pearl Street Mall.

CONTACTS Regional Transportation District (RTD). ☎ *303/299–6000, 800/366–7433* 🌐 *www.rtd-denver.com.*

CAR

Interstate 25, the most direct route from Denver to Fort Collins, is the north–south artery that connects the cities in the urban corridor along the Front Range. From Denver, U.S. 36 runs through Boulder, Lyons, and Estes Park to Rocky Mountain National Park. If you're driving directly to Fort Collins or Estes Park and Rocky Mountain National Park from Denver International Airport, take the E–470 tollway to I–25. U.S. 36 between Boulder and Estes Park is heavily traveled, while Highways 119, 72, and 7 have much less traffic.

Gasoline and service are available in all larger towns and cities in the region. Bicyclists are common except on arteries; state law gives them the same rights and holds them to the same obligations as those using any other vehicle. Expect a fair amount of road construction along the northern Front Range; arterial routes, state highways, and city streets are being rebuilt to accommodate increasing traffic in the urban corridor. Although the state plows roads regularly, a winter snowstorm can slow traffic and create wet, slushy, or icy conditions. Note that you can't always count on having cell-phone service in sparsely populated or mountainous areas.

CONTACTS Colorado Department of Transportation Road Information. ☎ *303/639–1111* 🌐 *www.codot.gov.* **Colorado State Patrol.** ☎ *303/239–4501, *277 from cell phone to report an aggressive driver* 🌐 *www.colorado.gov/csp.*

Parks and Recreation Areas

Rocky Mountain National Park is known for its scenery, hiking, wildlife-watching, camping, and snowshoeing.

North central Colorado has six state parks: Eldorado Canyon, Barr Lake, and St. Vrain, all close to Boulder; and Boyd Lake, State Forest, and Lory, all close to Fort Collins. In Boulder and Fort Collins you can literally walk out your door, up the street, and into the mountains or foothills on a hiking trail. There are also plenty of riparian trails and open-space paths within the city limits that can take you for miles; these trails usually have plenty of access points. The northern Front Range is home to a small downhill-ski area: Eldora Mountain Resort, 21 miles west of Boulder. You can access some trails in the Indian Peaks Wilderness from Nederland.

Restaurants

Thanks to the influx of people from around the world, there are plenty of dining options here. Restaurants in north central Colorado run the gamut from simple diners with tasty, homey basics to elegant establishments with extensive wine lists. The hot trend continues to be organic and sustainable ingredients, with many restaurants offering dishes made from local produce. Some restaurants take reservations, but many, particularly those in the middle price range, seat on a first-come, first-served basis.

Hotels

The area's ever-popular mountain B&Bs, vintage cabins, and luxurious resorts are places to escape after having fun outdoors. In some mountain hotels, high elevations keep the climate cool, which means no air-conditioning—but you really don't need it. The region also has plenty of chain hotels and some unique boutique lodgings.

Restaurant and hotel reviews have been shortened. For full information, visit Fodors.com. Restaurant prices are the average cost of a main course at dinner or, if dinner is not served, at lunch, excluding 5.75%–8.46% tax. Hotel prices are the lowest cost of a standard double room in high season, excluding service charges and 5.75%–12.40% tax.

What It Costs

$	$$	$$$	$$$$
RESTAURANTS			
under $15	$15–$22	$23–$30	over $30
HOTELS			
under $125	$125–$200	$201–$300	over $300

Boulder

No place in Colorado better epitomizes the state's outdoor mania than Boulder, where sunny weather keeps locals busy through all seasons. The bicycle count rivals the car tally in this uncommonly beautiful and beautifully uncommon city. Boulder has more than 150 miles of trails for hiking, walking, jogging, and bicycling.

One of Boulder's most endearing features is its setting. In 1960 Boulder citizens voted to start buying land surrounding the city to protect it from urban sprawl and preserve its historic and ecological resources. Residents started taxing themselves in 1967 in order to buy a greenbelt, and the city now owns more than 45,000 acres of open space—145,000 acres if you lump in lands owned and managed by Boulder County Parks & Open Space. This means that there's three times as much protected land surrounding the city as developed land. Even in winter, residents bicycle to work and jog on the open-space paths. It's practically a matter of civic pride to spend a lunch hour playing Frisbee, going on a bike ride with coworkers, hiking with the family dog, and even rock climbing on the Flatirons.

Boulder is also a brainy and artsy place. The city has one of the highest concentrations of software engineers and PhDs per capita, as well as one of the largest numbers of working artists per capita. The University of Colorado at Boulder and Naropa University are here. In addition, Boulder is home to a large number of tech companies and more than a dozen national laboratories, including the National Center for Atmospheric Research (NCAR) and the National Oceanic and Atmospheric Administration (NOAA).

GETTING ORIENTED

One of the best places to take a first look at this beautiful town is from the scenic overlook on Davidson Mesa (pull out at the scenic overlook on westbound U.S. 36, at the crest of the hill about 8 miles outside of town). In the distance are the craggy (and often snowcapped) peaks in Roosevelt National Forest, Indian Peaks Wilderness, and Rocky Mountain National Park. Closer by, to the southwest, are Bear Peak and the Devil's Thumb on its left slope, near the entrance to Eldorado Canyon. Just north of there are Green Mountain and the trademark red-sandstone Flatirons, which you can see from many vantage points in town. These massive rock upthrusts, named for their flat faces, are popular among rock climbers and hikers. To the east are flat plains, dotted with parks and reservoirs.

In town, the red-tile roofs of the University of Colorado dominate the landscape on University Hill ("the Hill"), just south of downtown. Boulder Creek courses along the south side of downtown, with a multiuse path alongside it. At the northeastern end of town is Boulder Reservoir, a 700-acre park used for swimming, rowing, kayaking, sailing, stand-up paddleboarding, windsurfing, and waterskiing.

GETTING HERE AND AROUND

Although a 10-minute walk separates downtown from the Hill, each area has a distinct flavor. Downtown—particularly the Pearl Street pedestrian mall—bustles with families, street performers, upscale boutiques, and eateries, while the Hill pulsates with trendy shops, packed coffeehouses, bars and rock clubs, and restaurants geared more to students. Parking and driving in these sections of Boulder can be frustrating and time-consuming. Leave your car at the hotel and try the Hop (🌐 *bouldercolorado.gov/hopbus*), a bus that circulates in both directions through downtown, the Twenty Ninth Street Mall, the CU Boulder campus, and Boulder Junction for $3 (cash) one way. Buses run every 10 to 30 minutes.

Both Boulder Custom Rides and zTrip provide private car service within Boulder.

For a quick trip, borrow a bike from B-cycle, Boulder's bike-sharing service, which has more than 300 bikes and more than 45 stations all over town. Download the free app, pick your pass, take a bike from one station, and return it to any other. The rate structure encourages trips of 30 minutes or less.

CONTACTS Boulder B-cycle. ☎ *303/532–4412* 🌐 *boulder.bcycle.com.* **Boulder Custom Rides.** ☎ *303/906–0250* 🌐 *www.bouldercoloradousa.com/listings/boulder-custom-rides/1974/.* **zTrip.** ☎ *303/699–8747* 🌐 *www.ztrip.com/boulder.*

TOURS

Banjo Billy's Bus Tours

BUS TOURS | The company offers tours around Boulder aboard a bus that has been retrofitted to look like a shack. The tour's lighthearted, quirky commentary focuses on ghosts, history, beer, and crime stories. Your seat may be a saddle, couch, or bench upholstered with funky, mismatched fabrics. ✉ *Boulder* ☎ *720/938–8885* 🌐 *www.banjobilly.com* 🎟 *From $24.*

Historic Boulder

WALKING TOURS | This nonprofit organization works to preserve historic places in Boulder and offers heritage education including walking tours, house tours, architecture tours, lectures, outreach, and special events. Call or stop by the Pearl Street office or pick up a Boulder Historic Neighborhoods map in the kiosk just east of 13th Street on the Pearl Street Mall. ✉ *1200 Pearl St., Suite 70* ☎ *303/444–5192* 🌐 *www.historicboulder.org* 🎟 *Free and up.*

VISITOR INFORMATION

CONTACTS Boulder Convention & Visitors Bureau. ✉ *2440 Pearl St.* ☎ *303/442–2911* 🌐 *www.bouldercoloradousa.com.*

WHEN TO GO

Like the rest of the Front Range, Boulder has beautiful weather year-round. The city definitely feels livelier when school is in session, especially on big football weekends. Summer weekends often bring big crowds of tourists (including day-trippers from Denver).

Boulder Creek Festival

FESTIVALS | **FAMILY** | Held each Memorial Day weekend since 1987, the Boulder Creek Festival converts a stretch along Boulder Creek into a giant party, complete with carnival rides, live music, hundreds of vendors, food, and multiple beer gardens. The festival runs between Arapahoe Avenue and Canyon Boulevard between 9th and 14th Streets. ✉ *Boulder* 🌐 *www.bouldercreekfest.com.*

Sights

Boulder Museum of Contemporary Art

MUSEUM | View local and worldwide contemporary art exhibits and performance art at this innovative museum with frequently changing exhibitions. Admission is free during the farmers' market, which takes place in front of the museum from May to November on Saturday 8 am–2 pm, and from May to October on Wednesday 4 pm–8 pm. The museum usually closes every quarter between exhibitions. ✉ *1750 13th St.* ☎ *303/443–2122* 🌐 *www.bmoca.org* 🎟 *$2 (free during farmers' market)* ⏲ *Closed Mon.*

Celestial Seasonings

TOUR—SIGHT | Spicy aromas greet you in the parking lot of Celestial Seasonings, North America's largest herbal-tea producer (the company seals 10 million tea bags daily). The factory offers free 45-minute tours that include a jolting trip into the famous "Mint Room," waking your senses and clearing your sinuses. Before the tour, check out original paintings of tea-box art and sample more than 80 varieties of tea. You can also grab a bite to eat at the on-site café. ✉ *4600 Sleepytime Dr.* ✢ *8 miles northeast of downtown Boulder. Take Hwy. 119 to Jay Rd., turn right. After about 1 mile, turn left onto Spine Rd. After about ½ mile, turn left onto Sleepytime Dr.* ☎ *303/530–5300* 🌐 *www.celestialseasonings.com* 🎟 *Free.*

★ Chautauqua Park

CITY PARK | For some of Boulder's prettiest views, follow Baseline Road west from Broadway to Chautauqua Park, nestled at the base of the Flatirons. Grab a picnic or ice cream cone at the General Store and relax on the lawn, or use the park as a launching point to 40 miles of hiking trails. Historic Chautauqua is also home to a tasty restaurant, the historic Chautauqua Dining Hall, open year-round for brunch and dinner. Or attend a lecture, silent film, or concert at the auditorium, which hosts the Colorado Music Festival and internationally renowned concerts every year. For a bird's-eye view of Boulder, keep going west on Baseline (which turns into Flagstaff Road) 1 mile to Panorama Point, and then 3½ miles to Realization Point. ✉ *Grant St. and Baseline Rd.* 🌐 *www.bouldercolorado.gov/parks-rec/chautauqua-park* 🎟 *Free.*

CU Heritage Center

MUSEUM | Seven galleries of campus history sweep you into exploring the past, present, and future of university achievements and traditions. Warp into space with CU's astronauts, and see an Apollo 15 moon rock; strut to the tunes of master swing conductor, Glenn Miller; challenge yourself to building a 1.5-million Lego brick model of the Boulder campus; and see if you can name the school's latest Olympians. ✉ *Old Main Bldg., 459 UCB, 3rd Fl.* ☎ *303/492–6329* 🌐 *www.cuheritage.org* 🎟 *Free* ⏲ *Closed Sun.*

★ Downtown Boulder Historic District

HISTORIC SITE | The late-19th- and early-20th-century commercial structures of the Downtown Boulder Historic District once housed mercantile stores and saloons, but today the stores here cater to modern tastes, with fair-trade coffees and Tibetan prayer flags. The period architecture—including Queen Anne, Italianate, and Romanesque styles in stone or brick—has been preserved. ✉ *Boulder* ✢ *Bounded by the south side of Spruce St. between 10th and 16th Sts., Pearl St. between 9th and 16th Sts., and the north side of Walnut St. between Broadway and 9th St.* 🌐 *historicboulder.org.*

Eldorado Canyon State Park

NATIONAL/STATE PARK | With steep canyon walls, a rushing creek, verdant pine forests, 10 picnic sites with multiple tables, and 12 miles of trails, this park attracts thrill-seekers and nature lovers alike. Rock climbers scale the sandstone walls, kayakers charge the rapids of South Boulder Creek (if stream flow allows), and anglers cast lines for brown and rainbow trout. The **Streamside Trail** parallels South Boulder Creek for ½ mile (wheelchair accessible for 300 feet). The 1-mile (one-way) **Fowler Trail** is wheelchair accessible, with interpretive signs and great views for climbers. For Continental Divide views, take the 3½-mile

Boulder
A
B
C
D
E
F
1
2
3
4
5
6
7
8
9
North Street
Dewey Avenue
Portland Place
Concord Avenue
Maxwell Avenue
Mapleton Avenue
Highland Avenue
Sunshine Canyon Dr.
4th Street
5th Street
6th St.
7th Street
8th Street
Broadway
13th Street
14th Street
15th Street
16th Street
17th Street
Mapleton Avenue
Pine Street
Pine Street
Spruce Street
Spruce Street
Pearl Street Mall
Pearl Street
Pearl Street
Walnut Street
Canyon Boulevard
Canyon Boulevard
Grove Street
119
Boulder Creek
Boulder Creek
Arapahoe Avenue
Arapahoe Avenue
Marine Street
Marine Street
Grandview Ave.
Broadway
5th Street
6th Street
7th Street
University Avenue
University Ave.
Pleasant Street
Pleasant St.
Pennsylvania Avenue
College Avenue
Euclid Avenue
8th Street
Grant Place
9th Street
Lincoln Pl.
10th Street
11th Street
12th Street
13th Street
14th Street
15th Street
15th Street
Aurora Avenue
Flagstaff Road
6th Street
7th Street
Cascade Avenue
Baseline Road
15th Street
KEY
Exploring Sights
Restaurants
Quick Bites
Hotels
0
1,000 ft
0
200 m

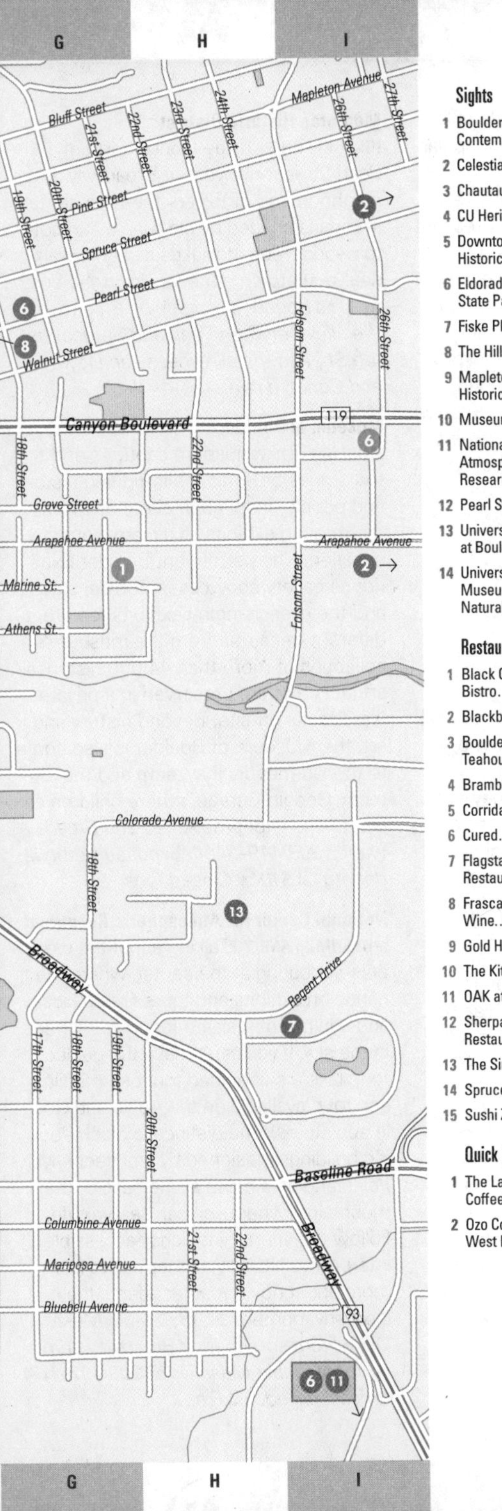

Sights

1 Boulder Museum of Contemporary Art....... E3
2 Celestial Seasonings.... I1
3 Chautauqua Park....... D8
4 CU Heritage Center...... F5
5 Downtown Boulder Historic District.......... E4
6 Eldorado Canyon State Park................ I9
7 Fiske Planetarium......... I7
8 The Hill.................... E6
9 Mapleton Historic District.......... F1
10 Museum of Boulder.... D2
11 National Center for Atmospheric Research.................. I9
12 Pearl Street.............. F2
13 University of Colorado at Boulder.............. H6
14 University of Colorado Museum of Natural History........... F6

Restaurants

1 Black Cat Farm to Table Bistro...................... E3
2 Blackbelly................ I4
3 Boulder Dushanbe Teahouse................. E3
4 Bramble & Hare.......... E3
5 Corrida.................. D3
6 Cured..................... G2
7 Flagstaff House Restaurant.............. A6
8 Frasca Food and Wine..................... G2
9 Gold Hill Inn............. A2
10 The Kitchen............. D3
11 OAK at fourteenth....... E3
12 Sherpa's Adventurers Restaurant & Bar....... D3
13 The Sink.................. F5
14 Spruce Farm & Fish..... E2
15 Sushi Zanmai............ E2

Quick Bites

1 The Laughing Goat Coffeehouse............. F2
2 Ozo Coffee West Pearl............... D3

Hotels

1 Basecamp Boulder Hotel........... G4
2 The Bradley Boulder Inn............... F2
3 Colorado Chautauqua............. D8
4 Foot of the Mountain Motel......... A4
5 Hotel Boulderado........ E2
6 Residence Inn by Marriott Boulder Canyon Boulevard........ I3
7 St Julien Hotel & Spa.............. D3

(round-trip) **Rattlesnake Gulch Trail,** which climbs 800 feet. Snowshoeing is popular here in winter. Mountain bikers crank on Rattlesnake Gulch Trail and the Walker Ranch Loop (accessed from the Crescent Meadows trailhead off Gross Dam Road). Hikers can climb the 3½-mile (one-way) **Eldorado Canyon Trail** to Crescent Meadows. The park is frequently at capacity on weekends and holidays, so weekday and evening visits are recommended. ✉ *9 Kneale Rd., Eldorado Springs* ✣ *Drive south on Broadway (Hwy. 93) 3 miles to Eldorado Canyon Dr. (Rte. 170); paved road ends at the village of Eldorado Springs. Drive through town to park entrance* ☎ *303/494–3943* 🌐 *cpw.state.co.us/placestogo/parks/EldoradoCanyon* 🎫 *$10 per vehicle.*

★ Fiske Planetarium

OBSERVATORY | This dome on the University of Colorado campus puts on planetarium shows and star talks, as well as laser shows choreographed to music by the likes of Pink Floyd, Bob Marley, and Queen. Showtimes vary somewhat, but generally laser shows take place on Thursday, Friday, and Saturday nights; and star shows are sprinkled throughout the week, including some family matinees. The planetarium hosts live talks on Thursday evenings. The Sommers–Bausch Observatory is open for free public viewing every Friday, weather permitting, when CU classes are in session. ✉ *2414 Regent Dr.* ☎ *303/492–5002* 🌐 *www.colorado.edu/fiske* 🎫 *$10.*

The Hill

NEIGHBORHOOD | Across Broadway from the University of Colorado campus is the Hill, a favorite student hangout. The neighborhood is home to restaurants, music venues, bars, coffeehouses, head shops, and boutiques. ✉ *Broadway and 13th St., between University Ave. and College Ave.*

Mapleton Historic District

HISTORIC SITE | Three blocks north of Pearl Street and west of Broadway, this neighborhood of turn-of-the-20th-century homes is shaded by old maple and cottonwood trees. It makes a scenic walk near downtown but away from the busy mall. ✉ *Bounded roughly by Broadway, the alley between Pearl and Spruce Sts., 4th St., and the alley between Dewey St. and Concord Ave.*

Museum of Boulder

MUSEUM | This museum captures and tells the stories of Boulder's intriguing history and people. Inspiration abounds, from the rotating exhibits to dynamic guest speakers. The permanent Boulder Experience gallery showcases Boulder's past, and the ever-changing exhibits feature different treasures from the museum's collection of more than 44,000 historical artifacts that are preserved in a private warehouse off-site. Beyond history and art, the Museum of Boulder is also home to the kid-friendly Playzeum and the techy Google Garage, where children can create and experiment. ✉ *2205 Broadway* ☎ *303/449–3464* 🌐 *museumofboulder.org* 🎫 *$10* 🕒 *Closed Tues.*

National Center for Atmospheric Research

MUSEUM | **FAMILY** | Talking about the weather is *not* boring at the center, where the hands-on exhibits and tours fire up kids' and adults' enthusiasm for what happens in the sky. If you can't make the guided tour, take a self-guided tour or a mobile app tour (available on the Apple and Google app stores). The distinctive blocky-looking buildings, designed by architect I. M. Pei, stand on a mesa at the base of the mountains, where you can see wildlife. Follow the short, wheelchair-accessible, interpretive NCAR Weather Trail to learn more about how weather affects the local environment. ✉ *1850 Table Mesa Dr.* ✣ *From southbound Broadway, turn right onto Table Mesa Dr.* ☎ *303/497–1174* 🌐 *ncar.ucar.edu* 🎫 *Free.*

One of Boulder's best places to gather is the pedestrian mall on Pearl Street.

★ Pearl Street

NEIGHBORHOOD | Between 8th and 20th Streets in the downtown area, Pearl Street is the city's hub, an eclectic collection of boutiques, bookstores, art galleries, cafés, bars, and restaurants. From 11th and 15th Streets is a pedestrian mall, with plenty of good people-watching and some of the most outrageous street performers you'll ever see. Regulars may include fire-eating contortionists, a man who plays the piano while hanging from his feet in a tree, and steampunk-style street bands. ✉ *Boulder* 🌐 *www.boulderdowntown.com.*

University of Colorado at Boulder

COLLEGE | The campus of the University of Colorado at Boulder began in 1876 with the construction of Old Main, which borders the Norlin Quadrangle, now on the National Register of Historic Places, a broad lawn where students hang out or play Frisbee between classes. The university's red sandstone buildings with tile roofs, built in the "Rural Italian" architectural style that Charles Z. Klauder created in the early 1920s, complement the campus's green lawns and small ponds. You can take a walking tour (reservations required) of the campus year-round. ✉ *University Memorial Center* ☎ *303/492–1411 CU main number, 303/492–6301 Admissions Office* 🌐 *www.colorado.edu/visit/admissions* 🎫 *Free tour.*

★ University of Colorado Museum of Natural History

MUSEUM | **FAMILY** | With more than 5 million objects, this museum is home to the largest natural history collection in the Rocky Mountain region. There are five galleries and a discovery corner for kids. Permanent and changing exhibits feature CU research, fossils, archaeological finds, dinosaur relics, plants, and invertebrates. Depending on your level of interest, you could spend anywhere from an hour to all day here. ✉ *Henderson Bldg., 15th and Broadway* ☎ *303/492–6892* 🌐 *www.colorado.edu/cumuseum* 🎫 *Free; $5 suggested donation.*

Restaurants

The variety of the restaurants here would be enviable in a city several times Boulder's size. Prices at the showier restaurants in town reflect their high quality and service, but because of the large student population many eateries offer up some excellent fare at more reasonable prices.

Black Cat Farm to Table Bistro

$$$$ | BISTRO | This intimate eatery delivers an authentic farm-to-table experience, with a French-influenced menu that changes daily, drawing from whatever the restaurant is harvesting from its 425-acre organic farm. Diners relax in leather couches at wall-side tables, with excellent views of the kitchen, while dining on options such as house-raised Tunis lamb and house-raised Mulefoot pork. **Known for:** excellent service; country's largest full-scale, farm-to-table operation—certified organic; wine pairings. *Average main: $34* *1964 13th St.* *303/444–5500* *www.blackcatboulder.com* *No lunch.*

★ Blackbelly

$$$ | AMERICAN | At the only independent restaurant in Boulder licensed to make and sell its own house-cured meats (you can see some in the windows), those seeking a sophisticated yet casual culinary experience away from downtown will delight in food known for farm-to-table freshness. Chef Hosea Rosenberg, a *Top Chef* winner, crafts a changing menu using ingredients from local farms and ranches. **Known for:** a hyper-seasonal menu that constantly changes; dry-aged beef, house-made sausages and salumi; seasonal pastas. *Average main: $26* *1606 Conestoga St., Unit 3* *303/247–1000* *www.blackbelly.com.*

★ Boulder Dushanbe Teahouse

$$ | INTERNATIONAL | Feast your eyes on the intricately carved walls, pillars, and ceiling at this unique teahouse, a gift from Boulder's sister city Dushanbe, Tajikistan; Tajik artisans decorated the building in a traditional style, with ceramic Islamic art and a riot of colorful wood. The menu presents a culinary cross section of the world, with dishes including North African harissa chicken, spicy Indonesian peanut noodles, and Tajik shish kebab. **Known for:** traditional afternoon tea service; nearly 100 varieties of tea; lovely patio. *Average main: $16* *1770 13th St.* *303/442–4993* *www.boulderteahouse.com.*

Bramble & Hare

$ | AMERICAN | Blending authentic farm-to-table with a cozy, old-fashioned farmhouse vibe, this small restaurant—sister to the Black Cat Farm to Table Bistro—boasts its own nearby organic farm, whose produce shapes the daily-evolving menu, even down to a special corn used to make polenta. The food is wildly innovative yet consistently delicious. **Known for:** its extensive organic farm; genius cocktails, including a farm-to-glass program; tasty deviled eggs. *Average main: $11* *1970 13th St.* *303/444–9110* *www.brambleandhare.com* *No lunch.*

Corrida

$$$$ | SPANISH | Perched on the rooftop level of a downtown building, this sleek, modern, Spanish-inspired steak house has one of Boulder's only unobstructed views of the Flatirons; grab a seat outdoors on the patio if you can. You can mix and match generous cuts of high-quality steak with seasonally rotating tapas for northern Spain flavor with a Boulder twist—think Vaca Vieja dry-aged tomahawk steak and a Basque-style cheesecake. **Known for:** tapas and sharable dishes; informed wine and sherry list, plus Spanish-style cocktails; queso asado served with Colorado honeycomb and fennel pollen. *Average main: $50* *1023 Walnut St., Unit 400* *303/444–1333* *www.corridaboulder.com* *No lunch.*

The Boulder Dushanbe Teahouse was carved and hand-painted by master artisans and gifted to Boulder by its sister city of Dushanbe, Tajikistan.

Cured

$$ | AMERICAN | Boulder's finest sandwich shop and the best place for a quick meal, this café–gourmet grocery store is small, with only a few tables, but impressive. Grab an exquisite charcuterie and cheese tray; European-style sandwiches; and premade dinners including roasted organic chicken. **Known for:** hand-rolled pasta; cute housewares and gifts; cheese-centric picnic lunches in wooden baskets. *Average main: $20 ✉ 1825 Pearl St., Suite B ☎ 720/389–8096 🌐 www.curedboulder.com.*

★ Flagstaff House Restaurant

$$$$ | AMERICAN | Boulder's most opulent restaurant has formal service and thoughtfully prepared food, served in a sophisticated space with oversized windows and tables with crisp, white tablecloths. Executive chef Chris Royster has fresh fish flown in daily and is noted for the exquisite combinations of ingredients on his daily-changing menu, which might include duck three ways; Colorado lamb rack, loin, and shank; or a hamachi crudo. **Known for:** stunning views overlooking the Front Range; award-winning wine list; fanciful food presentations. *Average main: $98 ✉ 1138 Flagstaff Rd. ✥ Drive west on Baseline Rd. and turn right onto Flagstaff Rd. Follow it up the hill for about ¾ mile; the restaurant is on your right. ☎ 303/442–4640 🌐 www.flagstaffhouse.com ⏲ No lunch.*

★ Frasca Food and Wine

$$$$ | ITALIAN | One of Boulder's best restaurants (with three James Beard honors) serves meticulously prepared food in the style of the Friuli-Venezia Giulia region of northeastern Italy, in a bustling dining room with a backlit wine wall. You choose from two prix-fixe tasting menus and might feast on dishes including an antipasto such as fish crudo; a house-made pasta with pork ragù; and lamb with hay-smoked potato. **Known for:** informed servers and warm hospitality; grappa cart for after-dinner libations; stellar wine service and pairings. *Average main: $110 ✉ 1738 Pearl St.*

☎ *303/442–6966* 🌐 *www.frascafoodanddwine.com* ⏲ *Closed Sun. No lunch.*

Gold Hill Inn

$$$$ | **AMERICAN** | About 10 miles from downtown Boulder on the dirt road going through the historic region of Gold Hill, this humble cabin hardly looks like a bastion of haute cuisine, but its six-course prix-fixe dinner (or three-course option) is outstanding. Entrées change daily but have a mountain gourmet theme, and may include roast duck or leg of lamb. **Known for:** generous portions well worth the price and drive; dish with trout that is broiled, smoked, and stuffed; bluegrass and roots music. $ *Average main: $39* ✉ *401 Main St., Gold Hill* ✣ *Take Mapleton Ave. west from Broadway up Sunshine Canyon Dr. to Gold Hill, then Main St.* ☎ *303/443–6461* 🌐 *www.goldhillinn.com* ⏲ *Closed Jan.–Apr.; Mon. and Tues. May–Oct.; weekdays Nov. and Dec. No lunch.*

The Kitchen

$$$$ | **AMERICAN** | A Boulder classic with a bright, cheery, and hip vibe, The Kitchen offers elegant, relaxed meals with great service, emphasizing local food in a community atmosphere. The menu changes seasonally, but you can always count on tasty combinations, such as salmon with bok choy or roasted carrots with locally sourced ricotta. **Known for:** an affiliated nonprofit that builds gardens for kids; menu perfect for sharing; one of the nation's greenest restaurants. $ *Average main: $45* ✉ *1039 Pearl St.* ☎ *303/544–5973* 🌐 *www.thekitchenbistros.com.*

OAK at fourteenth

$$$$ | **AMERICAN** | Foodies, first dates, and business diners flock to this bustling restaurant on Pearl Street Mall for seasonal cuisine that centers around a creatively used oak-fired oven and locally sourced meats and vegetables. The menu includes small and large plates, with staples like apple and kale salad and a roasted half chicken. **Known for:** some of Boulder's best cocktails; grilled double cheeseburger with Gruyère cheese and mushrooms; shrimp and grits. $ *Average main: $50* ✉ *1400 Pearl St.* ☎ *303/444–3622* 🌐 *www.oakatfourteenth.com.*

Sherpa's Adventurers Restaurant & Bar

$ | **NEPALESE** | A favorite of Boulder's many health-conscious athletes and world travelers, this homey restaurant in a historical house is owned and run by genuine Sherpas, and offers a voluminous menu with Himalayan favorites like curry and tandoori chicken. It oozes mountain culture and has a bar and library, and a chef who has summited Everest 10 times. **Known for:** saag dip with naan bread; one of Boulder's best patios; superfriendly but slow service. $ *Average main: $13* ✉ *825 Walnut St.* ☎ *303/440–7151* 🌐 *www.sherpas-restaurant.com* 💳 *No credit cards.*

The Sink

$$ | **AMERICAN** | Since 1923, students have flocked to this spot on the Hill, where Robert Redford worked briefly as a janitor in the 1950s while studying at CU; tables fill a labyrinth of rooms, and caricatures and murals decorate the walls. The broad pub-food menu includes the Sinkburger, smothered in barbecue sauce, and the POTUS pizza, named after former president Barack Obama, who ate here in 2012. **Known for:** Boulder's oldest bar and restaurant; Cowboy Reuben with 10-hour-smoked brisket; CU grads and patrons write their names on ceiling. $ *Average main: $15* ✉ *1165 13th St.* ☎ *303/444–7465* 🌐 *www.thesink.com.*

Spruce Farm & Fish

$$$ | **SEAFOOD** | Coffered ceilings, stained-glass windows, and mosaic tile floors create a classic setting for this fish-focused restaurant in the Hotel Boulderado. Savor happy hour at the spruce-wood bar with farm-fresh oysters and handcrafted cocktails, or stay for dinner in the dining room with its fully enclosed porch and sample a seasonal menu emphasizing local foods. **Known for:** its signature barrel-aged Manhattan; daily brunch with sweet and savory options; pan-seared Rocky Mountain trout. $ *Average main: $26* ✉ *Hotel Boulderado,*

2115 13th St. ☎ *303/442–4880* ⊕ *www.sprucebouldera do.com.*

Sushi Zanmai

$$$ | JAPANESE | Perennially popular, this restaurant with light-wood tables and simple decor serves delicious fish and other Japanese specialties to a packed house nightly, so grab a table or sit at the sushi bar. Try a Z No. 9 Roll, shrimp tempura wrapped in nori and rice, topped with salmon and avocado; Zanmai invented it, and other restaurants have copied it. **Known for:** fun, energetic atmosphere; Boulder's best sushi; hoppin' karaoke Saturday night. [$] *Average main: $30* ✉ *1221 Spruce St.* ☎ *303/440–0733* ⊕ *www.sushizanmai.com.*

 Coffee and Quick Bites

The Laughing Goat Coffeehouse

$ | CAFÉ | This bohemian-style café two blocks west of the pedestrian mall serves bagels, muffins, pastries, and oatmeal for breakfast, and panini sandwiches and soups for lunch; do try the locally roasted, organic espresso. This is where Boulder's creative community and young tech entrepreneurs rub shoulders, sometimes literally, thanks to the tight seating. **Known for:** open until 11 pm; patio with mountain views; coffee shop with nightlife vibe, with local beer and wine. [$] *Average main: $7* ✉ *1709 Pearl St.* ⊕ *www.thelaughinggoat.com.*

Ozo Coffee West Pearl

$ | AMERICAN | This Pearl Street café's locally roasted coffee is unmatched, with about a dozen blends, so you can expect all of Ozo's five locations to be packed. The decor is simple, centering around local art, and the food at the pastry counter is simple, too—coffee is the star. **Known for:** Cholaca Mocha with pure, liquid cacao; artfully crafted espresso and coffee drinks; tasty breakfast burritos. [$] *Average main: $7* ✉ *1015 Pearl St.* ☎ *303/645–4885* ⊕ *www.ozocoffee.com* ⏲ *No dinner.*

 Hotels

Boulder has luxurious resorts, historic hotels, and mountain inns, as well as some unexpected options, such as historic cottages at the base of the Flatirons and an adventure-themed hotel. You'll find a handful of chain hotels, but even those lean local, with Boulder-made artwork, beverages, and products in the rooms and shops.

Basecamp Boulder Hotel

$$$ | HOTEL | Per the name, this hotel in what looks like a two-level motel is designed to be the base camp for your adventures—and it's as unique as Boulder, with a bouldering wall in the lounge, kombucha and local beer on tap in the lobby bar, bicycles guests can borrow, a canvas map of Boulder on guest room walls, and a dry sauna. **Pros:** two beers included in your stay; furniture made out of recycled pine trees; free afternoon coffee and cookies. **Cons:** a bit off the main drag; expensive for a basic motel; small bathrooms. [$] *Rooms from: $224* ✉ *2020 Arapahoe Ave.* ☎ *303/449–7550* ⊕ *www.basecampboulder.com* *50 rooms* *No meals.*

The Bradley Boulder Inn

$$$ | B&B/INN | Elegant and contemporary, this downtown inn has a spacious, Craftsman-style great room with warm tones and an inviting stone fireplace, and original artwork is on display throughout the property. **Pros:** quiet inn one block from Pearl Street shopping and dining; daily wine-and-cheese hour; privileges at nearby gym. **Cons:** books up early; no children under 14; all rooms are not equal, and some bathrooms are small. [$] *Rooms from: $285* ✉ *2040 16th St.* ☎ *303/545–5200* ⊕ *www.thebradleyboulder.com* *12 rooms* *Free Breakfast.*

★ Colorado Chautauqua

$$$ | RENTAL | Surrounded by nature, this cluster of historic cottages plus two lodge buildings is at the base of the Flatirons in Chautauqua Park, one of the loveliest parts around Boulder. **Pros:** amazing views of town and mountains; arts, dining, and recreation on property; well-kept cabins. **Cons:** no maid service; park is crowded; cabins close together in busy park lack privacy. *Rooms from: $223* ✉ *900 Baseline Rd.* ☎ *303/952–1611* 🌐 *www.chautauqua.com* *15 rooms, 59 cottages* *No meals.*

Foot of the Mountain Motel
$$$ | **HOTEL** | Cute and no-frills, this mom-and-pop motel is adjacent to the Boulder Creek Path near the mouth of Boulder Canyon, far from Boulder's bustle yet a few minutes' walk from downtown. **Pros:** vintage property at the base of the mountain; quiet neighborhood; close to recreation. **Cons:** no-frills accommodations; no on-site restaurant; high price point for such casual lodging. *Rooms from: $229* ✉ *200 W. Arapahoe Ave.* ☎ *303/442–5688, 866/773–5489* 🌐 *www.footofthemountainmotel.com* *20 rooms* *Free Breakfast.*

★ **Hotel Boulderado**
$$$$ | **HOTEL** | This 1909 beauty beckons with a soaring stained-glass ceiling and large helpings of Victorian charm in its gracious lobby; opt for a room in the historic wing, with spacious quarters filled with period antiques and reproductions. **Pros:** well-maintained historic building; downtown location; excellent hotel restaurants. **Cons:** noisy streets; large, busy hotel; no fitness center, pool, or spa on-site. *Rooms from: $379* ✉ *2115 13th St.* ☎ *303/442–4344, 800/433–4344* 🌐 *www.boulderado.com* *160 rooms* *No meals.*

Residence Inn by Marriott Boulder Canyon Boulevard
$$$ | **HOTEL** | The sleek, modern extended-stay hotel opened in 2018, featuring Flatirons views from guest-room beds and easy access to the Twenty Ninth Street Mall. **Pros:** all rooms have kitchens; Flatirons views; spacious rooms. **Cons:** little local character; removed from the Pearl Street Mall action; most rooms have only showers versus tubs. *Rooms from: $209* ✉ *2550 Canyon Blvd.* ☎ *303/577–7300* 🌐 *www.marriott.com* *155 rooms* *Free Breakfast.*

★ **St Julien Hotel & Spa**
$$$ | **HOTEL** | Unwind in the luxury of this classy yet casual hotel and its stellar spa, in a building where the Colorado red-sandstone exterior reflects the local surroundings and the lobby features walnut floors, marble staircases, and a golden onyx bar. **Pros:** excellent service; close to downtown, outdoor activities, and mountains; dreamy spa with 12 treatment rooms, salon, and lounge. **Cons:** large hotel; quite busy, including special events; some rooms are small. *Rooms from: $299* ✉ *900 Walnut St.* ☎ *720/406–9696, 877/303–0900* 🌐 *www.stjulien.com* *201 rooms* *No meals.*

Nightlife

BARS AND LOUNGES

★ **The Bitter Bar**
BARS/PUBS | With an intimate, couch-lined space modeled after old-time speakeasies (complete with a secret back entrance), this could very well be Boulder's greatest bar, since the staff is passionate about handcrafted cocktails. They're not shy with advice—including the perfect ice shape to suit your booze. Eat before you go since food is limited to a few snacks. ✉ *835 Walnut St.* ☎ *303/442–3050* 🌐 *www.thebitterbar.com.*

Centro Mexican Kitchen
BARS/PUBS | Try happy hour with a Latin twist at this happening spot, which has one of Boulder's most vibrant patios—not to mention perhaps the best margarita in town. The long, wavy bar wraps around two sides, with large garage doors that open to the outside. ✉ *950 Pearl St.* ☎ *303/442–7771* 🌐 *www.centromexican.com.*

Corner Bar

BARS/PUBS | Business lunches and afterwork gatherings take place at the Hotel Boulderado's Corner Bar, a contemporary American pub with both indoor and spacious outdoor seating. The happy hour, from 3 to 6, brings good-value beers and martinis along with 40% off wines and appetizers. Don't miss the weekend brunch with expertly paired cocktails. ✉ *2115 13th St.* ☎ *303/442–4880* 🌐 *www.cornerbarboulderado.com.*

Pearl Street Pub & Cellar

BARS/PUBS | This laid-back pub has bucked the gentrification trend of downtown. Sidle up to the long wooden bar upstairs, or head to the basement for a game of pool, foosball, or darts. ✉ *1108 Pearl St.* ☎ *303/939–9900.*

Rio Grande Mexican Restaurant

BARS/PUBS | The margaritas at this festive place are so potent that there's a three-per-person limit, but that's not all the Rio offers. In addition to fresh citrus cocktails, the Rio has been serving classic and innovative TexMex food for more than 30 years. Request a table on the rooftop patio with unmatched mountain views. ✉ *1101 Walnut St.* ☎ *303/444–3690* 🌐 *www.riograndemexican.com.*

West End Tavern

BARS/PUBS | Beer and bourbon are the name of the game at this upscale pub, which also serves tasty barbecue and burgers. Try to nab a spot on the rooftop deck with mountain views. ✉ *926 Pearl St.* ☎ *303/444–3535* 🌐 *www.thewestendtavern.com.*

BREWPUBS AND BREWERIES

Avery Brewing Company

BREWPUBS/BEER GARDENS | Arguably the most famous brewery in Boulder, Avery has grabbed impressive awards for its innovative ales and lagers; the Avery IPA was Colorado's first packaged IPA. The brewpub offers a solid menu (complete with meat from the smoker), free brewery tours, and a dog-friendly patio. Try the White Rascal, which won silver for best Belgian-style witbier in the 2018 World Beer Cup competition. ✉ *4910 Nautilus Ct., Unit N* ☎ *303/440–4324* 🌐 *www.averybrewing.com.*

Mountain Sun Pub & Brewery

BREWPUBS/BEER GARDENS | There are always 20 beers on tap at this casual brewery, which crafts more than 100 beers throughout the year. A favorite is the FYIPA, a dry-hopped American IPA with a citrusy flavor. Stay for a cheeseburger and hand-cut fries, or for live music on Sunday night. Mountain Sun has three other Boulder locations, plus one each in Longmont and Denver. Brewery tours are available at Southern Sun, a location in south Boulder, upon request. ✉ *1535 Pearl St.* ☎ *303/546–0886* 🌐 *www.mountainsunpub.com.*

Sanitas Brewing Co.

BREWPUBS/BEER GARDENS | Delicious beers with distinctive personality are the hallmark of this brewery. Seventeen taps flow with regular brews, kombucha, and cold brew coffee, as well as a rotating cast of seasonal and short-run beers. Cheap eats are available from the McDevitt Taco Supply truck that parks alongside the spacious patio. Tours can be set up with an advance request. ✉ *3550 Frontier Ave., Unit A* ✥ *SE corner of the building* ☎ *303/442–4130* 🌐 *www.sanitasbrewing.com.*

West Flanders Brewing Company

BREWPUBS/BEER GARDENS | Handcrafting is the focus at this downtown brewpub, which specializes in pub-style, gourmet fare and Belgian-inspired beers. Locally owned since 2012, West Flanders has a casual atmosphere with serious offerings. Locals pack the house on Thursday night for live bluegrass jams. ✉ *1125 Pearl St.* ☎ *303/447–2739* 🌐 *www.wfbrews.com.*

GATHERING PLACES

★ Rayback Collective

GATHERING PLACES | **FAMILY** | A food-truck park, the Rayback Collective is a unique, authentic Boulder gathering place that brings an ever-rotating mix of food trucks, live music, events, and craft beverage menus to an open-air, indoor-outdoor space. Outside, sit by the firepit, play yard games, and chill with your dogs. Inside, drink a beer or coffee, with or without your kids, at a community table or private couch. The flexible space is popular from morning until night. ✉ *2775 Valmont Rd.* ☎ *303/214–2127* 🌐 *www.therayback.com.*

Performing Arts

ARTS FESTIVALS

Colorado Music Festival

CONCERTS | From July to early August, the Colorado Music Festival brings classical music, chamber music, music by contemporary composers, and more to the historic Chautauqua Auditorium. Since 1976, this long-running festival has hosted a variety of musical talent and has become a popular destination for music lovers. Evening meals are available in the dining hall, or you can picnic on the lawn to take in mountain views before the show. ✉ *Chautauqua Auditorium, 900 Baseline Rd.* ☎ *303/665–0599* 🌐 *www.comusic.org* 🎟 *From $5.*

★ Colorado Shakespeare Festival

FESTIVALS | This annual festival runs from early June to mid-August and presents the Bard's comedies and tragedies on the University of Colorado campus in the stunning Mary Rippon Outdoor Theater. ✉ *University of Colorado Campus* ☎ *303/492–8008 box office* 🌐 *www.coloradoshakes.org* 🎟 *From $20* 🕓 *Closed mid-Aug.–May.*

THEATER, FILM, MUSIC, AND DANCE

BDT Stage

THEATER | Since 1977, BDT Stage has been entertaining Boulder with four Broadway-quality musicals a year. An in-house chef prepares your dinner, and the stars of the show serve you at your table. ✉ *5501 Arapahoe Ave.* ☎ *303/449–6000* 🌐 *www.bdtstage.com* 🎟 *From $41, including dinner.*

Boulder Philharmonic Orchestra

CONCERTS | Boulder's professional orchestra presents its own concert season, frequently including some of the biggest names in classical music. The "Boulder Phil" also collaborates with the Boulder Ballet Ensemble to present the *Nutcracker* each holiday season. ✉ *University of Colorado, Macky Auditorium, 17th St. and University Ave.* ☎ *303/449–1343* 🌐 *www.boulderphil.org* 🎟 *From $15* 🕓 *Closed May–Aug.*

★ Boulder Theater

CONCERTS | The 1930s art deco–style Boulder Theater is a gem of a venue that hosts more than 200 events annually with national, international, and local artists, comedians, speakers, and a range of film events. ✉ *2032 14th St.* ☎ *303/786–7030* 🌐 *www.bouldertheater.com.*

Chautauqua Auditorium

CONCERTS | Concerts and more take place throughout the summer at this historic auditorium. Performers have included B.B. King, Melissa Etheridge, Lucinda Williams, the Indigo Girls, and Lyle Lovett. Former Vice President Al Gore and the Reverend Jesse Jackson are among those who have spoken here. ✉ *900 Baseline Rd.* ☎ *303/442–3282* 🌐 *www.chautauqua.com.*

College of Music

CONCERTS | The University of Colorado's superb College of Music presents hundreds of concerts each year, including chamber music by the internationally renowned Takács String Quartet and performances by a range of large and small orchestral, choral, new music, world music, and jazz ensembles. ✉ *301 UCB* ☎ *303/492–8008 CU Presents box office, 303/492–6352 College of Music* 🌐 *www.cupresents.org.*

Dairy Arts Center

ARTS CENTERS | Located in an old dairy building, this center is a hub for the arts community, housing multiple galleries and providing a venue for films as well as locally produced plays, music, and dance performances. ✉ *2590 Walnut St.* ✣ *Enter from 26th St.* ☎ *303/440–7826* 🌐 *www.thedairy.org.*

Department of Theatre and Dance

DANCE | The University of Colorado–Boulder's theater and dance department stages excellent student productions during the academic year. ✉ *University of Colorado Theater Building* ☎ *303/492–8008 CU Presents box office, 303/492–7355 administrative offices* 🌐 *www.colorado.edu/theatredance.*

Fox Theatre

ARTS CENTERS | A former movie palace, the Fox Theatre is now a premier live music venue in Boulder that holds just over 600 people and hosts a wide variety of musical talent, including fledgling groups that go on to become world-famous, as well as acts that are already legends. ✉ *1135 13th St.* ☎ *303/447–0095* 🌐 *www.foxtheatre.com.*

Shopping

The **Pearl Street Mall** (Pearl St. between 11th and 15th Sts.) is the heart of Boulder, a four-block pedestrian mall with upscale boutiques, art galleries, bookstores, shoe shops, and stores with home and garden furnishings. While you'll find some chains, 89% of downtown Boulder's businesses are locally owned and operated (96% of the dining is). Outside merchant doors, a slew of street performers, musicians, magicians, caricaturists, and a balloon artist keeps strollers amused. With upscale boutiques, art galleries, bookstores, shoe shops, and stores with home and garden furnishings, this is a shopping extravaganza.

Known as "the Hill," **University Hill** (13th St. between College Ave. and Pennsylvania St.) is a great place for smoking paraphernalia (both cannabis and vaping), new and used CDs, skateboards, apparel, and CU apparel. The Hill also offers tattoos and piercing, several small markets, and a tech repair shop.

ANTIQUES

The Amazing Garage Sale

ANTIQUES/COLLECTIBLES | You never know what you might discover here as you browse the glorious antique and midcentury furniture, home decor, jewelry, and other treasures. Inventory moves fast, so get it while you can. ✉ *4919 N. Broadway* ☎ *303/447–0417* 🌐 *www.theamazinggaragesale.com.*

Classic Facets Antique Jewelry

ANTIQUES/COLLECTIBLES | One of the most respected antique jewelry stores in the state features more than 20,000 one-of-a-kind treasures, some dating back to the 1700s. Look for famous pieces. In the past, it carried the jewelry that once belonged to Hollywood star Mae West. It's closed on Sunday and Monday. ✉ *942 Pearl St.* ☎ *303/938–8851* 🌐 *www.classicfacets.com.*

BOOKSTORES

Boulder has many used-book sellers, most on Pearl Street between 8th and 20th Streets.

★ **Boulder Book Store**

BOOKS/STATIONERY | Boulder's largest independent bookstore stocks thousands of new and used books, including a great selection of photography, history, and art books about Colorado. The bookstore hosts hundreds of community events each year. ✉ *1107 Pearl St.* ☎ *303/447–2074* 🌐 *www.boulderbookstore.net.*

Trident Booksellers and Cafe

BOOKS/STATIONERY | Channel your inner explorer here while browsing an eclectic collection of new and used books that focus on art, adventure, spirituality, poetry, culture, and literature. At the attached café, you can read while you sip tea in the back garden decorated with street art. Your barista is most likely an owner, too. ✉ *940 Pearl St.* ☎ *303/443–3133* 🌐 *www.tridentcafe.com.*

CLOTHING

Alpaca Connection

CLOTHING | The gorgeous alpaca garments here—including sweaters, hats, socks, and gloves—as well as cotton and linen dresses, are mostly from Peru. ✉ *1326 Pearl St.* ☎ *303/447–2047* 🌐 *www.alpaca-connection.us.*

Jacque Michelle

CLOTHING | Shop here for fashionably casual and unique women's clothing and accessories, as well as clever, appealing gifts. ✉ *2670 Broadway* ☎ *303/786–7628* 🌐 *www.jacquemichelle.com.*

CRAFTS AND ART GALLERIES

Art Source International

ANTIQUES/COLLECTIBLES | With more than 40 years in business, Colorado's largest antique print and map dealer is the place to go if you're looking for rare maps or historic photos of Colorado. Framing and puzzles are also available. ✉ *1237 Pearl St.* ☎ *303/444–4080* 🌐 *www.artsourceinternational.com.*

Boulder Arts & Crafts Gallery

CRAFTS | Owned and operated by 18 artists, the gallery features works by more than 100 Colorado artists. It's a popular place to find unique gifts and decorative items, such as photographs, pottery, hand-painted silk scarves, leather handbags, furniture, and glass objets d'art. ✉ *1421 Pearl St.* ☎ *303/443–3683* 🌐 *www.boulderartsandcrafts.com.*

SmithKlein Gallery

ART GALLERIES | At this expansive, fine art gallery on the Pearl Street Mall, you can browse an eclectic mix of contemporary and traditional art, including glass, bronze sculpture, jewelry, and paintings from some of the most distinguished artists in the nation. ✉ *1116 Pearl St.* ☎ *303/444–7200* 🌐 *www.smithklein.com.*

GIFTS

Bliss

GIFTS/SOUVENIRS | Locally owned and operated, this gift shop is a treasure trove of trendy collectibles and unique home accents from around the globe. ✉ *1643 Pearl St.* ☎ *303/443–0355* 🌐 *www.bliss-boulder.com.*

Two Hands Paperie

GIFTS/SOUVENIRS | Elegant European stationery, handmade paper, and handcrafted, leather-bound journals are among the finds here. The store cultivates a sense of community through art classes, craft parties, and community-making events. It carries a large selection of items from local artists. ✉ *803 Pearl St.* ☎ *303/444–0124* 🌐 *www.twohandspaperie.com.*

Where the Buffalo Roam

GIFTS/SOUVENIRS | Come here for quirky T-shirts, CU and Colorado souvenirs, and a variety of trinkets. ✉ *1320 Pearl St.* ☎ *303/938–1424* 🌐 *www.wherethebuffaloroam.com.*

HOME AND GARDEN

Peppercorn

HOUSEHOLD ITEMS/FURNITURE | A Boulder mainstay, this shop offers a dizzying selection of crockery, cookware, table linens, and kitchen utensils, as well as upscale food items and cookbooks. Kids love the balloon artist who often lingers outside the front door (although he's not affiliated with the store). ✉ *1235 Pearl St.* ☎ *303/449–5847* 🌐 *www.peppercorn.com.*

MARKETS

★ Boulder County Farmers Market

OUTDOOR/FLEA/GREEN MARKETS | FAMILY | This bustling farmers' market brings a hive of activity to 13th Street between Arapahoe Avenue and Canyon Boulevard on Wednesday afternoon from early May to early October, and on Saturday, from April through mid-November. This growers-only market, which has been named the No. 1 farmers' market in the country, features produce, baked goods, flowers, wines and spirits, cheeses, meats, and more straight from the local producers (cherries and peaches are prime in late summer). ✉ *13th St. between Canyon Blvd. and Arapahoe Ave.* ☎ *303/910–2236* 🌐 *www.bcfm.org.*

SPORTING GOODS

McGuckin Hardware

SPORTING GOODS | A Boulder institution, McGuckin Hardware stocks home appliances and gadgets, hardware, and a mind-boggling array of outdoor merchandise. The seemingly omniscient salespeople know where everything is. ✉ *Village Shopping Center, 2525 Arapahoe Ave., Unit D1* ☎ *303/443–1822* 🌐 *www.mcguckin.com.*

★ Neptune Mountaineering

SPORTING GOODS | Among Boulder's many outdoor equipment stores, Neptune is the longtime local favorite that has been outfitting Boulderites for rock climbing, skiing, camping, and mountaineering since 1973. It's the real deal, and shopping here comes with a direct view of the Flatirons. The shop is home to one of the largest selections of climbing gear in the country, and it displays one of the largest collections of mountaineering artifacts in the world in its on-site museum. Bonus: Refuel on food, local beer, and coffee at the Neptune Cafe and Bar. ✉ *633 S. Broadway* ☎ *303/499–8866* 🌐 *www.neptunemountaineering.com.*

TOYS

Grandrabbit's Toy Shoppe

TOYS | FAMILY | A Boulder institution since 1977, Grandrabbit's is every kid's dream come true, with shelves stocked from floor to ceiling. The independently owned specialty toy store has grown to three Colorado locations and is known as the place to go to find toys that contribute to learning and development. It's not uncommon to find adults wandering the aisles, sans children, enjoying the offerings. ✉ *The Village, 2525 Arapahoe Ave.* ☎ *303/443–0780* 🌐 *www.grtoys.com.*

Into the Wind

TOYS | FAMILY | In addition to carrying traditional and out-of-the-ordinary kites, this shop carries an imaginative selection of unique toys and quirky gifts. ✉ *1408 Pearl St.* ☎ *303/449–5356* 🌐 *www.intothewind.com.*

Activities

BICYCLING

BIKE TRAILS

Betasso Preserve

BICYCLING | For a fun mountain-bike ride, head to Betasso Preserve, about 6 miles outside Boulder to the west. The Canyon Loop Trail (moderate to difficult) is 3¼ miles, with the option to add the 2½-mile Benjamin Loop (moderate). Note: No bikes are allowed on the trails on Wednesday and Saturday, except for the Betasso Link. ✉ *Boulder* ✣ *Trailhead: From the western edge of Boulder, drive west on Canyon Blvd./Hwy. 119 for about 4 miles, then turn right at Sugarloaf Rd. After about a mile, turn right onto Betasso Rd. Look for the turnout on the left* 🌐 *www.bouldercounty.org/open-space/parks-and-trails/betasso-preserve* ⏲ *Closed to bikes on Wed. and Sat.*

★ Boulder Creek Path

BICYCLING | Winding through town for about 5½ miles, from Boulder Canyon in the west to the Gerald Stazio Softball Fields (near the intersection of Arapahoe and 55th) in the east, this multiuse path connects to more than 100 miles of city and greenbelt trails and paths. You can access paths from nearly every cross street in town, but don't always count on parking nearby. Find maps and other resources on the website. ✉ *Boulder* ⊕ *Trailheads: From downtown, the best access points are behind the public library parking lot on south side of Canyon Blvd. between 9th St. and Broadway or in Central Park on 13th St., between Canyon Blvd. and Arapahoe Ave.* 🌐 *www.bouldercolorado.gov/goboulder.*

Marshall Mesa/Community Ditch/Doudy Draw/Greenbelt Plateau Trails

BICYCLING | On this moderate 8-mile mountain-bike loop, you go up through pine stands and over a plateau where you can look down on Boulder, with the Flatirons and the Rockies in full view. Start from the Marshall Mesa Trailhead. Head right toward Highway 93, cross through the underpass, and continue along Community Ditch. Turn left on the Doudy Draw Trail, then left up Flatirons Vista to circle back via the Greenbelt Plateau and cross back over 93. Grab a trail map before heading out since you can add on other trails for a longer ride. ✉ *Boulder* ⊕ *Trailhead: Just east of intersection of Hwy. 93 and Marshall Rd. Parking available* 🌐 *www.bouldercolorado.gov/osmp/marshall-mesa-trailhead.*

Switzerland Trail

BICYCLING | An easy, scenic spin that's not too technical, the Switzerland Trail is a 14-mile ride one way that follows the route of an old narrow-gauge railroad, taking you past the mining ghost town of Sunset. ✉ *Boulder* ⊕ *Take Mapleton Ave. up Sunshine Canyon past Gold Hill. Follow Gold Hill Rd./County Rd. 52 about 2½ miles west of Gold Hill.*

Walker Ranch Loop

BICYCLING | For a moderate mountain-bike ride, head 9 miles west of Boulder to Walker Ranch. The 7¾-mile loop has several big climbs and two extended descents. ✉ *Boulder* ⊕ *Trailhead: Off Flagstaff Rd., about 9 miles west of Broadway* 🌐 *www.bouldercounty.org.*

BIKE RENTALS

Full Cycle

BICYCLING | Conveniently located Full Cycle sells a full selection of bicycles and gear, and also offers townie-, road-, and mountain-bike rentals (helmets and locks included) by the day, with discounts for weeklong periods. ✉ *1795 Pearl St.* ☎ *303/440–1002* 🌐 *www.fullcyclebikes.com.*

University Bicycles

BICYCLING | FAMILY | Stop here to rent town, mountain, road, electric, and kids' bikes for one day to one week. Rental fee includes helmet, lock, and map. ✉ *839 Pearl St.* ☎ *303/444–4196* 🌐 *www.ubikes.com.*

BIRD-WATCHING

Eldorado Canyon State Park

BIRD WATCHING | Red-tailed hawks, peregrine falcons, bald eagles, and golden eagles soar along the steep cliffs of Eldorado Canyon State Park. Owls, chickadees, nuthatches, and woodpeckers are at home in the pine forests along South Boulder Creek in the park. Wild turkeys have been sighted in Crescent Meadows and other trails. ✉ *9 Kneale Rd., Eldorado Springs* ⊕ *Drive south on Broadway (Hwy. 93) 3 miles to Eldorado Canyon Dr. (Rte. 170); paved road ends at the village of Eldorado Springs. Drive through town to park entrance* ☎ *303/494–3943* 🌐 *cpw.state.co.us/placestogo/parks/Eldorado-Canyon* 🎫 *$10 per vehicle.*

Walden Ponds Wildlife Habitat

BIRD WATCHING | Bring your binoculars (and bug repellant) to stroll the grounds of these former gravel pits, which attract songbirds, waterfowl, raptors, and other wildlife. Explore the nearly 3 miles of trails, including boardwalks through wetland habitat with interpretive signs. Dawn and dusk are best for species-spotting, especially in April and May when many birds migrate through the Front Range on their way to summer homes. ✉ *Jay Rd. and N. 75th St.* ✥ *Drive north on 28th St. (U.S. 36) and turn right at Valmont Rd. Drive east 4 miles and turn left at 75th St. Sign marking ponds is about ½ mile farther* 🌐 *www.bouldercounty.org.*

FISHING

Eldorado Canyon State Park offers excellent fly-fishing. Fish generally measure between 6 and 12 inches long. See 🌐 *cpw.state.co.us/placestogo/parks/EldoradoCanyon* for more information.

OUTFITTERS

Rocky Mountain Anglers

FISHING | Buy some flies here or sign up for a guided tour. The guides have access to private ranches and know where to find secluded fishing holes on public lands, including Rocky Mountain National Park. Fees include transportation and all your gear—plus lunch on full-day trips. You'll need a fishing license, available at the store. ✉ *1904 Arapahoe Ave.* ☎ *303/447–2400* 🌐 *www.rockymtanglers.com* 🎟 *From $225 for a half-day trip.*

GOLF

Indian Peaks Golf Course

GOLF | FAMILY | Designed by Colorado native Hale Irwin, this public championship golf course is a local favorite, partially owing to its views of the high peaks of the Continental Divide, which aren't visible from Boulder. Wildlife like great blue herons, birds of prey, and foxes also love this place, due to its numerous trees, six lakes, and two winding creeks. The well-maintained course has excellent greens and plays well for low and high handicappers. It's also a great spot to learn, with six sets of tees. ✉ *2300 Indian Peaks Trail, Lafayette* ✥ *Baseline Rd. to Indian Peaks Trail, 10 miles east of Boulder* ☎ *303/666–4706* 🌐 *www.indianpeaksgolf.com* 🎟 *$49 Mon.–Thurs., $61 Fri.–Sun.* ⛳ *18 holes, 5486 yards, par 72.*

HIKING

Boulder has hiking trails of all levels and lengths, from a short walk up the grassy slope between **Chautauqua Park** and the base of the mountains to a more grueling trek up the steep trails near **Mount Sanitas.**

City of Boulder's Open Space and Mountain Parks

HIKING/WALKING | The City of Boulder manages 155 miles of trails, with 37 trailheads and 76 access points in and around Boulder, offering a vast array of opportunities to commune with nature. Most trails are open to dogs, provided they are leashed or under voice and sight control and registered with the city's Voice and Sight Tag Program. Some don't allow dogs at all, so make sure you check the website before heading out. Most trailheads are free; a few require a $5 parking permit for nonresident vehicles. You can purchase a daily pass either at self-serve kiosks at trailheads or at the Open Space and Mountain Parks administration office on Cherryvale Road. ✉ *66 S. Cherryvale Rd.* ☎ *303/441–3440* 🌐 *www.bouldercolorado.gov/osmp.*

RECOMMENDED TRAILS

★ Boulder Creek Path

HIKING/WALKING | A relaxing 5½-mile amble with pleasant scenery, this path winds from west of Boulder through downtown and past the university to the eastern part of the city. Access the multiuse trail from almost any cross street. Within the eastern city limits, the path winds past wetlands and prairie-dog colonies. People-watching is also great, with everyone from cyclists in full spandex to parents pushing their babies in jogging strollers. Walk west along the path from Broadway to Boulder Canyon for views of kayakers and inner-tubers cooling off in the summer heat. Downtown delivers great mountain views. ✉ *Boulder* 🌐 *bouldercolorado.gov/parks-rec.*

★ Chautauqua Trailhead

HIKING/WALKING | Forty miles of trails snake up into the hills from the Chautauqua Trailhead. For a nice intro, hike up through the meadow on the Chautauqua Trail, turn left onto the Bluebell/Baird Trail, and then left again to return to the parking lot via the Mesa Trail, roughly a 1½-mile loop. The trail is a long slope at the beginning, but once you're in the trees you won't gain much more elevation. There are many other hiking options here as well. Study the map at the trailhead or stop in at the park's visitor center (next to the main parking lot). ✉ *Trailhead at main parking lot, Grant St. and Baseline Rd.* 🌐 *www.bouldercolorado.gov/osmp/chautauqua-trailhead.*

Flagstaff Mountain

HIKING/WALKING | There are many hiking options here—you can start from the base of Flagstaff Road and climb to the top of the mountain on foot, or drive 3½ miles up to the summit road and access trails. Park at Gregory Canyon to access the Flagstaff Trail from town. From the amphitheater, the **Boy Scout Trail** is an easy ¾-mile jaunt to May's Point, with views of high-alpine peaks. ✉ *Boulder* ✥ *Trailhead: Drive west on Baseline Rd. to sharp curve to right that is Flagstaff Rd. (turn left for the Gregory Canyon trailhead). Or drive 3½ miles to the Summit Rd. The Boy Scout Trail starts from the parking area about ½ mile in* 🌐 *www.bouldercolorado.gov/osmp/flagstaff-trailhead* 🎫 *$5 parking fee for nonresident vehicles.*

Green Mountain

HIKING/WALKING | Beginning at the Gregory Canyon trailhead, you can string together a variety of trails to climb this 8,144-foot peak, which rewards ambitious hikers with vistas of the Front Range and the Indian Peaks. Make a 5-mile loop with more than 2,000 feet of elevation gain by heading up the Gregory Canyon and Ranger trails, then returning via the E. M. Greenman (no dogs allowed) and Saddle Rock trails. Allow three to four hours. Or drive 4½ miles up Flagstaff Road to the West Ridge Trail to shave the journey hike to less than 3 miles. ✉ *Flagstaff Rd. and Baseline Rd.* ✥ *Trailhead (Gregory Canyon Trail): Drive west on Baseline Rd. to Flagstaff Rd., and turn left immediately after curve. Parking area is at end of short road where trail starts* 🌐 *www.bouldercolorado.gov/osmp/gregory-canyon-trailhead* 🎫 *$5 parking fee for nonresident vehicles.*

Royal Arch Trail

HIKING/WALKING | The roughly 3¼-mile round-trip hike to Royal Arch Trail provides an up-close look at Boulder's own rock arch. It is definitely worth the steep hike (1,400 feet of elevation gain) for views of the foothills and cities of the Front Range. The trail spurs off the Chautauqua Trail loop and follows the base of the Flatirons before a steep climb. Go under the arch to the precipice for the best views. If you turn around, the arch frames a couple of Flatirons for a good photo. This trail remains icy from late fall into early summer, so be prepared with traction devices. ✉ *Trailhead at main parking lot, 900 Baseline Rd.* 🌐 *www.bouldercolorado.gov/osmp.*

Sanitas Valley Loop

HIKING/WALKING | Known locally as Mount Sanitas, this challenging 3-mile hike has stunning views of snowcapped peaks to the west and Boulder to the east. From the trailhead, head left to climb the western ridge, which starts with steep steps and maintains a steady incline up 1,300 feet to the 6,863-foot summit. Descend the East Ridge Trail, with rugged switchbacks that drop down to Sanitas Valley, then take the Sanitas Valley Trail, or veer left onto Dakota Ridge Trail, which parallels the valley back to the parking lot. Don't take the sharp left at the Dakota Ridge intersection, which leads downhill to town. Allow two hours. ✉ *Boulder* ✥ *Trailhead: Mapleton Ave., 1 mile west of Broadway on the left* 🌐 *bouldercolorado.gov/osmp/mount-sanitas-trailhead.*

Settler's Park/Red Rocks

HIKING/WALKING | Carry a picnic and enjoy the mountain and city views from this mountain park, which includes a series of interconnected trails that skirt around a scenic rock outcropping. Head up from Settler's Park at the west end of Pearl and find your way to a lovely bench overlook east of the rocks, about ¼ mile. If you have time, continue down the other side to Sunshine Canyon and come back the same way or pick a different route. The trails are considered easy to moderate. ✉ *Boulder* ✣ *Trailhead: Settler's Park, where Pearl and Canyon meet at the western edge of town* 🌐 *www.bouldercolorado.gov/osmp/settlers-park-trailhead.*

KAYAKING AND CANOEING

Serious kayakers run the slaloms in Lefthand Canyon, but Boulder Creek—from within Boulder Canyon midway into the city—is one of the locals' favorites. Water in the creek can create Class II–III rapids when summer conditions are right.

Boulder Reservoir

CANOEING/ROWING/SKULLING | If calm waters are what you want, you can rent a canoe, kayak, or stand-up paddleboard at the Boulder Reservoir, a 700-acre recreation area with photo-worthy Flatirons views. ✉ *5565 N. 51st St.* ✣ *6 miles northeast of downtown. Drive northeast on Hwy. 119 and turn left at Jay Rd. Turn right immediately onto 51st St. and follow it to sign for entrance station* ☎ *303/441–3461* 🌐 *www.bouldercolorado.gov/parks-rec/boulder-reservoir* 🎟 *$7 entrance fee residents/$9 nonresidents, not including boat rentals* ⏲ *Closed Labor Day–Memorial Day.*

OUTFITTERS

Colorado Wilderness Rides and Guides

BICYCLING | This Boulder outfitter provides many fly-fishing and float trips for anglers but also offers bike and mountain-bike tours, rock climbing, backpacking, multiday camping, ziplining, white-water rafting, snowshoeing, ski tours, and even sightseeing and photo tours. The company can help you find just about any kind of outdoor adventure—whatever your level of experience, whatever the season. ✉ *6560 Odell Pl., Unit D* ☎ *720/242–9828* 🌐 *www.coloradowildernessridesandguides.com.*

Longmont

15 miles northeast of Boulder via Hwy. 119.

With more than 165 restaurants, some of Colorado's best breweries, a distinct local arts scene, and more than 2,000 acres of open space and parks, "the gem city of the St. Vrain Valley" offers everything visitors love about Colorado—in short: great brews and views. The lively downtown area offers free summer concerts, the work of local artists in galleries and coffee shops, and more than 70 places to shop. Beyond downtown, there are three public golf courses, five skateparks, and branches of large, high-tech companies. The St. Vrain Greenway links numerous parks and runs eight miles along St. Vrain Creek. Amid all the excitement of this thriving city, Longmont retains a sweet, small-town charm.

TOURS

★ **Brewhop Trolley**

SPECIAL-INTEREST | Colorado's only hop-on hop-off brewery tour, the Brewhop trolley makes a loop throughout Longmont from noon to 9 pm every Saturday and noon to 8 pm on Sundays, visiting nine craft breweries, two distilleries, and a local cidery. The hop-on hop-off service returns to each location along the route, allowing patrons to visit tasting rooms, enjoy guided tours, and shop for souvenirs before moving onto the next point, or pint.
The trolley also offers private charters for special events. ✉ *Longmont* ☎ *720/209–8505* 🌐 *www.brewhoptrolley.com* 🎟 *From $15.*

Sights

Union Reservoir

BODY OF WATER | FAMILY | One of only a few natural lakes in Colorado, this 736-acre body of water is known as one of the best windsurfing spots on the Front Range, with easy waterfront access. It's also quickly becoming one of Colorado's finest walleye fishing spots. Rent paddleboards and kayaks, swim, or watch dogs swim—the reservoir has one of the biggest dog swim beaches in northern Colorado. ✉ *461 County Rd. 26, Longmont* 🌐 *www.longmontcolorado.gov* 🕓 *Swim beach closed early Sept.–late May.*

Restaurants

Jefe's Tacos and Tequila

$ | MEXICAN | Serving up arguably the best street tacos in Boulder County, this colorful, upbeat restaurant is a popular spot with locals who appreciate the old-school hip-hop soundtrack and daily happy hour from 3 to 5 pm when street tacos are just a buck. The Squashacado (made with roasted butternut squash) is a vegetarian taco so tasty that it's almost as requested as the best-seller carne asada. **Known for:** chorizo queso appetizer; fresh fruit margaritas; tacos with meat from a local family farm. 💲 *Average main: $14* ✉ *246 Main St., Longmont* ☎ *303/827–3790* 🌐 *www.jefeslongmont.com.*

Nightlife

BREWPUBS

★ Left Hand Brewing Company

BREWPUBS/BEER GARDENS | Longmont's first brewery has been pouring innovative, independent craft brews since 1993. Left Hand first garnered attention for introducing America's first nitro bottle and now is an industry leader in stouts and nitros; its Milk Stout Nitro is especially lauded. This brewery is one of the most awarded breweries in Colorado, with more than 29 Great American Beer Festival medals, 11 World Beer Cup awards, and nine European Beer Star awards. Reserve a brewery tour or just stop in to enjoy a few pints out on the Tasting Room patio, which features 33 taps. Sit indoors or on one of four patios with Rocky Mountain views. ✉ *1265 Boston Ave., Longmont* ☎ *303/772–0258* 🌐 *www.lefthandbrewing.com.*

Wibby Brewing

BREWPUBS/BEER GARDENS | Wibby's craft lagers are brewed with German malt, American hops, and Rocky Mountain water. A cult fave is the seasonal Lightshine Radler, a blend of the gold-medal-winning Lightshine Helles and housemade raspberry lemonade. Beyond the brew, the taproom is a wunderbar: indoor and outdoor spaces are packed with yard games, a basketball hoop, shuffleboard, and more. Take a tour or ask your beertender to show you around. ✉ *209 Emery St., Longmont* ☎ *303/776–4594* 🌐 *www.wibbybrewing.com.*

Shopping

Cheese Importers

FOOD/CANDY | This family-run business boasts the largest walk-in refrigerator of cheese and cured meat in Colorado. With more than 350 types of cheese, Cheese Importers is the best place in the state to stock up on cheesy goodness. After shopping the massive selection of imported kitchen and household items, perfumes, and soaps, grab a latte and lunch in the European bistro, known for its French onion soup and fresh-baked goods, including macaroons. ✉ *103 Main St., Longmont* ☎ *303/772–9599* 🌐 *www.cheeseimporters.com.*

Nederland

16 miles west of Boulder via Hwy. 119.

A former mining and mill town at the top of Boulder Canyon and on the scenic Peak to Peak Highway, "Ned" embodies that small, mountain-town spirit in look and attitude: laid-back, independent, renegade, and friendly. Nederland is quite possibly quirkier than Boulder, with its famous "frozen dead guy" in a storage shed, community-wide coffin races, and unusual art throughout town. The town got its name from a Dutch company that owned several mines in the area: "Nederland" is Dutch for "Netherlands," or low lands. The downtown retains the character of its silver-mining days, and has several good bars, cafés, restaurants, and shops. Nederland is the gateway to skiing at Eldora Mountain Resort and high-altitude hiking in the Indian Peaks Wilderness.

GETTING HERE AND AROUND

Nederland is an easy drive from Boulder. Take Highway 119 (Canyon Boulevard) west.

VISITOR INFORMATION

CONTACTS Nederland Area Visitor Center. ✉ *4 W. 1st St.* ☎ *303/258–3936.*

FESTIVALS

Frozen Dead Guy Days

FESTIVALS | Inspired by a guy who wanted to be kept on ice after his death (his body is in a Tuff Shed near Nederland), this quirky festival brings out the oddball spirit of this town. The three-day event in March includes live music, a hearse parade, coffin races, icy turkey bowling, a salmon toss, and a charity polar plunge into (usually frozen) Chipeta Park Pond. ✉ *Nederland* ☎ *303/506–1048* 🌐 *frozendeadguydays.org* 🎟 *Free.*

Sights

Carousel of Happiness

CAROUSEL | FAMILY | No visit to Nederland is complete without a dollar spin on the nonprofit Carousel of Happiness, a restored 1910 carousel featuring 56 hand-carved, hand-painted animals running around to the sounds of a 1913 Wurlitzer band organ. The complex includes a gift shop and a puppet theater. ✉ *20 Lakeview Dr.* ☎ *303/258–3457* 🌐 *www.carouselofhappiness.org* 🎟 *$2.*

Peak to Peak Scenic and Historic Byway

SCENIC DRIVE | The byway (Highways 119, 72, and 7), a 55-mile stretch that winds from Central City north through Nederland to Estes Park, is not the quickest route to the eastern gateway to Rocky Mountain National Park, but it's certainly the most scenic. You'll pass through the old mining towns of Ward and Allenspark and enjoy spectacular mountain vistas. Mount Meeker and Longs Peak rise magnificently behind every bend in the road. The descent into Estes Park provides grand vistas of snow-covered mountains and green valleys. ✉ *Nederland* ✥ *From Central City, drive north on Hwy. 119. From Nederland, drive north on Hwy. 72. Turn left at intersection with Hwy. 7 and continue to Estes Park* 🌐 *www.codot.gov/travel/scenic-byways.*

Restaurants

Kathmandu Restaurant

$ | INDIAN | Prices are reasonable at this casual, bustling Nepali and Indian restaurant with dark wood walls, red booths, and a wood bar in the center of the room. Kathmandu has received accolades for its vegetarian food, but everything is good on a full traditional menu that spans the gamut from starters like momos (dumplings) and samosas to *aloo gobi* (cauliflower and potatoes), tandoori chicken and lamb, and curries. **Known for:** authentic food from family recipes; all-you-can-eat lunch buffet; chicken tikka masala. 💲 *Average main: $11* ✉ *110 N. Jefferson St.* ☎ *303/258–1169* 🌐 *www.kathmandurestaurant.us.*

The Train Cars Coffee and Yogurt Company

$ | **AMERICAN** | **FAMILY** | As the name hints, the café is set up inside three repurposed train cars, including an old circus train from the late 1800s. It serves locally roasted coffee, frozen yogurt, and light food, such as a grilled cheese and pesto sandwich. **Known for:** pick your own toppings for fresh-made mini-doughnuts; spicy green chile, Colorado's favorite dish; affogato with hot espresso over frozen yogurt. 💲 *Average main: $7* ✉ *101 Hwy. 119* ☎ *303/258–2455* 🌐 *www.thetraincarscoffee.com* ⏲ *No dinner.*

Boulder Creek Lodge

$$ | **B&B/INN** | Built in 1995 with rough-hewn timber, this rustic yet modern lodge is an excellent choice for those who want to be smack dab in the middle of Nederland, 10 minutes from Eldora Ski Resort. **Pros:** property has mountain style; guest rooms are quiet; good value for location. **Cons:** Nederland can feel remote unless you're spending a lot of time hiking and skiing; on a heavily traveled road; no pool or hot tub. 💲 *Rooms from: $160* ✉ *55 Lakeview Dr.* ☎ *303/258–9463* 🌐 *www.thebouldercreeklodge.com* *23 rooms* *No meals.*

HIKING

Caribou Ranch

HIKING/WALKING | At Caribou Ranch Open Space, the DeLonde Trail to Blue Bird Loop is an easy 4½-mile walk (allow two hours) through forests and wildflower-filled meadows. An elk herd resides on the open space, so listen for bugling in fall. The 1¼-mile DeLonde Trail starts to the left of the trailhead and connects to the Blue Bird Loop just before the former DeLonde homestead site. Take a break at the picnic table overlooking the pond before continuing on the loop to the former Blue Bird Mine complex. No dogs or bikes are allowed, and the loop closes April–June to protect migratory birds and calving elk. ✉ *Nederland* ✣ *Trailhead: From Nederland, drive north on Hwy. 72 to County Rd. 126, turn left, and go 1 mile* ☎ *303/678–6200* 🌐 *www.bouldercounty.org/open-space/parks-and-trails/caribou-ranch.*

★ Indian Peaks Wilderness

HIKING/WALKING | Offering some of the area's most popular hiking, Indian Peaks Wilderness encompasses more than 50 lakes, 133 miles of trails, and six mountain passes crossing the Continental Divide. Wildflowers are prolific and peak in late July and early August, when columbine (the state flower) and others mix in a mosaic of colors. Parking at trailheads is limited, so start out early. There's no central access point; contact the U.S. Forest Service or check the Arapaho and Roosevelt National Forests website for trail information and driving directions. Permits are required for camping, and dogs must be on leash. ✉ *Boulder Ranger District Office, Arapaho National Forest, 2140 Yarmouth Ave., Boulder* ☎ *303/541–2500* 🌐 *www.fs.usda.gov.*

SKIING AND SNOWBOARDING

Brainard Lake Recreation Area

SNOW SPORTS | In Roosevelt National Forest, Brainard Lake Recreation Area is the most popular destination in the Boulder Ranger District, with well-marked trails and gorgeous views of the snow-covered Indian Peaks and Continental Divide. You can snowshoe at the lake, which is set in a picturesque, glacier-carved valley. It's about 23 miles from Boulder up Lefthand Canyon. ✉ *Brainard Lake Rd., Ward* ✣ *Drive west on Hwy. 119 to Nederland*

and turn north at Hwy. 72 at Ward ☎ *303/541–2500* 🌐 *www.fs.usda.gov.*

Eldora Mountain Resort

SKIING/SNOWBOARDING | Boulder's backyard ski resort, Eldora Mountain Resort offers ski and snowboard terrain to suit every ability, as well as four terrain parks and a Nordic Center with 25 miles (40 km) of groomed trails. Eldora's summit is 10,600 feet, and it's often windy, so dress warmly. Head for the Indian Peaks Lodge for ski rentals and ski school, and to Timbers Lodge for the cafeteria and bar. The resort offers lessons for children and adults. There's no lodging on-site, so set up home base in Nederland or Boulder. **Facilities:** 66 trails; 680 acres; 1,400-foot vertical drop; 10 lifts. ✉ *2861 Eldora Ski Rd.* ✥ *5 miles west of Nederland off Hwy. 119 and Eldora Rd.* ☎ *303/440–8700* 🌐 *www.eldora.com* 🎫 *Lift ticket $99.*

Lyons

17 miles north of Boulder via U.S. 36.

Lyons is a peaceful, down-to-earth community of 2,000 residents that's tucked inside the red-sandstone foothills at the confluence of the North St. Vrain and South St. Vrain creeks. Founded in 1881, it's crammed with historic buildings—there are 15 structures here listed in the National Register of Historic Places—and the whole downtown area feels like a turn-of-the-20th-century frontier outpost. The cafés, restaurants, art galleries, and antiques stores attract lots of visitors, who also come for the recreation opportunities and top-notch music festivals.

GETTING HERE AND AROUND

To drive to Lyons from Boulder, travel north on U.S. 36.

VISITOR INFORMATION

CONTACTS Lyons Area Chamber of Commerce. ☎ *303/823–6622* 🌐 *www.lyonschamber.org.*

FESTIVALS

The summer outdoor music season kicks off in June, followed by the **Lyons Good Old Days** festival, and goes into September with midweek concerts in Sandstone Park (at 4th and Railroad Avenues). RockyGrass and the Planet Bluegrass Folks Festival are two large festivals held annually here. Cafés and restaurants host bands regularly. Check the Chamber of Commerce website for event schedules.

Planet Bluegrass

CONCERTS | At the end of July, Planet Bluegrass presents RockyGrass—an internationally renowned bluegrass festival that features a combination of legendary artists as well as up-and-comers. The venue—an idyllic outdoor setting under red-rock cliffs on the banks of the St. Vrain River—is also host to FolksFest in August. In addition, Planet Bluegrass's indoor Wildflower Pavilion stages about a dozen concerts in the spring and fall. ✉ *500 W. Main St.* ☎ *303/823–0848, 800/624–2422* 🌐 *www.bluegrass.com.*

LaVern M. Johnson Park

CITY PARK | Located along the banks of the St. Vrain River, this lovely park has something for everyone, from picnic areas and a playground to a winter-season ice-skating rink. Bird-watchers come from all over to see eagles nesting in the sandstone cliffs here. There's also a white-water park for kayakers and tubers, a splash pad, tubing on the river, and camping. ✉ *600 Park Dr.* ☎ *303/823–6622* 🌐 *www.townoflyons.com.*

Lyons Classic Pinball

LOCAL INTEREST | **FAMILY** | You wouldn't expect such a pinball extravaganza in tiny Lyons, but there it is, behind the Oskar Blues brewpub, with more than 50 classic pinball games. The change machines (and fellow gamers) make it a simple and fun evening stop. ✉ *339-A Main St.*

303/823–6100 *www.lyonspinball.com* *Closed Mon.–Wed.*

Restaurants

Oskar Blues Grill & Brew

$ | **AMERICAN** | The first American craft brewery to can its beer, Oskar Blues is a Lyons hot spot for beer, pub grub, and music. Try Dale's Pale Ale or any of the other robust beers brewed nearby in small (20-barrel) batches. **Known for:** creative burgers; Cajun dishes; bourbon balls for dessert. *Average main: $14* *303 Main St.* *303/823–6685* *www.oskarblues.com.*

Hotels

WeeCasa Tiny House Resort

$$ | **RENTAL** | Instead of a traditional hotel, stay close to nature at the country's largest tiny-house resort, with uniquely decorated private houses (all 400 square feet or less) that have varying floor plans. **Pros:** tons of personality in themed homes; private kitchens; immediate river and nature access. **Cons:** small spaces (starting at 135 square feet); limited hot water in showers; homes are packed close together. *Rooms from: $189* *501 W. Main St.* *720/460–0239* *www.weecasa.com* *22 units* *No meals.*

Activities

HIKING AND MOUNTAIN BIKING

Hall Ranch

HIKING/WALKING | Nearly 14 miles of trails at Hall Ranch are open to hikers, mountain bikers, and equestrians (but not dogs). The **Bitterbrush Trail/Nelson Loop** follows the Bitterbrush Trail for 3¾ miles, climbing 914 feet through meadows, pines, and rock outcroppings. It connects to the 2¼-mile Nelson Loop, which leads to the Nelson Ranch House. The loop's slight 300-foot elevation gain brings you onto a plateau with great mountain views. Allow five to six hours to hike. Mountain bikers can avoid the rocks by approaching the Nelson Loop via the **Antelope Trail,** which climbs a mile from the trailhead off Apple Valley Road. Note: The Nighthawk Trail (4.7 miles) is only open to hikers and equestrians. *Lyons* *¾ mile west of Lyons on Hwy. 7* *www.bouldercounty.org.*

Heil Valley Ranch

BICYCLING | The **Picture Rock Trail** leads up to Heil Valley Ranch from the Lyons side. It's a rocky 5¼ miles up 983 feet to join the other trails on this open-space property. You can continue on the 3-mile **Wild Turkey Loop,** and tack on even more mileage by biking or walking the 2½-mile **Ponderosa Loop.** No matter what you choose, you'll enjoy peacefully moving through the trees. *Lyons* *Picture Rock Trailhead: Drive ½ mile up Hwy. 7 out of Lyons, turn left onto Old St. Vrain Rd., and left again on Red Gulch Rd.* *303/678–6200* *www.bouldercounty.org.*

Ron Stewart Preserve at Rabbit Mountain

HIKING/WALKING | The preserve has several easy to moderate trails with great views of the High Rockies and the plains. Pick up the map at the trailhead that explains the history of the area, including the dramatic metamorphosis of Rabbit Mountain from a tropical swamp inhabited by dinosaurs to the present-day, mile-high desert that's home to raptors, prairie dogs, and coyotes. The 3-mile round-trip **Little Thompson Overlook Trail** forks off to the left before you come to the gravel road and climbs 400 feet to the point where you can see Longs Peak, the plains to the east, and Boulder Valley to the south. The 3½-mile **Eagle Wind Trail** loop has short spurs to viewpoints. From the parking area, head out on the trail to the gravel road and then right onto the single-track loop. *Lyons* *8 miles east of Lyons. Follow Hwy. 66 east out of Lyons for 4 miles, turn left on N. 53rd St., which turns into N. 55th St. The parking lot and trailhead are on the right* *www.bouldercounty.org* *Free.*

Fort Collins

65 miles north of Denver; 45 miles north of Boulder.

The city sits on the cusp of the high plains of eastern Colorado, but is sheltered on the west by the lower foothills of the Rockies, giving residents plenty of nearby hiking and mountain biking opportunities. By plugging a couple of gaps in the foothills with dams, Fort Collins created Horsetooth Reservoir, which you can't see from town. To view the high mountains, you'll need to head up into Lory State Park or Horsetooth Mountain Park, just west of town. A walk through Old Town Square and the neighborhoods to its south and west demonstrates Fort Collins's focus on historic preservation and the arts—music is everywhere, especially during summer. The city has more than 20 microbreweries and produces 70% of Colorado's craft beer, earning it the title of Craft Beer Capital of Colorado.

The city was established in 1868 to protect traders from the natives, while the traders negotiated the treacherous Overland Trail. After the flood of 1864 swept away Camp Collins—a cavalry post near today's town of LaPorte—Colonel Will Collins established a new camp on 6,000 acres where Fort Collins stands today. The town grew on two industries: education (Colorado State University was founded here in 1879) and agriculture (rich crops of alfalfa and sugar beets). Today there are plenty of shops and art galleries worth visiting in this relaxed university city.

GETTING HERE AND AROUND

From Boulder, take U.S. 36 east to Interlocken Loop/Storage Tek Drive, follow for about ½ mile, then get onto Northwest Parkway for about 8½ miles. Take I–25 north for about 41 miles and get off at the Prospect Road exit. Head west on East Prospect Road for about 4 miles. No commercial flights go here, but there's a local taxi service, and the city's bus system, Transfort, operates more than a dozen routes throughout the city, which run primarily Monday to Saturday. However, downtown is walkable, and the city also offers scooters for rent.

CONTACTS Transfort. ☎ *970/221–6620* 🌐 *www.ridetransfort.com.* **zTrip.** ☎ *970/224–2222* 🌐 *www.ztrip.com/northern-colorado.*

VISITOR INFORMATION

CONTACTS Visit Fort Collins. ✉ *19 Old Town Sq., Suite 137* ☎ *970/232–3840, 800/274–3678* 🌐 *www.visitftcollins.com.*

WHEN TO GO

Fort Collins's outdoor recreation and cultural pursuits attract visitors year-round, but it is definitely a college town, so expect a decidedly different atmosphere depending on whether CSU is in session.

FESTIVALS

Bohemian Nights at NewWestFest

FESTIVALS | Fort Collins's largest community festival, this music-centered event is a proud showing of the bustling Colorado music community, which has produced the Fray, Tennis, 3OH!3, OneRepublic, Nathaniel Rateliff, and others. Dozens of bands play on multiple stages during the free three-day event in August. Bohemian Nights also hosts Thursday night concerts downtown during the summer. ✉ *Old Town Sq.* ☎ *970/484–6500 Downtown Fort Collins Business Association* 🌐 *www.bohemiannights.org.*

Colorado Brewers' Festival

During the last full weekend of June, more than 10,000 people flock to downtown Fort Collins to sample beers from more than 50 Colorado brewers at this event, the state's first craft beer festival, established in 1989. You can roam the festival grounds for free, or pay a set price (usually cheaper in advance) to sample beer. Enjoy a rotating lineup of live music by Colorado artists while you sip. ✉ *Downtown Fort Collins, main entrance at Laporte Ave. and Howes St. ☎ 970/484–6500 Downtown Fort Collins Business Association 🌐 www.downtownfortcollins.com.*

Sights

★ Anheuser-Busch Fort Collins Brewery
WINERY/DISTILLERY | Learn about the large-scale Budweiser brewing process at Anheuser-Busch during one of the free tours, which start every 45 minutes and last about an hour and 15 minutes. You can also go behind the scenes on a two-hour Brewmaster Tour (fee, reservations required). Relax in the Biergarten and take in the mountain views. On special occasions, you can meet the famous Clydesdales. ✉ *3823 Mountain Vista Dr.* ☎ *970/490–4691* 🌐 *www.budweisertours.com* 🎟 *Free; $35 for Brewmaster Tour* ⏲ *No tours Tues. and Wed.; Biergarten and gift shop closed Tues.*

1879 Avery House
HISTORIC SITE | The stately sandstone Avery House was built in 1879 by Franklin Avery, who set the tone for Old Town's broad streets when he surveyed the city in 1873. You can tour the inside on weekends. The Avery House is just one of 36 sites on the Poudre Landmark Foundation's historic walking-tour map, which includes several self-guided options. ✉ *328 W. Mountain Ave.* ☎ *970/221–0533* 🌐 *www.poudrelandmarks.org* 🎟 *Free* ⏲ *Closed weekdays.*

Fort Collins Museum of Discovery
MUSEUM | **FAMILY** | The museum entertains and informs visitors of all ages with interactive science, history, music, and natural history exhibits. The OtterBox Digital Dome Theater screens a mix of planetarium space shows and captivating educational films on its 35-foot dome screen. Also, meet the two resident black-footed ferrets. This is the only museum in the world to host these endangered animals. ✉ *408 Mason Ct.* ☎ *970/221–6738* 🌐 *www.fcmod.org* 🎟 *$12.50.*

Old Town Square
ARTS VENUE | **FAMILY** | A National Historic District, Fort Collins' Old Town was the inspiration for Disneyland's Main Street USA, and Old Town Square is a bustling pedestrian zone with sculptures, fountains, a firepit, and historic buildings that house shops, galleries, bars, and, of course, breweries. Restaurants and cafés here have plenty of shaded outdoor seating. Musicians perform during the summer on a stage, and in the winter, the square is home to Santa's Workshop and an ice-skating rink. ✉ *Mountain and College Aves.* ☎ *970/484–6500* 🌐 *www.downtownfortcollins.com.*

Restaurants

Canino's
$$ | **ITALIAN** | **FAMILY** | Since 1976, Canino's has served hearty, traditional Italian specialties in a 1905 four-square house that has original stained-glass windows and cozy wood-trim rooms with tables on burgundy carpets. The casual setting is the perfect backdrop for appetizers like fried calamari and steamed mussels, and entrées including pastas and pizza, plus chicken Marsala, veal parmigiana, and seafood and vegetarian options. **Known for:** family-recipe cheesecake and other house-made desserts; bread recipe from current owner's grandfather; flower-trimmed patio. 💲 *Average main: $18* ✉ *613 S. College Ave.* ☎ *970/493–7205* 🌐 *www.caninositalianrestaurant.com.*

★ The Emporium: An American Brasserie
$$ | **AMERICAN** | This farm-to-table restaurant inside the Elizabeth Hotel has a full wine market, so you can select bottles on-site at retail price for your meal. It all adds to the homey yet hip, slightly retro vibe and look—complete with tile floor and wood throughout—that matches well with food that is some of the city's best, including the Wagyu beef burger, bison bourguignonne, and elk Wellington with puff pastry. **Known for:** perfect charcuterie board; the Bowerbird Coffee

Shop by day, unpretentious wine market by night; weekend brunch. *Average main: $20* *Elizabeth Hotel, 378 Walnut St.* *970/493–0024* *www.emporium-ftcollins.com.*

The Farmhouse at Jessup Farm

$$$ | **AMERICAN** | With a name like The Farmhouse, it's only fitting that this cozy, farm-style restaurant in a 130-plus-year-old home has its own quarter-acre chicken coop. Savor seasonal, locally inspired menus with tasty, from-scratch comfort food like fried chicken and biscuits, skillet chicken potpie, and green chile mac and cheese. **Known for:** pork-belly bites with grits and molasses gravy; brunch with blue-corn pancakes; s'mores doughnuts. *Average main: $23* *1957 Jessup Dr.* *970/631–8041* *www.farmhousefc.com.*

★ Jax Fish House & Oyster Bar

$$$ | **SEAFOOD** | At this seafood hot spot, the butcher paper–covered tables, exposed brick walls, and unique light fixtures encourage a cool, festive vibe. Explore Jax's delicious culinary creations by digging into a plate of peel 'n' eat shrimp, then moving on to seasonal combinations like citrus-glazed salmon, spiced tuna with aioli, or the staple fried fish po'boy. **Known for:** marvelous cocktails; oysters flown in fresh daily; commitment to sustainable seafood. *Average main: $25* *123 N. College Ave.* *970/682–2275* *www.jaxfish-house.com/fort-collins* *No lunch.*

Rio Grande Mexican Restaurant

$$ | **MEXICAN** | Like its other Front Range brethren, the Fort Collins branch of this six-location restaurant always satisfies with favorites such as tacos, quesadillas, burritos, and fajitas. The spacious location in the heart of Old Town has exposed brick walls, hand-painted tables, and old storefront windows. **Known for:** potent margaritas with a limit of three; 60-plus hand-selected tequilas; from-scratch black beans and handmade tortillas. *Average main: $20* *143 W. Mountain Ave.* *970/224–5428* *www.riogran-demexican.com.*

Silver Grill Cafe

$ | **AMERICAN** | **FAMILY** | For comfort food in a historic atmosphere, stop by this charming, bustling café with diner counters, some boxy booths, dozens of tables, and an inviting, year-round patio. Operating in its current location since 1933, it serves a wide selection of breakfast food all day, such as omelets, Benedicts, biscuits and gravy, hotcakes, steak and eggs, and burritos, while lunch features delicious sandwiches, soups, salads, and burgers. **Known for:** legendary cinnamon rolls; top-notch breakfasts including homemade hash browns; award-winning Bloody Marys. *Average main: $11* *218 Walnut St.* *970/484–4656* *www.silvergrill.com* *No dinner.*

Coffee and Quick Bites

Starry Night Espresso Café

$ | **CAFÉ** | Espresso drinkers sip their sustenance here while sitting on leather chairs or at tables. Beyond breakfast, the café serves delicious quiches, salads, and sandwiches at lunch and dinnertime. **Known for:** the popular cappuccino cake; unique drinks like Colorado honey and rose latte; great people-watching. *Average main: $9* *112 S. College Ave.* *970/493–3039.*

Hotels

The Armstrong Hotel

$$$ | **HOTEL** | In a 1923 building that's on the National Register of Historic Places, the boutique Armstrong Hotel (renovated in 2020) offers historic character in the heart of town, including a lobby that charms with its original terrazzo floor, pressed-tin ceiling, and leaded prismatic glass windows. **Pros:** the Ace Cafe, a patio café in front of the hotel; downtown location near restaurants and bars; cocktails and live music at Ace Gillett's Supper Club and Music Lounge in the basement.

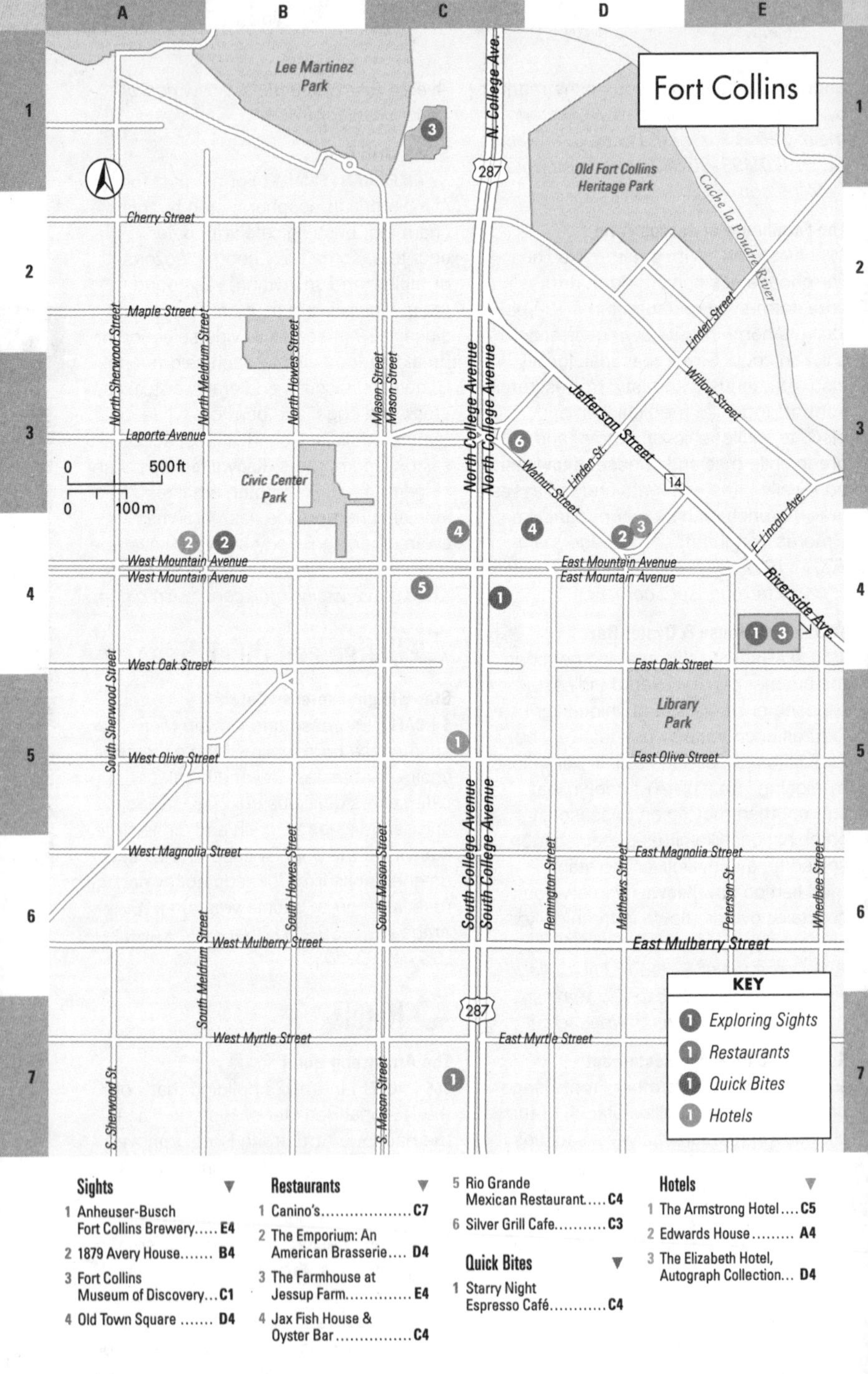

Sights

1 Anheuser-Busch Fort Collins Brewery..... **E4**

2 1879 Avery House....... **B4**

3 Fort Collins Museum of Discovery... **C1**

4 Old Town Square **D4**

Restaurants

1 Canino's.................. **C7**

2 The Emporium: An American Brasserie.... **D4**

3 The Farmhouse at Jessup Farm............. **E4**

4 Jax Fish House & Oyster Bar.............. **C4**

5 Rio Grande Mexican Restaurant..... **C4**

6 Silver Grill Cafe........... **C3**

Quick Bites

1 Starry Night Espresso Café............ **C4**

Hotels

1 The Armstrong Hotel.... **C5**

2 Edwards House......... **A4**

3 The Elizabeth Hotel, Autograph Collection... **D4**

Cons: can hear other guests; some rooms have limited storage space; passing trains can be loud. *Rooms from: $250 259 S. College Ave. 970/484–3883, 866/384–3883 www.thearmstronghotel.com 54 rooms No meals.*

Edwards House

$$$ | **HOTEL** | Quiet and intimate, this impeccably furnished and maintained Victorian inn is just three blocks from downtown. **Pros:** on a busy but quiet street near downtown; helpful and professional staff; pleasant grounds. **Cons:** small inn can fill up quickly; those seeking completely Victorian style won't find it here; old building has thin walls and creaky floors. *Rooms from: $220 402 W. Mountain Ave. 970/493–9191, 800/281–9190 www.edwardshouse.com 8 rooms Free Breakfast.*

★ The Elizabeth Hotel, Autograph Collection

$$ | **HOTEL** | Opened in 2017, this stylish, music-themed hotel pays tribute to the city's heritage with music-inspired artwork and a record library in the lobby; you can even borrow instruments for the night. **Pros:** central location, walking distance to downtown; mountain views on west side; great on-site dining and bars. **Cons:** can be noisy due to music bar; close to train tracks; no on-site spa. *Rooms from: $199 111 Chestnut St. 970/490–2600 www.theelizabethcolorado.com 164 rooms No meals.*

Nightlife

BARS AND CLUBS

Lucky Joe's Sidewalk Saloon

BARS/PUBS | College students and young adults line the bar at Lucky Joe's Sidewalk Saloon for live music by local bands Wednesday through Saturday nights. Sunday is open-mic night. *25 Old Town Sq. 970/493–2213 www.luckyjoes.com.*

Mishawaka Amphitheater

MUSIC CLUBS | This intimate outdoor venue on the banks of the Poudre River, about 25 miles outside Fort Collins, is a local staple and usually presents an eclectic mix of bands. Most shows are in the evening, but some are during the afternoon. Plan on reserving a shuttle from Fort Collins in advance, as parking is discouraged due to limited space along the highway; the website has details. *13714 Poudre Canyon Hwy., Bellvue 25 miles northwest of Fort Collins on Rte. 14 970/482–4420 www.themishawaka.com.*

Social

BARS/PUBS | Head down, down, down to this sexy, underground cocktail bar in Old Town with trendy industrial decor. Social feels like a speakeasy, with its expert cocktails, a curated wine list, and more absinthe than anyone should ever try. Absorb it all with a charcuterie plate. Both casual and fancy attire fit in fine here. *1 Old Town Sq., Unit 7 970/449–5606 www.socialfortcollins.com.*

BREWPUBS AND MICROBREWERIES

CooperSmith's Pub & Brewery

BREWPUBS/BEER GARDENS | After touring CooperSmith's brewery (free; by appointment only), you can enjoy a meal from the seasonally rotating menu in the pub, with its gleaming wood floors and exposed brick walls. Or you can chow down on pizza while shooting pool across the alley at CooperSmith's Poolside. Quaff a Punjabi Pale Ale (an IPA) or one of the other 14 to 18 beers on tap. *5 Old Town Sq. 970/498–0483 www.coopersmithspub.com.*

New Belgium Brewing Company

BREWPUBS/BEER GARDENS | The taproom of the fourth-largest brewer of craft beer in the United States offers an exceptional lineup featuring beers from the iconic Belgian Collection and brands such as Fat Tire and Voodoo Ranger IPA, as well as special-release small-batch brews. Events include live music, bike-in movies, and yoga with beer. During the day, bikes crowd the racks outside this pedal-friendly brewery, where visitors can sample a variety of brews and take a free 90-minute tour. These popular tours are first come, first served, so reserve online. The brewery is north of Old Town, near Cache la Poudre River and its popular trail system. ✉ *500 Linden St.* ☎ *970/221–0524* 🌐 *www.newbelgium.com* 🎫 *Free.*

Odell Brewing Co.

BREWPUBS/BEER GARDENS | You can take in the brewing process on a free tour at one of Colorado's oldest craft breweries. Sample favorites like 90 Shilling Ale, Odell IPA, and Sippin' Pretty (or try seasonal brews like winter's Isolation Ale) in a taproom that has long wooden tables as well as a massive outdoor patio. Odells hosts festivals, parties, and live music, and there are yard games and regular food trucks. Don't miss Odell's urban winery next door; the OBC Wine Project shares an outdoor patio space with the brewery. ✉ *800 E. Lincoln Ave.* ☎ *970/498–9070, 888/887–2797* 🌐 *www.odellbrewing.com.*

The historic buildings in Old Town Square and adjacent Linden Street house galleries, bookshops, cafés, brewpubs, and shops. Various Old Town art galleries host the **First Friday Gallery Walk** on the first Friday of each month—no matter the weather—with appetizers and music from 6 to 9 pm.

Alpine Arts—The Colorado Showcase

CRAFTS | The family-owned Alpine Arts is the place to go for unique apparel, hats, and souvenirs, as well as beautiful handcrafted pottery, carved wooden boxes, jewelry, and other gifts—most made by Colorado artists and all embodying the state. ✉ *112 N. College Ave.* ☎ *970/493–1941* 🌐 *www.alpineartscolorado.com.*

Northern Front Range Breweries

The Front Range boasts several brewing firsts. In 1959 Coors, located in Golden, introduced the first beer in an aluminum can. Boulder Beer is Colorado's first microbrewery, founded in 1979. The Great American Beer Festival, which started in 1981 in Boulder (now held in Denver), was the nation's first beer festival. For a list of the operators that offer tours of local breweries as well as the individual breweries, visit 🌐 www. *colorado.com/colorado-breweries.*

Clothes Pony and Dandelion Toys

TOYS | **FAMILY** | The shopkeepers here enjoy playing with the toys as much as their young customers do. This independent shop carries books, imported toys, games, and classics like marbles, dolls, and stuffed animals, as well as adorable clothing. ✉ *111 N. College Ave.* ☎ *970/224–2866* 🌐 *www.clothespony.com.*

Nature's Own

GIFTS/SOUVENIRS | **FAMILY** | You can browse an extensive collection of rocks, fossils, educational games, gifts, and beautiful onyx bowls here. There are also branches in Boulder, Nederland, and Breckenridge. ✉ *201 Linden St.* ☎ *970/484–9701* 🌐 *www.naturesown.com.*

Nuance Chocolate

FOOD/CANDY | **FAMILY** | Family-run, this bean-to-bar chocolate shop claims to have the world's biggest selection of single-origin chocolate, meaning the beans come from one region in the world and aren't blended. Beans are ground nearby in Old Town to produce more than 20 single-origin bars. Nuance also makes indulgent truffles with local ingredients. You can sit inside or outside at a few tables to sample a flight of chocolate or sip rich hot chocolate. ✉ *214 Pine St.* ☎ *970/484–2330* 🌐 *www.nuancechocolate.com.*

Trimble Court Artisans

CRAFTS | At this co-op gallery, more than 50 Colorado member-artists sell their paintings, jewelry, weavings, and pottery. ✉ *118 Trimble Ct.* ☎ *970/221–0051* 🌐 *www.trimblecourt.com.*

BICYCLING

Both paved-trail cycling and single-track mountain biking are within easy access of town.

For short, single-track rides, Pineridge (for beginners) and Maxwell (for technical riders) trails do not disappoint, and they connect to other trails for longer adventures. Head west on Drake Road to where it bends right and becomes South Overland Trail; turn left on County Road 42C and drive almost 1 mile to the signed parking lots.

Horsetooth Mountain Park

BICYCLING | Serious bike gearheads crank at Horsetooth Mountain Park on the southwest side of Horsetooth Reservoir, where several single-track trails provide challenges. No motorized vehicles are allowed. Park at the upper lot and head out on the **South Ridge Trail** to link to other trails. ✉ *6550 W. County Rd. 38E* ✣ *Drive west on Harmony Rd., which becomes West County Rd. 38E. Follow for about 6 miles to park entrance* 🌐 *www.larimer.org/naturalresources* 🎫 *$9 per vehicle.*

Poudre Trail

BICYCLING | This paved multiple-use trail winds more than 10 miles along the Poudre River. The best access points with parking are at the Lee Martinez Park or Lions Open Space for the western part of the trail, and the CSU Environmental Learning Center for the east end of the trail. ✉ *Fort Collins* 🌐 *www.larimer.org/naturalresources.*

RENTALS

Recycled Cycles

BICYCLING | Rent city bikes for $30 a day or electric bikes for $50 per day. Lock, helmet, and bike map included. The company has multiple locations. ✉ *4031 S. Mason St.* ☎ *970/223–1969* 🌐 *www.recycled-cycles.com.*

FISHING

The Cache la Poudre River is renowned for excellent fishing. Find ample pond fishing along the river's corridor, too. See the state's web site (🌐 *www.cpw.state.co.us/thingstodo/Pages/Fishing.aspx*) for more information on fishing licenses.

St. Peter's Fly Shop

FISHING | The knowledgeable folks at this full-service fly shop in Old Town arrange half-day to full-day guided or instructional wade and float trips in northern Colorado and southern Wyoming that can include permits for waters not open to the public. The store also sells and rents gear, and staff members gladly provide information on conditions to independent anglers. ✉ *202 Remington St.* ☎ *970/498–8968* 🌐 *www.stpetes.com* 🎫 *From $275 for a half day.*

GOLF

Mariana Butte Golf Course

GOLF | This undulating public course in Loveland, about 15 miles south of Fort Collins, follows the banks of the Big Thompson River and delights with stunning scenery, including expansive views of mountain peaks. Designed by Dick Phelps, the course delivers plenty of challenges, skirting rock outcroppings and ponds. ✉ *701 Clubhouse Dr., Loveland* ✣ *Go west on 1st St., take a right onto Rossum Dr. and another quick right onto Clubhouse Dr.* ☎ *970/667–8308 pro shop, 970/669–5800 tee times* 🌐 *www.golfloveland.com/mariana-butte* 🎫 *$23.50 for 9 holes, $47 for 18 holes* 🏌 *18 holes, 6718 yards, par 72.*

HIKING

Horsetooth Mountain Park

HIKING/WALKING | Twenty-nine miles of trails in Horsetooth Mountain Park offer easy to difficult hikes, with views of the mountains to the west and the plains to the east. An easy 2¼-mile round-trip walk to **Horsetooth Falls** is a good way to explore the foothills for a couple of hours. From the upper parking area, head up the Horsetooth Falls Trail and keep right at the junction with the Soderberg Trail. Go left at the next junction to get to the falls. Arrive early, as the parking lot fills by 9 am on weekends. ✉ *6550 W. County Rd. 38E* ✣ *Drive west on Harmony Rd., which becomes West County Rd. 38E. Follow for about 6 miles to park entrance* ☎ *970/679–4570* 🌐 *www.larimer.org/parks* 🎫 *$9 per vehicle.*

Lory State Park

HIKING/WALKING | About 15 minutes west of downtown, Lory State Park is home to a vibrant diversity of wildlife, songbirds, and springtime wildflowers. Arrive before 10 or 11 am to avoid weekend crowds. For gorgeous views of the Front Range and the city from 7,000-foot Arthur's Rock, take **Arthur's Rock Trail**, which climbs fast up switchbacks before leveling off in a meadow, a welcome breather before the steep approach to the summit. Allow about two hours to hike the trail (3½ miles round-trip and about 1,100 feet gain in elevation). ✉ *708 Lodgepole Dr., Bellvue* ✣ *Drive north on Overland Trail and turn left on Bingham Hill Rd. Turn left at County Rd. 23 north, go 1¼ miles to County Rd. 25G and turn right. It's 1½ miles to park entrance* ☎ *970/493–1623* 🌐 *cpw.state.co.us/placestogo/parks/Lory* 🎫 *$9 per vehicle.*

RAFTING AND KAYAKING

The Cache la Poudre River is famous for its rapids, and river trips fill fast. It's wise to book with an outfitter at least two weeks in advance.

A1 Wildwater Rafting

WHITE-WATER RAFTING | This long-standing outfitter will take you rafting on the nearby Poudre and North Platte rivers. With advance notice, it can accommodate large groups. Trips range from family-friendly mild to Class IV wild. ✉ *2801 N. Shields St.* ☎ *970/224–3379* 🌐 *www.a1wildwater.com* 🎫 *From $62.*

Rocky Mountain Adventures

FISHING | White-water raft trips, kayaking instruction, river sports retail, and gear rental are offered by this outfitter. ✉ *1117 N. U.S. 287* ☎ *970/493–4005* 🌐 *www.shoprma.com.*

Chapter 9

ROCKY MOUNTAIN NATIONAL PARK

WITH ESTES PARK AND GRAND COUNTY

Updated by
Lindsey Galloway

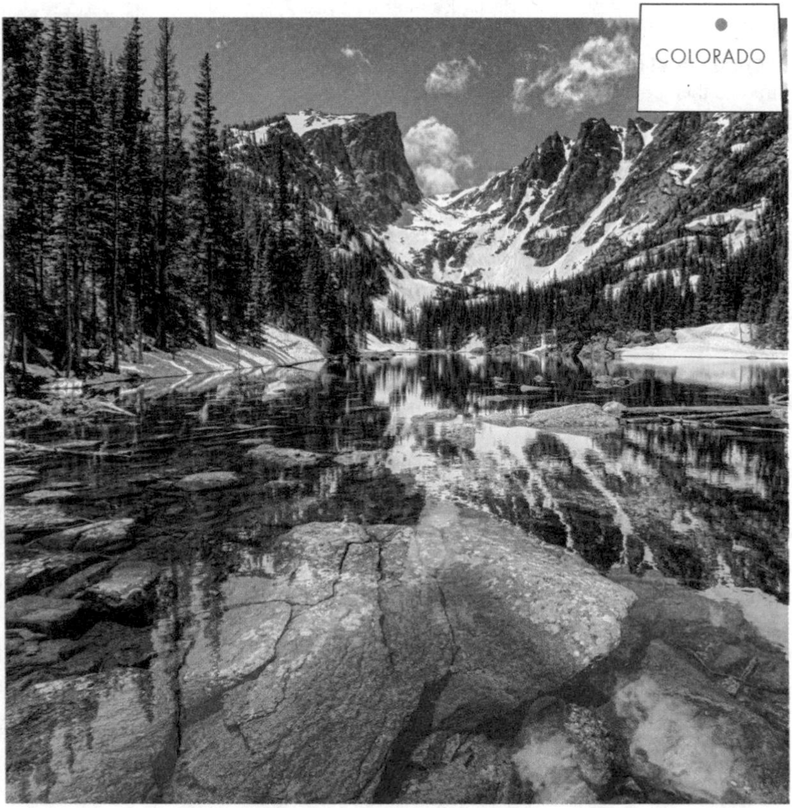

COLORADO

★★★★★

★★★☆☆

★★★★☆

★★☆☆☆

★★☆☆☆

WELCOME TO ROCKY MOUNTAIN NATIONAL PARK

TOP REASONS TO GO

★ **Awesome ascents:** Seasoned climbers can trek to the summit of 14,259-foot Longs Peak or attack the rounded granite domes of Lumpy Ridge. Novices can summit Twin Sisters Peaks or Mount Ida, both reaching more than 11,000 feet.

★ **Continental Divide:** Straddle this great divide, which cuts through the western part of the park, separating water's flow to either the Pacific or Atlantic Ocean.

★ **Gorgeous scenery:** Peer out over more than 100 lakes, gaze up at majestic mountain peaks, and soak in the splendor of lush wetlands, pine-scented woods, forests of spruce and fir, and alpine tundra in the park's four distinct ecosystems.

★ **More than 355 miles of trails:** Hike on dozens of marked trails, from easy lakeside strolls to strenuous mountain climbs.

★ **Wildlife viewing:** Spot elk and bighorn sheep, along with moose, otters, and more than 280 species of birds.

1 Moraine Park. This area offers easy access to several trailheads, the park's largest campground, and the Beaver Meadows Visitor Center near the east side entrance.

2 Bear Lake. One of the park's most photographed places is the hub for many trailheads and a stop on the park's shuttle service.

3 Longs Peak. The park's highest (and toughest to climb) peak, this Fourteener pops up in many park vistas. A round-trip summit trek takes 10 to 15 hours; most visitors opt for a (still spectacular) partial journey.

4 Trail Ridge Road. Alpine tundra is the highlight here, as the road—the nation's highest continuous highway—climbs to over 12,000 feet (almost 700 feet above timberline).

5 Timber Creek. The park's far western area is much less crowded than other sections, though it has evening programs, 98 camping sites, and a visitor center.

6 Wild Basin Area. Far from the crowds, this southeastern quadrant has lovely subalpine forest punctuated by streams and lakes.

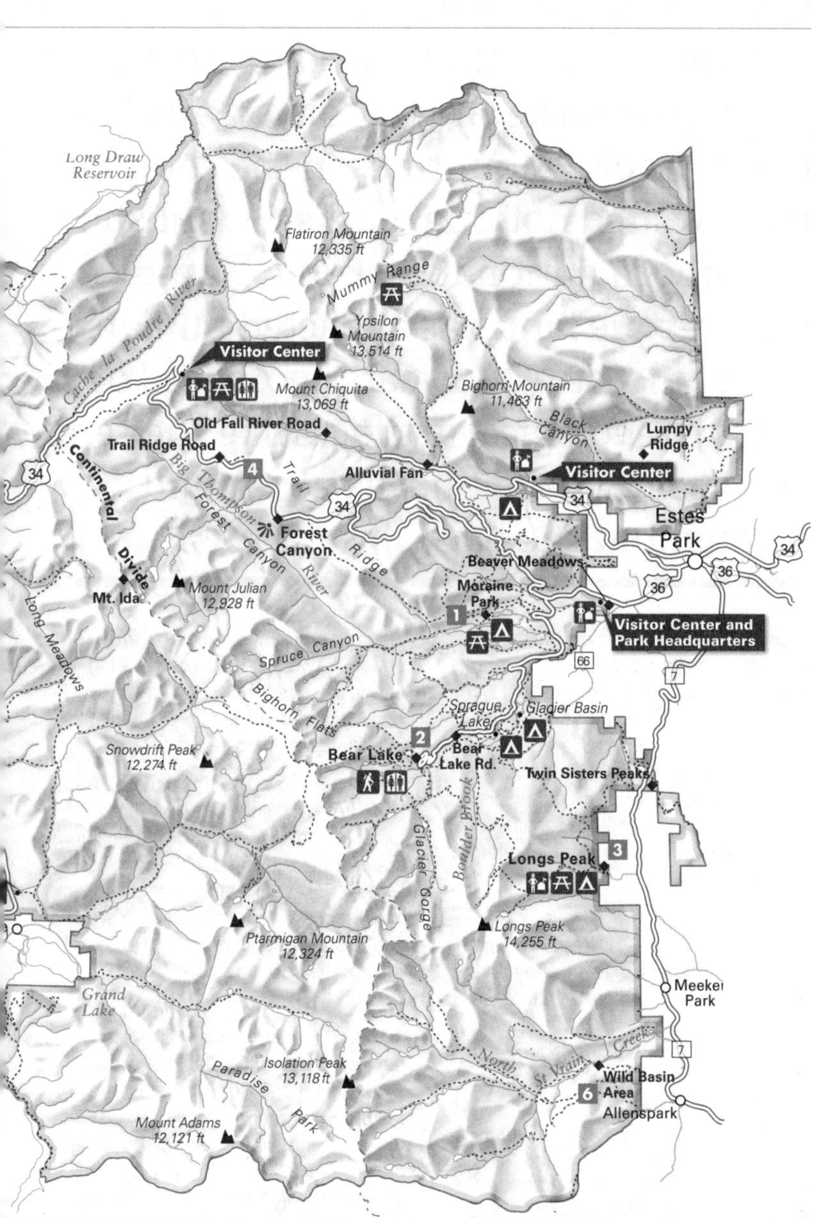
Long Draw Reservoir
Flatiron Mountain 12,335 ft
Mummy Range
Ypsilon Mountain 13,514 ft
Cache la Poudre River
Visitor Center
Mount Chiquita 13,069 ft
Bighorn Mountain 11,463 ft
Black Canyon
Lumpy Ridge
Old Fall River Road
Trail Ridge Road
Continental Divide
Big Thompson River
Trail Ridge
Alluvial Fan
Visitor Center
34
4
Forest Canyon
Forest Canyon
Estes Park
Beaver Meadows
36
Mt. Ida
Mount Julian 12,928 ft
Moraine Park
1
Visitor Center and Park Headquarters
Long Meadows
Spruce Canyon
66
7
Bighorn Flats
Sprague Lake
Glacier Basin
2
Bear Lake
Bear Lake Rd.
Snowdrift Peak 12,274 ft
Twin Sisters Peaks
Boulder Brook
Glacier Gorge
Longs Peak
3
Longs Peak 14,255 ft
Ptarmigan Mountain 12,324 ft
Meeker Park
Grand Lake
North St Vrain Creek
Isolation Peak 13,118 ft
Paradise Park
Wild Basin Area
6
Allenspark
Mount Adams 12,121 ft

With its towering mountains, active and abundant wildlife, and crystal clear lakes and rivers, Rocky Mountain attracts nearly 5 million visitors per year, trailing only the Grand Canyon and the Great Smoky Mountains in the country's most visited national parks. Established as the 10th national park in 1915, the picturesque land has attracted humans since at least 11,000 years ago, based on the archaeological artifacts like shelters and speartips that have been found throughout the park.

These ancient people used the very same trail as today's visitors: the 48-mile Trail Ridge Road. With an apex of 12,183 feet, the road travels from the east side Estes Park entrance, across the Continental Divide, to the west side Grand Lake entrance, giving even nonhikers a close look at the montane, subalpine, and alpine ecosystems found at different areas of the park.

Those who do hike have their pick of more than 355 miles of trails, with paths suited for every ability level. The park's high altitude—the lowest elevation starts at 7,000 feet above sea level—often affects out-of-towners, but a good night's sleep and healthy hydration go a long way. The park is famous for its robust elk population, especially active in "Elk-tober" when the elk come to lower elevations for their annual mating season. Moose are more common on the west side near the Kawuneeche Visitor Center and near rivers and lakes, while bighorn sheep are best spotted in late spring and early summer at the appropriately named Sheeps Lake in Horseshoe Park.

Rocky Mountain has more than 1,000 archaeological sites and 150 buildings of historic significance; 47 of the buildings are listed in the National Register of Historic Places. Most buildings at Rocky Mountain are done in the rustic style, which strives to incorporate nature into man-made structures.

Though the park has year-round access and activities, most visitors come between late spring and mid-autumn when Trail Ridge Road remains open. In the high summer months, the east side entrance and lower elevation trails can become quite congested, so beat the crowds by using the west entrance or

AVERAGE HIGH/LOW TEMPERATURES					
JAN.	**FEB.**	**MAR.**	**APR.**	**MAY**	**JUNE**
39/16	41/17	45/21	53/27	62/34	73/41
JULY	**AUG.**	**SEPT.**	**OCT.**	**NOV.**	**DEC.**
78/46	76/45	70/38	60/30	46/23	40/18

arriving before 8 am. *In 2020, a pair of devastating fires swept across approximately 30,000 acres, around 9% of the park, primarily in the west and far north part of the park, so check the latest conditions and closures on the park's website before setting off.*

Planning

When to Go

More than 80% of the park's annual 4.7 million visitors come in summer and fall. For thinner high-season crowds, come in early June or September. But there is a good reason to put up with summer crowds: only from late May to mid-October will you get the chance to make the unforgettable drive over Trail Ridge Road (note that the road may still be closed during those months if the weather turns bad).

Spring is capricious—75°F one day and a blizzard the next (March sees the most snow). June can range from hot and sunny to cool and rainy. July typically ushers in high summer, which can last through September. Up on Trail Ridge Road, it can be 15°F–20°F cooler than at the park's lower elevations. Wildlife viewing and fishing is best in any season but winter. In early fall, the trees blaze with brilliant foliage. Winter, when backcountry snow can be 4 feet deep, is the time for cross-country skiing, snowshoeing, and ice fishing.

FESTIVALS AND EVENTS

Elk Fest. In early autumn, the calls of bulls fill the forest as elk head down from the mountains for mating season. Estes Park celebrates with elk bugle contests, live music, and elk educational seminars. 🌐 *www.visitestespark.com/events-calendar/special-events/elk-fest.*

Longs Peak Scottish-Irish Highland Festival. A traditional tattoo (drum- and bugle-filled parade) kicks off this fair of ancient Scottish athletic competitions. There's also Celtic music, Irish dancing, and events for dogs of the British Isles (such as terrier racing and sheepdog demonstrations). 🌐 *www.scotfest.com.*

Rooftop Rodeo. Consistently ranked one of the top small rodeos in the country (and a tradition since 1908), this six-day event features a parade and nightly rodeo events, such as barrel racing and saddle bronc riding. 🌐 *www.rooftoprodeo.com.*

Getting Here and Around

AIR

The closest commercial airport is **Denver International Airport** (DEN). Its **Ground Transportation Information Center** (☎ *800/247–2336 or 303/342–4059* 🌐 *www.flydenver.com*) assists visitors with car rentals, door-to-door shuttles, and limousine services. From the airport, the eastern entrance of the park is 80 miles (about two hours). **Estes Park Shuttle** (☎ *970/586–5151* 🌐 *www.estesparkshuttle.com*; reservations essential) serves Estes Park and Rocky Mountain from both Denver International Airport and Longmont/Boulder.

Rocky Mountain in One Day

Starting out in Estes Park, begin your day at the **Bighorn Restaurant**, a classic breakfast spot and a local favorite. While you're enjoying your short stack with apple-cinnamon-raisin topping, you can put in an order for a packed lunch (it's a good idea to bring your food with you, as dining options in the park consist of a single, seasonal snack bar at the top of Trail Ridge Road).

Drive west on U.S. 34 into the park, and stop at the **Beaver Meadows Visitor Center** to watch the orientation film and pick up a park map. Also inquire about road conditions on Trail Ridge Road, which you should plan to drive either in the morning or afternoon, depending on the weather. If possible, save the drive for the afternoon, and use the morning to get out on the trails, before the chance of an afternoon lightning storm.

For a beautiful and invigorating hike, head to Bear Lake and follow the route that takes you to **Nymph Lake** (an easy 1/2-mile hike), then onto **Dream Lake** (an additional 0.6 miles with a steeper ascent), and finally to **Emerald Lake** (an additional 0.7 miles of moderate terrain). You can stop at several places along the way. The trek down is much easier, and quicker, than the climb up. **■ TIP→ If you prefer a shorter, simpler (yet still scenic) walk, consider the Bear Lake Nature Trail, a 0.6-mile loop that is wheelchair and stroller accessible.**

You'll need the better part of your afternoon to drive the scenic **Trail Ridge Road.** Start by heading west toward Grand Lake, stop at the lookout at the Alluvial Fan, and consider taking Old Fall River Road the rest of the way across the park. This single-lane dirt road delivers unbeatable views of waterfalls and mountain vistas. You'll take it westbound from Horseshoe Park (the cutoff is near the Endovalley Campground), then rejoin Trail Ridge Road at its summit, near the Alpine Visitor Center. If you're traveling on to Grand Lake or other points west, stay on Trail Ridge Road. If you're heading back to Estes Park, turn around and take Trail Ridge Road back (for a different set of awesome scenery). End your day with a ranger-led talk or evening campfire program.

BUS

Rocky Mountain has limited parking, but offers three free shuttle buses, which operate daily from 7 am to 8 pm, late May to early October. All three shuttles can be accessed from a large Park & Ride located within the park, 7 miles from the Beaver Meadows entrance. Visitors who don't want to drive into the park at all can hop on the Hiker Shuttle at the Estes Park Visitor Center. The shuttle, which runs every half hour during peak times, makes stops at the Beaver Meadows Visitor Center and the Park & Ride, where visitors can switch to one of the other two shuttles, which head to various trailheads. The Moraine Park Route shuttle runs every 30 minutes and stops at the Moraine Park Visitor Center and then continues on to the Fern Lake Trailhead. The Bear Lake Route shuttle runs every 10 to 15 minutes from the Park & Ride to the Bear Lake Trailhead.

CAR

Estes Park and Grand Lake are the Rocky Mountains' gateway communities; from these you can enter the park via U.S. 34 or 36 (Estes Park) or U.S. 34 (Grand

Lake). U.S. 36 runs from Denver through Boulder, Lyons, and Estes Park to the park; the portion between Boulder and Estes Park is heavily traveled—especially on summer weekends. Though less direct, Colorado Routes 119, 72, and 7 have much less traffic (and better scenery). If you're driving directly to Rocky Mountain from the airport, take the E-470 tollway from Peña Boulevard to Interstate 25.

The **Colorado Department of Transportation** (for road conditions ☎ *303/639–1111* 🌐 *www.cotrip.org*) plows roads efficiently, but winter snowstorms can slow traffic and create wet or icy conditions. In summer, the roads into both Grand Lake and Estes Park can see heavy traffic, especially on weekends.

WITHIN THE PARK

The main thoroughfare in the park is Trail Ridge Road (U.S. 34); in winter, it's closed from the first storm in the fall (typically in October) through the spring (depending on snowpack, this could be at any time between May and June). During that time, it's plowed only up to Many Parks Curve on the east side and the Colorado River trailhead on the west side. (For current road information: ☎ *970/586–1222* 🌐 *www.codot.gov*.)

The spectacular Old Fall River Road runs one way between the Endovalley Picnic Area on the eastern edge of the park and the Alpine Visitor Center at the summit of Trail Ridge Road, on the western side. It is typically open from July to September, depending on snowfall. It's a steep, narrow road (no wider than 14 feet), and trailers and vehicles longer than 25 feet are prohibited, but a trip on this 100-year-old thoroughfare is well worth the effort. For information on road closures, contact the park: ☎ *970/586–1206* 🌐 *www.nps.gov/romo*.

Inspiration

A Lady's Life in the Rocky Mountains, by Isabella L. Bird, has long been a favorite with Colorado residents and visitors to the park.

Hiking Rocky Mountain National Park: The Essential Guide, by Erik Stensland, matches your hiking ability and time allotted to find the perfect trail.

The Magnificent Mountain Women, by Janet Robertson, gives historical accounts of early pioneers.

Park Essentials

ACCESSIBILITY

All visitor centers are accessible to wheelchair users. The Sprague Lake, Coyote Valley, Lily Lake, and Bear Lake trails are all accessible loops of hard-packed gravel, ½ to 1 mile long. The Bear Lake trail is not entirely flat and is considered the most challenging of the accessible trails. A backcountry campsite at Sprague Lake accommodates up to 12 campers, including six in wheelchairs. The Moraine Park and Timber Creek campgrounds also offer some accessible sites and restroom facilities. All in-park shuttles and bus stops are wheelchair accessible.

PARK FEES AND PERMITS

Entrance fees are $25 per automobile for a one-day pass or $35 for a seven-day pass. Those who enter via foot or bicycle can get a seven-day pass for $20. Motorcyclists can get a seven-day pass for $30. An annual pass to Rocky Mountain costs $70, while the National Parks' America The Beautiful pass costs $80 and grants admission to more than 2,000 sites across the United States.

Wilderness camping requires a permit that's $30 per party from May through October, and free the rest of the year. Visit 🌐 *www.nps.gov/romo/planyourvisit/wilderness-camping.htm* before you go for a planning guide to backcountry camping. You can get your permit online, by phone (☎ *970/586–1242*), or in person. In person, you can get a day-of-trip permit year-round at one of the park's two backcountry offices, located next to the Beaver Meadows Visitor Center and in the Kawuneeche Visitor Center.

PARK HOURS

The park is open 24/7 year-round; some roads close in winter. It is in the Mountain time zone.

CELL PHONE RECEPTION

Cell phones work in some sections of the park, and free Wi-Fi can be accessed in and around the Beaver Meadows Visitor Center, Fall River, and the Kawuneeche Visitor Center.

Hotels

Bed-and-breakfasts and small inns in north central Colorado vary from old-fashioned fluffy cottages to sleek, modern buildings with understated lodge themes. If you want some pampering, guest ranches and spas will fit the bill.

In Estes Park, Grand Lake, and other nearby towns, the elevation keeps the climate cool, and you'll scarcely need (and you'll have a tough time finding) air-conditioned lodging. For a historic spot, try the Stanley Hotel in Estes Park, which dates to 1909. The park itself has no hotels or lodges. *Hotel reviews have been shortened. For full information, visit Fodors.com.*

Restaurants

Restaurants in north central Colorado run the gamut from simple diners with tasty, homey basics to elegant establishments with extensive wine lists. Some restaurants take reservations, but many—particularly midrange spots—seat on a first-come, first-served basis. In the park itself, the Trail Ridge Store next to the Alpine Visitor Center has a café and coffee bar open from late May to October. The park also has a handful of scenic picnic areas, all with tables and pit or flush toilets. *Restaurant reviews have been shortened. For full information, visit Fodors.com.*

What It Costs

$	$$	$$$	$$$$
RESTAURANTS			
under $13	$13–$18	$19–$25	over $25
HOTELS			
under $121	$121–$170	$171–$230	over $230

Tours

Green Jeep Tours

ADVENTURE TOURS | **FAMILY** | From the back of an open-air, neon-green Jeep on these tours, you can enjoy the majestic scenery while your experienced guide points out wildlife along the way. Green Jeep Tours also offers a three-hour tour in September and October that focuses on finding elk. Admission includes the cost of the one-day pass into the park. ✉ *157 Moraine Ave., Estes Park* ☎ *970/577–0034* 🎟 *From $90.*

Wildside 4x4 Tours

DRIVING TOURS | This company's most popular tour, the "Top of the World," takes visitors in an open-top vehicle all the way to Old Fall River Road and back down Trail Ridge. A waterfall tour and sunset valley tour offer great wildlife spottings at lower elevations. ✉ *212 E. Elkhorn Ave., Estes Park* ☎ *970/586–8687* 🌐 *www.wildside4x4tours.com* 🎟 *From $80.*

★ Yellow Wood Guiding

ADVENTURE TOURS | Guided photo safaris, offered year-round, ensure visitors leave the Rocky Mountain National Park with more than just memories. Customized for either beginners or experts, the tours offer the use of professional digital cameras for visitors who don't have their own. ✉ *404 Driftwood Ave., Estes Park* ☎ *303/775-5484* 🌐 *www.ywguiding.com* 🎫 *From $175.*

Visitor Information

CONTACTS Rocky Mountain National Park. ✉ *1000 U.S. 36, Estes Park* ☎ *970/586–1206* 🌐 *www.nps.gov/romo.*

Moraine Park

The starting point for most first-timers, the easternmost part of the park is easy to access via car or park shuttle. A number of popular trailheads originate here, particularly suited for half-day hikes, and a large campground accommodates those who want to stay overnight. It's also where you'll find the Beaver Meadows Visitor Center.

Sights

PICNIC AREAS

Hollowell Park

LOCAL INTEREST | In a meadow near Mill Creek, this lovely spot for a picnic has 10 tables and is open year-round. It's also close to the Hollowell Park and Mill Creek Basin Trailheads. ✉ *Off Bear Lake Rd., about 2½ miles from Moraine Park Visitor Center, Rocky Mountain National Park.*

TRAILS

Cub Lake Trail

TRAIL | This 4.6-mile, three-hour (round-trip) hike takes you through meadows and stands of aspen trees and up 540 feet in elevation to a lake with water lilies. *Moderate.* ✉ *Rocky Mountain National Park* ⊕ *Trailhead: at Cub Lake, about 1¾ miles from Moraine Park Campground.*

Deer Mountain Trail

TRAIL | This 6-mile round-trip trek to the top of 10,083-foot Deer Mountain is a great way for hikers who don't mind a bit of a climb to enjoy the views from the summit of a more manageable peak. You'll gain more than 1,000 feet in elevation as you follow the switchbacking trail through ponderosa pine, aspen, and fir trees. The reward at the top is a panoramic view of the park's eastern mountains. *Difficult.* ✉ *Rocky Mountain National Park* ⊕ *Trailhead: at Deer Ridge Junction, about 4 miles west of Moraine Park Visitor Center, U.S. 34 at U.S. 36.*

Fern Lake Trail

TRAIL | Heading to Odessa Lake from the north involves a steep hike, but on most days you'll encounter fewer other hikers than if you had begun the trip at Bear Lake. Along the way, you'll come to the Arch Rocks; the Pool, an eroded formation in the Big Thompson River; two waterfalls; and Fern Lake (3.8 miles from your starting point). Less than a mile farther, Odessa Lake itself lies at the foot of Tourmaline Gorge, below the craggy summits of Gabletop Mountain, Little Matterhorn, Knobtop Mountain, and Notchtop Mountain. For a full day of spectacular scenery, continue past Odessa to Bear Lake (9 miles total), where you can pick up the shuttle back to the Fern Lake Trailhead. *Moderate.* ✉ *Rocky Mountain National Park* ⊕ *Trailhead: off Fern Lake Rd., about 2½ miles south of Moraine Park Visitor Center.*

Sprague Lake

TRAIL | With virtually no elevation gain, this ½-mile, pine-lined looped path near a popular backcountry campground is wheelchair accessible and provides views of Hallet Peak and Flattop Mountain. *Easy.* ✉ *Rocky Mountain National Park* ⊕ *Trailhead: at Sprague Lake, Bear Lake Rd., 4½ miles southwest of Moraine Park Visitor Center.*

One of the easiest trails in the park is the loop around stunning Bear Lake.

 Restaurants

Café at Trail Ridge

$ | **AMERICAN** | The park's only source for food, this small café offers snacks, sandwiches, hot dogs, and soups. A coffee bar also serves fair-trade coffee, espresso drinks, and tea, plus water, juice, and salads. **Known for:** quick bite; fair-trade coffee; no-frills food. *Average main: $7 Trail Ridge Rd., at Alpine Visitor Center, Rocky Mountain National Park 970/586–3097 www.trailridgegiftstore.com Closed mid-Oct.–late-May. No dinner.*

 Shopping

Trail Ridge Store

CLOTHING | This is the park's only official store (though you'll find a small selection of park souvenirs and books at the visitor centers). Trail Ridge stocks sweatshirts and jackets, postcards, and assorted craft items. *Trail Ridge Rd., adjacent to Alpine Visitor Center, Rocky Mountain National Park www.trailridgegiftstore.com.*

Bear Lake

Thanks to its picturesque location, easy accessibility, and the good hiking trails nearby, this small lake below Flattop Mountain and Hallett Peak is one of the park's most popular destinations.

 Sights

PICNIC AREAS

Sprague Lake

LOCAL INTEREST | **FAMILY** | With 27 tables and 16 pedestal grills, this alfresco dining spot is open year-round, with flush toilets in the summer and vault toilets the rest of the year. *About ½ mile from intersection of Bear Lake Rd. and U.S. 36, 4 miles from Bear Lake, Rocky Mountain National Park.*

SCENIC DRIVES

Bear Lake Road

SCENIC DRIVE | This 23-mile round-trip drive offers superlative views of Longs Peak (14,259-foot summit) and the glaciers

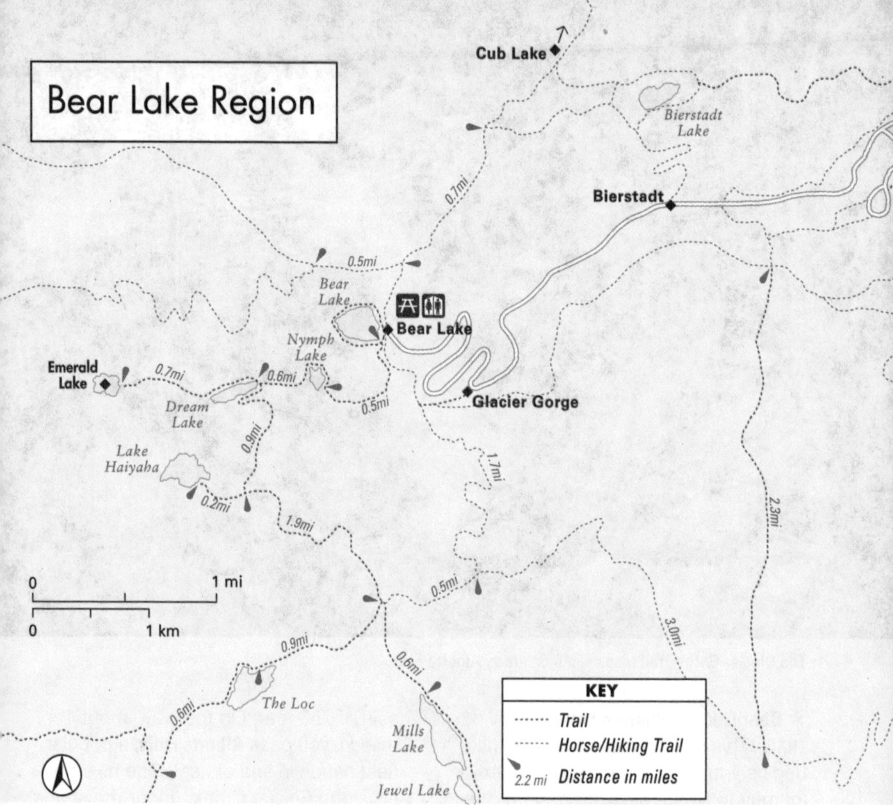

surrounding Bear Lake, winding past shimmering waterfalls shrouded with rainbows. You can either drive the road yourself (open year-round) or hop on one of the park's free shuttle buses. ✉ *Runs from the Beaver Meadow Entrance Station to Bear Lake, Rocky Mountain National Park.*

SCENIC STOPS

Farview Curve Overlook

VIEWPOINT | At an elevation of 10,120 feet, this lookout affords a panoramic view of the Colorado River near its origin and the Grand Ditch, a water diversion project dating from 1890 that's still in use today. You can also see the once-volcanic peaks of Never Summer Range along the park's western boundary. ✉ *Trail Ridge Rd., about 14 miles north of Kawuneeche Visitor Center, Rocky Mountain National Park.*

Forest Canyon Overlook

VIEWPOINT | Park at a dedicated lot to disembark on a wildflower-rich, 0.2-mile trail. Easy to access for all skill levels, this glacial valley overlook offers views of ice-blue pools (the Gorge Lakes) framed by ragged peaks. ✉ *Trail Ridge Rd., 6 miles east of Alpine Visitor Center, Rocky Mountain National Park.*

TRAILS

Bear Lake Trail

TRAIL | The virtually flat nature trail around Bear Lake is an easy, 0.6-mile loop that's wheelchair and stroller accessible. Sharing the route with you will likely be plenty of other hikers as well as songbirds and chipmunks. *Easy.* ✉ *Rocky Mountain National Park* ✣ *Trailhead: at Bear Lake, Bear Lake Rd.*

The Glacier Gorge Trail takes you past pretty Alberta Falls.

★ Bear Lake to Emerald Lake

TRAIL | This scenic, calorie-burning hike begins with a moderately level, ½-mile journey to **Nymph Lake.** From here, the trail gets steeper, with a 425-foot elevation gain, as it winds around for 0.6 miles to **Dream Lake.** The last stretch is the most arduous part of the hike, an almost all-uphill 0.7-mile trek to lovely **Emerald Lake,** where you can perch on a boulder and enjoy the view. All told, the hike is 3.6 miles, with an elevation gain of 605 feet. Allow two hours or more. *Moderate.* ✉ *Rocky Mountain National Park* ⊕ *Trailhead: at Bear Lake, off Bear Lake Rd., 8 miles southwest of the Moraine Park Visitor Center.*

★ Glacier Gorge Trail

TRAIL | The 2.8-mile hike to **Mills Lake** can be crowded, but the reward is one of the park's prettiest lakes, set against the breathtaking backdrop of Longs Peak, Pagoda Mountain, and the Keyboard of the Winds. There's a modest elevation gain of 750 feet. On the way, about 1 mile in, you pass **Alberta Falls,** a popular destination in and of itself. The hike travels along Glacier Creek, under the shade of a subalpine forest. Give yourself at least four hours for hiking and lingering. *Easy.* ✉ *Rocky Mountain National Park* ⊕ *Trailhead: off Bear Lake Rd., about 1 mile southeast of Bear Lake.*

Mills Lake

TRAIL | From this popular spot, you can admire the Keyboard of the Winds, a jagged ridge connecting Pagoda and Longs Peaks that looks like the top of a spiny reptile's back. The 5.6-mile hike gains 750 feet in elevation as it takes you past Alberta Falls and Glacier Falls en route to the shimmering lake at the mouth of Glacier Gorge. *Moderate.* ✉ *Rocky Mountain National Park* ⊕ *Trailhead: at Glacier Gorge Junction, about 1 mile from Bear Lake.*

Longs Peak

At 14,259 feet above sea level, Longs Peak has long fascinated explorers to the region. Longs Peak is the northernmost of the Fourteeners—the 53 mountains in Colorado that reach above the 14,000-foot mark—and one of more than 114 named mountains in the park that are higher than 10,000 feet. The peak, in the park's southeast quadrant, has a distinctive flat-topped, rectangular summit that is visible from many spots on the park's east side and on Trail Ridge Road.

Explorer and author Isabella L. Bird wrote of it: "It is one of the noblest of mountains, but in one's imagination it grows to be much more than a mountain. It becomes invested with a personality." It was named after Major Stephen H. Long, who led an expedition in 1820 up the Platte River to the base of the Rockies. Long never ascended the mountain—in fact, he didn't even get within 40 miles of it—but a few decades later, in 1868, the one-armed Civil War veteran John Wesley Powell climbed to its summit.

The ambitious climb to Longs summit is recommended only for those who are strong climbers and well acclimated to the altitude. If you're up for the 10- to 15-hour climb, begin before dawn so that you're down from the summit prior to typical afternoon thunderstorms.

Sights

TRAILS

Chasm Lake Trail

TRAIL | Nestled in the shadow of Longs Peak and Mount Meeker, Chasm Lake offers one of Colorado's most impressive backdrops, which also means you can expect to encounter plenty of other hikers on the way. The 4.2-mile Chasm Lake Trail, reached via the Longs Peak Trail, has a 2,360-foot elevation gain. Just before the lake, you'll need to climb a small rock ledge, which can be a bit of a challenge for the less sure-footed; follow the cairns for the most straightforward route. Once atop the ledge, you'll catch your first memorable view of the lake. *Difficult.* ✉ *Rocky Mountain National Park* ✣ *Trailhead: at Longs Peak Ranger Station, off Rte. 7, 10 miles from the Beaver Meadows Visitor Center.*

Longs Peak Trail

TRAIL | Climbing this 14,259-foot mountain (one of 53 "Fourteeners" in Colorado) is an ambitious goal for almost anyone—but only those who are very fit and acclimated to the altitude should attempt it. The 16-mile round-trip climb requires a predawn start (3 am is ideal), so that you're off the summit before the typical summer afternoon thunderstorm hits. Also, the last 2 miles or so of the trail are very exposed—you have to traverse narrow ledges with vertigo-inducing drop-offs. That said, summiting Longs can be one of the most rewarding experiences you'll ever have. The Keyhole route is the most popular means of ascent, and the number of people going up it on a summer day can be astounding, given the rigors of the climb. Though just as scenic, the Loft route, between Longs and Mount Meeker from Chasm Lake, is less crowded but not as clearly marked and therefore more difficult to navigate. *Difficult.* ✉ *Rocky Mountain National Park* ✣ *Trailhead: at Longs Peak Ranger Station, off Rte. 7, 10 miles from Beaver Meadows Visitor Center.*

Trail Ridge Road

The park's star attraction and the world's highest continuous paved highway (topping out at 12,183 feet), this 48-mile road connects the park's gateways of Estes Park and Grand Lake. The views around each bend—of moraines and glaciers, and craggy hills framing emerald meadows carpeted with columbine —are truly awesome. As it passes through three ecosystems—montane, subalpine, and arctic tundra—the road climbs 4,300 feet.

You can complete a one-way trip across the park on Trail Ridge Road in two hours, but it's best to give yourself three or four hours to allow for leisurely breaks at the overlooks. Note that the middle part of the road closes with the first big snow (typically by mid-October) and most often reopens around Memorial Day, though you can still drive up about 10 miles from the west and 8 miles from the east.

HISTORIC SIGHTS

Lulu City

ARCHAEOLOGICAL SITE | The remains of a few cabins are all that's left of this onetime silver-mining town, established around 1880. Reach it by hiking the 3.6-mile Colorado River Trail. Look for wagon ruts from the old Stewart Toll Road and mine tailings in nearby Shipler Park (this is also a good place to spot moose). ✉ *Off Trail Ridge Rd., 9½ miles north of Grand Lake Entrance Station, Rocky Mountain National Park.*

PICNIC AREAS

Endovalley

LOCAL INTEREST | With 32 tables and 30 fire grates, this is the largest picnic area in the park. Here, you'll find aspen groves, nice views of Fall River Pass—and lovely Fan Lake a short hike away. ✉ *Rocky Mountain National Park* ✣ *Off U.S. 34, at beginning of Old Fall River Rd., about 4½ miles from Fall River Visitor Center.*

SCENIC DRIVES

Old Fall River Road

SCENIC DRIVE | More than 100 years old and never more than 14 feet wide, this road stretches from the park's east side to the Fall River Pass (11,796 feet above sea level) on the west. The drive provides a few white-knuckle moments, as the road is steep, serpentine, and lacking in guardrails. Start at West Horseshoe Park, which has the park's largest concentrations of sheep and elk, and head up the gravel road, passing Chasm Falls. ✉ *Runs north of and roughly parallel to Trail Ridge Road, starting near Endovalley Campground (on east) and ending at Fall River Pass/Alpine Visitor Center (on west), Rocky Mountain National Park.*

TRAILS

Chapin Pass

TRAIL | This is a tough hike, but it comes with great views of the park's eastern lower valleys. It's about 3½ miles one way, including a 2,874-foot gain in elevation to the summit of Ypsilon Mountain (elevation 13,514 feet); you pass the summits of Mount Chapin and Mount Chiquita on the way. From the trailhead, the path heads downhill to Chapin Creek. For a short distance after leaving the trailhead, keep a sharp eye out to the right for a less obvious trail that heads uphill to the tree line and disappears. From here head up along the steep ridge to the summit of Mount Chapin. Chiquita and Ypsilon are to the left, and the distance between each peak is about 1 mile and involves a descent of about 400 feet to the saddle and an ascent of 1,000 feet along the ridge to Chiquita. From Ypsilon's summit you'll look down 2,000 feet at Spectacle Lakes. You may wish to bring a topo map and compass. *Difficult.* ✉ *Rocky Mountain National Park* ✣ *Trailhead: at Chapin Pass, off Old Fall River Rd., about 6½ miles from the Endovalley Picnic Area.*

Timber Creek

Located along the Colorado River, the west part of the park attracts fewer people and more wildlife in its valleys, especially moose. The towering mountain vistas are fewer here than in the east, but the expansive meadows, rivers, and lakes offer their own peaceful beauty. Unfortunately, wildfires in 2020 destroyed many acres of forest and damaged trails here, so check conditions and closures before setting off.

Sights

HISTORIC SITES

Holzwarth Historic Site

ARCHAEOLOGICAL SITE | FAMILY | A scenic ½-mile interpretive trail leads you over the Colorado River to the original dude ranch that the Holzwarth family, some of the park's original homesteaders, ran between the 1920s and 1950s. Allow about an hour to view the buildings—including a dozen small guest cabins—and chat with a ranger. Though the site is open year-round, the inside of the buildings can be seen only June through early September. ✉ *Off U.S. 34, about 8 miles north of Kawuneeche Visitor Center, Estes Park.*

TRAILS

Colorado River Trail

TRAIL | This walk to the ghost town of Lulu City on the west side of the park is excellent for looking for the bighorn sheep, elk, and moose that reside in the area. Part of the former stagecoach route that went from Granby to Walden, the 3.7-mile trail parallels the infant Colorado River to the meadow where Lulu City once stood. The elevation gain is 350 feet. *Moderate.* ✉ *Rocky Mountain National Park* ✣ *Trailhead: at Colorado River, off Trail Ridge Rd., 1¾ miles north of the Timber Creek Campground.*

Continental Divide National Scenic Trail

TRAIL | This 3,100-mile corridor, which extends from Montana's Canadian border to the southern edge of New Mexico, enters Rocky Mountain National Park in two places, at trailheads only about 4 miles apart and located on either side of the Kawuneeche Visitor Center on Trail Ridge Road, at the park's southwestern end. Within the park, it covers about 30 miles of spectacular montane and subalpine terrain and follows the existing Green Mountain, Tonahutu Creek, North Inlet, and East Shore Trails. *Moderate.* ✉ *Rocky Mountain National Park* ✣ *Trailheads: at Harbison Meadows Picnic Area, off Trail Ridge Rd., about 1 mile inside park from Grand Lake Entrance, and at East Shore Trailhead, just south of Grand Lake.*

Elk Bugling

In September and October, there are traffic jams in the park as people drive up to listen to the elk bugling. Rangers and park volunteers keep track of where the elk are and direct visitors to the mating spots. The bugling is high-pitched, and if it's light enough, you can see the elk put their heads in the air.

East Inlet Trail

TRAIL | An easy hike of 0.3 miles from East Inlet trailhead, just outside the park in Grand Lake, will get you to **Adams Falls** in about 15 minutes. The area around the falls is often packed with visitors, so if you have time, continue east to enjoy more solitude, see wildlife, and catch views of **Mount Craig** from near the East Meadow campground. Note, however, that the trail beyond the falls has an elevation gain of between 1,500 and 1,900 feet, making it a more challenging hike. *Easy.* ✉ *Grand Lake* ✣ *Trailhead: at East Inlet, end of W. Portal Rd. (CO 278) in Grand Lake.*

Wild Basin

This section in the southeast region of the park consists of lovely expanses of subalpine forest punctuated by streams and lakes. The area's high peaks, along the Continental Divide, are not as easily accessible as those in the vicinity of Bear Lake; hiking to the base of the divide and back makes for a long day. Nonetheless, a visit here is worth the drive south from Estes Park, and because the Wild Basin trailhead is set apart from the park hub, crowding isn't a problem.

Elk are some of the park's most famous residents.

Sights

TRAILS

Bluebird Lake Trail

TRAIL | The 6-mile climb from the Wild Basin trailhead to Bluebird Lake (2,478-foot elevation gain) is especially scenic. You pass Copeland Falls, Calypso Cascades, and Ouzel Falls, plus an area that was burned in a lightning-instigated fire in 1978—today it's a mix of bright pink fireweed and charred tree trunks. *Difficult.* ✉ *Rocky Mountain National Park* ✣ *Trailhead: at Wild Basin Ranger Station, about 2 miles west of Wild Basin Entrance Station off Rte. 7, 12¾ miles south of Estes Park.*

Copeland Falls

TRAIL | **FAMILY** | The 0.3-mile hike to these Wild Basin Area falls is a good option for families, as the terrain is relatively flat (there's only a 15-foot elevation gain). *Easy.* ✉ *Rocky Mountain National Park* ✣ *Trailhead: at Wild Basin Ranger Station.*

Activities

BICYCLING

There are no bike paths in the park, and bikes are not allowed on trails. Bicyclists are permitted on Trail Ridge Road, but it's too strenuous for most people due to its enormous changes in elevation. Those who have an extra lung or two to spare, however, might tackle a ride up the gravel 9-mile Old Fall River Road, then a ride down Trail Ridge Road.

BIRD-WATCHING

Spring and summer, early in the morning, are the best times for bird-watching in the park. **Lumpy Ridge** is a nesting ground for several kinds of birds of prey. Migratory songbirds from South America have summer breeding grounds near the **Endovalley Picnic Area.** The **alpine tundra** is habitat for white-tailed ptarmigan. The **Alluvial Fan** is the place for viewing broad-tailed hummingbirds, hairy woodpeckers, ouzels, and the occasional raptor.

CAMPING

The park's five campgrounds accommodate campers looking to stay in a tent, trailer, or RV (only three campgrounds accept reservations—up to six months in advance at 🌐 *www.recreation.gov* or 🌐 *www.reserveamerica.com*; the others fill up on a first-come, first-served basis).

Aspenglen Campground. This quiet, east-side spot near the north entrance is set in open pine woodland along Fall River. There are a few excellent walk-in sites for those who want to pitch a tent away from the crowds but still be close to the car. Reservations are recommended in summer. ✉ *Drive past Fall River Visitor Center on U.S. 34 and turn left at the campground road.*

Glacier Basin Campground. This spot offers expansive views of the Continental Divide, easy access to the free summer shuttles to Bear Lake and Estes Park, and ranger-led evening programs in the summer. Reservations are essential. ✉ *Drive 5 miles south on Bear Lake Rd. from U.S. 36* ☎ *877/444–6777.*

Longs Peak Campground. Open May to November, this campground is only a short walk from the Longs Peak trailhead, making it a favorite among hikers looking to get an early start there. The tent-only sites, which are first come, first served, are limited to eight people; firewood, lighting fluid, and charcoal are sold in summer. ✉ *9 miles south of Estes Park on Rte. 7.*

Moraine Park Campground. The only campground in Rocky Mountain open year-round, this spot connects to many hiking trails and has easy access to the free summer shuttles. Rangers lead evening programs in the summer. You'll hear elk bugling if you camp here in September or October. Reservations are essential from mid-May to late September. ✉ *Drive south on Bear Lake Rd. from U.S. 36, 1 mile to campground entrance.*

Timber Creek Campground. Anglers love this spot on the Colorado River, 10 miles from Grand Lake village and the only east-side campground. In the evening you can sit in on ranger-led campfire programs. The 98 campsites are first come, first served. ✉ *1 Trail Ridge Rd., 2 miles west of Alpine Visitor Center.*

Wilderness Camping, Rocky Mountain National Park. Experienced hikers can camp at one of the park's many designated backcountry sites with advance reservations or a day-of-trip permit (which comes with a $30 fee in May through October). Contact the Wilderness Office before starting out to get a sense of current conditions. ✉ *Beaver Meadows Visitor Center, Kawuneeche Visitor Center* ☎ *970/586–1242.*

FISHING

Rocky Mountain is a wonderful place to fish, especially for trout—German brown, brook, rainbow, cutthroat, and greenback cutthroat—but check at a visitor center about regulations and closures. No fishing is allowed at Bear Lake. To avoid the crowds, rangers recommend angling in the more remote backcountry. To fish in the park, anyone 16 and older must have a valid Colorado fishing license, which you can obtain at local sporting-goods stores. See 🌐 *www.cpw.state.co.us* for details.

Estes Angler

FISHING | This popular fishing guide arranges fly-fishing trips from two to eight hours into the park's quieter regions, year-round. The best times for fishing are generally from April to mid-November. Equipment is also available for rent. ✉ *338 W. Riverside Dr., Estes Park* ☎ *970/586–2110, 800/586–2110* 🌐 *www.estesangler.com* 🎫 *From $149.*

Kirks Fly Shop

CAMPING—SPORTS-OUTDOORS | This Estes Park outfitter offers various guided fly-fishing trips, as well as backpacking, horseback, and llama pack trips. The store also carries fishing and backpacking gear. ✉ *230 E. Elkhorn Ave., Estes Park* ☎ *970/577–0790, 877/669–1859* 🌐 *www.kirksflyshop.com* 🎫 *From $149.*

Scot's Sporting Goods

FISHING | This shop rents and sells fishing gear, and provides instruction trips daily from May through mid-October. Clinics, geared toward first-timers, focus on casting, reading the water, identifying insects for flies, and properly presenting natural and artificial flies to the fish. ✉ *870 Moraine Ave., Estes Park* ☎ *970/586–2877 May–Sept., 970/443–4932 Oct.–Apr.* 🌐 *www.scotssportinggoods.com* 🎫 *From $220.*

HIKING

Rocky Mountain National Park contains more than 355 miles of hiking trails, so you could theoretically wander the park for weeks. Most visitors explore just a small portion of these trails—those that are closest to the roads and visitor centers—which means that some of the park's most accessible and scenic paths can resemble a backcountry highway on busy summer days. The high-alpine terrain around Bear Lake is the park's most popular hiking area, and although it's well worth exploring, you'll get a more frontierlike experience by hiking one of the trails in the less-explored sections of the park, such as the far northern end or in the Wild Basin area to the south.

Keep in mind that trails at higher elevations may have some snow on them, even in late summer. And because of afternoon thunderstorms on most summer days, an early morning start is highly recommended: the last place you want to be when a storm approaches is on a peak or anywhere above the tree line.

HORSEBACK RIDING

Horses and riders can access 260 miles of trails in Rocky Mountain National Park.

Glacier Creek Stable

HORSEBACK RIDING | **FAMILY** | Located within the park near Sprague Lake, Glacier Creek Stable offers 2- to 10-hour rides to Glacier Basin, Odessa Lake, and Storm Pass. ✉ *Glacier Creek Campground, off Bear Lake Rd. near Sprague Lake* ☎ *970/586–3244 stables, 970/586–4577 off-season reservations* 🌐 *sombrero.com* 🎫 *From $70.*

Moraine Park Stable

HORSEBACK RIDING | **FAMILY** | Located inside the park just before the Cub Lake Trailhead, Moraine Park Stable offers two- to eight-hour trips to Beaver Meadows, Fern Lake, and Tourmaline Gorge. ✉ *549 Fern Lake Rd.* ☎ *970/586–2327 stables, 970/586–4577 off-season reservations* 🌐 *www.sombrero.com* 🎫 *From $70.*

National Park Gateway Stables

HORSEBACK RIDING | **FAMILY** | Guided trips into the national park range from two-hour rides to Little Horseshoe Park to half-day rides to Endo Valley and Fall River. The six-hour ride to the summit of Deer Mountain is a favorite. Preschool-aged children can take a 10- or 30-minute pony ride on nearby trails. ✉ *4600 Fall River Rd., Estes Park* ☎ *970/586–5269* 🌐 *www.skhorses.com* 🎫 *From $80.*

ROCK CLIMBING

Experts as well as novices can try hundreds of classic and big-wall climbs here (there's also ample opportunity for bouldering and mountaineering). The burgeoning sport of ice climbing also thrives in the park. The Diamond, Lumpy Ridge, and Petit Grepon are the places for serious rock climbing, while well-known ice-climbing spots include Hidden Falls, Loch Vale, and Emerald and Black lakes.

★ Colorado Mountain School

CLIMBING/MOUNTAINEERING | **FAMILY** | Guiding climbers since 1877, Colorado Mountain School is the park's only official provider of technical climbing services. They can teach you rock climbing, mountaineering, ice climbing, avalanche survival, and many other skills. Take introductory half-day and one- to five-day courses on climbing and rappelling technique, or sign up for guided introductory trips, full-day climbs, and longer expeditions. Make reservations a month in advance for summer climbs. ✉ *341 Moraine Ave., Estes Park* ☎ *720/387-8944, 303/447-2804* 🌐 *coloradomountainschool.com* 🎫 *From $199.*

WINTER ACTIVITIES

Each winter, the popularity of snowshoeing in the park increases. It's a wonderful way to experience Rocky Mountain's majestic winter side, when the jagged peaks are softened with a blanket of snow and the summer hordes are nonexistent. You can snowshoe any of the summer hiking trails that are accessible by road; many of them also become well-traveled cross-country ski trails. Two trails to try are Tonahutu Creek Trail (near Kawuneeche Visitor Center) and the Colorado River Trail to Lulu City (start at the Timber Creek Campground).

Estes Park Mountain Shop
CLIMBING/MOUNTAINEERING | You can rent or buy snowshoes and skis here, as well as fishing, hiking, and climbing equipment. The store is open year-round and gives four-, six-, and eight-hour guided snowshoeing, fly-fishing, and climbing trips to areas in and around Rocky Mountain National Park. ✉ *2050 Big Thompson Ave., Estes Park* ☎ *970/586-6548, 866/303-6548* 🌐 *www.estesparkmountainshop.com* 🎫 *From $95.*

Never Summer Mountain Products
CAMPING—SPORTS-OUTDOORS | This well-stocked shop sells and rents all sorts of outdoor equipment, including cross-country skis, hiking gear, kayaks, and camping supplies. ✉ *919 Grand Ave., Grand Lake* ☎ *970/627-3642* 🌐 *www.neversummermtn.com.*

Estes Park

2 miles east of Rocky Mountain National Park via U.S. 36E.

The vast scenery on the U.S. 36 approach to Estes Park gives little hint of the grandeur to come, but if ever there was a classic picture-postcard Rockies view, Estes Park has it. The town sits at an altitude of more than 7,500 feet, at the foot of a stunning backdrop of 14,259-foot Longs Peak, the majestic Stanley Hotel, and surrounding mountains.

GETTING HERE AND AROUND

To get to Estes Park from Boulder, take U.S. 36 north through Lyons and the town of Pinewood Springs (about 38 miles). You can also reach Estes Park via the Peak to Peak Scenic and Historic Byway. To reach the byway from Boulder, take Highway 119 west to Nederland and turn right (north) onto Highway 72, or follow Sunshine Canyon Drive/Gold Hill Road into Ward, and pick up Highway 72 there.

Estes Park's main downtown area is walkable, which is good news on summer weekends, when traffic can be heavy (and parking can be challenging). Keep an eye out for parking signs throughout town, as the public lots are your best chance for a close-in spot.

The National Park Service operates a free bus service in and around Estes Park and between Estes Park and Rocky Mountain National Park. Buses operate daily from early June to Labor Day, then on weekends until the end of September.

VISITOR INFORMATION Estes Park Visitor Center. ✉ *500 Big Thompson Ave.* ☎ *970/577-9900, 800/443-7837* 🌐 *www.visitestespark.com.*

Sights

Estes Park Museum

MUSEUM | The museum showcases Ute and pioneer artifacts, displays on the founding of Rocky Mountain National Park, and changing exhibits. It also publishes a self-guided walking tour of historic sites, which are mostly clustered along Elkhorn Avenue downtown. *200 4th St. 970/586–6256 www.estes.org/museum Free.*

MacGregor Ranch Museum

HISTORIC SITE | This working ranch, homesteaded in 1873, is on the National Register of Historic Places and provides a well-preserved record of typical ranch life. Take a guided tour of the 1896 ranch house, then explore the outbuildings and machinery on your own as you take in views of the Twin Owls and Longs Peak. *180 MacGregor La. 1½ miles north of town on U.S. 34. Turn right on MacGregor La., a dirt road 970/586–3749 www.macgregorranch.org $7.*

Restaurants

Bighorn Restaurant

$ | **AMERICAN** | **FAMILY** | An Estes Park staple since 1972, this family-run outfit is where the locals go for breakfast. Try a double-cheese omelet, huevos rancheros, or grits before heading into the park in the morning. **Known for:** hearty breakfast; huge portions; picnic lunches to-go. *Average main: $12 401 W. Elkhorn Ave. 970/586–2792 www.estesparkbighorn.com.*

Estes Park Brewery

$ | **AMERICAN** | If you want to sample some local brews, check out the Estes Park Brewery, which has been crafting beer since 1993. The food is no-frills (beer chili is the specialty), and the menu includes things like pizza, burgers, sandwiches, and house-made bratwurst. **Known for:** local beer; pool tables; laid-back atmosphere. *Average main: $11 470 Prospect Village Dr. 970/586–5421 www.epbrewery.com.*

Mama Rose's

$$ | **ITALIAN** | **FAMILY** | An Estes Park institution since 1989, Mama Rose's consistently serves no-nonsense Italian meals, including the house specialty: hearty lasagna concocted with house-made meatballs and sausage. There are also plenty of lighter options, including vegetarian and gluten-free entrées, as well as build-your-own pasta from three noodles, six sauces, and nine meats and vegetables. *Average main: $16 338 E. Elkhorn Ave. 970/586–3330 www.mamarosesrestaurant.com Closed Jan.*

Poppy's Pizza & Grill

$ | **PIZZA** | **FAMILY** | This casual riverside eatery serves creative signature pizzas. Try the spinach, artichoke, and feta pie made with sun-dried tomato pesto. **Known for:** create-your-own pizza; riverfront patio; vegan- and gluten-free-friendly. *Average main: $10 342 E. Elkhorn Ave. 970/586–8282 www.poppyspizzaandgrill.com Closed Jan.*

★ Seasoned

$$$$ | **AMERICAN** | With a menu that changes monthly, Seasoned takes its name to heart with its always-changing ingredients from local farms. The creative dishes, created by chef-owner and Michelin-star veteran Rob Corey, reflect influences from North, South, and Central America and feature Colorado specialties like lamb, trout, and bass. **Known for:** creative cuisine; Colorado lamb, trout, and bass; attentive service. *Average main: $30 205 Park La. 970/586-9000 seasonedbistro.com Closed Mon.*

Hotels

Boulder Brook

$$$$ | **HOTEL** | Watch elk stroll past your spacious luxury suite at this smart, secluded spot on the river amid towering pines. **Pros:** scenic location; quiet area; attractive grounds. **Cons:** not within

walking distance of attractions; no nearby dining. $ *Rooms from: $250* ✉ *1900 Fall River Rd.* ☎ *970/586–0910, 800/238–0910* 🌐 *www.boulderbrook.com* 🛏 *20 suites* 🍽 *No meals.*

Glacier Lodge

$$ | **RESORT** | **FAMILY** | Families are the specialty at this secluded, 22-acre guest resort on the banks of the Big Thompson River. **Pros:** great place for families; attractive grounds on the river; on free bus route. **Cons:** not within walking distance of attractions; along rather busy road. $ *Rooms from: $160* ✉ *2166 Hwy. 66* ☎ *800/523–3920* 🌐 *www.glacierlodgeonline.com* ⏲ *Closed Nov.–Apr.* 🛏 *30 cabins* 🍽 *No meals.*

★ **The Maxwell Inn**

$$ | **HOTEL** | Within walking distance of downtown, this family-run spot features small but comfortable rooms decorated with arts and crafts–style furnishings and locally built custom wood furniture. **Pros:** walking distance to downtown; relatively affordable for Estes Park; clean and comfortable. **Cons:** rooms are small; fairly basic accommodations. $ *Rooms from: $145* ✉ *553 W. Elkhorn Ave.* ☎ *970/586-2833* 🌐 *www.themaxwellinn.com* ⏲ *Closed Jan. and Feb.* 🛏 *21 rooms* 🍽 *Free Breakfast.*

★ **Stanley Hotel**

$$$$ | **HOTEL** | Perched regally on a hill, with a commanding view of town, the Stanley is one of Colorado's great old hotels, featuring Georgian colonial–style architecture and a storied, haunted history, inspiring Stephen King's novel *The Shining* and daily "ghost" tours. **Pros:** historic hotel; many rooms have been updated; good restaurant. **Cons:** some rooms are small and tight; building is old; no air-conditioning. $ *Rooms from: $299* ✉ *333 Wonderview Ave.* ☎ *970/577–4000, 800/976–1377* 🌐 *www.stanleyhotel.com* 🛏 *140 rooms* 🍽 *No meals.*

YMCA of the Rockies – Estes Park Center

$$ | **RESORT** | **FAMILY** | Surrounded on three sides by Rocky Mountain National Park, this 860-acre family-friendly property has attractive, clean lodge rooms (with either queen, full, or bunk beds), simple cabins for two to four people, and larger cabins that can sleep as many as 88 people. **Pros:** good value for large groups and longer stays; lots of family-oriented activities and amenities; stunning scenery. **Cons:** very large, busy, and crowded property; fills fast; location requires vehicle to visit town or the national park. $ *Rooms from: $169* ✉ *2515 Tunnel Rd.* ☎ *970/586–3341, 888/613–9622 family reservations, 800/777–9622 group reservations* 🌐 *www.ymcarockies.org* 🛏 *770 rooms* 🍽 *Some meals.*

Nightlife

Lonigans

BARS/PUBS | This fun Irish pub has karaoke on Wednesday, Friday, and Saturday nights starting at 9 pm, and the occasional theme party like "Freaky Friday" and "International Night," featuring plentiful drink specials. ✉ *110 W. Elkhorn Ave.* ☎ *970/586–4346* 🌐 *www.lonigans.com.*

Shopping

Shopping in Estes Park focuses around several T-shirt and souvenir shops, a labyrinth of sweets shops (taffy, caramel corn, and chocolate, oh my!), plus a number of more upscale gift shops and art galleries.

CRAFTS AND ART GALLERIES

Earthwood Collections

ART GALLERIES | This fine art and handicrafts shop sells a wide assortment of art, including ceramics, frames, jewelry, oil paintings, and more. ✉ *141 E. Elkhorn Ave.* ☎ *970/577–8100* 🌐 *www.earthwoodcollections.com.*

Images of Rocky Mountain National Park
ART GALLERIES | This shop showcases photographer Erik Stensland's stunning images of the park—a must-see collection of local photography. ✉ *203 Park La.* ☎ *970/586–4352* 🌐 *www.imagesofrmnp.com.*

Patterson Glassworks of Estes Park
ART GALLERIES | Watch glassblowing in action and browse a wide variety of glass creations. ✉ *323 W. Elkhorn Ave.* ☎ *970/586–8619* 🌐 *www.glassworksofestespark.com.*

Wild Spirits Gallery
ART GALLERIES | Shop for limited-edition prints, photographs, and paintings of the West and Rocky Mountain National Park. Custom framing and shipping are also available. ✉ *148 W. Elkhorn Ave.* ☎ *970/586–4392* 🌐 *wildspiritsgalleryestespark.com.*

Grand Lake

1½ miles west of Rocky Mountain National Park via U.S. 34.

The tiny town of Grand Lake, known to locals as Grand Lake Village, is doubly blessed by its surroundings. It's the western gateway to Rocky Mountain National Park and also sits on the shores of its namesake, the state's largest natural lake and the highest-altitude yacht anchorage in America. With views of snowy peaks and verdant mountains from just about any vantage point, Grand Lake is adored by Coloradans for sailing, canoeing, waterskiing, and fishing. In winter it's *the* snowmobiling and ice-fishing destination.

GETTING HERE AND AROUND

Grand Lake is about 60 miles from Boulder or 96 miles from Denver, as the crow flies, but to get here by car you have to circle around the mountains and travel more than 100 miles from Boulder and 171 miles from Denver. You've got two options: Take the highway the whole way (U.S. 36, CO Highway 93, I–70, U.S. 40, and U.S. 34) or take the scenic route (U.S 36 north to Estes Park, then U.S. 34 across Rocky Mountain National Park). The section of U.S. 34 that passes through Rocky Mountain National Park, known as Trail Ridge Road, is the highest paved road in America, and you can stop for a photo op at the Continental Divide sign. Trail Ridge Road closes every winter, typically between mid-October and late May.

You can explore most of the town on foot, including the historic boardwalk on Grand Avenue, with more than 70 shops and restaurants. Traffic and parking aren't a problem here.

VISITOR INFORMATION Grand Lake Chamber of Commerce and Visitor Center. ✉ *14700 U.S. 34* ☎ *970/627–3402, 800/531–1019* 🌐 *www.grandlakechamber.com.*

Sights

Colorado River Headwaters Scenic & Historic Byway
SCENIC DRIVE | Whether you're staying in Grand Lake or merely stopping on your way to another destination, the 80-mile (one way) Colorado River Headwaters Scenic & Historic Byway between Grand Lake and State Bridge is worth a side trip. The route takes you along the Colorado River, past hot springs, ranches, and reservoirs, through wide spaces with views of mountains, along deep canyons, and through a seemingly incongruous sage-covered desert. Along the turnouts within Gore Canyon, you can get a good look at the roaring Colorado River and train tracks below. Stop by the viewing platform at the Gore Canyon Whitewater Park at Pumphouse to see paddlers and boarders playing in the waves. ✉ *Grand Lake* ☎ *303/757–9786.*

Grand Lake
BODY OF WATER | According to Ute legend, the fine mists that shroud Grand Lake at dawn are the risen spirits of women and children whose raft capsized as

Grand Lake is the largest and deepest natural lake in the state.

they were fleeing a marauding party of Cheyennes and Arapahos. Grand Lake is the largest and deepest natural lake in Colorado. It feeds into two much larger man-made reservoirs, Lake Granby and Shadow Mountain Lake, and these three water bodies as well as Monarch Lake and Willow Creek and Meadow Creek reservoirs are called the "Great Lakes of Colorado." ✉ *Grand Lake.*

Restaurants

Cy's Deli

$ | **DELI** | The aroma of homemade bread and soup hint at the loving care this sandwich shop infuses into its food. Grab a quick breakfast burrito or sandwich to take out on the trail, or stay and snag a table inside the cheerful blue deli or on the sunny patio. **Known for:** quick lunch; green and red chile breakfast burritos; fresh-bread sandwiches. *Average main: $9* ✉ *717 Grand Ave.* ☎ *970/627–3354* 🌐 *www.cysdeli.com* ⏲ *Closed Nov.–mid-May.*

★ Fat Cat Cafe

$ | **CAFÉ** | Located on the boardwalk, this cozy family-run café serves up hearty helpings, as well as advice on local sightseeing. The weekend breakfast buffet includes nearly 50 items—including biscuits and gravy, huevos rancheros casserole with house-made green chile sauce, and a wide selection of scones, pastries, and pies that are baked in-house. **Known for:** sprawling brunch buffet; homemade pies; homey decor. *Average main: $10* ✉ *916 Grand Ave.* ☎ *970/627–0900* ⏲ *Closed Tues. No dinner.*

★ Sagebrush BBQ & Grill

$ | **SOUTHERN** | Falling-off-the-bone, melt-in-your-mouth barbecue pork, chicken, and beef draw local and out-of-town attention to this homey café. Munch on peanuts (and toss the shells on the floor) while dining at tables with cowhide-patterned tablecloths set against a backdrop of license plates from across the country. **Known for:** peanut shell–lined floor; wild game burgers and sausage; rotating daily specials. *Average main: $12* ✉ *1101*

Grand Ave. ☎ *970/627–1404* 🌐 *www.sagebrushbbq.com.*

Hotels

Grand Lake Lodge

$$ | **HOTEL** | Built in 1920 and on the National Register of Historic Places, this lodge is perched on the hillside overlooking Grand Lake and has 70 cabins, a swimming pool, hot tub, picnic tables, a playground, and sundecks. **Pros:** stunning views of Grand Lake; historic charm; near Rocky Mountain National Park. **Cons:** service can be lacking; some rooms are small. Ⓢ *Rooms from: $170* ✉ *15500 U.S. 34* ✥ *Drive up Trail Ridge Rd. toward Rocky Mountain National Park and turn right on Tonahutu Ridge Rd.* ☎ *970/627–3967, 855/585–0004* 🌐 *www.highwaywestvacations.com/properties/grand-lake-lodge* ⏲ *Closed mid-Oct.–mid-May* *70 cabins* 🍴 *No meals.*

★ Historic Rapids Lodge & Restaurant

$ | **HOTEL** | This handsome lodgepole-pine structure, which dates to 1915, is tucked on the banks of the Tonahutu River and features seven lodge rooms decorated with antique furnishings. **Pros:** in-house restaurant; condos are great for longer stays; quiet area of town. **Cons:** unpaved parking area; lodge rooms are above restaurant; all lodge rooms are on second floor and there's no elevator. Ⓢ *Rooms from: $98* ✉ *210 Rapids La.* ☎ *970/627–3707* 🌐 *www.rapidslodge.com* ⏲ *Closed Apr. and Nov.* *31 rooms* 🍴 *No meals.*

Mountain Lakes Lodge

$ | **HOTEL** | **FAMILY** | Families and dog lovers enjoy these comfortable, charming, whimsically decorated log cabins, which have such unique touches as cow-spotted walls, canoe-paddle headboards, and wooden ducks swimming on the ceiling. **Pros:** dog-friendly; close to fishing; good value. **Cons:** outside of town (and services); two-night minimum; no daily housekeeping. Ⓢ *Rooms from: $99* ✉ *10480 U.S. 34* ☎ *970/627–8448* 🌐 *www.grandlakelodging.net* ⏲ *Closed for 10 days in Apr.* *12 rooms* 🍴 *No meals.*

Western Riviera Lakeside Lodging and Events

$$$ | **HOTEL** | This friendly property offers lakeside motel rooms, cabins, and condos, as well as a second block of cabins clustered around a courtyard a few blocks up the road. **Pros:** helpful and friendly staff; lake views; clean rooms. **Cons:** rooms and bathrooms can be a little cramped; lobby is a bit small; no elevator. Ⓢ *Rooms from: $175* ✉ *419 Garfield Ave.* ☎ *970/627–3580* 🌐 *www.westernriv.com* *40 units* 🍴 *No meals.*

Nightlife

Lariat Saloon

BARS/PUBS | A local hot spot, this rustic bar has pinball, pool, and video games, plus live music on summer weekends. It's also the only spot in town for late-night eats. Look for the buffalo and dreadlock-adorned fox amid the eclectic Western decor. ✉ *1121 Grand Ave.* ☎ *970/627–9965.*

Shopping

Shopping in Grand Lake tends toward the usual resort-town souvenir shops, although a handful of stores stand out.

Never Summer Mountain Products

CLOTHING | Gear up with kayaks and SUPs in summer or snowshoes in winter at this year-round shop. ✉ *919 Grand Ave.* ☎ *970/627–3642* 🌐 *www.neversummermtn.com.*

Activities

BICYCLING

Willow Creek Pass

BICYCLING | This route covers about 25 miles (one way) from Granby and climbs 1,748 feet to the summit of one of the gentler passes on the Continental Divide, rewarding with stunning views of the Never Summer Range. The ride takes you through quiet aspen and pine forests where you might encounter moose and deer, which are often spotted just off the road. ✉ *The route starts on U.S. 40 in Granby and then follows Hwy. 125 north for 23 miles.*

BIRD-WATCHING

The islands in Shadow Mountain Reservoir and Lake Granby are wildlife refuges that attract osprey and many other migrating birds. The best way to get close to them is by canoe or foot trail. Be sure to take binoculars, because you're not permitted to land on the islands.

East Shore Trail

BIRD WATCHING | Good bird-spotting opportunities await along the East Shore and Knight Ridge trails, which follow the shores of Shadow Mountain Reservoir and Lake Granby for 13 miles. ✉ *Grand Lake* ✣ *Access trails either from Grand Lake between Grand Lake and Shadow Mountain Reservoir, or from Green Ridge Campground at the south end of Shadow Mountain Reservoir* ☎ *970/887–4100 Sulphur Ranger District.*

BOATING AND FISHING

There's plenty of water to share here. Anglers enjoy plentiful catches of rainbow trout, brown trout, mackinaw (lake trout), and kokanee salmon; recreational sailors and water-skiers ply acres of water; and paddlers can still canoe in peace. Ice fishers will not want to miss the big Three Lakes Ice Fishing Contest held in January. Contestants aim to catch four different species of fish, and winners collect from a booty of more than $20,000 in cash and prizes. A fishing license is required. See 🌐 *www.wildlife.state.co.us/fishing* for information on how to get one.

OUTFITTERS

Beacon Landing Marina

BOATING | On the north shore of Lake Granby, Beacon Landing Marina rents pontoon boats and fishing equipment. ✉ *1026 County Rd. 64* ☎ *970/627–3671* 🌐 *www.beaconlanding.us.*

Trail Ridge Marina

BOATING | The Trail Ridge Marina is on the western shore of Shadow Mountain Lake, which is connected to Grand Lake by a channel. The marina rents pontoon, pleasure, and fishing boats, as well as kayaks and stand-up paddleboards. ✉ *12634 U.S. 34* ☎ *970/627–3586* 🌐 *www.trailridgemarina.com* 🕓 *Closed Oct.–Apr.*

HIKING

A hike here can be a destination in itself: generally speaking, the trails on this side of the Continental Divide are longer than those on the Western Slope, meaning you'll trek farther and higher than you might expect to reach your destination. Many trails take you 5 miles one way before you reach a lake or peak. If you hike in the backcountry, be prepared for adverse weather. For those who'd rather not venture quite so far, there are many shorter hikes in and around Grand Lake, all of which offer gorgeous scenery and wonderful relaxation, as the trails here tend to have fewer hikers than those near Estes Park.

Adams Falls

HIKING/WALKING | This short hike is a must-do that rewards with a gorgeous 55-foot waterfall. You can access it from the East Inlet Trailhead at the West Portal of Grand Lake. There are no dogs allowed. ✉ *East Inlet Trailhead* ✣ *From downtown Grand Lake, drive west on W. Portal Rd. for 2½ miles.*

Indian Peaks Wilderness

HIKING/WALKING | **FAMILY** | At the southeast end of Lake Granby, the Monarch Lake Trailhead is a popular access point for hiking to Indian Peaks Wilderness, located within the Arapaho National Recreation Area. The area around Monarch Lake is popular with families for the selection of trails and the views of the Indian Peaks and the Continental Divide. Trails range in distance from 1½ to 10¾ miles one way. The easy **Monarch Lake Loop** is just over

3¾ miles and a mere 110 feet in elevation gain. ✉ *Grand Lake* ✢ *Take U.S. 34 south to County Rd. 6. Follow the lakeshore road about 10 miles* ☎ *970/887–4100.*

NORDIC SKIING AND SNOWSHOEING

Grand Lake Metropolitan Recreation District
SKIING/SNOWBOARDING | With nearly 22 miles (35 km) of cross-country ski trails, 15 miles of hiking and biking trails, and the Grand Lake Golf Course, the local recreation district offers year-round affordable ways to take in views of the Never Summer Range and the Continental Divide. ✉ *1415 County Rd. 48* ☎ *970/627–8872* 🌐 *www.grandlakerecreation.com.*

RENTALS

Never Summer Mountain Products
SKIING/SNOWBOARDING | Rent skis and snowshoes in the winter, or buy backpacks, tents, and other camping equipment for summer sports. Rocky Mountain National Park requires backpackers to use bear canisters (for overnight food storage), which Never Summer rents for $5 for 24 hours. ✉ *919 Grand Ave.* ☎ *970/627–3642* 🌐 *www.neversummermtn.com.*

Granby

20 miles south of Grand Lake via U.S. 34.

The small, no-nonsense town of Granby (elevation 7,935 feet) serves the working ranches in Grand County, and you'll see plenty of cowboys. What the town lacks in attractions it makes up for with its views of Middle Park and the surrounding mountains of the Front and Gore ranges, and with its proximity to outdoor activities, particularly its top-class golf courses just south of town.

GETTING HERE AND AROUND

Granby is 20 minutes from Rocky Mountain National Park and 15 minutes from the ski resorts Winter Park and Mary Jane and the mountain-biking trails of the Fraser Valley.

To get here from Grand Lake, take U.S. 34 south for 20 miles. From Boulder, you'll drive about 18 miles south on CO–93, 28 miles west on I–70, then take U.S. 40 north about 46 miles. From Denver, take I–70 west (about 30 miles) to U.S. 40, then drive north about 45 miles. The town is pretty small, and you can easily find a parking spot and walk from one end to the other.

Sights

Arapaho and Roosevelt National Forests and Pawnee National Grassland
FOREST | The Arapaho and Roosevelt National Forests and Pawnee National Grassland, an enormous area that encompasses 1.5 million acres, has fishing, sailing, canoeing, and waterskiing, as well as hiking, mountain biking, birding, and camping. Contained within the Arapaho National Forest is the **Arapaho National Recreation Area (ANRA)**, a 35,000-acre expanse adjacent to Rocky Mountain National Park that contains Lake Granby, Shadow Mountain Lake, Monarch Lake, and Willow Creek and Meadow Creek reservoirs. Toss in neighboring Grand Lake and you have what's known as Colorado's Great Lakes. ✉ *USDA Forest Service Sulphur Ranger District, 9 Ten Mile Dr.* ☎ *970/887–4100* 🌐 *www.fs.usda.gov/main/arp.*

Flying Heels Arena
RODEO | Watch cowboys demonstrate their rodeo skills at the Flying Heels Arena, held a couple of weekends in early summer. The rodeo finale and fireworks show is on the Saturday nearest July 4. ✉ *63032 U.S. 40, 1½ miles east of Granby* ☎ *970/887–2311* 🌐 *www.granbyrodeo.com* 🎟 *$10.*

Hotels

★ C Lazy U Ranch
$$$$ | **RESORT** | **FAMILY** | Secluded in a broad, verdant valley, this deluxe dude ranch offers a smorgasbord of activities as well as plush, Western-style accommodations with wood-paneled walls,

beautiful furnishings, and bathrooms with copper sinks and custom vanities. **Pros:** kid- and family-friendly; helpful staff; deluxe in every respect. **Cons:** distant from other area attractions; strict meal times; very expensive. *Rooms from: $600 3640 Hwy. 125 3½ miles north on Hwy. 125 from U.S. 40 junction 970/887–3344 www.clazyu.com 40 rooms All-inclusive.*

Activities

BIRD-WATCHING

Windy Gap Watchable Wildlife Area

BIRD WATCHING | On the path alongside the reservoir at Windy Gap Watchable Wildlife Area, you're likely to spot geese, pelicans, swans, eagles, killdeer, osprey, and more. The park has information kiosks, spotting scopes, viewing areas, covered picnic tables, and a nature trail that's wheelchair accessible. *Granby 5 miles west of Granby on U.S. 40 where it meets Rte. 125 970/725–6200 www.northernwater.org/what-we-do/deliver-water/windy-gap-project/windy-gap-watchable-wildlife.*

GOLF

The scenery and wildlife-viewing opportunities at Grand County's four golf courses make good excuses for being distracted during a critical putt or drive. You can expect secluded greens, expansive vistas, and an occasional interruption from deer, foxes, elk, or even a moose.

Golf Granby Ranch

GOLF | Tucked back in a valley at the end of a gravel road, this Jack Nicklaus–designed course delivers beautiful views of meadows and mountains, weaving through native grasses and wetlands along the meandering Poudre River. *2579 County Rd. 894 Turn off U.S. 40 onto Village Rd. Immediately after the Silver Creek Inn, turn left on Ten Mile Dr. Stay to the right on North Ranch Rd. and follow it to the clubhouse 970/887–2709, 888/850–4615 www.granbyranch.com $90 18 holes, 6601 yards, par 70 Reservations essential.*

Grand Elk Golf Club

GOLF | Designed by PGA great Craig Stadler, this challenging mountain course is reminiscent of traditional heathland greens in Britain yet brings its own blend of Colorado style, with expansive views of sagebrush-covered hills, aspen groves, and the Continental Divide. *1300 Tenmile Dr. 970/887–9122 www.grandelk.com $85 weekdays, $90 weekends 18 holes, 7144 yards, par 71 Closed mid-Oct.–mid-May Reservations essential.*

MOUNTAIN BIKING

Indian Peaks Wilderness Area is not open to mountain biking, but there are moderate and difficult trails in the **Arapaho National Forest** (*970/887–4100 www.fs.usda.gov/arp*). In addition, Grand County has several hundred miles of easy to expert-level bike trails, many of which are former railroad rights-of-way and logging roads.

Doe Creek Trail

BICYCLING | This roughly 3¼-mile one-way trail is a good workout of uphill climbs (and descents) with plenty of forest scenery. *Granby From Granby, take U.S. 34 to County Rd. 6 (Arapaho Bay Rd.) and follow it for about 3 miles. The trailhead is on your right.*

SKIING AND SNOWBOARDING

Ski Granby Ranch

SKIING/SNOWBOARDING | **FAMILY** | Two miles south of Granby, this small ski area features beginner, intermediate, and expert runs, which all end at the same place, making it an ideal place to teach the family to ski or snowboard. The resort also has a terrain park and two Nordic-trail networks for cross-country skiing and snowshoeing. **Facilities:** 41 trails; 406 acres; 1,000-foot vertical drop; 5 lifts. *1000 Village Rd. 888/850–4615 www.granbyranch.com Lift ticket $89 Closed mid-Apr.–mid-Dec.*

Hot Sulphur Springs

10 miles west of Granby via U.S. 40.

The county seat, Hot Sulphur Springs (population 639), is a faded resort town whose hot springs were once the destination for trains packed with people, including plenty of Hollywood types in the 1950s.

GETTING HERE AND AROUND

From Boulder, take U.S. 36 about 43 miles north to Estes Park. Take U.S. 34 west to Granby (53½ miles), then take U.S. 40 west for another 9 miles. From Fort Collins, take U.S. 287 south to Loveland (about 10 miles), then head west on U.S. 34 into Estes Park and then across Rocky Mountain National Park and into Granby (about 54 miles). Turn onto U.S. 40 and drive about 9 miles west.

You'll need a car to explore this area, as attractions, dining, and lodgings are spread out.

Sights

Hot Sulphur Springs Resort & Spa

HOT SPRINGS | Soak or pamper yourself with a massage, wrap, or salt glow at the Hot Sulphur Springs Resort & Spa. Twenty-one open-air pools are sprinkled up the hillside, with temperatures ranging from 95°F to 112°F. The seasonal swimming pool is just right for recreation, at a comparatively frigid 80°F, and the resort also has four private, indoor pools (two reserved for spa treatments). Bring sandals if you have them, especially during snowy months when rock salt is used on icy walkways. ✉ *5609 County Rd. 20* ✣ *From U.S. 40, head north onto Aspen St., go left onto Grand Ave. and follow signs to the resort* ☎ *970/725–3306* 🌐 *www.hotsulphursprings.com* 🎟 *$18.50.*

Pioneer Village Museum

MUSEUM | The old Hot Sulphur Schoolhouse—built in 1924—houses the Pioneer Village Museum. Artifacts depict Grand County history dating back 8,500 years, including tools, clothing, a railroad snowplow, and the old Winter Park Ski Train caboose. ✉ *110 E. Byers Ave.* ☎ *970/725–3939* 🌐 *www.grandcountyhistory.org* 🎟 *$6.*

Hotels

Hot Sulphur Springs Resort & Spa

$ | **HOTEL** | The basic, no-nonsense rooms here have comfortable lodgepole beds and showers en suite; rates include unlimited use of the pools during your stay. **Pros:** quick access to hot pools and spa; close enough that a visit can be tacked onto an outdoor activity. **Cons:** trains passing through at night are noisy; no breakfast and most restaurants are at least 15 minutes away; very basic accommodations. $ *Rooms from: $108* ✉ *5609 County Rd. 20* ☎ *970/725–3306* 🌐 *www.hotsulphursprings.com* 🛏 *19 rooms* 🍴 *No meals.*

Latigo Ranch

$$$$ | **RESORT** | **FAMILY** | This all-inclusive guest ranch offers views of the Continental Divide, complete seclusion, and superb trails. **Pros:** stunning scenery; quiet and secluded area; babysitting available for young children. **Cons:** no nearby restaurants or other attractions; three-bedroom cabins have only one bathroom. $ *Rooms from: $2995* ✉ *County Rd. 1911* ☎ *970/724–9008, 800/227–9655* 🌐 *www.latigotrails.com* 🕒 *Closed Apr., May, Oct., and Dec.* 🛏 *10 cabins* 🍴 *All-inclusive.*

Chapter 10

STEAMBOAT SPRINGS AND NORTHWEST COLORADO

Updated by
Kyle Wagner

Sights ★★★★☆ Restaurants ★★★☆☆ Hotels ★★☆☆☆ Shopping ★★★☆☆ Nightlife ★★★☆☆

WELCOME TO STEAMBOAT SPRINGS AND NORTHWEST COLORADO

TOP REASONS TO GO

★ **Colorado National Monument:** Gaze out over Grand Junction toward the Book Cliffs along the 23-mile Rim Rock Drive or hike one of the many trails through sandstone canyons.

★ **Dinosaur National Monument:** Wander among thousands of fossilized skeletons that remain embedded in the rugged hillsides or take a raft trip down the Green or Yampa rivers.

★ **Grand Junction and Palisade wine tasting:** More than two dozen local wineries have garnered attention for their grapes grown in the unique high-altitude soil.

★ **Steamboat Springs horseback riding:** Choose from an authentic dude ranch experience, a pack trip into the wilderness, or a gentle alpine trail ride.

★ **Strawberry Park Hot Springs:** Though it takes some work to get here, it's well worth the effort to soak away what ails you in the rustic, rock-lined setting.

1 **Grand Junction.** The meeting place of the Colorado and Gunnison rivers.

2 **Palisade.** Home to Colorado's best wine and best peaches.

3 **Colorado National Monument.** Stunning red rock cliffs that offer gorgeous views.

4 **Grand Mesa.** The world's largest flat-topped mountain.

5 **Cedaredge.** The gateway to the Grand Mesa.

6 **Steamboat Springs.** A mountain village famous for its hot springs and its Olympic skiers.

7 **Meeker.** A sleepy town with an army and a sheepdog history.

8 **Craig.** A small town with excellent fishing.

9 **Dinosaur National Monument.** One of the country's best collection of fossils that you can actually touch.

10 **Rangely.** Home to a fascinating collection of ancient petroglyphs from the Fremont tribe.

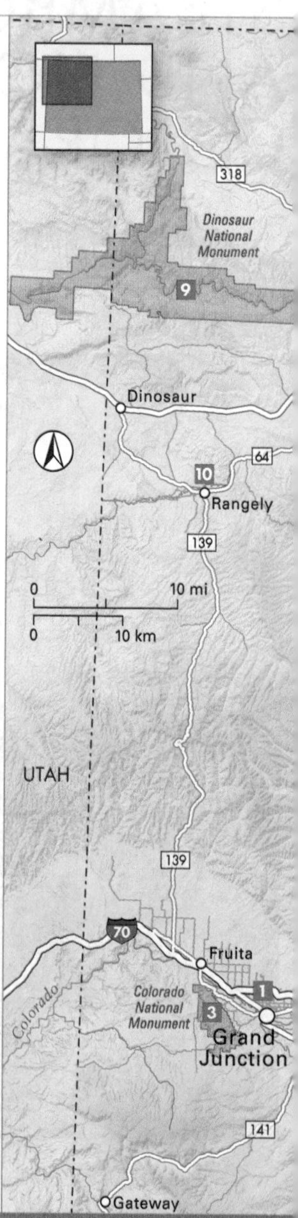

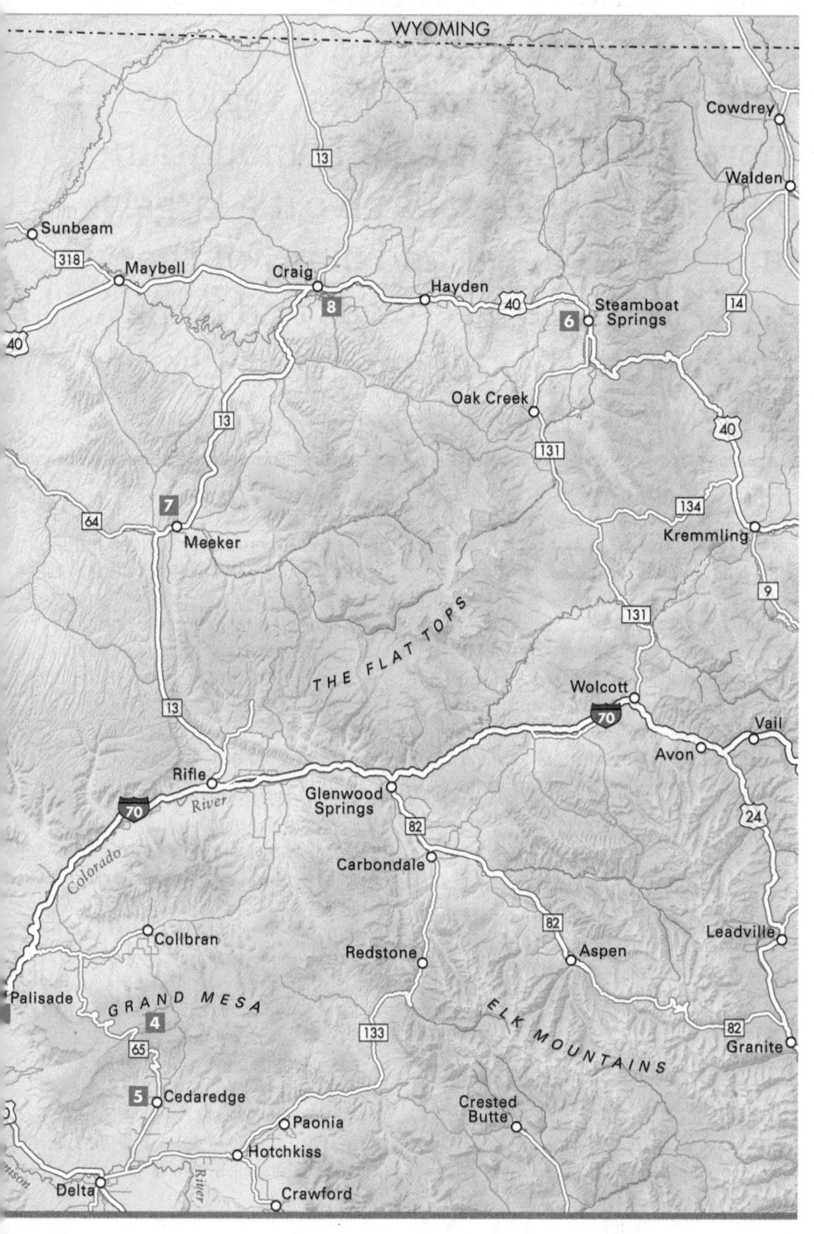

WYOMING
Cowdrey
Walden
Sunbeam
318
Maybell
Craig
13
Hayden
40
Steamboat Springs
14
8
6
40
Oak Creek
13
131
40
134
7
64
Meeker
Kremmling
9
131
THE FLAT TOPS
Wolcott
70
13
Vail
Avon
Rifle
River
Glenwood Springs
70
24
82
Colorado
Carbondale
82
Collbran
Leadville
Redstone
Aspen
Palisade
GRAND MESA
4
ELK MOUNTAINS
133
82
Granite
65
5
Cedaredge
Crested Butte
Paonia
Hotchkiss
River
Delta
Crawford

Varied terrain attracts bold outdoors enthusiasts, and genteel towns are tucked among the craggy cliffs for those seeking quieter pursuits. Whatever your choice, the northwest region's more remote location and mountain-dominated landscape give it a largely undiscovered feel, and many of the activities lack the crowds and frenzy attached to those in more heavily populated areas.

Adventures in these far-western and northern regions of the state might range from a bone-jarring mountain-bike ride on Kokopelli's Trail—a 142-mile route through remote desert sandstone and shale canyon from Grand Junction to Moab—to a heart-pounding raft trip down the Green River, where Major John Wesley Powell made his epic exploration of this continent's last uncharted wilderness in 1869. Colorado National Monument and Dinosaur National Monument have endless opportunities for hiking. For the less adventurous, a visit to the wine country makes for a relaxing afternoon, or try your hand at excavating prehistoric bones from a dinosaur quarry. Rich in more recent history as well, the area is home to the Museums of Western Colorado and Escalante Canyon, named after Spanish missionary explorer Francisco Silvestre Velez de Escalante, who with Father Francisco Atanasio Dominguez led an expedition through the area in 1776.

Farther east, flanked by mountains with some of the softest snow in the world, even the cowboys don skis. Steamboat Springs is Colorado at its most authentic, where pastures are dotted with hay bales and cattle, McMansions are regarded with disdain, high-schoolers compete in local rodeos, deer hang from front porches during hunting season, and high fashion means clean jeans. Steamboat Ski Resort has none of the pretensions of the glitzier Colorado resorts.

Even the less visited corners of the region have plenty of cultural opportunities for those willing to seek them out. Art galleries, antiques shops, and many small eateries with alfresco seating underscore the charming quality of the setting. People are friendly and share plenty of tourist tips just for the asking. As for quirky festivals, you might have a hard time choosing between the Olathe Sweet Corn Festival, Country Jam, or the Mike the Headless Chicken Festival. The laid-back lifestyle here is the perfect example to follow—chill out and explore the region at your own pace.

MAJOR REGIONS

Grand Junction and Around. With its mild climate and healthy economy, Grand Junction and the surrounding area make northwestern Colorado an inviting destination. A thriving retirement community and mountain-biking headquarters, the Grand Valley also counts superior soil and top-notch ranching among its assets. The contrast between the sandstone of the Book Cliffs and the canyons of the Colorado National Monument with the greenery of the lush orchards below, particularly in nearby Palisade with its peaches and wines, makes for a pleasant road trip.

Steamboat Springs. Unlike some of the other ski towns, Steamboat has always been a "real" town. With its touch of the Old West and plenty of cowboys still hanging around, visitors are usually torn—hot springs, horseback riding, or skiing?

Northwest Corner. The world's largest flat-topped mountain, the Grand Mesa, has a 55-mile Scenic Byway that feels a little like Land of the Lost. Meanwhile, Dinosaur National Monument offers thousands of fossils and hiking trails. Stop in nearby Craig or Rangely to refuel yourself and your vehicle. The towns are small and sleepy, but their inhabitants, many devoted to fishing, hunting, and other area outdoor pursuits, could not be more welcoming.

Planning

When to Go

The region has four distinct seasons. The heaviest concentration of tourists is in summer, when school is out and families hit the road for a little together time. Temperatures in summer frequently reach into the high 80s and 90s, although the mercury has been known to top triple digits on occasion. You might have a hard time finding a hotel room during late May and late June thanks to the National Junior College World Series and Country Jam music festival, both in Grand Junction. Hotels fill quickly in fall, which brings an explosion of colors. Days are warm, but nights are crisp and cool. There's still time to enjoy activities like fishing, hiking, and backpacking before the snow flies. Grand Mesa is a winter favorite among locals looking for a quick fix for cabin fever. Powder hounds can't wait to strap on their newly waxed skis and hit the slopes at Steamboat and Powderhorn ski resorts.

Getting Oriented

A little planning goes a long way when visiting this region. Grand Junction, the largest city between Denver and Salt Lake City, makes an ideal hub for exploring. Many of the sights, except for Steamboat Springs, are less than two hours from Grand Junction. You can make the loop from Delta to Cedaredge and Grand Mesa to Palisade easily in a day. If you want to break up the trip, stop in Cedaredge. The loop in the opposite direction—including Meeker, Craig, Dinosaur National Monument, and Rangely—is longer, but there's decent lodging along the way, with the exception of Dinosaur National Monument, where there's only one nearby motel and camping.

If you're headed to Steamboat Springs from Denver in winter, exercise caution on Highway 40. It sees less traffic than I–70, but it can be treacherous in the Berthoud Pass stretch during snowstorms.

Planning Your Time

The remoteness of northwest Colorado makes it appealing for those looking to escape the big crowds of more heavily visited areas of the state, but it also requires more careful planning.

Steamboat Springs is a good place to start and usually requires two–three days to explore, particularly if hiking, biking, skiing, horseback riding, or other adventure activities are on the itinerary, with optional day trips to Craig. From there, it's a commitment to spend time at Dinosaur National Monument, but one that is well worth the effort if dinosaurs or white-water rafting are on your must-do list.

Dropping down to Grand Junction is possible from Dinosaur through Rangely—which gives you the chance to do a little fishing—or you can skip the fossil tour and go through Meeker, secure in the knowledge that you'll still get your dino fix around this part of the Western Slope. Plan on several days to explore Grand Junction, with wine tasting in Palisade and the extensive outdoors options on the Grand Mesa nearby.

Getting Here and Around

AIR

Grand Junction Regional Airport (GJT) is served by Allegiant Air, American, Delta Airlines, United, and US Airways.

Yampa Valley Regional Airport (HDN) is in Hayden, 22 miles from Steamboat Springs. United flies nonstop year-round from various gateways during ski season, while Alaska, American, JetBlue, and Southwest fly here from mid-December to March.

Taxis and shuttle services are available in Grand Junction and Steamboat Springs.

AIRPORT CONTACTS Grand Junction Regional Airport (GJT). ✉ *2828 Walker Field Dr., Grand Junction* ☎ *970/244–9100* 🌐 *www.gjairport.com.* **Yampa Valley Regional Airport (HDN).** ☎ *970/276–5000* 🌐 *www.flysteamboat.com.*

CAR

In northwestern Colorado, I–70 (U.S. 6) is the major thoroughfare, accessing Grand Junction and Grand Mesa (via Route 65, which runs to Delta). Meeker is reached via Route 13, and Rangely and Dinosaur via Route 64. U.S. 40 east from Utah is the best way to reach Dinosaur National Monument and Craig.

From Denver, Steamboat Springs is about a three-hour drive northwest via I–70 and U.S. 40. The route traverses some high-mountain passes, so it's a good idea to check road conditions before you travel.

Grand Junction has gas stations that are open 24 hours. Most gas stations in the smaller towns are open until 10 pm in summer, and even some automated credit-card pumps shut down at that hour.

Most roads are paved and in fairly good condition. Summer is peak road-construction season, so expect some delays. Be prepared for winter driving conditions at all times. Enterprise car rental is in downtown Grand Junction, with free pickup. Alamo, Avis-Budget, Enterprise, Hertz, and National Car Rental are in the Grand Junction Airport terminal. Depending on where you're traveling, you might want a four-wheel-drive vehicle. Avis also has car rentals in Steamboat Springs.

TRAIN

Amtrak provides daily service to the East and West Coasts through downtown Grand Junction.

Parks and Recreation Areas

The blushing red-rock cliffs of the **Colorado National Monument** are easily accessible by winding roads that open to miles of hiking trails. **Dinosaur National Monument** holds a stunning cache of fossils as well as spectacular scenery aboveground for family-friendly hiking.

Browns Park Wildlife Refuge
A bird-watcher's destination with species from ducks to bald eagles, the remote Browns Park Wildlife Refuge northwest of Maybell can be navigated by car or horseback, or on foot. *www.fws.gov/brownspark*.

Flat Tops Wilderness
This alpine mesa has good stream and lake fishing and excellent deer and elk hunting. It's southwest of Steamboat Springs. *www.fs.fed.us/r2/whiteriver*.

Grand Mesa National Forest
This forest shimmers with peaceful alpine lakes and great fishing and hiking in summer, along with trails for snowmobiling in winter. *www.fs.usda.gov/gmug*.

Medicine Bow/Routt National Forests
Steamboat Springs is surrounded by the Medicine Bow/Routt National Forests, which stretch across northern Colorado and into southern Wyoming, embracing more than half a dozen mountain ranges, including the Gore, Flat Tops, Park, Medicine Bow, Sierra Madre, and Laramie. *www.fs.usda.gov/mbr*.

Restaurants

The usual chain restaurants ring Grand Junction, but they're joined by eclectic gourmet pizza joints and authentic Mexican restaurants. Look for made-from-scratch delicacies at mom-and-pop bakeries—especially worth seeking out during summer fruit harvests. In season, Palisade peaches, Olathe sweet corn, and Cedaredge apples find their way onto menus, and they're sometimes paired with a multitude of local wines. For something traditional, it's hard to beat a great hand-battered chicken-fried steak smothered in creamy gravy—which is available in just about any town in the area.

The town of Steamboat Springs, in the heart of cattle country, has far more carnivorous delights—including elk, deer, and bison—than you're likely to find in the trendier resorts of Aspen, Telluride, and Vail. The Steamboat ski resort, separated geographically from town, is more eclectic, with small sushi bars and Mediterranean cafés hidden among the boutiques.

Hotels

In Grand Junction, Horizon Drive has the largest concentration of hotels and motels, conveniently near the airport and within walking distance of a handful of restaurants. For the budget-conscious, there are many no-frills motels as well as hotel branches of the well-known chains. History buffs might enjoy a stay at a dude ranch, one of the many rustic cabin rentals, or the famed Meeker Hotel, once frequented by Teddy Roosevelt. For those looking for the comforts of home, the area has a nice selection of bed-and-breakfasts; be sure to ask for off-season lodging rates, which could save you a bundle.

Steamboat Springs is unique in the state because it has high-end dude ranches and ranch resorts, which are less abundant in resort areas like Aspen, Summit County, and Vail.

Restaurant and hotel reviews have been shortened. For full information, visit Fodors.com. Restaurant prices are the average price of a main course at dinner or, if dinner is not served, at lunch, excluding 6.5%–8.4% tax. Hotel prices are the lowest cost of a standard double room in high season, excluding service charges and 9.4%–10.65% tax.

What It Costs			
$	$$	$$$	$$$$
RESTAURANTS			
under $15	$15–$22	$23–$30	over $30
HOTELS			
under $125	$125–$200	$201–$300	over $300

Grand Junction

255 miles west of Denver via I–70.

Grand Junction is where the mountains and desert meet at the confluence of the mighty Colorado and Gunnison rivers—a grand junction indeed. No matter which direction you look, there's an adventure waiting to happen. The city, with a population of more than 59,000, is nestled between the picturesque Grand Mesa to the south and the towering Book Cliffs to the north. It's a great base camp for a vacation—whether you're into art galleries, boutiques, hiking, horseback riding, rafting, mountain biking, or winery tours.

The Art on the Corner exhibit showcases leading regional sculptors, whose latest works are installed on the Main Street Mall. Passersby may find their faces reflected in an enormous chrome buffalo (titled *Chrome on the Range II*) or, a few streets down, encounter an enormous cactus made entirely of rusted (but still prickly) chainsaw chains.

GETTING HERE AND AROUND

A Touch With Class has regular limo service into Grand Junction and outlying communities. Sunshine Taxi serves Grand Junction. Amtrak runs the California Zephyr round-trip from San Francisco to Chicago, which stops in Grand Junction, Glenwood Springs, Winter Park, and Denver. Grand Valley Transit operates 11 public bus routes that are geared to commuters between Grand Junction, Palisade, Clifton, Orchard Mesa, and Fruita.

TRANSPORTATION CONTACTS A Touch With Class. ☎ *970/245–5466* 🌐 *www.colorado-limo.com.* **Amtrak.** ☎ *800/872–7245* 🌐 *www.amtrak.com.* **Grand Valley Transit.** ☎ *970/256–7433* 🌐 *www.gvt.mesacounty.us.* **Sunshine Taxi.** ✉ *1321 Ute Ave.* ☎ *970/245–8294* 🌐 *sunshinetaxigj.com.*

FESTIVALS

Country Jam

Country Jam is held every June and draws the biggest names in country music, such as Carrie Underwood and Toby Keith. ✉ *Jam Ranch, 1065 Hwys. 6 and 50, Mack* ☎ *855/821–9210* 🌐 *countryjam.com.*

ESSENTIALS

VISITOR INFORMATION Grand Junction Visitor & Convention Bureau. ✉ *740 Horizon Dr.* ☎ *800/962–2547, 970/244–1480* 🌐 *www.visitgrandjunction.com.*

TOURS

Dino Digs

ARCHAEOLOGICAL SITE | **FAMILY** | Ever wonder what it's like to be on a dinosaur expedition? Here's your chance. The Museums of Western Colorado sponsors one- to five-day Dino Digs all over northwestern Colorado, and folks find fresh fossils all the time. The area includes some rich Late Jurassic soil, Morrison Formation sites, and other well-preserved zones that make for impressive discoveries. You never know what might be unearthed. ✉ *Grand Junction* ☎ *888/488–3466, 970/242–0971* 🌐 *www.dinodigs.org* 🎫 *From $75.*

Dinosaur Journey

SPECIAL-INTEREST | This company leads one- to five-day paleontological treks that include work in a dinosaur quarry. ✉ *550 Jurassic Ct., Fruita* ☎ *970/858–7282* 🌐 *www.dinosaurjourney.org* 🎫 *From $9.*

Sights

The Art Center

MUSEUM | This center rotates a fine permanent collection of Native American tapestries and Western contemporary art, including the only complete series of lithographs by noted printmaker Paul Pletka. The fantastically carved doors—done by a WPA artist in the 1930s—alone are worth the visit. Take time to view the elegant historic homes along North 7th Street afterward. Admission is always free for children under 12; it's also free on Tuesdays for everyone. ✉ *1803 N. 7th St.* ☎ *970/243–7337* 🌐 *www.gjartcenter.org* 🎟 *$3* 🕒 *Closed Sun. and Mon.*

★ Little Book Cliffs Wild Horse Range

NATURE PRESERVE | One of just three ranges in the United States set aside for wild horses, this range encompasses 36,113 acres of rugged canyons and plateaus in the Book Cliffs. Between 90 and 150 wild horses roam the sagebrush-covered hills. Most years new foals can be spotted with their mothers in spring and early summer on the hillsides just off the main trails. Local favorites for riding include the Coal Canyon Trail and Main Canyon Trail, where the herd often goes in winter. Vehicles are permitted on designated trails. ✉ *Grand Junction* ✣ *About 8 miles northeast of Grand Junction* ☎ *970/244–3000, 800/417–9647* 🌐 *www.co.blm.gov* 🎟 *Free.*

Museums of Western Colorado

MINE | The museums of Grand Junction have banded together as the Museums of Western Colorado, which comprises the Museum of the West, the Dinosaur Journey Museum, and the Cross Orchards Living History Farm. The Museum of the West relates the history of the area since the 1880s, with a time line, a firearms display, and a Southwest pottery collection. The area's rich mining heritage is perfectly captured in the uranium mine that educates with interactive sound and exhibit stations, and the museum also oversees paleontological excavations. ✉ *462 Ute Ave.* ☎ *970/242–0971* 🌐 *www.museumofwesternco.com* 🎟 *$7.*

Restaurants

Dos Hombres

$$ | **MEXICAN** | **FAMILY** | Casual and colorful, Dos Hombres serves the usual variety of combination platters and Mexican specialties, and loads up the plates for low prices. The fajitas and enchiladas are particularly well made, with quality meats and a noticeable lack of grease, and they have an unusually large menu of interesting salads (check out the Cancun version, with pineapple and fried tortilla strips). **Known for:** sangria brunch; freshly fried, salt-free chips; margarita happy hour. [$] *Average main: $15* ✉ *421 Brach Dr.* ☎ *970/434–5078* 🌐 *www.go2dos.com.*

Il Bistro Italiano

$$$ | **ITALIAN** | With a chef hailing from the birthplace of Parmigiano-Reggiano, this restaurant's authenticity is assured, down to that perfectly delivered final shredded topping. Diners are greeted by a case of pasta made fresh daily and assisted by a staff that knows the origins of each home-style dish. **Known for:** signature "Rosetta" noodle and ham dish; wine from Italy and Colorado; menu that changes weekly. [$] *Average main: $29* ✉ *400 Main St.* ☎ *970/243–8622* 🌐 *www.ilbistroitaliano.com* 🕒 *Closed Sun. and Mon. No lunch.*

★ Pablo's Pizza

$ | **PIZZA** | **FAMILY** | Drawing inspiration from Pablo Picasso's artwork, the pizzas at this funky joint make for a diverse palette of flavors and fun. Specialties include creations such as Popeye's Passion (featuring spinach and "olive oyl") or Dracula's Nemesis (studded with roasted garlic). **Known for:** locally sourced ingredients; party atmosphere; local wines and beers. [$] *Average main: $10* ✉ *319 Main St.* ☎ *970/255–8879* 🌐 *www.pablospizza.com.*

The Winery
$$$$ | **AMERICAN** | This is *the* place for that big night out and other special occasions in the area. The menu isn't terribly adventuresome, but the kitchen does turn out fresh-fish specials and top-notch steak, chicken, prime rib, and shrimp in simple, flavorful sauces. **Known for:** obscure, rare wines; top-notch steak; inviting wood-lined bar. *Average main: $40* *642 Main St.* *970/242–4100* *www.winery-restaurant.com* *No lunch.*

Hotels

DoubleTree by Hilton
$$ | **HOTEL** | **FAMILY** | At this sprawling full-service property, service begins with a warm cookie at check-in, and the attention to detail continues from there; many of the large rooms have vast mountain views, along with a long list of amenities. **Pros:** outdoor heated pool and hot tub; kid-friendly atmosphere; sports facilities. **Cons:** restaurant and room service food is so-so; feels like a chain; big groups can make it noisy. *Rooms from: $136* *743 Horizon Dr.* *970/241–8888, 800/222–8733* *www.doubletreegrandjunction.com* *273 rooms* *No meals.*

Fairfield Inn & Suites Grand Junction
$$ | **HOTEL** | Well situated in the middle of the downtown shopping district, this Marriott-owned property is ideal for business travelers, with spacious rooms that sport small sitting areas and large desks. **Pros:** downtown locale; cavernous rooms; quiet at night. **Cons:** chain-hotel atmosphere; extra $7 charge for parking; breakfast is average. *Rooms from: $130* *225 Main St.* *970/242–2525* *www.marriott.com* *70 rooms* *Free Breakfast.*

Grand Vista Hotel
$ | **HOTEL** | **FAMILY** | Plush high-back chairs invite visitors to relax in the spacious lobby of this hotel that lives up to its name. **Pros:** unbeatable views; complimentary bike storage; low price. **Cons:** mediocre breakfast buffet; service is patchy; rooms feel dated. *Rooms from: $80* *2790 Crossroads Blvd.* *970/241–8411, 800/800–7796* *www.grandvistahotel.com* *158 rooms* *Free Breakfast.*

Two Rivers Winery & Chateau
$ | **B&B/INN** | Open a bottle of wine inside the vineyard where it was created at this rustic French-styled inn set among acres of vines. **Pros:** idyllic locale; tasty wines always at hand; expansive continental breakfast. **Cons:** winery and functions make this noisier than the usual B&B; rooms are chilly in winter; walls are thin. *Rooms from: $92* *2087 Broadway* *970/241–3155, 866/312–9463* *www.tworiverswinery.com* *10 rooms* *Free Breakfast.*

Nightlife

Bistro 743 Lounge
BARS/PUBS | This lounge inside the DoubleTree by Hilton serves beverages, appetizers, and light snacks. On weekends, entertainers perform in the bar, and occasionally outside on the beer-garden stage. *743 Horizon Dr.* *970/241–8888* *doubletreegrandjunction.com.*

Blue Moon Bar and Grille
BARS/PUBS | This local bar, which serves decent wings, sandwiches, and other typical (albeit above-average) pub grub, is a popular spot for patrons to nurse their favorite brew while catching up with colleagues and friends. *120 N. 7th St.* *970/242–4506* *www.bluemoongj.com.*

Rockslide Brewery
BREWPUBS/BEER GARDENS | This brewery has won awards for its ales, porters, and stouts. The menu of burgers and other sandwiches, steaks, and pastas has something for just about everyone. The patio is open in summer. *401 Main St.* *970/245–2111* *www.rockslidebrewpub.com.*

Performing Arts

Avalon Theatre

DANCE | The Avalon Theatre is one of the largest performing arts complexes in western Colorado, offering traveling lectures, dance, theater, and other cultural performances. The popular monthly "Dinner and a Movie" Tuesday nights bring classic and popular old blockbusters to the big screen, with receipts from a meal in town garnering free admission. ✉ *645 Main St.* ☎ *970/263–5700* 🌐 *www.avalontheatregj.com.*

Grand Junction Symphony

MUSIC | The highly regarded, 95-piece Grand Junction Symphony performs in venues throughout the city, including the Avalon Theatre, Sherwood Park, Stocker Stadium, and area vineyards. ✉ *Grand Junction* ☎ *970/243–6787* 🌐 *www.gjso.org.*

Shopping

Enstrom Candies

FOOD/CANDY | **FAMILY** | The sweetest deal in town, Enstrom Candies is known for its scrumptious candy and renowned toffee. ✉ *701 Colorado Ave.* ☎ *970/683–1000* 🌐 *enstrom.com.*

Heirlooms for Hospice

CLOTHING | The cute but upscale boutique Heirlooms for Hospice has great secondhand designer clothing and shabby-chic furniture. ✉ *635 Main St.* ☎ *970/254–8556, 866/310–8900* 🌐 *www.heirloomsforhospice.com.*

Working Artists Studio and Gallery

ART GALLERIES | This studio and gallery carries prints, pottery, stained glass, and unique gifts. ✉ *520 Main St.* ☎ *970/256–9952* 🌐 *www.workingartistsgallery.com.*

Activities

GOLF

The Golf Club at Redlands Mesa

GOLF | The 18-hole, Jim Engh–designed championship course sits in a natural desert setting at an elevation of 4,600 feet in the shadows of the Colorado National Monument, just minutes from downtown. Sunset across the monument is spectacular, and the game is a challenge of red-rock walls and sloping stone formations. ✉ *2325 W. Ridges Blvd.* ☎ *970/255–7400, 866/863–9270* 🌐 *www.redlandsmesa.com* 🎟 *$79* ⛳ *Monument Course: 18 holes, 7007 yards, par 72; Redlands Course: 18 holes, 6486 yards, par 72; Canyon Course: 18 holes, 5281 yards, par 72; Desert Course: 18 holes, 4890 yards, par 72* ✍ *Reservations essential.*

MOUNTAIN BIKING

Several routes through Grand Junction are well suited to bicycle use. The city also has designated bike lanes in some areas. You can bike along the Colorado Riverfront Trails, a network that winds along the Colorado River, stretching from the Redlands Parkway to Palisade.

Colorado Plateau Mountain Bike Trail Association

BICYCLING | Those interested in bike tours should contact the Colorado Plateau Mountain Bike Trail Association. ✉ *Grand Junction* ☎ *970/901–4121* 🌐 *www.copmoba.org.*

Kokopelli's Trail

BICYCLING | This trail links Grand Junction with the famed Slickrock Trail outside Moab, Utah. The 142-mile stretch winds through high desert and the Colorado River Valley before climbing La Sal Mountains. ✉ *Loma.*

OUTFITTERS

Brown Cycles

BICYCLING | This company rents road, mountain, and hybrid bikes that start around $60 a day. It also sells and fixes bikes, and offers a full line of tandems for families, with expanded kid options for rent and sale, as well. Aficionados should allow some extra time to check out the interesting bike museum, with models from as early as the 1860s. ✉ *549 Main St.* ☎ *970/245–7939* 🌐 *www.browncycles.com.*

Over the Edge Sports

BICYCLING | Over the Edge Sports offers mountain-biking lessons and half- or full-day customized bike tours. ✉ *202 E. Aspen Ave., Fruita* ☎ *970/858–7220* 🌐 *www.otesports.com.*

Ruby Canyon Cycles

BICYCLING | This outfitter rents high-end, 29-inch, full-suspension mountain bikes for $80 the first day and $65 on subsequent days. The cycle shop also sponsors weekly evening rides around the area. ✉ *301 Main St.* ☎ *970/241–0141* 🌐 *www.rubycanyoncycles.com.*

Palisade

12 miles east of Grand Junction via I–70.

Palisade is Colorado's version of Napa Valley, with the highest concentration of wineries in the state. It's an easy day trip from Grand Junction; meander through the vineyards and stop for lunch in the tiny, slow-paced town framed by stately Victorian homes and sweetened by homespun festivals. The orchards also are a big draw; the long, frost-free growing season intensifies the fruit sugars, resulting in intensely flavorful peaches, cherries, apricots, and nectarines. At harvest time the area sees a steady flow of visitors stopping by the orchards themselves, many of which have on-site sales, as well as the roadside stands that pop up seasonally to sell preserves, salsas, pies, and other fruit-based products.

GETTING HERE AND AROUND

A car is the best way to get to and around Palisade. Public transportation options are limited.

WHEN TO GO

A variety of produce is available through the summer months, but the peaches and other fruits famous in the Palisade area are at the height of their season from late June to early October.

FESTIVALS

Colorado Mountain Winefest

FESTIVALS | September brings the annual Colorado Mountain Winefest. ✉ *Palisade* ☎ *800/704–3667* 🌐 *www.coloradowinefest.com* 🎟 *From $50.*

Grande River Vineyards

FESTIVALS | In summer Grande River Vineyards hosts a concert series featuring classical, country, blues, and rock music. The natural landscape contributes to the good acoustics, not to mention the spectacular sunsets. Concertgoers lounge in lawn chairs, enjoying picnics and dancing barefoot on the grass, and sometimes the concerts are held in the cellars. ✉ *787 N. Elberta Ave.* ☎ *970/464–5867* 🌐 *www.granderivervineyards.com* 🎟 *From $15.*

Palisade Peach Festival

FESTIVALS | Palisade celebrates the harvest for four days every August during the Palisade Peach Festival, most of which is held at Riverbend Park. ✉ *Palisade* ☎ *970/464–7458* 🌐 *www.palisadepeachfest.com* 🎟 *From $7.*

ESSENTIALS

VISITOR INFORMATION Palisade Chamber of Commerce. ✉ *305 S. Main St.* ☎ *970/464–7458* 🌐 *www.palisadecoc.com.*

Sights

★ Winery Tours

TOUR—SIGHT | One of Colorado's best-kept secrets is its winery tours. It's a great way to see how your favorite wine goes from vineyard to glass. You can learn about the grape-growing process and what varieties of grapes grow best in western Colorado's mild climate. Depending on the time of year, you may also see the grape harvesting and crushing process. For a self-guided tour, visit Grand Junction's website for maps and directions to the wineries. If you're taking the self-guided route, call to reserve tours that take you beyond the tasting room and into the wine-making process. Of course, the best part of the tour is sampling the wines. ✉ *Palisade* 🌐 *www.visitgrandjunction.com.*

Restaurants

Palisade Café and Wine Bar

$$$ | **SPANISH** | Changing artwork decorates the light and airy Palisade Café, which offers a nice selection for breakfast (only on weekends), as well as farm-to-table Spanish- and Peruvian-influenced lunch and dinner choices, including small plates and vegetarian dishes. Area wineries comprise the entire, and extensive, wine list, making it a good choice for sampling local offerings. **Known for:** authentic paella; Sunday brunch; fried cheese curds. [$] *Average main: $25* ✉ *113 W. 3rd St.* ☎ *970/464–2888* 🌐 *www.palisadecafeandwinebar.com* ⏲ *Closed Mon. and Tues.*

★ Slice O' Life Bakery

$ | **CAFÉ** | **FAMILY** | Aromatic goodies are baked with whole grains and fresh local fruits at this down-home–style bakery known around the region for its melt-in-your-mouth pastries, "jamocha" brownies, and fresh-fruit cobblers. Owners Tim and Mary Lincoln have made their fruitcakes craveable commodities, studding them with fresh Palisade peaches and mailing them around the country (in fact, they do lots of great things with peaches, including pie). **Known for:** good coffee; famous peach fruitcakes and raspberry cinnamon rolls; creative sandwich combinations. [$] *Average main: $6* ✉ *105 W. 3rd St.* ☎ *970/464–0577* ⏲ *Closed Sun. No dinner.*

Hotels

Wine Country Inn

$$$ | **B&B/INN** | A well-established vineyard surrounds this inn, giving an upscale feel to what's an appealingly casual and welcoming farmhouse-style lodging. **Pros:** convenient location off the interstate, close to wine properties; outdoor heated pool with views; afternoon wine tastings. **Cons:** nearby truck traffic can be noisy; spotty service, especially when the place is full; some rooms still feel dated. [$] *Rooms from: $220* ✉ *777 Grande River Dr.* ☎ *888/855–8330, 970/464–5777* 🌐 *www.coloradowinecountryinn.com* *86 rooms* *Free Breakfast.*

Shopping

Alida's Fruits

FOOD/CANDY | This market sells a wide range of fresh and dried fruits, including cherries, pears, apricots, and peaches, as well as chocolate-dipped fruits, nuts, and locally produced jams, jellies, and syrups. During the growing season, the market sells fresh produce as well. There's a second location in Grand Junction. ✉ *3402 C 1/2 Rd.* ☎ *970/434–8769* 🌐 *www.alidasfruits.com.*

Talbott Farms Mountain Gold Market

FOOD/CANDY | This market puts out nearly two dozen kinds of peaches, as well as apples and pears and the juices of all three annually from mid-July through the end of December. The huge, fourth generation–run operation sells local products and will take you on a tour of the place if you ask. ✉ *3782 F 1/4 Rd.* ☎ *970/464–5943* 🌐 *www.talbottfarms.com.*

Colorado National Monument is filled with dramatic overlooks.

Colorado National Monument

23 miles west of Grand Junction via Rte. 340.

Colorado's version of red rock is nowhere more spectacularly on display than at Colorado National Monument. Created between 65 and 225 million years ago, the monument was designated in 1911 and has been popular with photographers, hikers, and those eager to drive its paved road, Rim Rock Drive, ever since.

GETTING HERE AND AROUND

From I–70 westbound, take Exit 31 (Horizon Drive) and follow signs through Grand Junction; eastbound take Exit 19 (Fruita) and drive south 3 miles on Highway 340 to the west entrance.

FESTIVALS

Fruita Fat Tire Festival

FESTIVALS | The town's Fat Tire Festival brings mountain bikers from all over together to take on the area's trails every May. ☎ *970/858–7220* 🌐 *fruitafattirefestival.com.*

Mike the Headless Chicken Days

FESTIVALS | The town of Fruita celebrates Mike the Headless Chicken Days every June with the Chicken Dance and the Run Like A Headless Chicken 5K Race. ✉ *Fruita* ☎ *970/858–0360* 🌐 *www.mikethe headlesschicken.org.*

TOURS

American Spirit Shuttle

GUIDED TOURS | American Spirit Shuttle offers scheduled and customized tours of Colorado National Monument. ✉ *204 4th St., Clifton* ☎ *970/240–0813* 🌐 *www.americanspiritshuttle.com* *From $50.*

Sights

★ Colorado National Monument

MEMORIAL | Sheer red-rock cliffs open to 23 miles of steep canyons and thin monoliths that sprout as high as 450 feet from the floor of Colorado National Monument. This vast tract of rugged, ragged terrain was declared a national monument in 1911 at the urging of an eccentric visionary named John Otto. Now it's popular for rock climbing, horseback riding, cross-country skiing, biking, and camping. Cold Shivers Point is just one of the many dramatic overlooks along **Rim Rock Drive,** a 23-mile scenic route with breathtaking views. The town of Fruita, at the base of Colorado National Monument, is a haven for mountain bikers and hikers. It makes a great center for exploring the area's canyons—whether from the seat of a bike or the middle of a raft, heading for a leisurely float trip. ✉ *Fruita* ☎ *970/858–3617* 🌐 *www.nps.gov/colm* 🎫 *$15 per wk per vehicle. Visitors entering on motorcycle pay $10; bicycle or foot pay $5 for weekly pass.*

Dinosaur Journey

MUSEUM | FAMILY | Roaring robotic stegosaurs and meat-shredding animatronic allosaurs prowl Dinosaur Journey, a fun, informative attraction just off I–70 a few minutes from the western entrance to Colorado National Monument. Unlike many museums, this one encourages kids to touch everything—friendly paleontologists may even allow kids to hold a chunk of fossilized dino dung. In addition to the amazing lifelike replicas, there are more than 20 interactive displays. Children can stand in an earthquake simulator; dig up "fossils" in a mock quarry (the pit is made of crushed walnut shells); or make dino prints in dirt, along with reptile and bird tracks for comparison. The museum also sponsors daily digs nearby, where many of the fossils were found. Local volunteers are at work cleaning and preparing fossils for study. ✉ *550 Jurassic Ct., Fruita* ☎ *970/858–7282* 🌐 *museumofwesternco.com/dinosaur-journey* 🎫 *$9.*

★ McInnis Canyons National Conservation Area

NATURE PRESERVE | Ten miles west of Grand Junction, stretching from Fruita to just across the Utah border, the McInnis Canyons National Conservation Area (formerly Colorado Canyons National Conservation Area) is rife with natural arches, along with numerous rock canyons, caves, coves, and spires. **Rattlesnake Canyon** has nine arches, making it the second-largest concentration of natural arches in the country. The canyon can be reached in summer from the upper end of Rim Rock Drive with four-wheel-drive vehicles or via a 7-mile hike by the intrepid.

Though much of the territory complements the red-dirt canyons of Colorado National Monument, McInnis Canyons is more accessible to horseback riding, mountain biking, all-terrain vehicle and motorcycle trails, and for trips with dogs (most of these activities aren't allowed at the monument). Designated in 2000 by Congress, the conservation area was created from a desire of nearby communities to preserve the area's unique scenery while allowing multiple-use recreation. Be prepared for biting gnats from late May to late July. Contact the Bureau of Land Management for a map before venturing out. ✉ *2815 H Rd., Grand Junction* ☎ *970/244–3000* 🌐 *www.blm.gov/programs/national-conservation-lands/colorado/mcinnis-canyons* 🎫 *Free.*

Restaurants

Fiesta Guadalajara Restaurant

$ | MEXICAN | FAMILY | Authentic and family-friendly, this Mexican restaurant serves good food in huge portions. Try the chiles rellenos, super nachos, and especially the Chile Colorado: fork-tender beef simmered in a savory red-pepper sauce. **Known for:** great margaritas; Mexican pizza; house-made horchata. 💲 *Average main: $14* ✉ *103 Hwys. 6 and 50, Fruita* ☎ *970/858–1228* 🌐 *fiestaguadalajaraco.com.*

The Legacy of Mike the Headless Chicken

It all started with a run-in with a Fruita farmer who had bad aim, or so the tale goes. The year was 1945 and Mike, a young Wyandotte rooster, was minding his own business in the barnyard when farmer Lloyd Olsen snatched him from the chicken coop to prepare him for dinner. Just like he had done countless times before with other chickens, farmer Olsen stretched Mike's neck across the chopping block and whacked off his head. Apparently undaunted by the ordeal, Mike promptly got up, dusted off his feathers and went about his daily business pecking for food, fluffing his feathers, and crowing, except Mike's crow was now reduced to a gurgle. Scientists surmised that Mike's brain stem was largely untouched, leaving his reflex actions intact while a blood clot prevented him from bleeding to death. The headless chicken dubbed "Miracle Mike" toured the freak-show circuit, where the morbidly curious could sneak a peek at his nogginless nub for a quarter. Mike's incredible story of survival (he lived for 18 months without a head!) soon hit the pages of two national magazines, *Time* and *Life*. The headless wonder, who was fed with an eyedropper, eventually met his demise in an Arizona motel room, where he choked to death. His legacy lives on in Fruita, where the tiny town throws a gigantic party every June to celebrate Mike's life. Even in death, Mike is still making headlines.

Hotels

Comfort Inn

$ | HOTEL | FAMILY | Some rooms at this Southwestern-style budget motel have views of the Colorado National Monument. **Pros:** very affordable; great views; close to the monument. **Cons:** rooms and furniture are showing age; chain-hotel feel; breakfast is just so-so. *Rooms from: $74* ✉ *400 Jurassic Ave., Fruita* ☎ *970/858–1333* 🌐 *www.choicehotels.com* *64 rooms* *Free Breakfast.*

Activities

HIKING

Colorado National Monument Hiking Trails

HIKING/WALKING | A good way to explore Colorado National Monument is by trail. There are more than 40 miles of short and backcountry trails, with more than a dozen well-marked hikes ranging from a ¼ mile to 14 miles. ✉ *Fruita* ☎ *970/858–2800* 🌐 *www.nps.gov/colm.*

Otto's Trail

HIKING/WALKING | An easy 30-minute stroll with sweeping canyon views, Otto's Trail greets hikers with breezes scented by sagebrush and juniper, which stand out from the dull red rock and sand. The trail leads to stunning sheer drop-offs and endless views. At the end of the half-mile trail at Otto's Overlook you can hear the wind in the feathers of birds as they soar out of the canyon. ✉ *Fruita* *Trailhead: Rim Rock Dr., 1 mile from western gate visitor center.*

Serpents Trail

HIKING/WALKING | This trail has been called the "Crookedest Road in the World" because of its more than 50 switchbacks. The fairly steep but rewarding trail, which ascends several hundred feet, takes about two hours to complete, depending on your ability (and the heat). *Trailhead: Serpents Trail parking lot, ¼ mile from east gate.*

HORSEBACK RIDING

Rimrock Adventures

HORSEBACK RIDING | This company runs horseback rides near Colorado National Monument as well as through Little Book Cliffs Wild Horse Preserve. Rimrock Adventures also runs a variety of rafting excursions and easygoing float trips. ✉ *927 Hwy. 340, Fruita* ☎ *970/858–9555, 888/712–9555* 🌐 *www.rradventures.com.*

RAFTING

Adventure Bound River Expeditions

WHITE-WATER RAFTING | This company runs trips on the Colorado, Green, and Yampa rivers—the latter through the canyons of Dinosaur National Monument. ✉ *Grand Junction* ☎ *970/247–4789, 800/423–4668* 🌐 *www.adventureboundusa.com.*

ROCK CLIMBING

The stunning stark sandstone and shale formations of Colorado National Monument are a rock climber's paradise. Independence Monument is a favorite climb.

Glenwood Climbing Guides

CLIMBING/MOUNTAINEERING | This company offers a variety of climbing excursions in the canyons of Colorado National Monument, including rappelling and canyoneering. It also offers guides and climbing instruction elsewhere around western Colorado and eastern Utah, including Moab. ☎ *970/319–0656* 🌐 *www.glenwoodclimbingguides.com.*

Grand Mesa

47 miles southeast of Grand Junction via I–70 and Hwy. 65.

Small, quiet towns along the 63-mile Grand Mesa Scenic and Historic Byway (Highway 65) provide just enough support for the plethora of outdoor opportunities available in the diverse range of ecosystems on the world's largest flat-topped mountain.

GETTING HERE AND AROUND

A car is needed to explore Grand Mesa. In northwestern Colorado, I–70 (U.S. 6) is the major thoroughfare, accessing Grand Junction and Grand Mesa (via Route 65, which runs to Delta).

ESSENTIALS

TRANSPORTATION CONTACTS Grand Junction Regional Airport (GJT). ✉ *2828 Walker Field Dr., Grand Junction* ☎ *970/244–9100* 🌐 *www.gjairport.com.*

VISITOR INFORMATION Parachute/Battlement Mesa Area Visitor Center/Chamber of Commerce. ✉ *200 Green St.* ☎ *970/285–7934* 🌐 *www.battlementmesacolorado.com.*

Sights

Grand Mesa National Forest

FOREST | The world's largest flattop mountain towers nearly 11,000 feet above the surrounding terrain and sprawls an astounding 53 square miles. Grand Mesa National Forest attracts the outdoor enthusiast who craves the simple life: fresh air, biting fish, spectacular sunsets, a roaring campfire under the stars, and a little elbow room to take it all in. The landscape is filled with more than 300 sparkling lakes—a fisherman's paradise in summer. The mesa, as it's referred to by locals, offers excellent hiking and camping (try Island Lake Campground) opportunities. There is also a handful of lodges that rent modern cabins. You can downhill ski at Powderhorn Resort, cross-country ski, snowshoe, snowmobile, or ice fish. ✉ *2250 Hwy. 50, Delta* ☎ *970/874–6600* 🌐 *www.fs.usda.gov/gmug.*

Grand Mesa Scenic Byway

SCENIC DRIVE | This byway is 63 miles long and winds its way along Highway 65 through meadows sprinkled with wildflowers, shimmering aspen groves, aromatic pine forests, and endless lakes. Scenic overlooks (Land-O-Lakes is a standout), rest areas, and picnic areas are clearly marked. There are two visitor centers on the byway, which has endpoints at I–70 near Palisade and in Cedaredge. ☎ *970/471–9621* 🌐 *www.grandmesabyway.com.*

Hotels

Alexander Lake Lodge

$ | HOTEL | The mirror-calm Alexander Lake reflects towering pine trees that also overlook the majority of this resort's cozy cabins, which are designed for tranquility and hold as many as 12 people. **Pros:** fishing and snowmobiling right on the property; quiet and peaceful; cabins are well stocked. **Cons:** rather remote and winter driving can be rough; cabins are sparsely decorated; issues can take a while to fix because of remote location. 💲 *Rooms from: $95* ✉ *21221 Baron Lake Dr., Cedaredge* ✣ *17 miles north of Cedaredge, 2 miles from Grand Mesa visitor center on Forest Rd. 121* ☎ *970/856–2539, 800/850–7221* 🌐 *www.alexanderlakelodge.co* *7 cabins* 🍽 *Free Breakfast.*

Activities

DOWNHILL SKIING

Powderhorn Mountain Resort

SKIING/SNOWBOARDING | The slopes at this resort intriguingly follow the fall line of the mesa, carving out natural bowls. Those bowls on the western side are steeper than they first appear. Lift tickets are reasonable, the skiing is surprisingly good, and the addition of a halfpipe and an improved terrain park have gone a long way toward modernizing the resort. Powderhorn averages 250 inches of snowfall per year. **Facilities:** 42 trails; 1,600 acres; 1,650-foot vertical drop; 5 lifts. ✉ *Rte. 65, 48338 Powderhorn Rd., Mesa* ☎ *970/268–5700* 🌐 *www.powderhorn.com* 🎟 *Lift ticket $79.*

FISHING

The more than 300 lakes and reservoirs provide some of the best angling opportunities in Colorado for rainbow, cutthroat, and brook trout.

HIKING

Grand Mesa Discovery Trail

HIKING/WALKING | FAMILY | This trail is a great beginning hike for kids and adults attempting to acclimate themselves to the altitude—and the slow-paced attitude—of the mesa. Pick up a brochure at the visitor center for information on the landscape. The gently sloping 20-minute trail offers a taste of what to expect on longer hikes. ✉ *Trailhead: Grand Mesa visitor center, near intersection of Hwy. 65 and Trickel Park Rd.*

Cedaredge

15 miles south of Grand Mesa via Hwy. 65.

Cedaredge is called the gateway to the Grand Mesa, the world's largest flat-topped mountain. An elevation of 6,100 feet makes for a mild climate that is perfect for ranching, as well as for growing apples, peaches, and cherries. It's also rich in galleries, gift shops, antiques stores, and wineries.

GETTING HERE AND AROUND

Driving is the best way to get around the area; the small town is best explored on foot.

Sights

Pioneer Town

MUSEUM VILLAGE | The town site was originally the headquarters of a cattle spread, the Bar-I Ranch. Pioneer Town, a cluster of 23 authentic buildings that re-create turn-of-the-20th-century life, includes a country chapel, the Lizard Head Saloon, original silos from the Bar-I Ranch, and a working blacksmith shop. ✉ *336 S. Grand*

Mesa Dr. ☎ *970/856–7554* 🌐 *www.pioneertown.org* 🎫 *$7* ⏲ *Closed Sun. and early Oct.–Memorial Day.*

Shopping

★ Apple Shed

CRAFTS | Once an apple-packing shed, the Apple Shed has been restored and remodeled into a series of unusual gift shops and arts and crafts galleries. An attached tasting room features their own locally produced Williams Cellars wines and Snow Capped Ciders, while the deli serves breakfast Thursday through Sunday and Mexican fare and sandwiches and salads for lunch and dinner daily. ✉ *250 S. Grand Mesa Dr.* ☎ *970/856–7007* 🌐 *www.theappleshed.net.*

Steamboat Springs

42 miles east of Craig; 160 miles west of Denver.

Steamboat got its name from French trappers who, after hearing the bubbling and churning hot springs, mistakenly thought a steamboat was chugging up the Yampa River. Here Stetson hats are sold for shade and not for souvenirs, and the Victorian-era buildings, most of them fronting the main drag of Lincoln Avenue, were built to be functional, not ornamental.

Steamboat Springs is aptly nicknamed Ski Town, U.S.A., because it has sent more athletes to the Winter Olympics than any other town in the nation (and also more than some small countries). When sizing up the mountain, keep in mind that the part that's visible from below is only the tip of the iceberg—much more terrain lies concealed in back. Steamboat is famed for its eiderdown-soft snow; in fact, the term "champagne powder" was coined (and amusingly enough registered as a trademark) here to describe the area's unique feathery drifts, the result of Steamboat's fortuitous position between the arid desert to the west and the moisture-magnet of the Continental Divide to the east, where storm fronts duke it out.

The mountain village, with its maze of upscale condos, boutiques, and nightclubs, is certainly attractive, but spread out and a little lacking in character. To its credit, though, this increasingly trendy destination has retained much of its down-home friendliness.

GETTING HERE AND AROUND

Yampa Valley Regional Airport (HDN) is in Hayden, 22 miles from Steamboat Springs. Go Alpine and Storm Mountain Express provide door-to-door service to Steamboat Springs from Yampa Valley Regional Airport. A one-way trip with either starts at $36.

Steamboat Springs Transit (SST) provides free shuttle service between the ski area and downtown Steamboat year-round. Most of the major properties also provide shuttles between the two areas for their guests.

From Denver, Steamboat Springs is about a three-hour drive northwest via I–70 and U.S. 40. The route traverses some high-mountain passes, so it's a good idea to check road conditions before you travel.

TRANSPORTATION CONTACTS Go Alpine Taxi. ☎ *800/343–7433, 970/879–2800* 🌐 *www.goalpine.com.* **Steamboat Springs Transit.** ☎ *970/879–3717* 🌐 *steamboatsprings.net/transit.* **Storm Mountain Express.** ☎ *970/879–1963* 🌐 *www.stormmountainexpress.com.* **Yampa Valley Regional Airport (HDN).** ✉ *11005 County Rd. 51A, Hayden* ☎ *970/276–5000* 🌐 *flysteamboat.com.*

WHEN TO GO

A popular year-round destination, Steamboat becomes most dramatic in mid-September, when the leaves turn brilliant gold in the forests along the highways and the air cools considerably.

Did You Know?
Steamboat Springs is called Ski Town, U.S.A., because it has sent more athletes to the Winter Olympics than any other place in the country.

By the first week of November, the ski season has begun, and it doesn't end until mid-April.

FESTIVALS

Hot Air Balloon Rodeo and Annual Art in the Park

FESTIVALS | FAMILY | Every year since 1980, mid-July in Steamboat has meant hot-air balloons and fine art, a combination that draws folks from miles around to watch more than 40 balloons float out over the valley from Bald Eagle Lake each morning. The rest of the weekend is devoted to the display and sale of hundreds of works of art from all over the world at West Lincoln Park. ✉ *35565 S. Hwy. 40* ☎ *970/879–0880* 🌐 *www.steamboat-chamber.com.*

Strings in the Mountains Music Festival

MUSIC FESTIVALS | The focus is on chamber music and chamber-orchestra music presented by more than 150 musicians, including Grammy winners and other internationally renowned talents, throughout summer, primarily in the tent on the weekends. But Strings also offers big names in jazz, country, big band, bluegrass, and world music (Pink Martini, Lyle Lovett, and Dirty Dozen Brass Band, to name a few), as well as free concerts during its "Music on the Green" lunchtime series at Yampa River Botanic Park on Thursday in summer. ✉ *Steamboat Springs Music Festival Tent at the corner of Mt. Werner and Pine Grove Rds.* ☎ *970/879–5056* 🌐 *www.stringsmusicfestival.com.*

ESSENTIALS

VISITOR INFORMATION Steamboat Ski & Resort Corporation. ✉ *2305 Mount Werner Circle* ☎ *970/879–7300, 800/922–2722* 🌐 *www.steamboat.com.* **Steamboat Springs Chamber Resort Associationcom.** ✉ *125 Anglers Dr.* ☎ *970/879–0880* 🌐 *www.steamboat-chamber.com.* **Steamboat Springs Snow Report.** ☎ *970/879–7300* 🌐 *www.steamboat.com/the-mountain/daily-snow.*

TOURS

Sweet Pea Tours

BOAT TOURS | Steamboat's Sweet Pea Tours visits nearby hot springs. The ride takes about 25 minutes each way, and rates are higher in winter and on weekends. ✉ *Steamboat Springs* ☎ *970/879–5820* 🌐 *www.sweetpeatours.com* 🎟 *From $30.*

Sights

Medicine Bow/Routt National Forests

NATURE PRESERVE | In summer Steamboat serves as the gateway to the magnificent Medicine Bow/Routt National Forests, with a wealth of activities from hiking to mountain biking to fishing. Among the nearby attractions are the 283-foot **Fish Creek Falls** and the splendidly rugged **Mount Zirkel Wilderness Area.** To the north, two sparkling man-made lakes, **Steamboat** and **Pearl,** each in its own state park, are a draw for those into fishing and sailing. In winter the area is just as popular. Snowshoers and backcountry skiers are permitted to use the west side of Rabbit Ears Pass, whereas snowmobilers are confined to the east side. ✉ *Hahns Peak–Bears Ears Ranger District Office* ☎ *970/870–2187* 🌐 *www.fs.usda.gov/mbr.*

Old Town Hot Springs

HOT SPRINGS | FAMILY | There are more than 150 mineral springs of varying temperatures in the Steamboat Springs area, including this one, in the middle of town. Old Town Hot Springs gets its waters from the all-natural Heart Spring. The modern facility has a lap pool, relaxation pool, climbing wall, and health club. Two waterslides are open noon to 6 pm in summer and 4 to 8 pm in winter; they require an additional $7 fee. The inflatable playground called The Wibit is open Friday to Sunday from noon to 6 pm between June and September, and also requires an additional $7 fee. ✉ *136 Lincoln Ave.* ☎ *970/879–1828* 🌐 *www.steamboathotsprings.org* 🎟 *$25.*

A visit to Strawberry Park Hot Springs is charming in all four seasons.

★ Strawberry Park Hot Springs

HOT SPRINGS | About 7 miles west of town, the Strawberry Park Hot Springs is a bit remote and rustic, although only the winter drive on the gravel portion on the road is challenging. The way the pool is set up to offer semi-privacy makes for an intimate setting and relaxation. It's family-oriented during the day, but after dark clothing is optional, and no one under 18 is admitted. Feel free to bring food to eat in the picnic areas. A variety of massages, including aquatic-style, are offered next to the pools. ✉ *Strawberry Park Rd., 44200 County Rd. #36* ☎ *970/879–0342* 🌐 *www.strawberryhotsprings.com* 🎫 *$20, cash or check only.*

Tread of Pioneers Museum

MUSEUM | In a restored Queen Anne–style house, the Tread of Pioneers Museum is an excellent spot to bone up on local history on Fridays and Saturdays. It includes ski memorabilia dating to the turn of the 20th century, when Carl Howelsen opened Howelsen Hill, still the country's preeminent ski-jumping facility. ✉ *800 Oak St.* ☎ *970/879–2214* 🌐 *www.treadofpioneers.org* 🎫 *$6* 🕒 *Closed Sun.–Thurs.*

Restaurants

★ Aurum Food & Wine

$$$$ | **MODERN AMERICAN** | Situated along the Yampa River, with an expansive deck and couch seating that juts out over the water, Aurum serves seasonal modern American fare made from locally sourced ingredients. Inside, the pretty space features dark woods, lots of fresh flowers, and expansive windows to showcase the view. **Known for:** stunning views; good happy hour; jumbo lump crab cakes. 💲 *Average main: $41* ✉ *811 Yampa St.* ☎ *970/879–9500* 🌐 *aurumsteamboat.com* 🕒 *No lunch.*

★ Cafe Diva

$$$$ | **MODERN AMERICAN** | A pretty, egg-yolk yellow but unfussy dining room is an ideal backdrop for fresh, locally sourced modern American dishes. The menu lists a significant number of vegan and gluten-free options that put some effort into their creation, such as quinoa risotto with butternut squash and mushroom jus. **Known for:** by-the-glass wine list; venison tenderloin; elegant atmosphere that's not fussy. *Average main: $43 1855 Ski Time Square Dr. 970/871–0508 www.cafediva.com No lunch.*

Carl's Tavern

$$ | **AMERICAN** | Named after Karl Hovelsen, the Norwegian ski jumper who brought the sport to Colorado in the early 1900s and who also lent his name to Steamboat's Howelsen Hill, this modern tavern serves updated takes on comfort food, with an emphasis on locally sourced ingredients and as many items produced in-house as possible. Local favorites include chicken-fried steak, three-cheese mac, and lemon icebox pie, but it's also tough to pass up the pot roast made from Angus beef or the banana-chocolate bread pudding. **Known for:** half-price happy hour; Tuesday night prime rib; well-crafted cocktails. *Average main: $18 700 Yampa Ave. 970/761–2060 www.carlstavern.com Closed Mon. and Tues.*

Creekside Café & Grill

$$ | **AMERICAN** | **FAMILY** | This café's hearty breakfasts and lunches, which are crafted to get folks through a day of skiing or biking, are served in a casual atmosphere that's family—and group—friendly. The most popular item on the menu, and for good reason, is the roster of a dozen eggs Benedict choices, including "the Mountain Man," with smoked bacon, ham, and chorizo. **Known for:** bustling atmosphere; rotating local art; "the Mountain Man" eggs Benedict with smoked bacon, ham, and chorizo. *Average main: $16 131 11th St. 970/879–4925 www.creekside-cafe.com No dinner.*

★ Harwigs

$$$$ | **FRENCH** | Steamboat's most intimate restaurant is in a building that once housed Harwig's Saddlery and Western Wear. The classic French cuisine, with subtle Asian influences, is well crafted, and the menu changes monthly. **Known for:** wine cellar with more than 10,000 bottles; lamb sliders; duck and seafood dishes. *Average main: $49 911 Lincoln Ave. 970/879–1919 www.harwigs.com Closed Sun. and Mon. No lunch.*

Johnny B. Good's Diner

$ | **AMERICAN** | **FAMILY** | Between the appealing kids' menu and the memorabilia that suggests Elvis has not left the building, Johnny's is all about fun and family. Breakfast (until 2 pm), lunch, and dinner are served daily, and they are all budget minded and large portioned. **Known for:** kid-friendly locals hangout; reasonable prices; burgers and milkshakes. *Average main: $13 738 Lincoln Ave. 970/870–8400 www.johnnybgoods-diner.com.*

★ Laundry Kitchen & Cocktails

$$$$ | **MODERN AMERICAN** | Small plates are the way to go in this convivial, casual setting, which was indeed the Steamboat Laundry from 1910 to 1977 but now serves tasty modern American tidbits such as fried shoestring potatoes sprinkled with duck-fat powder and house-smoked trout with goat cheese in a jar (the "jar" offering routinely changes). The dining room is rustic and cozy—exposed brick and original wood—and the service is spot-on. **Known for:** house-cured meats; inviting bar; specialty cocktails. *Average main: $40 127 11th St. 970/870–0681 www.thelaundryrestaurant.com No lunch.*

Alpine Rose Bed and Breakfast

$ | **B&B/INN** | Views of Strawberry Park and an easy walk into town make the Alpine Rose a wonderful alternative to pricey hotels, especially during ski season. **Pros:** close to town; relatively close to ski area (five-minute drive); reasonably priced. **Cons:** not right next to ski area; two-night minimum can be an issue; kids can stay only in the suites. $ *Rooms from: $100* ✉ *724 N. Grand St.* ☎ *970/879–1528* 🌐 *www.alpinerosesteamboat.com* *6 rooms* 🍴 *Free Breakfast.*

Hotel Bristol

$$$ | **HOTEL** | **FAMILY** | A delightful small hotel nestled in a 1948 building, the Bristol—which is now owned by the Magnuson Hotels chain—not only has its location working for it, but also old-fashioned personalized service. **Pros:** families and groups can stay comfortably for a little bit extra; convenient location; ski lockers. **Cons:** rooms may seem uncomfortably small, bathrooms even more so; thin walls; in-house restaurant noise can be heard from some rooms. $ *Rooms from: $217* ✉ *917 Lincoln Ave.* ☎ *970/879–3083* 🌐 *www.steamboathotelbristol.com* *24 rooms* 🍴 *No meals.*

Inn at Steamboat

$$$ | **B&B/INN** | Rustic knotty pine, leather furniture, comfortable linens, and panoramic views of the Yampa Valley make this inn a good choice for visitors looking to stay somewhere that feels like a mountain lodge at lower-than-ski-resort prices. **Pros:** magnificent views, even from the heated pool and particularly in fall; spacious rooms; house-baked cookies and pastries. **Cons:** not ski-in ski-out; not walking distance to downtown; property feels dated. $ *Rooms from: $229* ✉ *3070 Columbine Dr.* ☎ *970/879–2600* 🌐 *www.innatsteamboat.com* *33 rooms* 🍴 *Free Breakfast.*

Mountain Resorts

$$$ | **RENTAL** | This vacation rental company manages condominiums at more than two dozen locations. **Pros:** some properties are very upscale; some have pools and fitness facilities; accommodating staff. **Cons:** properties vary wildly in price and decor; some properties are dated; some are relatively far from slopes or town. $ *Rooms from: $280* ✉ *2145 Resort Dr., Suite 100* ☎ *888/686–8075* 🌐 *www.mtn-resorts.com* *378 condos* 🍴 *No meals.*

Ptarmigan Inn

$$$ | **HOTEL** | **FAMILY** | Situated on the slopes, this laid-back lodging couldn't have a more convenient location. **Pros:** great location; ski-in ski-out; mountain views. **Cons:** chain-hotel vibes; decor feels dated; late-night slope grooming can be noisy. $ *Rooms from: $221* ✉ *2304 Après Ski Way* ☎ *888/236–2163* 🌐 *www.theptarmigan.com* *77 rooms* 🍴 *No meals.*

Rabbit Ears Motel

$$ | **HOTEL** | **FAMILY** | The playful, pink-neon bunny sign outside this motel has been a local landmark since 1952, making it an unofficial gateway to Steamboat Springs. **Pros:** great location; family- and pet-friendly; huge rooms. **Cons:** beds may be uncomfortable; kitschy and nothing fancy; it can be noisy along the main drag. $ *Rooms from: $169* ✉ *201 Lincoln Ave.* ☎ *970/879–1150, 800/828–7702* 🌐 *www.rabbitearsmotel.com* *65 rooms* 🍴 *Free Breakfast.*

★ Sheraton Steamboat Resort & Villas

$$$$ | **HOTEL** | **FAMILY** | This bustling high-rise is one of Steamboat's few ski-in ski-out properties; the amenities are classic resort-town, with a ski shop, golf course, an outdoor heated pool, and four rooftop hot tubs with sweeping views of the surrounding ski slopes. **Pros:** convenient location, with the slopes, three restaurants and a market, and town right there; large size means lots of amenities; cozy hangout areas. **Cons:** lobby areas can be chaotic; prices now on par with major ski areas; decor a bit bland. $ *Rooms from: $417* ✉ *2200 Village End Ct.* ☎ *970/879–2220* 🌐 *www.marriott.com* *281 rooms* 🍴 *No meals.*

Steamboat Mountain Lodge

$$ | **B&B/INN** | **FAMILY** | River or mountain views await at this budget-minded spot, which counts a river-rock fireplace surrounded by cozy couches and a Jacuzzi on the deck among its charms. **Pros:** great views; spacious rooms; bargain prices. **Cons:** very simple decor; breakfast is nothing special; property feels

dated. Ⓢ *Rooms from: $170* ✉ *3155 S. Lincoln St.* ☎ *970/871–9121* 🌐 *www.steamboatmountainlodge.com* 🛏 *38 rooms* 🍴 *Free Breakfast.*

★ Vista Verde Guest Ranch

$$$$ | B&B/INN | On a working ranch, the luxurious Vista Verde provides city slickers with an authentic Western experience; lodge rooms are huge and beautifully appointed, with lace curtains, Western art, and lodgepole furniture, while the spacious cabins are more rustic, with pine paneling and old-fashioned wood-burning stoves, plus refrigerators, coffeemakers, and porches. **Pros:** authentic dude ranch experience; lots of amenities; good packages available. **Cons:** pricey compared to other area lodging; remote location; can be snowed-in during winter. Ⓢ *Rooms from: $632* ✉ *31100 County Rd. 64, Clark* ☎ *970/879–3858* 🌐 *www.vistaverde.com* 🕒 *Closed late Mar.–early June and mid-Oct.–mid-Dec.* 🛏 *12 rooms* 🍴 *All-inclusive.*

Wyndham Vacation Rentals

$$$ | RENTAL | Torian Plum slope-side is just one of the properties managed by Wyndham Vacation Rentals (now the clearinghouse for most of the rental condos in the area); properties include elegant one- to six-bedroom units in a ski-in ski-out location and units sprinkled around town. **Pros:** secure rooms for ski storage; free shuttles to town; some rentals have hot tubs. **Cons:** properties vary in comfort and style; often completely booked during ski season; units can be cramped. Ⓢ *Rooms from: $276* ✉ *1855 Ski Time Sq.* ☎ *800/467–3529* 🌐 *www.wyndhamvacationrentals.com* 🛏 *347 condos* 🍴 *No meals.*

Nightlife

Mahogany Ridge Brewery & Grill

BREWPUBS/BEER GARDENS | Mahogany Ridge Brewery & Grill serves superior pub grub and pours an assortment of its own ales, lagers, porters, and stouts. Live music is a nice bonus on weekends. ✉ *435 Lincoln Ave.* ☎ *970/879–3773* 🌐 *www.mahoganyridgesteamboat.com.*

Old Town Pub

BARS/PUBS | Located in a 1904 building, this pub serves juicy burgers and fiery wings accompanied by music from some great bands. A limited bar menu and homemade pizza is served until 1 am. ✉ *600 Lincoln Ave.* ☎ *970/879–2101* 🌐 *www.theoldtownpub.com.*

Shopping

At the base of the ski area are three expansive shopping centers—Ski Time Square, Torian Plum Plaza, and Gondola Square.

BOOKSTORES

Off the Beaten Path

BOOKS/STATIONERY | Off the Beaten Path is a throwback to the Beat Generation, with poetry readings, lectures, and concerts. It has an excellent selection of New Age works, in addition to the usual best sellers and travel guides. The on-site coffee shop is the best in town, with fresh baked goods and sandwiches. Hours vary by season so call ahead to confirm. ✉ *68 9th St.* ☎ *970/879–6830* 🌐 *www.steamboatbooks.com.*

BOUTIQUES AND GALLERIES

Jac Romick Gallery

LOCAL SPECIALTIES | A former member of the U.S. Ski Team and a veteran of the rodeo circuit, Jace Romick has shifted from crafting splendid textured lodgepole furniture at his now-closed Into the West shop and focuses instead solely on his photography there, which features contemporary Western images for sale. ✉ *837 Lincoln Ave.* ☎ *970/879–8377* 🌐 *www.jaceromickgallery.com.*

Silver Lining

CRAFTS | This shop displays beautifully designed jewelry from around the world, such as Peruvian opal necklaces, as well as locally crafted Western pieces using turquoise and silver. They carry an extensive and well-organized selection of beads and found objects for making your own, which you can do on a small scale at one end of the tiny store. They also offer jewelry repair and pearl knotting. ✉ *Torian Plum Plaza, 1865 Ski Time Sq. Dr.* ☎ *970/879–7474* 🌐 *www.steamboat-mountainvillage.com.*

Wild Horse Gallery

ART GALLERIES | Native American images, local landscapes, and wildlife adorn the walls of the Wild Horse Gallery. This shop across from the Steamboat Art Museum is the place to buy artwork, jewelry, and blown glass. ✉ *802 Lincoln Ave.* ☎ *970/879–5515* 🌐 *www.wild-horsegallery.com.*

SHOPPING CENTERS

Old Town Square

SHOPPING CENTERS/MALLS | Downtown Steamboat's Old Town Square is a collection of upscale boutiques and retailers. There are also plenty of places to sit and people-watch or get a good cup of coffee. ✉ *7th St. and Lincoln Ave.*

SPORTING GOODS

Ski Haus

SPORTING GOODS | If you need to be outfitted for the slopes, look no further than Ski Haus, which has a full line of winter gear and also offers rentals. The Ski Haus Bike Shop rents bikes directly across the street. ✉ *1457 Pine Grove Rd.* ☎ *844/878–0385* 🌐 *www.skihaussteamboat.com.*

Straightline Sports

SPORTING GOODS | This sporting-goods store is a good bet for downhill necessities. ✉ *744 Lincoln Ave.* ☎ *970/879–7568* 🌐 *www.straightlinesports.com.*

WESTERN WEAR

F.M. Light and Sons

CLOTHING | Owned by the same family for four generations, F.M. Light and Sons caters to the cowpoke in all of us. If you're lucky you'll find a bargain on Western wear here. ✉ *830 Lincoln Ave.* ☎ *970/879–1822* 🌐 *www.fmlight.com.*

Activities

BACKCOUNTRY SKIING

The most popular area for backcountry skiing around Steamboat Springs is Rabbit Ears Pass, southeast of town. It's the last pass you cross if you're driving from Denver to Steamboat. Much of the appeal is its easy access to high-country trails from U.S. 40. There are plenty of routes you can take.

Hahns Peak Ranger Office

SKIING/SNOWBOARDING | A popular backcountry spot is Seedhouse Road, about 26 miles north of Steamboat, near the town of Clark. A marked network of trails across the rolling hills has good views of distant peaks. For maps and information on snow conditions, contact the Hahns Peak Ranger Office. ✉ *400 Seedhouse Rd.* ☎ *970/870–2299* 🌐 *www.steamboat-chamber.com.*

Ski Haus

SKIING/SNOWBOARDING | Touring and telemarking rentals are available at ski shops in the Steamboat area. One of the best is the Ski Haus. ✉ *1457 Pine Grove Rd.* ☎ *844/878–0385* 🌐 *www.skihaussteamboat.com.*

Steamboat Ski Touring Center

SKIING/SNOWBOARDING | Arrangements for backcountry tours can be made through Steamboat Ski Touring Center. Trail passes cost $23. ✉ *Steamboat Springs* ✣ *Left on Steamboat Blvd. from Mt. Werner Rd.; second right at Steamboat Ski Touring Center sign* ☎ *970/879–8180* 🌐 *www.nordicski.net.*

DOWNHILL SKIING AND SNOWBOARDING

Howelsen Hill Ski Area

SKIING/SNOWBOARDING | The tiny Howelsen Hill Ski Area, in the heart of Steamboat Springs, is the oldest ski area still open in Colorado. Howelsen, with 4 lifts, 17 trails, 9 Nordic trails, 1 terrain park, and a 440-foot vertical drop, is home to the Steamboat Springs Winter Sports Club, which has more than 800 members. The ski area not only has an awesome terrain park, but has night skiing as well. It's the largest ski-jumping complex in America and a major Olympic training ground. **Facilities:** 17 trails; 50 acres; 440-foot vertical drop; 4 lifts. ✉ *845 Howelsen Pkwy.* ☎ *970/879–4300* 🌐 *www.steamboat-springs.net/ski* 🎫 *Lift ticket $35.*

★ Steamboat Springs Ski Area

SKIING/SNOWBOARDING | The Steamboat Springs Ski Area is perhaps best known for its tree skiing and "cruising" terrain—the latter term referring to wide, groomed runs perfect for intermediate-level skiers. The abundance of cruising terrain has made Steamboat immensely popular with those who ski once or twice a year and who aren't looking to tax their abilities. On a predominantly western exposure—most ski areas sit on north-facing exposures—the resort benefits from intense sun, which contributes to the mellow atmosphere. In addition, one of the most extensive lift systems in the region allows skiers to get in lots of runs without having to spend much time waiting in line. The Storm Peak and Sundown high-speed quads, for example, each send you about 2,000 vertical feet in less than seven minutes. Do the math: a day of more than 60,000 vertical feet is entirely within the realm of possibility.

All this is not to suggest, however, that Steamboat is a piece of cake for more experienced skiers. Pioneer Ridge encompasses advanced and intermediate terrain. Steamboat is renowned as a breeding ground for top mogul skiers, and for good reason. There are numerous mogul runs, but most are not particularly steep. The few with a vertical challenge, such as Chute One, are not especially long. If you're looking for challenging skiing at Steamboat, take on the trees. The ski area has done an admirable job of clearing many gladed areas of such nuisances as saplings, underbrush, and fallen timber, making Steamboat tree skiing much less hazardous than at other areas. The trees are also where advanced skiers—as well as, in some places, confident intermediates—can find the best of Steamboat's much-ballyhooed powder. Statistically, Steamboat doesn't report significantly more snowfall than other Colorado resorts, but somehow snow piles up here better than at the others. Ask well-traveled Colorado skiers, and they'll confirm that when it comes to consistently good, deep snow, Steamboat is hard to beat. Also, when conditions permit, the ski area opens up for night skiing. **Facilities:** 165 trails; 2,965 acres; 3,668-foot vertical drop; 21 lifts. ✉ *2305 Mount Werner Circle* ☎ *877/783–2628* 🌐 *www.steamboat.com* 🎫 *Lift ticket $145.*

LESSONS AND PROGRAMS

Half-day group lessons begin at $199; all-day lessons are $299. Clinics in moguls, powder, snowboarding, and "hyper-carving"—made possible by the design of shaped skis—are available.

Snowcat skiing—where a vehicle delivers you to hard-to-reach slopes—has been called the poor man's version of helicopter skiing, although at $525 a day that's probably a misnomer. It's true that snowcat users don't have to worry about landing, and can get to places that would be inaccessible by helicopter.

Kids' Vacation Center

SKIING/SNOWBOARDING | **FAMILY** | Programs for children from two years, six months to kindergarten age are offered through the Kids' Vacation Center. Day care is also available. ✉ *Steamboat Springs* ☎ *800/922–2722.*

Steamboat Powder Cats

SKIING/SNOWBOARDING | Buffalo Pass, northeast of Steamboat, is one of the snowiest spots in Colorado, and that's why it's the base for Steamboat Powder Cats. There's a maximum of 12 skiers per group, so the open-meadow skiing is never crowded. ✉ *1724 Mt. Werner Circle* ☎ *970/879–5188* 🌐 *www.steamboatpowdercats.com* 🎫 *From $625.*

Steamboat Ski and Resort Corporation

SKIING/SNOWBOARDING | General information about the Steamboat Springs ski areas is available through the Steamboat Ski and Resort Corporation. ✉ *Steamboat Springs* ☎ *970/879–6111, 877/783–2628 reservations* 🌐 *www.steamboat.com.*

RENTALS

Steamboat Central Reservations

SKIING/SNOWBOARDING | Equipment packages are available at the gondola base as well as at ski shops in town. Packages (skis, boots, and poles) average about $55 a day, less for multiday and advance online rentals. Call Steamboat Central Reservations for rental information. ✉ *Steamboat Springs* ☎ *800/922–2722* 🌐 *www.steamboat.com.*

GOLF

Haymaker Golf Course

GOLF | Three miles south of Steamboat Springs, this public-access 18-hole Keith Foster course has a pro shop and café, the Haymaker Patio Grill ($$). The challenging, rolling course has hills, streams, and native grasses, as well as exceptional views. The course is noted for being well maintained, with large greens and a 10,000-square-foot putting green. ✉ *34855 U.S. 40* ☎ *970/870–1846* 🌐 *www.haymakergolf.com* *$135* *Silver course: 18 holes, 7308 yards, par 72; Blue course: 18 holes, 5059 yards, par 72; Gold course: 18 holes, 6728 yards, par 72; White course: 18 holes, 6151 yards, par 72* *Reservations essential.*

Rollingstone Ranch Golf Club at the Sheraton Steamboat Resort

GOLF | Expect to see plenty of wildlife on this 18-hole championship course, which was designed by the legendary Robert Trent Jones Jr. The extensive practice facilities include a driving range, a bunker, and a putting green. The Fish Creek Grille ($$) serves lunch daily. ✉ *1230 Steamboat Blvd.* ☎ *970/879–1391* 🌐 *www.rollingstoneranchgolf.com* *$129* *Black course: 18 holes, 6902 yards, par 72; Green course: 18 holes, 5205 yards, par 72* *Reservations essential.*

HORSEBACK RIDING

Because of the ranches surrounding the Yampa and Elk rivers, Steamboat is full of real cowboys as well as visitors trying to act the part. Horseback riding is popular here for good reason: seeing the area on horseback is not only easier on the legs, but it also allows riders to get deeper into the backcountry—which is crisscrossed by a web of deer and elk trails—and sometimes closer to wildlife than is possible on foot.

Del's Triangle 3 Ranch

HORSEBACK RIDING | This facility can organize rides from hour-long tours to journeys lasting several days. It's about 20 miles north of Steamboat via Highway 129. ✉ *55675 County Rd. 62, Clark* ☎ *970/879–3495* 🌐 *www.steamboathorses.com.*

Howelsen Rodeo Grounds

HORSEBACK RIDING | Every Friday and Saturday evening in summer, rodeos are held at the Howelsen Rodeo Grounds. ✉ *5th St. and Howelsen Pkwy.* ☎ *970/879–1818* 🌐 *steamboatprorodeo.com* *$20.*

MOUNTAIN BIKING

Steamboat Springs' rolling mountains, endless aspen glades, mellow valleys, and miles and miles of Jeep trails and single-track make for great mountain biking. In summer, when Front Range trails are baking in the harsh summer sun and cluttered with mountain bikers, horse riders, and hikers, you can pedal some of the cool backcountry trails in Steamboat without passing a single cyclist.

Gore Pass Loop

BICYCLING | The 27½-mile Gore Pass Loop takes you through aspen and pine forests, with gradual hill climbs and long, sweet descents. ✉ *Hwy. 134 and Forest Rd. 185* *Trailhead: Follow Hwy. 134 to Gore Pass Park.*

Orange Peel Bicycle Service

BICYCLING | This bike shop offers a sweet line of demos that cost about double the regular rental rates, which start at $60 for a half day. It's a good deal if you're in the market for a new bike. ✉ *1136 Yampa St.* ☎ *970/879–2957* 🌐 *www.orangepeelbikes.com.*

RAFTING

Bucking Rainbow Outfitters

WHITE-WATER RAFTING | This outfitter runs rafting excursions to the Yampa, Elk, Colorado, North Platte, and Eagle rivers. Half-day to two-day trips are available for all levels. ✉ *730 Lincoln Ave.* ☎ *970/879–8747* 🌐 *www.buckingrainbow.com* 🎫 *From $50.*

SNOWMOBILING

Steamboat Snowmobile Tours

SNOW SPORTS | This company offers guided snowmobile tours. A shuttle serves most hotels. ✉ *Steamboat Springs* ☎ *970/879–6500* 🌐 *www.steamboatsnowmobile.com.*

TRACK SKIING

Steamboat Ski Touring Center

SKIING/SNOWBOARDING | Laid out on and along the Sheraton Steamboat Golf Club, Steamboat Ski Touring Center has a relatively gentle 18½-mile trail network. A good option for a relaxed afternoon of skiing is to pick up some vittles at the Picnic Basket in the main building and enjoy a picnic along Fish Creek Trail, a 3-mile-long loop that winds through pine and aspen groves. Rental packages (skis, boots, and poles) are available. ✉ *1230 Steamboat Blvd.* ☎ *970/879–8180* 🌐 *www.steamboatnordiccenter.com* 🎫 *Trail fee $23.*

Vista Verde Guest Ranch

SKIING/SNOWBOARDING | This guest ranch has a well-groomed network of tracks (about 9 miles), as well as access to the adjacent national forest. ✉ *58000 Cowboy Way, Clark* ☎ *970/879–3858* 🌐 *www.vistaverde.com.*

Meeker

43 miles north of Rifle via Rte. 13.

Once an outpost of the U.S. Army, Meeker is still a place where anyone in camouflage is in fashion. Famous for its annual sheepdog championships—a sheepdog statue keeps watch over the sleepy town—it remains a favorite spot for hunting, fishing, and snowmobiling. Interesting historical buildings include the Meeker Hotel on Main Street, where Teddy Roosevelt stayed.

GETTING HERE AND AROUND

Meeker is fairly isolated, and nearly equidistant between Grand Junction and Steamboat Springs. There is no public transportation in town, and a car is needed.

ESSENTIALS

VISITOR INFORMATION Meeker Chamber of Commerce. ✉ *710 Market St.* ☎ *970/878–5510* 🌐 *www.meekerchamber.com.*

Sights

White River Museum

MUSEUM | This museum is housed in a long building that served as a barracks for U.S. Army officers. Inside are exhibits such as a collection of guns dating to the Civil War and the plow used by Nathan Meeker to dig up the Ute's pony racetrack. ✉ *565 Park Ave.* ☎ *970/878–9982* 🌐 *www.meekercolorado.com/museum.htm* 🎫 *Free.*

Hotels

Meeker Hotel and Cafe

$ | HOTEL | The lobby is lined with framed broadsheet biographies of famous figures—such as Teddy Roosevelt—who stayed in this landmark, which is on the National Register of Historic Places. **Pros:** delightful decor; delicious food in the café; balcony suite has views of Main

Street. **Cons:** the café can get crowded and noisy; the walls are paper-thin; some furnishings are worn. *Rooms from: $80 560 Main St. 970/878–5255 www.meekerhotel.com 15 rooms No meals.*

Wendll's

CLOTHING | In this remodeled 1904 building on Market Street, you can buy an eclectic mix of clothing, housewares, body-care products, greeting cards, Brighton jewelry, and Native American turquoise and sterling silver from Arizona. The coffee shop has morning comfort foods like oatmeal and biscuits and gravy, as well as lunchtime sandwiches until 6 pm weekdays and 4 pm Saturday. *206 Market St. 970/878–3688 www.wendlls.com.*

FISHING

JML Outfitters

FISHING | The White River valley is home to some of the best fishing holes in Colorado, including Meeker Town Park, Sleepy Cat Access, and Trappers Lake. Some of the best fishing is on private land, so you need to ask permission, and you might have to pay. Your best bet—if you don't want to go it alone—is to hire a guide familiar with the area, such as JML Outfitters, which has been in the outfitting business for three generations, offering photography and wildlife-viewing trips, kids' camps, and trail rides. Rates vary by excursion. *300 County Rd. 75 970/878–4749 www.jmloutfitters.com From $150.*

SNOWMOBILING

Welder Outfitting Services

SNOW SPORTS | One of Meeker's best-kept secrets is the fantastic snowmobiling through pristine powder in the backcountry, which some say rivals Yellowstone—without the crowds. Trail maps for self-guided rides are available through the Chamber of Commerce or the U.S. Forest Service, or from Welder Outfitting Services, a hunting and fishing service that also organizes snowmobile trips in the White River National Forest and Flat Tops Wilderness. Rates vary by excursion. *Meeker 970/878–9869 www.welderoutfitters.com From $165.*

Craig

48 miles north of Meeker via Rte. 13; 42 miles west of Steamboat Springs via U.S. 40.

Craig is home to some of the best fishing in the area. Guided trips to the hottest fishing spots are available, as are horseback pack trips into the wilderness. Depending on the season, you might spot bighorn sheep, antelope, or nesting waterfowl, including the Great Basin Canada goose.

GETTING HERE AND AROUND

U.S. 40 west from Denver or east from Utah is the best way to reach Craig. All Around Taxi provides service in town.

TRANSPORTATION CONTACTS All Around Taxi. *970/824–1177.*

ESSENTIALS

VISITOR INFORMATION Craig Chamber of Commerce. *775 Yampa Ave. 970/824–5689 www.craig-chamber.com.*

Marcia Car

MUSEUM | One of Craig's most prized historical possessions, the Marcia Car in City Park was the private Pullman car of Colorado magnate David Moffat, who at one time was full or partial owner of more than 100 gold and silver mines. Moffat was also instrumental in bringing railroad transportation to northwest Colorado. He used his private car to inspect construction work on the Moffat

Railroad line. Named after his only child, the car has been restored and makes for an interesting tour. ✉ *360 E. Victory Way* ☎ *970/824–5689* 🌐 *www.craig-chamber.com* 🎫 *Free.*

Museum of Northwest Colorado

MUSEUM | This museum elegantly displays an eclectic collection of everything from arrowheads to a fire truck. The upstairs of this restored county courthouse holds the largest privately owned collection of working cowboy artifacts in the world. Bill Mackin, one of the leading traders in cowboy collectibles, has spent a lifetime gathering guns, bits, saddles, bootjacks, holsters, and spurs of all descriptions. ✉ *590 Yampa Ave.* ☎ *970/824–6360* 🌐 *www.museumnwco.org* 🎫 *Free, donations accepted* ⏱ *Closed Sun.*

Restaurants

Gino's Neighborhood Pizzeria & Grill

$ | **ITALIAN** | **FAMILY** | The staff is friendly and the pizzas are excellent, thin-crust, and "Philly-style," which means they also offer that town's famous stromboli with the same thin, crispy crust. If you'd rather have pasta, the homemade lasagna is a rare treat. **Known for:** large patio; Philly-style stromboli; exposition kitchen. $ *Average main: $11* ✉ *572 Breeze St.* ☎ *970/824–6323.*

Hotels

Quality Inn & Suites

$ | **HOTEL** | The amenities at Craig's largest hotel include a recreational center with a pool, whirlpool, and exercise and game rooms, all inside a lush atrium. **Pros:** on-site restaurant; hot breakfast included; comfortable beds. **Cons:** area can be noisy at night; rooms need updating; not all rooms have microwaves and fridges. $ *Rooms from: $76* ✉ *300 Rte. 13 S* ☎ *970/824–4000* 🌐 *www.choicehotels.com* *171 rooms* *Free Breakfast.*

Activities

FISHING

Sportsman's Center at the Craig Chamber of Commerce

FISHING | The Yampa and Green rivers, Trappers Lake, Lake Avery, and Elkhead Reservoir are known for pike and trout. Contact the Sportsman's Center at the Craig Chamber of Commerce for information. ✉ *775 Yampa Ave.* ☎ *970/824–5689* 🌐 *www.craig-chamber.com.*

Dinosaur National Monument

90 miles west of Craig via U.S. 40.

Overlapping the border between Colorado and Utah, Dinosaur National Monument offers river runners and dinosaur enthusiasts a remote and magnificent attraction that more than rewards the effort to get here. Colorful canyons and endless opportunities to examine fossils and bones make the monument a unique destination, and the Yampa and Green rivers provide cooling relief from what is much of the year a hot and dry desert landscape.

GETTING HERE AND AROUND

U.S. 40 west from Denver or east from Utah is the best way to reach Dinosaur National Monument. You also can take Highway 139 and Route 64 from Grand Junction. The town of Dinosaur, with a few somewhat dilapidated concrete dinosaur statues watching over their namesake town, merits only a brief stop on the way to the real thing: the bones at Dinosaur National Monument.

Sights

★ Dinosaur National Monument

NATURE SITE | **FAMILY** | Straddling the Colorado–Utah border, Dinosaur National Monument is a must for any dinosaur enthusiast. A two-story hill teeming with

At Dinosaur National Monument, you can see a wide variety of different dinosaur fossils.

fossils—many still in the complete skeletal shapes of the dinosaurs—greets visitors at one of the few places in the world where you can touch a dinosaur bone still embedded in the earth. The Colorado side of the park offers some of the best hiking in the West, along the Harpers Corner and Echo Park Drive routes and the ominous-sounding Canyon of Lodore (where the Green River rapids buffet rafts). The drive is accessible only in summer—even then, four-wheel drive is preferable—and some of the most breathtaking overlooks are well off the beaten path. *4545 E. Hwy. 40, Dinosaur 435/781–7700 www.nps.gov/dino $25 per vehicle; $15 per individual.*

Dinosaur Quarry

NATURE SITE | The Dinosaur Quarry Exhibit Hall showcases an estimated 1,500 dinosaur bones that date to the late Jurassic Period still embedded in the clay. Open daily, the Exhibit Hall is ranger-guided only in the winter; check the website or call ahead for shuttle hours and access availability. Fossils are visible only from the Utah side of the monument, not the Colorado side. A half mile away is a massive 7,595-square-foot visitor center. *Visitor center: 7 miles north of Jensen, Utah, on Rte. 139, Dinosaur 970/374–3000 Canyon Visitor Center in Colorado, 435/781–7700 Quarry Visitor Center in Utah nps.gov/dino $25 per vehicle; $15 per individual.*

Restaurants

BedRock Depot

$ | **AMERICAN** | **FAMILY** | New batches of homemade ice cream show up almost every day at this roadside shop, where the walls are a gallery for the owners' photography and artwork. The shop sells fresh sandwiches—including a terrific roast beef on house-baked rolls—and specialty coffees, bottled root beer, cream soda, and ginger ale. **Known for:** "Mochasaurus" coffee; convivial atmosphere; kitschy souvenir gift shop. *Average main: $8 214 W. Brontosaurus Blvd., Dinosaur 970/374–2336 www.bedrockdepot.com Closed Thurs. No dinner Sun.*

Massadona Tavern & Steak House

$$ | AMERICAN | A restaurant and bar, Massadona is small, homey, and rustic, with a smattering of Western decor items and a mixture of tables and booths. It's also a casual, inviting, and relaxing place to stop after a day of digging around in dinosaur dirt, even if it's kind of in the middle of nowhere (20 minutes east of Dinosaur and a half-hour drive from the monument). **Known for:** bacon cheeseburger; weekly fish taco special; friendly owners. *Average main: $16* *22927 Hwy. 40, Dinosaur* *970/374–2324* *Closed Mon. year-round and Sun.–Thurs. in Nov.–Mar. No lunch weekdays Apr.–Oct.*

Activities

HIKING

Desert Voices Nature Trail

HIKING/WALKING | FAMILY | This nature trail is near the Dinosaur Quarry. The 1½-mile loop is moderate in difficulty and has a series of trail signs produced for kids by kids. *Split Mountain area, across from boat ramp, Dinosaur* *nps.gov/dino.*

RAFTING

Adventure Bound River Expeditions

WHITE-WATER RAFTING | One of the best ways to experience the rugged beauty of the park is on a white-water raft trip. Adventure Bound River Expeditions runs two- to five-day excursions on the Colorado, Yampa, and Green rivers. *Grand Junction* *800/423–4668, 970/247–4789* *www.adventureboundusa.com.*

Rangely

20 miles southeast of Dinosaur National Monument; 96 miles northwest of Grand Junction via Rte. 139 and I–70.

The center of one of the last areas in the state to be explored by European settlers, Rangely was dubbed an "isolated empire" by early pioneers. You can search out the petroglyphs left by Native American civilizations or just stroll the farmers' market in Town Square. If you enjoy back-road mountain biking, the Raven Rims have an abundance of trails. You may even spot elk, mules, deer, coyotes, and other wildlife as you spin your wheels through the multihued sandstone rims and mesas north of town. Kenney Reservoir 5 miles north of town offers fishing and swimming, and a trip on the Cathedral Bluffs trail gives new definition to "isolated empire."

GETTING HERE AND AROUND

U.S. 40 west from Denver or east from Utah and then Route 64 south is the best way to get to Rangely. You can also take Highway 139 from Grand Junction. There are no transportation services in town.

ESSENTIALS

VISITOR INFORMATION Rangely Chamber of Commerce. *255 E. Main St.* *970/675–5290* *www.rangelychamber.com.*

Sights

Canyon Pintado National Historic District

ARCHAEOLOGICAL SITE | One of Rangely's most compelling sights is the superb Fremont petroglyphs—carved between AD 600 and 1300—in Douglas Creek canyon, south of town along Route 139. This stretch is known as the Canyon Pintado National Historic District, and the examples of rock art are among the best-preserved in the West; half the fun is clambering up the rocks to find them. A brochure listing the sights is available at the Rangely Chamber of Commerce. *Rangely* *970/878–3800* *www.blm.gov* *Free.*

Giovanni's Italian Grill

$ | ITALIAN | FAMILY | Between the thick, hearty pizzas, big-as-your-head stromboli, and overflowing plates of pasta, it's hard to walk out of this friendly, casual eatery without feeling stuffed. The sauces are homemade, and the red sauce in particular is flavorful and authentic. **Known for:** the "Tank" pizza; family-friendly atmosphere; extensive beer roster. *Average main: $12* ✉ *855 E. Main St.* ☎ *970/675–2670* 🌐 *giovannisitaliangrill.letseat.at* 🕑 *Closed Sun.*

Blue Mountain Inn & Suites

$ | HOTEL | Rooms are simple but spacious at this reliable hotel, which is next to a grocery store. **Pros:** heated indoor pool and hot tub; pleasant lobby with soft, cozy chairs; centrally located. **Cons:** has a chain feel; rooms are sparsely decorated; breakfast is pretty basic. *Rooms from: $89* ✉ *37 Park St.* ☎ *970/675–8888* 🌐 *www.bluemountaininnrangely.com* *50 rooms* *Free Breakfast.*

Sweetbriar

GIFTS/SOUVENIRS | A wood-burning stove graces the front of charming Sweetbriar, a little store that sells a variety of gifts and home decor. ✉ *713 E. Main St.* ☎ *970/675–5353* 🌐 *sweetbriaronline.com.*

FISHING

Kenney Reservoir

FISHING | Just below Taylor Draw Dam, Kenney Reservoir draws anglers in search of black crappie, channel catfish, and rainbow trout. The best fishing is right below the dam. If you hook one of Colorado's endangered pikeminnow, you'll have to throw it back. You can also go camping, boating, waterskiing, wildlife-watching, and picnicking. Locals come to the reservoir to watch the sun's last rays color the bluffs behind the lake. ✉ *Rangely* 🌐 *www.rangelychamber.com/kenney-reservoir.*

MOUNTAIN BIKING

Town of Rangely

BICYCLING | The best mountain-biking trails north of town are in the Raven Rims, named in honor of the abundant population of the large, noisy birds that live in the area. Contact the Town of Rangely for trail information. ✉ *209 E. Main St.* ☎ *970/675–8476* 🌐 *www.rangely.com.*

Chapter 11

TELLURIDE AND SOUTHWEST COLORADO

WITH THE SAN JUAN MOUNTAINS AND BLACK CANYON OF THE GUNNISON

Updated by
Aimee Heckel
and Kellee Katagi

Sights ★★★★☆ | Restaurants ★★★☆☆ | Hotels ★★☆☆☆ | Shopping ★★☆☆☆ | Nightlife ★★★☆☆

WELCOME TO TELLURIDE AND SOUTHWEST COLORADO

TOP REASONS TO GO

★ **Skiing and snowboarding in Telluride:** There's never much of a wait to take a lift up to the sweeping, groomed trails and challenging tree and mogul runs at this world-famous ski area.

★ **Driving the Million Dollar Highway:** The scenery is unparalleled on this narrow, hairpin-turning road that winds over Red Mountain Pass between Ouray and Silverton.

★ **Exploring Black Canyon of the Gunnison:** Play it safe, but edge as close to the canyon rim as you dare and peer over into an abyss that's more than 2,700 feet deep in some places.

★ **Hiking the Colorado Trail:** Bike, hike, or photograph along the nearly 500 miles of volunteer-maintained trails traversing eight major mountain ranges, seven national forests, and six wilderness areas.

★ **Mountain biking in Crested Butte:** The town is one of the birthplaces of fat-tire biking, and it's completely surrounded by up-close mountain scenery.

1 **Crested Butte.** A former mining town.

2 **Gunnison.** A hub for outdoor lovers.

3 **Black Canyon of the Gunnison National Park.** An awe-inspiring canyon.

4 **Montrose.** The gateway to Black Canyon of the Gunnison.

5 **Paonia.** One of the area's best wine and harvest towns.

6 **Lake City.** A town with historic Victorian buildings.

7 **Creede.** Once Colorado's rowdiest mining camp.

8 **Telluride.** A mining town turned celebrity ski resort.

9 **Ridgway.** The setting for many Hollywood Westerns.

10 **Ouray.** A former mining town within a gorgeous landscape.

11 **Silverton.** An old historic mining town.

12 **Durango.** Once a cultural crossroads in the Old West.

13 **Pagosa Springs.** A major center for outdoor sports.

14 **Cortez.** A base for visiting Mesa Verde National Park.

15 **Dolores.** A small town with big landscapes.

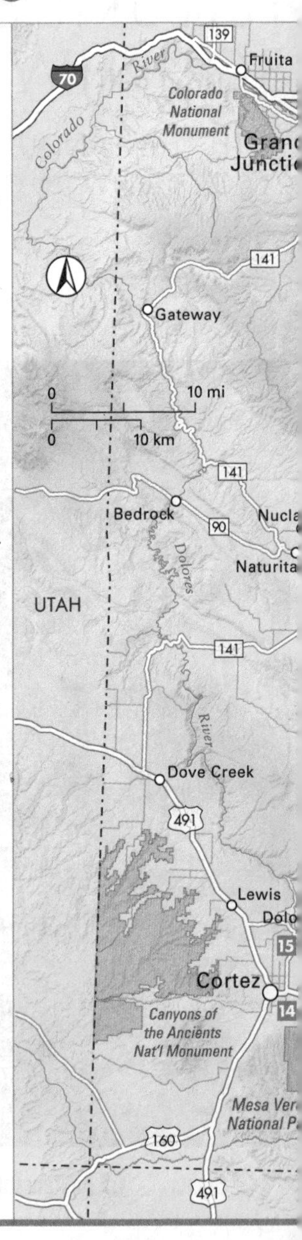

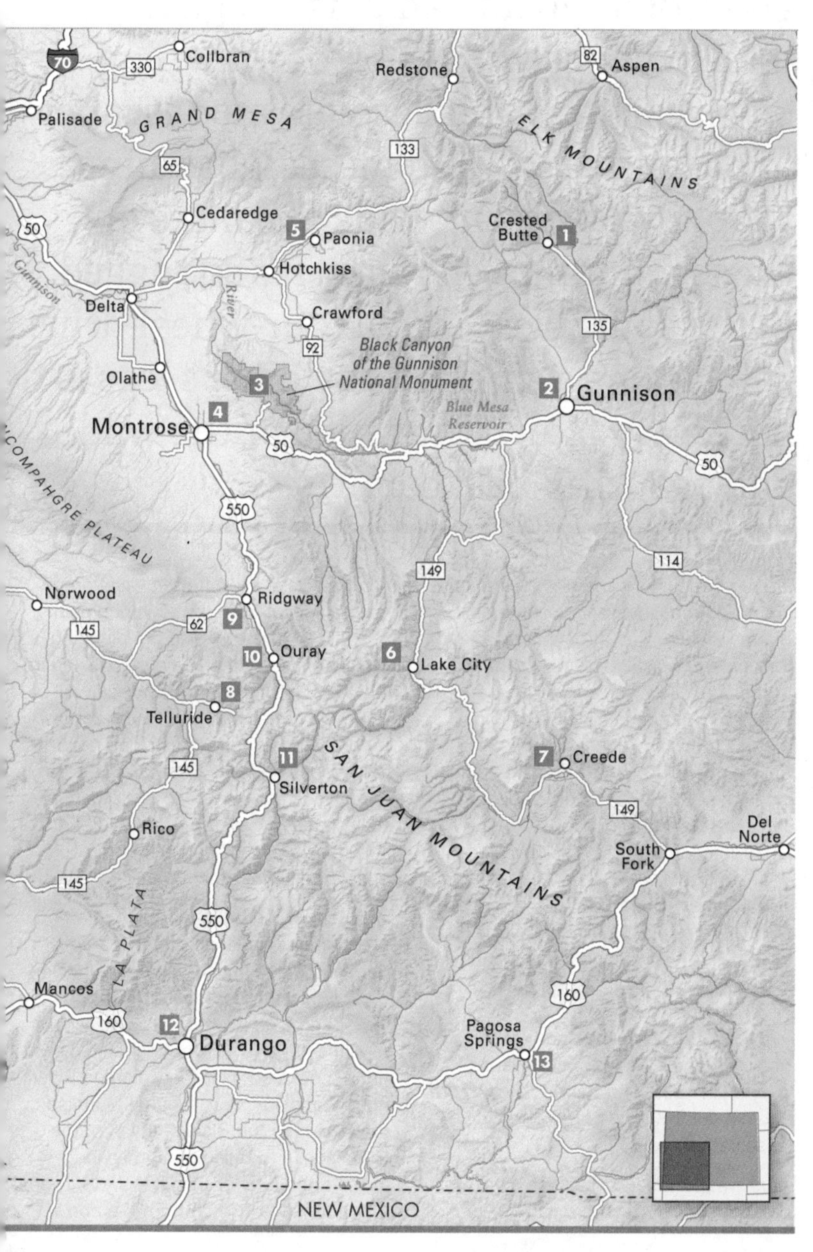

70
330
Collbran
Palisade
GRAND MESA
65
Cedaredge
50
Gunnison
Delta
River
Olathe
Montrose
UNCOMPAHGRE PLATEAU
Redstone
133
5
Paonia
Hotchkiss
Crawford
92
Black Canyon of the Gunnison National Monument
3
4
50
82
Aspen
ELK MOUNTAINS
Crested Butte
1
135
2
Gunnison
Blue Mesa Reservoir
50
550
149
114
Norwood
145
62
9
Ridgway
10
Ouray
6
Lake City
8
Telluride
145
11
Silverton
SAN JUAN MOUNTAINS
7
Creede
149
Del Norte
South Fork
Rico
145
LA PLATA
550
160
Mancos
160
12
Durango
Pagosa Springs
13
550
NEW MEXICO

The reddish rocks found in much of the state, particularly in the southwest, give Colorado its name. The region's terrain varies widely—from yawning black canyons and desolate moonscapes to pastel deserts and mesas, glistening sapphire lakes, and wide expanses of those stunning red rocks. It's so rugged in the southwest that a four-wheel-drive vehicle or a pair of sturdy hiker's legs is necessary to explore much of the wild and beautiful backcountry.

The region's history and people are as colorful as the landscape. Southwestern Colorado, as well as the "Four Corners" neighbors of northwestern New Mexico, northeastern Arizona, and southeastern Utah, was home to the Ancestral Pueblos formerly known as Anasazi, meaning "ancient ones." These people, ancestors of today's Pueblo peoples (including the Zuni and Hopi tribes) constructed impressive cliff dwellings in what are now Mesa Verde National Park, Ute Mountain Ute Tribal Park, and other nearby sites. This wild and woolly region, dotted with rowdy mining camps and boomtowns, also witnessed the antics of such notorious outlaws as Butch Cassidy, who embarked on his storied career by robbing the San Miguel Valley Bank in Telluride in 1889, and Robert "Bob" Ford, who hid out in Creede after shooting Jesse James in 1882.

Southwest Colorado has such diversity that, depending on where you go, you can have radically different vacations. You can spiral from the towering peaks of the San Juan range to the plunging Black Canyon of the Gunnison, taking in alpine scenery along the way, as well as the eerie remains of old mining camps, before winding through striking desert landscapes and Old West railroad towns. Even if you're not here to ski or golf in the resorts of Crested Butte, Durango, or Telluride, you'll still find plenty to experience in this part of the state.

MAJOR REGIONS

Crested Butte and Gunnison. This area is dominated and shaped by the Gunnison River, which gathers water from the Taylor and East rivers at Almont, meets the Uncompahgre River near Delta, and finally hooks up with the Colorado River near Grand Junction. West of Gunnison, the river cuts the Black Canyon of the Gunnison, a forbidding, 48-mile-long abyss often deeper than it is wide. The Elk Mountains stretch from the northern edge of the Black Canyon through Crested Butte. Almont, off Highway 135 between Crested Butte and Gunnison, is a still-rustic fly-fishing hideaway. Explore this mountain paradise on single-track in summer and Nordic track in winter. The Taylor and Gunnison rivers round out the adventure possibilities, with white-water rafting, kayaking, and great fly-fishing.

Black Canyon of the Gunnison National Park. The town of Montrose makes a great base for exploring the majestic canyon, which plunges 2,000 feet down sheer vertical cliffs to the roaring Gunnison River.

Lake City and Creede. Route 149 meanders south from the Black Canyon of the Gunnison through a scattering of cozy, laid-back communities with deep mining roots. Both Lake City and Creede have colorful histories and excellent access to the many hiking and mountain-biking trails in the Gunnison National Forest and the Rio Grande National Forest. If you're driving through here, especially on the Silver Thread Scenic Byway or the Alpine Loop Scenic Byway, allow plenty of time, because you'll want to keep stopping to take pictures of the surrounding mountains.

Telluride and the San Juan Mountains. The San Juan Mountains cover more than 12,000 square miles of southwestern Colorado. This striking mountain range ranks as one of the most rugged in the country, and is defined by the hundreds of peaks rising to an elevation of 13,000 feet or more. Former mining camps, including Silverton, Ouray, and Telluride, now welcome adventurers seeking other riches—wilderness trekking, rugged four-wheeling, mountain biking, skiing, ice climbing, and horseback riding.

Durango and Mesa County. Durango is an ideal springboard for exploring nearby Mesa County and its star attraction, Mesa Verde National Park. It's also a college town known for eclectic eateries and historic hotels, as well as its many hiking and mountain-biking options. You can ride the rails on the Durango & Silverton Narrow Gauge Railroad, raft the Animas River, explore 2,000 miles of hiking and biking trails, and ski at Purgatory Resort.

Planning

When to Go

Like the rest of the state, southwestern Colorado is intensely seasonal. Snow typically begins falling in the high country in late September or early October, and by Halloween seasonal closures turn some unpaved alpine roads into routes for snowmobiles. The San Juan Mountains see average annual snowfalls approaching 400 inches in the highest spots. Winter lingers well into the season that the calendar calls spring—the greatest snowfalls generally occur in March and April.

Skiing winds down in early April, as the snow in the higher elevations begins to melt. Some resort towns shut down almost completely from mid-April until late May, when cresting streams fill up for thrilling, if chilling, summer white-water rafting and kayaking. Hiking and biking trails become accessible, and wildflowers begin their short, intense season of show. Summer is glorious in the mountains, with brilliant sunshine and cobalt-blue skies. But it also brings brief and often intense showers on many an afternoon, sometimes accompanied by dramatic thunder and lightning. Summer tourism winds down after Labor Day, although fluttering, golden aspens increasingly draw leaf-peepers to the region in September and early October. After that, some resort towns take another hiatus for a few weeks. The mountains are popular year-round, but spring and fall are the best times to visit the hot, dry climate of the Mesa Country around the Four Corners.

Getting Oriented

Southwest Colorado is the land beyond the interstates. Old mining roads, legacies of the late 19th and early 20th centuries, when gold and silver mining was ascendant, lead through drop-dead-gorgeous mountain valleys and rugged high country. Much of this part of the state is designated as a wilderness area, which means that no roads may be built and no wheeled or motorized vehicles are permitted. A federal road known as U.S. 550 or the Million Dollar Highway corkscrews over Red Mountain Pass, around cliff-hugging turns and without the benefit of guardrails. While backcountry roads demand four-wheel-drive vehicles in summer and snowmobiles in winter, regular roads are no problem for passenger cars.

Planning Your Time

For the full southwestern Colorado experience, you'll need at least a week or 10 days. After all, there are no speedy interstates here—just winding two-lane highways over steep mountain passes.

If you're coming from Denver, start your visit with a couple of days in the mountain-biking, fishing, and skiing havens of Crested Butte and Gunnison. If time allows, take a day trip to the towns of Lake City and Creede for a taste of history and off-the-beaten-path beauty. Either way, for the next leg of your trip, travel west from Gunnison on U.S. 50 past the sprawling Curecanti National Recreation Area to the Black Canyon of the Gunnison. Be sure to carve out at least a few hours here (more if you love hiking) to take in the panoramic views.

From there, you'll head southwest to Telluride for a couple of relaxing days, enjoying the region's best cuisine, toniest hotels, and most rewarding scenery. Next, continue southwest (via Highways 145, 184, and 160) for a few days in Mesa Country. Plan to base yourself in Durango, with daytime excursions to Mesa Verde National Park (a must-see), Purgatory Resort, and the vast wilderness areas surrounding the town. Finally, head back north on U.S. 550, stopping for lunch in Silverton before the slow but ultrascenic trek over Red Mountain Pass, also known as the Million Dollar Highway (depending on whom you ask, the highway got its name from the views or from the precious metals under the mountain). Spend the night in Ouray—dubbed "The Switzerland of America" for its dramatic, jagged peaks—and take a soak in one of the town's hot springs before making your way back to Denver.

If you can't swing the full tour, consider basing yourself in either the Crested Butte/Gunnison area, Telluride, or Durango and taking day trips from there. Montrose is arguably the most central location, but accommodations and restaurants are more basic and limited than you'll find in resort towns.

Getting Here and Around

AIR

The Gunnison–Crested Butte Regional Airport (GUC) serves the nearby resort area. The closest regional airport to the Black Canyon of the Gunnison National Park is Montrose Regional Airport (MTJ).

The Durango–La Plata County Airport (DRO) is your closest option for Silverton, Durango, Pagosa Springs, Mesa Verde National Park, and the Four Corners region. ■ **TIP→ Depending on your final destination in the Four Corners region and airline schedules, you might want to consider flying to Albuquerque instead of Denver. The Albuquerque International Sunport (ABQ) is host to many of the major airlines and is closer than Denver.**

Several companies run transportation options between the airports and the resort towns of Telluride and Crested Butte. Shuttle fares vary; it's about $136 per person round-trip between Montrose Regional Airport and Telluride, and around $90 per person round-trip between Gunnison–Crested Butte Regional Airport and Crested Butte. To get to Crested Butte from Gunnison or Montrose, try Alpine Express. Telluride Express offers service to Telluride from Durango, Montrose, Cortez, Gunnison, and Grand Junction.

In addition, free shuttles operate between the towns of Crested Butte and Durango and their respective ski areas, although the Durango shuttle runs only once a day. The Crested Butte shuttle runs every 15 minutes in high season.

AIRPORT CONTACTS Albuquerque International Sunport (ABQ). ✉ *2200 Sunport Blvd. SE, Albuquerque* ☎ *505/244–7700* 🌐 *www.abqsunport.com.* **Durango–La Plata County Airport (DRO).** ✉ *1000 Airport Rd., Durango* ☎ *970/382–6050* 🌐 *www.flydurango.com.* **Gunnison–Crested Butte Regional Airport (GUC).** ✉ *711 Rio Grande Ave., Gunnison* ☎ *970/641–2304* 🌐 *www.flygunnisonairport.com.* **Montrose Regional Airport (MTJ).** ✉ *2100 Airport Rd., Montrose* ☎ *970/249–3203* 🌐 *www.flymontrose.com.*

AIRPORT TRANSFERS Alpine Express. ✉ *Gunnison Airport Terminal, 711 Rio Grande Ave., Gunnison* ☎ *970/641–5074, 800/822–4844* 🌐 *www.letsride.co.* **Buck Horn Limousine.** ☎ *970/769–0933* 🌐 *www.buckhornlimousine.com.* **Telluride Express.** ☎ *970/728–6000* 🌐 *www.letsride.co.*

CAR

Avis, Budget, Dollar, Enterprise, Hertz, National Alamo, Payless, and Thrifty have car-rental counters at the Montrose Regional Airport. Alamo, Avis, Enterprise, and Hertz/Dollar all have counters at Durango–La Plata County Airport. Gunnison–Crested Butte Regional Airport has Avis, Budget, and Hertz.

The main roads in the region are Highway 135 between Crested Butte and Gunnison; U.S. 50 linking Gunnison, Montrose, and Delta; Route 149 between Gunnison, Lake City, and Creede; U.S. 550 from Montrose to Ridgway, Ouray, Silverton, and Durango; Highway 62 and Route 145 linking Ridgway with Telluride, Dolores, and Cortez; and U.S. 160, which passes from Cortez to Durango to Pagosa Springs via Mesa Verde National Park. None of these roads officially close for winter, but be prepared at any time during snowy months for portions of the roads to be closed or down to one lane for avalanche control or to clear ice or snowdrifts.

TAXI

In the resort towns, you'll probably never need to call for a cab. You're most likely to use one to get to or from the airport.

Parks and Recreation Areas

Southwest Colorado includes a wealth of national and state parks and recreation areas. Three of the 11 rivers designated as "gold medal" waters by the Colorado Wildlife Commission—the Animas, Gunnison, and Rio Grande—are here. Blue Mesa and McPhee reservoirs, the state's largest bodies of water, are destinations for boaters, water-skiers, windsurfers, and anglers (including the ice-fishing kind). Up in rustic Almont, a small community near the Gunnison headwaters, they love—and live—fly-fishing. Anglers also love Ridgway State Park, with access to rainbow trout and other prize fish. **■ TIP→ Anyone 16 or older needs a Colorado fishing license, which you can obtain at local sporting-goods stores.**

The precipitous Black Canyon of the Gunnison National Park is a mysterious and powerful attraction. Also, some of the most intact remains of the ancient, little-known Ancestral Pueblo culture are inside Mesa Verde National Park and Canyons of the Ancients National Monument.

The San Juan Mountains stretch through 12,000 square miles of southwest Colorado, encompassing three national forests and seven wilderness areas. The enormous San Juan National Forest is a virtual paradise for all kinds of adventuring. Directly north, the Uncompahgre National Forest encompasses nearly a million acres of alpine wilderness and the picturesque peaks of Mount Sneffels and Lizard Head. To the east, the Rio Grande National Forest stretches from the magisterial Sangre de Cristo Mountains across the San Luis Valley.

Restaurants

With dining options ranging from creative international cuisine in the resort towns of Telluride, Crested Butte, and Durango to no-frills American fare in down-home communities like Montrose and Creede, no one has any excuse to visit a chain restaurant here. The leading chefs are tapping into the region's local bounty, so you can find innovative recipes for ranch-raised game, lamb, and trout. Many serve only locally raised, grass-fed meats. Olathe sweet corn is a delicacy enjoyed across the state (and found in grocery stores and roadside stands as well as restaurants). Seasonal produce is highlighted on the best menus.

Hotels

No matter what you're looking for in vacation lodging—luxurious slope-side condominium, landmark inn in a historic town, riverside cabin, guest ranch, country inn, budget motel, or chock-full-of-RVs campground—southwest Colorado has it in abundance. Rates vary season to season, particularly in the resort towns. Some properties close in fall once the aspens have shed their golden leaves, open in winter when the lifts begin running, close in spring after the snow melts, and open again in mid-May or early June.

Restaurant and hotel reviews have been shortened. For full information, visit Fodors.com. Restaurant prices are the average cost of a main course at dinner or, if dinner is not served, at lunch, excluding 5.9%–8.1% tax. Hotel prices are the lowest cost of a standard double room in high season, excluding service charges and 7.6%–9.9% tax.

What It Costs

	$	$$	$$$	$$$$
RESTAURANTS	under $15	$15–$22	$23–$30	over $30
HOTELS	under $125	$125–$200	$201–$300	over $300

Crested Butte

28 miles north of Gunnison via Hwy. 135; 92 miles northeast of Montrose via U.S. 50 and Hwy. 135.

Like Aspen, the town of Crested Butte was once a small mining village (albeit for coal, not silver). The Victorian gingerbread-trim houses remain, many of them now painted in whimsical shades of hot pink, magenta, and chartreuse. Unlike Aspen, however, Crested Butte has retained much of its small-town charm despite its development as a ski area.

The setting is serenely beautiful. The town sits at the top of a long, broad valley that stretches 17 miles south toward Gunnison. Mount Crested Butte, which looms over the town, is the most visible landmark. It's surrounded by the Gunnison National Forest and the Elk Mountain Range.

It's as an extreme-skiing playground that Crested Butte earned its reputation with some of the best skiers in the land. Over the years, Crested Butte has steadily increased its adventure-skiing terrain to

Crested Butte is considered the center of mountain biking in Colorado.

nearly 550 ungroomed acres. Although this area, known as the Extreme Limits, should only be attempted by experts, there are plenty of cruise-worthy trails for skiers of all levels. The groomed trails are rarely crowded, which allows for plenty of long, fast, sweeping turns.

Crested Butte is also popular in summer. Blanketed with columbine and Indian paintbrush, the landscape is mesmerizing. And the terrain makes it one of the country's major mountain-biking centers. Once the snow melts, mountain bikers challenge the hundreds of miles of trails surrounding the town.

GETTING HERE AND AROUND

Crested Butte is just over the mountain from Aspen, but there are no paved roads—just unpaved routes over the challenging Pearl, Taylor, and Schofield passes and hiking trails through White River National Forest. If you're coming from the north or west, the most direct route is over Kebler Pass. The drive is one of Colorado's prettiest, passing through one of the state's largest stands of aspens. If you're coming from the east, the beautiful Cottonwood Pass will deposit you on Highway 135, just south of town. Both graded gravel roads are closed in winter, making it necessary to take a circuitous route on U.S. 24 and U.S. 50 through Poncha Springs and Gunnison, and then up Highway 135 to Crested Butte.

Alpine Express will transport you between the Gunnison–Crested Butte Regional Airport and the resort for around $80 round-trip. Mountain Express is a reliable free shuttle bus that travels the 3 miles between the town and the resort throughout the year.

TRANSPORTATION CONTACTS Alpine Express. ☎ *970/641–5074, 800/822–4844* 🌐 *www.alpineexpressshuttle.com.* **Mountain Express.** ✉ *2 N. 8th St., Bldg. D* ☎ *970/349–5616* 🌐 *www.mtnexp.org.*

WHEN TO GO

Ski season—mid-December to mid-April—is definitely the busiest time in Crested Butte. The weeks between Memorial Day and Labor Day are hopping, as well. Things slow down dramatically in the in-between times, with some businesses closing completely.

FESTIVALS

Crested Butte Wildflower Festival

FESTIVALS | Such abundant foliage carpets the surrounding mountains that Crested Butte has been nicknamed the "Wildflower Capital of Colorado." For 10 glorious days in mid-July, the town celebrates this bounty with a varied event lineup: guided hikes, wildflower identification and photography workshops, classes on medicinal plants, and four-wheel-drive tours. ■ **TIP→ Check the website, because even if you can't make it on festival week, events run from June through the end of August.** ✉ *716 Elk Ave.* ☎ *970/349–2571* 🌐 *www.crestedbuttewildflowerfestival.com* 🎫 *Events start at $15.*

ESSENTIALS

VISITOR INFORMATION Crested Butte Snow Report. 🌐 *www.skicb.com/snow.* **Crested Butte Vacations.** ✉ *12 Snowmass Rd.* ☎ *855/969–3022* 🌐 *www.skicb.com.* **Crested Butte Visitor Center.** ✉ *601 Elk Ave.* ☎ *970/349–6438, 855/681–0941* 🌐 *www.cbchamber.com.*

Sights

Crested Butte Mountain Heritage Museum

MUSEUM | Housed in an 1893 hardware store, this museum showcases the essentials for life in an 1880s mining town, such as clothing, furniture, and household items. There's an intricate diorama of the town in the 1920s, complete with a moving train, plus exhibits on skiing, sledding, biking, and Flauschink, a quirky local ceremony that welcomes the return of spring. ✉ *331 Elk Ave.* ☎ *970/349–1880* 🌐 *www.crestedbuttemuseum.com* 🎫 *$5* ⏲ *Closed mid-Nov.*

Crested Butte Mountain Resort Adventure Park

AMUSEMENT PARK/WATER PARK | FAMILY | Make a day of it at Crested Butte Mountain Resort Adventure Park, where, for one ticket price, you can access unlimited lift-served hiking and biking, minigolf, bungee trampolines, a climbing wall, an inflated-bag jump, and a hands-on kids' mining exhibit. À la carte pricing and guided hiking are also available. The lift-served hiking and biking are summer-only, but the rest of the Adventure Park is open both winter and summer. ✉ *12 Snowmass Rd., Mt. Crested Butte* ☎ *855/969–3022* 🌐 *www.skicb.com* 🎫 *From $47, kids from $40* ⏲ *Closed early Apr.–late May and late Oct.–late Nov.*

Restaurants

Django's Kitchen

$$$ | MODERN AMERICAN | Delectable small plates and a wide-ranging wine list star at this sophisticated, modern eatery on the town's main street. The offerings change with the seasons but always include meat and seafood, as well as creative salads and veggie dishes. **Known for:** classy atmosphere; creek-side patio; tip included in prices. [$] *Average main: $30* ✉ *209 Elk Ave.* ☎ *970/765–8864* 🌐 *www.djangos.us* ⏲ *Closed Mon., Tues., mid-Apr.–early June, and Nov. No lunch.*

Montanya Distillers Tasting Room

$ | TAPAS | Stop here for artisanal cocktails and tasty tapas before dinner and it just might end up being your dinner spot. The rum is divine (ask for a free tasting)—there's a light and a dark, both skillfully distilled on-site in copper stills from Portugal using fresh local-spring water (come by between noon and 5 Wednesday through Saturday for a distillery tour). **Known for:** Maharaja cocktail; Asian-style rice and noodle bowls; live music. [$] *Average main: $12* ✉ *212 Elk Ave.* ☎ *970/799–3206* 🌐 *www.montanyarum.com.*

Secret Stash

$ | **PIZZA** | Sit inside beneath sweeping tapestries in a Japanese-style booth (seating on the floor) or opt for a table on the deck to enjoy amazing pizza in a mind-bending array of formulations—from the "Notorious F.I.G." (prosciutto, dried figs, and truffle oil) to the "Mac Daddy" (with Thousand Island, shaved rib eye, pickles, and a sesame seed crust). **Known for:** gluten-free crusts available; extensive bar menu; breakfast and brunch available. *Average main: $12* *303 Elk Ave.* *970/349–6245* *www.secretstash.com.*

The Slogar

$$$ | **AMERICAN** | In a lovingly renovated Victorian tavern awash in handmade lace and stained glass, this restaurant is just plain cozy. A menu with a comfort-food bent spotlights family-style options, such as skillet-fried chicken, rib-eye steak, and ribs, paired with sides like fresh biscuits, creamy mashed potatoes, gumbo, and mac 'n' cheese. **Known for:** family-style comfort food; Creole Sunday brunch; historic building. *Average main: $26* *517 2nd St., at Whiterock Ave.* *970/349–5765* *www.slogarcb.com* *Closed mid-Oct.–Nov. and mid-Apr.–mid-May. No lunch.*

★ **Soupçon**

$$$$ | **FRENCH** | "Soup's on" (get it?) occupies two intimate rooms in a historic cabin tucked away in an alley and dishes up five courses of nouveau American cuisine with a strong French accent. Organic herbs grown on the premises accent local produce, and everything, including soups, stocks, and sauces, is made from scratch. **Known for:** award-winning wine cellar; Colorado lamb; artistic presentation. *Average main: $50* *127A Elk Ave.* *970/349–5448* *www.soupcon-cb.com* *Closed Mon., Tues., Nov., and mid-Apr.–mid-May.*

Sunflower

$$$$ | **MODERN AMERICAN** | This small, simple-looking restaurant on Crested Butte's main street serves up perhaps the valley's best gourmet farm-to-table fare. New menus are printed regularly—creatively crafted to accommodate the fresh, organic meats and produce available that day from local farm suppliers—but they always feature a few delicious entrées, along with a generous selection of smaller plates. **Known for:** extremely fresh ingredients; a well-curated wine list; delicious homemade desserts. *Average main: $34* *214 Elk Ave.* *970/417–7767* *www.sunflowercb.com* *Closed Mon. No lunch.*

Teocalli Tamale

$ | **MEXICAN** | Known as "Teo's," this Mexican restaurant is housed in a small, historic building and is a local favorite for tasty takeout (or a claustrophobic eat-in experience). You can get a generous portion of tamales, burritos, or tacos for about $10. **Known for:** flavorful homemade salsas; mahimahi tacos; margaritas. *Average main: $11* *311 Elk Ave.* *970/349–2005* *www.teocallitamale.com.*

Hotels

Cristiana Guesthaus

$$ | **B&B/INN** | With a huge stone fireplace in a wood-beamed lobby, this alpine-style ski lodge provides a cozy, unpretentious haven. **Pros:** close to downtown and hiking, biking, and ski trails; knowledgeable hosts; hot tub on deck has mountain views. **Cons:** TV only in common area; no air-conditioning; no hot items at breakfast. *Rooms from: $145* *621 Maroon Ave.* *970/349–5326* *www.cristiana-guesthaus.com* *Closed early Apr.* *21 rooms* *Free Breakfast.*

Elevation Hotel & Spa

$$ | **HOTEL** | Top-notch service, mountain-modern luxury, and ample amenities make this upscale ski-in ski-out hotel worth the splurge. **Pros:** indoor and outdoor hot tubs; complimentary ski valet and storage; restaurant and beauty salon on-site. **Cons:** parking is $20 per day; pool is small; no meals included. *Rooms from: $186* *500 Gothic Rd., Mt. Crested Butte* *970/251–3000* *www.elevationresort.com* *311 rooms* *No meals.*

Elk Mountain Lodge

$$ | **B&B/INN** | Built in 1919 as a boardinghouse for miners, this historic hotel has been painstakingly renovated; step into the lobby and you will encounter a slower pace of life and extraordinary attention to detail. **Pros:** good, full breakfast; intimate feel; provides locked ski storage on-site and on-mountain. **Cons:** 3 miles from ski area; no elevator; stairs are a bit steep. *Rooms from: $200* *129 Gothic Ave.* *970/349–7533, 800/374–6521* *www.elkmountainlodge.com* *19 rooms* *Free Breakfast.*

Grand Lodge Crested Butte

$$ | **HOTEL** | A warm stone-and-log lobby with a huge fireplace welcomes guests to this comfortable lodge in the mountain's base village. **Pros:** close to ski lift; rooms have many amenities; terrific restaurant. **Cons:** some of the basic rooms are small; can feel impersonal; fitness center is small. *Rooms from: $199* *6 Emmons Loop, Mt. Crested Butte* *866/823–4446, 970/349–8000* *www.skicb.com* *228 rooms* *No meals.*

Old Town Inn

$ | **B&B/INN** | An excellent in-town location makes this a great base for adventures in town or the mountains, but the real draws are unique touches like the free-for-loan "townie" bikes, sleds, and snowshoes for guests' use; concierge services; and delicious homemade cookies each afternoon. **Pros:** good deluxe continental breakfast; outdoor hot tub; convenient location. **Cons:** no pool; no elevator to second story; ski storage on-mountain only. *Rooms from: $119* *708 6th St.* *970/349–6184, 888/349–6184* *www.oldtowninn.net* *33 rooms* *Free Breakfast.*

★ Pioneer Guest Cabins

$$$ | **B&B/INN** | On a creek-side meadow about 8 miles from Crested Butte, this pleasant getaway for outdoors lovers has rustic but comfortable two- and three-bed log cabins, and you can hike, bike, snowshoe, or cross-country ski from trails that start right at your door. **Pros:** secluded setting; close to trails and fishing; each cabin has a fully equipped kitchen and outdoor firepit. **Cons:** bedrooms are small; no restaurant, TVs, or phones; minimum stay required. *Rooms from: $229* *2094 Cement Creek Rd.* *970/349–5517* *www.pioneerguestcabins.com* *8 cabins* *No meals.*

Nightlife

Kochevar's Saloon and Gaming Hall

BARS/PUBS | An 1899 cabin built from hand-hewn logs, Kochevar's is a classic saloon where locals play pool. *127 Elk Ave.* *970/349–7117.*

Public House

BARS/PUBS | A classy, modern spin on a Western saloon, this pub has live music and serves draft beers and higher-end bar food, such as elk chili and cornbread. *202 Elk Ave.* *970/349–0173* *www.publichousecb.com.*

Wooden Nickel

BARS/PUBS | This popular place is packed for happy hour each day from 4 to 6. Stay for dinner, as the steaks are terrific. *222 Elk Ave.* *970/349–6350* *www.woodennickelcb.com* *Closed mid-Apr.–early May.*

Activities

BACKCOUNTRY SKIING

Crested Butte Nordic Center

SKIING/SNOWBOARDING | **FAMILY** | Crested Butte abounds with backcountry possibilities. You can rent cross-country skis or snowshoes, and then head out on one of the Forest Service roads that radiate from town—particularly Washington Gulch, Slate River Road, and Gothic Road. The Crested Butte Nordic Center offers half-day ski or snowshoe packages that include transportation, guides, and equipment. ✉ *620 2nd St.* ☎ *970/349–1707* 🌐 *www.cbnordic.org* 🎫 *Tours from $90.*

DOWNHILL SKIING AND SNOWBOARDING

Crested Butte Mountain Resort

SKIING/SNOWBOARDING | The skiing here has a split personality, which is plain to see when you check out the skiers who descend on the place year after year. Its mellow half is the network of trails on the front side of the mountain, characterized by long intermediate runs. Families flock to Crested Butte for these trails, as well as the children's ski-school facilities and the laid-back and friendly vibe.

The wilder side of Crested Butte's personality is the **Extreme Limits,** nearly 550 acres of backcountry-like terrain (all double black diamond), with steep bowls, gnarly chutes, and tight tree skiing. It's some of the toughest in-bounds skiing in North America. Sign up for one of the guided programs for expert instruction (and insider info on the best powder stashes on the mountain).

The best expert skiing on the front side of the mountain is off the Silver Queen high-speed quad, which shoots you up 2,078 vertical feet in one quick ride. For beginners there's a wonderful expanse of easy terrain from the Red Lady Express lift. **Facilities:** 121 trails; 1,547 acres; 2,755-foot vertical drop; 15 lifts. ✉ *12 Snowmass Rd.* ☎ *855/969–3022* 🌐 *www.skicb.com* 🎫 *Lift ticket from $117.*

LESSONS AND PROGRAMS

Crested Butte Ski and Ride School

SKIING/SNOWBOARDING | **FAMILY** | A half-day adult group lesson starts at $140 (lift ticket not included). For kids ages 5 through 17, Camp CB offers single all-day lessons starting at $175, which includes lunch. One-hour private lessons for three- and four-year-olds start at $135. ✉ *12 Snowmass Rd.* ☎ *855/969–3022* 🌐 *www.skicb.com.*

RENTALS

Crested Butte Rental and Demo Center

SKIING/SNOWBOARDING | Full rental packages (including skis, boots, helmet, and poles), as well as snowshoes, snowboard equipment, and tuning, are available at this outfitter. Packages start at $37 per day. **■ TIP→ For best prices, reserve ahead at rentskis.com.** ✉ *10 Crested Butte Way* ☎ *970/349–2240* 🌐 *www.skicb.com.*

FISHING

Almont

FISHING | Located where the East and Taylor rivers join to form the Gunnison River, this tiny angler-oriented hamlet is one of Colorado's top fly-fishing centers. It's also one of the most crowded. Local fishing outfitters rent equipment, teach fly-fishing, and lead guided wading or float trips to both public and private waters. ✉ *Almont.*

TOURS AND OUTFITTERS

Almont Anglers

FISHING | This outfitter and guide has a solid fly and tackle shop with an enormous selection. There are clinics for beginners as well as guided wading and float-fishing excursions on the East, Taylor, and Gunnison rivers. ✉ *10209 Hwy. 135, Almont* ☎ *970/641–7404* 🌐 *www.almontanglers.com* 🎫 *Lessons from $80; trips from $270.*

Dragonfly Anglers

FISHING | Crested Butte's oldest year-round guide service and fly-fishing outfitter, Dragonfly Anglers offers guided walk-wade trips and float trips to choice fly-fishing spots, including the famed

Gunnison Gorge. The shop sells a wide variety of rods and has a solid selection of reels, flies, and outdoor gear, including Patagonia items. ✉ *307 Elk Ave.* ☎ *970/349–1228, 800/491–3079* 🌐 *www.dragonflyanglers.com* 🎟 *From $295; from $425 for Black Canyon excursions.*

Willowfly Anglers at Three Rivers Resort
FISHING | A branch of Three Rivers Resort and Outfitting, the Orvis-endorsed Willowfly Anglers offers half- and full-day guided trips for all skill levels and has a full-service fly shop. Trip prices include all necessary equipment. ✉ *130 County Rd. 742, Almont* ☎ *970/641–1303, 888/761–3474* 🌐 *www.willowflyanglers.com* 🎟 *Trips start at $300.*

FOUR-WHEELING

Colorado Adventure Rentals
FOUR-WHEELING | Choose from a variety of one- to four-person ATVs to explore the rugged terrain around Crested Butte and Gunnison. Insurance, helmets, gas, and basic instruction are included, and snowmobiles are available in the winter. ✉ *23044 County Rd. 742, Almont* ☎ *970/641–3525* 🌐 *www.coloradoadventurerentals.com* 🎟 *From $139 for a two-hour rental.*

GOLF

★ The Club at Crested Butte
GOLF | Golf legend Robert Trent Jones Jr. designed this ravishing 18-hole course surrounded by gorgeous mountain peaks. The first nine holes follow a traditional format, but the back nine offer a Highlands-style surprise with a Scottish-links design. Water hazards are present on 14 of the 18 holes, so be sure to bring extra balls. The semiprivate course belongs to the country club, but it's open to the public daily after 11:30. The dress code bars denim and mandates stand-up collars for all. ✉ *385 Country Club Dr.* ☎ *970/349–8601* 🌐 *www.theclubatcrestedbutte.com* 🎟 *$99 for 9 holes, $179 for 18 holes* 🏌 *18 holes, 7208 yards, par 72* ✍ *Reservations essential* ☞ *Rates include golf cart and practice balls.*

HIKING

Judd Falls
HIKING/WALKING | **FAMILY** | One of the area's easiest—and most kid-friendly—hiking trails is the 2 miles round-trip to Judd Falls, located within the Gunnison National Forest near the former mining town of Gothic. The path slices through groves of aspen and, in summer, a crop of more than 70 local wildflower varieties. At the end, look over Judd Falls from a bench named after Garwood Judd, "the man who stayed" in the old mining town. ✉ *Gunnison National Forest, off Gothic Rd.* ☎ *970/874–6600* 🌐 *www.fs.usda.gov/gmug.*

HORSEBACK RIDING

Fantasy Ranch
HORSEBACK RIDING | **FAMILY** | Riding a horse is one of the best ways to see the Crested Butte area. Fantasy Ranch gives guided horseback tours into the Elk Mountains, Maroon Bells, and Gunnison National Forest. Trips range from 90-minute trail rides to full-day wilderness adventures. Riders must be at least 10 years old, but younger children can do 20-minute pony rides. ✉ *935 Gothic Rd., Mt. Crested Butte* ☎ *970/349–5425* 🌐 *www.fantasyranchoutfitters.com* 🎟 *From $75 in winter; from $85 spring through fall.*

ICE-SKATING

Crested Butte Nordic Center
ICE SKATING | **FAMILY** | If you're eager to practice a figure eight, the Crested Butte Nordic Center operates a covered, outdoor skating rink. Skating is free and open to the public when the rink isn't reserved for hockey. The center rents skates for $10–$20. ✉ *620 2nd St.* ☎ *970/349–1707* 🌐 *www.cbnordic.org* 🎟 *Free* 🕒 *Closed Mar.–Nov.*

KAYAKING AND RAFTING

Three Rivers Resort & Outfitting
KAYAKING | The rivers around Crested Butte are at their best from May through early August. Three Rivers offers rafting trips, kayaking lessons, and stand-up paddleboard rentals on the Taylor and

Gunnison rivers. ✉ *130 County Rd. 742, Almont* ☎ *970/641–1303, 888/761–3474* 🌐 *www.3riversresort.com* 💵 *Raft trips start at $55.*

MOUNTAIN BIKING

Crested Butte is the mountain-biking center of Colorado. This is a place where there are more bikes than cars, and probably more bikes than residents. Many locals own two: a cruiser (or "townie") for hacking around and a mountain bike for *serious* hacking around. Nearby Pearl Pass is known as the route that got the fat-tire craze started.

After a group of motorcyclists rode the rough old road from Aspen to Crested Butte, a few of the town's cyclists decided to do the same ride in reverse. They hopped onto their clunky two-wheelers—a far cry from today's sophisticated machinery—and with that, the sport had arrived. The 40-mile round-trip trek over Pearl Pass can be done in a day, but it's tough, and you must be in excellent condition and acclimatized to the elevation.

Crested Butte Mountain Bike Park

BICYCLING | Crested Butte Mountain Resort maintains 30 miles of downhill and cross-country single-track, from green to black diamond. There are also two skills zones for riders to work on fundamentals. ✉ *12 Snowmass Rd., Mt. Crested Butte* ☎ *855/969–3022* 🌐 *www.skicb.com* ⏲ *Closed Nov.–May.*

Upper Loop

BICYCLING | Great for beginners, the Upper Loop is a popular 1½-mile ride that will help orient you to the area. The views up the Slate River valley to the peaks of Paradise Divide are wonderful. **Tony's Trail** consists of a short, moderate climb leading to an intersection with the Upper Upper Loop Trail. Here you can take in the view of the town below and the mountains above, and then enjoy a fun descent or venture farther in either direction on the Upper Upper Loop. ✉ *Crested Butte* 🌐 *www.travelcrestedbutte.com.*

TOURS AND OUTFITTERS

Irwin Guides

BICYCLING | Guided rides on the area's legendary single-track trails are available for riders of all skill levels. Irwin offers instruction, half- and full-day tours, and overnight tours with meals, lodging, and transportation included. ✉ *330 Belleview Ave.* ☎ *970/349–5430* 🌐 *www.irwin-guides.com* 💵 *From $175 per person for a half day.*

RENTALS

Big Al's Bicycle Heaven

BICYCLING | This full-service downtown bike shop, a favorite with locals, sells and rents all manner of two-wheelers, from knock-around "townies" to state-of-the-art mountain bikes, as well as bike trailers to haul kids. The shop also carries road and cross-country bikes and a full line of clothing, helmets, and other necessities. Best of all, the staff is willing to share the inside scoop on local trails. ✉ *207 Elk Ave.* ☎ *970/349–0515* 🌐 *www.bigalsbicycleheaven.com.*

Crested Butte Sports

BICYCLING | Come here to rent Orbea and Transition mountain bikes, plus helmets and other gear. It also has a full repair shop. ✉ *35 Emmons Loop Rd.* ☎ *970/349–7516* 🌐 *crestedbuttesports.com* 💵 *From $50 for four hours.*

SPAS

Elevation Spa

SPA/BEAUTY | With an elevation of 9,385 feet, Mount Crested Butte can drain the life out of your skin. The energizing atmosphere and treatments of the Elevation Spa can bring it back. The 11,000-square-foot spa is simply decorated, but provides all the amenities you need to unwind: robes, sandals, steam rooms, and three relaxation rooms—men's, women's, and coed—plus a large, well-equipped fitness center overlooking the slopes. ✉ *500 Gothic Rd., Mt. Crested Butte* ☎ *970/251–3500* 🌐 *www.elevationspa.com* ☞ *$115 50-min massage, $295 2-hr massage and facial package.*

Hot tubs (indoor and outdoor), indoor pool, saunas, steam rooms. Gym with: cardiovascular machines, free weights, weight-training equipment. Services: body wraps and scrubs, facials, massage.

TRACK SKIING

Crested Butte Nordic Center

SKIING/SNOWBOARDING | **FAMILY** | The community-owned Crested Butte Nordic Center maintains 31 miles of cross-country ski and snowshoe trails, many of which start from town. The trails cover flat and moderately rolling terrain across meadows and through aspen groves. A one-day adult trail pass costs $20, although there are 6 miles of groomed trails that don't require a pass. Group classic lessons and private skate or classic lessons are offered daily, as well as training groups for adults and kids. You can also reserve a spot for a dinner at the Magic Meadows Yurt, which includes a 1-mile trek to a cozy yurt for a five-course dinner prepared by local chefs and accompanied by live music; the $185 per-person cost includes a trail pass, equipment rentals, and gratuity. You can also buy hot drinks, soups, and pastries every Sunday from 10 to 2 at the Magic Meadows Yurt. ✉ *620 2nd St.* ☎ *970/349–1707* 🌐 *www.cbnordic.org.*

RENTALS

The Alpineer

SKIING/SNOWBOARDING | This iconic Crested Butte shop rents top-notch backcountry and telemark equipment, as well as classic Nordic and skate skis. The staff offers expert advice on routes and snow conditions. ✉ *419 6th St.* ☎ *970/349–5210* 🌐 *www.alpineer.com* ⏲ *Closed Sun.*

ZIPLINING

Crested Butte Mountain Resort Zipline Tour

ADVENTURE TOURS | **FAMILY** | Friendly guides and superior views make this two-hour, five-line tour worth your time. The tour runs in the summer at the base of the mountain, where you can watch the bikers below as you zip from tree to tree. ✉ *12 Snowmass Rd., Mt. Crested Butte* 🌐 *www.skicb.com* 🎟 *From $65.*

Gunnison

64 miles east of Montrose via U.S. 50; 28 miles south of Crested Butte via Hwy. 135.

At the confluence of the Gunnison River and Tomichi Creek, Gunnison is an old mining and ranching community and college town. It's been adopted by nature lovers because of the excellent outdoor activities, including hiking, climbing, fishing, and hunting. In fact, long before any settlers arrived, the Ute Indians used the area as summer hunting grounds. Gunnison provides economical lodging and easy access to Crested Butte and Blue Mesa Reservoir. Locals (for good reason) call it "Sunny Gunny," despite its claim to fame of having recorded some of the coldest temperatures ever reported in the continental United States.

GETTING HERE AND AROUND

Getting in and out of Gunnison is a breeze. U.S. 50 travels right through town, heading east to I–25 in Pueblo and northwest to I–70 in Grand Junction. U.S. 50 goes by the name Tomichi Avenue as it travels 18 blocks through town. Western State Colorado University and the Pioneer Museum are on the east side of town, and the rodeo grounds and airport are to the south.

ESSENTIALS

VISITOR INFORMATION Gunnison County Chamber of Commerce. ✉ *500 E. Tomichi Ave.* ☎ *970/641–1501* 🌐 *www.gunnison-crestedbutte.com.*

Sights

Curecanti National Recreation Area

BODY OF WATER | This recreation area, part of the National Park Service, encompasses three reservoirs along 40 miles of the Gunnison River and can be accessed at the bottom of the East Portal Road. Blue Mesa, nearly 20 miles long, is the largest body of water in Colorado; Morrow Point and Crystal are fjordlike reservoirs set in the upper Black Canyon of the Gunnison. All three reservoirs provide water-based recreational opportunities, including fishing, boating, and paddling, but only Blue Mesa offers boat ramps. Excellent fly-fishing can be found upstream (east) of Blue Mesa Reservoir along the Gunnison River. A variety of camping and hiking opportunities are also available. The Elk Creek Visitor Center on U.S. 50 is available year-round for trip-planning assistance. *102 Elk Creek* *970/641–2337* *www.nps.gov/cure* *Free.*

Gunnison Pioneer Museum

MUSEUM | **FAMILY** | Anyone interested in the region's history shouldn't miss the Pioneer Museum. The complex spreads across 6 acres and includes an extensive collection of vehicles, from Model Ts to 1960s sedans. There are also two old schoolhouses; an impressive display of arrowheads; mining exhibits; and a train, complete with coal tender, caboose, and boxcar. *803 E. Tomichi Ave.* *970/641–4530* *www.gunnisonpioneermuseum.com* *$10* *Closed Oct.–mid-May* *Cash only.*

Hartman Rocks Recreation Area

PARK—SPORTS-OUTDOORS | This free recreation area is a haven for mountain bikers, hikers, horseback riders, rock climbers, and ATV riders in the summer and Nordic skiers and snowshoers in the winter. With 8,000 acres of public land, encompassing 40 miles of single-track trails and 33 miles of road, there's enough room for everyone. *Gunnison* *3 miles south of U.S. 50, via County Road 38* *www.blm.gov/visit/hartman_rocks.*

Restaurants

Blackstock Bistro

$$ | **CONTEMPORARY** | The atmosphere and food at this modern, airy bistro are about as sophisticated as you'll find in Gunnison. It serves an innovative selection of small and large plates, but the real gem is the happy hour (3 pm to 6 pm every day and from 9 to close Friday and Saturday), which offers hearty portions at very reasonable prices. **Known for:** delectable ramen bowls; innovative small plates; truffle fries. *Average main: $15* *122 W. Tomichi Ave.* *970/641–4394* *www.blackstockbistro.com* *Closed Sun. No lunch.*

Garlic Mike's

$$$ | **ITALIAN** | The menu at this unpretentious Italian spot is surprisingly rich and complex, featuring traditional favorites, as well as surprises like the scrumptious garlic-roasted prime rib. The atmosphere is especially delightful in summer, when you can dine on the outdoor patio overlooking the Gunnison River and enjoy an after-dinner libation at the River Bar. **Known for:** live music on Friday nights in summer; Float & Dine predinner raft trip; riverside patio. *Average main: $23* *2674 Hwy. 135* *970/641–2493* *www.garlicmikes.com* *No lunch.*

Hotels

The Inn at Tomichi Village

$$ | **HOTEL** | The rooms at this updated hotel feature modern-rustic decor, comfortable beds (including a variety of pillow styles to suit various tastes), and amenities such as refrigerators and microwaves. **Pros:** ample amenities; large indoor pool; on-site restaurant. **Cons:** motel-style entrances; bathrooms are a bit dated; a little outside of town. *Rooms from: $129* *41883 U.S. 50 E* *970/641–1131* *www.theinntv.com* *51 rooms* *Free Breakfast.*

Rockey River Resort

$ | **RESORT** | **FAMILY** | A tetherball on the turf, a riverside firepit, and welcoming front porches: these are just a few of the touches that make this old homestead a uniquely pleasant place to stay. **Pros:** close to fishing; a lot of activities available on the property; pet-friendly. **Cons:** 6 miles from Gunnison; TV only in common areas; some cabins are a bit dated. *Rooms from: $95 ✉ 4359 County Rd. 10 ☎ 970/641–0174 ⊕ www.gunnisoncabins.com ⏲ Closed Nov.–Apr. 14 cabins No meals.*

Activities

FISHING

Gunnison Sports Outfitters

FISHING | Take a guided fishing trip on the Gunnison River or the Blue Mesa Reservoir, which teems with brown trout, rainbow trout, and kokanee salmon. Full-day trips are $345 per person; half-day are $295. Kids 12 and younger are free with a paying adult. *✉ 201 W. Tomichi Ave. ☎ 970/641–1845 ⊕ www.gunnisonsportsoutfitters.com.*

HORSEBACK RIDING

Tenderfoot Outfitters

HORSEBACK RIDING | With a variety of guided backcountry trail rides ranging from three hours to a full day, Tenderfoot Outfitters also offers camping trips with comfortable tents and real beds, starting at $190, including meals. Rides start at $75. *✉ Gunnison ☎ 800/641–0504 ⊕ www.tenderfoot-outfitters.com.*

WATER SPORTS

At 20 miles long, with 96 miles of shoreline, Blue Mesa Reservoir ranks as Colorado's largest body of water. Located within Curecanti National Recreation Area, the reservoir was created in the mid-1960s when the Gunnison River was dammed as part of the Colorado River Storage Project. This cold-water reservoir has become a mecca for water-sports enthusiasts. Anglers are drawn by the 3 million stocked kokanee salmon, as well as rainbow, lake, brown, and brook trout.

Five boat ramps and two marinas operate through the summer with varying hours and amenities. Boat permits are required and are available at the Elk Creek Visitor Center. A two-day boat permit is $4, and a two-week permit is $10. Annual boat permits run $30.

Elk Creek Marina

WATER SPORTS | About 16 miles west of Gunnison, this marina on Blue Mesa Reservoir offers a range of services: boat and slip rentals, mechanical and towing services, gas, ice, bait, and supplies. You can also book guided fishing trips here. A small restaurant, Pappy's, is located above the dock, where you can enjoy a light meal while watching anglers try their luck. *✉ 24830 U.S. 50 ☎ 970/641–0707 ⊕ www.thebluemesa.com ⏲ Closed Oct.–Apr.*

Black Canyon of the Gunnison National Park

South Rim: 15 miles east of Montrose, via U.S. 50 and Rte. 347. North Rim: 11 miles south of Crawford, via Rte. 92 and North Rim Rd.

The Black Canyon of the Gunnison River is one of Colorado's most awe-inspiring places—a vivid testament to the powers of erosion, the canyon is roughly 2,000 feet deep. The steep angles of the cliffs allow little sunlight, and ever-present shadows blanket the canyon walls, leaving some of it in almost perpetual darkness and inspiring the canyon's name. And while this dramatic landscape makes the gorge a remarkable place to visit, it also has prevented any permanent occupation—there's no evidence that humans have ever taken up residence within the canyon's walls.

Spanish explorers encountered the formidable chasm in 1765 and 1776, and several other expeditions surveyed it from the mid-1800s to the early 1900s. The early groups hoped to find a route suitable for trains to transport the West's rich resources and the people extracting them. One such train—the Denver and Rio Grande narrow-gauge railroad, completed in 1882—did succeed in constructing a line through the far eastern reaches of the canyon, from Gunnison to Cimmaron, but ultimately concluded that the steepest and deepest part of the canyon, which is now the national park, was "impenetrable." Even so, the rail line's views were majestic enough and the passages narrow enough to earn it the moniker "Scenic Line of the World."

In the late 1800s Black Canyon explorers had another goal in mind: building a tunnel through the side of the canyon to divert water from the Gunnison River into the nearby Uncompahgre Valley, to nurture crops and sustain settlements, such as Montrose. To this day, water still flows through the tunnel, located at the Black Canyon's East Portal, to irrigate the valley's rich farmland.

Once the tunnel was complete, the focus shifted from esteeming the canyon for its resources to appreciating its aesthetic and recreational value. In 1933, Black Canyon of the Gunnison was designated a national monument, and from 1933–35, Civilian Conservation Corps crews built the North Rim Road, under the direction of the National Park Service. More than 60 years later, in 1999, the canyon was redesignated as a national park. Today, the canyon is far enough removed from civilization that its unspoiled depths continue, as an 1883 explorer wrote, to "arouse the wondering and reverent amazement of one's being."

GETTING ORIENTED

East Portal. The only way you can get down to the river via automobile in Black Canyon is on the steep East Portal Road. There's a campground and picnic area here, as well as fishing and trail access. Check the park website before you go, however; a repaving project will be closing the road for an extended time.

North Rim. If you want to access this side of the canyon from the South Rim, you will have to leave the park and wend around it to either the west (through Montrose and Delta) or to the east (via Hwy. 92); expect a drive of at least two hours. The area's remoteness and difficult location mean the North Rim is rarely crowded; the road is partially unpaved and closes in the winter. There's also a small ranger station here.

South Rim. This is the main area of the park. The park's only visitor center is here, along with a campground, a few picnic areas, and many hiking trails. The South Rim Road closes at Gunnison Point in the winter, when skiers and snowshoers take over.

WHEN TO GO

Summer is the busiest season, with July experiencing the greatest crowds. However, a spring or fall visit gives you two advantages: fewer people and cooler temperatures. In summer, especially in years with little rainfall, daytime temperatures can reach into the 90s. Winter brings even more solitude, as all but one section of campsites are shut down and only about 2 miles of South Rim Road, the park's main road, are plowed.

November through March is when the snow hits, with an average of about 3 to 8 inches of it monthly. March through April and July and August are the rainiest, with about an inch of precipitation each month. June is generally the driest month. Temperatures at the bottom of the canyon are about 8 degrees warmer than at the rim.

GETTING HERE AND AROUND

AIR

The Black Canyon of the Gunnison lies between the cities of Gunnison and Montrose, both with small regional airports.

CAR

The park has three roads. South Rim Road, reached by Route 347, is the primary thoroughfare and winds along the canyon's South Rim. From about late November to early April, the road is not plowed past the visitor center at Gunnison Point. North Rim Road, reached by Route 92, is usually open from April through Thanksgiving; in winter, the road is unplowed. On the park's south side, the serpentine East Portal Road descends abruptly to the Gunnison River below. The road is usually open from April through the end of November. Because of the grade, vehicles or vehicle-trailer combinations longer than 22 feet are not permitted. The park has no public transportation.

PARK ESSENTIALS

ACCESSIBILITY

South Rim Visitor Center is accessible to people with mobility impairments, as are most of the sites at South Rim Campground. Drive-to overlooks on the South Rim include Tomichi Point, the alternate gravel viewpoint at Pulpit Rock (the main one is not accessible), Chasm View (gravel), Sunset View, and High Point. Balanced Rock (gravel) is the only drive-to viewpoint on the North Rim. None of the park's hiking trails are accessible by car.

PARK FEES AND PERMITS

Entrance fees are $25 per week per vehicle. Visitors entering on bicycle, motorcycle, or on foot pay $15 for a weekly pass. To access the inner canyon, you must pick up a wilderness permit (no fee).

PARK HOURS

The park is open 24/7 year-round. It's in the Mountain time zone.

CELL-PHONE RECEPTION

Cell-phone reception in the park is unreliable and sporadic. There are public telephones at South Rim Visitor Center and South Rim Campground.

VISITOR INFORMATION

Black Canyon of the Gunnison National Park
✉ *Montrose* ✣ *7 miles north of U.S. 50 on CO Hwy. 347* ☎ *970/641–2337* 🌐 *www.nps.gov/blca.*

Sights

SCENIC DRIVES

The scenic South and North Rim roads offer deep and distant views into the canyon. Both also offer several lookout points and short hiking trails along the rim. The trails that go down into the canyon are steep and strenuous, and essentially unmarked, and so are reserved for experienced (and very fit) hikers.

East Portal Road

SCENIC DRIVE | The only way to access the Gunnison River from the park by car is via this paved route, which drops approximately 2,000 feet down to the water in only 5 miles, giving it an extremely steep grade. Vehicles longer than 22 feet are not allowed on the road. If you're towing a trailer, you can unhitch it near the entrance to South Rim campground. The bottom of the road is actually in the adjacent Curecanti National Recreation Area. There you'll find a picnic area, a campground, a primitive riverside trail, and beautiful scenery. A tour of East Portal Road, with a brief stop at the bottom, takes about 45 minutes. Immediately after arrival through the park's South entrance, take a right on East Portal Road. ⏲ *Closed mid-Nov.–mid.-Apr.*

South Rim Road

SCENIC DRIVE | This paved 7-mile stretch from Tomichi Point to High Point is the park's main road. The drive follows the canyon's level South Rim; 12 overlooks are accessible from the road, most via short gravel trails. Several short hikes along the rim also begin roadside. Allow between two and three hours round-trip.

SCENIC SIGHTS

The vast depths that draw thousands of visitors each year to Black Canyon have also historically prevented any extensive human habitation from taking root, so cultural attractions are largely absent here. But what the park lacks in historic sites it more than makes up for in scenery.

Chasm and Painted Wall Views

VIEWPOINT | At the heart-in-your-throat Chasm viewpoint, the canyon walls plummet 1,820 feet to the river, but are only 1,100 feet apart at the top. As you peer down into the depths, keep in mind that this section is where the Gunnison River descends at its steepest rate, dropping 240 feet within the span of a mile. A few hundred yards farther is the best place from which to see Painted Wall, Colorado's tallest cliff. Pinkish swaths of pegmatite (a crystalline, granitelike rock) give the wall its colorful, marbled appearance. ✉ *Black Canyon of the Gunnison National Park ✣ Approximately 3½ miles from the visitor center on South Rim Rd.*

Narrows View

VIEWPOINT | Look upriver from this North Rim viewing spot and you'll be able to see into the canyon's narrowest section, just a slot really, with only 40 feet between the walls at the bottom. The canyon is also taller (1,725 feet) here than it is wide at the rim (1,150 feet). ✉ *North Rim Rd., first overlook along the left fork of the North Rim Rd., Black Canyon of the Gunnison National Park.*

Warner Point

NATURE SITE | This viewpoint, at the end of the Warner Point Nature Trail, delivers awesome views of the canyon's deepest point (2,722 feet), plus the nearby San Juan and West Elk mountain ranges. ✉ *End of Warner Point Nature Trail, westernmost end of South Rim Rd., Black Canyon of the Gunnison National Park.*

VISITOR CENTERS

North Rim Ranger Station

INFO CENTER | This small facility on the park's North Rim is open sporadically and only in summer. Rangers can provide information and assistance and can issue permits for wilderness use and rock climbing. If rangers are out in the field, which they often are, guests can find directions for obtaining permits posted in the station. ✉ *North Rim Rd., 11 miles from Rte. 92 turnoff, Black Canyon of the Gunnison National Park* ☎ *970/641–2337.*

South Rim Visitor Center

INFO CENTER | The park's only visitor center offers interactive exhibits and an introductory film detailing the park's geology and wildlife. Inquire at the center about free informational ranger programs. ✉ *Black Canyon of the Gunnison National Park ✣ 1½ mile from the entrance station on South Rim Rd.* ☎ *970/249–1914.*

Activities

BICYCLING

Bikes are not permitted on any of the trails, but cycling along the South Rim or North Rim Road is a great way to view the park. ■ **TIP→ Be careful: the roads are fairly narrow.**

BIRD-WATCHING

The sheer cliffs of Black Canyon, though not suited for human habitation, provide a great habitat for birds. Peregrine falcons, white-throated swifts, and other cliff-dwelling birds revel in the dizzying heights, while at river level you'll find American dippers foraging for food in the rushing waters. Canyon wrens, which nest in the cliffs, are more often heard than seen, but their hauntingly beautiful songs are unforgettable. Dusky grouse are common in the sagebrush areas above the canyon, and red-tailed and Cooper's hawks and turkey vultures frequent the canyon rims. The best times for birding are spring and early summer.

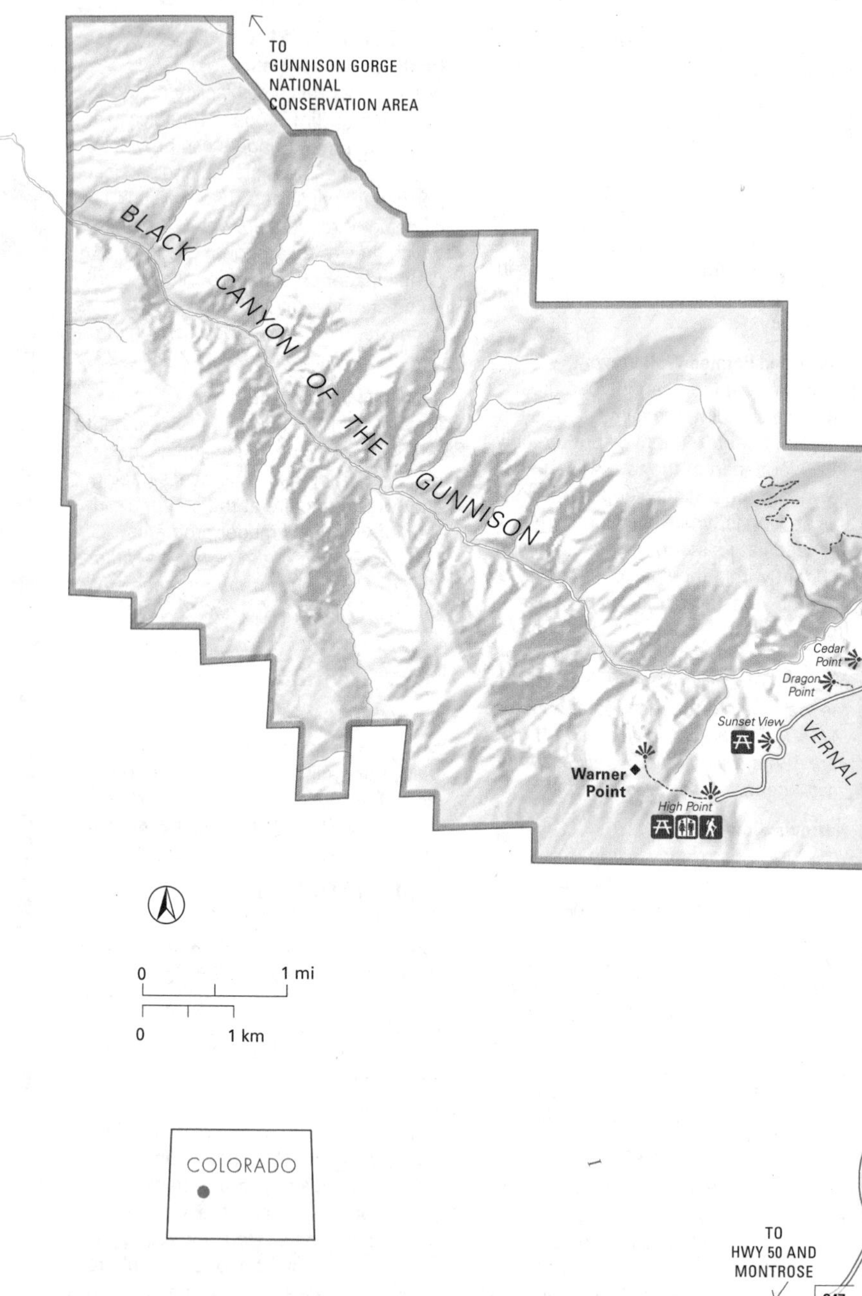

TO
GUNNISON GORGE
NATIONAL
CONSERVATION AREA
BLACK CANYON OF THE GUNNISON
Cedar Point
Dragon Point
Sunset View
VERNAL
Warner Point
High Point
0
1 mi
0
1 km
COLORADO
TO
HWY 50 AND
MONTROSE

Black Canyon of the Gunnison National Park

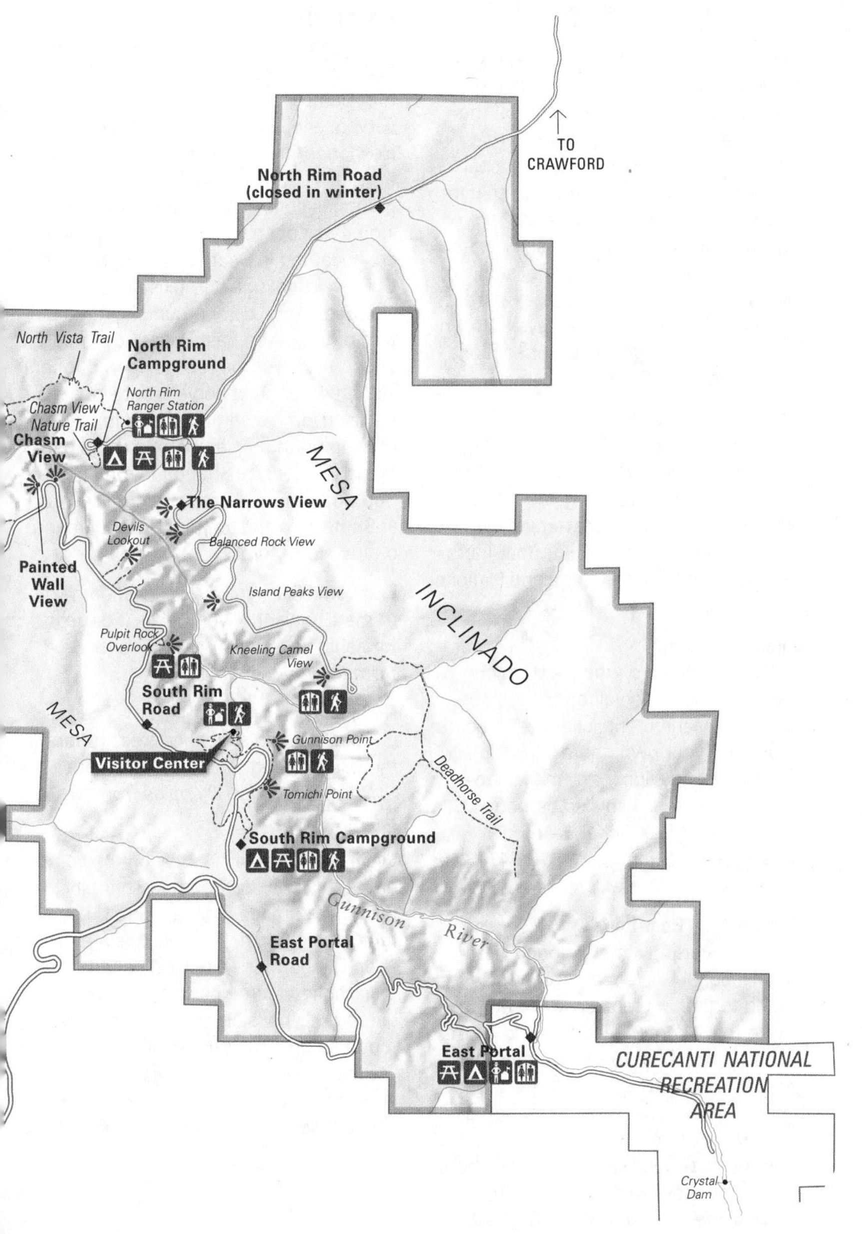

BOATING AND KAYAKING

With Class V rapids, the Gunnison River is one of the premier kayak challenges in North America. The spectacular 14-mile stretch of the river that passes through the park is so narrow in some sections that the rim seems to be closing up above your head. Once you're downstream from the rapids (and out of the park), the canyon opens up into what is called the Gunnison Gorge National Conservation Area. The rapids ease considerably, and the trip becomes more of a quiet float on Class I to Class IV water. Access to the Gunnison Gorge is only by foot or horseback. However, several outfitters offer guided raft and kayak trips in the Gunnison Gorge and other sections of the Gunnison River.

Kayaking the river through the park requires a wilderness use permit (and lots of expertise); rafting is not allowed. You can, however, take a guided pontoon-boat trip into the eastern end of the canyon via Morrow Point Boat Tours, which launch from the Curecanti National Recreation Area, east of the park.

Lake Fork Marina

BOATING | Located on the western end of Blue Mesa Reservoir off U.S. 92, the Lake Fork Marina rents all types of boats. If you have your own, there's a ramp at the marina and slips for rent. Guided fishing excursions can also be booked here. ✉ *Off U.S. 92, near Lake Fork Campground, Gunnison* ☎ *970/641–3048* 🌐 *www.thebluemesa.com.*

Morrow Point Boat Tours

BOATING | Starting in neighboring Curecanti National Recreation Area, these guided tours run twice daily (except Tuesday) in the summer, at 10 am and 1 pm. Morrow Point Boat Tours take passengers on a 90-minute trip into the Black Canyon via pontoon boat. Passengers must walk 1 mile in each direction to and from the boat dock (includes quite a few stairs), and reservations are required. ✉ *Pine Creek Trail and Boat Dock, U.S. 50, milepost 130, 25 miles west of Gunnison, Gunnison* ☎ *970/641–2337* 🌐 *www.nps.gov/cure* 🎟 *$25* 🕒 *Closed mid-Sept.–May.*

CAMPING

There are three campgrounds in Black Canyon National Park. The small North Rim Campground is first come, first served, and is closed in the winter. Vehicles longer than 35 feet are discouraged from this campground. South Rim Campground is considerably larger, and has a loop that's open year-round. Reservations are accepted in South Rim Loops A and B. Power hookups only exist in Loop B. The East Portal campground is at the bottom of the steep East Portal Road and is open whenever the road is open. It offers 15 first-come, first-served tent sites in a pretty, riverside setting. Water has to be trucked up to the campgrounds, so use it in moderation; it's shut off in mid-to-late September. Generators are not allowed at South Rim and are highly discouraged on the North Rim.

East Portal Campground. Its location next to the Gunnison River makes it perfect for fishing. ✉ *East Portal Rd., 5 miles from the main entrance.*

North Rim Campground. This small campground, nestled amid pine trees, offers the basics along the quiet North Rim. ✉ *North Rim Rd., 11¼ miles from Rte. 92.*

South Rim Campground. Stay on the canyon rim at this main campground right inside the park entrance. Loops A and C have tent sites only. The RV hookups are in Loop B, and those sites are priced higher than those in other parts of the campground. It's possible to camp here year-round (Loop A stays open all winter), but the loops are not plowed, so you'll have to hike in with your tent. ✉ *South Rim Rd., 1 mile from the visitor center.*

EDUCATIONAL OFFERINGS

Junior Ranger Program. Kids of all ages can participate in this program with an activities booklet to fill in while exploring the park. Inquire at the South Rim Visitor Center.

FISHING

The three dams built upriver from the park in Curecanti National Recreation Area have created prime trout fishing in the waters below. Certain restrictions apply: Only artificial flies and lures are permitted, and a Colorado fishing license is required for people ages 16 and older. Rainbow trout are catch-and-release only, and there are size and possession limits on brown trout (check at the visitor center). Most anglers access the river from the bottom of East Portal Road; an undeveloped trail goes along the riverbank for about three-quarters of a mile.

HIKING

All trails can be hot in summer and most don't receive much shade, so bring water, a hat, and plenty of sunscreen. Dogs are permitted, on leash, on Rim Rock, Cedar Point Nature, and Chasm View Nature trails, and at any overlook. Venturing into the inner canyon, while doable, is not for the faint of heart—or slight of step. Six named routes lead down to the river, but they are not maintained or marked, and they require a wilderness permit. In fact, the park staff won't even call them trails; they refer to them as "Class III scrambles" These supersteep, rocky routes vary in one-way distance from 1 to 2¾ miles, and the descent can be anywhere from 1,800 to 2,722 feet. Your reward, of course, is a rare look at the bottom of the canyon and the fast-flowing Gunnison. ■**TIP→ Don't attempt an inner-canyon excursion without plenty of water (the park's recommendation is 1 gallon per person, per day).** For descriptions of the routes and the necessary permit to hike them, stop at the visitor center at the South Rim or the North Rim ranger station. Dogs are not permitted in the inner canyon.

Wildlife in Black Canyon

You may spot peregrine falcons nesting in May and June. Other raptors (red-tailed hawks, Cooper's hawks, golden eagles) circle above year round. In summer, turkey vultures join the flying corps, and in winter, bald eagles. Mule deer, elk, and the very shy bobcat also call the park home. In spring and fall, look for porcupines among pinyon pines on the rims. Listen for the chirp of the yellow-bellied marmot on sunny, rocky outcrops. Though rarely seen, mountain lions and black bears also live in the park.

EASY

Cedar Point Overlook Trail

TRAIL | FAMILY | This 0.4-mile round-trip interpretive trail leads out from South Rim Road to two overlooks. It's an easy stroll, and signs along the way detail the surrounding plants. *Easy.* ✉ *Black Canyon of the Gunnison National Park* ✣ *Trailhead: off South Rim Rd., 4¼ miles from South Rim Visitor Center.*

Deadhorse Trail

TRAIL | Despite its name, the 6-mile Deadhorse Trail is actually a pleasant hike, starting on an old service road from the Kneeling Camel view on the North Rim Road. The trail's farthest point provides the park's easternmost viewpoint. From this overlook, the canyon is much more open, with pinnacles and spires rising along its sides. *Easy.* ✉ *Black Canyon of the Gunnison National Park* ✣ *Trailhead: at the southernmost end of North Rim Rd.*

MODERATE

Chasm View Nature Trail

TRAIL | The park's shortest trail (0.3 mile round-trip) starts at North Rim Campground and offers an impressive 50-yard walk right along the canyon rim as well as an eye-popping view of Painted Wall and Serpent Point. This is also an excellent place to spot raptors, swifts, and other birds. *Moderate.* ✉ *Black Canyon of the Gunnison National Park* ✣ *Trailhead: at North Rim Campground, 11¼ miles from Rte. 92.*

North Vista Trail

TRAIL | The round-trip hike to Exclamation Point is 3 miles; a more difficult foray to the top of 8,563-foot Green Mountain (a mesa, really) is 7 miles. The trail leads you along the North Rim; keep an eye out for especially gnarled pinyon pines—the North Rim is the site of some of the oldest groves of pinyons in North America, between 700 and 900 years old. *Moderate.* ✉ *Black Canyon of the Gunnison National Park* ✣ *Trailhead: at North Rim ranger station, off North Rim Rd., 11 miles from Rte. 92 turnoff.*

Rim Rock Nature Trail

TRAIL | The terrain on this 1-mile round-trip trail is primarily flat and exposed to the sun, with a bird's-eye view into the canyon. The trail connects the visitor center and the campground. There's an interpretive pamphlet, which corresponds to markers along the route, available at both destinations. *Moderate.* ✉ *Black Canyon of the Gunnison National Park* ✣ *Trailheads: at Tomichi Point overlook or Loop C in South Rim Campground.*

★ Warner Point Nature Trail

TRAIL | The 1½-mile round-trip hike starts from High Point. It provides fabulous vistas of the San Juan and West Elk mountains and Uncompahgre Valley. Warner Point, at trail's end, has the steepest drop-off from rim to river: a dizzying 2,722 feet. *Moderate.* ✉ *Black Canyon of the Gunnison National Park* ✣ *Trailhead: at the end of South Rim Rd.*

DIFFICULT

Oak Flat Loop Trail

TRAIL | This 2-mile loop is the most demanding of the South Rim hikes, as it brings you about 400 feet below the canyon rim. In places, the trail is narrow and crosses some steep slopes, but you won't have to navigate any steep drop-offs. Oak Flat is the shadiest of all the South Rim trails; small groves of aspen and thick stands of Douglas fir along the loop offer some respite from the sun. *Difficult.* ✉ *Black Canyon of the Gunnison National Park* ✣ *Trailhead: just west of the South Rim Visitor Center.*

HORSEBACK RIDING

Although its name might indicate otherwise, Deadhorse Trail is actually the only trail in the park where horses are allowed. Although no permit is required, the park has no riding facilities.

Elk Ridge Trail Rides

HORSEBACK RIDING | You can take 90-minute trail rides at this ranch just outside the Black Canyon National Park. ✉ *10203 Bostwick Park Rd., Montrose* ☎ *970/240–6007* 🌐 *www.elkridgeranchinc.com* 🎫 *$75. Reservations required.*

ROCK CLIMBING

Rock climbing in the park is for experts only, but you can do some bouldering at the Marmot Rocks area, about 100 feet south of South Rim Road between Painted Wall and Cedar Point overlooks (park at Painted Wall). Four boulder groupings offer a variety of routes rated from easy to very difficult; a pamphlet with a diagrammed map of the area is available at the South Rim Visitor Center.

Irwin Guides

CLIMBING/MOUNTAINEERING | Intermediate and expert climbers can take full-day rock-climbing guided tours in the Black Canyon on routes rated from 5.8 to 5.13. ✉ *330 Belleview Ave., Crested Butte* ☎ *970/349–5430* 🌐 *www.irwinguides.com* 🎫 *$550 for one person; $500 for two or more.*

WINTER ACTIVITIES

From late November to early April, South Rim Road is not plowed past the visitor center, offering park guests a unique opportunity to cross-country ski or snowshoe on the road. The Park Service also grooms a cross-country ski trail and marks a snowshoe trail through the woods, both starting at the visitor center. It's possible to ski or snowshoe on the unplowed North Rim Road, too, but it's about 4 miles from where the road closes, through sagebrush flats, to the canyon rim.

Montrose

15 miles west of Black Canyon of the Gunnison National Park; 64 miles west of Gunnison; 22 miles south of Delta, all via U.S. 50.

The "Home of the Black Canyon" sits amid glorious surroundings, but it's otherwise a typical Western town with a small historic center, where you'll find a smattering of trendy shops and restaurants, and a collection of truck stops, strip malls, and big-box stores along its outskirts. Montrose also has a small airport that's a major gateway for skiers heading to Telluride and Crested Butte.

GETTING HERE AND AROUND

U.S. 550 enters Montrose from the south; it's known as Townsend Avenue as it passes through town. At Main Street, U.S. 550 merges with U.S. 50, which continues north to Delta and east to Black Canyon of the Gunnison National Park and the town of Gunnison.

ESSENTIALS

VISITOR INFORMATION Montrose Visitor Center. ✉ *107 S. Cascade Ave.* ☎ *970/497–8558* 🌐 *www.visitmontrose.com.*

Sights

Museum of the Mountain West

MUSEUM | FAMILY | Run by a retired archaeologist, the museum depicts life in Colorado from the late 1800s to the 1940s. It features roughly 500,000 artifacts and 23 buildings, including a schoolhouse, church, carriage works, and jail cell, as well as homesteads and teepee replicas. ✉ *68169 E. Miami Rd.* ✥ *2 miles east of Montrose, off U.S. 50* ☎ *970/240–3400* 🌐 *www.museumofthemountainwest.org* 🎟 *$10* ⏲ *Closed Sun.*

Ute Indian Museum

MUSEUM | If you're interested in the lives of the region's original residents, stop by the renovated Ute Indian Museum, 3 miles south of town. The museum contains several dioramas and the most comprehensive collection of Ute materials and artifacts in Colorado. It's housed in the 1956 homestead of Ute Chief Ouray and his wife, Chipeta. Today, the complex includes the Chief Ouray Memorial Park, Chipeta's Crypt, a native plants garden, picnic areas, and shaded paths linked to the citywide walking trail. ✉ *17253 Chipeta Rd.* ☎ *970/249–3098* 🌐 *www.historycolorado.org* 🎟 *$6.*

Restaurants

Camp Robber

$$ | SOUTHWESTERN | This simply decorated restaurant serves some of Montrose's most creative cuisine, such as its famous green-chile chicken and potato soup or shrimp, avocado, and prosciutto pasta (gluten-free options available too). At lunch, salads with house-made dressings, hearty sandwiches, and blue-corn enchiladas fuel hungry hikers. **Known for:** New Mexican dishes; house-made salsa and desserts; shaded patio. [$] *Average main: $15* ✉ *1515 Ogden Rd.* ☎ *970/240–1590* 🌐 *www.camprobber.com* ⏲ *No dinner Sun.*

Colorado Boy Pizzeria & Brewery
$ | **PIZZA** | The dough is house-made (with Italian-imported flour) and the beer is home-brewed at this trendy downtown pizzeria with high ceilings, brick walls, and contemporary decor. Sit at the pizza bar in the back and enjoy an English-style ale while you watch the chefs craft your tasty pie. **Known for:** home-brewed ales; growlers and cans to go; house-made sausage. *Average main: $10 ✉ 320 E. Main St. ☎ 970/240–2790 ⊕ www.coloradoboy.com ⏲ No lunch weekdays.*

Hotels

Country Lodge
$ | **HOTEL** | A log cabin–style building and rooms ringing a pretty garden and pool make this hotel feel remote even though it's on Montrose's main drag. **Pros:** great value; intimate feel; nice pool and hot tub. **Cons:** small bathrooms and TVs; on main highway, so it can sometimes be noisy; breakfast is basic. *Rooms from: $90 ✉ 1624 E. Main St. ☎ 970/249–4567 ⊕ www.countrylodgecolorado.com 23 rooms Free Breakfast.*

Red Arrow Inn & Suites
$$ | **HOTEL** | This low-key establishment offers reasonable prices for one of the nicest lodgings in the area, mainly because of the large, pretty rooms filled with handsome wood furnishings. **Pros:** good breakfast; outdoor firepit; pleasant outdoor pool. **Cons:** motel-style entrances; next to busy street; decor doesn't offer much local flavor. *Rooms from: $140 ✉ 1702 E. Main St. ☎ 970/249–9641 ⊕ www.redarrowinn.com 59 rooms Free Breakfast.*

Activities

HIKING

Grand Mesa, Uncompahgre, and Gunnison National Forests
HIKING/WALKING | With some of the most spectacular scenery in the Colorado Rockies, this trio of national forests has a total of more than 3 million acres. The area contains many historic mining sites, 3,600 miles of streams, 3,500 miles of trails, and 300-plus lakes. *✉ 2250 U.S. 50, Delta ☎ 970/874–6600 ⊕ www.fs.usda.gov/gmug.*

Paonia

24 miles north of the north entrance of the Black Canyon of the Gunnison National Park.

Vineyards, orchards, and farms surround this small town, which encompasses a little over a square mile in the midst of a verdant valley. A pleasant but unassuming main street, called Grand Avenue, features shops and restaurants, many of which provide opportunities to enjoy the agricultural bounty of the area, including wines from some of the highest-altitude vineyards in the Northern Hemisphere.

VISITOR INFORMATION

North Fork Valley Tourism
✉ Hotchkiss ☎ 970/872–3226 ⊕ www.northforkvalley.net.

Sights

★ Big B's Delicious Orchards
FARM/RANCH | This lovely orchard 1 mile west of Paonia markets its own organic apples, apricots, cherries, peaches, pears, and plums throughout the summer. You can pick them yourself, along with a variety of other produce, or buy them in the shop in the form of homemade organic juices or hard cider; you'll

also find local wines, art, honey, and more. The café serves tasty sandwiches, salads, and Colorado-style Mexican entrées that can be enjoyed indoors or out. There's live music outdoors on many summer evenings, and kids will keep themselves entertained on the variety of tree swings. Camping is also available. ✉ *39126 Hwy. 133, Hotchkiss* ☎ *970/527–1110* 🌐 *www.bigbs.com* ⏲ *Closed Dec.–Mar.*

Orchard Valley Farms & Market and Black Bridge Winery
FARM/RANCH | Family fun takes an organic approach at this friendly farm. Take a stroll through the gardens and orchards and pick your own fruits and vegetables, or choose from a nice selection at the farm market, which also features a broad selection of other local products. Enjoy your bounty immediately at creek-side picnic tables. The on-site Black Bridge Winery offers $5 tastings of its Chardonnay, Riesling, Merlot, Pinot Noir, and other wines. ✉ *15836 Black Bridge Rd., Paonia* ☎ *970/527–6838* 🌐 *www.orchardvalleyfarms.com* ⏲ *Closed Nov.–late May.*

Stone Cottage Cellars
WINERY/DISTILLERY | This winery, 3 miles north of town (a mile of it up a steep, narrow dirt road), is in an idyllic setting, featuring old-world–style stone cottages the owner made himself. Specialties include Chardonnay, Merlot, Syrah, Pinot Noir, Pinot Gris, and Gewürztraminer varietals. Stop by for a free vineyard tour and wine tasting; don't miss the delicious small plates as well. If you plan ahead, you can book a night in the two-bedroom guest cottage. ✉ *41716 Reds Rd., Paonia* ☎ *970/527–3444* 🌐 *www.stonecottagecellars.com* ⏲ *Closed Nov.–Apr.*

Restaurants

Flying Fork Cafe & Bakery
$$ | ITALIAN | This charming café serves tasty Italian fare in a comfortable dining room and, in the summer, a shady outdoor garden. Local ingredients are used whenever possible, and the house-made fettuccine noodles are delicious. **Known for:** gluten-free pasta and pizza options; homemade fettuccine noodles; vegetarian lasagna. *Average main: $18* ✉ *101 3rd St., Paonia* ☎ *970/527–9075* 🌐 *www.flyingforkcafe.com* ⏲ *Closed Mon. and Tues.*

★ The Living Farm Café
$$ | ECLECTIC | Housed in a historic building at the end of the main drag, this farm-to-table eatery infuses local and organic fare throughout its menu—much of it from its own namesake farm nearby. There are salads, burgers, and sandwiches aplenty, along with a smattering of international selections, including Mexican, Indian, and Chinese. **Known for:** fresh-from-the-farm organic ingredients; vegan and gluten-free options aplenty; half portions available. *Average main: $17* ✉ *120 Grand Ave., Paonia* ☎ *970/527–3779* 🌐 *www.thelivingfarmcafe.com* ⏲ *Closed Tues. and Wed.*

Hotels

Bross Hotel
$$ | B&B/INN | On a quiet, shady street in downtown Paonia, this brick hotel was opened in 1906 by the local deputy sheriff. **Pros:** lovely hotel with genuine period ambience; excellent full breakfast in a large, classy breakfast room; outdoor hot tub and small fitness center. **Cons:** no a/c in the dog days of summer can be a drag; no elevator and narrow staircase; breakfast is at specific seating times versus at your leisure. *Rooms from: $155* ✉ *312 Onarga St., Paonia* ☎ *970/527–6776* 🌐 *www.paonia-inn.com* *10 rooms* *Free Breakfast.*

Lake City

45 miles from Ouray via Alpine Loop Scenic Byway (summer only); 55 miles southwest of Gunnison; 52 miles northwest of Creede.

Lake City—with its collection of lacy gingerbread-trim houses and other Victorian buildings—has one of the largest National Historic Districts in Colorado (more than 200 structures). Lake City is a quaint little town and a point of departure for superb hiking, fishing, and four-wheel driving in the Gunnison National Forest. A geological phenomenon known as the Slumgullion Earthflow occurred some 700 years ago, when a mountainside sloughed off into the valley, blocking the Lake Fork of the Gunnison River and creating Lake San Cristobal, the state's second-largest natural lake. There's a scenic overlook along Highway 149, just south of town, with a sign explaining how this happened.

GETTING HERE AND AROUND

Highway 149 turns into Gunnison Avenue as it passes through the seven blocks of Lake City. The majority of the town's shops and historic homes are one block west on Silver Street.

ESSENTIALS

VISITOR INFORMATION Lake City/Hinsdale County Chamber of Commerce. ✉ *800 Gunnison Ave.* ☎ *970/944–2527* 🌐 *www.lakecity.com.*

Sights

Alpine Loop Scenic Byway

SCENIC DRIVE | The inspiring 63-mile Alpine Loop Scenic Byway joins Lake City with Ouray and Silverton. The road, typically open late May or early June through early October, has unpaved sections that require a high-clearance, four-wheel-drive vehicle. Dizzily spiraling from 12,800-foot-high passes to gaping valleys, past seven ghost towns, the trip is well worth the effort. ✉ *Lake City.*

Silver Thread Scenic Byway

SCENIC DRIVE | Lake City used to be at the northern tip of the Silver Thread Scenic Byway, which has now been extended north to its intersection with U.S. 50 at Blue Mesa Reservoir, for a total of 117 miles. From Lake City, the byway (also called Highway 149) travels south 75 miles to South Fork, climbing over Slumgullion and Spring Creek passes. The route then overlooks the headwaters of the Rio Grande before dropping into the lush Rio Grande Valley. Along the way, you'll see plenty of old gold- and silver-mining camps and spectacular North Clear Creek Falls.

Activities

FISHING

Numerous high-alpine lakes and mountain streams make the area around Lake City an angler's heaven. Lake San Cristobal is known around the region for its rainbow and mackinaw trout, while the Lake Fork of the Gunnison attracts anglers for rainbow and brown trout.

The Sportsman Outdoors and Fly Shop

FISHING | This full-service outfitter offers half- and full-day guided fly-fishing trips, as well as lessons for both novice and advanced anglers. The Sportsman also runs hiking, four-wheel-drive, snowshoeing, and backcountry skiing trips. At the shop, you can buy and rent all manner of outdoor gear. ✉ *238 S. Gunnison* ☎ *970/944–2526* 🌐 *www.lakecitysportsman.com* 🎫 *Lessons from $130; fly-fishing tours from $260.*

HIKING

There are lots of trails in this region, with choices for all abilities. Many follow logging roads, so it's best to get the latest scoop on conditions before heading out. Ambitious hikers often overnight in Lake City before attempting five of Colorado's Fourteeners—Handies, Sunshine, Redcloud, Uncompahgre, and Wetterhorn peaks—all within about 15 miles of town. Sunshine and Redcloud are generally climbed together.

Creede

105 miles south of Gunnison via U.S. 50 and Rte. 149; 52 miles southeast of Lake City via Rte. 149.

Creede, a flash-in-the-pan silver town, was known in its heyday as Colorado's rowdiest mining camp. When silver was discovered here in 1889, hotels, saloons, banks, and brothels opened virtually overnight, often in tents and other makeshift structures. By 1892, Creede had become a collection of wood-framed buildings, at least 30 of which were saloons and dance halls. That year, Creede was immortalized in a poem written by the local newspaper editor Cy Warman: "It's day all day in daytime," he wrote, "and there is no night in Creede."

True, every other building back in the silver-boom days seems to have been a bar or bordello. Bob Ford, who killed Jesse James, was himself gunned down here; other notorious residents included Calamity Jane and Bat Masterson.

As delightful as the town's history may be, its location is even more glorious. Mineral County is almost entirely public land, including the nearby Weminuche Wilderness to the south and west and the Wheeler Geological Area to the east, where the unusual rock formations resemble playful abstract sculptures or M.C. Escher creations. The Colorado Trail and the Continental Divide Trail, two of the country's most significant long-distance recreational paths, pass through Mineral County.

GETTING HERE AND AROUND

Highway 149 (the Silver Thread Scenic and Historic Byway) connects with Main Street before it turns and heads out of Creede. The town encompasses about 15 blocks.

ESSENTIALS

VISITOR INFORMATION Creede & Mineral County Visitor Center and Chamber of Commerce. ✉ *904 S. Main St.* ☎ *719/658–2374* 🌐 *www.creede.com.*

Sights

Creede Historical Museum and Library
MUSEUM | Occupying the original Denver & Rio Grande Railroad Depot, the museum paints a vivid portrait of the town's rough-and-tumble early days. It also includes World War I and World War II exhibits. ✉ *15 Main St.* ☎ *719/658–2004* 🌐 *www.creede.com* 🎟 *$2* ⏲ *Closed Oct.–late May and weekdays in Sept.*

Creede Underground Mining Museum and Community Center
MUSEUM | This museum is housed in rooms that modern miners blasted out of solid rock to commemorate the lives of 1880s-era miners and trace the history of mining in the area. In summer, there are guided tours at 10 and 3 daily, but before 2:15 pm you can also take a self-guided audio tour. **■ TIP→ Reservations are recommended.** ✉ *503 Forest Service Rd. No. 9* ☎ *719/658–0811* 🌐 *www.undergroundminingmuseum.com* 🎟 *$8 self-guided tour, $15 guided tour.*

Hotels

Antler's Rio Grande Lodge
$$ | **B&B/INN** | **FAMILY** | Dating back to the late 1800s, this cozy lodge has rooms in the main building as well as rustic, secluded cabins with their own kitchens. **Pros:** hot tub on the river; 70 acres of open space; private fishing pond. **Cons:** a bit remote; restaurant is a bit spendy and closed Mondays; no lunch dining available. 💲 *Rooms from: $179* ✉ *26222 Hwy. 149* ☎ *719/658–2423* 🌐 *www.antlerslodge.com* ⏲ *Closed Oct.–Apr.* 🛏 *24 rooms* 🍽 *No meals.*

The Creede Hotel and Restaurant
$$ | **B&B/INN** | A relic of silver-mining days, this charming 1890s structure with a street-front balcony has been fully restored. **Pros:** in-town location; full breakfast; historic property with comfortable rooms. **Cons:** town can be noisy at night; closed in winter; one room's bathroom is at the end of the hall. *Rooms from: $145* ✉ *120 N. Main St.* ☎ *719/658–2608* 🌐 *www.thecreedehotel.com* *Closed Oct.–Mar.* *4 rooms* *Free Breakfast.*

Telluride

66 miles south of Montrose via U.S. 550 and Hwy. 62; 111 miles north of Durango via U.S. 160 and Rtes. 184 and 145.

Tucked away between the azure sky and the gunmetal mountains is Telluride, the colorful mining town–turned–ski resort famous for its celebrity visitors (Oprah Winfrey, Tom Cruise, and Oliver Stone spend time here).

Telluride's first mines were established in the 1870s, and by the early 1890s the town was booming. The allure of the place was such that Butch Cassidy robbed his first bank here in 1889. These days the savage but beautiful San Juan range attracts mountain people of a different sort—skiers, snowboarders, mountain bikers, and four-wheelers—who attack any incline, up or down, with abandon.

GETTING HERE AND AROUND

Although Telluride and the ski resort town of Mountain Village are two distinct areas, you can travel between them via a 2½-mile, over-the-mountain gondola ride, arguably one of the most beautiful commutes in Colorado. The gondola makes a car unnecessary, as both the village and the town are ski- and pedestrian-friendly.

The free Galloping Goose shuttle loops around Telluride every 10 minutes in winter, 20 minutes in summer, and less often in the off-season. The Dial-a-Ride shuttle, also free, serves the Mountain Village area during high season. Telluride Express, a private taxi company, serves Telluride Regional Airport and the rest of the surrounding area, including other regional airports.

At about 15 blocks long and 6 blocks wide, Telluride is easy to cover on foot. And interesting, too—it's made up of one pastel Victorian residence or frontier trading post after another. It's hard to believe that the lovingly restored shops and restaurants once housed gaming parlors and saloons known for the quality of their "waitressing." That party-hearty spirit lives on, evidenced by numerous annual summer celebrations.

TRANSPORTATION CONTACTS Dial-a-Ride. ✉ *Telluride Ski Resort* ☎ *970/728–8888.* **Galloping Goose.** ☎ *970/728–5700.* **Telluride Express.** ☎ *970/728–6000, 888/212–8294* 🌐 *www.tellurideexpress.com.*

WHEN TO GO

Telluride has two short off-seasons, when most restaurants and many lodgings take a breather. The town closes from late October until ski season gets going in late November. Many people also flee town during "mud season," leaving after the ski area shuts down in early April and returning in mid- to late May. But with the growing popularity of Mountainfilm, a film festival held over Memorial Day weekend, more places are staying open. Off-season rates offer you a chance to enjoy the town's charm for less. However, when the summer festivals are in full swing, prices skyrocket and rooms book up fast. The biggies are the Telluride Bluegrass Festival in June, the Telluride Jazz Festival in early August, the Telluride Film Festival over Labor Day weekend, and the Telluride Blues and Brews Festival in mid-September. Whenever you decide to go, you should check for upcoming events at least three months in advance.

A drive on the spectacular San Juan Skyway takes you past several mountains.

FESTIVALS

Highly regarded wine and film festivals alternate with musical performances celebrating everything from bluegrass to jazz to chamber music.

Telluride Bluegrass Festival

FESTIVALS | The Telluride Bluegrass Festival in June has gone far beyond its bluegrass roots and is now one of the country's premier acoustic folk–rock gatherings. ✉ *Telluride* ☎ *800/624–2422* 🌐 *www.bluegrass.com/telluride*.

★ Telluride Film Festival

FESTIVALS | Held each year over Labor Day, the Telluride Film Festival is up there with Sundance as one of the world's leading showcases for foreign and domestic films. ✉ *Telluride* ☎ *510/665–9494* 🌐 *www.telluridefilmfestival.org*.

ESSENTIALS

VISITOR INFORMATION Telluride Ski Resort. ✉ *565 Mountain Village Blvd.* ☎ *970/728–6900, 800/778–8581* 🌐 *www.tellurideskiresort.com.* **Telluride Visitors Center.** ✉ *236 W. Colorado Ave.* ☎ *970/728–3041, 800/525–3455* 🌐 *www.visittelluride.com.*

Sights

★ San Juan Skyway

SCENIC DRIVE | One of the country's most stupendously scenic drives, the 236-mile San Juan Skyway weaves through an impressive series of Fourteeners (peaks reaching more than 14,000 feet). From Telluride, it heads north on Route 145 to Placerville, where it turns east on Highway 62. On U.S. 550 it continues south to historic Ouray and over Red Mountain Pass to Silverton and then on to Durango, Mancos, and Cortez via U.S. 160. From Cortez, Route 145 heads north, passing through Rico and over lovely Lizard Head Pass before heading back into Telluride. In late September and early October, this route has some of the state's most spectacular aspen viewing. ✉ *Telluride.*

Telluride Bluegrass Festival

Bluegrass may have evolved from country's "Appalachian mountain music," but Telluride's Bluegrass Festival has added a distinctive Rocky Mountain note to the mix.

Since its inception in 1973, the festival has featured traditional bluegrass bands from across the nation, but when contemporary Colorado bands started adding the quintessential bluegrass instruments—mandolin, fiddle, guitar, upright bass, and banjo—to their lineups, their version of the "high lonesome sound" garnered national attention. It forced bluegrass to undergo several transformations, sometimes right before the Telluride audience's eyes, as the crowd's enthusiasm prompted more and more on-stage experimentation.

As the festival gained in popularity, it brought more bluegrass artists to Colorado, and crossover between bluegrass and other musical styles became more common. The festival earned the moniker "Woodstock of the West." Colorado bands such as String Cheese Incident, Leftover Salmon, and Yonder Mountain String Band performed regularly at the event, appealing to a younger audience and encouraging more experimentation.

Now the Telluride Bluegrass Festival often draws such popular acts as Emmylou Harris, Alison Krauss, Bonnie Raitt, Robert Plant, Janelle Monae, Mumford & Sons, Brandi Carlile, and Counting Crows—not exactly bluegrass purists. It has also boosted the popularity of other bluegrass gatherings around the state, including a sister festival held each July at Planet Bluegrass Ranch in Lyons, Colorado, a town of about 1,600 that has become a bluegrass artists' colony.

★ Telluride Historical Museum

MUSEUM | Housed in the 1896 Miner's Hospital, the Telluride Historical Museum hosts exhibits on the town's past, including work in the nearby mines, techniques used by local doctors, and an 860-year-old Native American blanket. It is one of only six Smithsonian-affiliated museums in Colorado. ✉ *201 W. Gregory Ave.* ☎ *970/728–3344* 🌐 *www.telluride-museum.org* 🎫 *$7.*

Restaurants

★ Allred's

$$$$ | **MODERN AMERICAN** | Unless you're planning some serious hiking, the town-to-mountain gondola is the only way to reach this high-end, sky-high eatery with a stone-walled dining room and panoramic windows. Locally inspired fare such as elk, bison, and lamb feature prominently on the menu. **Known for:** après-ski drinks and apps; excellent meats and fish; incredible views that make the high prices worth it. 💲 *Average main: $42* ✉ *Top of St. Sophia gondola station* ☎ *970/728–7474* 🌐 *www.allredsrestaurant.com* 🕒 *No lunch.*

Baked in Telluride

$ | **CAFÉ** | This Telluride institution turns out heavenly bagels, sandwiches made with baked-in-house bread, pizzas, hearty soups, and house-made pastas (try the Alfredo), as well as huge salads. Order your meal to go or grab a seat at one of the communal-style tables, where you can enjoy displays from a local art school. **Known for:** front porch with views; delicious breakfasts; reasonable prices. 💲 *Average main: $11* ✉ *127 S. Fir St.* ☎ *970/728–4775* 🌐 *bakedintel.com.*

Brown Dog Pizza

$ | **PIZZA** | This local hangout serves a mean pizza in a pub-style atmosphere, and is one of the few places in town that will feed your family for less than the cost of a lift ticket. Brown Dog specializes in Detroit-style square pizza (an international award winner), but it also offers gluten-free, classic American, and Roman-style pies. **Known for:** Detroit-style pizza; always-hopping atmosphere; gluten-free menu. *Average main: $13* *110 E. Colorado Ave.* *970/728–8046* *www.browndogpizza.com.*

The Butcher & The Baker

$$ | **CAFÉ** | Fresh farm-to-table fare and a modern-farmhouse feel define The Butcher & The Baker, a bustling café on the town's main strip where locals gather. The delectable baked goods and sandwiches, scrumptious salads, and house-made desserts do not disappoint. **Known for:** cocktail and espresso bar; pay-by-the-scoop deli salads; house-made soups. *Average main: $18* *201 E. Colorado Ave.* *970/728–2899* *www.butcherandbakercafe.com* *No dinner Sun.*

Cosmopolitan

$$$$ | **CONTEMPORARY** | The trendy Cosmopolitan lures guests with starters like sushi rolls and lobster corn dogs and keeps them here for some of Telluride's finest dining. Both surf and turf are expertly prepared and presented, and the wine selection is widely acclaimed. **Known for:** fresh fish dishes; excellent wines by the glass; lively atmosphere. *Average main: $60* *Hotel Columbia, 301 Gus's Way* *970/728–1292* *www.cosmotelluride.com* *No lunch. Closed Apr. and May.*

★ La Marmotte

$$$$ | **CONTEMPORARY** | It may be housed in one of Telluride's oldest buildings, but La Marmotte provides one of the city's most modern dining experiences, with menu offerings that expertly intertwine French and local influences. The candlelight-and-white-tablecloth atmosphere and simple, contemporary decor is, like the cuisine, sophisticated without being snooty. **Known for:** divine outdoor-patio seating; inspired wine list; romantic ambience. *Average main: $35* *150 W. San Juan Ave.* *970/728–6232* *www.lamarmotte.com* *No lunch.*

New Sheridan Chop House

$$$$ | **STEAKHOUSE** | This upscale steak house is arguably Telluride's best. Here you can choose your meat (sirloin, filet mignon, and succulent bison rib eye are among the choices), then your topping (think caramelized onions, blue cheese, or glazed wild mushrooms), and then your sauce (anything from béarnaise to chimichurri). **Known for:** high-quality beef and game; hearty daily brunch options; popular wine bar. *Average main: $100* *New Sheridan Hotel, 231 W. Colorado Ave.* *970/728–9100* *www.newsheridan.com* *Closed mid-Apr.–mid-May and mid-Oct.–late Nov.*

Oak, the New Fat Alley

$$ | **SOUTHERN** | Located within the Camel's Garden Hotel at Chair 8, Oak serves mouthwatering barbecue and Southern fare. Fill up on the likes of gumbo or a Carolina-smoked pulled pork shoulder sandwich, along with creative salads, veggie dishes, and Southern sides like fried okra and red beans and rice **Known for:** hopping patio next to gondola lift; bourbon, beer, and homemade sweet tea; lively atmosphere. *Average main: $15* *Camel's Garden Hotel, 250 San Juan Ave.* *970/728–3985* *www.oakstelluride.com* *Closed late Apr.*

221 South Oak

$$$$ | **EUROPEAN** | Housed in a beautifully restored Victorian, this classy bistro entices you to linger with its colorful artwork, two lovely garden patios, and scrumptious meals. The dinner menu changes frequently but always includes dishes made with locally sourced fish (like Rocky Mountain trout or Colorado striped bass) and meat (elk, lamb, or bison).

Known for: Sunday brunch in summer; full vegetarian menu; seasonal live music. *Average main: $70* *221 S. Oak St.* *970/728–9507* *www.221southoak.com* *Closed mid-Apr.–May and mid-Oct.–mid-Dec. No lunch.*

Hotels

Camel's Garden
$$$ | **HOTEL** | An ultramodern lodge that's all sharp lines, sleek surfaces, and colorful, contemporary art is just steps from the gondola and features huge rooms and suites. **Pros:** ski-in, ski-out location; full-service Aveda day spa; creek-side views. **Cons:** breakfast is generic; no amenities for kids; parking is $15 per day. *Rooms from: $295* *250 W. San Juan Ave.* *970/728–9300, 888/772–2635* *www.camelsgarden.com* *35 rooms* *Free Breakfast.*

Hotel Columbia Telluride
$$$$ | **HOTEL** | Conveniently located at the base of the gondola, this hotel has a crisp and contemporary vibe. **Pros:** spacious rooms with heated bathroom floors; steps from gondola; stunning views. **Cons:** expensive; some rooms can be noisy; valet parking is $35 per day. *Rooms from: $400* *301 W. San Juan Ave.* *970/728–0660, 855/318–7604* *www.hotelcolumbiatelluride.com* *21 rooms* *Free Breakfast.*

The Hotel Telluride
$$$ | **HOTEL** | With luxurious rooms, tasteful Western-style decor, and dramatic views from private patios or balconies, the Hotel Telluride is an ideal place to immerse yourself in mountain culture. **Pros:** free shuttle to the gondola; lots of amenities, including complimentary bikes; great views. **Cons:** $20 parking fee; a few blocks from downtown; restaurant not open for lunch. *Rooms from: $239* *199 N. Cornet St.* *970/369–1188* *www.thehoteltelluride.com* *59 rooms* *No meals.*

Telluride Lodging Alternatives

Telluride Rentals by Exceptional Stays. This agency books many of the town's and mountain's most luxurious properties, including private homes and condos. *209 E. Colorado Ave., Suite A* *800/970–7541, 970/519–2334* *www.telluriderentals.com.*

Telluride Resort Reservations. This central reservations system handles most of the properties at Telluride Mountain Village and several more in town. *Telluride* *970/728–7350, 800/778–8581* *www.tellurideskiresort.com.*

Inn at Lost Creek
$$ | **HOTEL** | A grand stone-and-wood structure, this luxury ski-in ski-out hotel in the Mountain Village resembles an alpine lodge with contemporary furnishings. **Pros:** tasty breakfast; upscale but friendly atmosphere; rooftop hot tubs. **Cons:** some bathrooms on the small side; $20 nightly fee for parking; hot tubs require reservations. *Rooms from: $200* *119 Lost Creek La., Mountain Village* *970/728–5678, 888/601–5678* *www.innatlostcreek.com* *Closed mid-Apr.–mid-May* *32 rooms* *Free Breakfast.*

★ Lumière with Inspirato
$$$$ | **HOTEL** | "Lumière" means "light" in French, and this luxury lodge lives up to its name—suites open onto dramatic mountain views, and the decor brings the outside in with a mountain-modern design. **Pros:** ski-in, ski-out location at the base of Lift 4 in Mountain Village; luxurious rooms with spacious bathrooms; warm-soak and cold plunge pools. **Cons:** very expensive; minimum stay during holidays; layout can be confusing. *Rooms from: $1750* *118 Lost Creek La.* *970/369–0400* *www.*

970/369–0400 www.lumierewithinspirato.com Closed Apr., May, Oct., and Nov. 18 rooms Free Breakfast.

Madeline Hotel and Residences
$$$$ | **HOTEL** | This spot blends the drama of a grand European hotel with the warmth of a mountain chalet. **Pros:** air-conditioning (rare for this region); ample amenities; incredible views from pool deck. **Cons:** $40 parking fee; no meals included; additional resort fee. *Rooms from: $550 568 Mountain Village Blvd. 970/369–0880 www.aubergeresorts.com/madeline Closed mid-Oct.–mid-May 137 rooms No meals.*

New Sheridan Hotel
$$$$ | **HOTEL** | Contemporary furnishings and historic black-and-white photos adorn this beautifully restored century-old landmark on Telluride's main drag. **Pros:** rooftop bar has great views; secure ski storage with boot warmers; guests receive a discount on breakfast and lunch and a permit for street parking. **Cons:** no hot tub; noise from the bar can drift upstairs at night; no fridge or microwave in rooms. *Rooms from: $350 231 W. Colorado Ave. 970/728–4351, 800/200–1891 www.newsheridan.com Closed mid-Apr.–mid-May and mid-Oct.–mid-Nov. 26 rooms No meals.*

Nightlife

Last Dollar Saloon
BARS/PUBS | A favorite après-ski destination, the Last Dollar (locals know it as "The Buck") has lots of beers, great margaritas, and a rooftop bar with phenomenal views. *100 E. Colorado Ave. 970/728–4800 www.lastdollarsaloon.com.*

New Sheridan Historic Bar
BARS/PUBS | The century-plus-old bar at the New Sheridan Hotel is a favorite hangout for skiers returning from the slopes and, in summer, for everybody else. There's live music weekly. *New Sheridan Hotel, 231 W. Colorado Ave. 970/728–9100 www.newsheridan.com.*

SideWork Speakeasy
BARS/PUBS | Classy cocktails, champagne, wine, and gourmet small and large plates in a refined mid-century American–style lounge make SideWork an ideal place for a nightcap. *225 S. Pine St. 970/728–5618 www.sideworkspeakeasy.com.*

There
BARS/PUBS | Tucked off the main strip, this tiny bar serves eclectic small plates, family-style entrées to share, and killer cocktails in a speakeasy atmosphere (complete with a blacklist drink menu delivered in a book). It's packed from 4:30 until 11:30 pm, so reserve a table in advance online. *627 W. Pacific Ave. 970/728–1213 www.experiencethere.com.*

Performing Arts

Sheridan Opera House
MUSIC | Miners built the opera house in 1913 as a venue primarily for vaudeville acts. Today the landmark opera house presents a variety of shows year-round, including live theater, concerts, and comedy acts. Over the years it has hosted performances by such popular artists as Jackson Browne, Jimmy Buffett, and Jewel. *110 N. Oak St. 970/728–6363 www.sheridanoperahouse.com.*

Telluride Theatre
THEATER | This semiprofessional group performs a variety of shows year-round in various venues. Productions include popular musicals, burlesque dancers, Shakespeare-in-the-park performances, and original, experimental shows. *134 E. Colorado Ave. 970/708–7629 www.telluridetheatre.org.*

Telluride was once famous for its challenging ski runs, but now welcomes skiers of all levels.

Shopping

BOOKS

Between the Covers Bookstore

BOOKS/STATIONERY | This locally owned bookstore is perfect for browsing through the latest releases while sipping a foam-capped cappuccino from the coffee bar at the back of the shop. You'll also find a good selection of field guides and books on local history. ✉ *224 W. Colorado Ave.* ☎ *970/728–4504* 🌐 *www.between-the-covers.com.*

CLOTHING

Telluride Trappings & Toggery

CLOTHING | Check The Toggery—the town's longest-standing retail store—for stylish Telluride and Colorado souvenir tees and sweatshirts. You'll also find a large selection of men's, women's, and children's clothing and shoes. ✉ *109 E. Colorado Ave.* ☎ *970/728–3338* 🌐 *www.thetellurídetoggery.com.*

Activities

DOWNHILL SKIING AND SNOWBOARDING

★ Telluride Ski Resort

SKIING/SNOWBOARDING | Dubbed "the most beautiful place you'll ever ski," Telluride Ski Resort once was known as an experts-only ski area. Indeed, the north-facing trails are impressively steep and long, and the moguls can be massive. Chairlift 9 services primarily expert terrain, including the famed Spiral Stairs and the Plunge, while Gold Hill, Bald Mountain, Black Iron Bowl, and Palmyra Peak provide challenging chutes and other double-diamond runs, as well as hiking options for expert skiers.

But then there is the other side—literally—of the ski area, the gently sloping valley called the Gorrono Basin, with long groomed runs excellent for intermediates and beginners. On the ridge that wraps around the ski area's core is the aptly named See Forever, a long cruiser that starts at 12,570 feet and delivers views over the San Juan Mountains and into Utah's La Sal mountain range. The best areas for beginners are the Meadows, off Lift 1, and Galloping Goose, a long winding trail off Lift 12 or 10. Near Gorrono Basin, off Lift 4 (the ski area's main artery), is another section that includes super-steep, double-diamond tree runs on one side and glorious cruisers on the other.

Midmountain, Lift 5 accesses a wealth of intermediate runs. From there, slide through a Western-style gate and you come to Prospect Bowl, a 733-acre area with a network of runs cut around islands of trees. Prospect Express (Lift 12) appeases not only experts—who can navigate double-diamond chutes, cliff bands, and open glades—but also beginners and intermediates, who can ski some of the highest green and blue terrain in North America.

Telluride also has three terrain parks for skiers and snowboarders of all levels. **Facilities:** 127 trails; 2,000 acres; 4,425-foot vertical drop; 16 lifts. ✉ *565 Mountain Village Blvd.* ☎ *800/778–8581* 🌐 *www.tellurideskiresort.com* 🎫 *Lift ticket $140.*

LESSONS AND PROGRAMS

Telluride Ski & Snowboard School

SKIING/SNOWBOARDING | At this well-regarded school, adult group lessons start at $160. Lessons are available for alpine and telemark skiers as well as snowboarders. Children's programs are $220 per day and include a lift ticket, lesson, and lunch. The school also offers Women's Week programs, which include three or five days of skills-building classes with female instructors. ✉ *565 Mountain Village Blvd.* ☎ *970/728–7540* 🌐 *www.tellurideskiresort.com.*

RENTALS

Bootdoctors

SKIING/SNOWBOARDING | Despite its name, Bootdoctors services go way beyond boots, renting all manner of skis, boots, and snowboards, along with backcountry gear and snowshoes. It also offers ski tuning, boot fitting, and repairs. It has two sister locations: one in Mountain Village and another on the city's main street that also serves as a year-round bike and paddleboard shop. ✉ *236 S. Oak St.* ☎ *970/728–4581* 🌐 *www.bootdoctors.com.*

Telluride Sports

SKIING/SNOWBOARDING | All manner of ski and snowboard rentals are available from the ubiquitous Telluride Sports, with 10 locations in Telluride and Mountain Village. The shop will deliver everything to your hotel for no extra charge via 🌐 *www.rentskis.com.* The Camel's Garden location has a ski valet. ✉ *150 W. Colorado Ave.* ☎ *970/728–4477* 🌐 *www.telluridesports.com.*

FOUR-WHEELING

For a short but very sweet four-wheel-drive trip, start at the east end of Colorado Avenue, where a 1¾-mile road from the old Pandora Mill leads to spectacular Bridal Veil Falls, which, at 365 feet, tumbles lavishly from the top of the box canyon. At the northern end of town, off of Oak Street, you'll find Tomboy Road, also known as Imogene Pass Road, which leads to one of the country's most interesting mining districts. The road has fabulous views of Bridal Veil Falls and Ingram Falls. After about 7 miles, it crests over 13,114-foot-high Imogene Pass, the highest pass road in the San Juans. If you continue down the other side, you end up in Yankee Boy Basin, near Ouray.

GOLF

Telluride Ski & Golf Club

GOLF | The soul-stirring, 360-degree mountain views at Telluride Golf Club may just elevate your game. Ease into play on the front nine, which includes downhill holes and a few par 3s. On the back nine, the holes lengthen, stretch uphill, and bend around doglegs for an invigorating challenge. Guests can also take advantage of a greatly expanded practice facility. The club is designated an Audubon

Cooperative Sanctuary for its wildlife-habitat protection and water and biodiversity conservation efforts. Green fees include cart rental. ✉ *The Peaks Resort & Spa, 136 Country Club Dr., Mountain Village* ☎ *970/728–2606* 🌐 *www.tellurideski-andgolfclub.com* 🎫 *$210* 🏌 *18 holes, 6574 yards, par 70.*

HIKING

The peaks of the rugged San Juan Mountains around Telluride require some scrambling, occasionally bordering on real climbing, to get to the top. A local favorite is Wilson Peak, which is one of the easier Fourteeners to climb if you take the Navajo Lake Approach. July and August are the most popular months on this 9½-mile round-trip hike.

Bear Creek Falls

HIKING/WALKING | An immensely popular trail leads to Bear Creek Falls, 2½ miles from the trailhead. It's a steady climb, but the destination is worth it. The route is also used by mountain bikers. ✉ *Telluride* ✣ *Trailhead at end of S. Pine St.*

Jud Wiebe Trail

HIKING/WALKING | This 3-mile loop is an excellent hike that is generally passable from spring until late fall. The first segment of the trail is fairly steep, so this is not the best choice for novices. It links with the Sneffels Highline Trail, a 13-mile loop that leads through wildflower-covered meadows. ✉ *Telluride* ✣ *Trailhead at north end of Aspen St.*

HORSEBACK RIDING

Telluride Horseback Adventures

HORSEBACK RIDING | Roudy Roudebush is a cowboy straight out of central casting (he starred in a television commercial and in Disney's 2004 film *America's Heart and Soul*). His company, Telluride Horseback Adventures, offers ultrascenic trail rides departing from his ranch in Norwood, 33 miles northwest of Telluride. You can also book sleigh rides in the winter. ✉ *4019 County Rd. 43ZS* ☎ *970/728–9611* 🌐 *www.ridewithroudy.com.*

MOUNTAIN BIKING

San Juan Hut System

BICYCLING | Having a fully equipped hut waiting at the end of a tough day of riding makes the San Juan Hut System a backcountry biker's dream come true. The company, which started out as a hut-to-hut service for backcountry skiers, operates a 190-mile route from Telluride to Moab, Utah, suitable for novice and intermediate riders. Trips run from June to October and last five or seven days, covering alpine meadows, desert slick rock, canyon country, and the Porcupine Rim Trail. Along the way, the six one-room huts are supplied with bunks, sleeping bags, heating and cooking stoves, food, and water. ✉ *618 N. Cora St., Ridgway* ☎ *970/626–3033* 🌐 *www.sanjuanhuts.com* 🎫 *From $795 per person.*

MULTI-TOUR OPERATORS

Telluride Outside

FISHING | Telluride's longest-running outfitter, this service offers a wealth of ways to experience the outdoors. Options include rafting trips, four-wheel-drive tours, paddleboarding tours, snowmobile trips, and guided fly-fishing outings from its store, the Telluride Angler. You can also buy fly-fishing gear here. ✉ *121 W. Colorado Ave.* ☎ *970/728–3895, 800/831–6230* 🌐 *www.tellurideoutside.com.*

SPAS

The Peaks Resort & Spa

SPA/BEAUTY | Plan for a full-day retreat at The Peaks, which at 42,000 feet is Colorado's largest spa. Its sheer size guarantees there is plenty to keep you occupied: a half-Olympic-size pool, indoor/outdoor pool with a two-story waterslide, full fitness center, a generous lineup of exercise classes, steam rooms, large Roman soaking tubs, saunas, an oxygen bar, and large, modern relaxation lounges, for a start. With 32 treatment rooms stretched down a long corridor, The Peaks looks a bit clinical, but your herbal massage with ginger, CBD massage, or other herbal remedy to combat stress will rub that feeling away. ✉ *136 Country Club*

Dr. ☎ *970/728–2590* 🌐 *www.thepeaksresort.com/spa-and-wellness* ☞ *$180 60-min massage. Hair salon, hot tubs (indoor and outdoor), oxygen inhalation, pools (indoor and outdoor), nail salon, saunas, steam rooms. Gym: cardiovascular machines, free weights, weight-training machines. Services: Body scrubs and wraps, facials, massage, hypnotherapy, nutrition counseling. Classes and programs: Conditioning and stretching, movement classes, personal training, Pilates, spinning (Peloton bikes), yoga.*

TRACK SKIING

Telluride Nordic Center

SKIING/SNOWBOARDING | Operated by the Telluride Nordic Association, the center offers cross-country ski lessons and a wealth of trail information. It also rents ski equipment, ice skates, snowshoes, and sleds for adults and children. ✉ *500 E. Colorado Ave.* ☎ *970/728–1144* 🌐 *www.telluridenordic.com* 🎫 *Group lessons start at $65 per person.*

TopAten Snowshoe and Nordic Area

SKIING/SNOWBOARDING | There are 6 miles of rolling trails groomed for cross-country skiing and snowshoeing, as well as a warming teepee, a picnic deck, and restroom facilities. To access TopAten, you'll need to buy a "foot passenger" lift ticket for $25. ✉ *Telluride Ski Resort* ✣ *Located near the unloading area for Chair 10* ☎ *970/728–7517* 🌐 *www.tellurideskiresort.com.*

Ridgway

40 miles from Telluride; 26 miles south of Montrose.

The 19th-century railroad town of Ridgway has been the setting for some classic Westerns, including *True Grit* (the original John Wayne version) and *How the West Was Won.* Though you'd never know it from the rustic town center, the area is also home to many swank ranches, including one belonging to fashion designer Ralph Lauren. It is also part of the Colorado Creative Corridor, a road-trip route that connects five mountain towns that are all "certified creative districts."

GETTING HERE AND AROUND

U.S. 550 runs along the eastern side of town, heading north to Montrose and south to Ouray. Highway 62 heads right through the middle of town on its way to Telluride. The rest of the main part of town encompasses all of seven blocks, making side travel a breeze.

Restaurants

Taco del Gnar

$ | **MEXICAN FUSION** | Inventive tacos, many with an Asian flavor profile, anchor the menu at this casual eatery with edgy, tattoo-parlor-style decor. Gnar's famous side of queso blanco tater tots pairs nicely with the tacos. **Known for:** unique, foodie-quality tacos; queso blanco tater tots; excellent margaritas. $ *Average main: $10* ✉ *630 Sherman St.* ☎ *970/626–9715* 🌐 *www.gnarlytacos.com* ⏲ *Closed Sun. and Mon.*

Hotels

Chipeta Solar Springs Resort & Spa

$$ | **HOTEL** | Enjoy the stunning views from the decks of the dramatic Southwestern-style adobe rooms and suites, which have rough-hewn log beds and hand-painted Mexican tiles. **Pros:** solar-heated swimming and soaking pools; nice on-site restaurant; ideal for outdoor activities. **Cons:** fills up on weekends; limited parking; not near ski resorts. $ *Rooms from: $175* ✉ *304 S. Lena St.* ☎ *970/626–3737, 800/633–5868* 🌐 *www.chipeta.com* 🛏 *29 rooms* 🍽 *No meals.*

BACKCOUNTRY SKIING

San Juan Hut System

SKIING/SNOWBOARDING | Among the better backcountry skiing routes is the San Juan Hut System. The route starts about 15 miles south of Ridgway in Ouray and leads toward Telluride along the Sneffels Range. The five huts in the system are about 7 miles apart, and are well equipped with bunks, wood-burning stoves, propane lights, and cooking stoves and utensils. Previous backcountry experience is highly recommended, and staff members can steer guests to terrain that best fits their backcountry knowledge and skill levels. Reservations are recommended at least two weeks in advance. ✉ *618 N. Cora St.* ☎ *970/626–3033.*

FISHING

Ridgway State Park

WATER SPORTS | At this peaceful state park, 4 miles north of Ridgway, the 5-mile-long reservoir is stocked with plenty of rainbow trout, as well as the larger and tougher brown trout. Anglers also pull up kokanee salmon and yellow perch. There's a boat ramp, swimming beach, picnic areas, playgrounds, and a campground. ✉ *28555 U.S. 550* ☎ *970/626–5822* 🌐 *www.cpw.state.co.us* 🎫 *$10 per vehicle.*

GOLF

Divide Ranch and Club

GOLF | This semiprivate 18-hole, Byron Coker–designed course twists through a maze of high-mesa forest, complete with mountain views and wildlife. It's long and often demanding, but at 8,000 feet your drives might go a little farther and higher than they do at sea level. ✉ *151 Divide Ranch Cir.* ☎ *970/626–5284* 🌐 *www.divideranchandclub.com* 🎫 *$65 weekdays, $75 weekends* ⛳ *18 holes, 7039 yards, par 72* ⏲ *Closed Mon. and mid-Oct.–mid-May.*

Ouray

10 miles south of Ridgway; 23 miles north of Silverton via U.S. 550.

The town of Ouray (pronounced *you-ray*) is nestled in a narrow, steep-walled canyon in the shadow of the San Juan Mountains. It was named for the great Southern Ute chief Ouray, labeled a visionary by the U.S. Army and branded a traitor by his people because he attempted to assimilate the Utes into white society. The former mining town is only a few blocks wide, but is filled with lavish old hotels, commercial buildings, and residences. More than 25 classic edifices are included in the walking-tour brochure issued by the Ouray County Historical Society and available at the town visitor center. Among the points of interest are the grandiose Wright's Opera House and the Western Hotel. The town's ultimate glory lies in its surroundings, and it has become an increasingly popular destination for climbers (both the mountain and ice varieties), mountain-bike fanatics, and hikers.

GETTING HERE AND AROUND

U.S. 550 runs straight through town and turns into Main Street for the six blocks from 3rd Avenue to 9th Avenue. The Ouray Visitors Center and the Hot Springs Park are on the north end of town, and the historic landmark hotel, the Beaumont, is smack in the middle of town between 5th and 6th Avenues. The Uncompahgre River runs parallel to Main Street just a couple of blocks west of town, and Box Cañon Park is just southwest of Main Street, at the confluence of Canyon Creek and the Uncompahgre River.

ESSENTIALS

VISITOR INFORMATION Ouray Visitors Center. ✉ *1230 Main St.* ☎ *970/325–4746, 800/228–1876* 🌐 *www.ouraycolorado.com.*

Sights

Bachelor-Syracuse Mine Tour
MINE | FAMILY | On this hour-long tour, visitors trek 1,500 feet into one of the region's great silver mines. Tour guides are actual miners and they explain various mining techniques and point out remaining silver veins and other mineral deposits. Tours depart every hour, and light jackets are wise year-round, as it's chilly in the mine. Gold-panning lessons in the adjacent stream are included in the tour price. **TIP→ On summer weekends, come early for a tasty, inexpensive breakfast.** *1222 County Rd. 14* *970/325–0220* *www.bachelorsyracusemine.com* *$16* *Closed Nov.–late May.*

Box Cañon Falls
BODY OF WATER | One particularly gorgeous jaunt is to Box Cañon Falls, where the turbulent waters of Clear Creek thunder 285 feet down a narrow gorge. A steel suspension bridge and well-marked trails afford breathtaking views. Birders flock to the park to see the rare black swift and other species, and a visitor center has interpretive displays. *Ouray* *West end of 3rd Ave. off U.S. 550* *970/325–7080* *www.ouraycolorado.com* *$5* *Closed Nov.–Apr.* *No pets allowed.*

Canyoning Colorado
CLIMBING/MOUNTAINEERING | For adventurous souls, the best way to explore the beautiful terrain around Ouray may be through the truly local sport of canyoning, which involves rappelling down waterfall-strewn gorges, swimming across pools of water, and an occasional jump off or slide down a cliff face. The minimum age is 10. *920 Main St.* *970/318–6492* *www.canyoningcolorado.com* *From $120.*

★ **Million Dollar Highway**
SCENIC DRIVE | Ouray is also the northern end of the Million Dollar Highway, the awesome stretch of U.S. 550 that climbs over Red Mountain Pass (arguably the most spectacular part of the 236-mile San Juan Skyway). As it ascends steeply from Ouray, the road clings to the cliffs hanging over the Uncompahgre River. Guardrails are few, hairpin turns are many, and behemoth RVs seem to take more than their share of road. This priceless road is kept open all winter by heroic plow crews. *Ouray.*

Ouray County Museum
MUSEUM | This small but surprisingly stocked museum housed in an 1887 hospital highlights the history of mining, ranching, and railroading in the San Juan Mountains. The basement features a life-size model mine tunnel, as well as an impressive collection of locally found gems and minerals. Other exhibits include Native American artifacts and depictions of domestic and commercial life in the late 1800s. *420 6th Ave.* *970/325–4576* *www.ouraycountyhistoricalsociety.org* *$7* *Closed mid-Nov.–mid-Apr., and Sun.–Wed. mid-Apr.–mid-May and Oct.–mid.-Nov.*

Ouray Hot Springs Pool
HOT SPRINGS | FAMILY | The massive, renovated Ouray Hot Springs Pool is brimming with a million gallons of naturally heated mineral water, kept between 78°F and 106°F. Kids love the two large waterslides, bouldering wall, volleyball net, and the inflatable obstacle course, while grown-ups can bask in peace in the adults-only pool. *1220 Main St.* *970/325–7073* *www.ourayhotsprings.com* *$18.*

The Wiesbaden Hot Springs Spa & Lodgings
HOT SPRINGS | At the source of several of Ouray's famed springs, this European-style spa and inn features rock-hewn vapor caves with a steamy soaking pool. In addition, there's a small outdoor pool, fed by continuously flowing hot-spring water. Massages and other treatments are offered at the spa. This is a strictly no-smoking facility, and no children under five are allowed in the caves. *625 5th St.* *970/325–4347* *www.wiesbadenhotsprings.com* *$20 for 3 hrs* *No pets allowed.*

Restaurants

Ouray Brewery
$$ | **AMERICAN** | This three-level brew-pub boasts an amazing rooftop patio, with great views of the surrounding canyon as well as the goings-on below on Main Street. The beers include four standards plus a few seasonal offerings while the food is typical pub fare, with a sprinkling of more interesting entrées like smoked beet Reuben sandwiches. **Known for:** acclaimed craft beers; swings for bar stools; always lively atmosphere. *Average main: $17 607 Main St. 970/325–7388 www.ouraybrewery.com.*

The Outlaw Restaurant
$$$ | **STEAKHOUSE** | Live ragtime piano music welcomes you most nights to this saloon-style eatery, specializing in steak, seafood, and pasta. Portions are generous and loaded with extras (each entrée comes with rice or potato, vegetables, and bread). **Known for:** great prime rib; homemade salad dressings; John Wayne's hat, which he left here in 1968. *Average main: $30 610 Main St. 970/325–4366 www.outlawrestaurant.com.*

Red Mountain Brewing
$$ | **AMERICAN** | Upscale versions of tavern comfort food—burgers, pork chops, gourmet grilled cheese, and the like—are served in an old-world–style pub, with wood and stone decor and arched doors. The house-brewed beers include red, wheat, pale, and cream ales. **Known for:** excellent ales; views from the patio; great starters like jumbo hot wings. *Average main: $20 400 Main St. 970/325–9858 www.redmountainbrewingouray.com.*

Hotels

Abram Inn & Suites
$ | **HOTEL** | This pleasantly renovated inn at the end of Main Street serves as a quiet but convenient base for area excursions. **Pros:** good value; free on-site parking; convenient but peaceful location. **Cons:** continental breakfast a bit lacking; no pool or hot tub; room decor a bit stale. *Rooms from: $99 407 Main St. 970/325–4589 www.abraminnandsuites.com 15 rooms Free Breakfast.*

★ **Beaumont Hotel and Spa**
$$ | **HOTEL** | No detail has been overlooked at this beautifully restored 1886 hotel, a gold-rush-era landmark that has hosted such VIPs as Theodore Roosevelt and Oprah Winfrey. **Pros:** sound-paneled rooms mean a quiet stay; good value; in-house spa. **Cons:** hot tubs cost extra; no children under 16; decor might be a bit old-fashioned for some. *Rooms from: $199 505 Main St. 970/325–7000 www.beaumonthotel.com 13 rooms No meals.*

Black Bear Manor Bed & Breakfast
$$ | **B&B/INN** | Tucked away on a quiet side street, this tidy B&B has terrific views of the surrounding San Juan Mountains from its outdoor decks. **Pros:** welcoming hosts; plenty of privacy; generous amenities. **Cons:** no children under 16; not all rooms have fireplaces and jetted tubs; breakfast served on the late side (9 am). *Rooms from: $190 118 6th Ave. 970/325–4219 www.blackbearmanor.com 9 rooms Free Breakfast.*

Box Canyon Lodge & Hot Springs
$$$ | **HOTEL** | If bathing with the masses at the local hot springs is not your cup of tea, opt for a semiprivate plunge at this friendly lodge with a great location off the main drag and near the stream. **Pros:** proximity to hot springs; terrific mountain views; off-the-beaten-path feel. **Cons:** a few blocks off Main Street; no-frills

rooms; no free breakfast. *Rooms from: $219* ✉ *45 3rd Ave.* ☎ *970/325–4981* 🌐 *www.boxcanyonouray.com* *39 rooms* *No meals.*

China Clipper Inn

$$ | **B&B/INN** | Although it was built in the mid-1990s, this stately inn fits in perfectly with its Victorian neighbors, but unlike nearly every other lodging in town, it isn't filled with Victorian- or Western-style trappings—it's tastefully decorated with Asian antiques. **Pros:** beautiful property; small and romantic; charming front porch and patio with a hot tub. **Cons:** minimum stay on some holidays and weekends; can be noisy between rooms; children under 12 not allowed. *Rooms from: $160* ✉ *525 2nd St.* ☎ *970/325–0565* 🌐 *www.chinaclipperinn.com* *13 rooms* *Free Breakfast.*

Activities

FOUR-WHEELING

Off-roaders delight in the more than 500 miles of four-wheel-drive roads around Ouray. Popular routes include the Alpine Loop Scenic Byway to the Silverton and Lake City areas, and Imogene Pass to Telluride.

Switzerland of America Jeep Rentals and Tours

FOUR-WHEELING | If you have the skill and confidence but not the four-wheel-drive vehicle, you can rent one from Switzerland of America Jeep Rentals and Tours. The company also operates guided 4x4 tours in custom, open-air vehicles and can provide private Jeep Safaris upon request. ✉ *226 7th Ave.* ☎ *970/325–4484, 866/990–5337* 🌐 *www.soajeep.com* *Tours from $58 for 3 hrs; rentals start at $185 per day.*

Yankee Boy Basin

FOUR-WHEELING | About the first 7 miles of the road to Yankee Boy Basin are accessible by regular cars, but it takes a four-wheel drive to reach the heart of this awesome alpine landscape. After leaving Ouray, the route climbs west into a vast basin ringed with soaring summits and carpeted with lavish displays of wildflowers. At 17 miles round-trip, this is one of the region's premier day-trip destinations. ✉ *County Rd. 361.*

HIKING

Ouray Perimeter Trail

HIKING/WALKING | For a glimpse of many of Ouray's most famous features—including Cascade Falls, Baby Bathtubs, the Potato Patch (where miners once grew potatoes), the Ouray Ice Park, Box Cañon Falls, and Ouray's old water tunnel—take this 6-mile trek around the town's outskirts. The trail starts at the Ouray Visitors Center, which is at about 7,800 feet. It climbs steeply at the beginning, but mostly undulates through the forests surrounding Ouray. The trail currently ends at South Pinecrest Street, but it's a beautiful walk back to your starting point past the Victorian homes on Oak Street. ■ **TIP→ You can also pick a smaller section of the trail like Baby Bathtubs or Lower Cascade Falls for a short, family-friendly hike.** ✉ *Ouray Visitors Center, 1230 Main St.* ☎ *970/325–4746* 🌐 *www.ouraycolorado.com.*

Uncompahgre River Trail

HIKING/WALKING | This 2-mile loop follows the riverbank of the Uncompahgre River, just north of Ouray. The terrain is relatively flat, and the trail meanders past stands of trees, a wildflower-filled meadow, and interpretive signs about the river ecosystem from its trailhead to the city's north boundary. Trail entry points are located near the Ouray Visitors Center, the north corridor hotel locations, and along Oak Street. ✉ *Ouray Visitors Center, 1230 Main St.* ☎ *970/325–4746* 🌐 *www.ouraycolorado.com.*

ICE CLIMBING

Ouray Ice Park

CLIMBING/MOUNTAINEERING | Ouray is known in ice-climbing circles for its abundance of frozen waterfalls, albeit man-made ones. The Ouray Ice Festival, held each January, helped to cement the town's reputation as America's ice-climbing mecca. The Ouray Ice Park is the world's first facility dedicated to the sport. In the Uncompahgre Gorge, just south of town, the Ice Park has 11 climbing areas with more than 150 routes. ✉ *280 County Rd. 361* ☎ *970/325–4288* 🌐 *www.ourayicepark.com.*

Ouray Mountain Sports
CLIMBING/MOUNTAINEERING | This outfitter sells and rents all sorts of outdoor-sports equipment, including ice-climbing gear. The staff will also sharpen your ice screws, generally within a day or two, using the only Grivel sharpening machine in North America. ✉ *732 Main St.* ☎ *970/325–4284* 🌐 *www.ouraymountainsports.com.*

NORDIC SKIING

Ironton Park
SKIING/SNOWBOARDING | Managed by the Ouray County Nordic Council, Ironton Park is a marked trail system for Nordic skiers and snowshoers. About 9 miles south of town, it has several interconnecting loops of beginner to intermediate difficulty that let you spend a day on the trails. Find trail maps online, at the trailhead, and at local sporting goods stores. ✉ *9 miles south of Ouray, Hwy. 550* 🌐 *www.ouraynordic.org* 🎫 *Free.*

Silverton

23 miles south of Ouray; 47 miles north of Durango.

Glorious peaks surround Silverton, an old mining community. The town reputedly got its name when a miner exclaimed, "We ain't got much gold but we got silver by the ton!" Silverton is the county seat, as well as the only remaining town, in San Juan County. The last mine here went bust in 1991 (which is recent as such things go), leaving Silverton to boom in summer, when the Durango & Silverton Narrow Gauge Railroad deposited three trainloads of tourists a day (which it still does today). But the addition of the Silverton Mountain ski area helped the town to shake off its long slumber, and now increasingly more businesses stay open year-round. Now winter in Silverton is lively, with an annual sled dog race, winter carnival, and the Silverton Splitfest for splitboarding enthusiasts. There's also the Silverton Skijoring and Snowscape Winter Carnival, featuring pro and amateur skijoring contests (that's where a horse and rider team pulls a skier at breakneck speeds through a course of jumps and obstacles).

The downtown area has been designated a National Historic Landmark District. Be sure to pick up the walking-tour brochure that describes—among other things—the most impressive buildings lining Greene Street: Miners' Union Hall, Teller House, the Town Hall, the San Juan County Courthouse (home of the county historical museum), and the Grand Imperial Hotel. These structures have historical significance, but more history was probably made in the raucous red-light district along Blair Street.

GETTING HERE AND AROUND

U.S. 550 North and U.S. 550 South meet at a junction in front of the Silverton Chamber of Commerce and Visitor Center. At the intersection, Greene Street—with the main stores, restaurants, hotels, and the only paved street in town—heads northeast from 6th Street to 15th Street before splitting into County Road 110 heading to the Silverton Mountain Ski Area to the north and County Road 2 heading to the Old Hundred Gold Mine and the Mayflower Gold Mill to the east.

ESSENTIALS

VISITOR INFORMATION Silverton Chamber of Commerce and Visitor Center. ✉ *414 Greene St.* ☎ *970/387–5654, 800/752–4494* 🌐 *www.silvertoncolorado.com.*

Sights

Christ of the Mines Shrine

RELIGIOUS SITE | If you look north toward Anvil Mountain, you'll see the Christ of the Mines Shrine, the centerpiece of which is a 12-ton statue of Jesus carved out of Italian marble. The shrine was erected in 1959, and has been credited with a handful of miracles over the subsequent years. A moderately strenuous 1-mile hike leads to the shrine, which has memorable views of the surrounding San Juan Mountains. ✉ *Silverton* ✣ *Trailhead at end of 10th St.*

Mayflower Mill

HISTORIC SITE | Northeast of Silverton, the Mayflower Mill (also known as the Shenandoah-Dives Mill) is a beautifully restored landmark with tours that explain how precious gold, silver, and other metals were extracted and processed. ✉ *135 County Rd. 2* ☎ *970/387–0294* 🌐 *www.sanjuancountyhistoricalsociety.org* 🎫 *$8* ⏲ *Closed Oct.–early June.*

Old Hundred Gold Mine Tour

HISTORIC SITE | A mine train takes you 1,500 feet underground into the Old Hundred Gold Mine for a tour of one of the area's oldest mining facilities. Your miner-guide follows the vein and operates authentic equipment to show you how mining was done in the old days. Old Hundred operated for about a century, from the first strike in 1872 until the last haul in the early 1970s. Temperatures remain at a steady 47°F, so be sure to bring a sweater or a jacket. Guided tours leave every hour on the hour 10 am–4 pm (arrive 15 minutes early to secure your spot). Your ticket price also covers panning for gold, silver, copper, and gemstones in the sluice boxes outside the mine. ✉ *721 County Rd. 4A* ✣ *5 miles southeast of Silverton* ☎ *970/387–5444, 800/872–3009* 🌐 *www.minetour.com* 🎫 *$28* ⏲ *Closed early Oct.–mid-May.*

★ San Juan County Historical Society Mining Heritage Center

MUSEUM | This large, well-kept museum houses an assortment of mining memorabilia, minerals, and local artifacts, including walk-in mining-tunnel replicas. The museum also includes the old San Juan County Jail, built in 1902. Here you can get a glimpse of turn-of-the-20th-century life in the region. ✉ *1557 Greene St.* ☎ *970/387–5609* 🌐 *www.sanjuancountyhistoricalsociety.org* 🎫 *$10* ⏲ *Closed mid-Oct.–late May.*

Restaurants

Handlebars Food & Saloon

$$ | **AMERICAN** | As much a museum as an eatery, this restaurant is crammed with mining artifacts, odd antiques, and taxidermied animals. The hearty menu includes steaks, ribs, hamburgers, chicken, pasta, prime rib, and chicken-fried steak, all with homemade sides and sauces. **Known for:** baby back ribs and elk burgers; house-made barbecue sauces; packaged soup and chili mixes. 💲 *Average main: $16* ✉ *1323 Greene St.* ☎ *970/387–5395* 🌐 *www.handlebarssilverton.com* ⏲ *Closed Nov.–Apr.*

Hotels

The Wyman Hotel

$$$ | **HOTEL** | Set in a renovated 100-year old landmark stone building, the Wyman Hotel offers all the benefits of a remote alpine retreat while maintaining the comforts and amenities of an urban boutique hotel. **Pros:** quiet; centrally located; gorgeous design. **Cons:** no meals on-site; no televisions or phones in rooms; Wi-Fi and cell phone reception iffy. 💲 *Rooms from: $275* ✉ *1371 Greene St.* ☎ *970/799–4952* 🌐 *www.thewyman.com* 🛏 *15 rooms* 🍽 *No meals.*

DOWNHILL SKIING AND SNOWBOARDING

Kendall Mountain Recreation Area

SKIING/SNOWBOARDING | FAMILY | Run by the town, Kendall Mountain Recreation Area is a single-lift ski center open Friday through Sunday during ski season, weather permitting. It's not a challenging slope, so it's perfect for beginners. You can also skate, sled, snowshoe, and cross-country ski here. Rentals are available. ✉ *1 Kendall Mountain Pl.* ☎ *970/387–5522* 🌐 *www.skikendall.com* 🎫 *$25* ⏲ *Closed Apr.–Nov.*

Silverton Mountain

SKIING/SNOWBOARDING | About 6 miles north of town, Silverton Mountain is one of the country's simplest yet most innovative ski areas. Open to expert skiers and boarders only, Silverton Mountain operates one double lift that accesses more than 1,800 acres of never-groomed backcountry steeps. It's the highest ski area in North America, as well as the steepest. The mountain sets a limit of roughly 80 people per day, and most of the time you feel like you have the mountain to yourself. There's no fancy lodge, either—in fact, there's no running water, but you can buy bottled water, along with simple lunches, at the base area. You can rent equipment, including a mandatory avalanche beacon, and other gear. Guided and unguided excursions are available. The ski area also now offers helicopter skiing seven days a week by reservation, which expands the skiable territory to more than 20,000 acres. **Facilities:** 69 trails; 1,819 acres; 3,000-foot vertical drop; 1 lift ✉ *6226 Hwy. 110* ☎ *970/387–5706* 🌐 *www.silvertonmountain.com* 🎫 *Lift ticket from $89; heli-skiing from $179.*

FOUR-WHEELING

Silverton provides easy access to such popular four-wheel-drive routes as Ophir Pass to the Telluride side of the San Juans, Stony Pass to the Rio Grande Valley, and Engineer and Cinnamon passes, components of the Alpine Loop. With an all-terrain vehicle you can see some of Colorado's most famous ghost towns, remnants of mining communities, and jaw-dropping scenery. The four-wheeling season is May to mid-October, weather permitting. In winter these unplowed trails are transformed into fabulous snowmobile routes.

Silver Summit RV Park and Jeep Rentals

FOUR-WHEELING | You can rent a four-wheel-drive vehicle starting at $175 per day. ✉ *640 Mineral St.* ☎ *970/387–0240, 970/946–0775 in winter* 🌐 *www.silversummitrvpark.com.*

ICE-SKATING

Silverton Town Rink

ICE SKATING | FAMILY | At the Kendall Mountain Recreation Area, the Silverton Town Rink lets you skate for free, weather permitting. Rentals are available. ✉ *Kendall Mountain Recreation Area, 1 Kendall Mountain Pl.* ☎ *970/387–5522* 🌐 *www.skikendall.com.*

NORDIC SKIING

The local snowmobile club grooms nearly 170 miles of cross-country skiing and snowshoeing trails around Silverton, so the route is flat, easy, and safe. Molas Pass, 6 miles south of Silverton on U.S. 550, has a variety of Nordic routes, from easy half-milers in broad valleys to longer, more demanding ascents.

St. Paul Lodge & Hut

SKIING/SNOWBOARDING | This place is an incredible find for anyone enchanted by remote high country. Above 11,000 feet and about a 40-minute ski-in from the summit of Red Mountain Pass (between Ouray and Silverton), the St. Paul Lodge (a converted mining camp) & Hut provide access to above–tree-line exploring via telemark or cross-country skis, snowboard, or snowshoes. The Hut is also available in summer, when you can reach the property via four-wheel-drive vehicle (or by hiking in). The hut has two bedrooms and sleeps six, and the lodge offers dormitory-style accommodations for larger groups; both buildings have shared baths. Reservations are essential, and pets are not allowed. ✉ *Silverton* ✣ *Top of Red Mountain Pass* ☎ *970/946–4807* 🌐 *www.stpaulhut.com* 🎫 *$180.*

Durango

47 miles south of Silverton via U.S. 550; 45 miles east of Cortez via U.S. 160; 60 miles west of Pagosa Springs via U.S. 160.

Wisecracking Will Rogers had this to say about Durango: "It's out of the way and glad of it." His statement is a bit unfair, considering that as a railroad town Durango has always been a cultural crossroads and melting pot (as well as a place to raise hell). Resting at 6,500 feet along the winding Animas River,with the San Juan Mountains as backdrop, the town was founded in 1879 by General William Palmer, president of the all-powerful Denver & Rio Grande Railroad, at a time when nearby Animas City haughtily refused to donate land for a depot. Within a decade, Durango had completely absorbed its rival. The booming town quickly became the region's main metropolis and a gateway to the Southwest.

A walking tour of the historic downtown offers ample proof of Durango's prosperity during the late 19th century, although the northern end of Main Avenue has the usual assortment of cheap motels and fast-food outlets.

About 27 miles north of town, the down-home ski resort of Purgatory welcomes a clientele that includes cowboys, families, and college students. The mountain is named for the nearby Purgatory Creek, a tributary of the River of Lost Souls.

GETTING HERE AND AROUND

Durango Transit operates regular trolleys and bus service throughout town. Purgatory Resort runs a $10 skier shuttle between the town and the mountain on weekends and holidays during the winter. Buck Horn Limousine is your best bet for airport transfers.

CONTACTS Buck Horn Limousine. ☎ *970/769–0933* 🌐 *www.buckhornlimousine.com.* **Durango Transit.** ☎ *970/259–5438* 🌐 *www.durangotransit.com.* **Purgatory Resort Skier Shuttle.** ☎ *970/426–7282* 🌐 *www.purgatoryresort.com.*

VISITOR INFORMATION

CONTACTS Durango Welcome Center. ✉ *802 Main Ave.* ☎ *970/247–3500, 800/525–8855* 🌐 *www.durango.org.*

Sights

★ Durango & Silverton Narrow Gauge Railroad

TRANSPORTATION SITE (AIRPORT/BUS/FERRY/TRAIN) | FAMILY | The most entertaining way to relive the Old West is to take a ride on the Durango & Silverton Narrow Gauge Railroad, a nine-hour round-trip journey along the 45-mile railway to Silverton. Travel in comfort in restored coaches or in the open-air cars called gondolas as you listen to the train's shrill whistle. A shorter excursion to Cascade Canyon in heated coaches is available in winter. The train departs from the Durango Depot, constructed in 1882 and beautifully restored. Next door is the Durango & Silverton Narrow Gauge Railroad Museum, which is free and well worth your time. ✉ *479 Main Ave.* ☎ *970/247–2733, 877/872–4607* 🌐 *www.durangotrain.com* 🎫 *$91–$199.*

Durango Hot Springs Resort & Spa

HOT SPRINGS | FAMILY | Come to this newly renovated, luxurious hot springs resort to soak your aching bones after a day of hiking or skiing. The complex includes an Olympic-size, saltwater swimming pool infused with aquagen, and 27

Durango's Purgatory Resort offers activities for all four seasons.

total natural mineral pools ranging from 98°F to 110°F; all are open year-round. The pools are outdoors, perched at the base of the mountain and thoughtfully designed to blend in with nature. The grounds also feature a spa, sauna, reflexology path, food carts and firepit, stage for live music, stream, separate adults-only area, and a hydrotherapy "yin-yang" pool. ✉ *6475 County Rd. 203* ✣ *About 5 miles north of Durango* ☎ *970/247–0111* 🌐 *www.durangohotspringsresortandspa.com* 🎟 *$20.*

Main Avenue National Historic District

HISTORIC SITE | The intersection of 13th Street and Main Avenue marks the northern edge of Durango's Main Avenue National Historic District. Old-fashioned streetlamps line the streets, casting a warm glow on the elegant buildings filled with upscale galleries, restaurants, and shops. Dating from 1887, the Strater Hotel is a reminder of the time when this town was a stop for many people headed west. ✉ *Main Ave., between 13th St. and 12th St.* 🌐 *www.durango.org.*

★ **Purgatory Resort**

Purgatory does summer better than just about any Colorado ski resort, especially for kids. In the past, activities have included a new mountain coaster, an off-road go-kart track, an alpine slide, a family-friendly ropes course, a short zipline, pony rides, bungee trampolines, an airbag jump, lift-served hiking and biking, and, of course, the obligatory climbing wall and minigolf course. ✉ *1 Skier Pl., Purgatory* ☎ *970/247–9000* 🌐 *www.purgatoryresort.com* 🎟 *$79 for 10 activities, $59 for 5, or choose à la carte pricing. Subject to change.*

Restaurants

Carver Brewing Co.

$$ | **AMERICAN** | The "Brews Brothers," Bill and Jim Carver, have about 12 beers on tap at any given time at this Durango favorite. If you're hungry, try one of the signature handmade bread bowls filled with green chile, soup, or chicken stew. **Known for:** hearty, creative breakfasts; lovely shaded patio out back; elevated pub cuisine. $ *Average main: $15 ✉ 1022 Main Ave. ☎ 970/259–2545 🌐 www.carverbrewing.com.*

Chimayo Stone Fired Kitchen

$$$ | **CONTEMPORARY** | The former chef for Michael Andretti's racing team runs this trendy bistro, in which every dish is cooked in one of two stone-fired ovens. The house specialty is artisanal pizza (try the four-mushroom variety and add the house fennel sausage), although pizza is only a small part of the menu. **Known for:** delectable cornbread and focaccia bread; specialty cocktails; classy decor. $ *Average main: $28 ✉ 862 Main Ave. ☎ 970/259–2749 🌐 www.chimayodurango.com ⏲ Closed Mon. and Tues. No lunch.*

Dandelion Cafe

$$$ | **MEDITERRANEAN** | In warm weather you can sit on the large garden patio, and the rest of the year you'll have to cozy up to your fellow diners in the 10-table Dandelion Cafe, housed in a quaint, sparsely decorated Victorian a block off Main Avenue. Mediterranean food receives a fresh and healthy treatment, including free-range chicken, sustainably sourced seafood, and locally grown ingredients whenever possible. **Known for:** live music; falafel and gyros; outdoor dining in summer. $ *Average main: $23 ✉ 725 E. 2nd Ave. ☎ 970/385–6884 🌐 www.dandelioncafedurango.com ⏲ Closed Sun. in winter.*

East by Southwest

$$$ | **ASIAN FUSION** | Asian food gets a bit of a Latin treatment in this inviting space. The menu has a strong Japanese bent, with sushi and sashimi, tempura, beef, and other traditional dishes elegantly presented and layered with complementary, often Southwest-inspired flavors. **Known for:** vegan and vegetarian options; bento boxes and poke bowls for lunch; sake, beer, wine, and tea lists. $ *Average main: $23 ✉ 160 E. College Dr. ☎ 970/247–5533 🌐 www.eastbysouthwest.com ⏲ No lunch Sun.*

11th Street Station

$ | **FAST FOOD** | Seven locally owned food trucks, serving cuisine from Thailand to breakfast burritos to pizza to sushi, surround an outdoor courtyard with picnic-table seating. Ernie's Bar anchors the eating collective and offers craft beers, tap cocktails, and a wide tequila and mezcal selection. **Known for:** moderately priced eats; variety; fresh, contemporary vibes. $ *Average main: $12 ✉ 1101 Main Ave. ☎ 970/422–8482 🌐 www.11thstreetstation.com.*

Ken & Sue's

$$ | **MODERN AMERICAN** | Plates are big and the selection is creative at Ken & Sue's, one of Durango's favorite restaurants. Locals are wild for the contemporary American cuisine with an Asian flair, served in an intimate space. **Known for:** large, pretty patio out back; worth-it desserts; pistachio-crusted grouper with vanilla-rum butter. $ *Average main: $18 ✉ 636 Main Ave. ☎ 970/385–1810 🌐 www.kenandsues.com ⏲ No lunch weekends.*

★ Ore House

$$$$ | **STEAKHOUSE** | Durango is a meat-and-potatoes kind of town, and the rustic Ore House is a splurge-worthy place to indulge (just ask the locals). The steaks are fantastic, and there are plenty of expertly prepared seafood and vegetarian selections as well. **Known for:** chateaubriand; cornbread with bacon butter; deep whiskey and wine lists. $ *Average main: $39 ✉ 147 E. College Dr. ☎ 970/247–5707 🌐 www.orehouserestaurant.com.*

★ Sow's Ear

$$$ | **STEAKHOUSE** | This airy eatery in Silverpick Lodge is known for providing "the best steaks on the mountain," topped with incredible au poivre, which it does with aplomb. It also serves up the best views of thick aspen groves. **Known for:** lovely views of mountains and cliffs; three-season alfresco patio open nightly, weather permitting; steak au poivre. $ *Average main:*

$30 ✉ 48475 U.S. 550 ☎ 970/247–3527 🌐 www.sowseardurango.com ⏲ No lunch. Closed Mon. and Tues.

Steamworks Brewing Co.

$$ | **AMERICAN** | Widely acclaimed craft brews and above-standard sandwiches, burgers, pizzas, and salads raise Steamworks beyond usual pub grub. It's no surprise that the large, high-ceilinged venue is nearly always overflowing and has been a Durango favorite for more than two decades. **Known for:** skillfully brewed beer; daily drink specials ($3 pints, $11 pitchers, and more); back patio with mountain views. *$ Average main: $16 ✉ 801 E. 2nd Ave. ☎ 970/259–9200 🌐 www.steamworksbrewing.com.*

Coffee and Quick Bites

James Ranch Grill

$ | **AMERICAN** | **FAMILY** | For a delicious summer detour, head 10 miles north of town to James Ranch, where you'll find a pleasant organic farm, with an outdoor grill that features homemade cheeses and homegrown meats and produce grown on-site. The menu keeps things simple, featuring a short list of burgers, sandwiches, and salads. **Known for:** ample outdoor seating; organic, homegrown ingredients; Signature Burger with rosemary-garlic mayo. *$ Average main: $13 ✉ 33846 U.S. 550 ☎ 970/676–1023 🌐 www.jamesranch.net.*

Hotels

Apple Orchard Inn

$$ | **B&B/INN** | This quiet B&B sits on five acres in the lush Animas Valley with an apple orchard, flower gardens, and trout ponds on the grounds. **Pros:** beautiful views; peaceful and quiet setting; cottages are intimate and romantic. **Cons:** no dinner on-site; several miles from town; rooms in the house are all upstairs (no elevator). *$ Rooms from: $160 ✉ 7758 County Rd. 203 ✣ About 8 miles north of downtown Durango ☎ 970/247–0751, 800/426–0751 🌐 www.appleorchardinn.com 4 rooms, 6 cottages 🍽 Free Breakfast.*

General Palmer Hotel

$$ | **HOTEL** | The General Palmer Hotel is a faithfully restored historic property in downtown Durango with a clean, bright look, as well as period furniture and Victorian touches that reinforce an old-timey feel. **Pros:** central location; some rooms have balconies; free off-street parking. **Cons:** no restaurant or bar; cramped elevator; pricey in season. *$ Rooms from: $200 ✉ 567 Main Ave. ☎ 970/247–4747 🌐 generalpalmerhotel.com 39 rooms 🍽 Free Breakfast.*

Purgatory Lodge

$$$$ | **HOTEL** | **FAMILY** | This mountain-luxe slope-side hotel provides an upscale retreat at a down-home resort, featuring roomy two- to four-bedroom suites decorated with contemporary furnishings. **Pros:** slope-side location; good restaurants; ample amenities. **Cons:** can be pricey; far from town; no meals included. *$ Rooms from: $350 ✉ Purgatory Resort, 24 Sheol St. ☎ 970/385–2100, 800/525–0892 🌐 www.purgatoryresort.com 37 suites 🍽 No meals.*

Rochester Hotel & Leland House

$$ | **B&B/INN** | The Rochester Hotel is a historic, boutique hotel that features paraphernalia and posters from movies filmed in the Durango area. **Pros:** free guest parking; amazing outdoor space; close to the action, yet off the main drag. **Cons:** no on-site food; no counter space in bathrooms; no pool or hot tub. *$ Rooms from: $199 ✉ 726 E. 2nd Ave. ☎ 970/385–1920, 800/664–1920 🌐 www.rochesterhotel.com 27 rooms 🍽 Free Breakfast.*

★ Strater Hotel

$$$ | **HOTEL** | Still the hottest spot in town, this Western grande dame opened for business in 1887 and has been visited by Butch Cassidy, Louis L'Amour (he wrote many of the *Sacketts* novels here),

Francis Ford Coppola, John Kennedy, and Marilyn Monroe (the latter two stayed here at separate times). **Pros:** right in the thick of things; free guest parking; filled with gorgeous antiques. **Cons:** breakfast not included in all rates; noisy bar; Wi-Fi is spotty. *Rooms from: $220 699 Main Ave. 970/247–4431, 800/247–4431 www.strater.com 88 rooms No meals.*

Nightlife

BARS AND CLUBS

The Bookcase & Barber

BARS/PUBS | There's more to this traditional working barbershop than meets the eye. Drop the right password (hint: it's subtly displayed on their website), and you'll be ushered through the bookcase into a Gatsby-worthy speakeasy. Sure, it's a bit gimmicky, but the excellence of the ever-changing house-original cocktails and small plates more than makes up for it. *601 E 2nd Ave. 970/764–4123 www.bookcaseandbarber.com.*

Diamond Belle Saloon

BARS/PUBS | Awash in flocked wallpaper and lace, the Diamond Belle Saloon is dominated by a gilt-and-mahogany bar. With its prime location—on the ground floor of the historic Strater Hotel—plus live ragtime piano music and servers dressed in period costumes, the Diamond Belle can really pack them in. Try the Brazilian mint martini; if you're hungry, order the much-hailed Diamond burger. **TIP→ Ask for the "secret menu."** *699 Main Ave. 970/247–4431 Strater Hotel strater.com/dining/diamond-belle-saloon.*

★ Ska Brewing Company

BARS/PUBS | Beer fans shouldn't miss Ska Brewing, a homegrown brewery that boasts a large "tasting room" with 20 taps. The decor is bowling-alley inspired, including tables crafted with wood from former lanes at a Denver bowling alley. If the weather allows, you can sip your beer of choice on the parklike patio or second-story deck, beneath enormous, metal brew tanks. Pair your beer with a sandwich or artisanal pizza from The Container restaurant, made from two repurposed shipping containers attached to the brewery. **TIP→ Stop by on a Thursday night for live music or 4 pm Monday through Saturday for a brewery tour.** *225 Girard St. 970/247–5792 www.skabrewing.com.*

Performing Arts

ARTS VENUES

Durango Arts Center

ART GALLERIES—ARTS | You can see stage productions as well as visual arts exhibits, concerts, and films at the Durango Arts Center. *802 E. 2nd Ave. 970/259–2606 www.durangoarts.org Closed Sun.–Mon.*

DINNER SHOWS

Bar D Chuckwagon Suppers

MUSIC | **FAMILY** | This old-style-cowboy venue, about 10 miles from Durango, serves steaks, barbecued beef and chicken, and biscuits under the stars every summer evening. After supper, the Bar D Wranglers entertain the crowd with guitar music, singing, and corny comedy. Reservations are required. *8080 County Rd. 250 970/247–5753 www.bardchuckwagon.com From $29 Closed Labor Day–Memorial Day.*

Shopping

BOOKS

Joyful Nook Gallery

SPECIALTY STORES | Joyful Nook uses original art from local artists to handcraft high-quality wooden puzzles that make for wonderful souvenirs. You'll also find decorative papers and stationery products here. *546 E. College Dr. 970/764–4764 www.jngpuzzles.com.*

FOOD

Honeyville

FOOD/CANDY | About 10 miles north of Durango, Honeyville sells honey, jams, jellies (try the wild chokecherry), syrups, sauces, and other goodies. You can watch the bees go about their work in a glass hive and, on weekdays, view honey being processed and bottled. Then taste honey-made spirits at the in-house Honey House Distillery. ✉ *33633 U.S. 550* ☎ *970/247–1474* 🌐 *www.honeyvillecolorado.com.*

GIFTS

Toh-Atin Gallery

ART GALLERIES | Recognized as one of the region's best Native American galleries, Toh-Atin specializes in vintage and contemporary Navajo weavings and authentic Native American jewelry. There's also a wide range of paintings, pottery, baskets, and sculptures made by the artisans of many Southwestern tribes. ✉ *145 W. 9th St.* ☎ *970/247–8277* 🌐 *www.toh-atin.com.*

SPORTING GOODS

Mountain Bike Specialists

BICYCLING | Although everybody in town seems to be an expert, the staff at this shop can help direct you to the trail of your dreams and outfit you for the excursion. They also do expert repairs. ✉ *949 Main Ave.* ☎ *970/247–4066* 🌐 *www.mountainbikespecialists.com* ⏲ *Closed Sun.*

BICYCLING

With a healthy college population and a generally mild climate, Durango is extremely bike-friendly and a popular destination for single-track enthusiasts. Many locals consider bikes to be their main form of transportation. The bike lobby is active, the trail system is well developed, and mountain biking is a particularly popular recreational activity.

Animas River Trail

BICYCLING | This 7-mile paved path parallels the river from Animas City Park south to Dallabetta Park in one smooth stroke. It's the main artery, linking up with several of the town's other trail systems. ✉ *Durango.*

Durango Mountain Bike Tours

BICYCLING | Take a guided, private ride tailored to your skill level and interests with Durango Mountain Bike Tours. Rides range from a two-hour "Town & Trails" tour for beginners, complete with riding instruction, to full-day excursions on the area's most challenging single-track. Ask about guided tours at Phil's World, the famous single-track trail network a few miles outside of Mesa Verde. If you don't have a bike, you can rent one here. ✉ *Durango* ☎ *970/367–7653* 🌐 *www.durangobiketours.com* 🎟 *From $90.*

Hermosa Creek Trail

BICYCLING | This single-track trail travels roughly 19 miles from Purgatory Resort to the lower Hermosa parking area. It's an intermediate-to-difficult ride with a couple of steep spots and switchbacks along with mellow rolls through open meadows and towering aspen and pine forests. The trail hugs the steep riverbank at a few places and there are a few creek crossings, so you shouldn't try it too early in the season, while the snow is still melting (the water can be waist-high in the spring and early summer). To minimize the fight against gravity, you can leave your car at the lower trailhead and catch a shuttle to the top—even so, there will still be plenty of climbing. ✉ *Durango* ✥ *Trailhead: 2 miles from Purgatory's upper parking lot.*

TOURS AND EXPEDITIONS

San Juan Hut Systems

BICYCLING | Having a fully equipped hut waiting at the end of a tough day of riding makes the San Juan Hut System a backcountry biker's dream come true. The company, which started out as a hut-to-hut service for backcountry skiers, operates a 215-mile route from Durango to Moab, Utah, suitable for intermediate and advanced riders. Trips run from June to October and last five or seven days, covering alpine meadows, desert slick rock, canyon country, and the famous Whole Enchilada Trail. Along the way, the six one-room huts are supplied with bunks, sleeping bags, heating and cooking stoves, food, and water. *970/626–3033 www.sanjuanhuts.com From $795 per person.*

GOLF

Dalton Ranch Golf Club

GOLF | About 6 miles north of Durango, this semiprivate 18-hole championship course delivers inspiring views of the Animas River Valley and surrounding San Juans. Swing, the clubhouse's full-service restaurant and bar, is a popular hangout for golfers and locals who like watching the resident elk herd take its afternoon stroll. *589 County Rd. 252, off U.S. 550 970/247–7921 www.daltonranch.com $125, includes cart 18 holes, 6934 yards, par 72 Closed Nov.–Mar. Reservations essential.*

Hillcrest Golf Club

GOLF | Since 1969, a relaxed atmosphere, affordable rates, and gorgeous views have attracted golfers to this 18-hole public course, perched on a mesa near the campus of Fort Lewis College. Carts are $16 per person for 18 holes, but the tee-to-green distance is relatively short, so most patrons opt to walk. *2300 Rim Dr. 970/247–1499 www.golfhillcrest.com $48 for 18 holes late May–early Sept. midweek only and $50 weekends; $37/$39 early Sept.–late May 18 holes, 6727 yards, par 71 Closed Dec.–Mar. Reservations essential.*

HIKING

Hiking trails are everywhere in and around Durango. Many trailheads at the edges of town lead to backcountry settings, and the San Juan Forest has plenty of mind-boggling walks and trails for those with the urge to explore.

Across from the Fort Lewis College Recreation Complex is a kid-friendly hike called **Lion's Den Trail.** It connects with the **Chapman Hill Trail** for a nice moderate hike, climbing switchbacks that take you away from town and hook up with the **Rim Trail.**

Animas Overlook Trail

TRAIL | If you're looking for a great view without the effort, try the ¾-mile Animas Overlook Trail. It takes you past signs explaining local geology, flora, and fauna before bringing you to a precipice with an unparalleled view of the valley and the surrounding Needle Mountains. It's the only wheelchair-accessible trail in the area. From town, it's a 45-minute drive up Junction Creek Road. *Durango Trailhead: at Forest Rd. 171, milepost 8.*

★ The Colorado Trail

TRAIL | Junction Creek to Gudy's Rest Junction Creek is the southern terminus for the Colorado Trail and one of Durango's best trails for hiking, mountain biking, and trail running. Located just 4 miles or so from downtown, this 8-mile out-and-back day hike rises and falls at a relatively gentle grade, so it's achievable for most hikers. The trail eventually winds its way up to Gudy's Rest, named after Gudy Gaskill, the "Mother of the Colorado Trail." This high spot is a great place to sit and take in the views of Durango and the San Juan Mountains. Instead of hiking all the way up to Gudy's Rest, you can make the hike a 5-mile round-trip by turning back at the wooden footbridge, which is a great goal for first-timers. *Trailhead off County Rd. 204 From town, take 25th St. west; it turns into Junction St. and continues on to the lower parking lot www.coloradotrail.org.*

HORSEBACK RIDING

Rapp Corral

HORSEBACK RIDING | At the entrance to Haviland Lake, about 20 miles north of town, Rapp Corrall offers a variety of trail rides into San Juan National Forest. Trips range from one-hour jaunts to day-long treks to above-timberline trails on Engineer Mountain, or you can combine horseback riding with cave exploration. In winter, they offer sleigh rides. ✉ *51 Haviland Lake Rd.* ☎ *970/247–8454* 🌐 *www.rappcorral.com* 🎫 *From $75.*

RAFTING

Durango Rivertrippers and Adventure Tours

WHITE-WATER RAFTING | This outfitter runs day trips down the Animas River and other multiday options around the area. You can up your adrenaline output by swapping the raft for an inflatable kayak when the river conditions are right. Or ask about discount packages that combine rafting with Jeep tours or other rentals. ✉ *724 Main Ave.* ☎ *970/259–0289* 🌐 *www.durangorivertrippers.com.*

Mild to Wild Rafting and Jeep Tours

WHITE-WATER RAFTING | **FAMILY** | The Lower Animas is a mostly mellow stretch of river, with a few livelier rapids thrown in, making it a good choice for families. Mild to Wild offers trips of various lengths, and also rents out inflatable kayaks. You can book Jeep tours here as well. ✉ *50 Animas View Dr.* ☎ *800/567–6745, 970/247–4789* 🌐 *www.mild2wildrafting.com* 🎫 *Raft trips start at $33. Jeep tours start at $76 for a half day.*

ROCK CLIMBING

East Animas

CLIMBING/MOUNTAINEERING | East Animas, just a few miles east of town, serves up some of the area's best multipitch traditional climbing on the "Watch Crystal" rock formation, a favorite with locals. You'll also find excellent bolted sport lines. The parking area is on the east side of the road. ✉ *Off County Rd. 250, 2 miles east of U.S. 550.*

The Rock Lounge

CLIMBING/MOUNTAINEERING | **FAMILY** | Stop in at this friendly gym to practice bouldering and climbing techniques before heading out to the real deal. You can also take classes or arrange private lessons here. In the summer, you can enroll your child in half- or full-day indoor and outdoor climbing camps. ✉ *111 E. 30th St.* ☎ *970/764–4505* 🌐 *www.rockloungeclimbing.com* 🎫 *Day pass $14; kids' camps start at $60 for a half day.*

San Juan National Forest

CLIMBING/MOUNTAINEERING | There are plenty of opportunities for climbing in the Columbine Ranger District of the San Juan National Forest, just outside of Durango. Some of the more popular spots are Cascade Canyon, Golf Wall, and Fume Wall. ✉ *U.S. Forestry office, 15 Burnett Ct.* ☎ *970/247–4874* 🌐 *www.fs.usda.gov/sanjuan.*

X-Rock

CLIMBING/MOUNTAINEERING | Just north of town, X-Rock offers a little bit of everything—slab, sport and crack climbs, bouldering—for novice and intermediate climbers. It's also a great place to learn (or just brush up on) basic climbing skills. One look at the distinctive natural cracks that cross its face will tell you how it got its name. ✉ *Off U.S. 550, just north of 38th St.*

SKIING AND SNOWBOARDING

★ Purgatory Resort

SKIING/SNOWBOARDING | This unpretentious ski resort 27 miles north of Durango has plenty of intermediate runs and gladed tree skiing, but what's unique about it is its stepped terrain: lots of humps and dips and steep pitches followed by virtual flats. Purgatory is just plain fun, and return visitors like it that way. It's not all old-school, however: A high-speed quad on the back side (Lift 8) conveys skiers to the top of the mountain in five minutes and accesses three advanced trails. The ski area is perfect for families and those who are open to other diversions, such as horse-drawn sleigh rides, snowshoeing, cross-country skiing, and snowmobiling. **Facilities:** 105 trails; 1,635 acres; 2,029-foot vertical drop; 12 lifts. ✉ *1 Skier Pl., Purgatory* ☎ *970/247–9000, 800/525–0892* 🌐 *www.purgatoryresort.com* 🎫 *Lift ticket $109.*

LESSONS AND PROGRAMS

Adult & Teen Ski and Ride School

SKIING/SNOWBOARDING | On the second level of the Village Center, the Adult & Teen Ski and Ride School runs full-day and half-day group lessons during the season. The school also provides private lessons, as well as specialty clinics for telemark and bump skiers of all levels. ✉ *Village Center, Purgatory* ☎ *970/385–2149* 🌐 *www.purgatoryresort.com* 🎫 *From $69 for two hours; $95 for four hours.*

Kids Ski and Ride School

SKIING/SNOWBOARDING | Getting kids onto the slopes is a cinch at the Kids Ski and Ride School, which offers programs for skiers and snowboarders ages 4 to 12. Choose from a full-day package—which includes lunch, a lesson, equipment rental, and a lift ticket—or a half-day package. Also check out the strider snowbike lessons for kids. ✉ *Village Center, Purgatory* ☎ *970/385–2149* 🌐 *www.purgatoryresort.com* 🎫 *From $69 for a half day; $95 for a full day.*

Purgatory Snowcat Adventures

SKIING/SNOWBOARDING | Out-of-bounds types can explore 35,000 acres of untamed wilderness with Purgatory Snowcat Adventures. A day of guided snowcat skiing or riding includes safety gear and a hearty lunch. ✉ *Village Center, Purgatory* ☎ *970/385–2115* 🌐 *www.purgatoryresort.com* 🎫 *$429.*

RENTALS

Expert Edge

SKIING/SNOWBOARDING | This is the go-to shop at the base village for demos, retail, and repair. It features top-of-the-line men's and women's skis, boots, bindings, poles, and more from top brands. Expert Edge also does custom boot fitting, ski tuning, and equipment repair. ✉ *Village Center, Purgatory* ☎ *970/385–2181* 🌐 *www.purgatoryresort.com.*

SNOWMOBILING

Snowmobile Adventures

SNOW SPORTS | With access to more than 75 miles of trails traversing mountain passes, old stagecoach roads, and mining sites, Snowmobile Adventures leads two- and three-hour tours from the base area of Purgatory Resort. Rides are available daily during ski season between 9 and 3. ✉ *Village Center, Purgatory* ☎ *970/205–9595, 888/210–9864* 🌐 *www.purgatoryresort.com* 🎫 *From $150.*

Pagosa Springs

60 miles east of Durango; 165 miles south of Gunnison.

Although not a large town, Pagosa Springs is home to the world's deepest hot springs and has become a major center for outdoor sports. Hiking, biking, and cross-country skiing opportunities abound here, and there's excellent downhill skiing and snowboarding at the nearby Wolf Creek ski area.

GETTING HERE AND AROUND

Highway 160 turns into Pagosa Street when it enters the town limits and serves as the main drag, with the majority of restaurants, shops, and hotels.

ESSENTIALS

VISITOR INFORMATION Pagosa Springs Visitor Center. ✉ *105 Hot Springs Blvd.* ☎ *800/252–2204* 🌐 *www.visitpagosasprings.com.* **Wolf Creek Snow Report.** ☎ *800/754–9653* 🌐 *www.wolfcreekski.com.*

Chimney Rock National Monument

ARCHAEOLOGICAL SITE | About 16 miles west of Pagosa Springs, State Highway 151 heads south to Chimney Rock National Monument. Twin spires of rock loom over the ruins of more than 100 homes and ceremonial buildings built about 1,000 years ago on a high mesa.

The area offers self-guided walking tours of the two trails affording access to the archaeological sites. The Great House Pueblo Trail is short, but steep and exposed, so bring plenty of water. The Mesa Village Trail loop is paved and mostly level. *Off Hwy. 151* *970/883–5359, 877/444–6777 for reservations* *www.chimneyrockco.org* *$12 tour* *Closed Oct.–mid-May.*

★ The Springs Resort & Spa

HOT SPRINGS | FAMILY | In a beautiful setting overlooking the San Juan River, the Springs Resort draws from the Guinness World Record–verified deepest geothermal hot spring to heat its 24 outdoor pools, ranging in temperature from 89°F to 114°F. The multitiered layout includes several waterfalls; a large, cooler-water swimming pool; a jetted tub; a goldfish pond; and plenty of lounge chairs and shaded tables for taking breaks from the steamy pools. There is also a full-service spa on-site. *323 Hot Springs Blvd.* *866/338–7404, 970/264–4168* *www.pagosahotsprings.com* *$35.*

Restaurants

Kip's Grill & Cantina

$ | SOUTHWESTERN | Locals pack out this small restaurant, famous for its Baja-style tacos. Favorites include the Dos Dynamite Diablos: two roasted Hatch green chilies stuffed with mozzarella cheese and hormone- and antibiotic-free top sirloin. **Known for:** homemade sauces; live music; outdoor dining in summer. *Average main: $10* *121 Pagosa St.* *970/264–3663* *www.kipsgrill.com.*

Hotels

★ The Springs Resort and Spa

$$$ | HOTEL | Wrap yourself in a big white spa robe and head directly for the 24 soaking pools that are terraced on several levels overlooking the San Juan River; as a hotel guest you'll have 24-hour access. **Pros:** access to hot springs; tranquil setting; on-site spa. **Cons:** service can be indifferent; no breakfast; some rooms are more basic than those in the newest building. *Rooms from: $209* *323 Hot Springs Blvd.* *970/264–4168, 866/338–7404* *www.pagosahotsprings.com* *79 rooms* *No meals.*

Activities

DOWNHILL SKIING AND SNOWBOARDING

Wolf Creek Ski Area

SKIING/SNOWBOARDING | With more than 430 average inches of snow annually, Wolf Creek Ski Area is Colorado's best-kept secret. The trails accommodate all ability levels offering a variety of terrain, from beginner to wide-open bowls and steep glades, with commanding views of remote valleys and towering peaks. Because there are no slope-side accommodations, Wolf Creek has a reputation as a laid-back place for those with an aversion to the long lift lines and the other hassles of faster-paced, better-known ski areas. The quaint mountain towns of Pagosa Springs, which is home to the healing waters of the Pagosa Hot Springs, and South Fork offer comfortable and affordable accommodations.

At 2 miles, the longest run at Wolf Creek is Navajo Trail. The Raven Chairlift has great beginner runs for new skiers. Skiers and snowboarders can start on the Raven chairlift to Upper Bunny Hop or Kelly Boyce Trail; both hook up with the Lower Bunny Hop back down the hill.

The best area for advanced skiers stretches back to the Waterfall area, serviced by the Alberta lift. The more intrepid will want to climb the Knife Ridge Staircase to the more demanding Knife Ridge Chutes and out to the Horseshoe Bowl. **Facilities:** 77 trails; 1,600 acres; 1,604-foot vertical drop; 10 lifts. *U.S. 160* *970/264–5639* *www.wolfcreekski.com* *Lift ticket $80* *Closed mid-Apr.–early Nov.*

LESSONS AND PROGRAMS

Wolf Creek Ski School

SKIING/SNOWBOARDING | FAMILY | Wolf Creek offers individual and group private lessons, starting at $115 for one hour for a single and $495 for a half day of up to five people. Also ask about group lessons, which can be less expensive, and the Wolf Pups program for children five and older. In the past, Wolf Creek has offered the Hot Shots program for kids ages 9 to 12, which took both skiers and boarders for about $84 per day. ✉ *Wolf Creek Ski Area, U.S. 160* ☎ *970/264–5639* 🌐 *www.wolfcreekski.com.*

GOLF

Pagosa Springs Golf Club

GOLF | The 27 championship holes here can be played in three combinations, essentially creating three different 18-hole courses. A bonus at this public course is the gorgeous mountain scenery. Cart rental is included in the green fee, and reservations are recommended. ✉ *1 Pines Club Pl.* ☎ *970/731–4755* 🌐 *www.golfpagosa.com* 🎫 *Late May–mid-Sept., $55 for 9 holes, $89 for 18 holes; mid-Sept.–late May, $43 for 9 holes, $68 for 18* ⛳ *Meadows-Pinon Course: 18 holes, 6412 yards, par 72; Pinon-Ponderosa Course: 18 holes, 6134 yards, par 72; Meadows-Ponderosa Course: 18 holes, 6026 yards, par 72* ⏲ *Closed mid-Sept.–May.*

HIKING

Pagosa Springs sits in a wondrous landscape, and there's no better way to enjoy its isolated natural beauty than to experience it from a trail. Surrounded by more than 2½ million acres of national forest and wilderness areas, Pagosa Springs features more than 650 miles of trails. Around here, trails pass through green forests and along cold mountain streams with expansive mountain views.

Continental Divide Trail

HIKING/WALKING | Serious hikers in the Pagosa Springs area head to the Continental Divide Trail, which has a major access point near Wolf Creek Pass. The trail can be an out-and-back day hike (that starts at 10,600 feet) or the starting point for a longer backcountry trip. ✉ *Pagosa Springs* ✢ *Trailhead directly off Hwy. 160 at the Continental Divide marker on Wolf Creek Pass; access also at the top of Lobo Overlook, Forest Service Rd. 402* 🌐 *www.continentaldividetrail.org.*

Piedra Falls Trail

HIKING/WALKING | FAMILY | This popular trail delivers an easy 1¼-mile (round-trip) hike through conifer and aspen forest to the falls, which tumble in two big steps down a narrow wedge cut through volcanic rocks. ✉ *Pagosa Springs* ✢ *Trailhead at end of East Toner Rd. (Forest Rd. 637)* ☎ *800/252–2204* 🌐 *www.visitpagosasprings.com.*

Cortez

45 miles west of Durango via U.S. 160; 78 miles southwest of Telluride via Hwy. 145.

The northern escarpment of Mesa Verde to the southeast and the volcanic blisters of La Plata Mountains to the east dominate the views around sprawling Cortez. With its Days Inns, Dairy Queens, and Best Westerns, the town has a layout that seems to have been determined by neon-sign and aluminum-siding salesmen of the 1950s. Hidden among these eyesores, however, are fine galleries, shops showcasing Native American art, and a host of secondhand shops that can yield surprising finds.

The gently rising hump to the southwest of town is Sleeping Ute Mountain, which resembles the reclining silhouette of a Native American, complete with headdress. This site is sacred to the Ute Mountain tribe, as it represents a great warrior god who, after being mortally wounded in a titanic battle with evil gods, lapsed into eternal sleep, his flowing blood turning into the life-giving Dolores and Animas rivers.

GETTING HERE AND AROUND

Cortez sits at the junction of Highway 160 and Highway 145, making it a busy town for people heading north to Dolores and Telluride, south into New Mexico and Arizona, and east to Durango. Highway 491 turns into Broadway heading north, and Highway 160 splits off due east, turning into Main Street as it passes through the center of town on its way to Durango.

VISITOR INFORMATION

CONTACTS Colorado Welcome Center. ✉ *928 E. Main St.* ☎ *970/565–4048.*

Sights

Cortez Cultural Center

ART GALLERIES—ARTS | The cultural center has exhibits on regional artists and Ancestral Pueblo culture, as well as events and fairs. Summer evening programs may include Native American dances and storytelling. ✉ *25 N. Market St.* ☎ *970/565–1151* 🌐 *www.cortezculturalcenter.org* ⏲ *Closed Sun.*

★ Four Corners Monument

LOCAL INTEREST | This interesting landmark is located about 42 miles from Cortez, 65 miles southeast of Bluff, and 6 miles north of Teec Nos Pos, Arizona. The Four Corners Monument Navajo Tribal Park is owned and operated by the Navajo Nation. On the Colorado side is the Ute Mountain Ute of the Corners. Primarily a photo op, you'll also find Navajo and Ute artisans selling authentic jewelry and crafts, as well as traditional foods. It's the only place in the United States where you can be in six places at one time: four states and two tribal parks meet at one single point. Bring plenty of water. ✉ *Four Corners Monument Rd., off U.S. 160, Teec Nos Pos* 🌐 *www.navajonationparks.org* 🎟 *$5–$10.*

★ Ute Mountain Ute Tribal Park

ARCHAEOLOGICAL SITE | The only way to see this spectacular 125,000-acre park, located inside the Ute reservation, is by taking a guided tour. Expert tribal guides lead strenuous daylong hikes into this dazzling repository of Ancestral Pueblo ruins, including beautifully preserved cliff dwellings, pictographs, and petroglyphs. There are also less demanding half-day tours, as well as private and custom tour options. Tours meet at the Tribal Park Visitor Center at the junction of Highways 160 and 491, 20 miles south of Cortez. ✉ *Hwy. 160/491* ☎ *970/565–9653* 🌐 *www.utemountaintribalpark.info* 🎟 *From $29* ⏲ *Closed Sun. and major tribal and national holidays* ☞ *No pets allowed.*

Restaurants

Absolute Bakery and Cafe

$ | CAFÉ | It's 20 minutes east of Cortez, but this from-scratch bakery and café is absolutely worth the drive. Breakfast offerings are traditional and scrumptious; lunch options include flavorful soups, salads, pastas, and sandwiches; and the home-baked breads, pastries, and desserts are heavenly. **Known for:** local, organic ingredients; house-specialty gluten-free macaroons; great value. 💲 *Average main: $10* ✉ *110 S. Main St., Mancos* ☎ *970/533–1200* 🌐 *www.absolutebakery.com* ⏲ *Closed Mon. No lunch Sun.*

Nightlife

Ute Mountain Casino

CASINOS | At the base of Sleeping Ute Mountain, the state's first tribal casino rings with the sound of more than 780 slot machines. Ute Mountain Casino also draws crowds for bingo, blackjack, roulette, and poker. The resort is 11 miles south of Cortez on U.S. 160. ✉ *3 Weeminuche Dr., Towaoc* ☎ *970/565–8800, 800/258–8007* 🌐 *www.utemountaincasino.com.*

Shopping

CRAFTS AND ART GALLERIES

Notah-Dineh Trading Company and Museum
CERAMICS/GLASSWARE | This store specializing in Navajo rugs has the largest collection in the area. There are also handmade baskets, beadwork, pottery, and jewelry. If you stop in the free museum you can see relics of the Old West. ✉ *345 W. Main St.* ☎ *800/444–2024* 🌐 *www.notahdineh.com.*

Activities

HORSEBACK RIDING

Rimrock Outfitters
HORSEBACK RIDING | **FAMILY** | This stable offers guided horseback rides ranging from gentle one-hour tours to four-day pack trips into Ute Mountain Tribal Park or the La Plata Mountains. There are also breakfast and dinner trips (with steaks served on the open range). In the winter, they offer sleigh rides. ✉ *12175 County Rd. 44, Mancos* ☎ *970/533–7588* 🌐 *www.rimrockoutfitters.com* 🎫 *From $50.*

Dolores

11 miles northeast of Cortez via Rte. 145.

On the bank of the Dolores River, just downstream from the McPhee Reservoir, the tiny town of Dolores is midway between Durango and Telluride on State Highway 145. The river runs along the south edge of town, while beautiful cliffs flank the northern edge. Dolores attracts visitors with its spectacular scenery, fabulous fly-fishing, water sports, mountain hiking, biking, and other outdoor adventures.

Sights

★ Canyons of the Ancients National Monument
ARCHAEOLOGICAL SITE | Spread across 176,000 acres of arid mesa and canyon country, the Canyons of the Ancients National Monument holds more than 20,000 archaeological sites, the greatest concentration anywhere in the United States. Some sites, like apartment-style cliff dwellings and hewn-rock towers, are impossible to miss. Others are as subtle as evidence of agricultural fields, springs, and water systems. They are powerful evidence of the complex civilization of the Ancestral Pueblo people. **Lowry Pueblo,** in the northern part of the monument, is a 40-room pueblo with eight kivas (round chambers used for sacred rituals). Its Great Kiva is one of the largest known in the Southwest.

Exploring the monument area can be a challenge: roads are few, hiking trails are sparse, and visitor services are all but nonexistent. The visitor center, which is also a museum, is 3 miles west of Dolores on Highway 184. The best bet is a guided hike with the nonprofit Southwest Colorado Canyons Alliance. ✉ *27501 Hwy. 184* ↔ *3 miles west of Dolores* ☎ *970/882–5600* 🌐 *www.blm.gov* 🎫 *Monument free; museum $3.*

Galloping Goose Historical Museum
MUSEUM | Housed in a replica of the town's 1880s-era train station, this museum displays Galloping Goose No. 5, one of only seven specially designed engines built in the 1930s. The "Geese" were motored vehicles built from touring-car bodies that could operate for much less than steam-powered engines. ✉ *421 Railroad Ave.* ☎ *970/882–7082* 🌐 *www.gallopinggoose5.com* 🎫 *Free* ⏲ *Closed Sun. mid-May–mid-Oct.; closed Fri.–Mon. mid-Oct.–mid-May.*

Hovenweep National Monument

ARCHAEOLOGICAL SITE | Straddling the Colorado–Utah border, this monument is known for distinctive square, oval, round, and D-shape towers that were engineering marvels when they were built around AD 1200. The buildings are spread throughout a series of ancient villages, once home to 2,500 people. The visitor center is on the Utah side of the monument. **■ TIP→ Per rangers, don't attempt to use your GPS to find Hovenweep. Most devices will take you either over rough dirt roads or to more remote parts of the monument.** *From Dolores, take Hwy. 184 west to U.S. 491, then head west onto County Rd. CC for 9 miles* *970/562–4282* *www.nps.gov/hove* *Free.*

McPhee Reservoir

BODY OF WATER | In 1985, crews completed construction of an irrigation dam across the Dolores River, forming the McPhee Reservoir, the second largest in the state. It draws anglers looking to bag a variety of warm- and cold-water fish along its 50 miles of shoreline, which is surrounded by spectacular specimens of juniper and sage as well as large stands of pinyon pine. There are two boat ramps. The area also has camping, hiking, and a relatively easy mountain-bike trail, and the mesa offers panoramic views of the surrounding San Juan National Forest. *Forest Service Rd. 271, off Hwy. 184* *About 9 miles northwest of Dolores* *Free* *Marina closed Nov.–Apr.*

Restaurants

Dolores River Brewery

$$ | AMERICAN | Stop in here for what's fittingly billed as "thought-provoking beer." Choose from a wide selection of craft ales and stouts to wash down a slice of tasty wood-fired pizza. **Known for:** house-brewed craft ales; live, local bands–especially in summer; pleasant back patio. *Average main: $15* *100 S. 4th St.* *970/882–4677* *www.doloresriverbrewery.com* *Closed Mon. No lunch.*

Activities

RAFTING

Dvorak Expeditions

WHITE-WATER RAFTING | The outfitter offers rafting trips through the Gunnison Gorge, just northwest of the Black Canyon. Excursions last from one to three days and can be combined with fishing- or photography-focused excursions. *17921 U.S. 285, Nathrop* *719/539–6851, 800/824–3795* *www.dvorakexpeditions.com* *From $229.*

Chapter 12

MESA VERDE NATIONAL PARK

Updated by
Aimee Heckel

Sights ★★★★★ | Restaurants ★★★☆☆ | Hotels ★★☆☆☆ | Shopping ★★☆☆☆ | Nightlife ★☆☆☆☆

WELCOME TO MESA VERDE NATIONAL PARK

TOP REASONS TO GO

★ **Ancient artifacts:** Mesa Verde is a time capsule for the Ancestral Pueblo culture; more than 4,000 archaeological sites and 3 million objects have been unearthed here.

★ **Bright nights:** Mesa Verde's lack of light and air pollution, along with its high elevation, make for spectacular views of the heavens.

★ **Active adventures:** Get your heart pumping outdoors with hiking, biking, and exploring on trails of varying difficulties.

★ **Cliff dwellings:** Built atop the pinyon-covered mesa tops and hidden in the park's valleys are 600 ancient dwellings, some carved directly into the sandstone cliff faces.

★ **Geological marvels:** View the unique geology that drew the Ancient Pueblo to the area: protected desert canyons, massive alcoves in the cliff walls, thick bands of sandstone, continuous seep springs, and soils that could be used for both agriculture and architecture.

1 **Morefield.** The only campground in Mesa Verde, Morefield includes a village area with a gas station and store, and is close to the main visitor center and some of the best hiking trails in the park.

2 **Far View.** Almost an hour's drive from Mesa Verde's entrance, Far View is the park's epicenter, with several restaurants and the park's only overnight lodge. The fork in the road here takes you west toward the sites at Wetherill Mesa or south toward Chapin Mesa.

3 **Chapin Mesa.** Home to the park's most famous cliff dwellings and archaeological sites, the Chapin Mesa area includes the famous 150-room Cliff Palace and Spruce Tree House dwellings and other man-made and natural wonders, as well as the Chapin Mesa Archeological Museum.

4 **Wetherill Mesa.** See Long House, Two Raven House, Kodak House, and the Badger House Community.

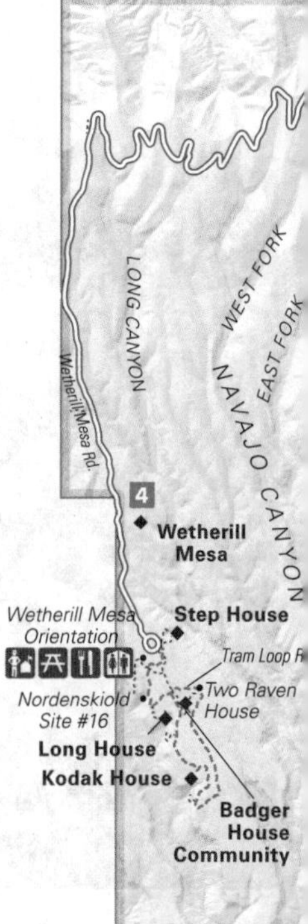

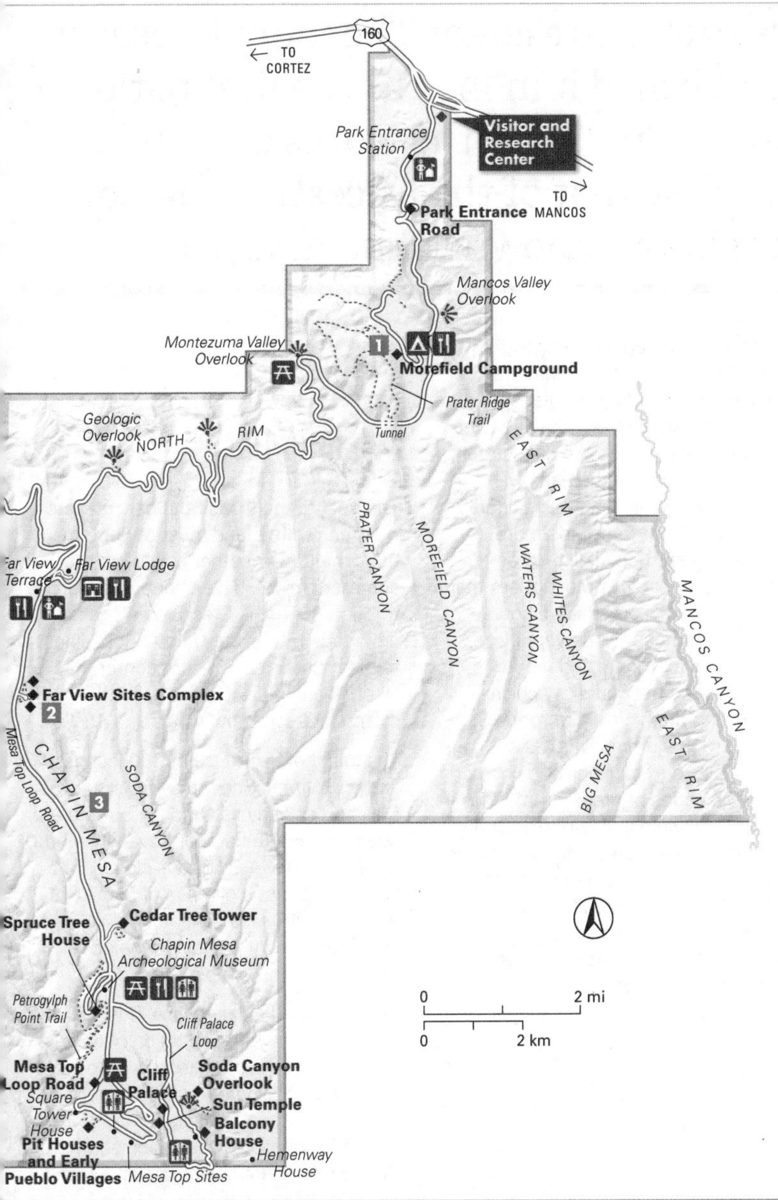

160
TO CORTEZ
Visitor and Research Center
Park Entrance Station
TO MANCOS
Park Entrance Road
Mancos Valley Overlook
Montezuma Valley Overlook
1
Morefield Campground
Prater Ridge Trail
Tunnel
Geologic Overlook
NORTH RIM
EAST RIM
PRATER CANYON
MOREFIELD CANYON
WATERS CANYON
WHITES CANYON
MANCOS CANYON
Far View Terrace
Far View Lodge
Far View Sites Complex
2
Mesa Top Loop Road
CHAPIN MESA
3
SODA CANYON
BIG MESA
EAST RIM
Spruce Tree House
Cedar Tree Tower
Chapin Mesa Archeological Museum
Petroglyph Point Trail
Cliff Palace Loop
Mesa Top Loop Road
Cliff Palace
Soda Canyon Overlook
Sun Temple
Square Tower House
Balcony House
Pit Houses and Early Pueblo Villages
Mesa Top Sites
Hemenway House
0
2 mi
0
2 km

Unlike the other national parks, Mesa Verde earned its status from its ancient cultural history rather than its geological treasures. President Theodore Roosevelt established it in 1906 as the first national park to "preserve the works of man," in this case that of the Ancestral Pueblo, previously known as the Anasazi.

They lived in the region from roughly 550 to 1300; they left behind more than 4,000 archaeological sites spread out over 80 square miles. Their ancient dwellings, set high into the sandstone cliffs, are the heart of the park. Mesa Verde (which in Spanish means, literally, "Green Table," but translates more accurately to something like "green flat-topped plateau") is much more than an archaeologist's dreamland, however. It's one of those windswept places where man's footprints and nature's paintbrush—some would say chisel—meet. Rising dramatically from the San Juan Basin, the jutting cliffs are cut by a series of complex canyons and covered in several shades of green, from pines in the higher elevations down to sage and other mountain brush on the desert floor. From the tops of the smaller mesas, you can look across to the cliff dwellings in the opposite rock faces. Dwarfed by the towering cliffs, the sand-color dwellings look almost like a natural occurrence in the midst of the desert's harsh beauty.

Planning

When to Go

The best times to visit the park are late May, early June, and most of September, when the weather is fine but the summer crowds have thinned. Mid-June through August is Mesa Verde's most crowded time. In July and August, lines at the museum and visitor center may last half an hour. Afternoon thunderstorms are common in July and August.

The park gets as much as 100 inches of snow in winter. Snow may fall as late as May and as early as October, but there's rarely enough to hamper travel. In winter, the Wetherill Mesa Road is closed, but you can still get a glimpse of some of the Wetherill Mesa sandstone dwellings, sheltered from the snow in their cliff coves, from the Chapin Mesa area.

Ute Mountain Ute Bear Dance. This traditional dance, the local version of a Sadie Hawkins (in which the women choose their dance partners—and the selected men can't refuse), is held in May or June on the Towaoc Ute reservation south of Cortez. The event celebrates spring and

AVERAGE HIGH/LOW TEMPERATURES					
JAN.	**FEB.**	**MAR.**	**APR.**	**MAY**	**JUNE**
37/16	41/20	49/26	57/31	67/39	79/49
JULY	**AUG.**	**SEPT.**	**OCT.**	**NOV.**	**DEC.**
84/55	81/53	74/46	61/36	48/25	38/18

the legacy of a mythical bear that taught the Ute people her secrets. It's part of a multiday festival that includes music, races, and softball games, and culminates with an hour-long dance that's over when only one couple remains. 🌐 *www.utemountainutetribe.com*

Durango Fiesta Days. A parade, one of the oldest rodeos in the state, barbecue, street dance, cook-offs, live music, and more come to the Durango Fairgrounds in July. 🌐 *www.downtowndurango.org*

Durango Cowboy Poetry Gathering. A parade accompanies art exhibitions, poetry readings, music, theater, and storytelling in this four-day event run by the Durango Cowboy Poetry Gathering, a nonprofit set up to preserve the traditions of the American West. It's held the first weekend in October. 🌐 *www.durangocowboypoetrygathering.org*

Getting Here and Around

AIR

The cities of Durango (36 miles east of the park entrance) and Cortez (11 miles to the west) have airports.

CAR

The park has just one entrance, off U.S. 160, between Cortez and Durango in what's known as the Four Corners area (which spans the intersection of Colorado, New Mexico, Arizona, and Utah). Most of the roads at Mesa Verde involve steep grades and hairpin turns, particularly on Wetherill Mesa. Vehicles over 8,000 pounds or 25 feet are prohibited on this road. Trailers and towed vehicles are prohibited past Morefield Campground. Check the condition of your vehicle's brakes before driving the road to Wetherill Mesa. For the latest road information, tune to 1610 AM, or call ☎ *970/529–4461*. Off-road vehicles are prohibited in the park. At less-visited Wetherill Mesa, you must leave your car behind and hike or bike to the Long House, Kodak House, and Badger House Community.

Inspiration

Mesa Verde National Park: Shadows of the Centuries, by Duane A. Smith, discusses the history and current issues facing the park.

Ancient Peoples of the American Southwest, by Stephen Plog, is an archaeologist's account of the Ancestral Pueblo people and two other cultures.

Mesa Verde: Ancient Architecture, by Jesse Walter Fewkes, tells the stories behind the park's dwellings.

Park Essentials

PARK FEES AND PERMITS

Admission is $25 per vehicle for a seven-day permit. An annual pass is $40. Ranger-led tours of Cliff Palace, Long House, and Balcony House are $5 per person. You can also take ranger-guided bus tours from the Far View Lodge, which last between 3½ and 4 hours and cost $55 ($33 for kids; under five free). Backcountry hiking and fishing are not permitted at Mesa Verde.

Mesa Verde in One Day

For a full experience, take at least one ranger-led tour of a major cliff dwelling site, as well as a few self-guided walks. Arrive early and stop first at the Visitor and Research Center, where you can purchase tickets for Cliff Palace and Balcony House tours on Chapin Mesa. If it's going to be a hot day, you might want to take an early-morning or late-afternoon bus tour. Drive to the **Chapin Mesa Museum** to watch a 25-minute film introducing you to the area and its history. Just behind the museum is the trailhead for the ½-mile-long **Spruce Tree House Trail**, which normally leads to the best-preserved cliff dwelling in the park. While the Spruce Tree House is temporarily closed for restabilization, you can still view it from up top. Then drive to **Balcony House** for an hour-long, ranger-led tour.

Have lunch at the Spruce Tree Terrace Café or the Cliff Palace picnic area. Afterward take the ranger-led tour of **Cliff Palace** (one hour). Use the rest of the day to explore the overlooks and trails off the 6-mile loop of **Mesa Top Loop Road.** Or when the Spruce Tree House is open, head back to the museum and take **Petroglyph Point Trail** to see a great example of Ancestral Pueblo rock carvings. A leisurely walk along the Mesa Top's **Soda Canyon Overlook Trail** (off Cliff Palace Loop Road) gives you a beautiful bird's-eye view of the canyon below. On the drive back toward the park entrance, be sure to check out the view from **Park Point.**

PARK HOURS

Mesa Verde's facilities each operate on their own schedule, but most are open daily, from Memorial Day through Labor Day, between about 8 am and sunset. The rest of the year, they open at 9. In winter, the Spruce Tree House is open only to offer a few scheduled tours each day. Wetherill Mesa (and all the sites it services) is open from May through October, weather depending. Far View Center, Far View Terrace, and Far View Lodge are open between April and October. Morefield Campground and the sites nearby are open from mid-April through mid-October (and until early November for limited camping with no services). Specific hours are subject to change, so check with the visitor center upon arrival.

CELL-PHONE RECEPTION AND INTERNET

You can get patchy cell service in the park. Best service is typically at the Morefield Campground area, which is the closest to the neighboring towns of Cortez and Mancos. Public telephones can be found at all the major visitor areas (Morefield, Far View, and Spruce Tree). You can get free Wi-Fi throughout the Far View Lodge and at the Morefield Campground store.

Restaurants

Dining options in Mesa Verde are limited inside the park, but comparatively plentiful and varied if you're staying in Cortez, Mancos, or Durango. In surrounding communities, Southwestern restaurants, farm-fresh eateries, and steak houses are common options.

Hotels

All 150 rooms of the park's Far View Lodge, open mid-April through late October, fill up quickly—so reservations are recommended, especially if you plan to visit on a weekend in summer. Options in the surrounding area include chain hotels, cabins, and bed-and-breakfast inns. Although 40 minutes away, Durango in particular has a number of hotels in fine old buildings reminiscent of the Old West.

Restaurant and hotel reviews have been shortened. For full information, visit Fodors.com. Restaurant prices are the average cost of a main course at dinner or, if dinner is not served, at lunch. Hotel reviews are the lowest cost of a standard double room in high season, excluding taxes and service charges.

What It Costs

$	$$	$$$	$$$$
RESTAURANTS			
under $13	$13–$18	$19–$25	over $25
HOTELS			
under $121	$121–$170	$171–$230	over $230

Tours

BUS TOURS

Aramark Tours

GUIDED TOURS | FAMILY | If you want a well-rounded visit to Mesa Verde's most popular sites, consider a group tour. The park concessionaire provides all-day and half-day guided tours of the Chapin Mesa and Far View sites, departing in buses from either Morefield Campground or Far View Lodge. Tours are led by Aramark guides or park rangers, who share information about the park's history, geology, and excavation processes. Cold water is provided, but you'll need to bring your own snacks. Buy tickets at Far View Lodge, the Morefield Campground, or online. Tours sell out, so reserve in advance. ✉ *Far View Lodge, 1 Navajo Hill, mile marker 15* ☎ *970/529–4422 Far View Lodge, 800/449–2288 Aramark* 🌐 *www.visitmesaverde.com* 🎫 *From $41* 🕓 *700 Years Tour closed late Oct.–mid-Apr. Far View Explorer Tour closed mid-Aug.–late May.*

GUIDED TOURS

Ranger-Led Tours

GUIDED TOURS | The cliff dwellings known as Balcony House, Cliff Palace, and Long House can be explored only on ranger-led tours; the first two last about an hour, the third is 90 minutes. Buy tickets at the Mesa Verde Visitor and Research Center. These are active tours and may not be suitable for some children; each requires climbing ladders without handrails and squeezing through tight spaces. Be sure to bring water and sunscreen. Site schedules vary so check ahead. ✉ *Mesa Verde National Park* ☎ *970/529–4465* 🌐 *www.nps.gov/meve/planyourvisit/visit-cliffdwelling.htm* 🎫 *$5 per site* 🕓 *Closed: Cliff Palace: Oct./Nov.–late May. Balcony House: early Oct.–late Apr. Long House: mid-Oct.–mid-May.*

Visitor Information

PARK CONTACT INFORMATION Mesa Verde National Park. ☎ *970/529–4465* 🌐 *www.nps.gov/meve.*

Morefield

Sights

PICNIC AREAS

Montezuma Valley Overlook Picnic Area

LOCAL INTEREST | FAMILY | There is only one picnic table (and no services) here, but the view is excellent. ✉ *5 miles west of park entrance.*

SCENIC DRIVES

Park Entrance Road

NATIONAL/STATE PARK | The main park road, also known as SH 10, leads you from the entrance off U.S. 160 into the park. As a break from the switchbacks, you can stop at a couple of pretty overlooks along the way, but hold out for Park Point, which, at the mesa's highest elevation (8,572 feet), gives you unobstructed, 360-degree views. Note that trailers and towed vehicles are not permitted beyond Morefield Campground. ✉ *Mesa Verde National Park.*

TRAILS

Knife Edge Trail

TRAIL | Perfect for a sunset stroll, this easy 2-mile (round-trip) walk around the north rim of the park leads to an overlook of the Montezuma Valley. If you stop at all the flora identification points that the trail pamphlet suggests, the hike takes about 1½ to 2 hours. The patches of asphalt you spot along the way are leftovers from old Knife Edge Road, built in 1914 as the main entryway into the park. *Easy.* ✉ *Mesa Verde National Park* ✥ *Trailhead: Morefield Campground, 4 miles from park entrance.*

Prater Ridge Trail

TRAIL | This 7.8-mile round-trip loop, which starts and finishes at Morefield Campground, is the longest hike you can take inside the park. It provides fine views of Morefield Canyon to the south and the San Juan Mountains to the north. About halfway through the hike, you'll see a cutoff trail that you can take, which shortens the trip to 5 miles. *Difficult.* ✉ *Mesa Verde National Park* ✥ *Trailhead: west end of Morefield Campground, 4 miles from park entrance.*

VISITOR CENTERS

Mesa Verde Visitor and Research Center

INFO CENTER | **FAMILY** | The visitor center is the best place to go to sign up for tours, get the information you need to plan a successful trip, and buy tickets for the Cliff Palace, Balcony House, and Long House ranger-led tours. The sleek, energy-efficient research center is filled with more than 3 million artifacts and archives. The center features indoor and outdoor exhibits, a gift shop, picnic tables, and a museum. Find books, maps, and videos on the history of the park. ✉ *Park entrance on the left, 35853 Rd H.5, Mancos* ☎ *970/529–4465* 🌐 *www.nps.gov/meve/planyourvisit/meve_vc.htm.*

 Restaurants

Knife Edge Cafe

$ | **CAFÉ** | **FAMILY** | Located in the Morefield Campground, this simple restaurant in a covered outdoor terrace with picnic tables serves a hearty all-you-can-eat pancake breakfast with sausage every morning. Coffee and beverages are also available. **Known for:** lively gathering spot; breakfast burritos; large coffees with free refills all day. [$] *Average main: $10* ✉ *4 miles south of park entrance* ☎ *970/565–2133* 🌐 *www.nps.gov/meve/planyourvisit/restaurants.htm* ⏲ *Closed mid-Sept.–late Apr.*

Far View

 Sights

HISTORIC SITES

Far View Sites Complex

ARCHAEOLOGICAL SITE | **FAMILY** | This was probably one of the most densely populated areas in Mesa Verde, comprising as many as 50 villages in a ½-square-mile area at the top of Chapin Mesa. Most of the sites here were built between 900 and 1300. Begin the self-guided tour at the interpretive panels in the parking lot, then proceed down a ½-mile, level trail. ✉ *Park entrance road, near the Chapin Mesa area* 🌐 *www.nps.gov/meve* 🎫 *Free* ☞ *In winter, access by parking at the gate and walking in.*

TRAILS

Farming Terrace Trail

TRAIL | FAMILY | This 30-minute, ½-mile loop begins and ends on the spur road to Cedar Tree Tower, about 1 mile north of the Chapin Mesa area. It meanders through a series of check dams, which the Ancestral Pueblo built to create farming terraces. *Easy.* ✉ *Mesa Verde National Park* ✥ *Trailhead: park entrance road, 4 miles south of Far View Center.*

Restaurants

Far View Terrace Café

$ | AMERICAN | This full-service cafeteria offers great views, but it's nothing fancy. Grab a simple coffee here or head across the dining room to Mesa Mocha for a latte. **Known for:** beautiful views; lattes; great gift shop. $ *Average main: $12* ✉ *Across from Far View Center* 🌐 *www.visitmesaverde.com/lodging-camping/dining/far-view-terrace-cafe* ⏲ *Closed late Oct.–mid-Apr.*

Metate Room Restaurant

$$$ | AMERICAN | The park's rugged terrain contrasts with this relaxing space just off the lobby of the Far View Lodge. The well-regarded dining room is upscale, but the atmosphere remains casual. **Known for:** Native American artwork; cheese and cured meats board; great views. $ *Average main: $25* ✉ *Far View Lodge, 1 Navajo Rd., across from Far View Center, 15 miles southwest of park entrance* ☎ *970/529–4422* 🌐 *www.visitmesaverde.com/lodging-camping/dining/metate-room-restaurant* ⏲ *Closed late Oct.–mid-Apr. No lunch.*

Hotels

★ Far View Lodge

$$ | HOTEL | Talk about a view—all rooms have a private balcony, from which you can admire views of the neighboring states of Arizona, Utah, and New Mexico up to 100 miles in the distance. **Pros:** close to the key sites; views are spectacular; small on-site fitness center. **Cons:** simple rooms and amenities, with no TV; walls are thin and less than soundproof; no cell-phone service. $ *Rooms from: $151* ✉ *Across from Far View Center, 1 Navajo Rd., 15 miles southwest of park entrance* ☎ *800/449–2288* 🌐 *www.visitmesaverde.com* ⏲ *Closed late Oct.–mid-Apr.* *150 rooms* *No meals.*

Shopping

Far View Terrace Shop

CLOTHING | In the same building as the Far View Terrace Café, this is the largest gift shop in the park, with gifts, souvenirs, Native American art, toys, and T-shirts galore. ✉ *Mesa Top Loop Rd., 15 miles south of park entrance* ☎ *800/449–2288* *Aramark.*

Chapin Mesa

Sights

HISTORIC SIGHTS

★ Balcony House

ARCHAEOLOGICAL SITE | The stonework of this 40-room cliff dwelling is impressive, but you're likely to be even more awed by the skill it must have taken to reach this place. Perched in a sandstone cove 600 feet above the floor of Soda Canyon, Balcony House seems suspended in space. Even with modern passageways and trails, today's visitors must climb a 32-foot ladder and crawl through a narrow tunnel. Look for the intact balcony for which the house is named. The dwelling is accessible only on a ranger-led tour. ✉ *Cliff Palace/Balcony House Rd., 10 miles south of Far View Center, Cliff Palace Loop* 🌐 *www.nps.gov/meve/learn/historyculture/cd_balcony_house.htm* *$5* ⏲ *Closed early Oct.–late Apr.*

Did You Know?

Balcony House was most likely once home to up to 30 people. It would've received little warmth from the sun during the winter, so its residents probably considered other needs (like water access) more important.

★ Cliff Palace

ARCHAEOLOGICAL SITE | This was the first major Mesa Verde dwelling seen by cowboys Charlie Mason and Richard Wetherill in 1888. It is also the largest, containing about 150 rooms and 23 kivas on three levels. Getting there involves a steep downhill hike and three ladders. **■ TIP→ You may enter Balcony House or Cliff Palace by ranger-guided tour only so purchase tickets in advance.** The 90-minute, small-group "twilight tours" at sunset present this archaeological treasure with dramatic sunset lighting. Tour tickets are only available in advance at the Visitor and Research Center, Morefield Ranger Station, Durango Welcome Center, and online at ⊕ *www.recreation.gov.* ✉ *Mesa Verde National Park* ✣ *Cliff Palace Overlook, about 2½ miles south of Chapin Mesa Archeological Museum* ⊕ *www.nps.gov/meve/learn/historyculture/cd_cliff_palace.htm* 🎫 *Regular tickets $5; twilight tours $20.* ⏲ *Closed Oct./Nov.–late May; loop closes at sunset.*

Pit Houses and Early Pueblo Villages

ARCHAEOLOGICAL SITE | Three dwellings, built on top of each other from 700 to 950, at first look like a mass of jumbled walls, but an informational panel helps identify the dwellings—and the stories behind them are fascinating. The 325-foot trail from the walking area is paved, wheelchair accessible, and near a restroom. ✉ *Mesa Top Loop Rd., about 2½ miles south of Chapin Mesa Archeological Museum* 🎫 *Free.*

Spruce Tree House

ARCHAEOLOGICAL SITE | FAMILY | This 138-room complex is the best-preserved site in the park; however, the alcove surrounding Spruce Tree House became unstable in 2015 and was closed to visitors. Until alcove arch support is added, visitors can view but not enter this site. You can still hike down a trail that starts behind the Chapin Mesa Archeological Museum and leads you 100 feet down into the canyon to view the site from a distance. Because of its location in the heart of the Chapin Mesa area, the Spruce Tree House trail and area can resemble a crowded playground during busy periods. When allowed inside the site, tours are self-guided (allow 45 minutes to an hour), but a park ranger is on-site to answer questions. ✉ *Mesa Verde National Park* ✣ *At the Chapin Mesa Archeological Museum, 5 miles south of Far View Center* ⊕ *www.nps.gov/meve/learn/historyculture/cd_spruce_tree_house.htm* 🎫 *Free* ⏲ *Tours closed for reconstruction.*

Sun Temple

ARCHAEOLOGICAL SITE | Although researchers assume it was probably a ceremonial structure, they're unsure of the exact purpose of this complex, which has no doors or windows in most of its chambers. Because the building was not quite half finished when it was left in 1276, some researchers surmise it might have been constructed to stave off whatever disaster caused its builders—and the other inhabitants of Mesa Verde—to leave. ✉ *Mesa Top Loop Rd., about 2 miles south of Chapin Mesa Archeological Museum* ⊕ *www.nps.gov/meve/history-culture/mt_sun_temple.htm* 🎫 *Free.*

PICNIC AREAS

Chapin Mesa Picnic Area

LOCAL INTEREST | FAMILY | This is the nicest and largest picnic area in the park. It has about 40 tables under shade trees and a great view into Spruce Canyon, as well as flush toilets. ✉ *Mesa Verde National Park* ✣ *Near Chapin Mesa Archeological Museum, 5 miles south of Far View Center.*

SCENIC DRIVES

Mesa Top Loop Road

SCENIC DRIVE | This 6-mile drive skirts the scenic rim of Chapin Mesa and takes you to several overlooks and short, paved trails. You'll get great views of Sun Temple and Square Tower, as well as Cliff Palace, Sunset House, and several other cliff dwellings visible from the Sun Point Overlook. ✉ *Mesa Verde National Park.*

The landscapes of Mesa Verde are beautiful no matter the season.

SCENIC STOPS

Cedar Tree Tower

ARCHAEOLOGICAL SITE | A self-guided tour takes you to, but not through, a tower and kiva built between 1100 and 1300 and connected by a tunnel. The tower-and-kiva combinations in the park are thought to have been either religious structures or signal towers. ✉ *Mesa Verde National Park* ✣ *Near the four-way intersection on Chapin Mesa; park entrance road, 1½ miles north of Chapin Mesa Archeological Museum* 🌐 *www.nps.gov/meve/learn/historyculture/mt_cedar_tree_tower.htm* 🎫 *Free.*

Soda Canyon Overlook

CANYON | Get your best view of Balcony House here. You can also read interpretive panels about the site and the surrounding canyon geology. ✉ *Cliff Palace Loop Rd., about 1 mile north of Balcony House parking area* ☞ *Access in winter by walking the Cliff Palace Loop.*

TRAILS

★ Petroglyph Point Trail

TRAIL | Scramble along a narrow canyon wall to reach the largest and best-known petroglyphs in Mesa Verde. If you pose for a photo just right, you can manage to block out the gigantic "don't touch" sign next to the rock art. A map—available at any ranger station—points out three dozen points of interest along the trail. However, the trail is not open while Spruce Tree House is closed; check with a ranger for more information. *Moderate.* ✉ *Mesa Verde National Park* ✣ *Trailhead: at Spruce Tree House, next to Chapin Mesa Archeological Museum.*

Soda Canyon Overlook Trail

TRAIL | **FAMILY** | One of the easiest and most rewarding hikes in the park, this little trail travels 1½ miles round-trip through the forest on almost completely level ground. The overlook is an excellent point from which to photograph the Chapin Mesa–area cliff dwellings. *Easy.* ✉ *Mesa Verde National Park* ✣ *Trailhead:*

Plants and Wildlife in Mesa Verde

Mesa Verde is home to 640 species of plants, including a number of native plants found nowhere else. Its lower elevations feature many varieties of shrubs, including rabbitbrush and sagebrush. Higher up, you'll find mountain mahogany, yucca, pinyon, juniper, and Douglas fir. During warmer months, brightly colored blossoms, like the yellow perky Sue, blue lupines, and bright-red Indian paintbrushes, are scattered throughout the park.

The park is also home to a variety of migratory and resident animals, including 74 species of mammals. Drive slowly along the park's roads; mule deer are everywhere. You may spot wild turkeys, and black bear encounters are not unheard of on the hiking trails. Bobcats, coyotes, and mountain lions are also around, but they are seen less frequently. About 200 species of birds, including threatened Mexican spotted owls, red-tailed hawks, golden eagles, and noisy ravens, also live here. On the ground, you should keep your eyes and ears open for lizards and snakes, including the poisonous—but shy—prairie rattlesnake. As a general rule, animals are most active in the early morning and at dusk.

Many areas of the park have had extensive fire damage over the years. In fact, wildfires here have been so destructive they are given names, just like hurricanes. For example, the Bircher Fire in 2000 consumed nearly 20,000 acres of brush and forest, much of it covering the eastern half of the park. It will take several centuries for the woodland there to look as verdant as the area atop Chapin Mesa, which escaped the fire. But in the meantime, you'll have a chance to glimpse nature's powerful rejuvenating processes in action; the landscape in the fire-ravaged sections of the park is already filling in with vegetation.

Cliff Palace Loop Rd., about 1 mile north of Balcony House parking area ☞ *Access in winter via Cliff Palace Loop.*

Spruce Canyon Trail

TRAIL | While Petroglyph Point Trail takes you along the side of the canyon, this trail ventures down into its depths. It's only 2.4 miles long, but you descend about 600 feet in elevation. Remember to save your strength; what goes down must come up again. The trail is open even while Spruce Tree House is closed. Still, check with a ranger. *Moderate.* ✉ *Mesa Verde National Park* ✣ *Trailhead: at Spruce Tree House, next to Chapin Mesa Archeological Museum* ☞ *Registration required at trailhead.*

VISITOR CENTERS

Chapin Mesa Archeological Museum

MUSEUM | This is an excellent first stop for an introduction to Ancestral Pueblo culture, as well as the area's development into a national park. Exhibits showcase original textiles and other artifacts, and a theater plays an informative film every 30 minutes. Rangers are available to answer your questions. The shop focuses on educational materials, but you can also find park-themed souvenirs. The museum sits at the south end of the park entrance road and overlooks Spruce Tree House. Nearby, you'll find park headquarters, a gift shop, a post office, snack bar, and bathrooms. ✉ *Park entrance road, 5 miles south of Far View Center, 20 miles from park entrance* ☎ *970/529–4465*

You'll find ancient petroglyphs in many places throughout the park.

General information line 🌐 *www.nps.gov/meve/planyourvisit/museum.htm* 🎫 *Free.*

Restaurants

Spruce Tree Terrace Café

$ | **AMERICAN** | This small cafeteria has a limited selection of hot food, coffee, salads, burgers, and sandwiches. The patio is pleasant, and it's conveniently located across the street from the museum. **Known for:** Southwest specialties; soup of the day specials; Navajo tacos. 💲 *Average main: $10* ✉ *Near Chapin Mesa Archeological Museum, 5 miles south of the Far View Center* ☎ *970/529–4465* 🌐 *www.visitmesaverde.com/lodging-camping/dining/spruce-tree-terrace-cafe* ⏲ *No dinner in off-season.*

Shopping

Chapin Mesa Archeological Museum Shop

BOOKS/STATIONERY | Books and videos are the primary offering here, with more than 400 titles on Ancestral Pueblo and Southwestern topics. You can also find a selection of touristy T-shirts and hats. Hours vary throughout the year. ✉ *Spruce Tree Terrace, near Chapin Mesa Archeological Museum* ✣ *5 miles from Far View Center* ☎ *970/529–4445* 🌐 *www.nps.gov/meve/planyourvisit/museum.htm.*

Wetherill Mesa

Sights

HISTORIC SIGHTS

Badger House Community

ARCHAEOLOGICAL SITE | A self-guided walk along paved and gravel trails takes you through a group of four mesa-top dwellings. The community, which covers nearly 7 acres, dates back to the year 650, the Basketmaker Period, and includes a primitive, semisubterranean pit house and what's left of a multistory stone pueblo. Allow about 45 minutes to see the sites. The trail is 2.4 miles round-trip. ✉ *Wetherill Mesa Rd., 12 miles from Far View Center* 🌐 *www.nps.gov/meve/historyculture/*

mt_badger_house.htm 🎫 *Free* ⏲ *Closed late Oct.–early May; road closes at 6 pm.*

Long House

ARCHAEOLOGICAL SITE | This Wetherill Mesa cliff dwelling is the second largest in Mesa Verde. It is believed that about 150 people lived in Long House, so named because of the size of its cliff alcove. The spring at the back of the cave is still active today. The in-depth, ranger-led tour begins a short distance from the parking lot and takes about 90 minutes. You hike about 2 miles, including two 15-foot ladders. ✉ *On Wetherill Mesa, 29 miles past the visitor center, near mile marker 15* 🌐 *www.nps.gov/meve/learn/historyculture/cd_long_house.htm* 🎫 *Tours $5* ⏲ *Closed mid-Oct.–mid-May.*

Step House

ARCHAEOLOGICAL SITE | So named because of a crumbling prehistoric stairway leading up from the dwelling, Step House is reached via a paved (but steep) trail that's ¾ mile long. The house is unique in that it shows clear evidence of two separate occupations: the first around 626, the second a full 600 years later. The self-guided tour takes about 45 minutes. ✉ *Wetherill Mesa Rd., 12 miles from Far View Center* 🌐 *www.nps.gov/meve/historyculture/cd_step_house.htm* 🎫 *Free* ⏲ *Closed mid-May–mid-Oct.; hrs vary seasonally.*

PICNIC AREAS

Cliff Palace Picnic Area

$ | LOCAL INTEREST | | FAMILY |LOCAL INTEREST | FAMILY | At this picnic area, there are several wooden tables under shade trees, plus restrooms, but no running water. The area is wheelchair accessible, although the nearby Cliff Palace dwellings are not. ✉ *2½ miles south of Chapin Mesa Archeological Museum* 🌐 *www.nps.gov/meve* ⏲ *Not plowed in the winter. Closed after sunset.*

Wetherill Mesa Picnic Area

LOCAL INTEREST | FAMILY | A handful of benches and tables near drinking water, a covered kiosk, and restrooms make this a pleasant spot for lunch in the Wetherill area. ✉ *Mesa Verde National Park* ✣ *12 miles southwest of Far View Center.*

SCENIC DRIVES

Wetherill Mesa Road

SCENIC DRIVE | This 12-mile mountain road, stretching from the Far View Center to the Wetherill Mesa, has sharp curves and steep grades (and is restricted to vehicles less than 25 feet long and 8,000 pounds). Roadside pull-outs offer unobstructed views of the Four Corners region. At the end of the road, you can access Step House, Long House, and Badger House. ✉ *Mesa Verde National Park* ⏲ *Closed late Oct.–early May.*

SCENIC STOPS

Kodak House Overlook

VIEWPOINT | Get an impressive view into the 60-room Kodak House and its several small kivas from here. The house, closed to the public, was named for a Swedish researcher who absentmindedly left his Kodak camera behind here in 1891. ✉ *Wetherill Mesa Rd.* 🌐 *www.nps.gov/meve* ⏲ *Closed late Oct.–May.*

Coffee and Quick Bites

Wetherill Mesa Snack Bar

$ | AMERICAN | There's little on offer here, just chips, soft drinks, and concessions served on picnic tables under an awning, but it's the only choice on Wetherill Mesa. 💲 *Average main: $7* ✉ *12 miles southwest of the park entrance* ☎ *970/529–4465* 🌐 *www.nps.gov/meve* 💳 *No credit cards* ⏲ *Closed Sept.–May.*

Activities

At Mesa Verde, outdoor activities are restricted, due to the fragile nature of the archaeological treasures here. Hiking (allowed on marked trails only) is the best option, especially as a way to view some of the Ancestral Pueblo dwellings.

BICYCLING

Bicycles are allowed on paved roads in the park except the twisty Wetherill Mesa Road, but there are no bike lanes and very narrow shoulders. During periods of low visibility (or when traveling through the tunnel on the main park road), bicycles must be fitted with a white light on the front and a red light (or reflector) on the back. Bikes are not allowed off-road or on trails.

BIRD-WATCHING

Turkey vultures soar between April and October, and large flocks of ravens hang around all summer. Among the park's other large birds are red-tailed hawks, great horned owls, and a few golden eagles. The Steller's jay (the male looks like a blue jay with a dark hat on) frequently pierces the pinyon-juniper forest with its cries, and hummingbirds dart from flower to flower in the summer and fall. Any visit to cliff dwellings late in the day will include frolicking white-throated swifts, which make their home in rock crevices overhead.

Pick up a copy of the park's "Checklist of the Birds" brochure or visit the National Park Service's website (🌐 *www.nps.gov/meve/planyourvisit/birdwatching.htm*) for a detailed listing of the feathered inhabitants here.

CAMPING

Morefield Campground is the only option within the park, and it's an excellent one. Reservations are accepted; it's open mid-April through mid-October, and through early November with no services. In nearby Mancos, just across the highway from the park entrance, there's a campground with full amenities (but no electrical hookups), while the San Juan National Forest offers backcountry camping.

Morefield Campground and Village. With 267 campsites, including 15 full-hookup RV sites, access to trailheads, a pet kennel, and plenty of amenities (including a gas station and a grocery store), the only campground in the park is an appealing mini-city for campers. It's a 40-minute drive to reach the park's most popular sites. Reservations are recommended, especially for RVs. ✉ *4 miles south of park entrance* ☎ *970/564–4300, 800/449–2288* 🌐 *www.visitmesaverde.com.*

HIKING

A handful of trails lead beyond Mesa Verde's most visited sites and offer more solitude than the often-crowded cliff dwellings. The best canyon vistas can be reached if you're willing to huff and puff your way through elevation changes and switchbacks. Carry more water than you think you'll need, wear sunscreen, and bring rain gear—cloudbursts can come seemingly out of nowhere. Certain trails are open seasonally, so check with a ranger before heading out. No backcountry hiking is permitted in Mesa Verde, and pets are prohibited.

STARGAZING

There are no large cities in the Four Corners area, so there is little artificial light to detract from the stars in the night sky. Far View Lodge and Morefield Campground are great for sky watching.

Chapter 13

COLORADO SPRINGS AND SOUTH CENTRAL COLORADO

WITH GREAT SAND DUNES NATIONAL PARK

Updated by
Whitney Bryen

Sights	Restaurants	Hotels	Shopping	Nightlife
★★★★☆	★★★☆☆	★★★☆☆	★★★☆☆	★★★☆☆

WELCOME TO COLORADO SPRINGS AND SOUTH CENTRAL COLORADO

TOP REASONS TO GO

★ **Hike a fourteener:** Coloradans collect hikes to the summit of Fourteeners—mountains that top 14,000 feet above sea level—like trophies.

★ **Play on the sand dunes:** At Great Sand Dunes, one of nature's most spectacular sandboxes, you'll feel like a kid again as you hike up a 750-foot dune then roll down (or sandboard) the other side.

★ **Raft on the Arkansas:** The Arkansas River is one of the most popular rivers for rafting and kayaking—from gentle floats to Class V rapids—in the United States.

★ **Ride up Pikes Peak:** Katharine Bates wrote "America the Beautiful" after riding to the top of Pikes Peak. Ride the Pikes Peak shuttle to the top for the same see-forever views.

★ **Visit the U.S. Air Force Academy:** Here you can learn more about the academy that trains future Air Force leaders and visit the stunning, nondenominational Cadet Chapel.

1 **Colorado Springs.** The second-largest city in the state and a major cultural hub and outdoor mecca.

2 **Cripple Creek.** A former mining and current gambling town.

3 **Florissant Fossil Beds.** A haven for dinosaur enthusiasts.

4 **Palmer Lake.** An artsy town with great hiking.

5 **Royal Gorge Region and Cañon City.** A dramatic canyon and its gateway city.

6 **Buena Vista.** A small community surrounded by the Collegiate Peaks.

7 **Salida.** A mountain town dominated by Mount Shavano.

8 **Pueblo.** A historical trading post.

9 **La Junta.** A small town with the fascinating Koshare Indian Museum.

10 **Trinidad.** A historic charming town.

11 **Cuchara Valley.** A true rural setting, home to San Isabel National Forest.

12 **Great Sand Dunes National Park and Preserve.** Colorado's unforgettable sand dunes.

13 **Alamosa.** The main city of San Luis Valley.

14 **San Luis and Fort Garland Loop.** A road trip or scenic railway ride through a beautiful region.

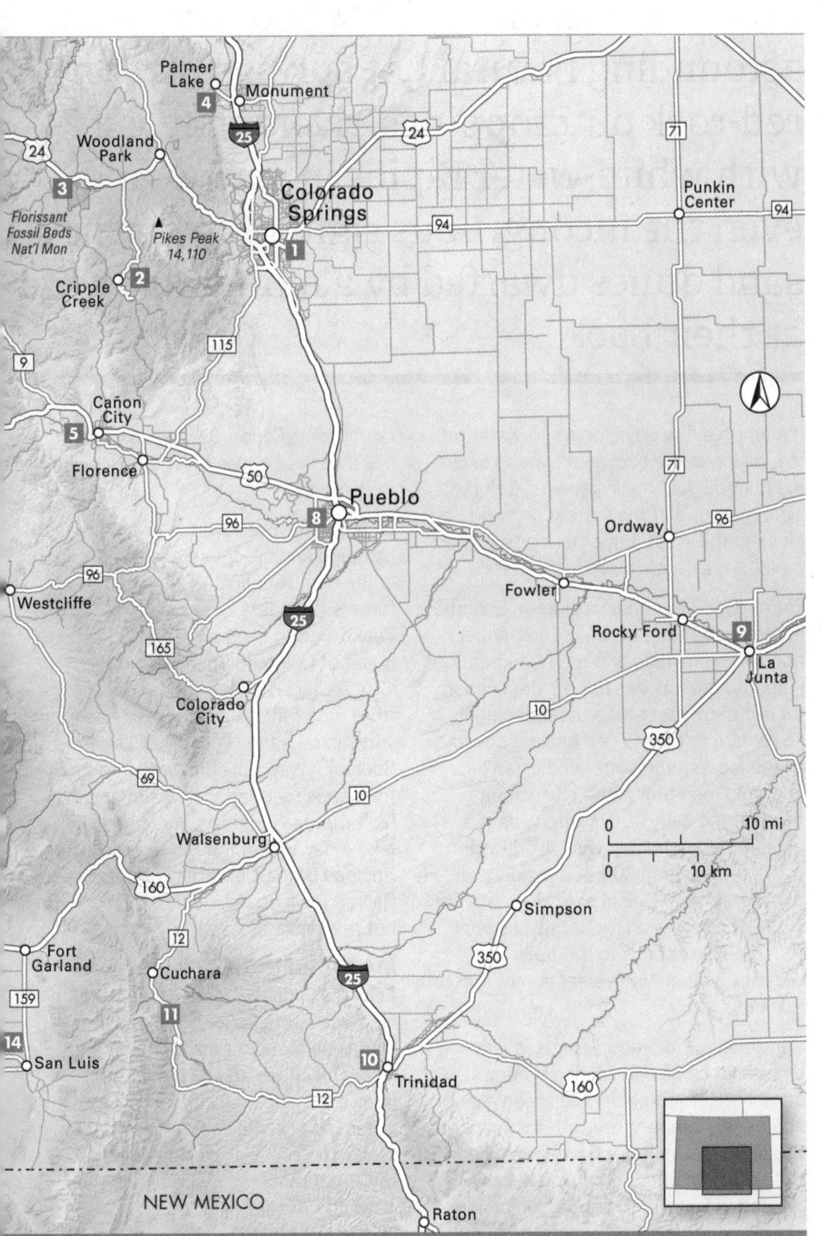
Palmer Lake
Monument
Woodland Park
Colorado Springs
Florissant Fossil Beds Nat'l Mon
Pikes Peak 14,110
Cripple Creek
Punkin Center
Cañon City
Florence
Pueblo
Ordway
Fowler
Westcliffe
Rocky Ford
La Junta
Colorado City
Walsenburg
Simpson
Fort Garland
Cuchara
San Luis
Trinidad
NEW MEXICO
Raton
0 10 mi
0 10 km

Stretching from majestic mountains into rugged, high desert plains, south central Colorado has plenty of 14,000-foot peaks, astounding natural hot springs, striking red-rock outcroppings, rivers that roll with white-water rapids in spring, and even the incongruous sight of towering sand dunes dwarfed by a mountain range at their back.

It's worth a few days for white-water rafting, hiking in the backcountry, and exploring historic gold-mining towns. Colorado Springs is one of the fastest growing cities in the West, but other parts of the area have a barely discovered feel.

Framed by Pikes Peak, Colorado Springs is the region's population center and a hub for the military and the high-tech industry. The city has been a destination for out-of-towners since its founding in 1870, due to the alleged healing power of the local spring water and clean air. The gold rush fueled the city's boom through the early 20th century, as the military boom did following World War II. With more than 700,000 residents in the metro area, Colorado Springs offers a mix of history and modernity, as well as incredible access to the trails and red-rock scenery in this section of the Rockies.

Surrounding Colorado Springs is a ring of smaller cities and alluring natural attractions. To the west, between alpine and desert scenery, are the Florissant Fossil Beds, the Royal Gorge, and Cripple Creek, which offers gambling in casinos housed in historic buildings. You can go rafting near Cañon City, while Pueblo has a dash of public art and history museums.

Outdoorsy types love the entire area: camping and hiking are especially superb in the San Isabel and Pike national forests. Climbers head to the Collegiate Peaks around Buena Vista and Salida (west of Colorado Springs) and the Cañon City area for a variety of ascents from moderate to difficult. Farther south, you can take the Highway of Legends Scenic Byway, which travels through the San Isabel National Forest and over high mountain passes. You can even take a day trip on the Rio Grande Scenic Railroad or the Cumbres & Toltec Scenic Railroad, which travels through regions not reachable by car.

MAJOR REGIONS

Colorado Springs. About 70 miles south of Denver, Colorado Springs is a comfortable base camp for travelers headed for high altitude and high adventure. Colorado's second-largest city has natural attractions like Pikes Peak and Garden of the Gods, and man-made additions like the Broadmoor luxury hotel and the U.S. Air Force Academy.

Side Trips from Colorado Springs. Easy day trips from Colorado Springs can lead you to Florissant Fossil Beds, a haven for geology buffs. If you like heights, head to Cañon City and walk over the Royal Gorge Bridge, or take a lunchtime ride on the train that runs on a track through the most dramatic part of the canyon. You could also gamble or visit a gold mine and learn more about the gold rush in Cripple Creek.

The Collegiate Peaks. Buena Vista and Salida provide easy access to the largest collection of 14,000-foot-or-higher peaks in Colorado, perfect for hiking, boating, river rafting, horseback riding, and mountain biking in wilderness areas. These towns are also favorites for folks who want to stay in rustic cabins or small mom-and-pop motels, perhaps take a rafting trip on the Arkansas River, and come home with their wallets still intact.

Southeast Colorado. Pueblo is the biggest city along I–25 between Colorado Springs and the New Mexico border. South of Pueblo, Trinidad is close to the state border, and there are a few small towns sprinkled around the region. West of I–25 there's easy access to the mountains along picturesque routes such as the Highway of Legends, a scenic byway that runs through the Cuchara Valley.

The San Luis Valley. The San Luis Valley is considered to be the world's largest alpine valley, sprawling on a broad, flat, dry plain between the San Juan and La Garita mountains to the west and the Sangre de Cristo range to the east. But equally important is that the valley, like much of the Southwest, remains culturally rooted in the early Hispanic tradition rather than the northern European one that early prospectors and settlers brought to central and northern Colorado. This area was settled first by the Ute, then by the Spanish, who left their indelible imprint in the town names and architecture. The oldest town (San Luis), the oldest military post (Fort Garland), and the oldest church (Our Lady of Guadalupe in Conejos) in the state are in this valley. Despite an average elevation of more than 7,500 feet, the San Luis Valley's sheltering peaks help to create a relatively mild climate. The area is also one of the state's major agricultural producers, with huge annual crops of potatoes, carrots, canola, barley, and lettuce. The large and sparsely populated valley contains some real oddities, including an alligator farm, a UFO-viewing tower, and the New Age town of Crestone, with its many spiritual centers.

Planning

When to Go

Colorado Springs is a good year-round choice because winters are relatively mild. Late spring or early summer is best if you want adrenaline-rush rafting, because the snowmelt feeds the rivers. Summer is tourist season everywhere in south central Colorado. Early fall is another good time to visit, especially when the aspen leaves are turning gold. Some of the lodging properties in the smaller towns are closed in winter, although there are always some open for the cross-country skiers who enjoy staying in the small high-mountain towns.

Getting Oriented

This region, which encompasses the south central section of Colorado, stretches from a collection of the state's 14,000-foot-high mountains in the heart of the Rockies eastward to Kansas, and from Colorado Springs south to the New Mexico state line. Pikes Peak, one of the most famous of Colorado's Fourteeners, forms the backdrop for Colorado Springs. Farther west, the Arkansas River towns of Buena Vista and Salida are within view of the Fourteeners of the Collegiate Peaks. Farther south, the Rio Grande runs through the flat San Luis Valley, which is lined by the Sangre de Cristo range. Cuchara Valley, just north of New Mexico, is framed by the Spanish Peaks.

Planning Your Time

If you have a short amount of time in the region, base yourself in Colorado Springs, or in neighboring Manitou Springs. On the first day, take the Pikes Peak Highway shuttle to the top of the mountain and explore the quirky artists' town of Manitou Springs. The following day, explore the "natural" sites, such as Cave of the Winds, Seven Falls, and Garden of the Gods. Visit the Broadmoor for a look at its palatial architecture, perhaps stopping for lunch or ending the day there in the Golden Bee. If the kids are along, try one of the outdoor settings above, then visit the Cheyenne Mountain Zoo and the Ghost Town Museum. End your stint by hiking in Red Rock Canyon park or visiting Cripple Creek if you enjoy gaming. Head to the Royal Gorge in Cañon City for a crowd-pleasing view of the deep canyon and its famous suspension bridge.

Getting Here and Around

AIR

Colorado Springs Airport (COS) is the major airport in the region, with more than a dozen nonstop destinations. Most south central residents south of Colorado Springs drive to this city to fly out.

Alternatively, you can choose to fly to Denver International Airport (DEN), which has a lot more nonstop flights from other major cities to Colorado. It's a 70-mile drive from Denver to the Springs, but during rush hour it might take a solid two hours, whether you're in your own car or in one of the Denver–Colorado Springs shuttles. It's fastest to take the E-470 toll road. Another option is Pueblo Memorial Airport (PUB), which has direct flights to Denver.

AIRPORT CONTACTS Colorado Springs Airport (COS). ☎ *719/550–1900* 🌐 *www.flycos.com.* **Denver International Airport (DEN).** ☎ *303/342–2000, 800/247–2336* 🌐 *www.flydenver.com.* **Pueblo Memorial Airport (PUB).** ☎ *719/553–2760* 🌐 *flypueblo.com.*

CAR

In Colorado Springs (whose airport has the typical lineup of car-rental agencies), the main north–south roads are I–25, Academy Boulevard, Nevada Avenue, and Powers Boulevard, and each will get you where you want to go in good time; east–west routes along Woodmen Road (far north), Austin Bluffs Parkway (north central), and Platte Boulevard (south central) can get backed up.

Running north–south from Wyoming to New Mexico, I–25 bisects Colorado and is the major artery into the area.

TRAIN

Amtrak's Southwest Chief stops in Trinidad and La Junta three days a week.

Parks and Recreation Areas

South central Colorado is chock-full of parks and recreational areas. Almost every chamber of commerce will have a list of trails in the near vicinity, so when you're asking for general information about the city, ask for a list of trails, too. The Arkansas River flows through this region, so every spring and summer people come here to raft through a mix of challenging white-water rapids interspersed with smoothly flowing sections. Pike, bass, and trout are plentiful in this region: popular fishing spots include Spinney Mountain Reservoir (between Florissant and Buena Vista), the Arkansas and South Platte rivers, and Trinidad Lake. Great Sand Dunes National Park and Preserve in the San Luis Valley is perfect for walking up (and sliding down) the dunes, hiking on mountain trails, kite flying, and wildlife viewing. Monarch, west of Salida, is the nearest ski area.

Arkansas Headwaters Recreation Area
This area is unique because it follows a 152-mile stretch of the Arkansas River, from the mountains near Leadville to Lake Pueblo. The Arkansas River is popular for rafting and kayaking, and fishermen love it for its brown trout. (Anglers near Salida reported good luck with 'hoppers, not to mention the "Mother's Day" caddis hatch every spring.) There are seven campgrounds along the river. ✉ *Arkansas Headwaters Recreation Area, 307 W. Sackett Ave., Salida* ☎ *719/539–7289* 🌐 *cpw.state.co.us/placestogo/Parks/ArkansasHeadwatersRecreationArea.*

Collegiate Peaks Wilderness
This wilderness region northwest of Buena Vista includes eight mountains above 14,000 feet and is known for superb hiking, mountain biking, and climbing, and a few ghost towns. ✉ *Leadville Ranger District, San Isabel National Forest, 810 Front St., Leadville* ☎ *719/486–0749* 🌐 *www.fs.usda.gov/recarea/psicc.*

Pike National Forest
This massive forest encompasses millions of acres of public land that stretch along the Front Range and go deep into the Rockies. Pikes Peak is the best-known 14,000-footer in Pike—and one of the most famous in the state. Forest entry is always free. ✉ *Forest Service Office, 2840 Kachina Dr., Pueblo* ☎ *719/553–1400* 🌐 *www.fs.usda.gov/psicc.*

Ring of the Peak
This collection of trails, four-wheel-drive roads, and a few paved roads circles Pikes Peak. Altitudes range between 6,400 and 11,300 feet. Check the website for trail access. 🌐 *www.friendsofthepeak.org/ring-the-peak-2.*

Restaurants

Many restaurants serve regional trout and game, as well as locally grown fruits and vegetables. In summer, look for cantaloupe from the town of Rocky Ford, the self-proclaimed "Sweet Melon Capital." Colorado Springs offers unique Colorado cuisine that zings taste buds without zapping budgets.

Hotels

The lodging star is the Broadmoor resort in Colorado Springs, built from the booty of the late-19th-century gold-rush days, but there are also predictable boxy-bed motel rooms awaiting travelers at the junctions of major highways throughout the region. Interspersed are quaint mom-and-pop motels, as well as bed-and-breakfasts and rustic lodges in tourist districts.

Restaurant and hotel reviews have been shortened. For full information, visit Fodors.com. Restaurant prices are for a main course at dinner, excluding 7.4% tax. Hotel prices are for two people in a standard double room in high season, excluding service charges and 9.4%–11.7% tax.

What It Costs

	$	$$	$$$	$$$$
RESTAURANTS	under $15	$15–$22	$23–$30	over $30
HOTELS	under $125	$125–$200	$201–$300	over $300

Colorado Springs

The contented residents of the Colorado Springs area believe they live in an ideal location, and it's hard to argue with them. To the west the Rockies form a majestic backdrop. To the east the plains stretch for miles. Taken together, the setting ensures a mild, sunny climate year-round, and makes skiing and golfing on the same day feasible with no more than a two- or three-hour drive. You don't have to choose between adventures here: you can climb the Collegiate Peaks one day and go white-water rafting on the Arkansas River the next.

The state's second largest city has a strong cultural scene, between the outstanding Colorado Springs Fine Arts Center, the Colorado Springs Philharmonic, and the variety of plays and musicals offered at several independent theaters.

The region abounds in natural and man-made wonders, from the red sandstone monoliths of the Garden of the Gods to the space-age architecture of the U.S. Air Force Academy's Cadet Chapel. The most indelible landmark is unquestionably Pikes Peak (14,115 feet), which is a constant reminder that this contemporary city is still close to nature. Purple in the early morning, snow-packed after winter storms, capped with clouds on windy days, the mountain is a landmark for directions and, when needed, a focus of contemplation.

GETTING HERE AND AROUND

It's easiest to explore this region in a private car because the attractions are spread out. If you're staying in the heart of town and don't intend to head out to Pikes Peak, the Air Force Academy, or other attractions farther away, you could use the Mountain Metropolitan Transit bus system or grab a taxi.

CONTACTS Colorado Springs Shuttle. ☎ *719/687–3456* 🌐 *www.coloradoshuttle.com.* **Mountain Metropolitan Transit.** ☎ *719/385–7433* 🌐 *www.coloradosprings.gov/mountain-metro.* **zTrip.** ☎ *719/766–4567* 🌐 *www.ztrip.com/colorado-springs.*

VISITOR INFORMATION Colorado Springs Parks, Recreation and Cultural Services Department. ☎ *719/385–5940* 🌐 *www.coloradosprings.gov/parks.* **Manitou Springs Chamber of Commerce.** ✉ *354 Manitou Ave.* ☎ *719/685–5089, 800/642–2567* 🌐 *www.manitousprings.org.* **Tri-Lakes Chamber of Commerce (Palmer Lake).** ✉ *166 2nd St., Monument* ☎ *719/481–3282* 🌐 *www.trilakeschamber.com.* **Visit Colorado Springs Information Center.** ✉ *515 S. Cascade Ave.* ☎ *719/635–7506, 800/888–4748* 🌐 *www.visitcos.com.*

Sights

Pikes Peak is a must-do and pairs nicely with an afternoon of poking around in the shops of Manitou Springs. The red rocks of Garden of the Gods and Cheyenne Cañon Park are the other natural show-stoppers—mix and match them with exploring the surrounding neighborhoods and tourist attractions. And don't forget the U.S. Air Force Academy, just north of town.

Access points for scaling the mighty Pikes Peak are in the Manitou Springs area, a quaint National Historic District that exudes an informal charm. Stop at the chamber for a free map of the eight mineral-springs drinking fountains and historic sites. On your self-guided tour, stop by 7 Minute Spring or Twin Springs for a spritz (it tastes and acts just like soda water).

Up in the Cheyenne Cañon section of town there are some terrific natural sites. Along the way you can view some of the city's exclusive neighborhoods and stop for lunch at the Broadmoor.

Depending on which museums you decide to visit, a tour of Garden of the Gods and urban Colorado Springs could take from two-thirds of a day to a full day to take everything in, from learning how the pioneers struggled to survive and thrive to strolling through the stunning red-rock cliffs and visiting the effortlessly educational and entertaining Trading Post at Garden of the Gods.

It takes a full day to visit Pikes Peak, explore Manitou Springs, and visit some of the attractions along U.S. 24, if you want to enjoy each without doing a marathon sprint. Whether you head up Pikes Peak in a car and stop for lunch at the top or take the train (which includes a stop at the summit), plan at least four hours. Visiting the variety of shops, which sell souvenirs to antiques, along historic Manitou Springs's main street, is a good way to stretch your legs after the journey to the peak. Heading underground into Cave of the Winds or visiting the Cliff Dwellings Museum will easily fill up the rest of the day.

ANA Money Museum

MUSEUM | **FAMILY** | The American Numismatic Association's fascinating Money Museum has a collection of old gold coins, an exhibit on the history of money, and currency from around the world. Tours are by reservation only. ✉ *818 N. Cascade Ave.* ☎ *800/367–9723, 719/632–2646* 🌐 *www.money.org/money-museum* 🎫 *$8.*

★ Cave of the Winds

CAVE | **FAMILY** | Discovered by two boys in 1880, the cave has been exploited as a tourist sensation ever since. The only way to enter the site is by purchasing a tour, but once inside the cave you'll forget the hype and commercialism of the gimmicky entrance. The cave contains examples of every major sort of limestone formation, from icicle-shaped stalactites and stump-like stalagmites to delicate anthodite crystals (or cave flowers), flowstone (or frozen waterfalls), and cave popcorn. Enthusiastic guides host easy 45-minute walking tours, adventurous cave expeditions, and lantern tours that last 1½ hours. An outdoor ropes course and rides like the Terror-dactyl, which swings riders off a 200-foot cliff, offer more fun outside of the cave. ✉ *100 Cave of the Winds Rd., off U.S. 24, Manitou Springs* ☎ *719/685–5444* 🌐 *www.caveofthewinds.com* 🎫 *Tours start at $23.*

Cheyenne Mountain Zoo

ZOO | **FAMILY** | America's only mountain zoo, at 6,700 feet, has more than 750 animals housed amid mossy boulders and ponderosa pines. You can hand-feed the giraffe herd in the zoo's African Rift Valley and check out the animals living in Primate World, Rocky Mountain Wild, or the Asian Highlands. ✉ *4250 Cheyenne Mountain Zoo Rd.* ☎ *719/633–9925* 🌐 *www.cmzoo.org* 🎫 *$29.75, includes same-day admission to Will Rogers Shrine.*

Colorado Springs Fine Arts Center

ARTS VENUE | This regional museum has a fine permanent collection of modern art and excellent rotating exhibits. Some highlight the cultural contributions of regional artists; others focus on famous artists such as the glassmaker Dale Chihuly and American pop artist Andy Warhol. Enjoy the view of Pikes Peak and the mountains from the patio in the summer. ✉ *30 W. Dale St.* ☎ *719/634–5581* 🌐 *fac.coloradocollege.edu* 🎫 *$10* 🕒 *Closed Mon.*

★ Garden of the Gods

NATURE SITE | These magnificent, eroded red-sandstone formations—from gnarled jutting spires to sensuously abstract monoliths—were sculpted more than 300 million years ago. Follow the road as it loops past such oddities as the Three Graces, the Siamese Twins, and the Kissing Camels or get an up-close look at the rocks with a guided climbing expedition booked at the visitor center. High Point, near the south entrance, provides camera hounds with the ultimate photo op: a formation known as Balanced Rock and jagged formations that frame Pikes Peak. The visitor center has maps of the trails

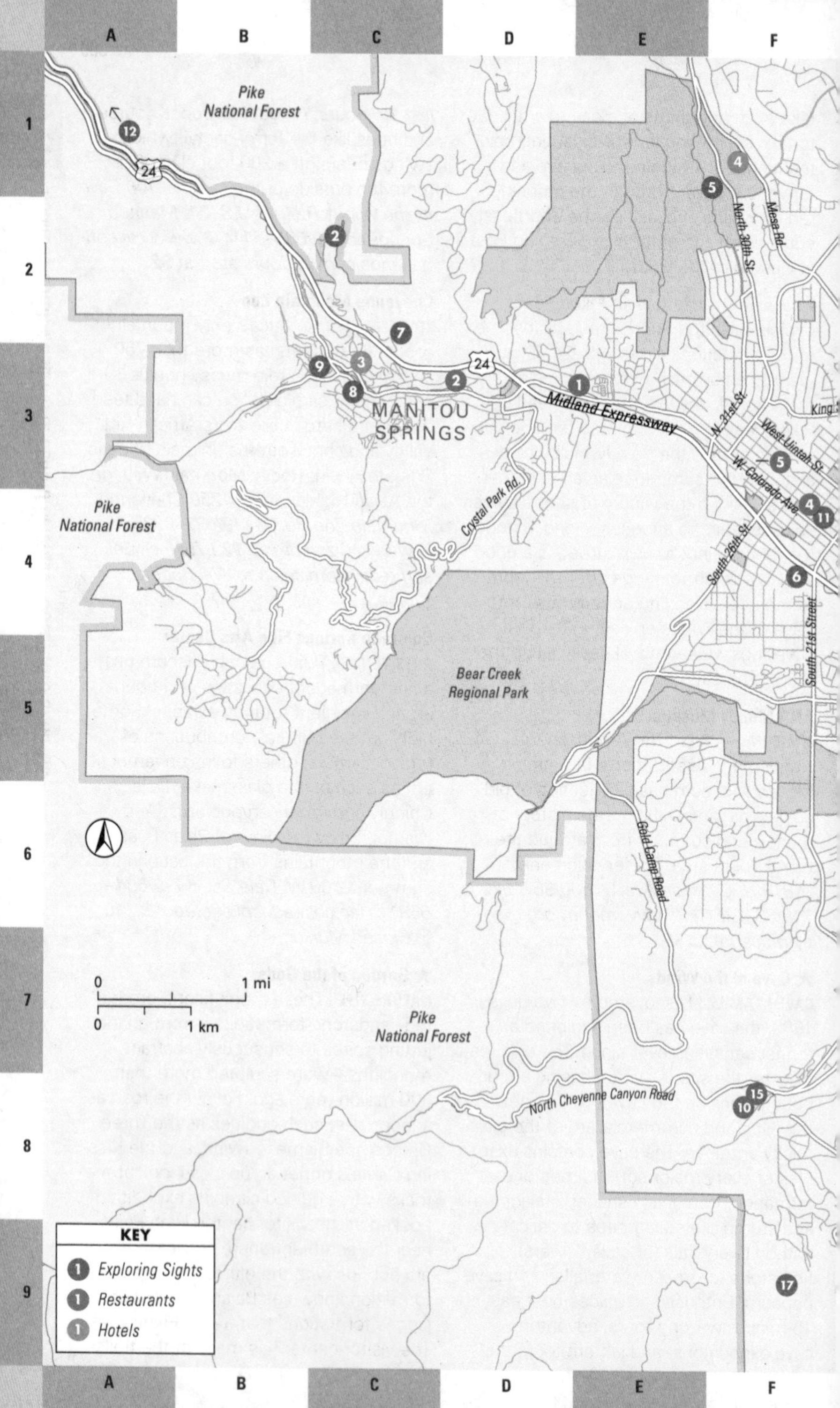
A
B
C
D
E
F
1
2
3
4
5
6
7
8
9
Pike
National Forest
24
MANITOU
SPRINGS
Midland Expressway
N. 31st St.
North 30th St.
Mesa Rd
King St
West Uintah St.
W. Colorado Ave.
South 26th St.
South 21st Street
Crystal Park Rd.
Pike
National Forest
Bear Creek
Regional Park
Gold Camp Road
0
1 mi
0
1 km
Pike
National Forest
North Cheyenne Canyon Road
KEY
Exploring Sights
Restaurants
Hotels

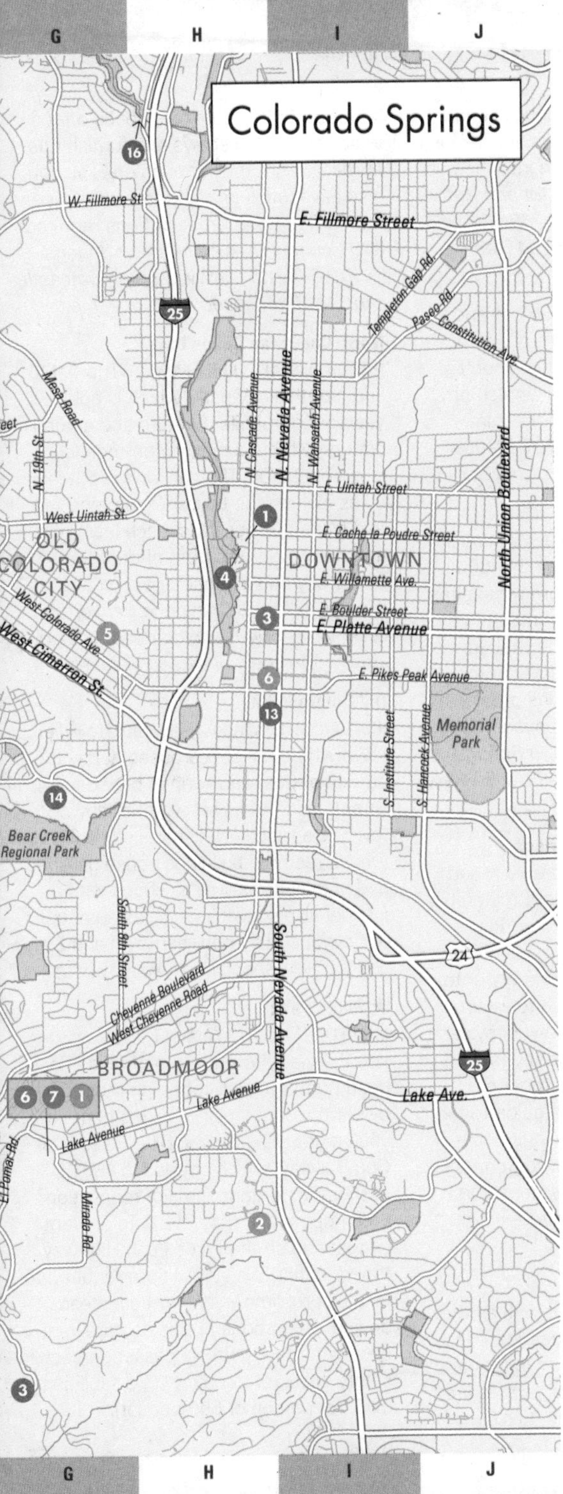

Sights

1 ANA Money Museum H4
2 Cave of the Winds C2
3 Cheyenne Mountain Zoo.......... G9
4 Colorado Springs Fine Arts Center.................... H4
5 Garden of the Gods................. F1
6 Ghost Town............................. F4
7 Manitou Cliff Dwellings C2
8 Manitou Springs Mineral Springs........................ C3
9 Miramont Castle Museum......... C3
10 North Cheyenne Cañon Park...... F8
11 Old Colorado City F4
12 Pikes Peak.............................. A1
13 Pioneers Museum H5
14 Seven Falls G5
15 Starsmore Visitor and Nature Center........................ F8
16 U.S. Air Force Academy H1
17 Will Rogers Shrine of the Sun..... F9

Restaurants

1 Adam's Mountain Café............. E3
2 Briarhurst Manor D3
3 Four by Brother Luck.............. H4
4 Front Range Barbeque............. F4
5 Paravicini's Italian Bistro F3
6 Penrose Room at the Broadmoor G8
7 Ristorante Del Lago at the Broadmoor G8

Hotels

1 The Broadmoor G8
2 Cheyenne Mountain Resort H8
3 Cliff House............................. C3
4 Garden of the Gods Club and Resort...................... F1
5 Holden House G4
6 The Mining Exchange.............. I5

and several geological, historical, and interactive hands-on displays, as well as a café. It's a short, paved hike into the park from the parking lot. ✉ *Visitor and Nature Center, 1805 N. 30th St.* ☎ *719/634–6666* 🌐 *www.gardenofgods.com* 🎟 *Free.*

Ghost Town

GHOST TOWN | **FAMILY** | You can see and hear a real player piano and a nickelodeon at this Western town with a sheriff's office, general store, saloon, and smithy. There's also gold panning in the summer. ✉ *400 S. 21st St.* ☎ *719/634–0696* 🌐 *www.ghosttownmuseum.com* 🎟 *$7.50.*

Manitou Cliff Dwellings

NATIVE SITE | Some Ancestral Pueblo cliff dwellings that date back nearly 1,000 years have been moved from other sites in southern Colorado to this museum. Two rooms of artifacts in the museum offer information on the history of the dwellings. Smartphone codes provide a free audio tour through the space. ✉ *10 Cliff Rd., off U.S. 24, Manitou Springs* ☎ *719/685–5242, 800/354–9971* 🌐 *www.cliffdwellingsmuseum.com* 🎟 *$12.*

Manitou Springs Mineral Springs

LOCAL INTEREST | The town grew around the springs, so there are eight mineral springs open to the public in or near downtown. Competitions to design the fountains that bring the spring water to the public ensured that each fountain design is unique. It's a bring-your-own-cup affair; the water (frequently tested) is potable and free. The chamber of commerce publishes a free guide to the springs and the Mineral Springs Foundation offers tours. ✉ *Manitou Springs* ☎ *719/685–5089* 🌐 *www.visitcos.com/areas/manitou-springs/manitou-mineral-springs* 🎟 *Free.*

Miramont Castle Museum

MUSEUM | Commissioned in 1895 as the private home of French priest Jean-Baptiste Francolon, this museum in Manitou Springs is still decorated, in part, as if a family lived here. More than 30 rooms in this 14,000-square-foot space offer a wide variety of displays and furnishings primarily from the Victorian era. You can also have lunch or high tea in the Queens Parlour Tea Room (reservations required). ✉ *9 Capitol Hill Ave., Manitou Springs* ☎ *719/685–1011* 🌐 *www.miramontcastle.org* 🎟 *$12* ⏲ *Closed Mon. in winter.*

North Cheyenne Cañon Park

NATIONAL/STATE PARK | **FAMILY** | The 1,600 acres of this city park, which is open year-round, manifest nature and natural history without a hint of commercialism—or charge. The canyon's moderate hikes include the Lower Columbine and Mount Cutler trails, each less than a 3-mile round-trip. Both afford a view of the city and a sense of accomplishment. ✉ *2120 S. Cheyenne Canyon Rd.* ☎ *719/385–5940* 🌐 *coloradosprings.gov/page/north-cheyenne-canon* 🎟 *Free.*

Old Colorado City

HISTORIC SITE | Once a separate, rowdier town where miners caroused, today the stretch of Colorado Avenue between 24th Street and 28th Street, west of downtown, is a kitschy National Historic District whose restored buildings house galleries and boutiques as well as shops with inexpensive souvenirs and restaurants. ✉ *Colorado Ave., between 24th and 28th Sts.* 🌐 *www.shopoldcoloradocity.com.*

★ Pikes Peak

MOUNTAIN—SIGHT | **FAMILY** | If you want to see the view from the top of Pikes Peak, head up this 14,115-foot-high mountain by shuttle or in a pair of hiking boots if you've got the stamina. (The Pikes Peak Cog Railway, which opened in 1891, has just undergone a major renovation and reopened in May 2021.) To prevent congestion on the Pikes Peak Highway, those visiting the summit are required to take a complimentary shuttle instead of driving. Exceptions to this rule are vehicles with more than six passengers, child safety seats, or people with disabilities ($15 per person or $50 per car).

Did You Know?

The famous Garden of the Gods is home to a large population of bighorn sheep.

Two shuttle options are available including a 32-mile round-trip that takes about 15 minutes to get to the top, or a 14-mile round-trip that takes about 30 minutes to the summit. Once at the top, stop for a doughnut at the Pikes Peak Summit House café and trading post. Whichever route you choose to take up the prominent peak, you'll understand why the pioneers heading West via wagon train used to say: "Pikes Peak or Bust." ✉ *U.S. 24* ✣ *5 miles west of Manitou Springs* ☎ *719/385–7325* 🌐 *www.coloradosprings.gov/pikes-peak-americas-mountain* 🎫 *$15 per person, $50 per vehicle; summit shuttle is free.*

Pikes Peak Cog Railway

MOUNTAIN—SIGHT | **FAMILY** | The world's highest cog train departs from Manitou Springs and follows a frolicking stream up a steep canyon, through stands of quaking aspen and towering lodgepole pines, before reaching the timberline, where you can see far into the plains until arriving at the summit. Advance reservations are recommended in summer and on weekends, as this three-hour trip sells out regularly. ✉ *515 Ruxton Ave.* ☎ *719/685–5401* 🌐 *www.cograilway.com* 🎫 *$37* ⛵ *Reservations essential.*

Pioneers Museum

MUSEUM | Once the Old El Paso County Courthouse, this repository has artifacts relating to the entire Pikes Peak area. The historic courtroom is absolutely elegant, and so perfectly appointed that it looks as if a judge will walk in any minute to start a trial. It's most notable for the special exhibits the museum puts together or receives on loan from other museums and institutions. ✉ *215 S. Tejon St.* ☎ *719/385–5990* 🌐 *www.cspm.org* 🎫 *Free.*

Starsmore Visitor and Nature Center

MUSEUM | At the mouth of the canyon off Cheyenne Boulevard, this center is chock-full of nature exhibits. ✉ *2120 S. Cheyenne Cañon Rd.* ☎ *719/385–6086* 🌐 *coloradosprings.gov/parks/page/starsmore-visitor-and-nature-center* ⏲ *Closed Mon. Labor Day–Memorial Day.*

Seven Falls

BODY OF WATER | Surrounded by towering red-rock canyon walls, these seven steep waterfalls plummet 181 feet into a tiny emerald pool that shimmers below. Hiking the steep 224 steps to the top of the falls is worth it for the view but you can also take an elevator to the Eagle's Nest look-out. Parking is free at the Penrose Equestrian Center where a shuttle will take passengers to and from the site. Guides at Soaring Adventures sail patrons across the nearby canyon on 10 ziplines and lead those daring enough to make the trip across rope bridges and on rappelling adventures that feature views of the falls. Restaurant 1858 serves Southern comfort food like shrimp and grits, roasted game, and local trout (Cajun style, barbecued, and fried) that is best enjoyed out on the patio overlooking the falls. ✉ *1045 Lower Gold Camp Rd.* ☎ *855/923–7272* 🌐 *www.broadmoor.com/broadmoor-adventures/seven-falls* 🎫 *$16.*

★ U.S. Air Force Academy

MILITARY SITE | The academy, which set up camp in 1954, is one of the most popular attractions in Colorado. Highlights include the futuristic design, 18,500 beautiful acres of land, and antique and historic aircraft displays. At the visitor center you'll find photo exhibits, a model of a cadet's room, a gift shop, a snack bar in the summer, and a film highlighting the history and bravery of the Air Force. Other stops on the self-guided tour include a B-52 display, sports facilities, and the chapel. Some days you can catch the impressive cadet lunch formation that begins between 11:30 and noon. The Air Force chapel, which can accommodate simultaneous Catholic, Jewish, and Protestant services, is easily recognized by its unconventional design, which features 17 spires that resemble airplane wings. Don't miss the smaller chapels,

The Will Rogers Shrine of the Sun is dedicated to America's favorite cowboy.

including the Buddhist room. Visitors can enter only through the North and South gates. *N. Gate Blvd., off I–25, Exit 156* *719/333–2025* *www.usafa.edu/visitors* *Free.*

★ Will Rogers Shrine of the Sun

MEMORIAL | FAMILY | This five-story tower was dedicated in 1937, after the tragic plane crash that claimed Rogers's life. Its interior is painted with all manner of Western murals in which Colorado Springs benefactor Spencer Penrose figures prominently, and is plastered with photos and homespun sayings of Rogers, America's favorite cowboy. In the chapel are 15th- and 16th-century European artworks. *4250 Cheyenne Mountain Zoo Rd.* *719/578–5367* *www.cmzoo.org/visit/will-rogers-shrine-of-the-sun* *$29.75, includes same-day admission to Cheyenne Mountain Zoo.*

Restaurants

Adam's Mountain Café

$$ | CAFÉ | Join the locals sitting at mismatched tables, viewing drawings by regional artists, and mingling at the community table. The food has an organic bent, with many vegetarian options. **Known for:** famous huevos rancheros; plenty of vegetarian and vegan options; local charm. *Average main: $15* *26 Manitou Ave.* *719/685–1430* *adamsmountaincafe.com* *No dinner Sun. and Mon.*

Briarhurst Manor

$$$$ | MODERN EUROPEAN | One of the most exquisitely romantic restaurants in Colorado, Briarhurst Manor has several dining rooms, each with its own look and mood like the book-lined library or the drawing room with an ornate chandelier. The menu regularly features lamb, poultry, fish, and wild game dishes, which change as the chef adds a seasonal flair. **Known for:** intimate atmosphere; historic estate; meat and wild game.

$ Average main: $32 ✉ 404 Manitou Ave. ☎ 719/685–1864 🌐 www.briarhurst.com ⏲ Closed Mon. and Tues. No lunch.

Four by Brother Luck

$$$$ | **MODERN AMERICAN** | With a focus on the historical cuisine of the Four Corners region where Utah, Arizona, New Mexico, and Colorado touch borders, chef Brother Luck's restaurant serves up creative tasting-style menus sure to impress his *Top Chef* fan base. Along with the Four Corners significance, the number four represents Luck's four key sources of ingredients—hunters, gatherers, farmers, and fishermen; the four seasonal menus; and the fact that Luck is the fourth generation in his family to have the name Brother Luck. **Known for:** lively atmosphere perfect for modern foodies; dirty farro creole dish inspired by the chef's father; chef's table. *$ Average main: $47 ✉ 321 N. Tejon St. ☎ 719/434–2741 🌐 www.fourbybrotherluck.com ⏲ No dinner Sun.*

Front Range Barbeque

$$ | **BARBECUE** | **FAMILY** | Tunes, brews, and barbecue attract visitors and locals to the outdoor patio at this causal smokehouse in Old Colorado City. Guests can be overheard arguing about which homemade sauce is best and singing along to the music of live acts from across the country that can be heard throughout the block. **Known for:** dry ribs; century-old pecan pie recipe; lively atmosphere. *$ Average main: $15 ✉ 2330 W. Colorado Ave. ☎ 719/632–2596 🌐 www.frbbq.com.*

Paravicini's Italian Bistro

$$ | **ITALIAN** | Named for the proprietor's grandmother, Paravicini lives up to its Italian name, which translates to "for the neighborhood." Locals of all ages gather in the colorful and well-lit space that provides a balance of fun and romance to sip glasses of wine and share the family-style salad, fresh bread, and heaping piles of noodles. Pasta reigns on this traditional Italian menu highlighting classic and surf-and-turf options. **Known for:** great spaghetti and meatballs; authentic Italian; perfect date-night setting. *$ Average main: $20 ✉ 2802 W. Colorado Ave. ☎ 719/471–8200 🌐 paravicinis.com 💳 No credit cards.*

Penrose Room at the Broadmoor

$$$$ | **MODERN AMERICAN** | Whatever number of courses you choose from the prix-fixe menu, you're guaranteed a memorable culinary experience at the award-winning Penrose Room where seasonal seafood, poultry, and red meat are served with French flair. Chef de cuisine Luis Young brings his background in American and French cuisine to the always evolving seasonal dishes. **Known for:** mountain and city views from the penthouse tower; smoked duck foie gras; chef's tasting menu with wine pairings. *$ Average main: $90 ✉ The Broadmoor South, 1 Lake Circle ☎ 719/577–5733, 844/727–8730 🌐 www.broadmoor.com/dining/penrose-room ⏲ Closed Sun. and Mon. No lunch 👔 Jacket required.*

Ristorante Del Lago at the Broadmoor

$$$$ | **ITALIAN** | With stunning views of Cheyenne Lake and the main hotel, this "restaurant of the lake" features an open kitchen and cozy lounge. Smaller portions allow guests to try a variety of authentic Italian dishes from antipasti and wood-fired pizzas to lasagne and house-made sausage. **Known for:** patio with lake view; imported Italian meats and cheese; impressive wine list. *$ Average main: $40 ✉ 1 Lake Ave. ☎ 719/577–5774, 866/381–8432 🌐 www.broadmoor.com/ristorante-del-lago ⏲ Closed Tues. No lunch.*

Hotels

★ The Broadmoor

$$$$ | **HOTEL** | With its old-world ambience that emits pure luxury—including the signature pink building with the Mediterranean-style towers—the Broadmoor continues to redefine itself with settings where guests can unwind

and be pampered. **Pros:** thoroughly pampering atmosphere; many excellent dining options; you won't need to leave the property with so many amenities available. **Cons:** very expensive; formal style might not be everyone's preference; rooms (especially with a view) book quickly. *Rooms from: $445 ✉ 1 Lake Circle ☎ 719/634–7711, 844/727–8730 🌐 www.broadmoor.com 784 rooms No meals.*

Cheyenne Mountain Resort
$$$ | RESORT | At this 217-acre resort on the slopes of Cheyenne Mountain, superb swimming facilities (including an Olympic-size pool), a variety of tennis courts, and a Pete Dye championship golf course tempt you to remain on-property, despite the easy access to the high country. **Pros:** resort ambience; outstanding views; large fitness center and spa. **Cons:** you must walk outside to get to the main lodge; can get crowded for conferences; few dining options nearby. *Rooms from: $249 ✉ 3225 Broadmoor Valley Rd. ☎ 719/538–4000, 800/588–0250 🌐 www.cheyennemountain.com 316 rooms No meals.*

Cliff House
$$ | HOTEL | This Victorian-era jewel was built in 1873 as a stagecoach stop between Colorado Springs and Leadville, and can name crown princes, presidents, and entertainers as past guests; their names live on as monikers for several distinctly different and extremely attractive suites: the Katharine Bates, the Teddy Roosevelt, and the Clark Gable are a few. **Pros:** convenient location; old-fashioned charm; luxurious amenities. **Cons:** might be a little too old-fashioned for some; price excludes resort fees; charge for valet parking with few other options. *Rooms from: $200 ✉ 306 Cañon Ave., Manitou Springs ☎ 719/685–3000, 888/212–7000 🌐 www.thecliffhouse.com 54 rooms Free Breakfast.*

Garden of the Gods Club and Resort
$$$$ | RESORT | The views are spectacular from this longtime private club overlooking the red rocks in the Garden of the Gods. **Pros:** great views; access to great golf on the Kissing Camels course; guests have exclusive access to the fitness center and infinity pool. **Cons:** a car is needed to get downtown; expensive; events and public amenities bring daytime traffic to the property. *Rooms from: $320 ✉ 3320 Mesa Rd. ☎ 719/632–5541, 800/923–8838 🌐 www.gardenofthegodsclub.com 56 rooms No meals.*

Holden House
$$ | B&B/INN | Innkeepers Sallie and Welling Clark realized their dream when they restored this 1902 home and transformed it into a B&B. **Pros:** good choice for travelers who want something homey; excellent breakfasts; friendly staff and owners. **Cons:** old-fashioned ambience may not suit all tastes; not suitable for young children; few on-site amenities. *Rooms from: $175 ✉ 1102 W. Pikes Peak Ave. ☎ 719/471–3980, 888/565–3980 🌐 www.holdenhouse.com 6 rooms Free Breakfast.*

The Mining Exchange
$$$ | HOTEL | Built as a stock exchange for local mining companies in 1902, this downtown hotel merges historic details, like an old vault and antique piano in the lobby, with modern amenities. **Pros:** historic charm; walkable, downtown location; lovely hotel courtyard. **Cons:** sometimes noisy from downtown crowds and traffic; mazelike hallways are difficult to navigate; some rooms are small. *Rooms from: $219 ✉ 8 S. Nevada Ave. ☎ 719/323–2000, 877/999–3223 for reservations only 🌐 www.wyndhamhotels.com 117 rooms No meals.*

BARS AND CLUBS

Cowboys

BARS/PUBS | This is a favorite hangout for country music lovers and two-steppers. ✉ *25 N. Tejon St.* ☎ *719/596–1212* 🌐 *www.cowboyscs.com.*

Golden Bee

BARS/PUBS | Remnants of a 19th-century English pub were discovered in a warehouse in New York City in the 1950s and moved to the Broadmoor site where the original mahogany bar, wood carvings, mirrors, and tin ceilings still define the Golden Bee's charm. The old-fashioned bar features a piano player leading sing-alongs. Watch out for the bees—as part of a long-standing tradition, they flick bee stickers into the audience during the show. ✉ *International Center at the Broadmoor, 1 Lake Circle* ☎ *719/634–7711* 🌐 *https://www.broadmoor.com/dining/golden-bee/.*

BREWPUBS

★ Ivywild School

BARS/PUBS | Student art still lingers on the bathroom walls of this historic elementary school turned hipster haunt. On one end of the 1916 school, Bristol Brewing Company schools patrons with its microwbrews while creative libations are shaken and stirred down the hall at The Principal's Office. Trendy locals flock to the historic site with large patios and lots of charm for the tastiest cafeteria grub around served up by Ivywild School Kitchen lining the art-covered hallway between the two bars. Axe and The Oak Whiskey House serve up spirits distilled from local grain at this popular hangout. ✉ *1604 S. Cascade Ave.* ☎ *719/368–6100* 🌐 *ivywildschool.com.*

Phantom Canyon Brewing Co.

BREWPUBS/BEER GARDENS | In a century-old brick building, this noted brewpub has shuffleboard and billiards in an upstairs hall. There's great pub grub, plus hop-infused desserts. ✉ *2 E. Pikes Peak Ave.* ☎ *719/635–2800* 🌐 *www.phantomcanyon.com.*

COMEDY

Loonees Comedy Corner

COMEDY CLUBS | This club showcases live stand-up comedy Thursday to Saturday evening. Some of the performers are nationally known. ✉ *1305 N. Academy Blvd.* ☎ *719/591–0707* 🌐 *www.loonees.com.*

Performing Arts

Pikes Peak Center

ARTS CENTERS | This downtown venue presents a wide range of musical events as well as touring theater and dance companies. ✉ *190 S. Cascade Ave.* ☎ *719/520–7469* 🌐 *www.pikespeakcenter.com.*

Shopping

Colorado Springs has a mix of upscale boutiques and chain stores. Many boutiques and galleries cluster in Old Colorado City and the posh Broadmoor One Lake Avenue Shopping Arcade.

Manitou Springs, a small town between Garden of the Gods and Pikes Peak, has a historic district, and large artists' population. Walk along Manitou Avenue and Ruxton Avenue, where you'll find a mix of galleries, quaint shops, and stores selling souvenirs.

ANTIQUES AND COLLECTIBLES

Ruxton's Trading Post

ANTIQUES/COLLECTIBLES | Look here for cowboy-era antiques and collectibles, Native American art, and nostalgia items from old TV programs and movies. ✉ *22 Ruxton Ave., Manitou Springs* ☎ *719/685–9024* 🌐 *www.ruxtons.com.*

CRAFT AND ART GALLERIES

Commonwheel Artists Co-Op

ART GALLERIES | This longtime co-op gallery is packed with art in various mediums, jewelry, paintings, sculpture, fiber, clay, and glass art. ✉ *102 Cañon Ave., Manitou Springs* ☎ *719/685–1008* 🌐 *www.commonwheel.com.*

Gallery 113

ART GALLERIES | Rotating exhibits by local artists keep visitors coming back to this popular co-op gallery on Tejon Street. Members display a variety of mediums, but vibrant paintings often dominate the gallery walls and space. You will also find locally created jewelry, pottery, and sculptures throughout. ✉ *125½ N. Tejon St.* ☎ *719/634–5299* 🌐 *www.gallery-113cos.com.*

Sculpture by Michael Garman

ART GALLERIES | This gallery in Old Colorado City carries the contemporary sculptures of renowned artist Michael Garman, including Western-themed pieces and a firefighter series. ✉ *2418 W. Colorado Ave.* ☎ *719/471–9391* 🌐 *www.michaelgarman.com.*

Activities

A number of activities are available within an hour or two of Colorado Springs, including hot-air ballooning, white-water rafting, and all-access Jeep tours. Riding in a Jeep is one way to view the backcountry; a horseback ride on trails through meadows and along mountainsides is another.

Some of the best choices for hiking in this region are the Barr Trail, which heads up Pikes Peak (and is for hardy, well-conditioned hikers), and the array of trails in North Cheyenne Cañon Park.

ADVENTURE TOURS

Adventures Out West

TOUR—SPORTS | This outfitter offers Jeep tours of Colorado Springs and Manitou Springs covering local sites like Garden of the Gods, Pike National Forest, and North Cheyenne Cañon Park. It can also arrange other activities, such as ballooning, horseback riding, ziplining, and climbing. ✉ *1680 S. 21st St.* ☎ *719/578–0935* 🌐 *advoutwest.com.*

HIKING

Barr Trail

MOUNTAIN—SIGHT | The 12-mile hike up Barr Trail gains nearly 8,000 feet in elevation before you reach the summit. About halfway up the steep trail is Barr Camp, where many hikers spend the night. Many of the trail's parking lots charge a fee. ✉ *Colorado Springs* 🌐 *www.visitcos.com/directory/barr-trail-pikes-peak.*

The Manitou Incline

TRAIL | Nearly 3,000 stairs stand between hikers at the bottom of this heart-pounding feat and the spectacular views above. Once a cable car track, now nearly a mile of steep steps and a 2,000 feet of elevation gain make this an advanced trail with rewarding views of Manitou and Colorado Springs. ✉ *10 Old Mans Trail, Manitou Springs* ✣ *Park at Hiawatha Gardens where a shuttle takes hikers to the trailhead* ☎ *719/385–5940* 🌐 *www.coloradosprings.gov/parks/page/manitou-incline.*

Pikes Peak Greenway Trail

HIKING/WALKING | The Pikes Peak Greenway offers 16 miles of multisurface hiking and biking trails running from Palmer Lake to the town of Fountain. On the north end, the trail connects with the Santa Fe Trail, which runs from Palmer Lake to the beautifully forested grounds of the U.S. Air Force Academy. For a scenic tour of the city, start at America the Beautiful Park in the heart of downtown and ride north to the Air Force Academy on 10 miles of open trail. You can also take the route west from the park for a 6-mile ride into Manitou Springs. ✉ *126 Cimino Dr.* ☎ *719/385–5940* 🌐 *www.trailsandopenspaces.org/trails/pikes-peak-greenwaysanta-fefountain-creekfront-range-trail.*

HORSEBACK RIDING

Academy Riding Stables

HORSEBACK RIDING | Year-round trail rides, most notably through the Garden of the Gods, are offered here. ✉ *4 El Paso Blvd.* ☎ *719/633–5667* 🌐 *www.academyridingstables.com.*

MOUNTAIN BIKING

Challenge Unlimited

BICYCLING | For nearly 30 years this outfitter has been leading bike tours throughout Colorado, including the daily 20-mile bike tour down Pikes Peak from May through mid-October. The tours include helmets and bikes, and breakfast and lunch. Other trips combine biking and ziplining. ✉ *204 S. 24th St.* ☎ *800/798–5954* 🌐 *www.pikespeakbybike.co.*

Pikes Peak Mountain Bike Tours

BICYCLING | The guides with this company will take you to the top of Pikes Peak, then let you ride all the way down on one of their lightweight mountain bikes. An alternative tour is the 20-mile tour on Upper Gold Camp Road, which is a self-paced downhill ride along an old railroad tract converted to a hiking–bicycling trail that cuts through the mountains. Another option allows you to saddle up and pedal down, a partnership with the Stables at the Broadmoor. ✉ *306 S. 25th St.* ☎ *719/337—5311* 🌐 *www.bikepikespeak.com.*

Cripple Creek

46 miles west of Colorado Springs via U.S. 24 and Hwy. 67.

One of Colorado's three legalized gambling towns, Cripple Creek once had the most lucrative mines in the state—and 10,000 boozing, brawling, bawdy citizens. Today the old-timey main street is lined with casinos housed in quaint Victorian buildings. Outside the central area, old mining structures and the stupendous curtain of the Collegiate Peaks are marred by slag heaps and parking lots.

Miners gathered around card games in most of the nearly 100 saloons in Cripple Creek, which opened during the wild years after Bob Womack discovered gold in the late 1800s. Today there's a lineup of casinos set into storefronts and buildings with exteriors retaining the aura they had a century ago. But today the casinos are chock-full of slot machines, video and live poker tables, roulette, craps, and blackjack tables.

Most of the casinos on East Bennett Avenue house predictable (albeit inexpensive) restaurants. Beef is the common denominator across all the menus. Some casinos also have hotel rooms.

GETTING HERE AND AROUND

The town is tiny, though a bit hilly off the main drag, so it's easy to walk around and explore. Drive here in a private car, or hitch a ride on one of the Ramblin' Express casino shuttles from Colorado Springs to Cripple Creek.

ESSENTIALS

TRANSPORTATION CONTACTS Ramblin' Express. ☎ *303/572–8687* 🌐 *www.casinoshuttle.com.*

VISITOR INFORMATION Cripple Creek Heritage and Information Center. ✉ *9283 S. Hwy. 67* ☎ *877/858–4653, 719/689–3461* 🌐 *www.visitcripplecreek.com.*

Sights

Bronco Billy's

CASINO—SIGHT | This longtime casino embodies the atmosphere of Cripple Creek's main drag with its Western theme and friendly staff. Known for its customer service, Bronco Billy's is a favorite among locals and tourists, with hotel rooms upstairs and restaurants on-site. ✉ *233 E. Bennett Ave.* ☎ *719/689–2142, 866/689–0353* 🌐 *www.broncobillyscasino.com.*

Cripple Creek District Museum

MUSEUM | The museum set in five historic buildings—including a vintage railway depot—contains a vast collection of artifacts, photos, and exhibits that provide a glimpse into mining life at the turn of the 20th century. ✉ *510 Bennett Ave.* ☎ *719/689–9540* 🌐 *cripplecreekmuseum.com* 🎫 *$8* 🕒 *Closed weekdays Labor Day–Memorial Day.*

Mollie Kathleen Gold Mine Tour

MINE | Descending 100 stories, the Mollie Kathleen Gold Mine Tour tours a mine that operated continuously from 1891 to 1961. The tours are fascinating, sometimes led by a former miner, and definitely not for the claustrophobic. Tours depart about every 30 minutes. ✉ *9388 Hwy. 67, northeast of town* ☎ *719/689–2466* 🌐 *www.goldmine-tours.com* 🎟 *$25.*

Florissant Fossil Beds

35 miles west of Colorado Springs via U.S. 24.

Florissant Fossil Beds is an excellent place to explore the nicely preserved fossils from the area.

GETTING HERE AND AROUND

From Colorado Springs, take U.S. 24 W. It's about 37 miles from town.

Florissant Fossil Beds National Monument

NATURE SITE | Once a temperate subtropical climate, Florissant Fossil Beds National Monument was perfectly preserved by volcanic ash and mud flow 34 million years ago. This little-known site is a haven for paleontologists. The visitor center offers a daily guided walk and ranger talks in the amphitheater in summer, or you can follow the more than 15 miles of well-marked hiking trails and lose yourself in the remnants of petrified redwoods from the Eocene epoch. ✉ *15807 Teller County Rd. 1, Florissant* ☎ *719/748–3253* 🌐 *www.nps.gov/flfo* 🎟 *$10.*

Palmer Lake

25 miles north of Colorado Springs via I–25 and Hwy. 105.

Artsy, and very sleepy, Palmer Lake is a magnet for hikers who set out for the evergreen-clad peaks at several in-town trailheads. There are more good restaurants and working artists than one would expect from a population of about 2,800. The town developed around the railroad tracks that were laid here in 1871—the lake itself was used as a refueling point for steam engines.

Colorado Renaissance Festival

FESTIVALS | **FAMILY** | The small town of Larkspur is home to just a couple hundred residents, but it knows how to throw a heck of a party—and a medieval one at that. The Colorado Renaissance Festival annually hosts throngs of families, chain mail–clad fantasy enthusiasts, tattooed bikers, and fun lovers of every other kind. Within about 350 wooded acres there are performers who deliver everything from juggling stunts and fire-eating to hypnotism and comedy. The big event happens three times a day, when knights square off in the arena for a theatrical joust. There are also more than 200 artisans selling their wares, games, rides, and myriad food and drink booths. ✉ *650 W. Perry Park Ave., off Larkspur Rd.* ✣ *Larkspur is 9 miles north of Palmer Lake via Spruce Mountain Rd.* ☎ *303/688–6010* 🌐 *www.coloradorenaissance.com* 🎟 *$24.*

Tri-Lakes Center for the Arts

ARTS VENUE | In a landmark Kaiser-Frazer building on the north fringe of town, the Tri-Lakes Center for the Arts hosts rotating exhibits, live music, and theater. Classes and workshops are offered, and several resident artists work from studios on-site. ✉ *304 Hwy. 105* ☎ *719/481–0475* www.trilakesarts.org Free Closed Sun. and Mon.

Restaurants

Bella Panini

$ | **ITALIAN** | This popular restaurant has a heavy Italian focus, but the chefs here aren't afraid to mix things up, whipping out such creative concoctions as crawfish-and-jalapeño pizza. The owner also hosts food and wine pairings. **Known for:** creative pizzas; local atmosphere; good service. *Average main: $13* *4 Hwy. 105* *719/481–3244* *www.bellapanini.com* *No credit cards* *Closed Sun. and Mon.*

Rock House Ice Cream

$ | **AMERICAN** | **FAMILY** | This is a popular stop for hikers on their way home. Choose from among more than 24 different types, including maple walnut, coconut-almond fudge, and—seasonally—pumpkin, for your cone, sundae, or milkshake. **Known for:** historic stone facade; seasonal ice cream specialties; friendly service. *Average main: $4* *24 Hwy. 105* *719/488–6917* *www.rockhouseicecream.com* *Closed Mon. and Tues. in winter.*

Activities

HIKING

Palmer Lake Reservoirs Trail

HIKING/WALKING | One of the most popular hiking trails between Denver and Colorado Springs, the Palmer Lake Reservoirs Trail begins near Glen Park. After a fairly steep incline, the 4-mile trail levels out and follows the shoreline of Upper and Lower Palmer Lake reservoirs between forested mountains. Bikes and leashed dogs are permitted. *Palmer Lake* *Trailhead starts at bottom of Old Carriage Rd.* *719/633–6884* *www.townofpalmerlake.com.*

Royal Gorge Region and Cañon City

45 miles southwest of Colorado Springs via Hwy. 115 and U.S. 50.

From the glut of adventure tours that line U.S. 50 west of the city and the nearby Royal Gorge—a dramatic crack that plunges more than 1,000 feet into the earth—to the strip mall veneer and juxtaposed revitalization of historic downtown buildings of Cañon City, the region is undeniably quirky. The Royal Gorge Region encompasses all of Fremont County, which is an outdoor adventure haven for some, but more commonly dubbed "Colorado's Correctional Capital" by others. In Cañon City and nearby Florence (also the "Antique Capital of Colorado") there are more than a dozen prisons, including ADX, the country's only federal supermax prison. Despite the prisons having pumped millions of dollars into the local economy, the prisons are not exactly a source of town pride, but locals hope a host of new hiking and biking trails, and local businesses aimed at tourists, will overshadow the city's reputation as a prison town.

GETTING HERE AND AROUND

The route from Colorado Springs to Cañon City (on Highway 115 and U.S. 50) goes through Red Rock Canyon, with lovely views. You'll need a car to get to Cañon City, where there are limited transportation options.

VISITOR INFORMATION Cañon City Chamber of Commerce. *424 Main St., Cañon City* *719/275–2331, 800/876–7922* *www.canoncitycolorado.com.*

Sights

Museum of Colorado Prisons

JAIL | Introduce yourself to life behind bars at the Museum of Colorado Prisons, which formerly housed the Women's State Correctional Facility and where many of the exhibits are housed in cells. The museum exhaustively documents prison life in Colorado through old photos and newspaper accounts, as well as with inmates' confiscated weapons and contraband. The gas chamber sits in the courtyard. While an important window into prison life, past and present, the museum can be disturbing for young kids and those with loved ones in the prison system. ✉ *201 N. 1st St., Cañon City* ☎ *719/269–3015* 🌐 *www.prisonmuseum.org* 🎫 *$10* ⏲ *Closed Mon. and Tues. in winter.*

Royal Gorge Bridge and Park

CITY PARK | Carved by the Arkansas River more than 3 million years ago, the Royal Gorge canyon walls tower up to 1,200 feet high. The site is known for the 1877 Royal Gorge War between the Denver & Rio Grand and Santa Fe railroads over the right-of-way through the canyon. Rival crews laid tracks during the day and would dynamite each other's work at night until the Denver & Rio Grande eventually prevailed. Today, a private company runs the Royal Gorge Bridge and Park featuring the highest **suspension bridge** in the country, constructed in 1929 as a tourist attraction. The 956-foot-high bridge sways on gusty afternoons and the river can be seen clearly between gaps in the boards, adding to the thrill of a crossing. You can cross the suspension bridge and ride the astonishing **aerial tram** (2,400 feet long and more than 1,000 feet above the canyon floor) or experience the Cloudscraper, America's highest zipline. Renovations to the park following a devastating wildfire in 2013 brought a Children's Playland with a playground, carousel, maze, and splash pad to the site. A ride on the **Royal Rush Skycoaster** ensures an adrenaline rush—you'll swing from a free-fall tower and momentarily hang over the gorge. Also on hand are outdoor musical entertainment in summer, and the usual assortment of food and gift shops. ✉ *4218 Fremont County Rd. 3A, Cañon City* ☎ *719/275–7507, 888/333–5597* 🌐 *www.royalgorgebridge.com* 🎫 *$29.*

Royal Gorge Route Railroad

TRANSPORTATION SITE (AIRPORT/BUS/FERRY/TRAIN) | **FAMILY** | A ride on the Royal Gorge Route Railroad takes you under the bridge and through one of the most dramatic parts of the canyon. From the Santa Fe depot in Cañon City, the train leaves several times a day for the two-hour ride. The breakfast, lunch, and dinner rides are pleasant, and the food is good, although not exactly "gourmet" as advertised. Seasonal rides like the Oktoberfest train and Santa Express offer additional entertainment. For an extra fee you can ride in the cab with the engineer. ✉ *330 Royal Gorge Blvd., Cañon City* ☎ *719/274–4000* 🌐 *www.royalgorgeroute.com* 🎫 *From $44.*

Westcliffe

SCENIC DRIVE | In a joint effort with neighboring Silver Cliff, this remote town at the base of the Sangre de Cristo Mountains became the state's first International Dark Sky Community in 2015. Nestled in quiet Custer County, mountains shade the town from light pollution to the east preserving the dark nights that provide a perfect backdrop for stargazing year-round. Once a mining town, Westcliffe's 600 residents now thrive mostly on agriculture and ranching, but spring and summer festivals attract tourists from around the world to the charming Main Street. ✣ *55 miles west of Pueblo via Hwy. 96 and 50 miles southwest of Cañon City via scenic Hwys. 50 and 69.*

Winery at Holy Cross Abbey

WINERY/DISTILLERY | The Benedictine monks once cloistered at Holy Cross Abbey came to Cañon City for spiritual repose. But for the faithful who frequent the winery on the eastern edge of the property, redemption is more easily found in a nice bottle of Revelation, a Bordeaux-style blend. For a truly divine experience, reserve a wine and cheese tasting ($35 per person) on the terrace that includes a private hostess, sampling of all wines, and an artisanal cheese, bread, fruit, and chocolate plate. ✉ *3011 E. U.S. 50, Cañon City* ☎ *719/276–5191, 877/422–9463* 🌐 *www.abbeywinery.com.*

Restaurants

Cañon City Brews & Bikes

$ | **AMERICAN** | Centrally located on Main Street, Cañon City Brews & Bikes offers an extensive craft beer menu and pub food that attracts hikers, bikers, and locals alike. The massive outdoor space, with tables and a beer garden, offers a perfect place to wind down from outdoor activities. **Known for:** extensive craft beer menu; outdoor beer garden; casual atmosphere. *Average main: $8* ✉ *224 Main St., Cañon City* ☎ *719/275–2472* 🌐 *www.canoncitybrewsandbikes.com* *Closed Mon. and Tues.*

Pizza Madness

$ | **PIZZA** | **FAMILY** | There is no shortage of fun or food at family-friendly Pizza Madness. Arcade games keep kids and adults entertained while you wait for your hand-tossed pie. **Known for:** central location; noisy and family-friendly atmosphere; speciality pizzas. *Average main: $10* ✉ *509 Main St., Cañon City* ☎ *719/276–3088* 🌐 *www.mypizzamadness.com.*

Hotels

★ Royal Gorge Cabins and Glamping Tents

$$$$ | **RENTAL** | With views of the Sangre de Cristo Mountains, these rustic but cozy cabins offer a comfy spot to rest your head without leaving the outdoor setting that brings visitors to the region. **Pros:** spectacular views; modern decor; spacious cabins. **Cons:** less expensive glamping tents lack restrooms; several miles from downtown restaurants; limited availability. *Rooms from: $435* ✉ *45054 W. U.S. 50, Cañon City* ☎ *800/748–2953* 🌐 *www.royalgorgecabins.com* *Glamping tents closed Nov.–Mar.* *9 cabins, 8 glamping tents* *No meals.*

Activities

BICYCLING

South Cañon Trails

BICYCLING | Nearly 12 miles of single-track trails offering the challenging "Great Escape" section and the more moderate "Mutton Bustin'" are located closer to town. Trails are accessed at the Riverwalk Trail near Centennial Park downtown. ✉ *221 Griffin Ave., Cañon City* 🌐 *www.singletracks.com/bike-trails/south-canon-trails.html.*

HIKING

Red Canyon Park

HIKING/WALKING | Cañon City–owned Red Canyon Park, 12 miles north of town, offers splendid easy to moderate hiking among the rose-color sandstone spires. The easy-to-find park features towering red-rock formations and fossils. ✉ *Red Canyon Rd. and Field Ave., Cañon City* 🌐 *www.royalgorgeregion.com/red-canyon-park-trail-map.*

Tunnel Drive Trail

HIKING/WALKING | **FAMILY** | This mild and flat section of the Arkansas Riverwalk Trail is less than 4 miles round-trip and features views of the Arkansas River and a series of tunnels that once housed the city's water delivery pipeline. ✉ *205 Tunnel Dr., Cañon City* 🌐 *www.royalgorgeregion.com/tunnel-drive-2.*

JEEP TOURS

Colorado Jeep Tours

DRIVING TOURS | **FAMILY** | See the Royal Gorge from a new perspective with a Jeep ride over the 956-foot-high suspension bridge with knowledgeable guides pointing out fun facts along the way. ✉ *2320 E. Main St., Cañon City* ☎ *719/275—6339* 🌐 *coloradojeeptours.com.*

RAFTING

TOURS AND OUTFITTERS

★ Royal Gorge Rafting and Zip Line Tours

WHITE-WATER RAFTING | This outfitter is truly a one stop shop for adventure tours in the Royal Gorge Region. Combine rafting with ziplining, ropes courses, and helicopter tours over the Royal Gorge available at the base on U.S. 50 for a full day of fun. Most packages include lunch at White Water Bar & Grill, which serves large portions of barbecue, smothered spuds, burgers, and libations for refueling. ✉ *45045 W. U.S. 50, Cañon City* ☎ *719/275–7238* 🌐 *www.royalgorgerafting.net.*

Buena Vista

94 miles west of Colorado Springs on U.S. 24.

Skyscraping mountains, the most impressive being the Collegiate Peaks, ring Buena Vista (pronounced *byoo*-na *vis*-ta by locals). The 14,000-foot, often snowcapped peaks were first summited by alumni from Yale, Princeton, Harvard, and Columbia, who named them for their respective alma maters. A small mining town–turned–casual resort community, Buena Vista's main street is lined with Wild West–style historic buildings. On U.S. 24, which bisects the town, there are inexpensive roadside motels. The town is also a hub for the white-water rafting industry that plies its trade on the popular Arkansas River, and a great central location for hiking, fishing, rafting, and horseback riding.

GETTING HERE AND AROUND

You'll need your own car to explore this region. Everything outdoors from hiking and mountain biking to rafting on the Arkansas is an easy drive from Buena Vista.

VISITOR INFORMATION Buena Vista Welcome Center. ✉ *343 U.S. 24* ☎ *719/395–6612* 🌐 *www.buenavistacolorado.org.*

Sights

Buena Vista Heritage Museum

MUSEUM | Before leaving downtown, meander through the Buena Vista Heritage Museum in the 1882 brick courthouse. Each room is devoted to a different aspect of regional history from the 1860s to the 1900s: one to mining equipment, another to fashions, and another to household utensils. There are working models of the three railroads that serviced the area in its heyday, a schoolroom, and historical photos in the archives. A rafting and kayaking exhibit will have you itching to experience the thrill of the area's water sports for yourself, and the mine and cave exhibit features a fluorescent mineral display. ✉ *506 E. Main St.* ☎ *719/395–8458* 🌐 *www.buenavistaheritage.org* 🎫 *$5* ⏲ *Closed late Oct.–early May.*

★ Collegiate Peaks Wilderness Area

NATIONAL/STATE PARK | Taking its own name from the many peaks named after famous universities, the 168,000-acre Collegiate Peaks Wilderness Area includes eight mountains that tower more than 14,000 feet high. Forty miles of the Continental Divide snake through the area as well. The most compelling reason to visit Buena Vista is for the almost unequaled variety of hikes, climbs, biking trails, and fishing streams here. (Keep an eye out for hot springs, too.) Two ranger offices, one in Leadville and one in Salida, handle inquiries about this region. ✉ *Leadville Ranger District, 810 Front St., Leadville* ☎ *719/486–0749* 🌐 *www.fs.usda.gov/recarea/psicc/recarea/?recid=80755.*

Mount Princeton Hot Springs Resort

HOT SPRINGS | To relax sore muscles after your outdoor adventure, visit Mount Princeton Hot Springs Resort, 8 miles from Buena Vista. The resort has four pools open year-round and a fifth in the summer, plus several "hot spots in the creek"—the water temperature ranges between 97°F and 108°F. The restaurant features mostly fish and steak entrées with creative seasonal specials and has a large stone fireplace and a dramatic view of the Chalk Cliffs. If you're too relaxed to drive home, stay in one of the resort's hotel rooms or log cabins beginning

Did You Know?
The Collegiate Peaks Wilderness Area gets its name from the region's mountain peaks that are named after famous universities.

at $180 per night during the summer. ✉ *15870 County Rd. 162, Nathrop ✣ 4½ miles west of U.S. 285 ☎ 719/395–2447 🌐 www.mtprinceton.com 🎟 $20 Mon.–Thurs.; $25 Fri.–Sun.*

St. Elmo

TOUR—SIGHT | If you want to see an authentic ghost town, head 15 miles west on County Road 162. Once the supply center for the Mary Murphy Mine and dozens of smaller mines, St. Elmo is the best-preserved ghost town in Colorado. It doesn't take long to walk along the main street and peer into some of the rickety old buildings. There is a B&B, as well as a general store that's open in the summer. ✉ *Western end of County Rd.162.*

Restaurants

★ Eddyline Restaurant & Brewery

$ | **AMERICAN** | This casual brewpub is located by South Main River Park, so after dining on wood-fired pizzas, steaks, or seafood, washed down with ales brewed on-site, you can tackle the nearby miles of hiking and biking trails. **Known for:** locally brewed craft beer; casual atmosphere; convenient location near the river. 💲 *Average main: $13* ✉ *926 S. Main St.* ☎ *719/966–6000* 🌐 *eddylinebrewing.com.*

House Rock Kitchen

$$ | **MEXICAN** | Outdoor adventurers both local and visiting gather to kick back and refuel on the fresh and healthy dishes at this lively spot on downtown's Main Street. Seasonal ingredients fill the bowls, salads, and sandwiches and are best enjoyed on the patio with a cold beer. **Known for:** downtown location; healthy dishes; outdoor patio. 💲 *Average main: $15* ✉ *421 E. Main St.* ☎ *719/966–2326* 🌐 *www.houserockkitchen.com.*

Hotels

Riverside Lodge

$$ | **B&B/INN** | On the banks of the Arkansas River, this fishing lodge–inspired B&B surrounded by 23 acres of woodland is just a mile north of downtown. **Pros:** gorgeous setting; river views (and sounds); close to downtown. **Cons:** not the best choice if you have young kids; despite central location it can be difficult to find; no river access. 💲 *Rooms from: $190* ✉ *30000 County Rd. 371* ☎ *719/395–3444, 888/542–7756* 🌐 *www.liarslodge.com* *5 rooms* *Free Breakfast.*

★ Surf Hotel and Chateau

$$ | **HOTEL** | This bright and thoughtfully decorated boutique hotel on the banks of the Arkansas River offers well-appointed, minimalist rooms; an enclosed central courtyard that encourages socializing after kayaking; and balconies and patios to maximize on its location on the water. **Pros:** modern, bright design; centrally located in the South Main neighborhood; large balcony with river and mountain views. **Cons:** no on-site parking; no pool or fitness center; shared balcony can be noisy. 💲 *Rooms from: $200* ✉ *1012 Front Loop* ☎ *719/966—7048* 🌐 *www.surfhotel.com* *62 rooms* *No meals.*

Nightlife

Deerhammer Distilling Company

GATHERING PLACES | Be sure to sit at the bar in this Main Street joint and chat up the local bartenders that serve up opinions on town politics and advice on where to eat, as well as delicious cocktails made from whiskey and gin distilled on-site. Bands liven up Main Street on weekends and throughout the summer, bringing in tourists and plenty of local flavor. ✉ *321 E. Main St.* ☎ *719/395–9464* 🌐 *www.deerhammer.com.*

Some of the state's best white-water rafting is on the Arkansas River.

The Jailhouse

BREWPUBS/BEER GARDENS | Nothing will raise your thirst like considering the former occupants of this very cool 1880s jailhouse-turned-craft-beer bar, complete with jailhouse knickknacks, stone walls, and bars on its windows. It's perfectly situated on Main Street, and the excellent beer selection, with a focus on local brews, attracts a lively crowd to the cozy inside nooks and crannies and the large outdoor patio. ✉ *412 E. Main St.* ☎ *719/966–5544* 🌐 *www.thejailhousebv.com.*

Activities

HORSEBACK RIDING

Mt. Princeton Hot Springs Stables

HORSEBACK RIDING | Here you can book trail rides along the dramatic Chalk Creek Cliffs; the cost is $45 per hour or day rides starting at $195 (including lunch). ✉ *14582 County Rd. 162* ☎ *866/877–3630, 719/395–3630* 🌐 *www.coloradotrailrides.com.*

RAFTING

Arkansas River

WHITE-WATER RAFTING | Adrenaline-charging rapids range from Class II to Class V on Colorado's Arkansas River, one of the most commercially rafted and challenging rivers in the world. Among the most fabled stretches of the Arkansas are the Narrows, the Numbers, and Browns Canyon, but extreme paddlers tend to jump on trips through the Royal Gorge, which the river has carved out over eons. Plan your trip for the early summer snowmelt for the biggest thrills. ✉ *Buena Vista.*

TOURS AND OUTFITTERS

★ River Runners

WHITE-WATER RAFTING | This long-respected outfitter offers rafting trips on the Arkansas River, including overnight trips, and to Browns Canyon or Bighorn Sheep Canyon, which offer family-friendly trips that are ranked beginner and intermediate. ✉ *24070 County Rd. 301* ☎ *800/723–8987* 🌐 *www.whitewater.net.*

Salida

25 miles south of Buena Vista; 102 miles southwest of Colorado Springs.

Imposing peaks, including 14,000-plus-foot Mount Shavano, dominate the town of Salida, which is on the Arkansas River. This small but artsy town is host to 20 art galleries and draws some of the musicians who appear at the Aspen Music Festival—classical pianists, brass ensembles, and the like—for its Salida–Aspen Concerts in July and August. The town's other big event is an annual white-water rafting rodeo in June, on a section of river that cuts right through downtown. It's been taking place since 1949.

GETTING HERE AND AROUND

You need a private car to explore this area. There's a compact, walkable downtown area, but you'll need to drive to most lodgings, rivers, attractions, and the trailheads in the mountains.

VISITOR INFORMATION Salida Colorado Chamber of Commerce. ✉ *406 W. U.S. 50* ☎ *719/539–2068, 877/772–5432* 🌐 *www.salidachamber.org.*

Restaurants

Amicas Pizza and Microbrewery

$ | PIZZA | The wood-fired pizzas and craft brews at this downtown grub hub come highly recommended by locals. Families stop in for a giant pie that can easily feed a family of four while white-water rafters, hikers, and bikers unwind at the next table with one of the brewery's well-known chili beers. **Known for:** the Michelangelo, a goat cheese pizza with sausage, pesto, green chilies, and caramelized onion; on-site microbrewery; downtown location. *$ Average main: $11* ✉ *127 F St.* ☎ *719/539–5219* 🌐 *amicas-salida.com* 💳 *No credit cards.*

The Fritz

$$ | MODERN AMERICAN | This hip small-plates restaurant is as trendy as Salida dining gets. The intimate bar and expansive patio are some of the region's best spaces for socializing. **Known for:** creative small plates; central location; trendy scene. *$ Average main: $15* ✉ *113 E. Sackett St.* ☎ *719/539–0364* 🌐 *www.thefritzsalida.com.*

Hotels

Tudor Rose

$$ | B&B/INN | With beautiful furnishings and an idyllic setting, this rustic mountain lodge sits on a 37-acre spread of pine forest and mountain ridges. **Pros:** owners will stable horses in their barn; perfect rustic retreat; beautiful deck with mountain views. **Cons:** not for guests with young children; no pool; a bit outside of town. *$ Rooms from: $125* ✉ *6720 County Rd. 104* ☎ *719/539–2002, 800/379–0889* 🌐 *www.thetudorrose.com* *6 rooms, 5 chalets* *Free Breakfast.*

Performing Arts

Salida Steam Plant Event Center

THEATER | In recent years, the former power plant overlooking the Arkansas River, now known as Salida Steam Plant Event Center, has become the arts and culture hub of town. The theater hosts several concerts and productions each summer, ranging from drama and comedy to music and cabaret, and two art galleries house exhibits featuring local and regional artists. ✉ *220 W. Sackett Ave.* ☎ *719/530–0933* 🌐 *www.salidasteamplant.com.*

Shopping

The Maverick Potter

ART GALLERIES | Brice Turnbill's wonderful blown-glass creations are at the Maverick Potter gallery, where the artist rents space. The gallery also displays work from owner Mark Rittmann, a brewer-turned-potter who has shown pieces all over the country. ✉ *119 F St.* ☎ *719/539–5112* 🌐 *www.maverickpotter.com.*

Rock Doc at Prospectors Village

LOCAL SPECIALTIES | Midway between Salida and Buena Vista, the Rock Doc is an enormous shop with gold-panning equipment, metal detectors, and rock art. ✉ *17897 U.S. 285, Nathrop* ☎ *719/539–2019* 🌐 *www.therockdoc.net.*

Activities

BICYCLING

Absolute Bikes

BICYCLING | This downtown shop rents cruisers starting at $25 per day and mountain bikes starting at $65 per day, and provides repair service, maps, and good advice. ✉ *330 W. Sackett Ave.* ☎ *719/539–9295* 🌐 *www.absolutebikes.com.*

DOWNHILL SKIING

Monarch Mountain

SKIING/SNOWBOARDING | A small, independently owned ski resort that tops out on the Continental Divide, Monarch Mountain is a family-friendly place with moderate pricing and discounts for advanced online purchases. The resort also offers 1,635 acres of snowcat skiing on steep runs off the divide, plus the 130 acres of hike-to skiing on extreme terrain in Mirkwood Basin. **Facilities:** 58 trails; 800 acres; 1,162-foot vertical drop; 7 lifts. ✉ *22720 U.S. 50* ✣ *18 miles west of Salida* ☎ *719/530–5000, 888/996–7669* 🌐 *www.skimonarch.com* 🎫 *Lift ticket $99.*

FISHING

The Arkansas River, as it spills out of the central Colorado Rockies on its course through the south central part of the state, reputedly supports a brown trout population exceeding 5,000 fish per mile. Some of the river's canyons are deep, and some of the best fishing locations are difficult to access, making a guide or outfitter a near necessity. See 🌐 *cpw.state.co.us/thingstodo/Pages/Fishing.aspx* for more information.

OUTFITTERS

ArkAnglers

FISHING | A good fly shop with an experienced staff, ArkAnglers offers guided float and wade trips, fly-fishing lessons, and equipment rentals. ✉ *7500 W. U.S. 50* ☎ *719/539–4223* 🌐 *www.arkanglers.com.*

RAFTING

The Salida area is a magnet for rafting aficionados, and there are dozens of outfitters. Salida jockeys with Buena Vista for the title of "Colorado's White-Water Capital."

Independent Whitewater

WHITE-WATER RAFTING | This family-owned company has been running the Arkansas River since the 1980s. Groups are small, and the take-out is at a private area after running Seidel's Suckhole and Twin Falls on regular half-day trips. ✉ *10830 County Rd. 165* ☎ *800/428–1479, 719/539–7737* 🌐 *www.independentrafting.com.*

SNOWMOBILING

All Season Adventures Inc.

SNOW SPORTS | Leisurely rides and snow-throwing thrills are both offered by this snowmobile outfitter. You can ride the Continental Divide with tours starting at $120 for a single and $165 for doubles. ✉ *10238 US 50, Poncha Springs* ☎ *719/530–0651* 🌐 *www.allseasonrentals.com.*

Pueblo

40 miles east of Cañon City via U.S. 50; 45 miles south of Colorado Springs via I–25.

In 1842 El Pueblo trading post, on the bank of the Arkansas River, was a gathering place for trappers and traders. Today the trading post is an archaeological dig set in a pavilion next to the El Pueblo History Museum. The thriving city of Pueblo surrounds the museum, and the Arkansas River runs through the city in a concrete channel, tamed by the Pueblo Dam.

Stroll through the Union Avenue Historic District, and take a ride on one of the tour boats leaving from the Historic Arkansas Riverwalk, an urban waterfront area that restored the Arkansas River channel to its original location. More than 682 acres of parkland, in addition to hiking and bicycling trails, help to define Pueblo as a sports and recreation center.

GETTING HERE AND AROUND

A car is the best way to explore this sprawling city.

VISITOR INFORMATION Pueblo Chamber of Commerce. ✉ *302 N. Santa Fe Ave.* ☎ *719/542–1704, 800/233–3446* 🌐 *www.pueblochamber.org.*

Sights

Bishop Castle

CASTLE/PALACE | This elaborate creation, which resembles a medieval castle replete with turrets, buttresses, and ornamental iron, is the prodigious (some might say monomaniacal) one-man undertaking of Jim Bishop, a self-taught architect who began work in 1959. Once considered a blight on pastoral Highway 165, the castle is now a popular attraction. Not yet complete, it is three stories high with a nearly 165-foot tower. Those who endeavor to climb into the structure must sign the guest book–cum–liability waiver. Bishop finances this enormous endeavor through donations and a gift shop. ✉ *12705 Hwy. 165* ☎ *719/564–4366* 🌐 *www.bishopcastle.org* 🎟 *Free.*

Buell Children's Museum

MUSEUM | **FAMILY** | Ranked among the best in the country, the Buell Children's Museum provides fun, interactive experiences for kids of all ages. The 12,000-square-foot facility has innovative exhibits on art, science, and history. It's in the same complex as the Sangre de Cristo Arts Center. ✉ *210 N. Santa Fe Ave.* ☎ *719/295–7200* 🌐 *www.sdc-arts.org/museum/about* 🎟 *$10* ⏲ *Closed Sun.–Tues.*

City Park

CITY PARK | **FAMILY** | The fine City Park has fishing lakes, playgrounds, a carousel, a mini train ride, and tennis courts and a swimming pool. ✉ *Pueblo Blvd. and Goodnight Ave.*

El Pueblo History Museum

MUSEUM | **FAMILY** | A nicely designed repository for the city's history, El Pueblo History Museum extends its scope to chronicle life on the plains dating back before Colorado statehood. It tells of Pueblo's role as a cultural and geographic crossroads, beginning when it was a trading post in the 1840s. Hands-on features—a giant teepee where guests can go inside and play historic drum replicas; a dress-up chest full of pioneer clothing and hats; and a covered wagon that is just the right height for small hands to discover the trinkets on board—make this museum fun for the whole family. Remnants of the original trading post are now an archaeological dig enclosed in a pavilion next to the museum. ✉ *301 N. Union Ave.* ☎ *719/583–0453* 🌐 *www.historycolorado.org* 🎟 *$5* ⏲ *Closed Sun. and Mon.*

Historic Arkansas Riverwalk of Pueblo

PROMENADE | Stroll on the paths or take to the water on a boat tour or in a paddleboat to explore this 32-acre urban waterfront park. Boat rides are available at the riverwalk center at 101 South Union Avenue. ✉ *Pueblo* ☎ *719/595–1589 boat reservations* 🌐 *www.puebloriverwalk.org.*

Pueblo-Weisbrod Aircraft Museum

MUSEUM | At the city's airport, the Pueblo-Weisbrod Aircraft Museum traces the development of American military aviation with nearly 35 aircraft in mint condition, ranging from a Lockheed F-80 fighter plane to a MiG-15. Curator Shawn Kirscht is restoring a Boeing B-29 Super Fortress of atomic-bomb fame on-site. Admission also includes entry to the International B-24 Memorial Museum, which is also on this site. ✉ *Pueblo Memorial Airport, 31001 Magnuson Ave.* ☎ *719/948–9219* 🌐 *www.pwam.org* 🎟 *$10.*

Pueblo Zoo

ZOO | FAMILY | In City Park, this biopark is home to African penguins, ringtail lemurs, and boa constrictors—housed separately of course. Favorites here include African painted dogs, lions, river otters, and the annual holiday feature ElectriCritters, an evening light display that involves more than 250,000 lights, which runs from late November through the end of the year. ✉ *3455 Nuckolls Ave.* ☎ *719/561–1452* 🌐 *www.pueblozoo.org* 🎟 *$12.*

Rocky Ford

TOWN | Leaving the Rockies far behind, U.S. 50 takes you toward the eastern plains, where rolling prairies give way to hardier desert blooms and the land is stubbled with sage and stunted pinyon pines. One fertile spot—50 miles along the highway—is the town of Rocky Ford, dubbed the "Sweet Melon Capital" for its famously succulent cantaloupes. ✉ *Rocky Ford.*

Rosemount Museum

MUSEUM | Exquisite maple, oak, and mahogany woodwork gleams throughout this splendid 37-room mansion, with ivory glaze and gold-leaf trim. Marble fireplaces, Tiffany-glass fixtures, and frescoed ceilings complete the opulent look. The top floor—originally servants' quarters—features the odd Andrew McClelland Collection: objects of curiosity this eccentric philanthropist garnered on his worldwide travels, including an Egyptian mummy. ✉ *419 W. 14th St.* ☎ *719/545–5290* 🌐 *www.rosemount.org* 🎟 *$8.*

Union Avenue Historic District

HISTORIC SITE | The century-old stores and warehouses of Union Avenue Historic District make for a commercial district filled with a mix of stores ranging from kitschy to good. Among the landmarks are the glorious 1889 sandstone-and-brick Union Depot. Pitkin Place, lined with fabulous gabled and turreted mansions, attests to the town's more prosperous times. Walking-tour brochures are available at the chamber of commerce. ✉ *Pueblo.*

Restaurants

dc's on b street

$$$ | AMERICAN | There are two dining areas in this restaurant, housed in the historic redbrick Coors building across from the Union Depot. At lunch you can order sandwiches, salads, and other light fare in a room with simple tables, brick walls, and a tin ceiling. **Known for:** good wine list; delicious steak and decadent sauces; intimate dining room. $ *Average main: $24* ✉ *115 B St.* ☎ *719/584–3410.*

★ Gray's Coors Tavern

$ | AMERICAN | Locals constantly debate where to find the city's best "slopper"—an open-faced burger smothered in cheese, red or green chile, and onions—but there is no question you will find an authentic Pueblo experience at this dive bar where the dish was first served. Bikers and families converge on the large outdoor patio during the summer to devour the messy burger. **Known for:** excellent Slopper (an open-faced burger smothered in red or green chile); ice-cold Coors served in large schooner glasses; old-school Pueblo atmosphere. $ *Average main: $9* ✉ *515 W. 4th St.* ☎ *719/544–0455* 💳 *No credit cards.*

Hotels

Station on the Riverwalk

$$ | HOTEL | Once Pueblo's police station and jail, this family-operated hotel features a modern design that pays homage to the building's past. **Pros:** central location; historic, jailhouse theme in every room; fireplaces in some rooms. **Cons:** bar next door can be noisy; no overnight staff; jailhouse theme not for everyone. $ *Rooms from: $170* ✉ *140 Central Main St.* ☎ *719/924–7904* 🌐 *www.stationontheriverwalk.com* *7 rooms* 🍽 *No meals.*

Shamrock Brewing Company

BARS/PUBS | This consistently jam-packed hot spot is a bar and grill with a good kitchen. They brew their own beer—six or seven varieties are usually on tap including the Irish Red Ale and PAPA, the Pueblo American Pale Ale. It's especially popular with the after-work crowd. ✉ *108 W. 3rd St.* ☎ *719/542–9974* 🌐 *www.shamrockbrewing.com.*

Broadway Theatre League

THEATER | This downtown theater company brings three touring Broadway blockbusters to the restored Memorial Hall every year. ✉ *Memorial Hall, 1 City Hall Place* ☎ *719/583–4961* 🌐 *www.broadwaytheatreleaguepueblo.com.*

Pueblo Symphony

MUSIC | The city's symphony performs all types of music, from pops to classical. Concerts are held at the Hoag Recital Hall on the Colorado State University–Pueblo campus. ✉ *Hoag Recital Hall, 2200 Bonforte Blvd.* ☎ *719/545–7967* 🌐 *www.pueblosymphony.com.*

Sangre de Cristo Arts Center

ART GALLERIES—ARTS | Rotating exhibits at this impressive performance and gallery center celebrate regional arts and crafts. The center also houses the superb Western art collection and a theater with a performing-arts series that ranges from plays to ballets. ✉ *210 N. Santa Fe Ave.* ☎ *719/295–7200* 🌐 *www.sdc-arts.org* 🎟 *$10.*

BICYCLING

Pueblo River Trail System

BICYCLING | An extensive network with more than 30 miles of hiking and biking trails loops around the city, following the Arkansas River for part of the way before heading out to the reservoir. There are paved portions of the trail that are popular in-line skating routes, too. You can get trail maps at the chamber of commerce. ✉ *Pueblo* 🌐 *www.pueblo.us/DocumentCenter/View/2580/City-Trail-System?bidId=.*

BOATING, KAYAKING, AND FISHING

Edge Ski, Paddle and Pack

BOATING | The Edge Ski, Paddle and Pack rents kayaks for use on the Arkansas River. ✉ *107 N. Union Ave.* ☎ *719/583–2021.*

Lake Pueblo State Park

CAMPING—SPORTS-OUTDOORS | There's excellent camping and fishing at Lake Pueblo State Park, as well as many other outdoor activities. ✉ *Hwy. 96* ✣ *8 miles west of downtown* ☎ *719/561–9320* 🌐 *cpw.state.co.us/placestogo/parks/LakePueblo.*

South Shore Marina

BOATING | At this marina in Lake Pueblo State Park, you can rent 10-passenger pontoon boats for $330 per half day. ✉ *Lake Pueblo State Park, Hwy. 96* ✣ *8 miles west of downtown* ☎ *719/564–1043* 🌐 *www.thesouthshoremarina.com.*

HIKING

San Isabel National Forest

HIKING/WALKING | You can hike in relative solitude on many trails threading the San Isabel National Forest, 45 minutes southwest of Pueblo. The forest service station in Pueblo is open 7:30 am–4:30 pm weekdays. ✉ *2840 Kachina Dr.* ☎ *719/553–1400* 🌐 *www.fs.usda.gov/psicc.*

La Junta

60 miles east of Pueblo via U.S. 50.

For an easy day trip from Pueblo into Colorado's past, head east to La Junta. The Koshare Indian Museum is in town, and Bent's Old Fort National Historic Site and the dinosaur tracks and ancient rock art of the canyonlands are nearby.

La Junta (which roughly translated from Spanish means "the meeting place") was founded as a trading post in the mid-19th century. It was a stop for the Santa Fe and Kansas Pacific railroads, and today is home to 7,000 residents.

GETTING HERE AND AROUND

Amtrak stops in La Junta but a private car is best to explore this remote area.

ESSENTIALS

VISITOR INFORMATION La Junta Chamber of Commerce. ✉ *110 Santa Fe Ave.* ☎ *719/384–7411* 🌐 *www.lajuntachamber.com.*

Sights

Bent's Old Fort National Historic Site
HISTORIC SITE | About 8 miles east of La Junta, Bent's Old Fort National Historic Site painstakingly re-creates what life was like in this adobe fort. The 1840s fort was situated along the commercially vital Santa Fe Trail, providing both protection and a meeting place for the soldiers, trappers, and traders of the era. The museum's interior reveals daily life at a trading post, providing looks at a smithy and carpenter's workshop and featuring educational films and guided tours. ✉ *35110 Hwy. 194* ☎ *719/383–5010* 🌐 *www.nps.gov/beol* 🎟 *$3.*

★ Koshare Indian Museum
MUSEUM | With Navajo silver and Hopi pottery, the Koshare Indian Museum contains extensive holdings of Native American artifacts and crafts. It also displays pieces from Anglo artists, such as Remington, known for their depictions of Native Americans. The Koshare Indian Dancers—actually local youth—perform regularly. ✉ *115 W. 18th St.* ☎ *719/384–4411* 🌐 *koshares.com* 🎟 *$5.*

Restaurants

Boss Hogg's
$ | BARBECUE | For a quick bite, try this Western-themed watering hole and barbecue-steak joint with a quirky personality. Boss Hogg's is a local institution. **Known for:** hand-cut steaks; quirky Western decor; friendly staff. 💲 *Average main: $14* ✉ *808 E. 3rd St.* ☎ *719/384–7879* 💳 *No credit cards.*

Activities

Comanche National Grassland
HIKING/WALKING | This vast 444,000-acre tract has a pair of canyon loops where there's a fair amount of rock art. Some of the largest documented sets of fossilized dinosaur tracks in the United States are in **Picket Wire Canyonlands,** a part of the grassland. There are tables for when you want an impromptu picnic. ✉ *Ranger Office, 1420 E. 3rd St.* ✥ *From La Junta, drive south on Hwy. 109 for 13 miles, west on County Rd. 802 for 8 miles, and south on County Rd. 25 for 6 miles. Turn left at Picket Wire Corrals onto Forest Service Rd. 2185 and follow signs to Withers Canyon Trailhead* ☎ *719/384–2181* 🌐 *www.fs.usda.gov/recarea/psicc.*

Trinidad

85 miles south of Pueblo and 13 miles north of New Mexico border.

If you're traveling on I–25 and want to stop for a night in a historic town with character instead of a motel on the outskirts of a bigger city, check out Trinidad. Walk around Corazon de Trinidad, the downtown creative district area where some of the streets still have the original bricks—instead of pavement—and visit a few of the town's superb museums, a remarkably large number for a town of barely more than 8,000 residents.

Trinidad was founded in 1862 as a rest-and-repair station along the Santa Fe Trail. Starting in 1878 with the construction of the railroad and the development of the coal industry, the town grew and expanded, but the advent of natural gas, coupled with the Depression, led to a gradual decline in population. Since the 1990s there's been a modest increase, though, and a major interest in the upkeep of the city's rich cultural heritage.

GETTING HERE AND AROUND

Amtrak stops here. You'll need a private car or you can take the free Trinidad Trolley between shops, restaurants, and museums downtown.

ESSENTIALS

VISITOR INFORMATION Trinidad & Las Animas Chamber of Commerce. ✉ *137 N. Commercial St., Suite 204* ☎ *719/846–9285* 🌐 *www.tlacchamber.org.*

Sights

Corazon de Trinidad (*Heart of Trinidad*)
HISTORIC SITE | Downtown Trinidad, called the Corazon de Trinidad, is a National Historic District, mixing historic original brick-paved streets and architecture with modern concerts, restaurants, shops, and festivals. Residents and officials recently launched a bit of a revival here with big plans for the creative district. ✉ *Trinidad* 🌐 *www.corazondetrinidad.org.*

Louden-Henritze Archaeology Museum
MUSEUM | On the other side of the Purgatoire River, this museum at Trinidad State Junior College takes viewers back millions of years to examine the true origins of the region, including early geological formations, plant and marine-animal fossils, and prehistoric artifacts. ✉ *Trinidad State Junior College, 600 Prospect St.* ☎ *719/846–5508* 🌐 *trinidadstate.edu/archaeology-museum/index.html* 🎫 *Free* ⏲ *Closed Fri.–Sun.*

Trinidad History Museum
GARDEN | This complex with three separate museums and a garden is a place to learn about the town's history. The first museum is **Baca House,** the 1870s residence of Felipe Baca, a prominent Hispanic farmer and businessman. Displays convey a mix of Anglo (clothes, furniture) and Hispanic (santos, textiles) influences. Next door, the 1882 **Bloom Mansion** was built by Frank Bloom, who made his money through ranching and banking. He filled his ornate Second Empire–style Victorian with fine furnishings and fabrics brought from the East Coast and abroad. The adjacent **Santa Fe Trail Museum** is dedicated to the effects of the trail and railroad on the community. Inside are exhibits covering Trinidad's heyday as a commercial and cultural center. Finish up with a stop in the **Historic Gardens,** which are open year-round and filled with native plants and grapevines similar to those tended by the pioneers. ✉ *312 E. Main St.* ☎ *719/846–7217* 🌐 *www.trinidadhistorymuseum.org* 🎫 *$5* ⏲ *Closed Sun. and Mon.*

Restaurants

Nana and Nano's Pasta House
$ | **ITALIAN** | The aroma of garlic and tomato sauce saturates this tiny, unpretentious eatery. Pastas, including standards like ravioli with homemade sauce and rigatoni with luscious meatballs, are consistently excellent. **Known for:** authentic Italian pasta dishes; deli with sandwiches and imported cheeses; informal and welcoming atmosphere. 💲 *Average main: $10* ✉ *418 E. Main St.* ☎ *719/846–2696* ⏲ *Closed Sun.–Tues.*

Hotels

Tarabino Inn

$$ | **B&B/INN** | This Italianate–Victorian B&B sits in the middle of the Corazon de Trinidad National Historic District. **Pros:** decorated with works by local artists; within walking distance of museums; historical building. **Cons:** not much privacy; decor a little old-fashioned; not suitable for young children. *Rooms from: $129* *310 E. 2nd St.* *719/846–2115, 866/846–8808* *www.tarabinoinn.com* *4 rooms* *Free Breakfast.*

Activities

Trinidad Lake State Park

PARK—SPORTS-OUTDOORS | There's hiking, fishing, horseback riding, and camping at this park in the Purgatoire River Valley. *Hwy. 12* *3 miles west of Trinidad* *719/846–6951* *cpw.state.co.us/placestogo/parks/TrinidadLake.*

Cuchara Valley

55 miles northwest of Trinidad and 64 miles southwest of Pueblo to the town of La Veta via I–25, U.S. 160, and Hwy. 12.

If you want a true mountain rural setting, head to the Cuchara Valley. From here or La Veta you can go camping or hiking in the San Isabel National Forest, go horseback riding on trails through the woods, or go fishing in streams.

GETTING HERE AND AROUND

The Cuchara Valley is along the Highway of Legends. You need a private car to get here and move around this region.

ESSENTIALS

VISITOR INFORMATION La Veta–Cuchara Chamber of Commerce. *719/742–3676* *www.lavetacucharachamber.com.*

Sights

Cokedale

HISTORIC SITE | This entire town is a National Historic District, and it's the most significant example of a turn-of-the-20th-century coal–coke camp in Colorado. As you drive through the area, note the telltale streaks of black in the sandstone and granite bluffs fronting the Purgatoire River and its tributaries, the unsightly slag heaps, and the spooky abandoned mining camps dotting the hillsides. *Hwy. 12, Cokedale* *9 miles west of Trinidad.*

Highway of Legends

SCENIC DRIVE | From Trinidad, the scenic Highway of Legends curls north through the Cuchara Valley. As it starts its climb, you'll pass a series of company towns built to house coal miners. The Highway of Legends, also known as Highway 12, takes you through some of the wildest and most beautiful scenery in southern Colorado. You can start the drive in Trinidad or La Veta. *www.codot.gov/travel/scenic-byways/southeast/highway-legends.*

La Veta

TOWN | The Highway of Legends passes through the tiny, laid-back resort town of La Veta before intersecting with U.S. 160 and turning east toward Walsenburg, another settlement built on coal and the largest town between Pueblo and Trinidad. *La Veta.*

San Isabel National Forest

FOREST | As you approach Cuchara Pass, several switchbacks snake through rolling grasslands and dance in and out of spruce stands whose clearings afford views of Monument Lake. You can camp, fish, and hike throughout this tranquil part of the San Isabel National Forest, which in spring and summer is emblazoned with a color wheel of wildflowers. Four corkscrewing miles later you'll reach a dirt road that leads to Bear Lake and Blue Lake. The resort town of Cuchara is about 4 miles from the Highway 12 turnoff to the lakes. 🌐 *www.fs.usda.gov/psicc.*

Spanish Peaks

NATURE SITE | In the Cuchara Valley you'll see fantastic rock formations with equally fanciful names, such as Profile Rock, Devil's Staircase, and Giant's Spoon. With a little imagination you can devise your own legends about the names' origins. There are more than 400 of these upthrusts, which radiate like the spokes of a wheel from the valley's dominating landmark, the Spanish Peaks. In Spanish they are known as *Dos Hermanos,* or "Two Brothers." In Ute, their name *Huajatolla* means "breasts of the world." The haunting formations are considered to be a unique geologic phenomenon for their sheer abundance and variety of rock types.

Restaurants

★ Alys' Restaurant

$$$ | **CONTEMPORARY** | Dinner at Alys' is a simple treat, where the "international eclectic" prix-fixe options feature lamb, steak, chicken, or seafood; fresh vegetables; potato, rice, or pasta; soup or salad; and soft drinks, tea, or coffee (vegetarian dinners are always available too). Wine is extra, and you'll appreciate the attentive care taken with the thoughtful wine list—you might even have the opportunity to ask chef Alys Romer what she recommends. **Known for:** affordable prix-fixe menus; impressive wine list and cocktail menu; excellent duck l'orange. *Average main: $30 ✉ 604 S. Oak St., La Veta ☎ 719/742–3742 🌐 www.alysrestaurant.com.*

Hotels

Inn at the Spanish Peaks Bed & Breakfast

$ | **B&B/INN** | This Southwestern-style B&B is set in an adobe-style home with open beams and high ceilings. **Pros:** mountain views; friendly owners; walking distance from downtown La Veta. **Cons:** you are really in the outback of Colorado; minimum two night weekend stays in summer; no pets. *Rooms from: $95 ✉ 310 E. Francisco St., La Veta ☎ 719/742–5313 3 suites 🍽 Free Breakfast.*

Great Sand Dunes National Park and Preserve

Created by winds that sweep the San Luis Valley floor, the enormous sand dunes that form the heart of Great Sand Dunes National Park and Preserve are an improbable, unforgettable sight. The dunes stretch for more than 30 square miles, solid enough to have withstood 440,000 years of Mother Nature.

Nomadic hunters followed herds of mammoths and prehistoric bison into the San Luis Valley, making them some of the first people to visit the dunes. The hills of sand marked a common route for Native American tribes and explorers who traveled between the plains and Santa Fe. Speculation that gold was hiding under the sand attracted droves of miners in the 19th and 20th centuries. By the 1920s, operations had sprung up along the seasonal Medano Creek at the eastern base of the dunes, alarming residents of the nearby Alamosa and Monte Vista communities. Members of the Ladies Philanthropic Educational Organization lobbied politicians to protect the landmark, and in 1932 it was designated a national monument. Seventy years later, it was discovered that a large inland lake once covered the San Luis Valley, but had dried up due to climate change. Residents again rallied to protect the local resource, wildlife, and unique ecosystems, and the area was expanded into a national park and preserve in 2004.

Today, more than half a million visitors flock to the region annually to gawk at and play on the vast mountains of sand framed by the low grasslands and high-reaching Sangre de Cristo peaks. The tallest sand dunes in North America are nestled among diverse ecosystems of wetlands, grasslands, forests, and a towering mountain range where visitors can fish alpine lakes, walk among wildflowers, listen to songbirds, and climb the soft sand in a single day. Pronghorn, elk, and bighorn sheep call the area home, while sandhill cranes flood the area twice a year during spring and fall migrations. From star designs to sharp, defined edges, the shapes of the dunes are as disparate as the geography surrounding them. Warmed by the sun or coated in snow, the sand hills, which tower as high as 750 feet, offer opportunities for sledding or climbing year-round. Adding to the awe of the unusual landscape, avalanches of sand can create a rare humming sound that inspired Bing Crosby's musical hit "The Singing Sands of Alamosa." Intrigue and inspiration continue to attract visitors from all around.

GETTING ORIENTED

Main Use Area. This relatively compact area contains all of the park's developed campgrounds, trails, and the visitor center.

Sand Dunes. The 30-square-mile field of sand has no designated trails. The highest dune in the park—and, in fact, in North America—is 750-foot-high Star Dune.

Sangre de Cristo Mountains. Named the "Blood of Christ" Mountains by Spanish explorers because of their ruddy color—especially at sunrise and sunset—the range contains 10 of Colorado's 54 Fourteeners (mountains taller than 14,000 feet); six mountains within the preserve are more than 13,000 feet tall.

Southern Grasslands. Wildlife, such as elk and bison, feed on the park's grassy areas, primarily found in the park's southern area and the Great Sand Dunes National Preserve.

Medano Creek Wetlands. Popular with a variety of birds and amphibians, these seasonal wetlands form in the area around Medano Creek, where cottonwood and willow trees also thrive.

WHEN TO GO

More than half a million visitors come to the park each year, most on summer weekends; they tend to congregate around the main parking area and Medano Creek. To avoid the crowds, hike away from the main area up to the High Dune. Or come in the winter, when the park is a place for contemplation and repose—as well as skiing and sledding.

Fall and spring are the prettiest times to visit, with the surrounding mountains still capped with snow in May, and leaves on the aspen trees turning gold in September and early October. In summer, the surface temperature of the sand can climb to 150°F in the afternoon, so climbing the dunes is best in the morning or late afternoon. Since you're at a high altitude—about 8,200 feet at the visitor center—the air temperatures in the park itself remain in the 70s most of the summer.

GETTING HERE AND AROUND

Great Sand Dunes National Park and Preserve is about 240 miles from both Denver and Albuquerque, and roughly 180 miles from Colorado Springs and Santa Fe. The fastest route from Denver is I–25 south to U.S. 160, heading west to just past Blanca, to Highway 150 north, which goes right to the park's main entrance. For a more scenic route, take U.S. 285 over Kenosha, Red Hill, and Poncha Passes, turn onto Highway 17 just south of Villa Grove, then take County Lane 6 to the park (watch for signs just south of Hooper). From Albuquerque, go north on I–25 to Santa Fe, then north on U.S. 285 to Alamosa, then U.S. 160 east to Highway 150. From the west, Highway 17 and County Lane 6 take you to the park. The park entrance station is about 3 miles from the park boundary, and it's about a mile from there to the visitor center; the main parking lot is about a mile farther.

PARK ESSENTIALS

PARK FEES AND PERMITS

Entrance fees are $25 per vehicle and are valid for one week from date of purchase. Pick up camping permits ($20 per night per site at Pinyon Flats Campground) and backpacking permits (free) online at 🌐 *www.recreation.gov.*

PARK HOURS

The park is open 24/7. It is in the Mountain time zone.

PHONES

Cell-phone reception in the park is sporadic.

VISITOR INFORMATION

PARK CONTACT INFORMATION Great Sand Dunes National Park and Preserve. ✉ *11999 Hwy. 150, Mosca* ☎ *719/378–6395* 🌐 *www.nps.gov/grsa.*

SCENIC STOPS

High Dune

TRAIL | This isn't the park's highest dune, but it's high enough in the dune field to provide a view of all the dunes from its summit. It's on the first ridge of dunes you see from the main parking area. ✉ *Great Sand Dunes National Park.*

VISITOR CENTERS

Great Sand Dunes Visitor Center

INFO CENTER | View exhibits and artwork, browse in the bookstore, and watch a 20-minute film with an overview of the dunes. Rangers are on hand to answer questions. Facilities include restrooms and a vending machine stocked with soft drinks and snacks, but no other food. (The Great Sand Dunes Oasis, just outside the park boundary, has a café that is open generally late April through early October.) ✉ *Near the park entrance, Great Sand Dunes National Park* ☎ *719/378–6395* 🌐 *www.nps.gov/grsa/planyourvisit/visitor-center.htm.*

BIRD-WATCHING

The San Luis Valley is famous for its migratory birds, many of which stop in the park. Great Sand Dunes also has many permanent feathered residents. In the wetlands, you might see American white pelicans and the American avocet. On the forested sections of the mountains there are goshawks, northern harriers, gray jays, and Steller's jays. And in the alpine tundra there are golden eagles, hawks, horned larks, and white-tailed ptarmigan.

CAMPING

Great Sand Dunes has one campground, open April through October. During weekends in the summer, it can fill up with RVs and tents by midafternoon. Black bears live in the preserve, so when camping there, keep your food, trash, and toiletries in the trunk of your car (or use bear-proof containers). There is one campground and RV park near the entrance to Great Sand Dunes, and several others in the area.

Pinyon Flats Campground. Set in a pine forest about a mile past the visitor center, this campground has a trail leading to the dunes. Sites must be reserved online; RVs are allowed, but there are no hookups. ✉ *On the main park road, near the visitor center* 🌐 *www.recreation.gov* ☎ *719/378–6399.*

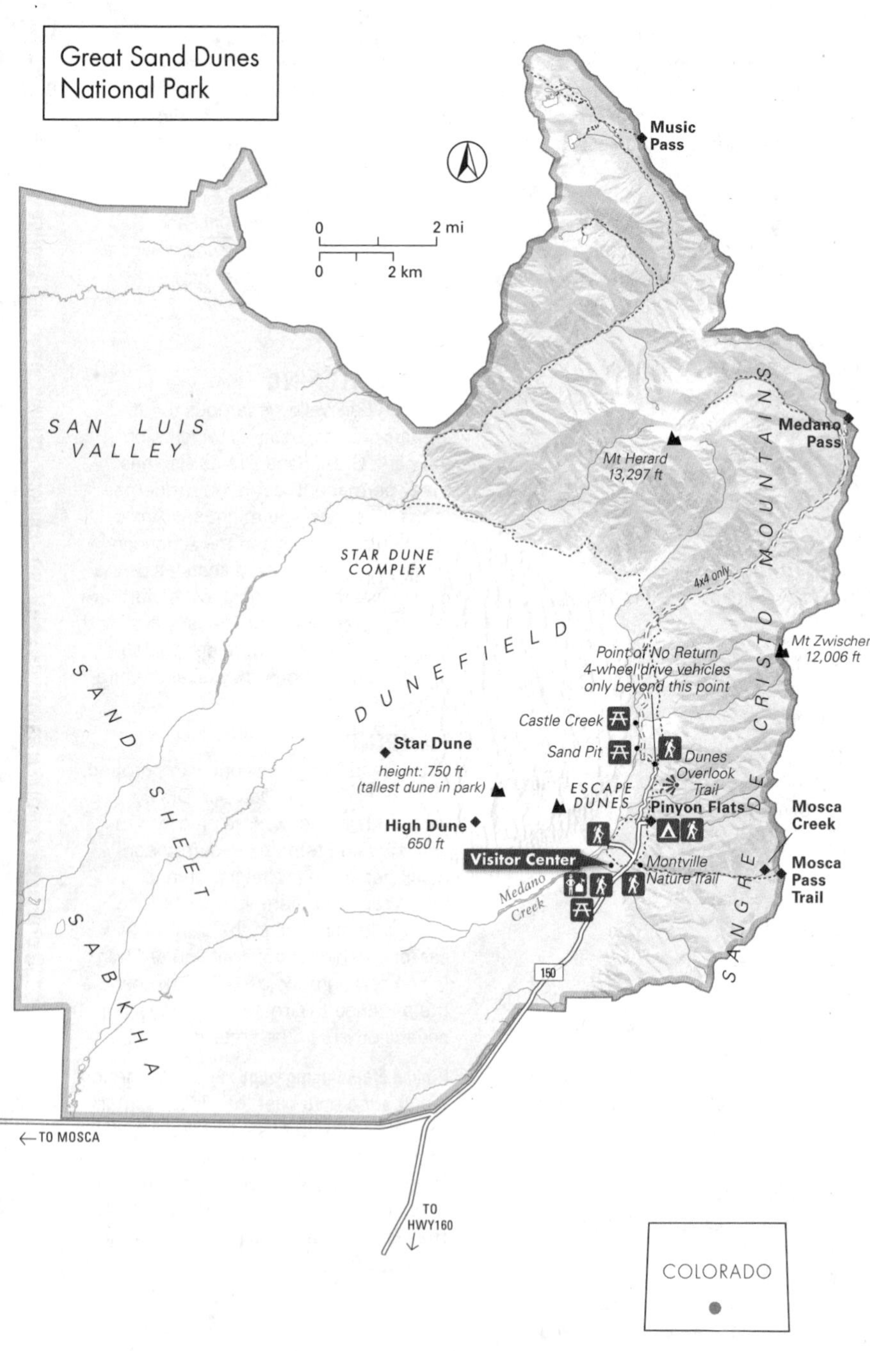
Great Sand Dunes National Park
Music Pass
0
2 mi
0
2 km
SAN LUIS VALLEY
Medano Pass
Mt Herard 13,297 ft
STAR DUNE COMPLEX
SANGRE DE CRISTO MOUNTAINS
4x4 only
DUNEFIELD
Mt Zwischen 12,006 ft
Point of No Return
4-wheel drive vehicles only beyond this point
Castle Creek
Sand Pit
Dunes Overlook Trail
SAND SHEET
Star Dune
height: 750 ft (tallest dune in park)
ESCAPE DUNES
Pinyon Flats
Mosca Creek
High Dune
650 ft
Visitor Center
Montville Nature Trail
Mosca Pass Trail
Medano Creek
SABKHA
150
← TO MOSCA
TO HWY160
COLORADO

The landspaces of Great Sand Dunes National Park are some of the country's most beautiful.

EDUCATIONAL OFFERINGS

Interpretive Programs

TOUR—SIGHT | FAMILY | Family-friendly nature walks designed to help visitors learn more about the Great Sand Dunes National Park are scheduled most days from late May through September, and sporadically in April and October. Call or drop in to ask about sunset walks, afternoon weekend tours, and evening stargazing programs. The Junior Ranger program is a favorite for children ages 3 to 12, who can earn their badge by completing a booklet of activities. ✉ *Programs begin at the visitor center, Great Sand Dunes National Park* ☎ *719/378–6395* 🎟 *Free.*

FISHING

Fly fishermen can angle for Rio Grande cutthroat trout in the upper reaches of Medano Creek, which is accessible by four-wheel-drive vehicle. It's catch-and-release only, and a Colorado license is required (☎ *800/244–5613*). There's also fishing in Upper and Lower Sand Creek Lakes, but it's a very long hike (3 or 4 miles from the Music Pass trailhead, located on the far side of the park in the San Isabel National Forest).

HIKING

Visitors can walk just about anywhere on the sand dunes in the heart of the park. The best view of all the dunes is from the top of High Dune. There are no formal trails because the sand keeps shifting, but you don't really need them: it's extremely difficult to get lost out here.

■ TIP→ Before taking any of the trails in the preserve, rangers recommend stopping at the visitor center and picking up the handout that lists the trails, including their degree of difficulty. The dunes can get very hot in the summer, reaching up to 150°F in the afternoon. If you're hiking, carry plenty of water; if you're going into the backcountry to camp overnight, carry even more water and a water filtration system. A free permit is required to backpack in the park. Also, watch for weather changes. If there's a thunderstorm and lightning, get off the dunes or trail immediately, and seek shelter. Before hiking, leave word with someone indicating where you're going to hike and when you expect to be back. Tell that contact to call 911 if you don't show up when expected.

EASY

Hike to High Dune

TRAIL | FAMILY | Get a panoramic view of all the surrounding dunes from the top of High Dune. Since there's no formal path, the smartest approach is to zigzag up the dune ridgelines traversing about 2½ miles round-trip. High Dune is 699 feet high, and to get there and back takes about two hours, or longer if there's been no rain for some time and the sand is soft. If you add on the walk to the 750-foot Star Dune, plan on another two or three hours and a strenuous workout up and down the dunes. *Easy to moderate.* ✉ *Great Sand Dunes National Park* ✣ *Start from main dune field.*

MODERATE

★ **Mosca Pass Trail**

TRAIL | This moderately challenging route follows the Montville Trail laid out centuries ago by Native Americans, which became the Mosca Pass toll road used in the late 1800s and early 1900s. This is a good afternoon hike, because the trail rises through the trees and subalpine meadows, often following Mosca Creek. Watch for grouse and turkey along the route and listen for songbirds and owls cooing at dusk. It is 3½ miles one way, with a 1,400-foot gain in elevation. Hiking time is about two hours each way. *Moderate.* ✉ *Great Sand Dunes National Park* ✣ *Trailhead: lower end of trail begins at Montville Trailhead, just north of visitor center.*

Alamosa

35 miles southwest of Great Sand Dunes via U.S. 160 and Rte. 150; 163 miles southwest of Colorado Springs.

The San Luis Valley's major city is a casual, central base from which to explore the region and visit the Great Sand Dunes.

VISITOR INFORMATION

CONTACTS Alamosa Convention & Visitors Bureau. ✉ *610 State Ave.* ☎ *800/258–7597, 719/589–4840* 🌐 *www.alamosa.org.*

Sights

Adams State University

COLLEGE | The campus here contains several superlative examples of 1930s WPA-commissioned murals in its administrative building. The college's **Luther Bean Museum and Art Gallery** displays European porcelain and furniture collections, and exhibits of regional arts and crafts. ✉ *Richardson Hall, Richardson and 3rd Sts.* ☎ *719/587–7151* 🌐 *www.adams.edu/lutherbean/* 🎟 *Free* ⏲ *Closed weekends.*

Alamosa National Wildlife Refuge

NATURE PRESERVE | FAMILY | Less than an hour's drive southwest of Great Sand Dunes is a sanctuary for songbirds, waterbirds, and raptors (it's also home to many other types of birds, along with mule deer, beavers, and coyotes). The Rio Grande runs through the park comprising more than 11,000 acres of natural and man-made wetlands. You can take a 4-mile hike round-trip along the river or a 3½-mile wildlife drive on the park's western side or a drive along Bluff Road to an overlook on the park's eastern side. The refuge office is staffed by volunteers sporadically from March through November and closed in winter, but a self-service kiosk provides visitor information year-round. ✉ *9383 El Rancho La., off U.S. 160* ☎ *719/589–4021* 🌐 *www.fws.gov/refuge/alamosa/* 🎟 *Free.*

The Greenhouse at Sand Dunes Pool

HOT SPRINGS | After a long day of hiking the dunes, take a dip in the soothing soaking tubs inside the 10,000-square-foot greenhouse at the Sand Dunes Pool. Just 30 minutes northwest of the park is a sanctuary that offers 70°F comfort year-round. Visitors 21 and older can soak in three hot tubs ranging from 103°F to 110°F, or take a dip in the large, 98°F swimming pool surrounded by lush gardens. A bar offers cocktails and sweet and savory small plates. For families, a giant outdoor pool with views of the Sangre de Cristo mountains is a popular amenity. ✉ *1991 County Rd. 63, Mosca* ☎ *719/378-2807* 🌐 *www.sanddunespool.com/greenhouse* 🎟 *$20 for adults* ⏲ *Closed Thurs.*

Monte Vista National Wildlife Refuge
NATURE PRESERVE | FAMILY | Just west of the Alamosa wildlife refuge is its sister sanctuary, the Monte Vista National Wildlife Refuge, a 15,000-acre park that's a stopping point for more than 20,000 migrating cranes in the spring and fall. It hosts an annual Crane Festival, held one weekend in mid-March in the nearby town of Monte Vista, and a children's Crane Festival in mid-October at the park with kid-friendly activities. You can see the sanctuary by foot, bike, or car via the 4-mile Wildlife Drive. ✉ *6120 Hwy. 15, Monte Vista* ☎ *719/589–4021* 🌐 *www.fws.gov/refuge/monte_vista* 🎟 *Free.*

Restaurants

Milagros Coffeehouse
$ | CAFÉ | The coffee is full-bodied at this coffeehouse and café where all profits go to local charities. Amish baked goods reign on the menu where local food dominates, which includes plenty of vegetarian and gluten-free options. **Known for:** vegetarian options; charitable donations; excellent coffee. Ⓢ *Average main: $7* ✉ *529 Main St.* ☎ *719/589–9299.*

Hotels

Best Western Alamosa Inn
$ | HOTEL | This sprawling, well-maintained complex is your best bet for reasonably priced lodgings. **Pros:** reliable accommodations; easy to find; good base for area activities. **Cons:** noisy street; nothing but fast food nearby; basic rooms. Ⓢ *Rooms from: $110* ✉ *2005 Main St.* ☎ *719/589–2567, 800/459–5123* 🌐 *www.bestwestern.com* *53 rooms* *Free Breakfast.*

Comfort Inn
$$ | HOTEL | This property is a few miles west of downtown Alamosa on a strip with other chain hotels and restaurants, several of which will deliver to the hotel. **Pros:** basic accommodations at a reasonable price; pets allowed; hot tub. **Cons:** on a noisy street; a car-ride away from downtown restaurants. Ⓢ *Rooms from: $145* ✉ *6301 W. Hwy. 160* ☎ *800/424–6423, 719/937–4002* 🌐 *www.comfortinn.com* *49 rooms, 3 suites* *Free Breakfast.*

San Luis and Fort Garland Loop

San Luis is 40 miles from Alamosa, 45 miles from Great Sand Dunes National Park; Fort Garland is 16 miles from San Luis, 30 miles from Great San Dunes National Park.

To get a real feel for this area, take an easy driving loop from Alamosa that includes San Luis and Fort Garland. In summer, take a few hours to ride one of the scenic railroads that take you into wilderness areas in this region.

Sights

Cumbres & Toltec Scenic Railroad
TRANSPORTATION SITE (AIRPORT/BUS/FERRY/TRAIN) | FAMILY | Take a day trip on the Cumbres & Toltec Scenic Railroad, an 1880s steam locomotive that chugs through portions of Colorado's and northern New Mexico's rugged mountains that you can't reach via roads. It's the country's longest and highest steam-operated railroad. The company offers round-trip train routes, several bus-and-train combinations, one-way trips, and themed rides. ✉ *5234 U.S. 285, Antonito* ☎ *888/286–2737* 🌐 *www.cumbrestoltec.com* 🎟 *$110–$216.*

Fort Garland

MILITARY SITE | One of Colorado's first military posts, Fort Garland was established in 1858 to protect settlers. It lies in the shadow of the Sangre de Cristo Mountains. The mountains were named for the "Blood of Christ" because of their ruddy color, especially at dawn. The legendary Kit Carson commanded the outfit, and some of the original adobe structures are still standing. The **Fort Garland Museum** features a re-creation of the commandant's quarters and period military displays. The museum is 16 miles north of San Luis via Highway 159 and 24 miles east of Alamosa via U.S. 160. ✉ *U.S. 160 and Hwy. 159, Fort Garland* ☎ *719/379–3512* 🌐 *www.museumtrail.org/fortgarlandmuseum.asp* 🎟 *$5.*

Manassa, San Luis, and Fort Garland Loop

SCENIC DRIVE | To get a real feel for this area, take an easy driving loop from Alamosa through much of the San Luis Valley (the whole trip is about 95 miles). Head east on U.S. 160 to Fort Garland, south on Highway 159 to San Luis, west on Highways 159 and 142 to Manassa, then north on U.S. 285 back to Alamosa. More than half of the route is part of the Los Caminos Antiguos Drive, one of Colorado's Scenic Byways.

San Luis

TOWN | Founded in 1851, San Luis is the oldest incorporated town in Colorado. Murals depicting famous stories and legends of the area adorn several buildings in the town. A latter-day masterpiece is the **Stations of the Cross Shrine,** created by renowned local sculptor Huberto Maestas. The shrine is formally known as La Mesa de la Piedad y de la Misericordia (Hill of Piety and Mercy), and its 15 stations with bronze statutes illustrate the last hours of Christ's life. The trail leads up to a chapel called La Capilla de Todos Los Santos. ✉ *San Luis.*

Hotels

Mountain View Motor Inn

$ | HOTEL | This cheerful, squeaky-clean motel is just a few miles south of the Great Sand Dunes, in the tiny town of Fort Garland, and makes a great base from which to visit the park and other San Luis Valley attractions. **Pros:** spotless, comfortable rooms; 20 minutes from park. **Cons:** no pool or other recreational amenities in hotel; no great eating options nearby. 💲 *Rooms from: $96* ✉ *411 U.S. 160, Fort Garland* ☎ *719/379–2993* 🛏 *22 rooms* 🍽 *No meals.*

Index

A

B

N

O

P

Photo Credits

Front Cover: Whit Richardson / Alamy Stock Photo [Description: Main Street, Telluride, Colorado.]. **Back cover, from left to right:** Kravka/Dreamstime.com, The World in HDR/Shutterstock, Jonathan Tung Photography/Shutterstock. **Spine:** Nick Fox/Shutterstock. **Interior, from left to right:** Jonathan Tung Photography/Shutterstock (1). thanasarn/Shutterstock (2). **Chapter 1: Experience Colorado:** Jeremy Janus/Shutterstock (8-9). Kevin Ruck/Shutterstock (10). Sopotnicki/Shutterstock (11). Nate Luebbe/Shutterstock (11). Doug Berry/iStockphoto (12). The Springs Resort & Spa, Pagosa Springs, CO (12). Michael Liggett/Shutterstock (12). Patrick Myers/NPS (13). Danica Bona - Sweet Tea Studios (13). Jay Krishnan/Shutterstock (14). Adeliepenguin | Dreamstime.com (14). Jack Affleck/Visit Glenwood Springs (14). Steve Boice/Shutterstock (14). RRuntsch/Shutterstock (15). f11photo/Shutterstock (15). Eric Limon/Shutterstock (15). Anton Foltin/Shutterstock (15). Zack Frank/Shutterstock (16). bjul/Shutterstock (16). Zach Maraziti/Aspen Chamber Resort Association (16). RoschetzkylstockPhoto/iStockphoto (17). Courtesy of WeldWerks (22). Courtesy of Colorado Lamb (23). arinahabich/iStockphoto (24). mistysprouse/iStockphoto (24). Courtesy of Visit Grand Junction (24). Breckenridge Tourism Office (24). Courtesy of Stranahan's Distillery (25). arinahabich/iStockphoto (26). MargaretW/iStockphoto (26). Courtesy of Visit Colorado Springs (26). Graddy Photography/coloradoranch.com (26). Aleksander Mirski/iStockphoto (27). grenierb/Shutterstock (27). Luke Koppa (27). Danica Bona - Sweet Tea Studios (27). Thomas Torget/Shutterstock (28). NPS photo by Russell Smith (28). Gary Gray/iStockphoto (28). Kerry Hargrove/iStockphoto (29). SWKrullImaging/iStockphoto (29). **Chapter 2: Travel Smart:** Emily Yoon/Shutterstock (55). **Chapter 3: Denver:** f11photo/Shutterstock (57). Sepavo | Dreamstime.com (68). Reedcody | Dreamstime.com (72). Arina P Habich/Shutterstock (82). Kitleong | Dreamstime.com (88). **Chapter 4: Side Trips from Denver:** Sparty1711/iStockphoto (107). Infinite_Eye/Shutterstock (114). Brandon Iwamoto/Shutterstock (119). Steve Boice/Shutterstock (125). Mikle15 | Dreamstime.com (128). **Chapter 5: Breckenridge and Summit County:** Photo Spirit/Shutterstock (131). sboice/iStockphoto (140). marekuliasz/iStockphoto (143). Margaret.Wiktor/Shutterstock (148). **Chapter 6: Vail Valley:** Paul Seftel/Shutterstock (155). Margaret619 | Dreamstime.com (167). Noamfein | Dreamstime.com (169). Chblueskye | Dreamstime.com (174). **Chapter 7: Aspen and the Roaring Fork Valley:** Jonathan Ross/iStockphoto (177). SeanXu/iStockphoto (187). David A Litman/Shutterstock (198). David A Litman/Shutterstock (201). Andy Konieczny/Shutterstock (204-205). ablokhin/iStockphoto (207). **Chapter 8: Boulder and North Central Colorado:** Adam Goldberg Photography/Shutterstock (211). randy andy/Shutterstock (223). littlenySTOCK/Shutterstock (225). **Chapter 9: Rocky Mountain National Park With Estes Park and Grand County:** Zhu_zhu | Dreamstime.com (251). Brendalynn6769 | Dreamstime.com (260). Mudwalker | Dreamstime.com (262). Virrage Images/Shutterstock (266). Markel Echaburu Bilbao/Shutterstock (273). **Chapter 10: Steamboat Springs and Northwest Colorado:** T.Schofield/Shutterstock (279). evanbrogan/iStockphoto (292). steve estvanik/Shutterstock (298). Teri Virbickis/Shutterstock (300). Deadendphoto | Dreamstime.com (310). **Chapter 11: Telluride and Southwest Colorado with the San Juan Mountains and Black Canyon of the Gunnison:** Kwiktor | Dreamstime.com (313). Andriy Blokhin/Shutterstock (321). Tristanbnz | Dreamstime.com (345). DBSOCAL/Shutterstock (350). KaraGrubis/iStockphoto (362). **Chapter 12: Mesa Verde National Park:** Sopotnicki/Shutterstock (375). Keifer | Dreamstime.com (384). John De Bord/Shutterstock (386). Dominic Gentilcore PhD/Shutterstock (388). **Chapter 13: Colorado Springs and South Central Colorado with Great Sand Dunes National Park:** ABDESIGN/iStockphoto (391). Pixelview Media/Shutterstock (403). Neil Podoll/Shutterstock (405). Swtrekker | Dreamstime.com (416). Camerashots | Dreamstime.com (418). F11photo | Dreamstime.com (431). **About Our Writers:** All photos are courtesy of the writers.

*Every effort has been made to trace the copyright holders, and we apologize in advance for any accidental errors. We would be happy to apply the corrections in the following edition of this publication.

Notes

Notes

Notes

Notes

Fodor's COLORADO

Publisher: Stephen Horowitz, *General Manager*

Editorial: Douglas Stallings, *Editorial Director;* Jill Fergus, Jacinta O'Halloran, Amanda Sadlowski, *Senior Editors*; Kayla Becker, Alexis Kelly, *Editors*

Design: Tina Malaney, *Director of Design and Production;* Jessica Gonzalez, *Graphic Designer;* Mariana Tabares, *Design and Production Intern*

Production: Jennifer DePrima, *Editorial Production Manager;* Elyse Rozelle, *Senior Production Editor;* Monica White, *Production Editor*

Maps: Rebecca Baer, *Senior Map Editor*; Mark Stroud (Moon Street Cartography), David Lindroth, *Cartographers*

Photography: Viviane Teles, *Senior Photo Editor;* Namrata Aggarwal, Ashok Kumar, Rebecca Rimmer, *Photo Editors*

Business and Operations: Chuck Hoover, *Chief Marketing Officer;* Robert Ames, *Group General Manager;* Devin Duckworth, *Director of Print Publishing;* Victor Bernal, *Business Analyst*

Public Relations and Marketing: Joe Ewaskiw, *Senior Director Communications and Public Relations*

Fodors.com: Jeremy Tarr, *Editorial Director;* Rachael Levitt, *Managing Editor*

Technology: Jon Atkinson, *Director of Technology;* Rudresh Teotia, *Lead Developer;* Jacob Ashpis, *Content Operations Manager*

Writers: Whitney Bryen, Lindsey Galloway, Aimee Heckel, Kellee Katagi, Kyle Wagner, Tim Wenger

Editors: Amanda Sadlowski, Laura Kidder, Doug Stallings

Production Editor: Jennifer DePrima

14th Edition

ISBN 978-1-64097-426-5

ISSN 0276–9018

Library of Congress Control Number 2018954453

All details in this book are based on information supplied to us at press time. Always confirm information when it matters, especially if you're making a detour to visit a specific place. Fodor's expressly disclaims any liability, loss, or risk, personal or otherwise, that is incurred as a consequence of the use of any of the contents of this book.

SPECIAL SALES

This book is available at special discounts for bulk purchases for sales promotions or premiums. For more information, e-mail SpecialMarkets@fodors.com.

PRINTED IN CANADA

10 9 8 7 6 5 4 3 2 1

About Our Writers

Whitney Bryen is a freelance journalist, hiking enthusiast, admirer of mountains, craft beer lover, and travel junkie. Her work has been featured in the *Denver Post, Boulder Daily Camera, Colorado Springs Independent,* and on Colorado Public Radio. Whitney updated the Aspen and Roaring Fork Valley and Colorado Springs and South Central Colorado chapters this edition.

Lindsey Galloway lives in Boulder, Colorado, and frequently overeats at the many restaurants on Pearl Street. Like any good Boulderite, she loves yoga and is particularly proud of her tree pose; however, the state of Colorado has threatened to revoke her license if she doesn't climb a Fourteener soon. She contributes regularly to BBC Travel and AOL Travel, and founded TravelPretty.com to document her perils in packing. Lindsey updated the Rocky Mountain National Park, Breckenridge and Summit County, and Vail Valley chapters this edition.

Aimee Heckel is a Colorado native who has been working at Colorado newspapers for nearly two decades. She's the head writer for TravelBoulder.com, the Colorado travel expert for Tripsavvy, and a book editor. Heckel also freelances for the *Boulder Daily Camera* and has worked as a regular travel writer for USA Today 10Best.com. Her passion for storytelling has brought her around the world as a journalist, but still, one of her favorite places to explore is the miraculous mountains in her home state. For this edition, she updated the Mesa Verde National Park, Boulder and North Central Colorado, and Telluride and Southwest Colorado chapters.

Kellee Katagi has lived in eight U.S. states, but Colorado is by far her favorite—not least because of the glorious scenery and the adventures to be had in its southwest region. A former managing editor of *SKI Magazine,* Katagi is now a freelance writer/editor specializing in travel, sports, fitness, health, and food. When not at her desk, she enjoys playing in the Colorado mountains with her husband, her three children (Shaelyn, David, and A.J.), and their trusty raft dubbed *K-5 Shark.* Kellee contributed to parts of the Telluride and Southwest Colorado chapter.

Kyle Wagner wrote about restaurants and food in Denver for 12 years, first for the alternative weekly *Westword* and then for the *Denver Post,* before being named travel editor for the *Post* in 2005, a position she held until 2014. The Denver resident, an avid mountain biker, river rafter, and skier, now writes freelance food and travel stories for regional and national magazines. For this edition, Kyle updated Denver, Side Trips from Denver, and Steamboat Springs and Northwest Colorado.

Tim Wenger is a Denver-based journalist who has worked as a reporter and editor at travel and culture publications in both the print and digital space. After finishing a BA in Communications from Fort Lewis College in 2007, Tim jumped into the back of a Ford Econoline and spent a few years traversing Colorado and beyond with a punk rock band, along the way falling in love with travel, good food, and local drink. He's been unable to rest his pen (or feet) ever since. An avid snowboarder and general outdoor enthusiast, he's documented his experiences and passion for Colorado across many platforms, including updating the Experience Colorado and Travel Smart sections for this Fodor's edition.